THE ROUTLEDGE HISTORY HANDBOOK OF CENTRAL AND EASTERN EUROPE IN THE TWENTIETH CENTURY

Statehood examines the extending lines of development of nation-state systems in Eastern Europe, in particular considering why certain tendencies in state development found a different expression in this region compared to other parts of the continent.

This volume discusses the differences between the social developments, political decisions and historical experience that have influenced processes of state-building, with a focus on the structural problems of the region and the different paths taken to overcome them. The book addresses processes of building social orders and examines the contribution of state institutions to social and cultural integration and disintegration. It analyzes institutional and personnel continuities that have outlasted the great political changes of the twentieth century and addresses the expansion of state activity in shaping property relations in agriculture and industry as well as in social security and family politics. Taking a comparative approach based on experiential history, allowing individual experience to be detached from specific national references, the volume delineates a transnational comparison of problems shared within the region as they have been passed down through history, providing definition to the specificity of Eastern Europe and situating the historical experience of the region within a pan-European context.

The second in a four-volume set on Central and Eastern Europe in the twentieth century, it is the go-to resource for those interested in statehood and state-building in this complex region.

Włodzimierz Borodziej is Professor of History at Warsaw University, Poland.

Sabina Ferhadbegović is Research Associate at Friedrich Schiller University Jena, Germany.

Joachim von Puttkamer is Professor of Eastern European History at the Friedrich Schiller University Jena, Germany and Co-Director of the Imre Kertész Kolleg, Germany.

The Imre Kertész Kolleg at the Friedrich Schiller University in Jena is an institute for the advanced study of the history of Eastern Europe in the twentieth century.

The Kolleg was founded in October 2010 as the ninth Käte Hamburger Kolleg of the German Federal Ministry for Education and Research (BMBF). The directors of the Kolleg are Professor Joachim von Puttkamer and Dr Michal Kopeček. Professor Włodzimierz Borodziej was the Kolleg's co-director from 2010 to 2016 and is now chairman of its advisory board.

THE ROUTLEDGE TWENTIETH CENTURY HISTORY HANDBOOKS

The Routledge History Handbook of Central and Eastern Europe in the Twentieth Century
Volume 1: Challenges of Modernity
Edited by Włodzimierz Borodziej, Stanislav Holubec and Joachim von Puttkamer

The Routledge History Handbook of Central and Eastern Europe in the Twentieth Century
Volume 2: Statehood
Edited by Włodzimierz Borodziej, Sabina Ferhadbegović and Joachim von Puttkamer

For more information about this series, please visit: www.routledge.com/The-Routledge-Twentieth-Century-History-Handbooks/book-series/RHHC20.

THE ROUTLEDGE HISTORY HANDBOOK OF CENTRAL AND EASTERN EUROPE IN THE TWENTIETH CENTURY

Volume 2: Statehood

Edited by
Włodzimierz Borodziej, Sabina Ferhadbegović
and Joachim von Puttkamer

LONDON AND NEW YORK

First published 2020
by Routledge
2 Park Square, Milton Park, Abingdon, Oxon OX14 4RN

and by Routledge
52 Vanderbilt Avenue, New York, NY 10017

Routledge is an imprint of the Taylor & Francis Group, an informa business

© 2020 selection and editorial matter, Włodzimierz Borodziej, Sabina
Ferhadbegović and Joachim von Puttkamer; individual chapters, the contributors

The right of Włodzimierz Borodziej, Sabina Ferhadbegović and Joachim von
Puttkamer to be identified as the authors of the editorial material, and of the
authors for their individual chapters, has been asserted in accordance with
sections 77 and 78 of the Copyright, Designs and Patents Act 1988.

All rights reserved. No part of this book may be reprinted or reproduced or
utilised in any form or by any electronic, mechanical, or other means, now
known or hereafter invented, including photocopying and recording, or in
any information storage or retrieval system, without permission in writing
from the publishers.

Trademark notice: Product or corporate names may be trademarks or registered
trademarks, and are used only for identification and explanation without
intent to infringe.

British Library Cataloguing-in-Publication Data
A catalogue record for this book is available from the British Library

Library of Congress Cataloging-in-Publication Data
Names: Borodziej, Włodzimierz, editor. | Ferhadbegović, Sabina, editor. |
Puttkamer, Joachim von, editor.
Title: The Routledge history handbook of Central and Eastern Europe in the
twentieth century / edited by Włodzimierz Borodziej, Sabina
Ferhadbegović and Joachim von Puttkamer.
Other titles: Central and Eastern Europe in the twentieth century
Description: New York : Routledge, 2019- | Series: Routledge twentieth
century history handbooks | Volume 1 title information from publisher's
website. | Includes bibliographical references and index. | Contents:
[Volume 1. The Challenges of Modernity]—Volume 2. Statehood—
Identifiers: LCCN 2019049033 (print) | LCCN 2019049034 (ebook) |
ISBN 9781138301665 (hardback) | ISBN 9780367822118 (ebook)
Subjects: LCSH: Europe, Central—Politics and government—1989- | Europe,
Eastern—Politics and government—1989- | Post-communism—Europe,
Central—History—20th century. | Post-communism—Europe, Eastern—
History—20th century.
Classification: LCC DAW1051 .R68 2019 (print) | LCC DAW1051 (ebook) |
DDC 943.009/04—dc23
LC record available at https://lccn.loc.gov/2019049033
LC ebook record available at https://lccn.loc.gov/2019049034

ISBN: 978-1-138-30166-5 (hbk)
ISBN: 978-0-367-82211-8 (ebk)
ISBN: 978-0-367-51865-3 (set)

Typeset in Bembo
by Swales & Willis, Exeter, Devon, UK

CONTENTS

Series introduction	*vii*
Włodzimierz Borodziej and Joachim von Puttkamer	
Acknowledgements	*ix*
List of figures	*x*
List of abbreviations	*xi*
List of contributors	*xii*
Volume introduction: statehood	*xv*
Włodzimierz Borodziej, Sabina Ferhadbegović and Joachim von Puttkamer	

1   Projections and representations of statehood   1
      Sabina Ferhadbegović

2   Towards a new quality of statehood: bureaucratization and
      state-building in empires and nation states before 1914   41
      Hannes Grandits, Pieter Judson and Malte Rolf

3   Deconstructing and reconstructing statehood: the impact
      of the World Wars (Part I) – the First World War   117
      Jochen Böhler

4   Statehood in Central, Eastern and Southeastern Europe:
      the interwar period   148
      Dietmar Müller

5   Deconstructing and reconstructing statehood: the impact
      of the World Wars (Part II) – the Second World War   194
      Jochen Böhler

Contents

6 Statehood in socialism 215
Ulf Brunnbauer and Claudia Kraft

7 1989 and beyond 291
Joachim von Puttkamer

Index *328*

SERIES INTRODUCTION

What were the central twentieth-century experiences for Eastern European societies? Depending on whom you ask and depending on which country their thoughts intuitively drift towards, the answer is likely to be quite different. The answer could refer to significant dates, such as the 1939 Molotov-Ribbentrop Pact, the 1956 Hungarian uprising, the Prague Spring of 1968 or the year of Solidarity in 1980–1981. It could also revolve around the experiences in various countries – the Stalinist deportations left deep scars in the Baltic states, as did the wars of the 1990s in former Yugoslavia. The thoughts of a Western European are likely to jump to 1989 and the collapse of communist rule – perhaps also to the disappointed (or at least unlikely) prospects of a unified Europe. Hopefully, he or she might learn something from this volume.

As that Western European will discover, there were particular as well as shared experiences. The volumes presented here focus on both, grouped around what the editors regard as central, overarching themes. To emphasize the experience of *Violence* (vol. 4) is just as obvious as prioritizing the manifold *Challenges of Modernity* (vol. 1) of a region that has often been described – and perceived by its own inhabitants – as the periphery of Europe. The need to address the transformation of *Statehood* (vol. 2) over the course of the century may initially seem less apparent, but it allows for an elucidation of profound changes and phenomena that are otherwise obscured in a discussion of the emergence and emancipation of modern nation-states. *Intellectual Horizons* (vol. 3) reflects the wealth of self-descriptions and self-localizations in and about the region.

What do these volumes offer the reader? Not an encyclopaedia of Central, Eastern and Southeastern Europe in the long twentieth century, but a series of essays written from different perspectives and life experiences. The authors live in Bulgaria, Germany, Canada, Austria, Poland, Romania, Serbia, Czechia, Hungary and the United States. They belong to different generations and milieus and often have vastly different conceptions of historiography and the writing of history. Therein lies – according to the editors – the appeal of these volumes.

The shared goal of these contributions is to tell the story of the 'suburbs' of Europe in the twentieth century; to tell how the story unfolded, how it was perceived within this region and how it can be interpreted today.

Series introduction

The authors were not given any methodological parameters to follow. Some contributions may seem conservative or even old-fashioned; others argue in the spirit of what, in many universities today, is considered mainstream. None of the authors, however, crosses the boundary beyond which they see traditional sources as nothing more than merely conceptual obstacles. If the present volumes provide a new impetus for a collective reflection on Eastern Europe, both in teaching and in research, then much will have been gained.

ACKNOWLEDGEMENTS

Thinking through trajectories of states and political regimes in the twentieth century sometimes demands a terminology of its own, and there is no need to deny that much of the inspiration for this volume has been drawn from both German and Eastern European research. To reiterate the words of Umberto Eco, the language of Europe is indeed translation. In this regard, we would like to acknowledge the translators who worked with us on this volume. David Burnett translated from German parts of the chapter *Towards a new quality of statehood: Bureaucratization and state-building in empires and nation states before 1914* as well as the entire chapters *Statehood in Central, Eastern and Southeastern Europe: The interwar period* and *Projections and representations of statehood*. Thomas Lampert and Jonathan Lutes co-translated the chapter *Statehood in socialism* and Adam Bresnahan translated the volume introduction, also from German. We are deeply grateful to all of them. We would also like to thank Raphael Utz for the acquisition of photographic material and copyright permissions. And finally, Jaime Elizabeth Hyatt was responsible for the entire editing process, and in doing so, she drew our attention to some terminological inconsistencies which only native speakers of German could have produced, and only native speakers of English would have noticed. We are deeply grateful for all of her work behind the scenes, the scope of which we are sure to have underestimated. The responsibility for any remaining errors and flaws, of course, rests with us.

Finally, we would like to thank the German Federal Ministry of Education and Research for generously providing the project funding which has thus allowed us the unique opportunity to develop each of the four volumes in this series.

FIGURES

1.1	Emperor Francis Joseph visiting the Provincial Government Building, Sarajevo 1910	2
1.2	The Hungarian pavilion at the Universal Exhibition of 1900 in Paris	7
1.3	The Russian pavilion at the Universal Exhibition of 1900 in Paris	10
1.4	Town hall of Szabadka/Subotica	13
1.5	Hungarian Parliament Building	14
1.6	Buda Castle	15
1.7	Old Palace, Belgrade	21
1.8	House of the National Assembly of Yugoslavia	23
1.9	Royal Palace, Belgrade	24
1.10	Palace of Soviets (Model), Moscow	26
1.11	Headquarters of the Central Committee of the Polish United Worker's Party, Warsaw	29
1.12	Headquarters of the Central Committee of the League of Communists of Yugoslavia	31
1.13	The Czechoslovak Pavilion at the Universal and International Exposition in Brussels (EXPO 58)	32
1.14	Federal Assembly of Czechoslovakia	34
1.15	House of the Republic, Bucharest	36

ABBREVIATIONS

CIAM – Congrès Internationaux d'Architecture Moderne/International Congress of Modern Architecture
CNSAS – Consiliul Naţional pentru Studierea Arhivelor Securităţii/National Council for the Study of Securitate Files
Comecon (CMEA) – Council for Mutual Economic Assistance
Cominform – Communist Information Bureau
Comintern – Communist International
CPC – Communist Party of Czechoslovakia
CPSU – Communist Party of the Soviet Union
CSCE – Conference on Security and Cooperation in Europe
ČSSR – Československá socialistická republika/Czechoslovak Socialist Republic
Fidesz – Fidesz – Magyar Polgári Szövetség/Hungarian Civic Alliance
GDP – Gross Domestic Product
GDR – German Democratic Republic
HDZ – Hrvatska Demokratska Zajednica/Croatian Democratic Union
ILO – International Labour Organization
IMF – International Monetary Fund
IPN – Instytut Pamięci Narodowej/Institute of National Remembrance
JDC – American Jewish Joint Distribution Committee
KOR – Komitet Obrony Robotników/Workers' Defence Committee
KPN – onfederacja Polski Niepodległej/Confederation of Independent Poland
MDF – Magyar Demokrata Fórum/Hungarian Democratic Forum
NATO – North Atlantic Treaty Organization
OECD – Organisation for Economic Co-operation and Development
POW – prisoner of war
PSL-Piast – Polskie Stronnictwo Ludowe Polskie 'Piast'/Polish People's Party
SED – Sozialistische Einheitspartei Deutschlands/Socialist Unity Party of Germany
SFRY – Socialist Federal Republic of Yugoslavia
USSR – Union of Soviet Socialist Republics
WIDF – Women's International Democratic Federation
ZOMO – Zmotoryzowane Odwody Milicji Obywatelskiej/Motorized Reserves of the Citizens' Militia

CONTRIBUTORS

Jochen Böhler has published two best-selling histories of German militarism in Poland: *Der Überfall: Deutschlands Krieg gegen Polen* ('Onslaught: Germany's war against Poland', Eichborn 2009) and *Auftakt zum Vernichtungskrieg: die Wehrmacht in Polen 1939* ('Prelude to the war of extermination: the Wehrmacht in Poland 1939', Fischer Taschenbuch 2006), and recently co-edited *War, Pacification, and Mass Murder, 1939: The Einsatzgruppen in Poland* (Rowman and Littlefield 2014). His most recent monograph *Civil War in Central Europe, 1918–1921: The Reconstruction of Poland* (Oxford University Press 2018) was awarded the ASEEES Kulczycki Book Prize 'for the best book in any discipline, on any aspect of Polish affairs, published in the previous calendar year' in 2019. Currently, he is acting Chair of Eastern European History at the Friedrich Schiller University of Jena and is co-editor of Volume 4 of this series, *Violence*.

Włodzimierz Borodziej is Professor of Modern History at Warsaw University. He was Co-Director of the Imre Kertész Kolleg in Jena (2010–2016) and is currently the chairman of the Kolleg's academic advisory board. His books include *The Warsaw Uprising of 1944* (English translation, Univ. of Wisconsin 2006), a seminal twentieth-century history of Poland (*Geschichte Polens im 20. Jahrhundert*, C.H. Beck 2010), and many key studies of Polish and Polish–German history. The two-volume monograph, which he co-authored with Maciej Górny, *Nasza Wojna. Imperia 1912–1916* (WAB 2014) and *Nasza Wojna: Narody 1917–1923* (WAB 2018) has been published in German as *Der Vergessene Weltkrieg: Europas Osten 1912–1923* (wbg Theiss 2018) and offers the most comprehensive account of the First World War in Central and Eastern Europe. An English translation is forthcoming.

Ulf Brunnbauer is Director of the Institute for East and Southeast European Studies at the University of Regensburg. He has published numerous monographs, co-edited volumes and articles on the history of migration, nationalisms, families, Muslim minorities and state socialism in Southeastern Europe, including *'Die sozialistische Lebensweise'. Ideologie, Politik und Alltag in Bulgarien 1944–1989* ('"The socialist way of life": ideology, politics and everyday life in Bulgaria, 1944–1989', Böhlau 2007). His most recent book is a comprehensive history of Southeast Europe *Geschichte Südosteuropas* (co-authored with Klaus Buchenau, Reclam 2018).

List of contributors

Sabina Ferhadbegović is the author of *Prekäre Integration. Serbisches Staatsmodell und regionale Selbstverwaltung in Sarajevo und Zagreb 1918–1929* ('Precarious integration: The Serbian state model and regional self-administration in Sarajevo and Zagreb', Oldenbourg 2008) and many articles on state- and nation-building processes in ex-Yugoslavia. She has been a research fellow of the Imre Kertész Kolleg in Jena and is co-editor of Volume II: *Statehood*. Currently, she is preparing a monograph on post-war trials in Bosnia.

Hannes Grandits is Professor for Southeast European History at the Humboldt University in Berlin. His recent books include *Local Dimensions of the Second World War in Southeastern Europe* (co-edited with Xavier Bougarel and Marija Vulesica, Routledge 2019), *The Ambiguous Nation: Case Studies from Southeastern Europe in the 20th Century* (co-edited with Ulf Brunnbauer, Oldenbourg 2013), *Conflicting Loyalties in the Balkans: The Great Powers, the Ottoman Empire and Nation-Building* (co-edited with Nathalie Clayer and Robert Pichler, Tauris 2011) and *Yugoslavia's Sunny Side: A History of Tourism in Socialism, 1950s–1980s* (co-edited with Karin Taylor, CEU Press 2010).

Pieter Judson is Professor of 19th and 20th Century History at the European University Institute in Florence, Italy and author of *Exclusive Revolutionaries: Liberal Politics, Social Experience, and National Identity in the Austrian Empire, 1848–1914* (University of Michigan Press 1996) and *Guardians of the Nation: Activists on the Language Frontiers of Imperial Austria* (Harvard University Press 2006). His latest book is the much-appraised monograph *The Habsburg Empire: A New History* (The Belknap Press of Harvard UP 2016).

Claudia Kraft is Professor of Contemporary History at Vienna University, with a special focus on the history of knowledge, culture and gender. Her wide range of publications includes a comparative study of Polish law in the interwar period, *Europa im Blick der polnischen Juristen* ('Europe from the perspective of Polish jurists', Oldenbourg 2002) and *Zwischen Geschlecht und Nation: Interdependenzen und Interaktionen in der multiethnischen Gesellschaft Polens im 19. und 20. Jahrhundert* ('Between gender and nation: Interdependencies and interactions in Poland's multi-ethnic society in the 19th and 20th Centuries', Fibre 2016). She has also published numerous edited volumes and articles on postcolonialism, gender relations and the history of migration in East Central Europe.

Dietmar Müller recently published *Property in East Central Europe: Notions, Institutions, and Practices of Landownership in the Twentieth Century* (co-edited with Hannes Siegrist, Berghahn Books 2015) and has authored many other books and articles on nation-building and minorities, agrarian politics and property rights, governance and statehood, and memory cultures and the politics of history in Eastern Europe. He is a research associate of the Centre for the History and Culture of East Central Europe at the University of Leipzig and the Southeastern Europe editor of *H-Soz-u-Kult*.

Malte Rolf is Professor of Central and Eastern European History at the University of Oldenburg. He is the author of *Imperiale Herrschaft im Weichselland: Das Königreich Polen im Russischen Imperium, 1864–1915* (Oldenbourg 2015, Polish edition: *Rządy imperialne w Kraju Nadwiślańskim. Królestwo Polskie i cesarstwo rosyjskie*, Wydawnictwa Uniwersytetu Warszawskiego 2016; English edition: *Russian Rule in the Kingdom of Poland, 1864–1915*, Univ. of Pittsburgh Press forthcoming) and *Das sowjetische Massenfest, 1927–1941* ('Soviet mass festivals', Hamburger Edition 2006).

List of contributors

Joachim von Puttkamer is Co-Director of the Imre Kertész Kolleg and Chair of Eastern European History at the Friedrich Schiller University of Jena. He has published widely on the histories of nationalism, state-building and statehood, education, and security apparatuses, as well as on cultures of memory and political thought in the region. He is the author of the survey history *Ostmitteleuropa im 19. und 20. Jahrhundert* ('East Central Europe in the 19th and 20th centuries', Oldenbourg 2010), *1956 – (nieco) inne spojrzenie* ('1956: A somewhat different perspective', co-edited with Jerzy Kochanowski, Neriton 2016) and is co-editor of numerous publications including *From Revolution to Uncertainty: The Year 1990 in Central and Eastern Europe* (Routledge 2019) and *Catastrophe and Utopia: Jewish Intellectuals in Central and Eastern Europe in the 1930s and 1940s* (De Gruyter 2017).

VOLUME INTRODUCTION: STATEHOOD

Włodzimierz Borodziej, Sabina Ferhadbegović and Joachim von Puttkamer

Introduction

The states of Central and Eastern Europe as we know them today are relatively young. Or at least it seems that way when we look at maps from the late nineteenth century. Indeed, there is hardly a political border that has not been redrawn since then. Some internal borders of the Habsburg Monarchy and the Ottoman Empire later became borders between sovereign states, and most of today's borders in the region were drawn only after 1918, 1945 or 1991. In Eastern Europe, millennial borders like the northern border of Switzerland or the eastern border of the Netherlands, are few and far between.

This observation has shaped the perception of modern statehood in the region. In 1946, just one year after the end of the Second World War, Hungarian political theorist István Bibó inquired as to what exactly was the ultimate cause of all the conflict in Central and Eastern Europe. In an influential essay, he maintains that the contention is the result of 'the historical states and the nations of the region' having been 'blown up' and the 'borders among its various nations' having become 'subject to dispute.'[1] Indeed, Bibó was writing about the art of good peace-making, which he believed would enable the establishment of nation states with democratic constitutions, ultimately winning the enduring support of their populations. To him, the concept of the modern nation hinged on the framework of a state which the people, 'through the power of democratized mass emotion, seek to take possession of and own.'[2]

As we know, things turned out differently after 1946, at least at first. Instead of liberal democratic nation states, communist one-party states were set up, and the feeling described by Bibó that Eastern Europe had gotten the short end of the stick in comparison with Western Europe persisted for another four decades. The fact that most states in the region have joined the European Union since 2004 has not diminished the significance of this political feeling, and the ethnic conflicts that have historically plagued the region have in no way subsided.

---

1 István Bibó, 'The Miseries of East European Small States', in *The Art of Peacemaking*, trans. Péter Pásztor, ed. Iván Zoltán Dénes (New Haven, CT: Yale University Press, 2015), 130–80, here 164.

2 Ibid., 130.

Volume introduction: statehood

This volume questions the popular notion that the state is nothing more than a neutral framework that constitutes a nation as a political entity. It draws inspiration from the 'politics as cultural history' [*Kulturgeschichte des Politischen*] debate that German historians have been discussing for some time now.[3] Rather than studying state institutions and their political effectiveness as such, this volume seeks to analyze historical notions about what exactly the state's task is and historical expectations about what the state can achieve. To be sure, these ideas and expectations underwent radical changes in Eastern Europe over the course of the twentieth century.

The state regulation of property relations and the state's active role in shaping population and society are two areas in which these shifts are particularly apparent. State institutions first began intervening in private property relations during the abolition of serfdom. The intensity of these measures gave the state an unprecedented local presence in Prussia, and even more so in the Habsburg Empire. It is precisely because the agrarian reforms of the interwar period were so closely linked to the emancipation of the serfs in the nineteenth century that this volume has to look back further into the nineteenth century than might normally be expected of a book dedicated to twentieth century history. Indeed, drawing these connections will help shine light on the history of the complex entanglements of state action, local elites and agrarian self-administration. Although these entanglements took different permutations from the Baltic to Southeastern Europe, they were gradually made more uniform in the first half of the twentieth century, reaching a climax in the post-1945 collectivizations, which ultimately sought to put farmers on the same level as workers and make them into de facto employees of the region's one-party states. The massive sell-off of the socialist agricultural collectives to private investors after 1989 brought Eastern European agriculture much closer to its Western counterpart than had been the case a century before. The comprehensive nationalization of industry and trade after the Second World War and similarly comprehensive privatization after 1989 have also had a serious impact. In the end, Eastern European expectations about what the state and its institutions can and should do now vary greatly from country to country.

A second key question concerns the state's active political role in shaping social relations, particularly through family and welfare policy. While there are similarities and differences between Eastern and Western Europe here too, most of the overlaps concern social developments that are comprehensively treated from another perspective in the volume *Challenges of Modernity*. In contrast, this volume seeks to analyze shifts in the state's claims about its role in organizing society and its capacity to make good on them.

Finally, this volume seeks to offer insights into Eastern Europe's political systems, their failures and transformations, moves towards democratization, and authoritarian backlash. At first glance, it might seem that researchers have pretty much exhausted this field. However, taking up perspectives from the politics as cultural history debate allows us to see just how close expectations about the efficacy of political participation were connected with concrete reforms and promises made by the respective states. This holds for the old continental empires on the eve of the First World War and for the revolutionary hopes at its end, for the early phases of communist dictatorships and the political changes after 1989. The kind of national mass emotion

---

3 Achim Landwehr, 'Diskurs – Macht – Wissen. Perspektiven einer Kulturgeschichte des Politischen', *Archiv für Kulturgeschichte* 85 (2003): 71–117; Thomas Mergel, 'Überlegungen zu einer Kulturgeschichte der Politik', *Geschichte und Gesellschaft* 28 (2002): 574–606.

xvi

Volume introduction: statehood

Bibó had in mind was in no way completely democratic. In fact, it was often the complete opposite of democratic. One way or the other, when the people took possession of the state as Bibó envisioned, their representatives always invested the takeover with promises of participation, justice and prosperity.

Included in this volume are studies of the representation of statehood in architecture and in the rituals and appearance of monarchic heads of state. This is another lesson from 'politics as cultural history' debate: the modern state and its institutions have not cut all ties with the past, but instead regularly draw on older forms of staging political power.

It might seem surprising that the volume's contributors rarely touch on classical fields of state activity like the police and military, taxes and expenditures, streets and schools, or even internal administration in general. However, this is simply due to the fact that the current state of research tells us that these areas are less conducive for giving us a robust understanding of the significant shifts undergone by statehood in the twentieth century, which, of course, might also be attributed to the relative lack of strong research on these shifts. Infrastructure is also treated in a different context in *Challenges of Modernity*. In this volume, the focus lies more on the role played by war and experiences of violence in the development of concepts of statehood and state-building in Eastern Europe.

This volume also says relatively little about what is generally termed 'political culture,' which encompasses everything from political mentalities to the observation of Swiss anthropologist Christian Giordano that Eastern European societies are, in contrast to their Western counterparts, societies of public distrust, a fact that has its roots in the experience of centuries of foreign rule, particularly in Southeastern Europe and divided Poland.[4] Historians have a more difficult time studying such mentalities than anthropologists, which also has something to do with their worry that the lack of good methodologies might lead them to speak in clichés. This volume's contributors hope that the individual chapters and the volume as a whole can help give us a better understanding of the historical transformations undergone by the region's state institutions and the tasks they have been vested with. In the end, this will make clear that the advent of democratic, constitutional nation states in Eastern Europe has in no way put an end to the question of what the tasks, goals and limits of the state are or should be in the region.

---

4 Christian Giordano, 'Privates Vertrauen und informelle Netzwerke: Zur Organisationskultur in Gesellschaften des öffentlichen Misstrauens: Südosteuropa im Blickpunkt', in *Soziale Netzwerke und soziales Vertrauen in den Transformationsländern: Ethnologische und soziologische Untersuchungen – Social networks and social trust in the transformation countries*, ed. Klaus Roth (Vienna: Lit, 2007), 21–49.

1

PROJECTIONS AND REPRESENTATIONS OF STATEHOOD

Sabina Ferhadbegović

Theoretical approach: presenting, representing, communicating

Josip Vancaš had just turned 24 years old when he left Vienna to go to Sarajevo.[1] Administrators, teachers, doctors and fortune-seekers of every kind flocked there from all corners of the monarchy after the occupation of Bosnia-Herzegovina.[2] Arriving in 1883 at the invitation of the joint Austro-Hungarian finance minister Benjámin von Kállay, Vancaš would, during the next thirty years, leave his mark on the new urban landscape unlike any other architect. While the Habsburg monarchy established itself in its newly occupied territories, Vancaš built the seat of the provincial government (Zgrada Zemaljske Vlade), the central post office, the regional bank and over one hundred other representative buildings, schools, banks and offices.

Before the seat of government was installed, the central organs of administration had been located in various old, and sometimes dilapidated, Ottoman-era buildings that Kállay, who was responsible for the administration of Bosnia, deemed 'undignified'.[3] He was very concerned that central state institutions be housed in appropriate structures, so that the local population would not get the impression that their new rulers were only temporary.[4] The new government building was to be representative, reflecting the character of the new administration while also

---

1 Dragan Damjanović, 'Arhitekt Josip Vancaš i katedrala s biskupskim sklopom u Đakovu' [The architect Josip Vancaš and the cathedral with the episcopal complex in Đakovo], *Scrinia Slavonica* 8 (2008): 177.

2 In 1881 there were 600 Austro-Hungarian civil servants working in Sarajevo. By 1897 the figure had risen to 7,000, a stark contrast to the number of Ottoman officials: only 120 at the time of occupation. See Emily Gunzburger Makaš, 'Sarajevo', in *Capital Cities in the Aftermath of Empires: Planning in Central and Southeastern Europe*, eds Emily Gunzburger Makaš and Tanja Damljanovic Conley (London: Routledge, 2010), 243.

3 See the website of the presidency of Bosnia-Herzegovina, which is now housed in the building: www.predsjednistvobih.ba/zgr-konak/?cid=8,2,1 (accessed 7 February 2014). More about Kállay in Jelena Milojković-Djurić, 'Benjamin von Kállay`s Role in Bosnia-Herzegovina 1882–1903: Habsburg`s Policies in an Occupied Territory', *Serbian Studies* 14 (2000): 211–20.

4 Božo Madžar, 'Sto godina vladine zgrade u Sarajevu (1885–1985)' [A hundred years of the government building in Sarajevo (1885–1985)], *Glasnik arhiva* 25 (1985): 249.

Figure 1.1 Emperor Francis Joseph visiting the Provincial Government Building, Sarajevo 1910
© Historijski Muzej Bosne i Hervegovine

lending the new administration a physical dimension. Vancaš' construction – which used more than three million bricks – resulted in a structure that outwardly resembled a Florentine palazzo, in the Historicist style quite widespread in Europe at that time.[5] Theatres and art museums in Prague and Budapest looked virtually identical, but the new seat of the provincial government on Ćemaluša Street was clearly something different in Sarajevo. The new rulers intended it to be an architectural symbol of their power. The provincial government building symbolized Kállay's own understanding of the new administration: uniform and efficient, dignified in its external appearance (reminiscent of the universal visual imagery of the Renaissance); structurally, it signified openness with clear lines of internal and external communication. It was thus fundamentally different from the other buildings around it and a departure from the Ottoman style of architecture; it was unmistakably new.

The Habsburgs left Bosnia after the First World War, and in the decades that followed, Vancaš' building was occupied by key institutions of the various successor states. With the dissolution of the Austro-Hungarian provincial government and the founding of the Kingdom of Serbs, Croats and Slovenes, the building became home to the government of the Sarajevo district and later served as the seat of government of the Drina Banovina province. In the socialist era, the president of the Republic of Bosnia-Herzegovina inhabited the building, and with the subsequent Bosnian independence it housed the supreme governing body, the Bosnian presidency.

On 7 February 2014 angry demonstrators broke through a police cordon, cut up antique carpets, smashed gold-framed mirrors to pieces and destroyed hand-carved walnut shelves. Their ire was directed at the corrupt political leadership. Vancaš' building burned that night, because in that moment the people perceived it as the symbol of a dysfunctional state whose failed political elites enriched themselves at the expense of the general public.[6] The

---

5 More about the building in Madžar, 'Sto godina vladine zgrade'; Ibrahim Krzović, *Arhitektura secesije u Bosni i Hercegovini* [Vienna secession in Bosnia and Herzegovina] (Sarajevo: Sarajevo Publishing, 2005).
6 See the essay of Bosnia writer Faruk Šehić, 'Fuck Them, They Make Three and a Half Thousand a Month', in http://bhprotestfiles.wordpress.com/2014/02/12/fuck-them-they-make-three-and-a-half-thousand-a-month/ (accessed on 14 February 2014).

Projections and representations of statehood

demonstrators acted like medieval iconoclasts, attacking the building as if it were a personification of the hated politicians.[7]

The destruction was a symbolic act of anger by the population: the end of non-violent communication with the state and the termination of their loyalty. Ironically, some of those who set the fire were the same people who had risked their lives on 2 May 1992 as unarmed protesters, opposing the tanks of the Yugoslav People's Army in order to protect the building. Back in 1992 the building mainly symbolized the independence of the Bosnian state – today, it symbolizes its failure.

The above examples of the projections and representations of statehood encompass the main focal points addressed in the current chapter: the question of representation, the performance and communication of state and statehood in Eastern Europe in the twentieth century, the experience of the state and the reactions to its forms of enactment.

Since antiquity, politics and statehood have been closely linked to communication and the form it takes in the media of the day. The modern state in particular gained influence by reproducing public rituals and performances; Indeed, it has always been dependent on cultural resources such as narratives, symbols and codes to create a sense of belonging.[8] The modern state was representative and presented itself like any other social organization. The self-representation of the state can manifest in a variety of ways, attaching itself to symbolic objects such as state architecture, or to individuals as in the case of the army.[9] It also follows a variety of aims. It can serve to stabilize the system and have an integrative function – with imagined unity playing an important role here – or it can demonstrate power. It is important, however, to bear in mind what Quentin Skinner says, 'that there has never been any generally acknowledged idea that can be captured by the word "state"'.[10] The concern is therefore not the theoretical approximation of a concept of state. Rather, following Philip Manow, it is the 'mythical convictions'[11] of various Eastern European societies that have served as the basis of their political orders and their transformation in the twentieth century. What does the self-representation of the state tell us about the concept of state, and the self-understanding of these countries, some of which are newly founded? Or to put it another way, if we follow Pierre Bourdieu and his notion that the state is a 'collective fiction',[12] a construct based on hidden 'principles of social order, of physical and at the same time symbolic rule as well as physical and symbolic force'[13] which has risen to a universalizing institution in twentieth-century Eastern Europe, then questions arise regarding what symbolic means these states used to legitimize and communicate this claim to power, how the symbolic legitimization of rule changed during the transition from imperial monarchical-absolutist rule to democracy, and which forms of representation justified the belief in these states. Ultimately, the ceremonial or representative aspect of state rule

---

7 More on the principle of iconoclasm in Horst Bredekamp, *Theorie des Bildaktes – Frankfurter Adorno-Vorlesungen 2007* (Frankfurt a.M.: Suhrkamp, 2010), 210.

8 More on this in Rudolf Schlögl, Bernhard Giesen and Jürgen Osterhammel, *Die Wirklichkeit der Symbole: Grundlagen der Kommunikation in historischen und gegenwärtigen Gesellschaften* (Constance: UVK, 2004).

9 Helmut Quaritsch, introduction to *Die Selbstdarstellung des Staates* (Berlin: Duncker Humblot, 1977), 5.

10 Quentin Skinner, *Die drei Körper des Staates* (Göttingen: Wallstein, 2012), 9.

11 Philip Manow, *Im Schatten des Königs: Die politische Anatomie demokratischer Repräsentation* (Frankfurt a.M.: Suhrkamp, 2008), 13.

12 Pierre Bourdieu, *Über den Staat – Vorlesungen am Collège de France 1989–1992* (Frankfurt a.M.: Suhrkamp, 2014), 24.

13 Bourdieu, *Über den Staat*, 24.

disappears neither with the emergence of bureaucratic institutions nor with democratization, but is merely perpetuated.[14]

Every society leaves traces of itself in its surroundings. Into the late eighteenth century, secular rulers used public space to display their power, building ever higher, bigger and more grandiose structures, the symbolic legitimization for which alternated between a celebration of their achievements and a focus on ancestral narratives. According to Peter Stachel, along with the nationalization of the masses, the forms of political representation fundamentally changed in Europe.[15] The public sphere became a stage for aspiring national identities, a controversial and contested battleground for various political programmes and claims to occupation.[16] This is especially true in twentieth-century Eastern Europe with its heterogeneous population and repeated political ruptures. Here, where the public sphere has been characterized by multiple codings and numerous occupations of space, it is warranted to inquire into the varied attributions of meaning and their integrative potential as well as the long-term evolution of the theatre of statehood.

In this context, it is hard to underestimate the importance of the state as an agent of integration. The state imposes patterns of meaning which draw on existing narratives or represent aesthetic constructs, and which ultimately develop their own hegemonic integrative force. Various media are suitable for conveying this, beginning with the classic symbols of the state such as emblems, flags, coins and anthems.[17] The breadth and scope of the state is made tangible by means of bureaucracy, two experiential examples of which are the birth certificate and tax certificate. Recognition is achieved through the use of signs and symbols whereby the state lends power and legitimacy to various objects, making them identifiable as institutions.[18] According to Michael Herzfeld, premodern metaphors such as 'blood', 'kin', 'birth' and 'fate' have managed to enter the symbolic repertoire of nation states and ensured their livelihood.[19] How does their adoption and adaptation in the modern states' language of signs work? What other symbols have established themselves as nation-unifying symbols in the states of Eastern Europe?

One way the state is visible is through its architecture; both larger administrative buildings and small-scale infrastructure can be symbolically charged. Various types of constructions

---

14 Barbara Stollberg-Rilinger has impressively demonstrated this in her work. See, e.g. 'Rituals of Decision-making? Early Modern European Assemblies of Estates as Acts of Symbolic Communication', in *Political Order and the Forms of Communication in Medieval and Early Modern Europe*, ed.Yoshihisa Hattori (Rome:Viella, 2014), 63–95; idem, '"Parlamentarische Kultur" und "Symbolische Kommunikation:" Grundsätzliche kommentierende Überlegungen', in *Parlamentarische Kulturen in Europa – Das Parlament als Kommunikationsraum*, eds Andreas Schulz and Andreas Wirsching (Düsseldorf: Droste, 2012), 91–102.

15 Peter Stachel, 'Stadtpläne als politische Zeichensysteme: Symbolische Einschreibungen in den öffentlichen Raum', in *Die Besetzung des öffentlichen Raumes: Politische Plätze, Denkmäler und Straßennamen im europäischen Vergleich*, eds Rudolf Jaworski and Peter Stachel (Berlin: Frank&Timme, 2007), 20–21.

16 Stachel, 'Stadtpläne als politische Zeichensysteme', 21.

17 Jürgen Hartmann, 'Selbstdarstellung der Bundesrepublik Deutschland in Symbolen, Zeremoniell und Feier', in *Staatsrepräsentation*, eds Jörg-Dieter Gauger and Justin Stagl (Berlin: Reimer, 1992), 178–86. See also Bredekamp's deliberations on national emblems, Horst Bredekamp, *Theorie des Bildakts* (Berlin: Suhrkamp, 2010), 192–3.

18 In the context of absolutist rule, see Albrecht Koschorke, 'Macht und Fiktion', in *Des Kaisers neue Kleider: Über das Imaginäre politischer Herrschaft, Texte – Bilder – Lektüren*, eds Thomas Frank, Albrecht Koschorke, Susanne Lüdemann and Ethel Matala de Mazza (Frankfurt a.M.: Fischer, 2002), 77–81. Or more fundamentally, Bourdieu, *Über den Staat*, 24–31.

19 Michael Herzfeld, *The Social Production of Indifference* (Chicago, IL: The University of Chicago Press, 1992), 26–44.

Projections and representations of statehood

help structure social space.[20] But architecture is more than just a symbolic shell tasked with providing an inexhaustible reservoir of attributions and meanings. Just as the identity of objects is produced socially and culturally and is context-dependent, architecture can only be gauged when its socially constitutive function is taken into consideration.[21] It 'shapes' political spaces, lends them political effectiveness and becomes the site of political communication.[22] If we follow Thomas Mergel in his understanding of Niklas Luhmann, and define politics as a mode of communication whose codes are aimed at creating collectively binding decisions,[23] the question arises as to the communicative process and function of these codes for erecting, stabilizing and dissolving social orders.

Political rule requires cultural justifications. In this context, the indeterminacy of symbolic communication enables the emergence of parallel attributions of meaning and the synthesis of contradictory narratives into something new. The imperfect determinacy of symbols proves to be an advantage, as symbolic communication keeps interpretive spaces open and their reading depends on which cultural semantics are activated.[24] The protagonists in this process always endeavour to minimize the complexity and ambiguity of symbols and assert a hegemonic interpretation.[25]

Only through culturally conditioned attributions of meaning are institutions institutionalized, i.e. perceived as social bodies. The widespread premodern notion of the 'two bodies of the king, the corporal mortal one and the eternal political one'[26] has remained widely influential to this day, manifesting itself in myriad ways, a fact which has been shown by a number of studies.[27]

In Eastern Europe, too, the fiction of the state as a social body accompanied the process of institution-building as a powerful metaphor, though not without irritation and conflict. After all, the nineteenth and twentieth centuries in this region were characterized by great territorial shifts and cultural transfers. Political rulers faced the ever-new challenge of organizing and legitimizing their rule in light of manifold cultural differences. Regarding their self-representation in particular, they often referred to patriarchal and monarchic forms of presentation from the premodern era which had weathered institutional change and political ruptures. The main focus of the current chapter is to investigate the continuity and discontinuity of these forms of representation and symbolic inscriptions, with a view to their functions as well. The emphasis is on their integrative and

---

20 On the concept of space, see Doris Bachmann-Medick, *Cultural Turns: Neuorientierungen in den Kulturwissenschaften* (Reinbeck: Rowohlt Verlag, 2006), 284–328.

21 On the various functions of architecture, see Heike Delitz, 'Gesellschaften der Städte und Gesellschaften der Zelte: Zur politischen Effektivität der Architektur', in *Politische Raumtypen: Zur Wirkungsmacht öffentlicher Bau- und Stadtstrukturen im 20. Jahrhundert*, ed. Ernst Seidl (Göttingen: Vandenhoeck & Ruprecht, 2009), 21.

22 Bredekamp's argument follows Alfred North Whitehead, assuming that images 'not only contain [communities] but create aims by dint of their politically revelatory character [*Vorscheincharakter*] for the sake of which they are negotiated'. Bredekamp, *Theorie des Bildakts*, 196.

23 Thomas Mergel, 'Überlegungen zu einer Kulturgeschichte der Politik', *Geschichte und Gesellschaft* 28 (2002): 587.

24 The category of indeterminacy plays a key role in the cultural semantics of Yuri Lotman, see Susi Frank, introduction to *Explosion und Peripherie: Jurij Lotmans Semiotik der kulturellen Dynamik revisited*, eds Susi Frank, Cornelia Ruhe and Alexander Schmitz (Bielefeld: transcript 2012), 8; For theoretical approaches to cultural studies, see Albrecht Koschorke, *Wahrheit und Erfindung: Grundzüge einer Allgemeinen Erzähltheorie* (Frankfurt a.M.: Fischer, 2012).

25 I am grateful to Malte Rolf for pointing this out to me.

26 Manow, *Im Schatten des Königs*, 8.

27 See Manow, *Im Schatten des Königs*; Frank et al., *Des Kaisers neue Kleider*; Albrecht Koschorke, Thomas Frank, Ethel Matala de Mazza and Susanne Lüdemann, *Der fiktive Staat: Konstruktionen des politischen Körpers in der Geschichte Europas* (Frankfurt a.M.: Fischer, 2007); Skinner, *Die drei Körper des Staates*.

system-stabilizing capacities. Ultimately, the state legitimizes its hegemonic order by enforcing it. We will also consider how the components of hegemonic semantics are dissolved and regrouped in the respective society and which counter-reactions they give rise to.

The seat of parliament, like no other building, expresses the builder's claim to and comprehension of parliamentarianism. And, like no other building, it specifically symbolizes the parliamentary form of government. The first modern parliaments of constitutional monarchies were built under conditions of 'competing claims to sovereignty by the monarch and the representative body of the people',[28] whereas with the democratization of the political system, an understanding of parliament gradually emerged that viewed it as the representative body of the people, expressing the sovereignty of the people, and not that of a ruler. Questions arise as to which 'architectonic visual schema'[29] underlie modern parliaments and how they are symbolically charged against the backdrop of legitimized constraints in the effort to distance themselves from previous regimes. What is important here is not only the self-symbolizing and self-enactment of parliaments but also the malfunctioning of legitimization and the establishment of counter-narratives.

According to Claude Rivière, state power follows specific aims in its self-representation: the legitimization of a transition of power, emphasizing power hierarchies and the inculcation of civic values.[30] Civic values produce shared feelings by 'regulating society through the repetition of an essential, fundamental event ... communicating security, the mobilization of participants.'[31]

In discussing the projections and representations of state and statehood in Eastern Europe, the primary focus is on the communicative and performative dimensions of the political. It is therefore not just about how various political systems have tried by means of their self-representation to pursue concrete symbolic policies, but also about the compatibility of cultural influences, the shaping of communication between state and society, and the question of what effects state self-representation has had on the integration and stabilization of a given society.

The architecture of statehood: on styles and places

Empires

Most of the Central, Eastern and Southeastern European states were not on the map of Europe at the turn of the twentieth century. Political power was focused in the imperial centres of Vienna, Berlin, Moscow and Istanbul, and the notion of statehood was strongly influenced by imperial structures.

Visitors to the World's Fair in Paris in 1900 could walk along the *Quai des Nations* and see all of Europe lined up in a row of pavilions.[32] Contemporary critics may have been sceptical – if not despairing – of the architectonic value of these structures, but the pavilions were nonetheless an interesting instance of self-representation, some of the builders having taken out horrendous

---

28 Andreas Biefang, 'Die Neuformierung der parlamentarischen Bilderwelt um 1800', in *Parlamentarische Kulturen vom Mittelalter bis in die Moderne: Reden – Räume – Bilder*, eds Jörg Feuchter and Johannes Helmrath (Düsseldorf: Droste, 2013), 142.

29 Philip Manow, 'Kuppel, Rostra, Sitzordnung: das architektonische Bilderprogramm moderner Parlamente', in *Parlamentarische Kulturen vom Mittelalter*, 115.

30 Claude Rivière, 'Politische Liturgien', in *Symbole und Rituale des Politischen: Ost- und Westeuropa im Vergleich*, eds Andreas Pribersky and Berthold Unfried (Frankfurt a.M.: P. Lang, 1999), 28.

31 Rivière, 'Politische Liturgien', 29.

32 Julius Meier-Greaffe, *Die Weltausstellung in Paris 1900* (Paris: Krüger, 1900), 41.

Projections and representations of statehood

loans to present their states in a positive light. The Habsburg monarchy erected three structures in strict accordance with the legal status of the monarchy's constituent states: an Austrian, a Hungarian and a Bosnian one, the latter sandwiched between the other two, just like in the day-to-day politics of the time. The Austrian one was built in the then ubiquitous Viennese Baroque style, whose design vocabulary was associated with the period of absolutism and hence symbolically charged. The Hungarian structure was markedly different from the Austrian one. It was an idiosyncratic composition of various architectural motifs, a mixture of fortress and church, and a testimony in stone to the greatness and otherness of Transleithania. The main tower was modelled after St. Catherine Church in Kremnica (in Slovakia), the three oriels were imitations

Figure 1.2 The Hungarian pavilion at the Universal Exhibition of 1900 in Paris
© akg-images

of the knights' hall of the Hunyad Castle (in Hunedoara, Romania), and the chapel was like-wise an allusion to both the Slovakian village Spišský Štvrtok and the Saint Michael Chapel in Košice. Parts of the façade were reminiscent of the Rákóczy House and the Klobusitzky Palace in Prešov, whereas the small tower was taken from the Serbian Chapel in Budapest.[33]

Viewed as a whole, the individual motifs were only discernible to experts; their symbolic effect could only be felt by a viewer who grasped the historical references. The numerous cata-logues published before and after the exhibition served as an aid to understanding the symbol-ism. As a new equal partner in the empire, Hungary emphasized its independence in the area of political symbolism as well, consciously choosing to stand out in its self-presentation.

What did this mean for the Habsburg monarchy, assuming that empires cannot afford to 'do without the symbolic visualization of imperial unity'[34] lest they threaten to disintegrate? What symbols did imperial statehood in Eastern Europe use to represent itself at the turn of the twentieth century, and how did the juxtaposition of hegemonic imperial state symbols with respective local ideas of statehood function in transnational systems of rule? In this regard, the focus in the following is on the question of dominant symbols of state and statehood, on the relationship between centre and periphery with continuously shifting power centres, as well as on the building and rebuilding of conceptual worlds.

Unlike formally defined state symbols like flags, emblems, seals and anthems or other nor-mative symbols, e.g. rules of ceremony, state architecture serves as a symbolic state metaphor.[35]

After the Compromise of 1867, Austria-Hungary was under pressure to legitimize itself and sought a new form of expression to symbolically emphasize the unity of its empire. In design-ing public buildings, architects resorted to what were perceived as 'genuine' Habsburg styles, reviving the 'Austrian' Baroque with its associations to Empress Maria Theresa and a vigor-ous state. This 'invention of tradition'[36] led to a situation where in a relatively short period of time numerous court and state structures were erected whose symbolic language visualized the 'authority' of the monarchy and the 'unity' of the state.[37] This architectural form of expression, referred to as 'Viennese Baroque', 'Neo-Baroque' or 'Maria Theresa style' henceforth signified the Habsburg monarchy. The buildings erected in this style marked its territory of rule and made it visible. Radiating from Vienna, the state erected seats for its institutions in Prague and Budapest, Zagreb and Brno, had theatres and museums built to carry out its cultural mission, and new barracks for its military. Empires always claim universality for their own culture.[38] It is not surprising that architects fanned out from Vienna, building uniform structures for the monarchy's royal and imperial administrative offices, regardless of which part of the Empire

---

33 Meier-Graeffe, *Die Weltausstellung*, 29.

34 Jürgen Osterhammel, 'Symbolpolitik und imperiale Integration: Das britische Empire im 19. Und 20. Jahrhundert', in *Die Wirklichkeit der Symbole: Grundlagen der Kommunikation in historischen und gegenwär-tigen Gesellschaften*, eds Rudolf Schlögl, Bernhard Giesen and Jürgen Osterhammel (Constance: UKP, 2004), 399.

35 Barbara Stollberg-Rilinger, '"Parlamentarische Kultur" und "Symbolische Kommunikation"', 94; Horst Bredekamp, 'Staat', in *Handbuch der politischen Ikonographie*, eds Uwe Fleckner, Martin Warnke and Hendrik Ziegler (München: Beck, 2011), 375.

36 Eric Hobsbawm, 'Introduction', *The Invention of Tradition*, eds Eric Hobsbawm and Terence Ranger (Cambridge: Cambridge University Press, 1983), 1.

37 Michaela Marek, 'Stil und Modi als symbolischer Politikdiskurs: Zur Architektur in der Habsburger-monarchie um 1900 aus kulturgeschichtlicher Perspektive', in *Die Wiener Hofburg und der Residenzbau in Mitteleuropa im 19. Jahrhundert: Monarchische Repräsentation zwischen Ideal und Wirklichkeit*, eds Werner Telesko, Richard Kurdiovsky and Andreas Nierhaus (Vienna: Böhlau, 2010), 178.

38 Osterhammel, 'Symbolpolitik und imperiale Integration', 398.

Projections and representations of statehood

they were located in. These architects succeeded in drawing from a wealth of historical forms to create a uniform expression for state institutions, oriented around the concepts of 'unity' and 'strength'. The focus of attention was tradition and history, as well as a unifying dynasty.

The monarchy and its monarchs played a special role in the symbolic presentation of statehood. Imperial rulers availed themselves of symbolic communication at various levels and for various reasons. The primary aim was always the preservation of the Empire by strengthening inner stability. Internal integration is more stable when state institutions are familiar.[39] The integrative effect of monarchy is not to be underestimated in this respect. The ruler, as head of state, was thought to embody and guarantee unity. But his symbolic representation underwent a transformation, challenged by the French Revolution, the republican United States of America and the idea of nationalism.[40]

Dynastic succession and the grace of God were no longer sufficient to uphold the fiction of the king as a symbol of political unity. Rulers adopted new motifs and created new networks of meaning. The Habsburg emperor Francis Joseph portrayed himself as a soldier of the state, or as its servant, working at his desk and directing the affairs of the empire.[41] Wherever his residences and monuments were located, where his busts and portraits were found, where people walked down streets named after him and paid with money bearing his countenance – in all of these places the head of state was a symbolic presence, projecting state power into the far reaches of the empire. His subjects were continually reminded of his presence and proximity even when he was not physically present. Rulers could assert integrative power in particular when they succeeded in linking themselves to local symbols and roles, or whenever local elites could be won over to the imperial project. Journeys to the provinces served to create a symbolic sense of community or revealed its limits, as in the case of Tsar Nicholas II's visit to Warsaw in 1897.[42]

The itinerary of this visit paid attention to every minute detail and attached great importance to staging the tsar's visit as a symbolic 'new beginning', in line with a new governing policy which focused on transforming Russian-Polish relations. Even though the organizers of this choreography planned numerous encounters between the young tsar and representatives of Polish society, so that elements of imperial 'grace and benevolence' were performed on the one hand and the 'love of loyalty of his subjects' on the other,[43] conflicts over the use of 'proper' symbols reinforced contradictions in the public perception of the tsar's visit and revealed different expectations about how Russian–Polish relations should be handled.

Only symbols that were undeniably 'Russian' were appropriate for representing statehood, and the symbols considered to be appropriate were Russian Orthodoxy, the Russian military and the Russian language. The Russian palace at the Paris World's Fair of 1900 was an

---

39 Bourdieu, *Über den Staat*, 78.

40 Andreas Biefang, 'Visualisierung des Parlamentarismus im 19. Jahrhundert: Ein Problemaufriss in europäischer Perspektive', in *Das Parlament als Kommunikationsraum*, eds Andreas Schulz and Andreas Wirsching (Düsseldorf: Droste, 2012), 358.

41 Ernst Bruckmüller, 'Die österreichische Revolution von 1848 und der Habsburgermythos des 19. Jahrhunderst: Nebst einigen Rand- und Fußnoten von und Hinweisen auf Franz Grillparzer', in *Bewegung im Reich der Immobilität: Revolutionen in der Habsburgermonarchie 1848–1849, Literarisch-publizistische Auseinandersetzungen*, eds Hubert Lengauer and Primus Heinz Kucher (Vienna: Böhlau, 2001), 23.

42 Malte Rolf, 'Der Zar an der Weichsel: Repräsentationen von Herrschaft und Imperium im fin de siècle', in *Imperiale Herrschaft in der Provinz: Repräsentationen politischer Macht im späten Zarenreich*, eds Jörg Baberowski, David Feest and Christoph Gumb (Frankfurt a.M.: Campus Verlag, 2008), 145–71.

43 Rolf, 'Der Zar an der Weichsel', 152.

Weltausstellung zu Paris: Die russisch-asiatische Ausstellung vor dem Trocadero.
Nach einer Photographie.

Figure 1.3 The Russian pavilion at the Universal Exhibition of 1900 in Paris
© akg-images

expression of this self-understanding. Architecturally modelled after the Moscow Kremlin, the pavilion combined elements of a fortress and an Orthodox church.[44] Built in a massive, uniform way, it symbolized greatness, unity and solidarity; the presence of a few, very small windows, strengthened this impression. This compacted monumentalism and outward uniformity – the pavilion covered a surface area of 6,000 square metres and the highest tower was 54 metres – was interrupted inside by a collection of ethnographic installations. Here, the architect permitted himself some references to the ethnic and cultural diversity of the Russian Empire, none of which was hinted at by the exterior. The structure seemed more like a bulwark or citadel, the embodiment of a uniform and unifying state policy. Its civilizational achievements in the East Asian reaches of the Empire were underscored by an official travel guide, citing Orthodoxy, Russian citizenship and the Russian state as the 'bearer of Christian-European culture'[45] in a single paragraph.

In this case, the Russian Empire – with an imperial self-understanding that asserted the superiority of its various civil institutions – was on a par with other European empires. While its self-representation shifted attention to the Asian parts of the Empire, its cultural claim was valid for the European periphery of Russia. The concept of amalgamating into a homogeneous state citizenry found its aesthetic expression in historicizing architecture and the so-called 'Russian' and 'neo-Russian' styles. From Tallinn and Warsaw all the way to Tashkent and even further east, numerous structures were erected in this style combining Byzantine and traditional Russian elements. Resorting to symbolic capital by structuring the public sphere can create a

---

44 Meier-Graefe, *Die Weltausstellung*, 39.
45 Dietmar Neutatz, *Träume und Alpträume: Eine Geschichte Russlands im 20. Jahrhundert* (München: Beck, 2013), 23.

Projections and representations of statehood

sense of trust and credibility, but it can also serve as a constant reminder of state authority and power.[46] Indeed, symbolic policies can have a cohesive effect, but they also harbour disintegrating forces and can have a destabilizing effect. The imperial self-representation of the Russian Empire, closely intertwined with tsarist representations of rule, reinforced the existing tensions and differences between the centre and the multinational periphery of the empire. It was an expression of Russian domination, reflected in particular in the conflicts over the construction of numerous Alexander Nevsky cathedrals on the western margins of the empire.[47] In a multi-denominational and multi-religious empire, these Orthodox churches symbolized the expansion of imperial power into the religious sphere, marking territorial conquest with no regard for local sensitivities. Religion thus became a symbol of military rule and state unity, paid homage to at key locations throughout the Empire.

The existence of alternative counter-semantics that developed in opposition to the hegemonic claims of the dominant centralized semantics allows us to describe interactions and interdependencies between the centre and the periphery. Conversely, it is also true that empires aim to adapt to local environments; they influence them and transform them from the locus of the periphery. Around the turn of the twentieth century, numerous architectonic styles were created in multi-ethnic regions, often by merging local motifs with classic styles, the results of which were interpreted as an expression of a specific national culture.[48] The invention of 'national styles' can be seen as an expression of artistic emancipation or as a rejection of the dominant style of the hegemonic power.

Unlike the Viennese Baroque with its clutter of 'German' symbols, Czech architects reinterpreted the Baroque by referencing French models, developing an alternative that was henceforth considered the Czech 'national style' and that emphasized their claims to cultural autonomy and political self-determination.[49] The construction of Czech styles – including the Czech Renaissance – must always be seen in the context of local German–Czech conflicts for supremacy in Bohemia, but also as a reaction to the symbolic policies of the centre. In the same way, the terms 'German style' and 'German Renaissance' stand for representative public buildings in regions of Bohemia with a German majority. The new town hall in the northern Bohemian city of Liberec (Reichenberg) is one example. On the one hand, it was meant to express the German-Bohemian contractor's cultural affinity with the German Empire and symbolically elevate the political claim to autonomy within the Habsburg monarchy.[50] On the other hand, it was a visible way of marking off supposed national territory. The strategies of national self-presentation were thus a symbolic demonstration of a conscious delimitation from a cultural as well as a political community.[51]

The conflict of nationalities in nineteenth-century multi-ethnic empires left myriad architectural traces. This architectural 'marking off' of supposed national territory was particularly

---

46 Jörg Baberowski, 'Vertrauen durch Anwesenheit: Vormoderne Herrschaft im späten Zarenreich', in *Imperiale Herrschaft in der Provinz: Repräsentationen politischer Macht im späten Zarenreich*, eds Jörg Baberowski, David Feest and Christoph Gumb (Frankfurt a.M.: Campus Verlag, 2008), 19.

47 Malte Rolf, 'Russische Herrschaft in Warschau: Die Aleksandr-Nevskij-Kathedrale im Konfliktraum politischer Kommunikation', in *Jenseits der Zarenmacht: Dimensionen des Politischen im Russischen Reich 1800–1917*, ed. Walter Sperling (Frankfurt a.M.: Campus, 2008), 173.

48 Marek, 'Stil und Modi', 171.

49 Marek, 'Stil und Modi', 187–8.

50 Michaela Marek, *Kunst und Identitätspolitik: Architektur und Bildkünste im Prozess der tschechischen Nationsbildung* (Köln: Böhlau, 2004), 311–5.

51 Marek, 'Stil und Modi', 171.

striking in the province of Posen, where the Prussian government erected numerous grandiose Wilhelmine buildings, especially the Emperor's Palace in Poznań.[52] Inspired by medieval castles, Emperor Wilhelm II erected a monument to 'German-ness' and the 'irrevocable bond between the province of Posen with the Prussian state and the German Empire'[53] which the Polish population couldn't fail to notice. The architect Franz Schwechten designed it as a gigantic, compact, fortress-like building in neo-Renaissance style that towered over every other structure around it. The palace henceforth dominated the cityscape and was a clear demonstration of power and an unmistakable symbol of the German claim to rule in Posen.

This imperial-national building policy was pursued quite offensively in Hungary, where a range of public buildings were erected in Hungarian national style – a mixture of Gothic, Indian and Oriental elements with the ornamentation of Hungarian folk art.[54] Hungarian building policy also had various symbolic levels. It was oriented towards Vienna and was also visibly distinct from the Cisleithanian half of the empire. But it was also oriented inward, towards its national minorities. The permeation of the multi-ethnic periphery with public buildings in the Hungarian style made it clear that Budapest defined the common state, namely, as a Hungarian one.

Compared with Subotica (Szabadka) or Timişoara (Temesvar), there was no question of Budapest's exceptional position, with the added importance of its position as the Hungarian royal seat and political capital. After the Compromise of 1867, the gain in political power vis-à-vis Vienna was visible in its urban landscape. In just a matter of years, Budapest transformed itself into a modern metropolis, quadrupled its population, massively expanded its infrastructure, and clearly staged itself in a number of symbolic acts and institutional structures as an equal centre of power. Two large-scale building projects from the period reflect this struggle for dominance and the symbolic occupation of space: the expansion of the Buda Castle (Budavári Palota) and the construction of a new parliament building. The Hungarian Parliament, completed in 1902, is an oft-cited example of parliamentary symbolism that works at various levels. Built in Gothic Revival style on the banks of the Danube, it is reminiscent of the Palace of Westminster in London. It stands directly opposite the castle, the imperial residence, which was expanded at the same time, strengthening their mutual references and intentional contrasts. The Viennese Baroque of the Royal Palace stands out in bold relief to the neo-Gothic eclectic style of Parliament, which initially sparked a backlash. The National Committee had given the architects free reign in terms of style, but did specify Gothic, Renaissance and Baroque as possible styles.[55] There was a heated debate in parliament about the use of Gothic elements on account of their 'German origins', and the press demanded that the architects employ a 'tried-and-tested' Renaissance style, but ultimately the deputies approved the government's decision through a roll-call vote and cleared the way for construction using the design of Imre Steindl.[56]

---

52 Heinrich Schwendemann and Wolfgang Dietsche, *Hitlers Schloss: Die 'Füherresidenz' in Posen* (Berlin: Ch. Links Verlag, 2003), 38.

53 Schwendemann and Dietsche, *Hitlers Schloss*, 39.

54 Ilona Sármány-Parsons, 'Rathausbauten in Ungarn um die Jahrhundertwende', in *Bürgerliche Selbstdarstellung: Städtebau, Architektur, Denkmäler*, eds Hanns Haas and Hannes Stekl (Vienna: Böhlau, 1995), 106.

55 József Sisa, '"Das Vaterland hat bereits sein Haus": Das ungarische Parlament in Budapest', in *Parlamentarische Repräsentationen: Das Bundeshaus in Bern im Kontext internationaler Parlamentsbauten und nationaler Strategien*, eds Anna Minta and Bernd Nivolai (Bern: Peter Lang, 2014), 169.

56 Alice Horváth, 'Entwürfe Imre Steindls zu dem ersten Architekturwettbewerb 1872 für das Gebäude des Berliner Reichstags', *Periodica Polytechnica Architecture* 32 (1988): 42.

Like Josip Vancaš, Steindl had also studied in Vienna under the famed architect of the New Town Hall, Friedrich von Schmidt, who established the Gothic Revival style there. The master must have been pleased with his pupil, because his neo-Gothic design was enormous. With 33,210 square metres of building space, the planned parliament building was much larger than any other of its day, including the Imperial Council Building in Vienna.[57] The building project was an infrastructural challenge. Hundreds of people worked day and night despite flooding from the Danube. Yet, the tight schedule had to be maintained since the building was supposed to be done before the millennium exhibition – the one-thousand-year celebration of the Hungarian conquest. They were only partly successful despite a doubling of construction costs, for only in 1902 did the government move into the building.[58]

At that time, the dome was a frequently used symbol taken from sacred architecture. Revolutionary French architects used this architectural device in order to lend their earthly order 'a cosmic authentication'.[59] The most influential instance, however, of the 'migration

Figure 1.4 Town hall of Szabadka/Subotica
© Arhiv Jugoslavije

---

57 [s.n.], 'Das neue Parlamentsgebäude in Budapest', *Schweizerische Bauzeitung* 33/34 (1899): 2.
58 Sisa, 'Das Vaterland', 174.
59 Manow, 'Kuppel, Rostra, Sitzordnung', 116.

Figure 1.5 Hungarian Parliament Building
© APA Austrian Presse Agentur

of this most prominent architectural formula of grandeur'[60] from a religious motif to its use in profane representative structures was the construction of the dome of the United States Capitol building. Numerous American states followed this example, and in Europe, too, the fashion prevailed in new parliament buildings from Bern to Berlin, including Budapest. The dome in Budapest was indeed enormous. Steindl himself saw in it a symbol of the crown, holding together the largely identical, and hence equal chambers, of a bicameral parliament.[61] However, the motif could have been interpreted differently, as a crowning of the parliament building.[62] With a height of 96 metres, the dome symbolically references the year AD 896. Its shape and the explicit height stood for the unity of the nation, referring to a long tradition of Hungarian statehood. Its iconographic programme was totally subordinate to the national idea, even if the 90 figures from Hungarian history adorning the external façade were barely recognizable. The statues inside the building were more important. In contemporary parliaments, glass domes emphasize the new legitimate centre of political power: the parliamentary

---

60 Wolfgang Sonne, 'Der lange Atem der Monarchie: Residenzbauten im Zeitalter der Metropolen', in *Die Wiener Hofburg und der Residenzbau in Mitteleuropa im 19. Jahrhundert: Monarchische Repräsentation zwischen Ideal und Wirklichkeit*, eds Werner Telesko, Richard Kurdiovsky and Andreas Nierhaus (Vienna: Böhlau, 2009), 20.
61 Horváth, 'Entwürfe Imre Steindls', 43.
62 Manow, 'Kuppel, Rostra, Sitzordnung', 121.

Projections and representations of statehood

Figure 1.6 Buda Castle
© APA Austria Presse Agentur

assembly hall.[63] Steindl's dome, however, was made of stone, and beneath it in the domed hall, stood the thousand-year-old history of Hungarian statehood, likewise made of stone – a national pantheon with a full statue gallery of Hungarian monarchs. On 6 June 1896, in honour of the first formal session of both houses of parliament, the ultimate historical relic of Hungary, the Holy Crown and the coronation insignia, were carried into Parliament.[64]

With its compact and polysemantic symbolism, the Hungarian Parliament referenced different narratives and evoked a variety of ideas. If some considered Gothic a 'German style', others associated the building with the Palace of Westminster in Britain, the cradle of modern parliamentarianism. It was also possible to construe it as a demonstration of Hungarian nationalism, liberalism and conservatism. The power of the symbolic unfolds at this level of sensory perception precisely because it reinforces value convictions, despite its ambiguity. Even the policy of employing only Hungarian artists, Hungarian master builders and Hungarian contractors, as well as the strict use of Hungarian building materials,[65] suggested unity and clarity where before there was none. The combined use of building materials taken from various regions is a commonly used method for the 'political representation of belonging'.[66] In this manner, the parliament became a national monument. Yet another symbolic reference to monarchy was the fact that Emperor Francis Joseph had ridden on horseback over Coronation Hill – an artificial mound containing earth from every Hungarian county – to be crowned as the King of Hungary.[67]

---

63 Ibid., 121.
64 Sisa, 'Das Vaterland', 174.
65 Sisa, 'Das Vaterland', 183.
66 Monika Wagner, 'Material, politisches', in *Handbuch der politischen Ikonographie*, eds Uwe Fleckner, Martin Warnke and Hendrik Ziegler (München: Beck, 2011), 126.
67 Árpád Klimo, *Nation, Konfession, Geschichte: Zur nationalen Geschichtskultur Ungarns im europäischen Kontext (1860–1948)* (München: Oldenbourg, 2003), 115.

Sabina Ferhadbegović

A competition ensued between the parliament building and the Royal Palace over which would have the highest political representation in the future. Its symbolism not only demonstrated the Hungarian elite's opposition to the 'official' representative style of the Habsburgs, the Viennese Baroque; it was also a clear signal of political power against Austrian supremacy. Its sacred pomp, its monumentality, and its reference to monarchic forms of presentation emphasized a new Hungarian self-awareness while illustrating the claim to power of the Hungarian elites. The new parliament building was above all a symbol of Hungarian 'statehood' and the Hungarian 'nation'. Croatian writer Miroslav Krleža wrote that the 'decorative Budapest dome stood for a parliamentarianism that defied Europe until its very downfall, like a symbol of the blatant denial of all European democratic principles'.[68]

Located on the top of Buda Hill above the Danube, the Royal Palace had a symbolic advantage in terms of topography. Its dominant position in the urban landscape was a symbol of monarchic supremacy, radiating its 'immense absolutist power across the Danube city'.[69] The Royal Palace was three times bigger after its reconstruction, underlining its claims to representation. The palace architect, Miklós Ybl and his successor Alajos Hauszmann, oriented their planning towards the new parliament building and also towards another residence, the newest wings of the Vienna Hofburg.[70] The aim was to demonstrate dynastic power in the Hungarian part of the empire on the one hand, and the equality of both royal capitals on the other. The adoption of the dome motif can be interpreted as a symbolic reference to the parliament building. But here too, varied attributions of meaning are possible. The tip of the palace dome was graced by a replica of the Crown of Saint Stephan,[71] interpretable as a demonstration to the Hungarian elites of the power-political significance of the royal capital. Moreover, the Crown of Saint Stephan was stored in the Royal Palace, marking it as the legitimate centre of political power. This crowning of the Royal Palace was rejected at first in Vienna, since it was possible to interpret the act as the subordination of the monarchic symbol of power to the symbol of Hungarian statehood.

This tension between meaning-creating symbolic presentation and the legitimization of rule is characteristic of the relationship between modern parliament buildings and monarchic or presidential seats. Mutual referencing or even the adoption of symbolic capital was commonplace and the 'parasitic participation in the king's claims to sacrality'[72] was a commonly used motif in parliament architecture. What's more, the frequent use of existing buildings was not only an adoption of monarchic property, since the history and symbolism of these structures continued to have an impact despite their repurposing.

Nations

Encouraged by the First World War and the subsequent revolutionary upheavals, nationalist counter-symbols gained ascendancy over imperial ones. This creeping antagonism led symbolically to a visible fracture, like in the Second Polish Republic when as of 1921, the new Polish

---

68 Miroslav Krleža, 'Stjepan Radić u Beogradu' [Stjepan Radić in Belgrade], in *Deset krvavih godina i drugi politički eseji* (Sarajevo: Svjetlost, 1990), 228.

69 Sonne, 'Der lange Atem', 28.

70 Peter Farbaky, 'Analogie und Antithese: Die Erweiterung des Budapester Königspalastes nach dem österreichisch-ungarischen Ausgleich von 1867', in *Die Wiener Hofburg und der Residenzbau in Mitteleuropa im 19. Jahrhundert: Monarchische Repräsentation zwischen Ideal und Wirklichkeit*, eds Werner Telesko, Richard Kurdiovsky and Andreas Nierhaus (Vienna: Böhlau, 2010).

71 Ibid., 246–7.

72 Manow, 'Kuppel, Rostra, Sitzordnung', 117.

Projections and representations of statehood

government began tearing down Alexander Nevsky cathedrals.[73] In newly founded nation states, new political centres were formed, which in turn became new loci of dominant semiotic systems. Which state symbols accompanied the process of nation state-building and the democratization of the interwar period? According to Bourdieu's structuralism, the formation of modern states, in particular, is accompanied by the development of categories of political thinking, and those meanings that are imprinted through habit and which everyone uses unconsciously, resulting in a state that remains as an 'unthought'.[74] Imagination and performativity are an integral part of the process of founding the state, and occurred in Eastern Europe under the banner of 'continuity, birth and new beginning', but the spirit of optimism and enthusiasm of the post-war period fizzled out quickly under the pressures of enormous social and national problems besetting such young states. The officially designated state symbols, flags and emblems triggered discussions in multi-religious and multi-ethnic states about the national hegemony of the majority nation and were only suitable to a limited extent as facilitators of cohesion. Modernity, with its new design vocabulary, would have been one way of emphasizing the symbolic difference between empires and the new, democratically legitimized constitutional states, and yet during the interwar period the first styles to predominate were defined as expressions of the respective nationality. In Poland, it was neoclassicism with its particular connotations of the Poniatowski era.[75] A popular architectonic element when it came to giving buildings a uniquely Polish face was the use of a Renaissance attic. Overall, the dominant style in interwar Poland was the national-romantic style, or *Styl swojski i dworkowy*, in which architects blended elements of modern architecture with motifs from folk art.[76] Further, when restoring and rebuilding ruined buildings – the First World War having left behind massive structural damage – local builders followed the 'native' style.[77] 'Reconstruction' was the catchword, and it referred not only to Polish statehood. The Polish cities being rebuilt were supposed to conform to notions of traditional Polish architecture. The use of historical motifs gave rise to new compositions whose established and well-known design vocabulary suggested authenticity and familiarity as well as cultural unity. Like the other national styles of the period, *Styl swojski i dworkowy* was a heterogeneous construct that only became 'Polish' by dint of its contextualization. It expressed the patriotism and pathos of this era and suggested the permanence and dependability of the old in a new context.

More often than erecting new structures, the new states made use of existing buildings, relocating new ministries and institutions into the buildings of their predecessors. New plaques were put up, old emblems chiselled away and new flags hoisted. The most prominent example of adapting inherited buildings was the use of the former royal seat in Prague by the new republican government. With the founding of the state of Czechoslovakia, President Tomáš Masaryk

---

73 Wlodzimierz Borodziej, *Geschichte Polens im 20. Jahrhundert* (München: Beck, 2010), 154.

74 Bourdieu, *Über den Staat*, 195–6.

75 Beate Störtkuhl, 'Gdynia: Meeresmetropole der Zweiten Polnischen Republik', in *Neue Staaten – neue Bilder? Visuelle Kultur im Dienst staatlicher Selbstdarstellung in Zentral- und Osteuropa seit 1918*, eds Arnold Bartetzky, Marina Dmitrieva and Stefan Troebst (Köln: Böhlau, 2005), 39.

76 Małgorzata Omilanowska, 'Searching for a National Style in Polish Architecture at the End of the 19th and Beginning of the 20th Century', in *Art and the National Dream: The Search for Vernacular Expression in Turn-of-the-Century Design*, ed. Nicola Gordon Bowe (Blackrock: Irish Academic Press, 1993), 111.

77 Małgorzata Omilanowska, '"Wie der märchenhafte Phönix aus der Asche werden sie auferstehen": Haltungen zum Wiederaufbau und zur Restaurierung von Baudenkmälern in Polen in den Jahren 1915–1925', in *Der Umgang mit dem kulturellen Erbe in Deutschland und Polen im 20. Jahrhundert*, ed. Andrea Langer (Warsaw: 2004), 88.

moved the presidential seat to Hradčany Castle, defining it as a historical monument representing independence and national sovereignty.[78] The state appropriation of the castle complex was likewise a demonstration of historical continuities and a new beginning, with historical preservation being focused on the medieval Royal Palace, where a crypt for the Bohemian kings was installed.[79] At the same time, the new president wanted the monarchic symbol to be artistically transformed so as to embody the 'symbolic idea of sovereignty and democracy'.[80] Slovenian architect Jože Plečnik, a Viennese pupil of Otto Wagner, opened up the castle towards the city, created new passageways, referenced classical models in his design vocabulary, paved the third castle yard with slabs of granite from various quarries throughout the republic, used Moravian firs for flagpoles, and originally planned to close the main entranceway, the Matthias Gate, and replace its imperial emblem with the Czechoslovak coat of arms. The latter would have been a more visible break with the previous system. Though not able to fully realize his plans, the measures eventually taken were sufficient to stylize the castle and new presidential seat as a symbol of the new republic and democracy. By linking the guiding principles of 'new beginning', 'opening' and 'democracy', he created numerous associations which in turn left many interpretive possibilities open.

The imperial emblem stayed in place, unlike in other regions of Eastern Europe, where new rulers resorted to radical solutions to obliterate the traces of their predecessors after attaining national independence. Whether in Belgrade, Sofia or Bucharest, entire neighbourhoods, along with their inhabitants, disappeared with the withdrawal of the Ottomans. The aim here was 'de-Orientalization',[81] the destruction of the old, with its associations of backwardness, in order to make room for the new. New structures were erected following the model of Central European cities, in a style based on traditional elements. One visitor to the Paris World's Fair of 1900 compared this style to a fantasy costume, remarking that 'It's as if it had found no time to clothe itself in a European uniform.'[82] Byzantine elements and Oriental ornamentation were reserved for sacred architecture. State institutions appeared in a classicist guise associated throughout Europe with concepts like dignity and authority. (Re)integration in the European system of norms needed to be visible in the public sphere.

Yugoslavia is a good example of the challenges and contradictions that accompanied this process. Emerging after the First World War and composed of states with different legal, political, religious and cultural traditions, from the very beginning it sought an aesthetic expression of shared statehood.

When Croatian writer Miroslav Krleža visited the former Serbian capital Belgrade in 1925, the Kingdom of Serbs, Croats and Slovenes had already existed for seven years. The Serbian

---

78 Jörg Stabenow, 'Eine kaiserliche Residenz als republikanisches Staatssymbol: der Hradschin in Prag', in *Die Wiener Hofburg und der Residenzbau in Mitteleuropa im 19. Jahrhundert: Monarchische Repräsentation zwischen Ideal und Wirklichkeit*, eds Werner Telesko, Richard Kurdiovsky and Andreas Nierhaus (Vienna: Böhlau, 2010), 206.

79 Stabenow, 'Eine kaiserliche Residenz', 207.

80 Arnold Bartetzky, 'Václav Havel und Tomáš G. Masaryk: Präsidentielle Kunstpatronage und visuelle Staatsrepräsentation auf der Prager Burg', in *Nation – Staat – Stadt: Architektur, Denkmalpflege und visuelle Geschichtskultur vom 19. bis zum 21. Jahrhundert* (Köln: Böhlau, 2012), 123.

81 Wolfgang Höpken, 'Schrittmacher der Moderne? Urbanisierung und städtische Lebensweise in den Metropolen Südosteuropas im 19. Und frühen 20. Jahrhundert', in *Die europäische Stadt im 20: Jahrhundert: Wahrnehmung – Entwicklung – Erosion*, eds Friedrich Lenger and Klaus Tenfelde (Köln: Böhlau, 2006), 73.

82 Georg Malkowsky, *Die Pariser Weltausstellung in Wort und Bild* (Berlin: Kirchhoff & Co, 1900), 30.

Projections and representations of statehood

Karađorđević dynasty shared power with the central parliament of the then united nation-state. Fierce disputes over its territorial and legal orientation, and generally diametrically opposed ideas of statehood from Serbian, Croatian and Slovenian political elites, combined with unresolved social problems, destabilized the country in a lasting way from the moment of its founding.[83] In particular, the vigorous opposition of the Croatian Agrarian Party to the concept of a triple-named Serbian-Croatian-Slovenian nation and to its monarchic, centralist form of government had a disintegrative effect, continually questioning the legitimacy of the common state. Only in the year of Krleža's visit to Belgrade did the party and its leadership accept the constitution proclaimed in 1921 and the institutions of the state, thus exercising their parliamentary mandates. Representatives met in the former cavalry barracks of Serbian prince Miloš Obrenović. Krleža recorded his impression of the converted parliamentary building in his essay 'Stjepan Radić in Belgrade':

> One should visit the Belgrade parliament with his head bowed ... this manège of the cavalry of Prince Miloš, this riding hall of the Obrenovićs where everything still reeks of horses and sawdust ... one should visit these barracks and witness the necromancy of deceased salon-coat and jacket wearers ... to reach most intensely the lowest point of one's own existence. ... The grey and filthy corridors of the Belgrade parliament are spat upon like the waiting room of a provincial train station, and remind one with their sooty iron stoves of a remote provincial tavern. ... Up front a smoky provincial tavern where the slivovitz is warmed up, in the back an old-fashioned waxworks – in this manège resound the cries of crazed grandpas, who act like proper pyromaniacs, hoping that once again the roof will burn over our heads.[84]

Though the leftist Krleža may have been partial in his views, he nonetheless addressed an important point. The public representation of parliamentarianism corresponded with the way in which it was perceived. Newspaper reports often described parliament as an 'open market stall' and parliamentarians as 'unqualified protégées', while denouncing corruption and other abuses.[85] Regular brawls and ferocious insults were the order of the day.[86] Parliament, which the deputies of the ruling parties pathetically stylized as the High Temple of the Serbian-Croatian-Slovenian people while disparaging the opposition parties as a new 'prison of nations', was tantamount to a drama or circus. There was no 'dignity', 'unity' or 'authority' to speak of.

The unification of Southern Slav nations into a common state was accompanied by much pathos and exalted symbolism. Quite a few referred to parliament itself as the people's temple, creating high expectations. The parliament building described in such detail by Krleža may have only been provisional, yet as a provisional solution it served as a symbol of the Yugoslav state at a particular moment in history, a state in which the provisional had become the rule and where a considerable discrepancy existed between the actions of those involved and their symbolic

---

83 Sabina Ferhadbegović, *Prekäre Integration: Serbisches Staatsmodell und regionale Selbstverwaltung in Sarajevo und Zagreb 1918–1929* (München: Oldenbourg, 2008), 104.

84 Krleža, 'Stjepan Radić', 230–1.

85 See the numerous articles in Yugoslav papers such as *Pravda*, 10 August 1928, *Pravda*, 26 April 1928; *Vreme* 13 May 1925.

86 *Vreme* 23 March 1925; *Vreme* 1 March 1928; *Vreme* 10 July 1925; *Pravda* 17 December 1927; *Pravda* 28 April 1928.

representation. Symbolic communication and symbolic actions create or strengthen the 'mutual expectations of participants'.[87] Normally, symbols will work as long as their consensus-creating power corresponds with the norms and values they represent. They only begin to break down when symbolic acts are degraded to the point of becoming mere outward conventions that are convincing to no one and are no longer observed.[88] By exercising their mandates and swearing an oath to parliament, Croatian deputies belatedly legitimized the joint parliament. Moreover, by recognizing an institution they had hitherto shied away from, they set an important symbolic example of their will to constructively cooperate in forming the first Yugoslav state. Their participation in the work of parliament buoyed expectations, but the loss of confidence suffered by the parliament was a harsh blow indeed.

Modern democratic parliaments are not secret institutions operating behind closed doors. The public is always present in the form of an audience, and it is this very moment of division between the spectators on the one side and the members of parliament on the other side that often leads to assemblies being compared to the theatre.[89] Krleža, however, came up with another metaphor: the popular assembly as a veritable circus. The aptness of this interpretation is evident – considering the Yugoslav parliament met in a former riding hall – upon taking a closer look at the circumstances surrounding the erection of the new building.

Construction work started as early as 1907 – the building had originally been intended to house the Popular Assembly of the Kingdom of Serbia at the end of the nineteenth century.[90] The change of dynasty, the Balkan wars, the First World War and the repeated lack of funds resulted in a situation where only the first floor had been built by the time the Kingdom of Serbs, Croats and Slovenes was established. The first design in eclectic style – a mixture of neo-Renaissance and classicism – was submitted in 1892 by Viennese architect Konstantin Jovanović, a pupil of Gottfried Sempers. Jovanović had designed the Bulgarian parliament in a similar style some years before. For the structure in Belgrade he used Viennese models as his inspiration, bearing in mind that its planned location was across from the royal seat, whose architecture evinced neo-Renaissance and classicist styles.[91]

The obligatory dome was there, but there was no reference to the local medieval Byzantine style that some considered the Serbian 'national style'. Jovanović's design was never implemented, having been conceived for the unicameral system in existence at that time. A new constitution and the introduction of the bicameral system made changes necessary, which led to a break in the already volatile relationship between the Serbian state and its architect. A new competition was held which was won by Jovan Ilkić, whose proposal was rather similar to that of Jovanović. Jovan Ilkić was a leading architect of the Kingdom of Serbia. Born in Zemun, then still a part of Austria-Hungary, he studied in Vienna under Theophil Hansen and collaborated on the Vienna parliament building. The ground-breaking ceremony was conducted by King Peter I Karađorđević, close to the spot where the first Grand National Assembly convened in 1830 and where autonomy from the Ottoman Empire was proclaimed in a *hatt-ı şerif*

---

87 Barbara Stollberg-Rilinger and Tim Neu, 'Einleitung' to *Alles nur symbolisch? Erträge und Grenzen der Erforschung symbolischer Kommunikation*, eds Barbara Stollberg-Rilinger, Christina Brauner and Tim Neu (Köln: Böhlau 2013), 20.
88 Stollberg-Rilinger and Neu, 'Einleitung', 19.
89 Bierfang, 'Visualisierung', 359.
90 *Politika*, 19 October 1936.
91 Tanja Damljanovic Conley, 'The Backdrop of Serbian Statehoods: Morphing Faces of the National Assembly in Belgrade', *Nationalities Papers* 41 (2013): 68.

Figure 1.7   Old Palace, Belgrade
© Arhiv Jugoslavije

(supreme edict).[92] The Grand National Assembly thus symbolized 'the beginning' of the modern Serbian state. This second Serbian 'act of instituting'[93] – the first of which was the Kosovo myth – references the constitutive elements of Serbian statehood, the struggle for freedom, the dynasty and the national assembly as the representative of the Serbian people. The new parliament building was supposed to lend itself to this and internalize this symbolism. The fact that the new *Skupština* was to be built on the ruins of the destroyed *Batal* Mosque reinforced the significance of the chosen location. It was not only a demonstration of power but part of an agenda of de-Ottomanization that extended to all areas of social life.[94] Obliterating the traces of the Ottoman Empire in the urban landscape of Belgrade and other Serbian cities illustrated that the new decision-makers interpreted the Ottoman era and its legacy primarily as something foreign. Rather than integrating this 'foreignness' into the cultural history of the nation, they tried to remove it.

---

92 Tanja Damljanovic Conley, 'Belgrade', in *Capital Cities in the Aftermath of Empires: Planning in Central and Southeastern Europe*, eds Emily Gunzburger Makaš and Tanja Damljanovic Conley (London: Routledge, 2010), 50.
93 Albrecht Koschorke, 'Götterzeichen und Gründungsverbrechen: Die zwei Anfänge des Staates', *Neue Rundschau* 1 (2004): 2.
94 Aleksandar Ignjatović, 'Architecture, Urban Development and the Yugoslavization of Belgrade, 1918–1941', *Centropa* 9 (2009): 115.

Ilkić did not see the completion of his project. He died in 1917, in the *Nezsider* internment camp. His son Pavle was commissioned to complete the building project in the newly founded Kingdom of Serbs, Croats and Slovenes, in what would become the popular assembly of the triadic Serbian-Croat-Slovenian nation. But the resumption of construction work was delayed again and again, leading to all manner of speculation and interpretation, including the belief – much popularized in the media – that the building was somehow cursed. In 1927, an anonymous author in the Serbian newspaper *Pravda* wrote: 'The building ... attracts no attention. It has been completely forgotten, and people now walk past it as if it were a horse stable.'[95] At this point in time, the exterior was largely finished and the focus was on the building's interior. However, seventy sculptures still needed to be completed to adorn the outside of the parliament. There was a plan to place three sculptures by the Croatian artist Robert Frangeš above the entrance, thus representing the Serb, the Croat and the Slovene as a symbol of national unity.[96] The unity of this triple nation was the main subject of public debate in the interwar period: various political viewpoints argued about what the nation was supposed to be and how it could find expression in the architecture of statehood. According to Aleksandar Ignjatović, the idea of a primordial Yugoslavism dominated both the political discourse as well as the artistic imagination of this triple nation.[97] According to this theory, Serbs, Croats and Slovenes were an ethnic group with a common origin that developed differently under different historic, political and cultural conditions, as reflected in the cultural and religious differences between the different members of the group. The narrative of a unified Serbian-Croatian-Slovenian people was supposed to find its unmistakable visual expression at the location of this people's democratic assembly. But Frangeš' sculptures were a temporary design, cast in plaster and not chiselled in stone. They were eventually lost or destroyed when King Alexander Karađorđević introduced a dictatorship in 1929. The completion of the new *Skupština* had no priority from his point of view. It was out of the question now to adorn the entranceway with sculptures of Serbs, Croats and Slovenes as a symbol of Yugoslav national unity at a time when all national designations were forbidden. King Alexander did not believe in a triple nation but in a single Yugoslav nation. Indeed, rather than finishing the parliament building, he was much more eager to complete the new royal residence begun by his father, *Novi dvor*, as well as the construction of his own new residence, *Kraljevski dvor*, on the highest point in the city, Dedinjes Hill.

Alexander's residence was built between 1924 and 1929 and is a symbol, hewn in stone, of Serbia's turn away from Austria-Hungary. The neo-Renaissance style of the old residence was now a thing of the past; the king was given a representative structure in the style of primordial Yugoslavism, made of white marble from the Croatian island of Brač.[98] The architects Živojin Nikolić and Nikolaj Krasnov followed the aesthetic models favoured by the court and state, created especially by Russian architects, like Krasnov himself, for representative state buildings of the period.[99] The official policy of unifying and homogenizing the southern Slavic 'tribes' evinced

---

95 Anonymous, 'Četrdeset gipsanih kipova čekaju svoj dan' [Forty plaster sculptures waiting for their moment], *Pravda*, 4 November 1927, 5.

96 The article incorrectly refers to Josip Frangeš. Anonymous, 'Četrdeset gipsanih kipova', 5.

97 Aleksandar Ignjatović, 'Images of Nation Foreseen: Ivan Meštrović`s Vidovdan Temple and Primordial Yugoslavism', *Slavic Review* 73 (2014): 828–58.

98 Ignjatović, 'Architecture, Urban Development', 115.

99 Aleksandar Ignjatović, 'Razlika u funkciji sličnosti: arhitektura ruskih emigranata u Srbiji između dva svetska rata i konstrukcija srpskog nacionalnog identiteta' [Difference as likeness: The Russian émigré architects in interwar Serbia and the construction of Serbian national identity] *Tokovi istorije* 1 (2011): 63–75.

Figure 1.8 House of the National Assembly of Yugoslavia
© Arhiv Jugoslavije

strong parallels to the Russian imperial concept of melting Slavic tribes together into a constitutive nation under Russian leadership. In the case of Yugoslavia, the founding of the Kingdom of Serbs, Croats and Slovenes meant that Serbs living on former Habsburg territory were living in their own state for the very first time.[100] Thus, the state policy of unification intended to culturally assimilate the Serbian nation, which prior to 1918 had lived under various state, legal and cultural conditions. In this context, the monarchy set a visible example, with the Russian architects adapting the design vocabulary of imperial classicism and erecting monumental administrative

---

100 Holm Sundhaussen, *Geschichte Serbiens: 19.–21. Jahrhundert* (Vienna: Böhlau, 2007).

Figure 1.9 Royal Palace, Belgrade
© Arhiv Jugoslavije

buildings that served to consolidate the idea of monarchism and visualize the fiction of a Serbian culture and a homogeneous Serbian nation.[101] While the parliament building remained unused, the Kingdom of Serbs, Croats and Slovenes was busy erecting the ministries of Finance, Forestry, Mines, Agriculture and Water, the palace of the General Staff, and numerous other representative administrative buildings, along with hundreds of Orthodox churches, mostly in the Serbian-Byzantine style. A theatre was built too: like the popular assembly, the theatre was originally housed in another former riding hall. After partly burning down in 1927, it was reconstructed by Nikolaj Krasnov in 1929. The theatre company only played there for two years, however, until parliament took over the building in 1931 – parliament had to abandon their own building after some Croatian deputies were murdered on site during a parliamentary debate.[102]

With the assassination of King Alexander In 1934, public debate about the first joint parliament of the Yugoslav people centred more on bad karma than on the architectural importance of the building or the parliament's re-election.[103] The construction site was a symbol for the condition of Yugoslav parliamentarianism, which remained an unfinished project. It is little wonder that when the building was completed in 1936 it failed to establish itself as a political or

---

101 Ignjatović, 'Razlika u funkciji', 70.
102 Mark Biondich, *Stjepan Radić, The Croat Peasant Party, and the Politics of Mass Mobilization, 1904–1928* (Toronto: University of Toronto Press, 2000), 239.
103 Damljanovic Conley, 'The Backdrop of Serbian Statehoods', 70.

Projections and representations of statehood

a symbolic centre of power. When Belgrade citizens gathered for protests, it was in the centre of town at the square in front of the National Theatre, and not outside of parliament. Following the putsch of 27 March 1941, thousands poured into the city-centre and occupied the streets, yet the square outside parliament remained empty.

At his first big speech in liberated Belgrade on 27 March 1945, partisan leader Josip Broz Tito spoke with great symbolic importance from the balcony of the National Theatre, because that's where the people had gathered. The first military parades, too, took place as un-choreographed happenings in the city centre. This does not mean that communist leaders eschewed the symbolic power of parliament. On the second anniversary of the first constitutive session of the Second Yugoslav Republic on 29 November 1945, the temporary legislative assembly met there to announce the end of the kingdom and proclaim the new Yugoslav republic. From that point on, however, the parliament was reduced to a mere backdrop. At important events, agitprop members would set up a huge stage outside the building for Tito and other powerful figures in Yugoslavia. They were preceded by military parades, and the parliament building behind them suggested a link to the people – or perhaps it served to disguise the absence of an actual parliament. The official imagery of the regime followed different patterns: the new rulers attached import to imperial monumentality. Tito moved into the former prince's palace of the royal residence *Beli dvor*, the White Court, which remained the most important centre of power under the communists. It is hardly surprising that Slobodan Milošević, as the president of rump Yugoslavia in 1997, also chose *Beli dvor* as his official residence, driving there with his family in Tito's Mercedes during his inauguration on 23 July, under the watchful eye of the media.[104] The second aesthetic reference point, at least in the early years of socialist Yugoslavia, was the design vocabulary of Soviet architecture. The new state planned representative buildings in New Belgrade to be an expression of its ties to the Soviet Union, in particular the building of the Central Committee of the Communist Party, a smaller Yugoslav version of the Palace of the Soviets.[105]

Communism

Just as late nineteenth-century tsarist Russia was dotted with Alexander Nevsky cathedrals, the Soviet sphere of influence after the Second World War was marked by palaces in the Socialist Classicist style. The Palace of Culture in Warsaw, and the Largo ensemble in Sofia, are just two prominent examples of the historicizing and politicizing concept of architecture signifying power and supremacy. Quite a bit has been written about architecture as a reflection of the ideological competition between the two superpowers in the early phase of the Cold War.[106] Whereas architectural ideas in the West reproduced themselves in pluralist discourses, centralized building projects in the Eastern bloc were firmly rooted in ideological considerations. The aesthetic model here was the Palace of Soviets that was never built; a radical and utopian vision to transform Moscow into the ideal type of a socialist city.

---

104 Vladan Jovanović, 'Malterisanje nacije' [Plastering the nation], *Peščanik*, 30 September 2013, http://pescanik.net/malterisanje-nacije/ (accessed 12 July 2017).

105 Vladimir Kulić, 'National, Supranational, International: New Belgrade and the Symbolic Construction of a Socialist Capital', *Nationalities Papers* 41 (2013): 41.

106 Annabel Jane Wharton, *Building the Cold War: Hilton International Hotels and Modern Architecture* (Chicago, IL: Chicago University Press, 2004); Greg Castillo, *Cold War on the Home Front: The Soft Power of Mid-century Design* (Minneapolis, MN: University of Minnesota Press, 2010).

Figure 1.10 Palace of Soviets (Model), Moscow
© akg-images

In the immediate post-war period, it looked as if the interwar period would continue its previous course. The baseline conditions of reconstruction were just too varied to predict any future developments. While wartime destruction in Poland and eastern Slovakia was enormous, Bulgaria and Romania were not severely affected. In Czechoslovakia, and to a lesser extent in Hungary, modernist architecture was the predominant style; in Romania and Bulgaria it was neoclassicism. The first post-war buildings reflected this pluralism. Only after 1948 did Socialist Realism prevail as the dominant art form and a counter-model to the modernism decried as 'cosmopolitan' and 'imperialistic'. The formula was succinct: 'socialist in content, national in form.' What did the hegemonic position of the Soviet Union and the attendant process of Sovietization mean for the forms of presentation of state and statehood in Eastern Europe after

Projections and representations of statehood

1945? Thomas Bohn summarized the different characteristics of a 'socialist city', the origins of which can easily be traced back to the Moscow General Plan:

(a) designing urban spaces with no regard for property relations; (b) structuring the city by means of straight transport axes and prominent high-rises; (c) erecting monumental administrative and governmental buildings in the centre; (d) laying out public spaces with ceremonial character.[107]

The centre of the socialist city was empty, ready to take in huge masses of people for future demonstrations and assemblies. The main thoroughfares radiated towards this centre – or away from it, depending on your perspective – and symbolized the focal point, the heart of the capital and the centre of power. The architects of absolutism placed their ceremonial axes following the same principle and with the same goal in mind: demonstrating power, but also to create controlled spaces of communication with the citizens. According to Malte Rolf, the performance and exercise of power are mutually dependent.[108] The beginning of large-scale building projects was often marked by a break or discontinuity. Buildings spared by the Second World War were destroyed by workers making room for the new. In Aleksandr Medvedkin's 1938 film *The New Moscow*, a euphoric Bolshevik presses the symbolic button that destroys old Moscow. While the heroes of labour build a newer, more beautiful city in the Socialist Classicist style, with palaces for the workers who have ousted the kings, it seems as if the amazed onlookers can't really believe in this fairy tale. The rapid transformation of socialist cities disabused them.

It is not difficult to interpret Stalinist architecture as mere propaganda or as a 'dictatorial offense against good taste'.[109] But what did its 'imperial compatibility',[110] its oppressive monumentality, mean for the development of public space? What images and ideas guided the planners in their designs? In the general plan for reconstructing Moscow in 1935, it was St. Petersburg, the well-ordered, planned European city that served as a model for the new Moscow.[111] The destruction of the old, chaotic, 'Asian' Moscow and the creative act of its rebirth as a modern, enlightened and progressive city stood for the communist belief in the victory of the Enlightenment, the superiority of order and technology. It stood for the belief in the malleability of the New Man. These beliefs can be traced back to the urban planning concepts of utopian modernists who found their aesthetic expression in the work of Le Corbusier.[112] The belief in the triumph of modernity, which James C. Scott called 'high-modernist ideology',[113] was not an exclusively communist phenomenon. In the case of the Soviet Union, an authoritarian

---

107 Thomas Bohn, intoduction to *Von der 'europäischen Stadt' zur 'sozialistischen Stadt' und zurück? Urbane Transformationen im östlichen Europa des 20. Jahrhunderts* (München: Oldenbourg, 2009), 9.

108 Malte Rolf, *Soviet Mass Festivals, 1917–1991* (Pittsburgh, PA: University of Pittsburgh Press, 2013), 1.

109 Harald Bodenschatz and Christiane Post, introduction to *Städtebau im Schatten Stalins: Die internationale Suche nach der sozialistischen Stadt in der Sowjetunion 1929–1935* (Berlin: Verlagshaus Braun, 2004), 7.

110 Philip Manow, 'Demokratie und Architektur', *Merkur* 69, no. 3 (2015): 46.

111 Monica Rüthers, *Moskau bauen von Lenin bis Chruscev: Öffentliche Räume zwischen Utopie, Terror und Alltag* (Vienna: Böhlau, 2007), 88.

112 On the influence of Le Corbusier on the architecture of the Soviet Union, see Bodenschatz and Post, *Städtebau im Schatten Stalins*, 88–91.

113 James C. Scott, *Seeing Like a State: How Certain Schemes to Improve the Human Condition Have Failed* (New Haven, CT: Yale University Press, 1998), 3.

state forced the radical reconstruction of public space; its functional efficiency was beholden to political demands. The destruction of entire neighbourhoods and their reconstruction in the monumental style of classicism was intended as an internal and external demonstration of power, of Soviet capabilities and importance. At the same time, however, this recognition-seeking architecture seemed woefully out of place, like the forced attempt of a parvenu to gain social prestige, the status symbol of a political elite on a *mission civilisatrice*.

At first glance, patterns of demolition and reconstruction such as those in line with the aesthetic guidelines of Socialist Classicism can be found in almost every socialist capital after 1945. But in fact, they were limited to specific, clearly defined spaces and did not affect the entire city. A much more common strategy was to redefine the urban landscape by setting clear symbolic accents. In Prague and Warsaw, government authorities moved into the former palaces of nobility, neutralizing the capitalist-imperialist legacy of these buildings.[114] At the same time these old buildings lent legitimacy to new institutions, signalling as they did, the permanence and seriousness of the new rulers housed in them.

The new people's assemblies moved mostly into historical parliament buildings. A different kind of symbolic takeover took place in Prague, where the former commodity exchanges were transformed into the seat of the new Czechoslovak national assembly. In general, old buildings were retrofitted more often than new ones were built. The adaptation of pre-existing buildings enabled new attributions of meaning and created points of identification with the new state. Spectacular new constructions were reserved for other institutions, with the ruling communist parties erecting new headquarters for themselves as central symbols of their power. Whether the *Dom Partii* in Warsaw, the *Fehér Ház* (White House) of the Hungarian Workers' Party in Budapest or *Partien dom* in Sofia, these were where the actual centres of social and political power were located and not in the still-convening but largely meaningless parliaments. Instead, the street took over the function of legitimization. According to Anders Aman, the regime used regular mass gatherings, state celebrations and parades as a source of ceremonial recognition.[115] As different as the new party headquarters may have been in their external form, they did have one thing in common. Built of marble or granite and with no visible entrances, they gave the outward impression of being sealed-off, inaccessible bulwarks, thus symbolizing the fundamentally undemocratic nature of the communist system. In his novel *The Palace of Dreams*, referring to the massive building of the Albanian Central Committee, Ismael Kadare described this feared and mysterious authority as the centre of a state that could even classify and examine the dreams of its citizens:

> So the Palace of Dreams is no mere whim or fancy; it is one of the pillars of the State. It is here, better than in any surveys, statements, or reports compiled by inspectors, policemen, or governors of pashaliks, that the true state of the Empire may be assessed … All that is murky and harmful, or that will become so in few years or centuries, makes its first appearance in men's dreams.[116]

---

114 Michaela Marek, 'Sozialismus in der alten Stadt. Oder: Ein Vorschlag zur kulturgeschichtlichen Erweiterung der sozialgeschichtlichen Stadtforschung', in *Von der 'europäischen Stadt' zur 'sozialistischen Stadt'*, 39–40; Borodziej, *Geschichte*, 274.

115 Andres Åman, *Architecture and Ideology in Eastern Europe during the Stalin Era: An Aspect of Cold War History* (Cambridge, MA: MIT Press, 1992), 88.

116 Ismael Kadare, *The Palace of Dreams* (New York: Arcade Publishing 1998), 25–6.

Projections and representations of statehood

Figure 1.11 Headquarters of the Central Committee of the Polish United Worker's Party, Warsaw
© PAP Polska Agencja Prasowa/Szyperko

Entering on one's own was impossible. Passers-by saw only a 'row of unused doors', all of which were closed. Heavily laden with symbolism, the buildings of communist-party headquarters generated a sense of oppression or even anxiety, like a fortress warding off intruders:

> Its two wings stretched away into the mist, while the main part of the building stood back a little as if recoiling from some threat. Mark-Alem felt his anxiety increase. Before him lay a long series of identical entrances, but when he got nearer he realized that all these great doors, wet from the sleet, were closed, and looked as if they hadn't been opened for some time.[117]

---

117 Kadare, *The Palace of Dreams*, 16.

The image of the fortress suggests safety and protection, but it also intimates separation and isolation. The new headquarters of the Communist Parties were built to last an eternity and have served to highlight the communist claim to power. Their monumental, monolith appearance has created the image of a wall dividing the common people from the party which was supposed to represent them.

Yugoslavia looked different, though. After his break with Stalin, Tito – following the binary logic of the Cold War – defected to the enemy camp. Under these new circumstances, the plans to build Yugoslav Central Committee headquarters in New Belgrade in the manner of the Palace of the Soviets were suddenly rendered obsolete. Starting in April 1948, volunteer brigades dumped almost 90 million cubic metres of debris and sand into the uninhabited swampland at the mouth of the river Sava in order to fill it.[118] Poets and politicians praised the power of these youth who created for 'all victorious Yugoslavs' a new symbol of their struggle for independence, a Yugoslav Moscow. The creation of a new political, administrative and representative centre for the new Yugoslav state was an event fraught with symbolism, a self-stylized demonstration of the strength, abilities and unity of the Yugoslav people. And now it had come to a standstill. The construction site lay idle for half a decade. The shell of the planned seat of government was there protruding from the foundations for anyone to see. The Yugoslavs had meanwhile found new aesthetic models to follow and new sponsors for their prestige project. In designing the new government building, the team of architects took their inspiration from Oscar Niemeyer. Light and airy, almost transparent modern architecture emerged on the old foundations, instead of classicist buildings made of stone (and, following Tito's imperial taste, adorned by Greek columns). Instead of Socialist Classicism, Yugoslavia was now copying the ultimate project of modernism: Brasilia. The Central Committee would reside from now on in a narrow glass tower with an 'American façade' and a clear aesthetic link to the Lever House in New York.[119] There was no red star crowning the building, no hammer and sickle, just a small bust of Lenin in the entranceway as a concession to communist symbolism. Instead, new technical solutions enabled ideological representation of another kind: special lights were used to shine the name of the new father of the state, Tito, on the façade of the building at night like a logo. This accent can be interpreted as a demonstration of power. In the context of political representation, the real question however, is how the dictator managed to maintain his personal rule. According to Philip Manow, it was essential to be 'everywhere and nowhere' at the same time in order to uphold his aura of omnipotence and omnipresence.[120] Tito therefore imitated imperial rulers and simulated his presence. His name was the most powerful symbol of Yugoslavia and was truly ubiquitous – in giant letters made of whitewashed stones piled up on meadows and hillsides, as graffiti on walls and fences, and now in illuminated letters on the building of the Central Committee. The Yugoslav state and Tito were one and the same. Every day Tito watched the Yugoslav people from his vantage point, and in turn, they observed him on state holidays as a gigantic photographic image displayed on prominent facades in almost every city in the country. In this regard, Yugoslavia implemented the Stalinist model of symbol politics better than a countrywide policy of Socialist Classicist architecture could have.

---

118 Kulić, 'National, International, Supranational', 42.

119 Vladimir Kulić, 'Land of the In-Between: Modern Architecture and the State in Socialist Yugoslavia 1945–6', (PhD diss., University of Texas at Austin), 283.

120 Manow, *Im Schatten*, 122.

Projections and representations of statehood

Figure 1.12 Headquarters of the Central Committee of the League of Communists of Yugoslavia
© Arhiv Jugoslavije

However, as already mentioned, hegemonic narratives are often challenged by subversive stories 'by making visible and explicit the connections between particular lives and social organization'.[121] Starting in 1969 with the Bosnian conceptual artist Braco Dimitrijević, then 21 years old, who photographed anonymous common people and printed their portraits on huge billboards in key public spaces. Instead of honouring Tito, Dimitrijević criticized his personality cult by reproducing the codes and the visual language of agitprop. Dimitrijević's performances intervened in the semantic structure of hegemonic narratives and caused irritation among 'puzzled early morning commuters, queuing for the tram', who 'asked themselves if there had been a sudden change of government'.[122]

With the end of Stalinism, communist architecture entered a phase of purpose-built modernism. But this aesthetic and conceptual opening did not mean a pluralization of architectural styles. Prefabricated panel housing was the prescribed method for dealing with the housing shortage. Individualized planning was reserved for large-scale prestige projects. The modern

---

121 Patricia Ewick and Susan S. Silbey, 'Subversive Stories and Hegemonic Tales: Toward a Sociology of Narrative', in *Law and Society Review* 29 (1995): 197.
122 Nena Dimitrijević, 'The Posthistorical Dimension', in *Tractatus Post Historicus (1976)*, by Braco Dimitrijević, ed. Aaron Levy (Philadelphia, PA: Slought Books 2009), 105.

Figure 1.13 The Czechoslovak Pavilion at the Universal and International Exposition in Brussels (EXPO 58)
© Česká Tisková Kancelář ČTK/Šaroch Jindřich

architecture disdained not long before now prevailed as the symbol of progress, especially in the case of representative projects. Czechoslovakia, in particular, whose architects had made considerable modifications in applying the Socialist Classicist model, rediscovered modernist traditions.[123] The World's Fair in Brussels in 1958 heralded the start of this process when Czechoslovakia won the Grand Prix for best national pavilion.[124]

František Cubr, Josef Hrubý and Zdeněk Pokorný, who were sent to Brussels as Czechoslovak delegates, worked for the state after 1948 like all Czech architects did. In the interwar period they were pupils of renowned avant-gardists, and after the war rarely designed buildings in the Socialist Classicist style. They had experience designing fairs and exhibits, both at home and abroad, which served them well because it led them to be elected as representatives of

---

123 Kimberly Elman Zarecor, *Manufacturing a Socialist Modernity: Housing in Czechoslovakia, 1945–1960* (Pittsburgh, PA: University of Pittsburgh Press, 2011), 150.
124 Vladimir Kulić and Kimberly Elman Zarecor, 'Socialism on Display: The Czechoslovak and Yugoslav Pavilions at the 1958 Brussels World's Fair', in *Meet me at the Fair: A World's Fair Reader*, eds Laura Hollengreen et al. (Pittsburgh, PA: ETC Press, 2014), 225.

Projections and representations of statehood

Czechoslovakia in Brussels. Their pavilion was composed of two parts, assembled like Lego blocks: an L-shaped ground floor and a two-story restaurant made of glass and anchored in the courtyard. The main entrance was also made of glass, with the sidewalls clad in opaque plastic panels. This contrast of classic and modern elements lent the structure a certain tension but also underlined its singularity.[125] Positive feedback in Brussels helped the Czechoslovak architects to ride a wave of success, resulting in the emergence of the so-called 'Brussels style', which was a clear break, but ultimately made possible by certain Soviet developments. Still, Czechoslovak architects celebrated it as the return to an international movement. Numerous public buildings were erected whose architects were guided by the concept of the EXPO pavilion, Karel Prager among them.

After myriad conflicts and the universal failure to build a new parliament building in the period between the wars, Prager was commissioned in 1964 to refunction the old commodity exchange then being used as a national assembly.[126] No other building in Prague unleashed such a controversy. Surveys have continuously singled it out as the 'ugliest building' in the city, which merely underscores its polarizing effect.[127] The site itself was a symbolic demonstration. Located not far from Wenceslas Square, between the National Museum and the Smetana Theatre, the Old Stock Exchange occupied a key position in the city. Built in 1938 by architect Jaroslav Rössler in the modern classicist style, it served in the Second World War as a military camp and hospital. The architects integrated the old structure by setting a box-like superstructure supported by four pillars on top of it.

A complicated technical procedure was used to raise the Vierendeel trusses, and the building, rather than symbolizing the parallel efforts to democratize Czechoslovak society, seemed to express an enthusiasm for technical progress.[128] The materials used, the interior decoration, the generous glass surfaces combined with metal – all of this was modern and radiated functionality. The spacious glass foyer suggests that the architect was invoking the idea of transparency, a popular motif in many public buildings in Western Europe at this time.

Prager's *Dům nad domem* (building above the building) concept was reminiscent of the EXPO structure. But thanks to its nesting principle, the new building towered over the Old Stock Exchange, nearly enveloping it. It is reported that Prager got his inspiration after seeing an Italian gallery. His main concern was to use a new design vocabulary to recode the historical city centre and open it up for a new application.[129] The idea was to use bridge structures to create new links between old and new, a concept he actually borrowed from Czech cubists of the interwar period. The intended result was the creation of a 'third dimension', expanding the city by means of new forms around its existing structures rather than

---

125 Martin Strakoš, 'Architektura Expo 58 v Bruselu a Československý pavilion' [The architecture of Expo 58 in Brussels and the Czechoslovak Pavilion], *Bruselský sen: československá účast na světové výstavě Expo 58 v Bruselu a životní styl 1. poloviny 60 let*, eds Vít Havránek and Marie Bergmanová (Prague: Arbor Vitae, 2008), 88–107.

126 Karel Ksandr, 'Nová budova Národního muzea' [New building of the National Museum], www.nm.cz/download/nova%20budova/letak_historie%20nb_1.pdf (accessed 13 July 2017).

127 ARTMarginis, interview with Rostislav Švácha from 11 July 2013, http://artmargins.com/index.php/interviews-sp-837925570/713-interview-with-rostislav-svacha (accessed 11 February 2016).

128 Joachim Amm, *Die Föderalversammlung der ČSSR: Sozialistischer Parlamentarismus im unitarischen Föderalismus 1969–1989* (Wiesbaden: Westdeutscher Verlag, 2001), 109.

129 Oldřich Ševčík and Ondřej Beneš, *Architektura 60. let: zlatá šedesátá léta v České architektuře 20. století* [Architecture of the 1960s: The golden 1960s of Czechoslovak architecture in the twentieth century] (Prague: Grada Publ., 2009), 64.

Figure 1.14   Federal Assembly of Czechoslovakia
© Česká Tisková Kancelář ČTK/Nosek Josef

into the suburbs. His parliament consistently applied this idea. At a time when prefabricated panel housing was popping up like mushrooms in Czechoslovakia, the building was an experimental attempt to start a new discussion about social and urban solutions to the problem of limited space.

And yet Prager failed in all of his aims. Contrary to his intentions, the building was effectively cut off from the public in the ensuing decades.[130] It is wedged between two arterial roads which act like ramparts, preventing its integration into the urban surroundings. It was always closed to visitors – yet another popular assembly that kept the people out. And while his vision of a *města nad městem* (city above the city) inspired other architects, most of his designs landed in the desk drawer on account of their costliness. Singular representative projects could not change the fact that neither Prager's *Laterna Magika* (magic lantern), nor Ivan Vitić's *Kockica* (little cube) housing the Croatian Central Committee, advanced to become the symbol of socialism. Instead, what became the face of socialism was the gigantic housing developments whose panelled apartment blocks were built as part of state housing projects. According to Juliana Maxim, the Romanian capital of Bucharest was primarily presented in post-war media

---

130 Ševčík and Beneš, *Architektura 60. let*, 64.

as 'a place of beauty, order, and healthy comforts' where 'ordinary people, after long struggles, built contented, wholesome lives'.[131] The images of modern housing developments suggested that the socialist state was a social-welfare state that assumed responsibility for the collective well-being of its people and raised their standard of living. The state was presented as a guarantee, and enabler, of progress. The semantic linking of progress with modernity, order and prosperity implied, conversely, that the old mode was tantamount to poverty, backwardness and inefficiency, thus undermining its value. The radical transformation of socialist societies functioned as a promise for the future, and fulfilling this promise meant a radical break with the past.

The 'House of the Republic' in Bucharest symbolized the realization of modernist fantasies and a drastic reconfiguration of urban space. This idea had existed in Romania since the 1930s, when King Carol II commissioned a new development plan. An ensemble of new modernist administrative buildings and historicizing monuments lined up on enormous boulevards and squares was supposed to lend expression to the country's progressive development.[132] The old, medieval city centre was to give way to a structurally different urban order perceived as being progressive. According to this early plan, a new administrative palace was scheduled to be built on *Dealul Spirii* (Spirea's Hill).[133] In its most radical sense – that of consciously destroying the old – the fulfilment of high-modernist ideology became reality under dictator Nicolae Ceauşescu. And the earthquake of 1977 offered a discursive justification for this megalomaniacal project. For his film *Autobiografia lui Nicolae Ceauşescu*, director Andrei Ujica sifted through one thousand hours of propaganda footage. He spliced together a biography of Ceauşescu, by chronologically arranging original footage of the dictator, his wife and his family, and by reconstructing his life as a Romanian head of state. In Ujica's version, the earthquake is followed by the death of Ceauşescu's mother. Images of the destroyed capital are followed by those of the mourning leader, the 'beloved son of the Romanian people', at his mother's wake. In the next sequence, we see Ceauşescu inspecting the ramshackle residential buildings in the centre of Bucharest and driving to the spectacular pavilion of the fair grounds. The entire floor of the pavilion is covered by a gigantic model of the city. The dictator, his wife and their entourage are borne aloft by a platform rising above the model of the city. The couple gives instructions, points to buildings and demonstrates that no force of nature and no stroke of fate can halt the progress of Bucharest and Romania. In the years that followed, excavators tore down every building in the city centre, an area totalling 485 hectares.[134] In the images captured on 25 June 1984, at the ground-breaking ceremony for this grandiose future administrative and political centre of Romania, as far as the eye could see the only buildings standing as symbolic markers of the future were the socialist skyscrapers.

---

131 Juliana Maxim, 'Bucharest: The City Transfigured', in *Sanctioning Modernism: Architecture and the Making of Post-war Identities*, eds Vladimir Kulic, Timothy Parker and Monica Penick (Austin, TX: University of Texas Press, 2014), E-Book, Pos. 341.

132 Robert Born, 'Römer und/oder Daker: Zur symbolischen Funktionalisierung der Antike in Rumänien von 1918 bis 1989', in *Neue Staaten – neue Bilder? Visuelle Kultur im Dienste staatlicher Selbstdarstellung in Zentral- und Osteuropa seit 1918*, eds Arnold Bartetzky, Marina Dmitrieva and Stefan Troebst (Vienna: Böhlau, 2005), 262.

133 Augustin Ioan, 'The Peculiar History of (Post) Communist Public Places and Spaces: Bucharest as a Case Study', in *The Post-Socialist City: Urban Form and Space Transformations in Central and Eastern Europe after Socialism*, ed. Kiril Stanilov (Dordrecht: Springer, 2007), 303.

134 Augustin Ioan, *The History of Nothing*, www.artmargins.com/index.php/8-archive/156-the-history-of-nothing-contemporary-architecture-and-public-space-in-romania (accessed 13 February 2016).

Figure 1.15 House of the Republic, Bucharest
© APA Austria Presse Agentur

The young architect Anca Petrescu, whose design won the architectonic competition for the rebuilding of the new city centre, used 700,000 tons of iron and bronze combined with a million cubic meters of marble, 3,500 tons of crystal and 900,000 cubic metres of wood, making the central building of the project, the House of the Republic, the heaviest building in the world.[135] All the building materials came from Romania – yet another symbolically charged decision suggesting national unity and solidarity,[136] just like the concerts at the construction site organized by the regime. Ceaușescu set store in the power of nationalism. He presumed that 'constructing an exceptional work of architecture ... would kindle national pride and restore his authority before his people and the entire world.'[137]

The use of Romanian building materials was meant to represent national unity. Ever since antiquity, the use of a variety of stone types and materials in the locus of power testified to the expansion of a leader's territory of rule and symbolized unity.[138] This kind of communal ritual was still common in the interwar period and was utilized by Jože Plečnik during the renovation of the Prague Castle and by Nikolaj Krasnov for the construction of the Serbian military cemetery in Thessaloniki after the First World War. By the 1980s, however, it seemed

---

135 http://www.guinnessworldrecords.com/world-records/heaviest-building/ (accessed on 13 February 2016).
136 Wagner, 'Material, politisches', 126.
137 Dana Vais, 'The (in)Famous Anca Petrescu: Authorship and Authority in Romanian Communist Architecture, 1977–1989', in *Ideological Equals: Women Architects in Socialist Europe 1945–1989*, eds Mary Pepchinski and Mariann Simon (London: Routledge 2017), 141.
138 Wagner, 'Material, politisches', 127.

Projections and representations of statehood

disturbing and out of place, as did the entire building complex. In the words of Romanian architect Augustin Ioan:

> The composition types and ornaments, the assemblages of classical/eclectic elements discharging an evocative/aesthetic function, the use of identities, a praise to the urban façade – are, undoubtedly, comparable to those celebrated by postmodern architecture. However, several essential ingredients are missing, e.g. irony, double encoding, cues to indicate the concessions meant to flatter kitsch mass culture. The complex is a stark set of buildings, designed to be taken quite seriously, although they are hilariously kitsch, just like the former Securitate secret agents, dressed in black suits, with dandruff specking their collars, and wearing white cotton socks in black lacquer shoes.[139]

Interpreted as such, the building is a belated work of Socialist Classicism. That is to say, an expression of contempt for the past, an attempt to create new realities, a gigantic Potemkin village intended to distract from the otherwise disastrous state of the country.

Thus, the symbol of the power, success, efficiency, modernity and unity of the Romanian people was reduced to mere appearances. It did not have the desired effect, because the people linked it to a drastic decline in their own quality of life, the bankrupt state having demanded considerable sacrifices from its people in order to finance this prestige project. 'Living in the dark and cold and lacking the most elementary provisions became the norm for most Romanians in the 1980s.'[140] And so the people revolted. The protests began in Timişoara, in the province. Ceauşescu, in his televised speech on state TV, referred to it as an attack against the state by 'isolated groups of hooligans'. He appealed to the citizens of Timişoara to stay calm and support the state, i.e. his regime. Just a few days later, the protesting masses stormed the party building, the dictator managing a last-minute escape by helicopter. He was caught by the military while attempting to flee the country and placed, together with his wife, before a military tribunal. Both were condemned to death and executed.

Post-1989

In his essay about democracy and architecture, Philip Manow asks if a 'democratic appropriation of political space'[141] is possible. He provides the answer himself, with a brief history of the public buildings in Washington DC. He argues that public space is always controversial and that only a public sphere gives it meaning. The meaning of representative buildings is always dependent on how they are perceived by those whom they claim to represent. Dietmar Müller has shown in detail how the discursive transformation of the Romanian 'House of the Republic' into a 'House of the People' and finally into a 'Palace of the Parliament' occurred.[142] But the transformation of this public space – or as architect Lebbeus Woods called it, 'scarred space' – and its actual democratic appropriation never took place. Augustin Ioan suggests that all Central, Eastern and Southeastern European cities that are marked by violent interventions

---

139 Ioan, *The History of Nothing*.
140 Vais, 'The (in)Famous Anca Petrescu', 141.
141 Manow, *Demokratie und Architektur*, 47.
142 Dietmar Müller, 'Strategien des öffentlichen Erinnerns in Rumänien nach 1989: Postkommunisten und postkommunistische Antikommunisten', in *Zwischen Amnesie und Nostalgie: die Erinnerung an den Kommunismus in Südosteuropa*, ed. Ulf Brunnbauer (Köln: Böhlau, 2007), 50.

in their urban architecture should be redesigned according to Woods' plans for Sarajevo after the Bosnian War of 1995. Woods describes how architecture in post-conflict societies can have a positive influence on the process of pacification:

> My answer was that architecture, as a social and primarily constructive act, could heal the wounds, by creating entirely new types of space in the city. These would be what I had called 'free-spaces,' spaces without predetermined programs of use, but whose strong forms demanded the invention of new programs corresponding to the new, post-war conditions. I had hypothesized that '90% of the damaged buildings would be restored to their normal pre-war forms and uses, as most people want to return to their old ways of living ... but 10% should be free-spaces, for those who did not want to go back, but forward.' The free-spaces would be the crucibles for the creation of new thinking and social-political forms, small and large. I believed then – and still do – that the cities and their people who have suffered the most difficult transitions in the contemporary world, in Sarajevo and elsewhere, have something important to teach us, who live comfortably in the illusion that we are immune to the demands radical changes of many kinds will impose on us, too.[143]

To be sure, this approach would require a radical public debate about the past, as well as a discussion of who, on what basis, and in what manner, has the right to design public space.

The parliaments of Eastern European states that became independent after 1989 have yet to discuss such questions. The newly proclaimed independent states drew on federal traditions from the communist era, and the now democratically elected representatives moved into pre-existing buildings. The buildings of the Slovakian National Council, the Lithuanian *Seimas*, and the Bosnian *Parlamentarna Skupština* were planned and built as regional parliaments in the communist era and are representative, in their own way, of modern socialist architecture of this period. The Croatian *Sabor* and the Macedonian *Sobranie* served as communist parliaments too but were built before 1945.

Just after the proclamation of Croatian independence, architect Miroslav Begović was commissioned with renovating the historical building of the *Sabor*, bringing it in line with modern technical requirements.[144] In 1907, when the Kingdom of Croatia, Slavonia and Dalmatia, still under Habsburg rule, awarded a contract to erect a new building for the *Sabor* on *Markov Trg* (St. Mark's Square), a place traditionally associated with political power, the winning design met with resistance on account of its strong references to the Viennese neo-historic Palladian style.[145] In 1908, commentators questioned the competence of the jury, bemoaning that 'the winners availed themselves of the colonial relations between Croatian culture and the imperial tendencies of Austria and Hungary'.[146] In 1991, Habsburg imperial tendencies were used to underline the European heritage of Croatia. The architects were asked to erase any traces of the Yugoslav era and try to restore the building's original state in their renovation work, the Habsburg past now being taken as a symbol of Croatian statehood.

---

143 Lebbeus Woods, *The Reality of Theory*, https://lebbeuswoods.wordpress.com/2008/02/06/the-reality-of-theory/ (accessed 14 February 2016).

144 Borka Bobovec, *Miroslav Begović* (Zagreb: HAZU/UHA, 2013), 240.

145 Olga Maruševski, 'Tradicija i suvremenost: U povodu obnove vijećnice u palači Hrvatskog Sabora 1995–1996' [Tradition and modernity: due to the reconstruction of the council hall in the palace of the Croatian parliament], *Život i umjetnost* 31, no. 59 (1997): 52.

146 Maruševski, 'Tradicija i suvremenost', 55.

Projections and representations of statehood

The notion of parliament as an imperial foreign body – this reproach seems unwarranted nowadays. At the same time, it documents the national and symbolic appropriation of political space or, following Philip Manow, it shows that the effects of public space never overlap completely with the intentions of their designers. Because 'spatial purposing [is] ambivalent in its effects; only through a public sphere acting in a political space does it acquire its particular meaning, which changes over time.'[147]

Further reading

Åman, Andres. *Architecture and Ideology in Eastern Europe during the Stalin Era: An Aspect of Cold War History* (Cambridge, MA: MIT Press, 1992).

Bachmann-Medick, Doris. *Cultural Turns: Neuorientierungen in den Kulturwissenschaften* (Reinbeck: Rowohlt Verlag, 2006).

Bartetzky, Arnold. *Nation – Staat – Stadt: Architektur, Denkmalpflege und visuelle Geschichtskultur vom 19. bis zum 21. Jahrhundert* (Köln: Böhlau, 2012).

Bartetzky, Arnold, Marina Dmitrieva, and Stefan Troebst, eds. *Neue Staaten - neue Bilder? Visuelle Kultur im Dienste staatlicher Selbstdarstellung in Zentral- und Osteuropa seit 1918* (Vienna: Böhlau, 2005).

Biondich, Mark. *Stjepan Radić, The Croat Peasant Party, and the Politics of Mass Mobilization, 1904–1928* (Toronto: University of Toronto Press, 2000).

Bodenschatz, Harald, and Christiane Post. *Städtebau im Schatten Stalins: Die internationale Suche nach der sozialistischen Stadt in der Sowjetunion 1929–1935* (Berlin: Verlagshaus Braun, 2004).

Bourdieu, Pierre. *Über den Staat – Vorlesungen am Collège de France 1989–1992* (Frankfurt a.M.: Suhrkamp, 2014).

Bowe, Nicola Gordon, ed. *Art and the National Dream: The Search for Vernacular Expression in Turn-of-the-Century Design* (Blackrock: Irish Academic Press, 1993).

Bredekamp, Horst. *Theorie des Bildaktes – Frankfurter Adorno-Vorlesungen 2007* (Frankfurt a.M.: Suhrkamp, 2010).

Castillo, Greg. *Cold War on the Home Front: The Soft Power of Mid-century Design* (Minneapolis, MN: University of Minnesota Press, 2010).

Ferhadbegović, Sabina. *Prekäre Integration: Serbisches Staatsmodell und regionale Selbstverwaltung in Sarajevo und Zagreb 1918–1929* (München: Oldenbourg, 2008).

Feuchter, Jörg, and Johannes Helmrath, eds. *Parlamentarische Kulturen vom Mittelalter bis in die Moderne: Reden – Räume – Bilder* (Düsseldorf: Droste, 2013).

Gauger, Jörg-Dieter, and Justin Stagl, eds. *Staatsrepräsentation* (Berlin: Reimer, 1992).

Herzfeld, Michael. *The Social Production of Indifference* (Chicago, IL: The University of Chicago Press, 1992).

Hobsbawm, Eric, and Terence Ranger, eds. *The Invention of Tradition* (Cambridge: Cambridge University Press, 1983).

Kadare, Ismael. *The Palace of Dreams* (New York: Arcade Publishing, 1998).

Koschorke, Albrecht, Thomas Frank, Ethel Matala de Mazza, and Susanne Lüdemann. *Der fiktive Staat: Konstruktionen des politischen Körpers in der Geschichte Europas* (Frankfurt a.M.: Fischer, 2007).

Kulić, Vladimir. 'Land of the In-Between: Modern Architecture and the State in Socialist Yugoslavia 1945–6', (PhD Dissertation, University of Texas at Austin 2009) https://repositories.lib.utexas.edu/handle/2152/11635.

Kulić, Vladimir, Timothy Parker, and Monica Penick, eds. *Sanctioning Modernism: Architecture and the Making of Post-war Identities* (Austin, TX: University of Texas Press, 2014).

Makaš, Emily Gunzburger, and Tanja Damljanovic Conley, eds. *Capital Cities in the Aftermath of Empires: Planning in Central and Southeastern Europe* (London: Routledge, 2010).

Malkowsky, Georg. *Die Pariser Weltausstellung in Wort und Bild* (Berlin: Kirchhoff & Co, 1900).

Manow, Philip. *Im Schatten des Königs: Die politische Anatomie demokratischer Repräsentation* (Frankfurt a.M.: Suhrkamp, 2008).

---

147 Manow, 'Demokratie und Architektur', 49.

Marek, Michaela. *Kunst und Identitätspolitik: Architektur und Bildkünste im Prozess der tschechischen Nationsbildung* (Köln: Böhlau, 2004).

Neutatz, Dietmar. *Träume und Alpträume: Eine Geschichte Russlands im 20. Jahrhundert* (München: Beck, 2013).

Pepchinski, Mary, and Mariann Simon, eds. *Ideological Equals: Women Architects in Socialist Europe 1945–1989* (London: Routledge, 2017).

Quaritsch, Helmut. *Die Selbstdarstellung des Staates* (Berlin: Duncker Humblot, 1977).

Rolf, Malte. *Soviet Mass Festivals, 1917–1991* (Pittsburgh, PA: University of Pittsburgh Press, 2013).

Rüthers, Monica. *Moskau bauen von Lenin bis Chruscev: Öffentliche Räume zwischen Utopie, Terror und Alltag* (Vienna: Böhlau, 2007).

Schlögl, Rudolf, Bernhard Giesen, and Jürgen Osterhammel. *Die Wirklichkeit der Symbole: Grundlagen der Kommunikation in historischen und gegenwärtigen Gesellschaften* (Constance: UVK, 2004).

Scott, James C. *Seeing Like a State: How Certain Schemes to Improve the Human Condition Have Failed* (New Haven, CT: Yale University Press, 1998).

Skinner, Quentin. *Die drei Körper des Staates* (Göttingen: Wallstein, 2012).

Stanilov, Kiril, ed. *The Post-Socialist City: Urban Form and Space Transformations in Central and Eastern Europe after Socialism* (Dordrecht: Springer, 2007).

Stollberg-Rilinger, Barbara. 'Rituals of Decision-making? Early Modern European Assemblies of Estates as Acts of Symbolic Communication', in *Political Order and the Forms of Communication in Medieval and Early Modern Europe*, ed. Yoshihisa Hattori (Rome: Viella, 2014), 63–95.

Telesko, Werner, Richard Kurdiovsky, and Andreas Nierhaus, eds. *Die Wiener Hofburg und der Residenzbau in Mitteleuropa im 19. Jahrhundert: Monarchische Repräsentation zwischen Ideal und Wirklichkeit* (Vienna: Böhlau, 2010).

Wharton, Annabel Jane. *Building the Cold War: Hilton International Hotels and Modern Architecture* (Chicago, IL: Chicago University Press, 2004).

Zarecor, Kimberly Elman. *Manufacturing a Socialist Modernity: Housing in Czechoslovakia, 1945–1960* (Pittsburgh, PA: University of Pittsburgh Press, 2011).

2

TOWARDS A NEW QUALITY OF STATEHOOD

Bureaucratization and state-building in empires and nation states before 1914

Hannes Grandits, Pieter Judson and Malte Rolf

Under the heading 'State' (*Állam*), volume one of *Révai's Encyclopedia*, published in Budapest in 1911, offered a comprehensive introduction to contemporary political science. The state, it said, was essentially defined by its territory and inhabitants, as well as by its sovereignty. It represented the highest form of social cooperation. Legally it had unlimited power over its citizens, to the point of annihilating the economic and physical existence of the individual, at least in theory, for 'the will of the state itself lays down the law.' The encyclopaedia went on to elaborate that opinions varied concerning the task of the state. Some thought its sole purpose was to preserve law and order, others saw it as being responsible for promoting the welfare of the population, e.g. through intervention in education and the economy; still others believed it was there to completely organize the production and distribution of material goods in line with theories of the socialist state, so that 'culture does not lead to the impoverishment of the majority in human society'.[1] There was also an idealistic concept in which the state was imagined to lead its citizens to moral perfection, making itself redundant in the process. The entry continued with deliberations on the rule of law, the constitutional state, the cultural state, and the various forms of government. The corresponding entry in *Enciclopedia Româna*, published a decade earlier, was much more concise. Valerian Urşianu, a Bucharest political scientist and expert in constitutional law, succinctly defined the state as the 'totality of inhabitants of a certain territory organized as a political body.'[2] The tasks of the state were outlined elsewhere under the heading 'Administration' and in the broader sense were said to encompass foreign affairs, war, finances and judicial affairs; in the narrower sense, every public matter that 'fundamentally informs the physical, intellectual and economic life of the nation', the responsibility for which

---

1 *Révai nagy lexikona. Az ismeretek enciklopédiája*, vol. 1, *A-Arany* (Budapest: Révai 1911), 374–6, quote on 374.

2 C. Diaconovich, ed., *Enciclopedia Română*, vol. 3, *Kemet – Zymotic* [Romanian encyclopaedia] (Sibiu: Editura şi tiparul lui W. Krafft, 1904), 1007f.

rested with the respective ministries of the Interior, Cultural Affairs and Education, Trade, Agriculture, Transportation and Public Works.[3]

Such definitions stemmed from an era that was marked by an enormous expansion of state activities and in which the discussion of 'socialist' ideas anticipated the 'total state', despite the fact that the latter term was only coined in the 1920s. The distinction between empires and nation states, on the other hand, played only a marginal role in these debates. *Révai's Encyclopedia* explained:

> *Birodalom* (lat. *imperium*, Ger. *Reich*, Engl. & Fr. *empire*): designation for a state extending over a larger area, e.g. the Roman Empire, the Russian Empire, the German Empire; one understanding of empire is particularly important from a legal perspective, referring to a state entity that is not a uniform but a composite state. See federal state.[4]

The Czech *Ottův Slovník* noted without further ado: '*Říše* (from the German *Reich*, in turn from the Latin *regnum*), essentially means state.'[5] More recent research, too, has concluded that the European continental empires were fundamentally similar to the emerging nation states of the nineteenth century, as they had a similar understanding of their state tasks and spheres of activity.[6] The German Empire, for example, did not qualify as an empire because Prussia had incorporated parts of Poland and used them, as Austria and Russia did, as a proving ground for ideal statehood, however much Prussia, in particular, occasionally exhibited an unmistakably colonial attitude. The key developments of the state in Eastern Europe were not limited to nationality politics, even though linguistic and ethnic diversity had an influence on state activity, giving rise to nationality conflicts in 'imperial borderlands' like these.

A deeper understanding of how statehood developed in the late nineteenth and early twentieth centuries is not possible without some consideration of longer-term developments. Of note here first and foremost are the long-term consequences of the emancipation of serfs. In Prussia, Austria and ultimately Russia, the state intervened profoundly in rural property relations, and did so despite the fact that it wasn't sufficiently present in many places. The extent to which a rapidly growing rural population made more sweeping agrarian reforms seem necessary was an issue well into the twentieth century. Closely linked to this were the new social-policy challenges in the cities and the countryside which industrialization presented. Here, too, the state acquired new spheres of activity going well beyond the poor relief of the early modern period and which gave birth to rapidly growing bureaucracies from the late nineteenth century onwards.

It is not so much these new spheres of activity themselves and their attendant implications that distinguished nation states from empires: for when, as in the Romanian definition (and elsewhere), the politically organized totality of inhabitants forms the basis of the state, the question arises as to who exactly is included in this 'totality' and how exactly they are organized politically. It was hence a question of citizenship and the constitution, and ultimately of political participation and rights. Only in the ideal nation state did the answer seem inherent to the concept itself. Citizenship and nationality were considered to be congruent. Yet, European states at the turn of the twentieth

---

3 C. Diaconovich, ed., *Enciclopedia Română*, vol. 1, *A – Copenhaga* (Sibiu: Editura și tiparul lui W. Krafft, 1898), 40.

4 *Révai nagy lexikona. Az ismeretek enciklopédiája*, vol. 3, *Béke – Brutto* [Révai's great lexicon: the encyclopaedia of knowledge] (Budapest: Révai, 1911), 332.

5 *Ottův slovník naučný*, vol. 21, *R (Ř)–Rozkoš* [Otto's scholarly dictionary] (Prague: J. Otto, 1904), 822.

6 Jörn Leonhard and Ulrike Hirschhausen, eds, *Comparing Empires: Encounters and Transfers in the Long Nineteenth Century*, Schriftenreihe der FRIAS School of History 1 (Göttingen: Vandenhoeck und Ruprecht, 2010); Stefan Berger and Alexei Miller, eds, *Nationalizing Empires* (Budapest: CEU Press, 2015).

century were far from achieving this congruence. The question was relevant, first of all, because former subjects were conscripted indiscriminately into military service and hence enjoyed the privileges and rights of citizens. This presented a difficult challenge to the Ottoman Empire and tsarist Russia. And yet, universal conscription was a relatively marginal issue when compared with the question of how a linguistically and religiously heterogeneous population should be represented politically by a parliamentary body. It was not just about linguistic and religious diversity: the question of whether women possessed full civic rights was controversial at best. The emancipation of Russian serfs presented a similar problem – the abolition of serfdom in 1861 was initially founded on the idea that Russian peasants would largely be left to their own devices and given over to self-rule. The Serbian state of the nineteenth century was based on peasant self-rule as well.

This rough sketch should make it abundantly clear that a history of statehood in Eastern Europe at the turn of the twentieth century, which in turn serves as an introduction to the history of the state in the twentieth century, must go back well into the nineteenth century. The Crimean War, a humiliating affair for the Ottoman and the Russian empires, was a major reason that the problems depicted here became politically relevant in Russia and the Ottoman Empire, resulting in sweeping reforms. The Habsburg monarchy and Prussia remained neutral in the Crimean War, but the revolutions of 1848 prompted similar questions for them. Key developments, similarities and differences will only become apparent with a view to the entire region. It is here that the present chapter begins.

Expansion of the state: developments up to the last third of the nineteenth century

The transition to 'modernity' as a challenge and an explanatory concept

The claim that reforms were the only alternative to making the state function in a more modern and appropriate way is surely the central characteristic of the development of governance and statehood in Eastern and Southeastern Europe in the second half of the nineteenth century, a claim which forms the focus of this chapter. For years historians have explained the changing state structures in these regions as a kind of 'Europeanization' or the progressive adoption of modern Western ideas, procedures and practices – as if these regions did not really follow the general European trends of the period. This explanation was closely linked to the ever greater economic as well as cultural and intellectual entanglement and integration of Southeastern and Eastern Europe in the overall European context throughout the course of the nineteenth century. Diana Mishkova and Roumen Daskalov aptly described this kind of transfer from the West with respect to Ottoman Southeastern Europe as follows:

> The imports from the 'West' ran the gamut from material goods to the mental and spiritual sphere: clothes, furniture and various products; knowledge, ideas and technical devices; and forms of social behavior, attitudes and values. This influence traveled through diverse channels, including tradesmen from within the Balkans and from émigré colonies, intellectuals educated abroad, foreign diplomats and travelers, Catholic and Protestant missionaries, invading armies and Ottoman reformers.[7]

---

7 Diana Mishkova and Roumen Daskalov, '"Forms without Substance": Debates on the Transfer of Western Models to the Balkans', in *Entangled Histories of the Balkans*, eds Roumen Daskalov and Diana Mishkova, vol. 2 of *Transfers of Political Ideologies and Institutions* (Leiden and Boston, MA: Brill, 2014), 1–97, here 1.

In the nineteenth century in particular, relations with other parts of Europe (understood as an imagined 'West') were indeed becoming more intense. For the Ottoman Empire, the Crimean War years were a zenith in terms of its interaction with the West. Hundreds of thousands of soldiers from the Western allies were sent to the Ottoman Empire between 1853 and 1856. Soldiers and their commanders, diplomats and people of varied professions who accompanied them went to the empire and remained there for years. Many thousands were stationed or resident in Istanbul; indeed, never in the preceding centuries had so many people from the West lived there.[8]

It goes without saying that relations with the rest of Europe likewise intensified during the period in question. But how accurate is it to explain this development as the polarization between a progressive 'Western' civilization and a backwards 'Eastern' one? Was there even a unified Western Europe at all (considering developments in Spain, Portugal, Ireland, Italy and rural France, for example) compared to a supposed East? Is it really unavoidable to describe the general structural changes that form the focus of this chapter as a transfer of Western civilization to the East?

This predominant tendency to explain the history of the social and state structures of the Balkan region – and of Eastern and Southeastern Europe in general – exclusively or primarily as the history of a delayed, incomplete or failed attempt at Westernization in the nineteenth century has been the subject of growing criticism. Maria Todorova offers an interesting new perspective in her essay 'The Trap of Backwardness', by investigating temporality as the dominant element in Western discourses of superiority (and of historiography into the present). She refers to a foundational narrative that emerged in the course of the nineteenth century, according to which the societies of the Balkans and especially the Ottoman Empire in the nineteenth century were suddenly thought to be living in the (remote) past. If they wanted to achieve modernity (or to live in modern times), so the narrative went, they had no choice but to 'catch up'.[9] The building of efficient administrations and infrastructures – in short, all those things that make a modern state 'modern' – has played a key role in this understanding down to the present day. Western historians have even conceded late tsarist Russia a pivotal role in this process of catching up.

This notion of an Ottoman or an Eastern European society existing in a 'different time' was and still is a central framework for historically contextualizing the process of state reform in the second half of the nineteenth century in Southeastern and Eastern Europe. It will not be used in the present chapter, however. Despite increasing economic, social and cultural entanglements at a European or global level encompassing the regions of Southeastern and Eastern Europe – and this at quite an accelerated pace in the second half of the nineteenth century – a polarized West–East framework of this sort falls short as an interpretative model, suggesting as it does an ever-deficient 'transformation'. It posits a 'civilizational' picture of an idealized (imagined) West that can never actually be attained. The image of being 'behind in times' is thus self-perpetuating. For, by the time they've caught up, the West will once again be ahead of them, continually upholding the fundamental motif of a failed modernization.

---

8 See a.o. the following literature: Candan Badem, *The Ottoman Crimean War 1853–1856* (Leiden and Boston, MA: Brill, 2010); Winfried Baumgart, ed., *Akten zur Geschichte des Krimkriegs*, 12 vols, (München: Oldenbourg, 1980–2011); Winfried Baumgart, *The Crimean War, 1853–1856* (London: Hodder Arnold, 1999); Orlando Figes, *The Crimean War: A History* (New York: Picador, 2011).

9 Maria Todorova, 'The Trap of Backwardness: Modernity, Temporality, and the Study of Eastern European Nationalism', *Slavic Review* 64, 1 (2005): 140–64.

Towards a new quality of statehood

Nathalie Clayer and Tassos Anastassiadis[10] have pointed out rather incisively that in writing the history of reform or the transformation of rule in Southeastern and Eastern Europe, it is necessary to abandon such rigid narrative patterns about a 'civilizational lag' as well as the cultural notion of a constant backwardness or social deficit. It is indeed extremely necessary to view reform and the transformation of rule in these regions in a more comprehensive explanatory context, and to bear in mind that not only the societies of Southeastern and Eastern Europe made enormous efforts and encountered considerable difficulties and conflicts in their efforts to implement politically, socially and economically a modern, bureaucratic or more rational statehood; indeed, every society both inside and outside of Europe has at some point faced similar challenges. Gale Stokes succinctly summarizes:

> In the modern era every society has had to find a way to confront the enormous energy produced by industrialism, the integrating and dominating power of capitalism, the corrosive ideal of equality, and the organizing demands of the state system. And no society has been able to choose an optimum way to face the challenge.[11]

One need only think of the pauperization of the lower classes and the class conflicts in an England marked by Manchester Capitalism, or of the mass emigration fuelled by famine in various regions of Scandinavia in the 1860s, or of the intra-societal conflicts in southern Italy at the turn of the twentieth century, to name just a few examples. Countless other contexts would serve to illustrate the abovementioned point that no society in Europe (and surely beyond) was able to find an 'optimal path' in meeting the enormous challenges of modernity. This is certainly true of the societies in question here in Southeastern and Eastern Europe during the second half of the nineteenth and early twentieth centuries. They too had enormous problems with the overwhelming challenges posed by state, social and economic reform. Yet no European society in the era under consideration was free of devastating and recurring social conflict. It therefore makes sense to reformulate the standard approach: the societies of Southeastern and Eastern Europe were not the only ones facing the immense challenges of modernity; the rest of Europe and the rest of the world had to deal with it as well. This shift did not occur in different eras, but rather simultaneously, each society with its respective problems, conflicts and degrees of success acting from within its own unique conditions. Only when we adopt this perspective, can we address the specific starting points, idiosyncrasies and enormous struggle experienced in the regions under investigation, as well as both their success and failure in coping with the manifold challenges of an emerging new 'modernity'.

The end of the feudal system of administration and the subsequent move towards bureaucratization

Probably the biggest challenge in these regions was the attempt to overcome a centuries-old feudal order and replace it with a new, state-sanctioned bureaucratic administration, even in the most remote rural areas. In the wake of the French Revolution and the Napoleonic Wars,

---

10 Nathalie Clayer and Tassos Anastassiadis, 'Beyond the Incomplete or Failed Modernization Paradigm', in *Society, Politics and State Formation in Southeastern Europe during the 19th Century*, eds Tassos Anastassiadis and Nathalie Clayer (Athens: Alpha Bank, 2011), 11–32.

11 Gale Stokes, *Three Eras of Political Change in Eastern Europe* (Oxford: Oxford University Press, 1997), 74–5.

the abolition of feudal laws – long a topic of debate – spread outwards from France to more states on the European continent, where it was implemented either in full, in stages or in some rudimentary form. But the process began to falter after the Congress of Vienna, as the feudal aristocracy was still exerting an enormous influence in regional politics. This was likewise true for post-1815 France and Spain, for various Italian territories and many states in the German Confederation (e.g. Bavaria and Prussia), as well as the Habsburg Empire.

The revolutionary year of 1848 brought with it a long-awaited breakthrough for many states across Europe, including the Habsburg Empire: namely, the emancipation of the serfs, which reform-oriented forces and the rural population had eagerly anticipated. The accompanying agrarian reform was implemented in full, in the Habsburg states as well. In almost every instance, however, this conflict-ridden and highly controversial process of replacing feudal property rights dragged out for decades to come, a point to which we shall return.

In the Ottoman and Russian empires, where the revolutions of 1848 had no particular impact, the Crimean War was the decisive factor in the efforts to end the feudal era. In the Russian Empire, the emancipation of the serfs became official in 1861, following years of intense debate about reform after Russia's defeat in the Crimean War. The old feudal administration, largely run by the landowning class, was to be replaced by a peasant-run system of local government. In the Ottoman Empire, the situation was a bit more complex, as no 'feudal system' in the narrow sense had ever really been established here. But there was an oppressive class of estate- and landowners, mostly urban and predominantly Muslim, who made life for rural peasants difficult. In this case, too, the end of the Crimean War brought with it considerable change, generally through legal measures. With the Ottoman Reform Edict of February 1856 (*Islâhat Hatt-ı Hümayun*), which the Great Powers had made a precondition to the Treaty of Paris, the Ottoman Empire had committed itself to numerous sweeping reforms, especially with regard to landownership rights and the conditions of the (non-Muslim) population in the countryside.

From this general European backdrop, let us now move to the more concrete characteristics accompanying the end of the feudal system in the regions of Central, Eastern and Southeastern Europe. The challenges common to that period could be described in the following way: in the nineteenth century, reformers aimed to establish a new and legal demarcation of property claims, which can aptly be described as a de-feudalization. This went hand in hand with the thrust towards bureaucratization in the structures of state power and was a basic precondition to the process in the first place. Ultimately, there was a tendency toward the (legal) equality or emancipation of political elites and other social groups who would be part of a future political order considered to be 'modern', or at least aspiring to be so. This order was rather open and largely undetermined, and also became the aim of various political programmes. De-feudalization and bureaucratization were the two particularly dominant and characteristic tendencies informing the period into the 1880s in the regions under discussion here. We will therefore address them first, taking an in-depth look at concrete developments in the three major empires: the Russian Empire (especially the Kingdom of Poland), the Ottoman Empire (including the Danubian Principalities and Serbia) and the Habsburg Empire. These empires, which underwent radical transformations in the 1850s and 1860s, covered the vast majority of the territory in question here.

The Russian Empire and the Kingdom of Poland

Following its defeat in the Crimean War, Russia was faced more urgently than ever with the question of internal reform in its multi-ethnic empire. The Crimean defeat made clear to Russia that its empire was inferior to the Western European powers not only in military and logistical

Towards a new quality of statehood

matters, but also that it was incapable of mobilizing support among its population. The debates about a necessary modernization of Russia were given a new impetus when Alexander II (who reigned from 1855 to 1881) ascended the throne. The debates resulted in a series of reforms that would go down in history as the Great Reforms. Over a period of almost 20 years, the tsar and his active team of reform bureaucrats instituted sweeping changes that would fundamentally alter the social and cultural landscape of the empire and likewise give a new foundation to the institutions of the state.[12]

The bundle of resolutions, which were intended to bring Russia more in line with the modern European powers, included the emancipation of the serfs (1861), judicial reform (1864), rural and municipal organs of self-government (1864 and 1870), education reform (1865), military service (1874), and throughout the 1860s and 70s, censorship practices and labour law. The France of Napoleon III and his efforts at centralization within the framework of the monarchy served as an exemplar in many instances. And yet, Russia was by no means following the nation state model, but rather trying to adapt its dynastic system of rule to a rapidly changing world. The imperial self-understanding of the Russian Empire as a multi-ethnic state, legitimized through dynasty, was never seriously questioned in the process.

The modernization project pursued in these reforms essentially followed three specific aims in terms of internal reorganization. First, as with other European powers, the emancipation of serfs in Russia was intended as a de-feudalization of rule over the country and its people. Second, the reforms aimed to expand the state and strove for an internal unification in administrative and legal terms. Third, (strictly monitored) institutions of civic participation were to enable social engagement, which in turn would help establish a broad stratum of loyal citizens. The centrepiece of these reforms was certainly the emancipation of the serfs: it was prepared by an energetic reform bureaucracy, supported by a liberal segment of the aristocracy and was implemented in the face of considerable resistance in 1861. Eleven million peasants were released into freedom, thus rolling back the authority of landowners over a large part of the population. At the same time, it opened up the potential for expansion of state structures and institutions of self-governance.[13]

Though the emancipation of the serfs undoubtedly unleashed the process of de-feudalization of local rule, it did not mean that statehood was immediately and palpably intensified in the farthest reaches of the Russian Empire. On the one hand, the obstinate weakness of state structures effectively stood in the way. On the other hand, the provisions of the emancipation edict bound the former serfs to their village community (*obshchina*), transporting them into a legal, administrative and cultural parallel universe of de-facto self-government. The lack of state institutions in the vast expanses of the empire was supposed to be compensated by rural organs of self-government;

---

12 On the Crimean War, see Robert B. Edgerton, *Death or Glory: The Legacy of the Crimean War* (Boulder, CO: Westview, 1999); Orlando Figes, *Crimea: The Last Crusade* (London: Penguin, 2010); Idem, *The Crimean War*. On the Great Reforms, see the still insightful W. Bruce Lincoln, *The Great Reforms: Autocracy, Bureaucracy, and the Politics of Change in Imperial Russia* (DeKalb, IL: Northern Illinois University Press, 1990); Ben Eklof, John Bushnell and Larisa Zakharova, eds, *Russia's Great Reforms 1855–1881* (Bloomington, IN: Indiana University Press, 1994).

13 On the emancipation of the serfs, see Carol Scott Leonard, *Agrarian Reform in Russia: The Road from Serfdom* (New York: Cambridge University Press, 2011); David A.J. Macey, *Government and Peasant in Russia, 1861–1906: The Prehistory of the Stolypin Reforms* (DeKalb, IL: Northern Illinois University Press, 1987); Christine D. Worobec, *Peasant Russia: Family and Community in the Post-Emancipation Period* (DeKalb, IL: Northern Illinois University Press, 1995); George L. Yaney, *The Urge to Mobilize: Agrarian Reform in Russia, 1861–1930* (Urbana, IL: University of Illinois Press, 1982).

these assemblies, however, disproportionately represented the aristocracy. Large landowners therefore remained a dominating power in the provinces of the empire for a long time to come, the state being dependent on them. To ensure the display of state power in Russia's far-reaching countryside, the institution of justice of the peace (*mirovoi posrednik*) was created to mediate disputes between landowners and peasants. The only suitable candidates for this office, however, were members of the local nobility, and so local state representation remained an affair of the noble estate, nevertheless, many of these officials of the first generation genuinely represented the concerns of the peasants. Even the position of land captain (*zemskii nachal'nik*), introduced by Alexander III in 1889, remained true to this principle. This long arm of governmental power in a local context was selected – at the governor's recommendation – from the body of local nobles.[14]

Although the reforms of the mid-nineteenth century did not succeed in implementing a consistent de-feudalization of the provincial order, they were nonetheless an important incentive for the domestic expansion of the state and the genesis of a new understanding of statehood. The reform bureaucrats under Alexander II saw the administrative-legal unification of the empire as a decisive key to the successful modernization of the country. The historically rooted structure of the composite monarchy with its numerous legal jurisdictions was comparable to a patchwork rug that appeared increasingly antiquated in the context of contemporary political thought. Accordingly, the Great Reforms always aimed to reduce special local provisions and privileges. The modern state was conceived of here, above all, as an internally homogeneous, legal-administrative order, and its unification became a core concern of the reformers.

The dynastic principle was never challenged as the glue that held the multi-ethnic empire together, and indeed, the emperor remained the central figure of integration. The internally homogeneous state, however, did become a new reference point in the concept of state during the reform era. The result was an increasing bureaucratization and formalization of rule, giving rise to a pronounced expansion of bureaucracy and a standardization of the administrative system. Whereas statistics recorded 112,000 civil servants in 1860, by 1900 their number had risen to 524,000. Hence, by the end of the century, more than half a million people were employed in the tsarist administrative apparatus. To be sure, the period of reform engendered a new type of civil servant, marked by an increasing degree of professionalization and work ethic. Though the upper echelons of the administrative hierarchy were reserved for individuals from the (high) aristocracy, who would preferably have had a military career behind them and a good relationship with the tsarist court, a middle stratum of civil servants was nonetheless in the making; these were officials who were increasingly expected to have a university education and who began to adopt a certain code of conduct. This new bureaucracy saw itself as a vehicle of modern statehood and reform. Conflicts with the new bodies of self-government, as well as with the landowning nobility and the independent courts established under judicial reform, were inevitable and had a formative influence on the administrative routine of these public officials. The expansion of ministerial bureaucracy also led to tensions within the civil service bureaucracy. The governors general in particular, who saw themselves in the tradition of tsarist viceroys reaching out to the provinces or the fringes of the empire, felt increasingly marginalized in light of the expanding authority of the Ministry of the Interior and its sprawling

---

14 See Jörg Baberowski, *Autokratie und Justiz: Zum Verhältnis von Rechtsstaatlichkeit und Rückständigkeit im ausgehenden Zarenreich 1864–1914* (Frankfurt a.M.: Klostermann, 1996), Chapter 4; Judith Pallot, ed., *Transforming Peasants: Society, State, and the Peasantry, 1861–1930* (Houndmills: Macmillan, 1998); and David Feest, *Ordnung schaffen: Bäuerliche Selbstverwaltungen und Obrigkeit im ausgehenden Zarenreich (1834–1889)* (Wiesbaden: Harrassowitz, 2018).

Towards a new quality of statehood

bureaucratic powers. Ultimately, at the local level, there was a parallel administration to the central and provincial level whose officials helped the state have a greater influence in the affairs of local communities.[15]

The process of bureaucratization affected other areas of the Great Reforms as well. The expansion of higher education was motivated not least of all by the fact that these educational institutions were supposed to produce the staff for a growing state apparatus. Indeed, in the second half of the nineteenth century, university degrees gradually became more common among those who wished to pursue a career as a civil servant. In this sense as well, state bureaucracy was becoming more and more professionalized.

Thus, the reform era of Alexander II can be characterized as a period of rapid state expansion in which statehood itself was being redefined. The state was increasingly understood as an autonomous institution, even though the autocratic principle of rule was never infringed upon.[16] These processes of the bureaucratization of rule continued after the death of Alexander II. Even in the 'counter-reform' era ushered in as of 1881 by his successor Alexander III, there were no attempts to reinstate some form of tsarist 'personal rule' of the kind seen under Nicholas I. The emergency regulations of 1881 illustrate how dominant the view was that even in times of crisis, control should be exercised with the aid of bureaucratic machinery and regulated levels of internal decision-making. The declaration of a state of emergency was no longer merely an expression of the sovereign will but occurred in a formalized way and was linked to the internal structures of the Ministry of the Interior and was hence subject to valid legal norms.[17]

---

15 On the transformation of state bureaucracy, see Dietrich Beyrau, 'Liberaler Adel und Reformbürokratie im Rußland Alexanders II', in *Liberalismus im 19. Jahrhundert*, ed. Dieter Langewiesche (Göttingen: Vandenhoeck und Ruprecht, 1988), 499–514; Dominic Lieven, *Russia's Rulers Under the Old Regime* (New Haven, CT: Yale University Press, 1989); Daniel T. Orlovsky, *Limits of Reform: Ministry of Internal Affairs in Imperial Russia, 1802–81* (Cambridge, MA: Harvard University Press, 1981); Raymond Pearson, *Russian Officialdom in Crisis: Autocracy and Local Self-Government, 1861–1900* (Cambridge: Cambridge University Press, 1989); Richard G. Robbins, *The Tsar's Viceroys: Russian Provincial Governors in the Last Years of the Empire* (Ithaca, NY: Cornell University Press, 1987); Malte Rolf, *Imperiale Herrschaft im Weichselland: Das Königreich Polen im Russischen Imperium (1864–1915)* (München: De Gruyter Oldenbourg, 2015); Malte Rolf, *Rządy imperialne w Kraju Nadwiślańskim. Królestwo Polskie i cesarstwo rosyjskie (1864–1915)* [Imperial government in the Vistula Land: the Kingdom of Poland and the Tsarist Empire (1864–1915)] (Warsaw: Wydawnictwa Uniwersytetu Warszawskiego, 2016); Malte Rolf, 'Between Imperial State-Building and Local Cooperation: Russian Rule in the Kingdom of Poland (1864–1915)', *Kritika: Explorations in Russian and Eurasian History* 18, 1 (2018): 385–416; Don Karl Rowney and Eugene Huskey, eds, *Russian Bureaucracy and the State: Officialdom from Alexander III to Vladimir Putin* (Houndmills: Palgrave Macmillan, 2009); Karl W. Ryavec, *Russian Bureaucracy: Power and Pathology* (Lanham, MD: Rowman & Littlefield, 2003); Leonid E. Shepelev, *Chinovnii mir Rossii XVIII – nachalo XX v.* [The world of the Russian bureaucrats from the 18th to the early 20th centuries] (St. Petersburg: Iskusstvo-SPB, 1999); D.N. Shilov, *Gosudarstvennye deiateli Rossiiskoi imperii: 1802–1917 – Biobibliograficheskii spravochnik* [Statesmen of the Russian Empire, 1802–1917: a biobibliographic guide] (St. Petersburg: Dmitrii Bulanin, 2002). The bureaucracy of the pre-reform period offers a marked contrast, see Susanne Schattenberg, *Die korrupte Provinz? Russische Beamte im 19. Jahrhundert* (Frankfurt a.M.: Campus Verlag, 2008).

16 See Jörg Ganzenmüller and Tatjana Tönsmeyer, eds, *Das Vorrücken des Staates in die Fläche im langen 19. Jahrhundert* (Köln: Böhlau, 2016).

17 In 1881, a three-stage emergency law was passed, which provided for a hierarchy of emergency levels and corresponding powers. After 'intensified' and 'exceptional protection' (*usilennaia* and *chrezvychainaia okhrana*), the ultimate level of protection, martial law, could be proclaimed. See, among others, Don C. Rawson, 'The Death Penalty in Late Tsarist Russia: An Investigation of Judicial Procedures', *Russian History* 1 (1984): 29–58, here 40–7; see also Baberowski, *Autokratie und Justiz*, particularly 691–721.

The expansion of state bureaucracy and its increasing importance, and thus its partially autonomous decision-making, continued under Alexander III. 'Restoration' tended to take place with a view to the participatory role of social self-determination. With regard to an ever more dirigiste state economic policy, there were even areas in which state activity further increased in the post-reform period.

This progressive expansion of state intervention in domestic affairs in the latter half of the nineteenth century had dramatic repercussions, particularly for the empire's peripheries. The process of state expansion and its internal administrative-legal homogenization fundamentally altered the special status of the peripheral provinces in Russia. The Great Reforms were St. Petersburg's attempt to dismantle the provinces' special status and push for an empire-wide standardization of administration and legislation. Achieving the model of an internally unified, and thus stabilized and more interventionist state, meant overcoming the diversity of administrative and legal jurisdictions in the empire. The aim was to transform the patchwork of strongly divergent particularist systems inherited from the premodern multi-ethnic empire – the result of territorial expansion and the co-opting of ever new territories along with their elites and privileges – into a unified whole.[18]

For the Kingdom of Poland, incorporated as it was into the Russian Empire, the reform era clearly represented a watershed. The January Uprising of 1863–64 in Poland deepened this break, but its suppression was by no means the only reason St. Petersburg set out in the 1860s and 70s to administratively reorganize this region of unrest. The expansion of central state structures in the Polish provinces must instead be viewed in the context of the Great Reforms. For the fundamental and guiding vision of these reforms – a homogenized state structure extending across the empire – demanded the alignment of administrative and legal structures in the peripheries of the empire as well.[19]

Intensified military subjugation, including more Russian troops in Warsaw and the Polish provinces, was only one result of the failed Polish uprising. The administration in the Kingdom of Poland likewise adapted to the Russian governorate structure. In the wake of this administrative reform, St. Petersburg progressively dissolved all Warsaw institutions previously administered by the Kingdom. Thus, in 1867, the State Council (*Gosudarstvennyi Sovet/Rada Stanu Królestwa*) and the Administrative Council (*Administrativnyi Sovet/Rada Administracyjna*) were disbanded. The individual administrative departments of interior, finance, judiciary and

---

18 See Jörg Baberowski, 'Auf der Suche nach Eindeutigkeit: Kolonialismus und zivilisatorische Mission im Zarenreich und der Sowjetunion', *Jahrbücher für Geschichte Osteuropas* 47, 3 (1999): 482–503, particularly 489–90; Andreas Kappeler, *Rußland als Vielvölkerreich: Entstehung, Geschichte, Zerfall* (München: C.H. Beck, 1992), 199–200; Andreas Kappeler, *The Russian Empire: A Multi-Ethnic History* (Essex: UK Pearson Education Limited, 2001); Rolf, 'Between Imperial State-Building and Local Cooperation'; Dov Yaroshevski, 'Empire and Citizenship', in *Russia's Orient: Imperial Borderlands and Peoples, 1700–1917*, eds Daniel R. Brower and Edward J. Lazzerini (Bloomington, IN: Indiana University Press, 1997), 58–79.

19 On the following, see also Rolf, *Imperiale Herrschaft im Weichselland*; Rolf, *Rządy imperialne w Kraju Nadwiślańskim*; Malte Rolf, 'Russifizierung, Depolonisierung oder innerer Staatsaufbau? Konzepte imperialer Herrschaft im Königreich Polen (1863–1915)', in *Kampf um Wort und Schrift: Russifizierung in Osteuropa im 19.–20. Jahrhundert*, ed. Zaur Gasimov (Göttingen: Vandenhoeck und Ruprecht, 2012), 51–88; Piotr S. Wandycz, *The Lands of Partitioned Poland 1795–1918* (Seattle, WA: University of Washington Press, 1974); Theodore R. Weeks, *Nation and State in Late Imperial Russia: Nationalism and Russification on the Western Frontier, 1863–1914* (DeKalb, IL: Northern Illinois University Press, 1996).

education were now directly subordinate to the respective ministries in St. Petersburg. By 1866 this process of administrative reconstruction was largely complete. The Kingdom, now often officially referred to as Vistula Land, was subsequently divided into ten administrative districts or 'guberniia', each of which was headed by a governor who was appointed by the tsar. The governors' offices were subordinate to the imperial viceroy (*namestnik*) in Warsaw, whose post was transferred to the office of the Warsaw governor general after the death of field marshal Fyodor Fyodorovich fon Berg in 1874. External governors and officials appointed by St. Petersburg took over the new bureaucratic apparatus and closely aligned the local administration to the directives of the ministries working at the imperial centre. Moreover, after the January Uprising, St. Petersburg made sure that the upper echelons of the state administration were not occupied by Polish officials. The same applied to the military hierarchies, the police force and the educational system. Hence, Vistula Land was ruled by a non-local civil service imported from the interior of the empire and usually Russian-Orthodox by faith. Russian became the official language of the administration, the courts, and very soon after, higher education as well. Further, countless laws were brought in line with the Russian legal system. The social and economic situation in the Kingdom of Poland was likewise becoming increasingly aligned with conditions in the centre. In 1864, the tsar decreed the emancipation of the serfs in the Kingdom, and the provinces lost their economic independence. Russian economic policy aimed to progressively integrate the periphery into the centre, a strategy exemplified in the formerly independent Bank of Poland being degraded to a branch of the centralized State Bank of the Russian Empire.

In overall terms, this reorganization of the administrative, legal and economic systems of the Kingdom of Poland aimed to incorporate the Polish provinces more fully into the imperial framework of Russia. From the perspective of St. Petersburg, these measures were a 'normalization' of internal state structures. The revolt accelerated a process of homogenization in the Polish provinces that in subsequent years would extend to other imperial peripheries. Once the uprising was quelled, there was no longer any need to abide by inherited legal traditions. The central government could pursue a policy of radical change with no regard for the voices of the local population, especially the indigenous elites. Undoubtedly, the measures were also intended as a punishment for the rebellious Poles, part of a long-term strategy of pacification and rule. But they were also a logical extension of the new reasons of state. In the political thinking of influential St. Petersburg officeholders, the internal unification of the state had become a value in its own right. The convergence of state structures in all parts of the empire promised modernity and progress, whereas their divergence recalled the fragmentation and stolidity of the ancien régime.

In the minds of Petersburg officials, the struggle with Polish insurgents only strengthened their conviction that the unification and centralization of the empire was the only way to secure its viability in the long run. The events of 1863–4 and the accompanying spectre of secession taught tsarist authorities the lesson that reforms could not stop at the inner-Russian borders but would have to be extended to the numerous administration and legal spheres of the peripheries as well. It was therefore not a break in the imperial policy of the reform period when Alexander III and Nicholas II pushed for the greater standardization of administrative and legal systems in the Baltic Sea provinces and Finland; rather, it was a logical continuation of it, using the insights gained in their struggle against the Poles. It could also be roughly summarized as follows: the ambitious project of ubiquitously transforming the premodern multi-ethnic empire into a modern one dates back to the crisis years of the Polish rebellion. The administrative measures undertaken in the Kingdom of Poland in the 1860s and 70s served as a model for how imperial state expansion would be organized in other peripheries of the Russian Empire.[20]

Ottoman Southeastern Europe: reforming the property and administration systems

The great Reform Edict of 1856 (*Islâhat Hatt-ı Hümayun*) at the end of the Crimean War announced a variety of reforms in the Ottoman Empire which the government of the sultan promised to implement without delay. One of the most comprehensive changes on the domestic front was initiated in 1858 with the newly proclaimed Land Code (*Arazi Kanunnâmesi*).[21] The law had several thrusts. By passing a new land law, the Sublime Porte was attempting to assert more regulatory power over the *çiftlik* estates. In many regions of Ottoman Southeastern Europe, the vast majority of the rural population lived in thrall to land- and estate owners (*çiftlik sahibi*), who were often referred to as 'agas' and 'beys' in everyday speech and administrative jargon.[22] Many peasant families, whom landowners perceived as something akin to 'tenant farmers', were under constant threat of being expelled from their respective *çiftlik*. But landowners did not exercise judicial or other functions over 'their' peasants. They also had no personal rights over them, and the peasants themselves were not restricted in their freedom of movement, meaning there was no real analogy here to the feudal manorial system.

The Sublime Porte used the Ottoman Land Code of 1858 to strengthen the rights of *çiftlik* peasants and set legal limits to the powers of landowners. The Land Code established certain basic principles. It was implemented step by step with separate agreements for each district, or *vilayet*, enforced by means of special decrees.

As a result, the new land system that emerged enabled rural families to buy their own land from the agas and beys. The psychological effect of this was significant. The emerging option of investing in property marked a turning point. Rural families now aspired to own their own piece of land with no obligations whatsoever to a *çiftlik sahibi*. To be sure, this shift in relations was a gradual one, the extent of property transactions being limited at first due to the reluctance of landowners to sell.

A key motivation of the Ottoman administration during the Tanzimat era – as the period of reformation in the Ottoman Empire is commonly called, especially from 1839 to the onset

---

20 On the Baltic Sea provinces, see especially Michael H. Haltzel, 'Triumphs and Frustrations of Administrative Russification, 1881–1914', in *Russification in the Baltic Provinces and Finland, 1855–1914*, ed. Edward C. Thaden (Princeton, NJ: Princeton University Press, 1981), 150–60; Edward C. Thaden, 'The Russian Government', in *Russification in the Baltic Provinces*, 15–110; indeed, see the entire volume edited by Thaden, *Russification in the Baltic Provinces*; Edward C. Thaden, *Russia's Western Borderlands, 1710–1870* (Princeton, NJ: Princeton University Press, 1984). On Finland, see Tuomo Polvinen, *Imperial Borderland: Bobrikov and the Attempted Russification of Finland, 1898–1904* (London: Hurst, 1995); Peter Waldron, 'Stolypin and Finland', *The Slavonic and East European Review* 63, 1 (1985): 41–55.

21 Donald Quataert, 'The Age of Reforms, 1812–1914', in *An Economic and Social History of the Ottoman Empire 1300–1914*, eds Halil İnalçık with Donald Quataert (Cambridge: Cambridge University Press, 1994): 759–943, here 856–61; see also Kemal Karpat, 'The Land Regime, Social Structure and Modernization in the Ottoman Empire', in *Beginnings of Modernization in the Middle East: The Nineteenth Century*, eds William Polk and Richard Chambers (Chicago, IL: University of Chicago Press, 1968): 69–90.

22 For a study of one exemplary context, see, e.g., Hannes Grandits, *Herrschaft und Loyalität in der spätosmanischen Gesellschaft: Das Beispiel der multikonfessionellen Herzegowina* (Weimar: Böhlau, 2008), especially 125–332.

Towards a new quality of statehood

of the reign of Abdülhamid II in 1876 – was the desire to generate more tax revenue from the large rural population, more than 80 per cent of which was rural-agricultural in most regions. One step in achieving this aim was to establish an efficient system of administration as well as to facilitate a more modern budget, both of which were defining characteristics of Ottoman policymaking in the final decades of the empire.[23] These efforts were not always consistent, however, and were often accompanied by various conflicts.

It is also necessary to keep in mind that there were considerable differences between the individual regions of 'European Turkey', as Ottoman Southeastern Europe was referred to by many contemporaries. Large parts of the Ottoman Balkans were mountainous, and many of these mountain regions were more reliant on livestock than agriculture. Thus, historically speaking, they were not or not so greatly affected by the *çiftlik* consolidation process that favoured local elites in other regions. Population density and the degree of penetration of various types of *çiftlik* estate farms varied greatly from region to region.[24]

Sparse settlement was a defining characteristic especially in many lowland areas. Mountainous areas, on the other hand, were usually more densely settled and were sometimes marked by tribal social structures, where landowning elites as well as the state – even in the period of intensive reform – had a hard time directly influencing the conditions of daily life.[25]

The de-feudalization tendencies in Ottoman Southeastern Europe discussed above in the context of the Land Code of 1858 need to be viewed against the backdrop of these regional differences. It is evident that these processes began even earlier (combatting and gradually eliminating the influence of all-powerful local *ayans* in the first decades of the century, disbanding the janissaries in 1826 and abolishing the *sipahi* system in the 1830s). But with the land ownership laws of 1858 (amended in the 1860s) the process was greatly accelerated. And yet, even in the 1850s and 60s, Ottoman reform bureaucracy never went so far as to fully distinguish between the ownership claims of the traditional landowning class in rural areas and those of the peasant *çiftlik* families. The reformers of the *Tanzimât*, despite their many initiatives, never planned to abolish the *çiftlik* system entirely. They had no intention of making enemies of the whole 'propertied class' (the majority of whom were Muslim), and so when it came to the agrarian question, they were not prepared to go any further than had the Land Code of 1858. There was no question of completely abolishing the *çiftliks*, so that in many regions the traditional landowning elites remained very powerful, at least economically.

Reforms were made in agriculture, albeit often preserving historical property relations. In another area, however, the Tanzimat reformers were more radical, following the trend of the day

---

23 See here the relevant views in Çağlar Keyder, ed., 'Ottoman Empire: Nineteenth-Century Transformations', *Review (Fernand Braudel Center)* 11, 2 (Spring, 1988).

24 For an excellent overview of the various types of *çiftlik* systems in the Ottoman Balkans, see especially Avdo Sućeska, 'O nastanku čifluka u našim zemljama' [On the emergence of the *çiftlik*-system in our region], *Godišnjak društva istoričara Bosne i Hercegovina God* XVI (1965): 37–57.

25 See here, e.g. the classic of Karl Kaser, *Hirten, Helden, Stammeskrieger: Ursprünge und Gegenwart des balkanischen Patriarchats* (Vienna: Böhlau 1992). But not all mountainous areas were out of the state's reach or poorly integrated in transregional economic relations. For an exemplary study, see e.g. Ulf Brunnbauer, *Gebirgsgesellschaften auf dem Balkan: Wirtschaft und Familienstrukturen im Rhodopengebiet (19./20. Jahrhundert)* (Vienna: Böhlau, 2004). For the empire-wide context and a look at older historical developments, see e.g. Fikret Adanır, 'Ottoman Peasantries c.1360–c.1860', in *The Peasantries of Europe from the Fourteenth to the Eighteenth Centuries*, ed. Tom Scott (London: Longman, 1998), 268–310; or with a view to transformation processes in the Ottoman Balkans, Fikret Adanır, 'Tradition and Rural Change in Southeastern Europe during Ottoman Rule', in *The Origins of Backwardness in Eastern Europe*, ed. Daniel Chirot (Berkeley, CA: University of California Press, 1989), 131–76.

more rigorously, namely, in their attempt to expand the modern administrative system down to the regional and communal level. The traditional elites (and religious institutions) influential up until that point, were increasingly expected to step aside in territorial administration and bow to the wishes of Tanzimat reformers. A new self-government at the local level along with a procedure more aligned with the vastly growing state bureaucracy were a first step in that direction. A new reform *vilayet* in Ottoman Southeastern Europe established in the 1860s, the so-called Danbue Vilayet,[26] was an essential indication of how this development would be implemented in practice.

The rather sprawling Danube Vilayet (Vilâyet-i Tuna) was created in 1864 from various territories south of the Danube and was a kind of model province for restructuring the Ottoman provincial order. The first *vali*, or governor, of the new *vilayet*, in office from 1864 to 1868, was Ahmed Şefik Midhat Pasha – the same Midhat Pasha who would go on to become a leading Ottoman statesman in the 1870s (and who was also active at the forefront of the constitutional movement of 1876). Attempts were made under Midhat Pasha to modernize, streamline and reform various parts of the economy and society. Of vital importance here was the establishment of a modern administrative organization, first implemented in the Danube Vilayet. Modelled after the French *departements* and *arrondissement* system, it was proclaimed in 1864 as a new *vilayet* system (the Vilayet Nizamnamesi, the Vilayet Law of 1864 which regulated the provinces and was followed by the Vilayet-i Umumiye Nazamnamesi, or the General Provincial System in 1867). This *vilayet* system was gradually introduced to other parts of the Ottoman Empire, including the Balkan provinces, for example in the Bosnian Vilayet, as early as 1865.[27]

The following excerpt from *Loi constitutive du département formé sous le nom de vilayet du Danube*, officially published by the authorities in French and Turkish, concerns the various levels of administration, beginning with the *vilayet* and covering the *sandshak* (translated as *arrondissement* in the official French document), the *kaza* (translated as *canton*) and administration at the communal level. The decrees on the latter included the following stipulations:

> Art. 58: In every village, two *mukhtars* will be elected by each community, conforming to the provisions of Art. V. Every community that consists of less than twenty houses is only entitled to elect one mukhtar.

> Art. 59. The mudir will be notified of the election of the mukhtars, and he will confirm it.

> ...

> Art. 67. Every Ottoman subject, regardless of the community to which he belongs, who has completed more than eighteen years of age, has an interest in the commune and pays more than at least fifty piasters in direct contributions per year, will take part in the college which assembles yearly in each village to elect the mukhtars and the elders.[28]

---

26 Milen V. Petrov, *Tanzimat for the Countryside: Midhat Paşa and the Vilayet of Danube 1864–1868* (Dissertation, Princeton University, 2006).

27 For a general account, see e.g. Standford J. Shaw and Ezel Kural Shaw, *History of the Ottoman Empire and Modern Turkey*, vol. 2, *Reform, Revolution, and Republic: The Rise of Modern Turkey, 1808–1975* (Cambridge: Cambridge University Press [1977] 2002), 91–5. For the Bosnian example, see Ahmed Aličić, 'Decree on the Organization of Vilayets 1867', in *Prilozi za orijentalnu filologiju* 36 (Sarajevo: Orijentalni Institute, 1986), 255–76; and Ahmed Aličić, *Uređenje bosanskog elayeta od 1789 do 1878 godine* [The organization of the Bosnian Eyalet from 1789 to 1878] (Sarajevo: Orijentalni Institute, 1983).

28 *Loi constitutive du département formé sous le nom de vilayet du Danube* (Constantinople: Imprimerie Centrale 1865), 10–11.

Towards a new quality of statehood

These provisions indicate that a system of elected local representatives was being established at the communal level. These *mukhtars* – as all village chiefs were now officially called, regardless of whether the villages were Muslim or Christian[29] – were to serve as contact persons to the state administration (to the *mudirs* in the *kazas* or to the *sandjak* and *vilayet* authorities). Active and passive voting rights, according to the excerpt above, were linked to how much one paid in taxes. The *vilayet* system also regulated the establishment of a council of elders (*ihtiyer meclis*), and in the towns and cities, too, communal administrations were elected with the view of fulfilling certain agendas. The electoral procedures in the *mahallas* in the urban context were similar to those described here.

The reform tendencies in communal administration established by the *vilayet* system are clear. First, the procedures for appointing representatives at the communal level were standardized. Well-defined procedures for electing *mukhtars* were meant to replace the *adets*, the customary rules in place up to that point. Second, the possibility of participating in the electoral process was linked to property in the form of tax payments.

The reforms outlined above considerably expanded the responsibilities and powers of *mukhtars* in local public affairs. But government officials also knew that the village chiefs could be held accountable now if something in the villages did not function the way the authorities wanted. Indeed, this new system of administration was increasingly consolidated throughout the 1860s, making this the decisive decade in the transition to a new quality and presence of statehood and/or state administration in the regions of Ottoman Southeastern Europe.

The abovementioned de-feudalization tendencies, however limited they may have been, thus went hand in hand with the establishment of a state administrative system organized according to modern principles and extending into the most remote villages and urban *mahallas* (quarters or districts). At least this was the state's enthusiastic aim, which turned out to be an immense challenge (proceeding with varying degrees of success given the great structural differences from region to region).[30]

Parallel to this development there was a considerable wave of bureaucratization, for the authorities at the *vilayet*, *sandshak* and *kaza* levels expanded infrastructure with new spheres of responsibility for financial administration, the judiciary and the police – some of it in cooperation with (e.g. the abovementioned councils), but more often in contrast to or in conflict with, the hitherto dominant local (primarily Muslim-religious) elites.[31]

This wave of bureaucratization, growing more relevant in the 1860s, must be viewed against the backdrop of general restructuring within the Ottoman Empire. In the wake of the great Tanzimat reform process, the empire had set out to (again) tighten, in a wholly new form, the authority and reach of the central governing powers. A new bureaucratic apparatus – as sketched above in the example of the *vilayet* system – was to extend into regional and local affairs, linking them to the Sublime Porte and its newly established ministries. In the imperial centre, a new bureaucratic apparatus was rapidly replacing the traditional work of the scribes employed by the

---

29 In daily usage, Christian village chiefs were traditionally still referred to as *knez* – or sometimes as *koca-başı* if these men were likewise representatives of the people in the *meclis* of the *kaza*.

30 See Abdulhamit Kırmızı, 'Taming the Governors: The Swinging Pendulum of Power over the Ottoman Provinces in the Nineteenth Century', *International Journal of Regional and Local Studies* 6, 1 Series 2, (2010): 4–23.

31 On this wave of bureaucratization in general, see especially Carter V. Findley, *Bureaucratic Reform in the Ottoman Empire: The Sublime Porte, 1789–1922* (Princeton, NJ: Princeton University Press, 1980); See also Karen Barkey, *Bandits and Bureaucrats: The Ottoman Route to State Centralization* (New York: Columbia University Press, 1997).

sultan. Civil servants with their own professional code of conduct, trained at special schools and pursuing a hierarchical career path, rapidly became the key representatives of the state in the second half of the nineteenth century. Like many historians of the Ottoman reforms, Carter V. Findley in his *Ottoman Civil Officialdom: A Social History* emphasizes the following:

> Ottoman civil officials had a social prominence different in kind from that of their western European counterparts. The traditional concept of Ottoman society as divided into 'ruling' and 'subject classes', and the fact that the ruling class was almost exclusively Muslim while the subject classes were religiously mixed, played a part in defining this prominence.[32]

We will address in more detail below the persistent religious issues in the Ottoman Empire, which for centuries was defined as an Islamic state but that now – according to the new reform edict – was supposed to be restructured into a modern state accommodating all of its citizens, at least theoretically. It was not only in this respect, however, that the transformation of a scribe-based system, already highly antiquated in the nineteenth century, into a uniform-wearing, professional and self-confident bureaucracy was an enormous cultural upheaval.

The rise of this new bureaucracy in the second half of the nineteenth century was astonishing in quantitative terms as well. It is difficult to put into numbers, but the following figures should offer an impression of how massive this development was: in the early nineteenth century, a group of little more than 2,000 scribes served the sultan and his government and were responsible for the bulk of the empire's administrative duties; yet, by the end of the nineteenth century, somewhere between 35,000 and 50,000 (higher-ranking) bureaucrats were running the Ottoman administration. This number does not include the many assistants and employees in subordinate positions.[33] If the officers and soldiers in the military were added to the equation, one can see just how much the public-service sector grew in a state with a population of approximately 25 million.

But these figures must still be put into perspective by comparing them with the even higher level of bureaucratization found, for instance, in the Habsburg administration, addressed in more detail below. The Ottoman Empire, despite the quantitative developments previously mentioned – and despite the many efforts of Sublime Porte reformers to make progress in constructing a modern state apparatus – was still under-bureaucratized by comparison at the end of the nineteenth century. Granted, the sultans and their governments were prepared to make considerable efforts and invest enormous resources, material and otherwise, to change this situation, which leads us to a special set of problems regarding the Ottoman Empire's emergence into a modern bureaucratic state order. As previously mentioned, the 1856 Treaty of Paris had guaranteed the Ottoman Empire's acceptance into the Concert of the European powers. Yet other international treaties were still in force (some of them decades old, or ever older) that gave various European powers extensive economic and commercial privileges in Ottoman territories. These so-called 'capitulation' treaties, once considered modernization initiatives, opened up Ottoman markets to Western industrial and commercial goods during the period in question here, even placing the citizens of other empires (e.g. Britain, France and Austria) outside of Ottoman jurisdiction. The share of Western investments and commercial offices on Ottoman territory – just

---

32 Carter V. Findley, *Ottoman Civil Officialdom: A Social History* (Princeton, NJ: Princeton University Press, 1989), here 11.

33 Kemal H. Karpat, *Ottoman Population, 1830–1914: Demographic and Social Characteristics*, (Madison, WI: University of Wisconsin Press, 1985), here 218.

Towards a new quality of statehood

like the number of 'foreigners' engaged in trade who enjoyed special protection on account of the capitulation treaties – rose steeply in the second half of the nineteenth century.[34] This was not necessarily advantageous to the 'domestic' economy in the Ottoman Empire; quite the contrary, in fact. Thus, with its growing entanglement in Western trade – which an emerging homegrown, mostly Christian, merchant bourgeoisie greatly profited from – the Ottoman economy increasingly became the object of Western (commercial) imperialism.[35]

What is more, in the two decades after the Crimean War, the Ottoman government insisted on financing its considerable armaments programme, state spending and especially the reform projects outlined above with massive loans from Western capital markets. By the late 1860s and particularly in the 1870s, this policy had plunged the Ottoman Empire into a serious debt crisis. Ever new loans helped at first to plug holes in the budget and maintain salary payments to the military and civil service (often with considerable delay). But with rising debt claims from Paris and London the state threatened to default as early as the 1870s. The spiralling debt of Ottoman state finances presented a growing challenge to the Ottoman Empire's ambitious modernization programme.[36]

Linked to this was yet another development that set in soon after the Treaty of Paris and became even more apparent in the 1860s: the progressive loss of Ottoman influence in the Danubian Principalities and the Principality of Serbia. Whereas the two decades after the Crimean War were described as a period of increased 'bureaucratic centralization' in the Ottoman Empire – the characteristic feature of the Sublime Porte during these years – such a description did not apply to the Danubian Principalities or to Serbia. To be sure, the contrary was true in these territories, whose leading elites endeavoured to rid themselves of Ottoman rule and gradually transform the internationally recognized rights of 'national' self-government outlined in the peace treaty of 1856 into independent statehood.

It is impossible here to give a detailed account of every aspect (and inherent contradiction) of this process of secession and independence. Essentially, it boiled down to a protracted legal battle with international repercussions. Escalating violence figured prominently in the Serbian case. In 1862, for example, a conflict with the Ottoman military forces stationed in the Belgrade fortress developed into a veritable civil war, resulting in the negotiation (with international arbitration) of the complete withdrawal of Ottoman troops stationed in the city (including most other cities in the principality) several years later. Though officially under Ottoman supremacy into the 1870s, in practice, these territories made considerable gains in asserting their own statehood.[37]

---

34 For an in-depth look at this situation and its development, see e.g. Jens–Oliver Schmitt, *Levantiner: Lebenswelten und Identitäten einer ethnokonfessionellen Gruppe im Osmanischen Reich im 'langen 19. Jahrhundert'* (München: Oldenbourg, 2005).

35 On general developments, see e.g., Matthew Smith Anderson, *The Eastern Question 1774–1923: A Study in International Relations* (London: Macmillan 1966); Şevket Pamuk, *The Ottoman Empire and European Capitalism, 1820–1913: Trade, Investment and Production* (Cambridge: Cambridge University Press, 1987); Reşat Kasaba, *The Ottoman Empire and the World Economy: The Nineteenth Century* (Albany, NY: State University of New York Press, 1988).

36 Edhem Eldem, 'Ottoman Financial Integration with Europe: Foreign Loans, the Ottoman Band and the Ottoman Public Debt', in *European Review* 13, 3 (Cambridge: Cambridge University Press, 2005): 431–45; Christopher Clay, *Gold for the Sultan: Western Bankers and Ottoman finance 1856–1881* (London: I.B. Tauris, 2000); Edhem Eldem, *A History of the Ottoman Bank* (Istanbul: Osmanlı Bankası, 1999).

37 See Holm Sundhaussen, *Geschichte Serbiens 19.-21. Jahrhundert* (Vienna: Böhlau, 2007); Nataša Mišković, *Basare und Boulevards: Belgrad im 19. Jahrhundert* (Vienna: Böhlau, 2008); and Viorel S. Roman, *Rumänien im Spannungsfeld der Grossmächte. Teil: Bd. 1., 1774–1878: die Donaufürstentümer vom osmanischen Vasallentum zur europäischen Peripherie* (Offenbach: Falk, 1987); Paul E. Michelson, *Romanian Politics 1858–1871: From Prince Cuza to Prince Carol* (Iaşi: Centrul de Studii Romaneşti, 1998).

Conflicts in the Ottoman Empire culminated in the summer of 1875 when, in addition to national debt and the regional independence movements in Serbia and the Danubian Principalities, local rebellions broke out in the Bosnia Vilayet along with revolutionary insurrections in the Danube Vilayet against Ottoman institutions.[38] In the Danube Vilayet in particular, Ottoman troops and local paramilitary forces used massive counter-violence to put down the 'guilty' insurrectionists. The great powers began to exert more diplomatic pressure. The Sublime Porte was exhorted to repay its debts as well as to improve the 'imperilled status of the Christians' in the areas of rebellion and the Ottoman Empire in general. This was soon accompanied by the great powers asserting their claims to protect the Christian population in the empire. A popular movement (e.g. with Russian volunteers) even led to the Principality of Serbia declaring war on the sultan – resulting in Serbia's quick defeat and considerable concessions. The crucial turning point, however, came in 1877 when the Russian government became militarily involved in the conflict.[39] The principalities under Ottoman suzerainty, i.e. Serbia, Romania (created through the merging of the two Danubian Principalities) and Montenegro, soon followed suit.

The Russo-Turkish War of 1877–8 claimed tens of thousands of military and civilian casualties. Even more were turned into refugees, especially inhabitants of the combat zone. Despite desperate attempts of the Ottoman army and its leadership, the conflict ended with their catastrophic defeat in the face of vigorous Russian offensives which stopped just short of Istanbul.[40] The defeat put an abrupt end to the First Constitutional Era (*Birinci Meşrutiyet*), which will be discussed in more detail below.

The peace framework of the Congress of Berlin, convened in the summer of 1878 to settle the 'Oriental Question', significantly curtailed Ottoman rule in the Balkans, a region so pivotal in the empire's history.[41] The principalities of Romania, Serbia and Montenegro now became internationally recognized independent states. The newly established Principality of Bulgaria became a state under Ottoman suzerainty. Moreover, the *vilayets* of Bosnia and Herzegovina were occupied by Habsburg troops, and from 1878 on, were under Austro-Hungarian administration. Thus, large parts of the Balkans were effectively divorced from Ottoman rule. And yet the Ottoman Empire still remained a ruling power in the Balkans. Direct Ottoman rule extended from Edirne and Thessaloniki in the south, across the Macedonian region and as far as Epirus in modern-day Greece as well as present-day Albania.[42]

---

38 On Bosnia-Herzegovina, see e.g. Hannes Grandits, 'Violent Social Disintegration: A Nation-Building Strategy in Late-Ottoman Hercegovina', in *Conflicting Loyalties in the Balkans: The Great Powers, the Ottoman Empire and Nation-Building*, eds Hannes Grandits, Nathalie Clayer and Robert Pichler (London: I.B. Tauris, 2011), 110–34. On the so-called April Uprising, see e.g. Alexander Vezenkov, 'Alexander in the Service of the Sultan, in the Service of the Revolution: Local Bulgarian Notables in the 1870s', in Grandits, Clayer and Pichler, *Conflicting Loyalties in the Balkans*, 86–106.

39 See Barbara Jelavich, *Russia's Balkan Entanglements 1806–1914* (Cambridge: Cambridge University Press, 1993); Bela Kiraly and Gale Stokes, eds, *Insurrections, Wars, and the Eastern Crisis in the 1870s* (New York: Columbia University Press, 1985).

40 Ömer Turan, *The Ottoman-Russian War of 1877–78* (Ankara: TDV, 2007).

41 For a contextualization and general discussion of the importance of the Balkans in the Ottoman imperial framework, see the concise summary in Nathalie Clayer, 'Balkans', *The Encyclopedia of Islam*, eds Kate Fleet, et al. (Leiden: Brill, 2015) 32–41; and for a more detailed account, Fikret Adanır and Suraiya Faroqui, eds, *The Ottomans and the Balkans: A Discussion of Historiography* (Leiden: Brill, 2002).

42 See Ralph Melville and Hans-Jürgen Schröder, eds, *Der Berliner Kongress von 1878: die Politik der Grossmächte und die Probleme der Modernisierung in Südosteuropa in der 2. Hälfte des 19. Jahrhunderts* (Wiesbaden: Steiner 1982).

Towards a new quality of statehood

The peace settlement of the Congress of Berlin reaffirmed the debt obligations of the Ottoman Empire. To 'stabilize' Ottoman finances (and ensure debt servicing) an international fiscal authority was set up in 1881, the so-called *Administration de la Dette Publique Ottomane*. It was this institution, with its several thousand employees, that would exercise broad rights of determination over Ottoman public finance management over the next three decades.[43] In other words, the status of the Ottoman Empire deteriorated considerably after the Congress of Berlin and during the transition to the 1880s. It had gone from being an empire in the European concert of great powers to being placed under the trusteeship of an international debt control commission, thus forfeiting its rights of sovereignty. To a certain extent the Ottoman Empire (once again) became the object of the 'imperial imagination' in Europe's age of New Imperialism. This was not without repercussions on the representation of rule, as will be seen in the following section. And yet, it was still a gigantic empire, stretching from Anatolia to Mesopotamia, all the way to Mecca and Medina. As far as the Balkans were concerned, however, the sultan was just one among several rulers, the Ottoman Empire just one among several states. A number of small independent states had emerged, whose statehood and its development will be discussed in more detail below.

The development of the Habsburg state, 1850–1880

The existential challenges posed to the Romanov and Ottoman empires by the Crimean War had produced a broad range of reform efforts initiated by Tsar Alexander II, Sultan Abdülmecid, and their successors. By contrast, not the Crimean War but rather the revolutions of 1848–49 had shaken the Habsburg Empire to its very foundations. For the sake of restoring domestic stability and of strengthening the empire's international position after the revolutions, the Habsburgs too pursued a broad and pronounced reform agenda starting in the 1850s. But they did so from a set of social, economic, political and cultural conditions that differed significantly from those experienced by their neighbours to the east and south. Unlike the situations in Russia and the Ottoman Empire, the Habsburg Empire had initiated massive state-building and de-feudalization efforts in the second half of the eighteenth century to address several of the crises now being faced by the other two empires. Those Habsburg reforms, however, had stalled significantly when the state was plunged into nearly 25 years of incessant warfare (1790–1815). Emerging from the Napoleonic Wars in 1815, as mentioned above, the cautious regime eschewed further reform even as many social groups expected and demanded the fulfilment of the government's earlier efforts.

The revolutionary upheavals of 1848–49, that neither Russia nor the Ottoman Empire had experienced, forced several European states including Austria to take decisive action with regard to two different continuing targets of popular protest. First was the as-yet incomplete process of de-feudalization that continued to rankle and radicalize peasant populations in several regions of Europe. In the Habsburg Monarchy peasant anger was especially strong in Galicia and parts of Hungary. Second were the growing demands, generally made by urban populations, to institutionalize meaningful forms of popular political participation. In France and several German states this meant reforming existing constitutions; in Austria, it meant achieving a constitution.

---

43 Murat Birdal, *The Political Economy of Ottoman Public Debt: Insolvency and European Financial Control in the Late Nineteenth Century* (London: Tauris Academic Studies, 2010).

The revolutions – particularly in the Habsburg Monarchy's Italian and Hungarian regions – also exposed the incompleteness of a process of territorial integration in the Habsburg Monarchy that had really only started a century earlier. In the spring of 1848 when the regime was vulnerable to protest (and the military was busy on the Italian peninsula), the Hungarian Estates under the leadership of Louis Kossuth had forced the Emperor's agreement to a set of constitutional laws that essentially made Hungary into a state separate from the Habsburgs' other holdings, although retaining a Habsburg ruler.[44] Independence in turn produced internal opposition in Hungary – tacitly fed by the Habsburgs – among elements of the populations of Croatia, the Vojvodina, Transylvania and northern Hungary (today's Slovakia) who opposed the revolutionary regime's emphasis on Hungarian language and Hungarian nationhood.[45] At the same time, Hungary's successful example emboldened town and city populations elsewhere in the empire that spring to demand constitutional rights and the ability to legislate. These efforts produced an Austrian Parliament elected by a remarkably broad franchise that met in the summer and autumn of 1848 to produce a constitution and end feudal relations on the land. The revolution also produced efforts in many crown lands to reform and liberalize local institutions like crown land diets and municipal councils. By March of 1849 a constitutional committee of the Austrian parliament was finishing a draft constitution for the empire, even as the Hungarian government prepared to declare full independence from the Habsburgs.

On 9 March 1849, the new Emperor Francis Joseph I, who had replaced his faltering uncle Ferdinand I in December 1848, dismissed the parliament and imposed a constitution on Austria that had been written by his minister of the interior, Count Francis Stadion. One noteworthy innovation this imposed constitution introduced was an attempt to make autonomous communes the basis for future popular participation in the political system. The idea of the autonomous commune was to make the citizen into an active, if junior, partner with the state bureaucracy by assigning a degree of administrative and political competencies to elected local municipal councils. It was hoped that this hybrid combination of state bureaucratic oversight with local initiative might create a restricted sphere into which the public might channel some limited activism.[46] Hungary, however, was a different matter. There a civil war raged, and it was only with the help of the Russian army that the Austrians eventually defeated the revolutionaries in August of 1849.

As disturbing as they were to the Habsburg elite, an examination of the revolutionary events of 1848–49 suggests to us today that with the major exception of the Hungarian Estates, the revolution was not directed against the existence of the composite Austrian state. More often the revolution seems to have been fought around the questions of just how the empire ought to be organized politically or which direction the empire ought to take, and not about whether the empire ought to exist in the first place. Many of the most articulate revolutionaries from different regions of the empire – from the Bohemian Czech nationalist František Palacký to the Adriatic Italian nationalist Niccolò Tommaseo – agreed on the critical necessity to maintain the

---

44 The so-called April Laws. István Deák, *The Lawful Revolution: Louis Kossuth and the Hungarians, 1848–1849* (New York: Columbia University Press, 1979).

45 The new laws stated that only those with knowledge of the Hungarian language could be elected to the Hungarian Diet. Robert John Weston Evans, 'Language and State Building: The Case of the Habsburg Monarchy', *Austrian History Yearbook* 35 (2004): 13.

46 On Stadion's 1849 constitution and the communal autonomy laws, see most recently John Deak, *Forging a Multinational State: State Making in Imperial Austria from the Enlightenment to the First World War* (Stanford, CA: Stanford University Press, 2015), especially 154–8.

empire.[47] The Empire benefited from too many regional and local interests to be itself an object of destruction. Rather, it was the way the empire was organized and run that engendered revolutionary passions. Moreover, it quickly became clear to most observers during the revolutionary year – both those sympathetic to and those opposed to revolution – that having obtained the end to their feudal obligations in regions where they still existed, the peasantry constituted a deep reservoir of loyalty both to the dynasty and to the state.

In the decade following 1848–49, the Habsburg Monarchy too pursued ambitious programmes of economic, political and social reform designed to build on these strengths (peasant loyalty, local and regional interests in maintaining empire) and to remove forms of potential political opposition. One major lesson Austria's rulers drew from the experience of revolution was the critical importance of effective institutional integration and centralization. The concession of the Hungarian April Laws and Hungary's later declaration of independence from the Habsburg state had laid bare the dangerous degree to which different parts of the empire remained subject to different laws, institutions and traditions often dictated by crown land nobilities. The regime had also learned that it could not rely even tacitly on its traditional alliance with the regional nobilities, privileged men and women who during the revolution had often pursued their own regional interests at the expense of the dynasty's. The instrument for asserting this new form of rule in the post-revolutionary decade was to be a vastly expanded bureaucracy with a powerfully renewed mission of reform, staffed with men (and later women) whose loyalties lay unquestionably with the imperial centre. As one disillusioned Bohemian aristocrat complained of the new regime, everything was now 'handed over without protection to the bureaucrats' and that 'what conservative institutions the revolution from below left intact, the revolution from above has continued to destroy.'[48]

The regime's first aims were 1) to address the remaining challenges of de-feudalization while 2) rapidly building state structures that would more effectively integrate the empire's different regions and peoples. Through strict policies of centralized administration, large-scale infrastructure development and social and educational reform, the post-revolution government hoped to immunize society from the kinds of internal instability it had recently experienced, while simultaneously rebuilding Austria's weakened position on the European stage. To accomplish these ends, however, demanded an ambitious degree of political centralization not attempted since the tumultuous reform era of the second half of the eighteenth century.

Empress Consort Queen Maria Theresa (ruled 1740–1780) and her sons Joseph II (1780–1790) and Leopold II (1790–1792) had already laid important foundations for most of these policies of the 1850s. They had ended the most extreme forms of serfdom, limiting the *robot*[49] and even occasionally making land available to peasants, but to very different extents in different regions of their monarchy. In Austria, the increasing number of common empire-wide laws and institutions jostled against a range of separate crown land customs, laws, traditions and administrative practices. This fact illustrates the degree to which Austria, like many European states in

---

47 On Tommaseo, see Dominique Kirchner Reill, *Nationalists Who Feared The Nation: Adriatic Multinationalism in Habsburg Dalmatia, Trieste, and Venice* (Stanford, CA: Stanford University Press, 2012); for Palacký's famous statement regarding Austria's existence in 1848, František Palacký, 'Letter to Frankfurt, 11 April 1848', in Balázs Trencsény and Michal Kopeček, eds, *Discourses of Collective Identity in Central and Southeast Europe (1770–1945)*, vol. 2 (Budapest: CEU Press, 2007), 327.

48 Quoted in Robert John Weston Evans, *Austria, Hungary, and the Habsburgs: Essays on Central Europe c. 1683–1867* (Oxford: Oxford University Press, 2006), 272.

49 The term *robot* refers to forced labour – usually a specified number of days per week – owed by the serf to the Lord.

the nineteenth century, remained to a great extent a composite monarchy.[50] In order to accomplish the dual processes of centralization and integration the state built an imperial bureaucracy separate from the traditional administration of each region. This growing bureaucracy in turn was increasingly staffed by the sons of the merchant and educated middle classes, rather than by the regional aristocracies (or at first, in addition to them).[51] A bureaucrat owed his unquestioning loyalty to the state, rather than to his class or to regional interests. He must therefore embody the highest Enlightenment ideal of dedicated citizenship, and 'to be a citizen meant, according to the Enlightenment ... active participation in the construction of the nation state' rather than any kind of noble status.[52] Every aspect of bureaucratic life came to favour the norms of educated middle-class life, from a range of office practices (the daily demands of punctuality) and dress codes to housing and modes of socializing outside of work (where nobles maintained status differences more successfully). And although Clemens von Metternich might famously continue to receive colleagues at home in his pyjamas well into the nineteenth century, the new trend for mid-level servants of the state emphasized a decidedly non-aristocratic separation of home and workplace. Qualifications such as a law degree also made state service more available to upwardly mobile members of the educated middle classes.

What we already see before the French Revolution is not only the development of a new concept of citizenship among the peoples of the Habsburg Monarchy, but also new assertions of uniformity, integration and equivalence among the territories that previously had little formal institutional relationship to each other. In 1811, the Austrian Civil Law Code (*Allgemeines bürgerliches Gesetzbuch*) stated that 'An individual earns his full enjoyment of his rights through his citizenship in the state' and 'every person has innate rights, clearly through reason, and is therefore to be regarded as a person. Slavery or servitude ... is not permitted in these countries.'[53]

After the Napoleonic Wars, the state's exhausted fiscal means had prevented it from undertaking large-scale economic, infrastructural, or social projects. During the period 1815–1848 most initiatives for social, economic or cultural reform in Austria – and there were many – originated from society, from individual entrepreneurs or from industrial, agricultural, educational and other reform associations that often combined aristocratic, noble and middle-class memberships. When those revolutions had exploded across Europe in 1848, peasantry, educated middle classes, including nobility and gentry in several regions had seen in them the opportunity to transform a dissatisfactory status quo. The violence, disorder and suffering experienced by many during the revolutionary period, however, also convinced many revolutionaries by 1849, that only an enlightened state could create effective reform without unleashing social instability.

---

50 On the concept of composite monarchy, John H. Elliot, 'A Europe of Composite Monarchies', *Past and Present* 137 (1992): 48–71. This type of state consisted of a union of distinct territories under the rule of one sovereign by which each territory retained distinctive laws and customs. In the Habsburg Monarchy, it was the laws and agreements promulgated in the early eighteenth century and referred to as the 'Pragmatic Sanction' that had first bound the territories together as one, to agree to the succession of a female heir. Paula Sutter Fichtner, *The Habsburg Monarchy 1490–1848* (New York: Palgrave, 2003), 61; Charles Ingrao, *The Habsburg Monarchy 1618–1815* (Cambridge: Cambridge University Press, 1994), 128–9.

51 In the period 1780–1811, the number of state bureaucrats in Vienna alone rose from 495 to 618. Their social composition included 41% from a commoner background and 41% from ennobled civil-service or military background. Waltraud Heindl, *Gehorsame Rebellen: Bürokratie und Beamte in Österreich 1780 bis 1848* (Vienna: Böhlau, 1990), 147.

52 Heindl, *Gehorsame Rebellen*, 23–34.

53 *Allgemeines bürgerliches Gesetzbuch*, accessed at www.ibiblio.org/ais/abgb1.htm#t1h1

Towards a new quality of statehood

Not two years after imposing his own constitution in March of 1849, however, the young Francis Joseph abrogated it and on 31 December 1851, he imposed a more ambitiously absolutist set of policies on Austria. Now the emperor stated that 'after careful consideration of every aspect we find ourselves pressed by our duty as sovereign to declare the ... constitutional document of 4 March 1849 to be annulled.' The announcement hastened to add, however that two critical and popular achievements of the revolution, 'the equality of all citizens before the law, as well as ... laws regarding the abolition of all peasant serfdom with compensation' remained in force.[54]

The ensuing decade saw Austria embark on an ambitious, and in many ways quite liberal programme of imposed economic, social and cultural renewal to strengthen the empire domestically and restore its foreign influence. An enlarged bureaucracy implemented a set of highly centralized and integrated institutions of rule. The programme of the 1850s did not reject the social, legal and economic accomplishments of many of the revolutionaries, but it pursued them in a politically absolutist way. And although these programmes were imposed from above, even contemporaries noted the degree to which the origins of many of them had been inspired by the creative efforts of the revolutionary activists. Some of those very revolutionaries, like the Minister of the Interior Alexander von Bach (1813–1893), even became mainstays of the authoritarian but also reform-minded regime that took hold in the 1850s.

The new regime initiated innovative policies to improve agriculture, transport and communications infrastructures, trade, as well as the spread of small credit banks to rural areas. In the crown lands where feudal relations had remained in force until 1848, peasants finally gained ownership of some of the land they had worked, and their obligations in kind, labour and services were cancelled. At the same time, the government created a complex formula to compensate landowners for lost labour, based on an estimate of their financial losses over a 20-year period. Outside of Hungary, for example, the value of lost peasant *robot* was set at one-third the value of free labour. The government then reduced this amount by a third since the state now assumed the burden of judicial and administrative functions for which local landowners had previously been responsible. Within Hungary the government set compensation at a full third of the value of the land now occupied by the peasants. In Bukovina, Galicia and Hungary the government itself financed the entire compensation process, while in the rest of the empire the provincial crown land governments shared the costs with the peasants (who were generally better off). This condition in turn produced an enormous demand for access to credit in the countryside.[55]

An 1853 law also gave large landowners the opportunity to buy up lands that had formerly been held in common in the peasant communities and which peasants had used to pasture animals or gather wood and other resources to help them survive the winter. This option gave lords in Galicia an effective strategy to force peasants in many communities to work for a wage on the lords' lands, in return for the assignment of a small part of those lands back to the village to use for common purposes. Not surprisingly, peasants often refused to recognize the loss of what they considered to be their own forests and pastures, and when they did, the police and military had to frequently intervene to force

---

54 *Allgemeines Reichs- Gesetz- und Regierungsblatt für das Kaiserthum Österreich* 1852, II. Stuck, 10 January, 25–6.

55 David Good, *The Economic Rise of the Habsburg Monarchy 1750–1914* (Berkeley, CA: University of California Press, 1984), 78–9; Christoph Stölzl, *Die Ära Bach in Böhmen: Sozialgeschichtliche Studien zum Neoabsolutismus 1849–1859* (München: R. Oldenbourg, 1971), 28; Roman Sandgruber, *Ökonomie und Politik: Österreichs Wirtschaftsgeschichte vom Mittelalter bis zur Gegenwart* (Vienna: Ueberreuter, 2005), 234–5.

their compliance. The complexity of these cases is demonstrated by the fact that it took a government commission, set up in 1855, 40 years to adjudicate the competing claims to formerly common lands in Galicia. As a consequence, peasants in several regions of Galicia remained suspicious of the opportunity to work for a wage on the lords' land, fearing a re-imposition of the hated *robot* obligations.[56]

If the reforms seem to have inadvertently maintained a status quo of low productivity and dissatisfaction in Galician villages, it had very different effects elsewhere in the monarchy. In Bohemia, for example, more well-to-do peasants, now freed from the *robot*, expanded their planting and profited from a rise in grain prices in the period 1850–1870, enabling them to pay off their share of the compensation within a decade. Moreover, as property owners, they often gained a critical voice in Stadion's municipal councils (which were retained), and this helped them to control the sales of formerly community lands, usually to themselves. Poorer or landless peasants in the Bohemian lands unable to make the payments often left the land for industrial work, (for which, however, there were far fewer opportunities in Galicia or Bukovina).

Other economic reforms transformed the empire into a single free-trade zone, finally ending the tariff barrier that had long separated Hungary from the rest of the empire. In the past, although they had hoped to remove the barrier, Austria's rulers had left it in place in order to compensate themselves for the tax-exempt status of the Hungarian nobility. Now such traditional privileges were swept aside (and even replaced with the imposition of an income tax). In order to coordinate economic policy more effectively and to coordinate developments in the different regions of the empire, Commerce Minister Karl Ludwig von Bruck (1798–1860) created elected Chambers of Commerce in each region. These 56 bodies sent regular reports to Vienna describing local economic conditions, regional transport needs, and evaluations of policy. They also had the power to act as local referees in disputes between firms or between employers and employees.[57] Members of the Chambers of Commerce worked hard to anchor their institutional status, not so much as the advisory bodies they originally intended to be, but rather as an influential set of interest groups throughout the empire. When parliamentary rule and full communal autonomy were restored in the 1860s, for example, the Chambers of Commerce gained the right as a separate curia to elect deputies to both the Austrian parliament and the crown land diets, as well as to some city councils.

At the same time, the government embarked on a massive effort to expand Austria's railway infrastructure. This effort in turn demanded a re-thinking of railway ownership and sources of capital for large government projects. Recognizing the key strategic commercial and military value of railways, the state owned and managed 70 per cent of them. However, the staggering sums required for investment, and the perceived failures of the railway during the costly mobilization for the Crimean War in 1853 persuaded the government to develop a new strategy. In 1854 the state decided to privatize the individual railway systems, selling them to private companies while at the same time sweetening the deal by offering stockholders lucrative guaranteed rates of return on their investments. Within five years the state had succeeded in selling off almost all of its directly-held railway holdings. Moreover, by extending the lucrative financial conditions to contracts for new railway concessions, the companies that bought existing lines

---

56 Kai Struve, *Bauern und Nation in Galizien: Über Zugehörigkeit und soziale Emanzipation im 19. Jahrhundert* (Göttingen:Vandenhoek & Ruprecht, 2005), 108–12.

57 Carl von Czörnig, *Österreichs Neugestaltung 1848–1858* (Stuttgart: Cotta, 1858), 206–9.

Towards a new quality of statehood

rushed to build new ones. The mobilization of credit required for the purchase, managing and extension of the railways was considerable, and demanded a transformation of the banking system as well. In the 1850s the government created new banks (such as the *Creditanstalt* in 1855) that could make far larger amounts of credit available to private firms. The rapid development of the provincial infrastructures in turn had an enormous effect on the lives of ordinary Austrians, especially through the connection of formerly economically isolated regions, and their creation of new commercial opportunities.[58]

All of these policies were also meant indirectly to help underwrite Austria's ambitious attempts to reassert its position as a dominant international power after the humiliations of 1848–49. In 1853, for example, Bruck concluded a treaty to liberalize trade with the states of the Prussian-led *Zollverein*, mirroring Prime Minister Prince Felix Schwarzenberg's (1800–1852) efforts to re-establish Austria as the pre-eminent state in the German Confederation.

In domestic affairs, the state pursued a high degree of bureaucratic centralization. Minister of the Interior Alexander von Bach, a commoner who had served on Vienna's revolutionary Committee of Public Safety in 1848, typified the belief among the regime's leading figures that only a reformed bureaucracy could accomplish the necessary modernization of state and society that the politics of the street had failed to accomplish in 1848. The regime might eventually permit organized participation by the citizenry (as in Bruck's Chambers of Commerce or Stadion's autonomous municipal councils) but that participation should be limited to the most local forums. Bach sought to develop a centralized and rational, but also effective and popular bureaucracy. Streamlining its structure throughout the empire, Bach created clearer command structures that ran from the centre to the provincial governments (the crown land governors or *Statthalter* now became direct servants of the Crown rather than mediators between Crown and diets). In particular, Bach sought to integrate Hungary completely into this system (often referring to it as 'the former Kingdom of Hungary'). He abolished Hungary's traditional self-governing counties and replaced them with newly drawn districts that better approximated Austria's districts in size. He replaced the local elites who had traditionally governed the counties with bureaucrats appointed from Vienna. These German-speaking bureaucrats – of Czech-, German-, Slovene-, Italian- or Polish-speaking background – came to be known contemptuously by bitter Hungarian nationalists as 'Bach Hussars', a term that associated them with the punitive military suppression of the Hungarian rebellion in 1849 (but also referred to the distinctive uniforms Bach had created for them). Bach also re-introduced German as the official language of the inner administration, a measure which did not end the use of vernacular languages in the administration and education, but which symbolically rankled local nationalists and produced accusations of Germanization against the regime.[59]

After a decade of these expansive – and extremely costly – policies, however, Austria was drawn into an expensive and disastrous war against France and Piedmont. Defeated in Italy in 1859, pushed again to the brink of bankruptcy and forced to seek new loans, the regime faced serious demands by the credit markets for some kind of institutional independent budgetary

---

58 On the railways and the credit banks, Good, *The Economic Rise of the Habsburg Monarchy*, 81–3; Burkhard Köster, *Militär und Eisenbahn in der Habsburgermonarchie 1825–1859* (München: De Gruyter Oldenbourg, 1999).

59 On Bach's reforms and plans, see excellent analysis in Waltraud Heindl, *Josephinische Mandarine: Bürokratie und Beamte in Österreich*, vol. 2, 1848–1914 (Vienna: Böhlau, 2013); and in Deak, *Forging a Multinational State*. Also, Karl Megner, *Beamte: Wirtschafts-und sozialgeschichtliche Aspekte des k.k. Beamtentums* (Vienna: Verlag der österreichischen Akademie der Wissenschaften, 1986); and Evans, *Austria, Hungary, and the Habsburgs*, 281–2.

review. The fiscal crisis was only compounded in 1862 when Austria joined Prussia in a successful war against Denmark. Finally, in 1866 Prussia challenged Austria directly in a lightning war that ended any hopes Austria entertained to unite Germany under its auspices. Each of these mobilizations plunged Austria into fiscal crisis, each crisis overshadowed the domestic achievements of the regime, and each undermined the legitimacy of the dynasty and the Emperor. During this next period from 1859 until 1867 the emperor reluctantly altered course several times to experiment with various types of parliamentary government, while maintaining his ongoing commitment to policies of centralization.

Patterns of participation, representations of rule and social resistance

As we have seen, de-feudalization and bureaucratization were essential features of state-building carried out by the ruling empires and monarchies in Central, Eastern and Southeastern Europe during the second half of the nineteenth century. Reforms, however, were increasingly guided by the realization that in order for the state to effectively penetrate society, it had to grant spaces for participation and 'progressive' development. Each state tended toward creating forms of legal citizenship that included fundamental legal equality for the citizens and possible – albeit minimal – forms of political participation for both the political elites and other influential social groups. These concessions were deemed necessary to establish a framework for a future modern political order. The realization that a modern state must be accompanied by at least the partial ability of society to participate in decision-making processes was in part motivated by purely pragmatic considerations. The wave of bureaucratization of state power structures notwithstanding, the network of administrative institutions in the nineteenth century remained woefully understaffed and full of loopholes. It therefore seemed advisable to build up parallel structures of social self-government from below that could cover areas of loopholes or bureaucratic weakness in the system. At the same time, these developments also expressed an increasingly new understanding of the state as an all-encompassing arena for the interaction of its subjects. The state was to be a place where new concepts of citizenship could unfold, that required an active commitment to the affairs of the state, at least in a limited local context. Such notions were mixed with older values such as service to the state or the loyalty of its subjects, while still allowing for the growth of new platforms for social development and popular participation in these monarchies. The next chapter will focus on how these new developments were sometimes in harmony, and sometimes in conflict, with a system of monarchic rule and a process of bureaucratization.

Austria-Hungary

After Austria's defeat in the Italian war of 1859 and its subsequent defeat by Prussia in 1866, Emperor Francis Joseph conceded constitutional power-sharing arrangements in order to restore both his own legitimacy and the state's credit. In 1860 and 1861 the October and February Patents revived the crown land diets and created an elected parliament for the Austrian Empire. Later with the Settlement (*Ausgleich*) of 1867 Francis Joseph conceded even greater powers to the Hungarian Diet. From the start, however, he believed that as Emperor he still held all of the important cards in the game, writing confidently to his mother in 1860 that, 'We shall indeed have a little parliamentary government, but the power remains in my hands.'[60] As things turned

---

60 Franz Schnürer, *Briefe Kaiser Franz Josefs an seine Mutter* (Salzburg: Kosel & Pustet, 1930), 302.

Towards a new quality of statehood

out, however, the Emperor was utterly mistaken about these constitutional experiments. The power did not remain in his hands but devolved instead to an Imperial Austrian Parliament, a Royal Hungarian Parliament, to a series of provincial crown land governments in Austria, and to an ever-expanding bureaucracy whose interests became increasingly aligned with those of political parties rather than with the person of the Emperor.

At the start of this renewed reform era, parliamentary experiments unleashed a fierce competition for power among the crown land aristocracies on the one hand, and the increasingly influential capitalist, educated and professional middle classes (especially Vienna's banking community) on the other. The former groups sought to replace the bureaucratic centralization of the past decade with a federal system that would return power to the regional crown land diets. The latter favoured maintaining a centralized system that nevertheless subjected the empire as a whole to a written constitution and to the policies of an elected parliament. The centralists wanted to impose a range of cultural and legal reforms on the empire, such as a bill of rights, the separation of the judiciary from the administration, a universal educational system that required school attendance for both boys and girls and the removal of the Catholic Church from political and social affairs. They did not, however, want to return to what they characterized as the political chaos of 1848–49, and they generally agreed that universal manhood suffrage (as it had been for the 1848 Austrian – but not the Hungarian – parliament) should be avoided for the new elected institutions, both local and national. Voting for the Austrian parliament, for the diets and for the municipal councils should, they agreed, be organized on a curial basis that privileged large landowners and tax payers (the urban and town upper bourgeoisie). Interestingly, the centralists maintained strong support for Stadion's municipal experiment that had guaranteed local communes a surprisingly high degree of local autonomy over issues of economic planning and social policy.[61]

The first reforms of the 1860s (the October Diploma of 1860 and the February Patent of 1861) made it possible for citizens to pursue their interests far more openly in a competitive political process, although given the curial voting process and high tax requirements for voting, that process clearly favoured some social groups over others.[62] The reforms also established several new public forums in which diverse social groups – including the un-enfranchised – could pursue their political interests ever more loudly and vigorously. In this they were aided by the rapid expansion of a less-censored press that enthusiastically engaged all manner of political causes and offered politicians opportunities to disseminate and popularize their ideas with a broader public.

Francis Joseph believed that by conceding limited reforms he could exercise firm control over political participation and gain greater popular support for the regime. In fact, he had unleashed a politics that – at least to him and to his allies – sounded unpleasantly loud, brash, bourgeois and combative, even if it was also highly loyal to the dynasty. Moreover, the newly empowered, socially elite politicians tended – annoyingly for the Emperor – to treat the reforms not as completed, but rather as a basis from which to build a much greater transformation of the Austrian system. Through legislative activism the politicians consistently pushed the emperor

---

61 Pieter M. Judson, *The Habsburg Empire: A New History* (Cambridge, MA: Harvard University Press, 2016), 251–5.

62 On the complex curial and suffrage arrangements, see Bernd Rottenbacher, *Das Februarpatent in der Praxis: Wahlpolitik, Wahlkämpfe und Wahlentscheidungen in den böhmischen Ländern der Habsburgermonarchie 1861–1871* (Frankfurt a.M.: Peter Lang, 2001).

to concede further structural reforms.[63] Their actions compare in a different way to Hungarian nationalists, many of whom saw the Vienna reforms as a reason to boycott the system unless the regime restored the independence they had gained with the laws of April 1848. Ultimately, Francis Joseph and the political leaders on whom he relied failed to persuade the Hungarians to participate in the new parliamentary institutions.

The Settlement of 1867 concluded after Austria's defeat by Prussia ended this period of structural political reform by finally resolving Hungary's political status. The Settlement created a new set of political/state structures that lasted – with some modifications along the way – until the fall of the empire at the end of the First World War. The Settlement created two independent states, a Kingdom of Hungary and an imperial state known officially as 'The Kingdoms and Territories Represented in the Imperial Council' but which for the sake of convenience I refer to as 'Austria'.[64] As Austria-Hungary, the two states shared a common diplomatic service, a common military and certain financial arrangements. Three so-called 'common ministers' presided over these shared institutions. Francis Joseph reigned now as the Emperor of Austria *and* King of Hungary. According to the Settlement, the arrangement would be renewed every ten years (with possible modifications to the economic clauses especially regarding the quota of the national debt assumed by each state). Delegates from both parliaments met annually to set budgets for their common affairs. Neither state could change the arrangement without the consent of the other. And although Emperor-King Francis Joseph retained the formal power to shape military and foreign policy independent of other political actors, over time the regular budget process that shaped policy in each state tended to constrain him in these areas as well.

From now on Austria and Hungary were constitutional monarchies but with very different constitutions, administrative and judicial systems, and even different requirements for citizenship.[65] The two states differed radically in other ways as well. Hungary's new rulers saw their state primarily as a nation state. Now that they controlled their national destiny, Hungary's political class institutionalized a highly centralized form of government that diminished the traditional powers of the counties and empowered bureaucrats and politicians in Budapest. They also developed political, educational and cultural policies of Magyarization that they imposed on those Hungarians who spoke Romanian, Slovak, Serb, German or Ukrainian, and who together made up over 50 per cent of Hungary's population in 1867. In the decades after 1867, Hungary's political class also refused to expand the suffrage – in fact they decreased it – largely fearing that new voters would disproportionately belong to Hungary's many linguistic minorities and pose a challenge to Hungarian rule. Hungary's new rulers did conclude a separate Settlement with the Kingdom of Croatia (the *Nagodba*) in 1868 that gave Croatians limited cultural, fiscal and administrative autonomy and the right to representation within the Hungarian Parliament. Still, it was the Hungarian

---

63 Pieter M. Judson, 'Forcing Constitutional Change through Parliamentary Practice in 1861', in *Hohes Haus! 150 Jahre moderner Parlamentarismus in Österreich, Böhmen, der Tschechoslowakei und der Republik Tschechien im mitteleuropäischen Kontext*, eds Franz Adlgasser, Jana Malínská, Helmut Rumpler and Luboš Velek (Vienna: Verlag der österreichischen Akademie der Wissenschaften, 2015), 119–33.

64 The emperor and many centralists did not want to use the name Austria to refer to the non-Hungarian half of the Dual Monarchy, since for them, Austria connoted the entirety of the Habsburgs' holdings.

65 Gerald Stourzh, 'Die dualistische Rechtsstruktur, Österreichbegriff und Österreichbewusstsein 1867–1918', in *Der Umfang der österreichischen Geschichte: Ausgewählte Studien, 1990–2010* (Vienna: Böhlau, 2011), 105–24.

government that chose the King's *Ban* or viceroy, and Croatians tended to view the *Ban* as subservient to Hungarian interests.[66]

The Austrian state, by contrast, in no way saw itself as a nation state. No language in the Austrian half of the Dual Monarchy was claimed in the census of 1880 by more than a third of Austria's population, although many nationalist politicians complained that the state privileged Austria's German-speaking populations because German remained the language of command in the military as well as of the inner civil service.[67] A general constitutional promise of linguistic equality in the State's Fundamental Law on the rights of the citizen ensured that the bureaucracy, judiciary and school systems, and even the nearly universal conscription-based military, became increasingly multilingual in the ensuing decades. After 1867, liberal education reforms – including requiring eight years of schooling for all boys and girls – increased the centrality of questions of language use within the schools. So too did the new military conscription law of 1868 that at least in theory called up young men from all social classes and regions (including Hungary) to experience a maximum of three years of common military service. Although recruits were required to learn a minimum of circa 80 commands in German, conscripts also had the right to be trained and to converse with their superiors (up to the rank of captain) in their own languages.[68]

In large part, the ever-increasing institutionalization of multilingualism in Austria, if not in Hungary, was also the product of an effective and increasingly mass-based politics organized around nationalist and linguistic claims in the different crown lands. Constitutional promises of linguistic equality in Austria were vague enough to create serious public debates and spaces for popular political activism. Did, for example, the constitutional requirement apply to post-primary school education as well? Did it justify demands for the creation of universities in languages other than German? By the 1880s politics in Austria was becoming dominated by specifically nationalist issues and parties that demanded greater institutional fairness and representation of different languages. Another factor that increased the nationalization of politics in Austria (and that differed profoundly from Hungary) were the regular franchise reforms that increased the numbers of voters for parliamentary elections in Austria – at least one per decade. In 1897, for example, all male citizens who fulfilled certain basic age and living requirements gained the

---

66 Under the terms of the *Nagodba*, Croatia also retained 45% of the taxes it collected for purely Croatian purposes. Additionally, Croatia elected 40 of the 442 deputies who sat in the Hungarian Parliament. Interestingly, Francis Joseph agreed that the diet of Dalmatia – located in the Austrian half of the empire, but claimed by many Croatian nationalists since before 1848 – could negotiate its incorporation into the Kingdom of Croatia. However, the Dalmatian Diet, dominated at this time by Italian nationalists, rejected the option. Later, with a Croatian nationalist majority it debated the question again. Carlile Aylmer Macartney, *The Habsburg Empire, 1790–1918* (London: Weidenfeld and Nicolson, 1969), 557–8; 645–6.

67 This is a more complicated issue than it may appear, since even within the military if a language was spoken by at least 20% of a regiment, then it was treated as a regimental language and could be used in daily communication, if not in terms of orders. Crown land and state civil services were obligated to use the local languages in which they had been addressed, if 20% of a district's population spoke that language. Similar rules pertained to languages of instruction in schools as well.

68 Tamara Scheer, 'Die K. und K. Regimentssprachen: Eine Institutionalisierung der Sprachenvielfalt in der Habsburgermonarchie (1867/8–1914)', in *Sprache, Gesellschaft und Nation in Ostmitteleuropa: Institutionalisierung und Alltagspraxis*, eds Klaas-Hinrich Ehlers, Martina Niedhammer and Marek Nekula (Göttingen: Vandenhoeck & Ruprecht, 2014), 75–92. On details of military service laws, Laurence Cole, *Military Culture and Popular Patriotism in Late Imperial Austria* (Oxford: Oxford University Press, 2014).

right to elect a small number of deputies to the lower house of parliament in a so-called 'general curia'. In 1907, curial voting itself was abolished for the Parliament. From now on, single constituencies with universal manhood suffrage elected the deputies. The rapid increase in voters over time had two significant effects on Austrian politics. In the first place, activists and parties increasingly sought to raise issues that could unite larger cross-class alliances and integrate the new voters into existing parties. Nationalist issues seemed to fit this bill substantially. Secondly, the turn to a nationalist politics produced a continuously radicalizing dynamic as parties within the same language communities battled each other for the same voters.

It is important to investigate the particular dynamics of this expanding politics, and to point out, that its nationalization did not necessarily reflect the prior existence of ethnic nations in Austria or the importance of nationalist issues in everyday life. Nor did this increasingly popular politics represent the success of self-styled national awakening activism as many nationalist activists claimed it did. In fact, the opposite was largely the case. The rise of nationalist politics was a product of activists' attempts to bring specifically political questions, viewpoints and arguments about nationhood into prominence in local communities where they had not been prominent before. One could as easily argue that it was nationalist politicians who created popular national communities during this period (1850–1880) rather than the other way around. Although nationalist politics became more noticeable, it is not clear that nationalism meant much in the everyday lives of most Austrians.[69]

Another critical dynamic in this rise of a politics focused on nationhood was that the ever-harsher rhetoric it produced was part of a complex series of activist performances directed at potential constituents rather than representing real hostility to neighbours or to other citizens who used different languages and therefore were seen to belong to other nations. Still, one longer-term result of this nationalization of politics in Austria was a growing belief that Austria's different people were indeed separated by more than simple questions of language use, and that those differences in language use reflected fundamental differences of culture and history.

The period 1850–1880 is noteworthy for two other developments related to state-building. The first was the self-conscious attempt by the Habsburg dynasty to position itself more effectively among the peoples of Austria-Hungary through calculated rituals, performances and visits that took place across the monarchy. Francis Joseph and other members of his family travelled more to the far corners of the empire than any other Habsburg since Joseph II. Moreover, the dynasty also took advantage of press coverage, of new technologies of photography and the rise of mass consumerism of small items (pictures, postcards, etc.) to control its image.[70] At the same time, it is noteworthy that many proponents of the empire and the dynasty also adopted the new nationalist rhetoric about cultural and linguistic differences among the empire's peoples, although for very different purposes. Especially after 1867, Emperor King Francis Joseph strove to position himself as a protector for all his people, for all language groups, for all cultures and especially for all confessional groups. This strategy presented the empire as one that fostered and protected the developments of different small nations in Central and Eastern Europe who,

---

69 Pieter M. Judson, *Guardians of the Nation: Activists on the Language Frontiers of Imperial Austria* (Cambridge, MA: Harvard University Press, 2006). On national indifference see also Tara Zahra, 'Imagined Noncommunities: National Indifference as a Category of Analysis', *Slavic Review* 69, 1 (2010): 93–119.

70 Daniel Unowsky, *The Pomp and Politics of Patriotism: Imperial Celebrations in Habsburg Austria 1848–1916* (West Lafayette, IN: Purdue University Press, 2005). On Empress Elizabeth's control over photography and her depiction of the media, Olivia Gruber Florek, 'The Modern Monarch: Empress Elizabeth and the Visual Culture of Femininity, 1850–1900' (PhD diss., Rutgers University, 2012).

Towards a new quality of statehood

without the aid of the Habsburgs, would find themselves victimized by Germany, Russia or the Ottoman Empire. This argument was of course more persuasive before the advent of the new nation states in the Balkans in the second half of the nineteenth century. But these strategies eventually made Francis Joseph remarkably popular, especially given how reviled he had been in the first decade of his reign. The second development might be called the rise of an imperial set of ideologies that mirrored the rise of nationalist ideologies. During this period, the empire developed several new legitimating ideologies, especially after it lost its position as hegemon in Germany and Italy. One of these was the idea mentioned above that imperial rule produced cultural, economic and social development for all the peoples of empire. Another related idea was that the empire would bring a higher degree of civilization to its less fortunate eastern and southern peoples. This vague set of ideologies found even more explicit expression thanks to the political and economic opportunities created for a range of entrepreneurs and civil servants by Austria-Hungary's occupation of the Ottoman provinces Bosnia and Herzegovina in 1878.[71] The same thinking took deeper scientific root in the ambitious 24-volume project to legitimate the empire known as the *Kronprinzenwerk* started in the 1880s, an attempt to catalogue and display for popular consumption the geography, flora, fauna and ethnography of each region.[72]

The Ottoman Empire and the post-Ottoman states in the Balkans

Despite the great reorganization and reforms (Tanzimat),[73] the religious representation of the sultans, who for centuries ruled the Ottoman state in the tradition of an Islamic empire, was still influential in many institutions. Though the religious dimension of staging power generally faded into the background during the reigns of sultans Mahmud II (1808–39), Abdülmecid I (1839–61) and Abdülaziz (1861–76), the traditional demonstration of the unity of the sultanate and caliphate played a very important role in the self-presentation of Abdülaziz's eventual successor, Abdülhamid II (1876–1909), before the Young Turk revolutionaries of 1908 shifted the focus once again to a decidedly 'secular' understanding of the state. In a sense, this development reflects the very same tendencies that held for representations of state power in the long

---

71 On the occupation of Bosnia Herzegovina as civilizing project, Robin Okey, *Taming Balkan Nationalism: The Habsburg 'Civilizing Mission' in Bosnia, 1878–1914* (Oxford: Oxford University Press, 2007).

72 On the *Kronprinzenwerk*, Zoltán Szász, 'Das "Kronprinzenwerk" und die hinter ihm stehende Konzeption', in *Nation und Nationalismus in wissenschaftlichen Standartwerken Österreich- Ungarns, ca. 1867–1918*, eds Endre Kiss, Csaba Kiss and Justin Stagl (Vienna: Böhlau, 1997), 65–70; Justin Stagl, 'Das "Kronprinzenwerk" – eine Darstellung des Vielvölkerreiches', in *Das entfernte Dorf. Moderner Kunst und ethnischer Artefakt*, ed. Akos Moravánsky (Vienna: Böhlau, 2002), 169–82; Regina Bendix, 'Ethnology, Cultural Reification, and the Dynamics of Difference in the Kronprinzenwerk', in *Creating the Other: Ethnic Conflict and Nationalism in Habsburg Central Europe*, ed. Nancy M. Wingfield (New York: Berghahn, 2003), 149–66; Hans Petschar, *Altösterreich: Menschen, Länder und Völker in der Habsburgermonarchie* (Vienna: Brandstätter, 2011). Historian Deborah Coen has repeatedly drawn scholars' attention to the critical work of amateur and professional scientists in shaping contemporary ideas of empire. See Coen, 'Climate and Circulation in Imperial Austria', *Journal of Modern History* 82, 4 (December 2010): 839–75; Coen, *The Earthquake Observers: Disaster Science from Lisbon to Richter* (Chicago, IL: University of Chicago Press, 2012). See also Peter Stachel, 'Ethnischer Pluralismus und wissenschaftliche Theoriebildung im zentraleuropäischen Raum: Fallbeispiele wissenschaftlicher und philosophischer Reflexion der ethnisch-kulturellen Vielheit der Donaumonarchie' (PhD diss. Karl- Franzens Universitat Graz, 1999).

73 R.H. Davison, 'Tanzimat', in *The Encyclopedia of Islam – New Edition*, vol. 10, eds P.J. Bearman, et al. (Leiden: Brill, 2000), 201–9.

nineteenth century. These representations were characterized by various phases and discontinuities, references to the state's Islamic founding principles sometimes varying considerably.

An important watershed moment in this overall development was the Russo-Turkish War
of 1877–1878 that ended so disastrously for the Ottoman Empire. Their catastrophic defeat,
accompanied by an enormous wave of refugees, resulted in drastic restrictions to Ottoman
power in the Balkans and diminished the Empire's international standing as one of the European
Great powers. The same was true with regard to the international peace settlement after the war
(the Congress of Berlin of 1878 and the establishment of an international debt control commission in 1881 as a regulatory body supervising Ottoman state finances), which the Ottoman
elite perceived as a humiliation. As Selim Deringil aptly describes in his book *The Well-Protected
Domains*, one reaction to this was that a greater emphasis was placed on Islamic symbolism
under Sultan Abdülhamid in the following decades.[74] And yet, at the same time, the sultan
still endeavoured to portray his empire to an international public as a great modern, as well as
European, state. This dual strategy will be discussed in more detail below.

But let us first turn to the challenges of religious equality between Muslims and non-Muslims
in the Ottoman state. This was the one area of policymaking that remained a thorny issue
throughout the period of great transformation. The same applied to the (dis)continued existence
of a multi-religious society in the Christian-oriented, post-Ottoman Balkan successor states. The
religious question became increasingly important in the progressively modernizing state of the
nineteenth century, especially with regard to the opportunities of political participation afforded
to its 'citizens'. It is well worth pointing out that religious equality and civic participation were
always closely intertwined in the Ottoman territories, both before and during the process of
liberation from Ottoman rule as well as in the post-Ottoman states of Southeastern Europe.

A look at historical developments reveals that the formal and legal guarantee of religious
equality extended to the sultan's subjects in the wake of the great Ottoman reform edicts of the
Tanzimat era (1839 and 1856) was not merely a promise, but it actually made great inroads into
the day-to-day life of these subjects. This was readily apparent in various spheres of public and
economic life, in particular after the Crimean War and during the 1860s. New and sometimes
rather imposing Christian churches were now being built in Ottoman cities, transforming city-
scapes in Southeastern Europe that were hitherto marked by mosques and other Islamic structures. Their construction was frequently subsidized by the sultan, along with donations from the
Christian population or from abroad. The intensification of international trade and the protections offered by new legislation in the area of commercial law (beginning with the Commerce
and Trade Code of 1850, but also the political and economic 'protection' of consulates set up
in many places by the great powers) helped establish an emerging economic bourgeoisie, predominantly among Orthodox, Armenian and Jewish communities, giving rise to a flourishing
cultural scene. But these tendencies had certain limitations and often met with considerable
scepticism on the part of many conservative Muslim elites. While it is true that state offices
were open to non-Muslims (and more recent research, such as that of Abdulhamit Kırmızı,[75]
indicates that the number of non-Muslims holding such offices had grown considerably in the
late Ottoman period), as a rule, the civil service remained primarily Muslim-dominated and
firmly in the hands of a Muslim 'bureaucratic bourgeoisie' that developed in the second half

---

74 Selim Deringil, *The Well-Protected Domains: Ideology and the Legitimation of Power in the Ottoman Empire,
1876–1909* (London: I.B. Tauris, [1998] new edition, 2011).

75 Abdulhamit Kırmızı, 'A Prosopographic Study of Christian Officials in the Late Ottoman Bureaucracy' (paper presented at the Forschungskolloquium Südosteuropa-HU–Berlin, 4 Nov. 2016).

Towards a new quality of statehood

of the nineteenth century, as Fatma Müge Göçek has shown.[76] There were other traditions as well that were very hard to break; for example, in the military. Recruitment for the Ottoman military (with the exception of certain niches such as the medical corps or the navy) was largely aimed at the Muslim population. The Christian population was for all intents and purposes excluded from military service, being subject to a military exemption tax instead, thus continuing a centuries-old tradition of a Muslim-run military.[77]

Relations between Muslim and non-Muslim elites at the local and regional levels varied, with rivalries and conflicts as well as cooperation and mutual adaptation.[78] Yet, despite the many efforts and increasing developments towards legal equality, religion was still an important factor in the everyday practice of state participation. But the realities and issues of emancipation were determined by local set-ups or by the extent to which Ottoman reform policies had penetrated individual regions, including the urban–rural divide.

The new states created in the Balkans during the post-Ottoman era were accompanied by a whole new dynamic. The citizenship laws and constitutions created in these states can serve as an illustration. The Principality of Serbia and the Principality of Romania, for example, had their own citizenship laws, even when these territories were still under Ottoman suzerainty. This had consequences for the rest of the empire. As Constantin Iordachi has shown,[79] the adoption of the Ottoman Nationality Law of 1869 could be seen as a reaction to the new state-building projects within the Ottoman Balkans which granted extensive civic rights to Orthodox inhabitants in the respective principalities, which were still under Ottoman suzerainty, and prompted Ottoman leaders to clarify the situation. It is therefore clear that developments in Ottoman, and later post-Ottoman, territories in Southeastern Europe must be viewed with an eye to their mutual influences.[80]

This was also true of developments regarding the political participation of citizens in the state. The (conflictive) process of gaining independence from Ottoman rule promoted the constitutional anchoring of political (co-)determination rights. The 1860s, in particular, saw a new quality of legislation. The decade witnessed the passage of constitutional amendments

---

76 Fatma Müge Göçek, *Rise of the Bourgeoisie, Demise of Empire: Ottoman Westernization and Social Change* (New York: Oxford University Press, 1996).

77 See, for example, Mehmet Hacısalihoğlu, 'Inclusion and Exclusion: Conscription in the Ottoman Empire', *Journal of Modern European History* 5 (2007): 264–86; Erik Jan Zürcher, 'Ottoman Conscription System in Theory and Practice, 1844–1918', in *Arming the State: Military Conscription in the Middle East and Central Asia, 1775–1925*, ed. Erik J. Zürcher (London: I.B. Tauris, 1999), 78–94; Fikret Adanır, 'Christliche Rekruten unter dem Halbmond: Zum Problem der Militärdienstpflicht für Nichtmuslime im spätosmanischen Reich', in *Von der Pruth-Ebene bis zum Gipfel der Ida: Festschrift zum 70. Geburtstag von Emanuel Turczynski*, ed. Gerhard Grimm (München: Südosteuropa-Gesellschaft, 1989), 153–64.

78 This is nicely demonstrated in various studies on Ottoman governors, which offer a good introduction to this topic. See, for example, Olivier Bouquet, *Les Pachas du sultan: Essai sur les agents supérieurs de L'Etat ottoman (1839–1909)* (Leuven: Peeters, 2007); or Abdulhamit Kırmızı, 'Experiencing the Ottoman Empire as a Life Course: Ferid Pasha, Governor and Grandvizier (1851–1914)', *Geschichte und Gesellschaft* 40 (2014): 42–66.

79 Constantin Iordachi, 'The Making of Citizenship in the Post-Ottoman Balkans: State Building, Foreign Models, and Legal-Political Transfers', in *Ottomans into Europeans: State and Institution Building in South-East Europe*, eds Alina Mungiu-Pippidi and Wim van Meurs (London: Hurst, 2010), 179–220.

80 See here the instructive works of Dietmar Müller, *Staatsbürger auf Widerruf: Juden und Muslime als Alteritätspartner im rumänischen und serbischen Nationalcode – Ethnonationale Staatsbürgerschaftskonzepte, 1871–1941* (Wiesbaden: Harrssowitz, 2005); Ioannis Zelepos, *Die Ethnisierung griechischer Identität 1870–1912: Staat und private Akteure vor dem Hintergrund der 'Megali Idea'* (München: R. Oldenbourg, 2002).

that did indeed offer opportunities for a broader distribution of political power and participation. Greece, the first country to free itself completely from Ottoman rule (albeit with a much smaller territory in the nineteenth century than would later be the case), was ruled in the first decades of independence by King Otto I (1832–62) from the Bavarian House of Wittelsbach. Installed by the great powers, he ruled in a largely authoritarian manner with the aid of a hand-picked government. Though forced by a military coup to adopt a first constitution in 1844, little changed in Otto's style of rule as he substantially marginalized parliamentary participation. It was during the crisis of state of 1862–4 that Otto was finally deposed and replaced by a new king from the Danish House of Schleswig-Holstein-Sonderburg-Glücksburg, enthroned as King George I (1863–1913). The appointment of a new royal dynasty was followed by the ratification of a modern constitution (1864), which granted real powers to an elected parliament chosen on the basis of male suffrage.[81]

Romania saw the introduction of a modern constitution at about the same time (1866), albeit under Ottoman suzerainty, laying the formal foundations for a new political system. This occurred in the wake of dramatic political developments and following the overthrow of a hitherto powerful ruler. In 1859, a local Moldavian boyar, Alexander Ion Cuza, was successively elected prince of both Danubian principalities by their respective elites (on the basis of an 'Organic Statute' dating from the 1830s), in compliance with the Treaty of Paris and under the protest of the sultan. In December 1861, he proclaimed the union of Moldavia and Wallachia, forming the single state of Romania. Following the French model, he began to modernize the government and push through extensive agrarian reforms which, among other things, nationalized the church's considerable property holdings and tried to limit the near omnipotence of boyar families. Ottoman rights of influence soon diminished to become merely symbolic. Cuza was brought down by a military coup in February 1866, resulting in a serious crisis of authority. Here, too, the installation of a new – likewise foreign – prince was part of the solution. Karl, Prince of Hohenzollern-Sigmaringen, became Prince Carol I (1866 to 1914, as of 1881, King Carol I). His appointment was paired with the creation of a constitution that established a power-sharing agreement and extensive parliamentary rights. But the traditionally dominant boyar class secured itself a key position in the Romanian principality once again, electoral law having divided the populace into four curiae to the benefit the landowning class, leaving the majority of the rural population with nothing but indirect voting rights.[82]

In Serbia, too, a modern constitution was established in the 1860s, likewise under Ottoman suzerainty. This occurred in 1869, and, just like in Romania, the crucial event was preceded by turbulent internal developments. The scope of influence of Ottoman supremacy was increasingly indirect in nature, especially since the Belgrade crises of 1858–60, 1862 and 1867, when the Muslim population and eventually the Ottoman occupiers were ultimately forced to leave. The political situation in the preceding decades had been marked by frequent internal power

---

81 Richard Clogg, *Geschichte Griechenlands im 19. und 20. Jahrhundert: Ein Abriß* (Köln: Romiosini, 1997); Gunnar Hering, *Die politischen Parteien in Griechenland 1821–1936*, 2 vols (München: Oldenbourg, 1992); John Petropoulos, *Politics and Statecraft in the Kingdom of Greece, 1833–43* (Princeton, NJ: Princeton University Press, 1968).

82 Edda Binder-Iijima, 'Creating Legitimacy: The Romanian Elite and the Acceptance of Monarchical Rule', in *Society, Politics and State Formation in Southeastern Europe during the 19th Century*, eds Tassos Anastassiadis and Nathalie Clayer (Athens: Alpha Bank, 2011) 177–203; Edda Binder-Iijima, *Die Institutionalisierung der rumänischen Monarchie unter Carol I, 1866–1881* (München: R. Oldenbourg, 2003); Paul Michelson, *Romanian Politics, 1859–1871: From Prince Cuza to Prince Carol* (Iaşi: Center for Romanian Studies, 1998); Keith Hitchins, *Rumania, 1866–1947* (Oxford: Oxford University Press, 1994).

Towards a new quality of statehood

struggles between Serbian princes and local 'oligarchs'. Yet, an essentially authoritarian form of princely rule prevailed for lengthy periods. With the assassination of Prince Mihailo Obrenović in 1868 a regency council briefly assumed the business of governing (for the underage Milan, who reigned from 1868 to 1889, as of 1882 as King Milan) and a new political era seemed imminent. The constitution, proclaimed in 1869, established a parliamentary monarchy in Serbia which would later be based on universal male suffrage. Various political parties now began to compete for power, and from their ranks emerged the leading figures of Serbian politics in the late nineteenth and early twentieth centuries.[83]

The dynamics described here with regard to Greece, Romania and Serbia were echoed a few years later in the Ottoman Empire itself. Here, too, a form of constitutional parliamentarianism was established in the wake of a massive state crisis. Uprisings in 1875–6 caused the situation to escalate in a number of Balkan provinces and, compounded by the looming threat of bankruptcy given the empire's considerable international debts, the sultan's authority began to waver. The 'year of three sultans', 1876, began with the forced abdication and subsequent murder of Sultan Abdülaziz (1861–76); his successor Murad V remained in office just a few months, before being replaced by Abdülhamid II (1876–1909). The new sultan, enthroned in the summer of 1876, began by supporting a liberal reform movement, led among others by Midhat Pasha. The movement declared a new constitution against the backdrop of an ongoing conference in Istanbul, where representatives of the great powers were meeting to discuss the debt and 'Oriental' crisis. Parliamentary elections were held throughout the country in 1877 and 1878. A General Assembly of the Ottoman Empire was the first attempt at a representative democracy at the imperial level. This so-called First Constitutional Era (*Birinci Meşrutiyet*) did not last long, however. Against the backdrop of a catastrophic defeat in the Russo-Turkish War, which broke out soon after the constitution was declared and would soon be followed by further wars against the Balkan states seceding from the imperial federation, Abdülhamid shut down the parliament in February of 1878. Over the next three decades, the sultan once again ruled in an authoritarian manner with the governments he himself appointed, using massive police force and censorship against growing demands for the re-establishment of parliamentary representation.[84]

In this crisis-ridden period of upheaval during the Russo-Turkish War, two other state-building projects made inroads into (post-)Ottoman territory, mostly at the instigation of Russia. The first was the creation of the Principality of Bulgaria as a consequence of the Russo-Turkish War and the subsequent Treaty of San Stefano in February 1878 and the resolutions of the Congress of Berlin a few months later. Though remaining under Ottoman suzerainty

---

83 Dubravka Stojanović, 'In the Quicksand: Political Institutions in Serbia at the End of the Long 19th Century', in *Society, Politics and State Formation in Southeastern Europe during the 19th Century*, eds Tassos Anastassiadis and Nathalie Clayer (Athens: Alpha Bank, 2011), 205–31; Holm Sundhaussen, *Geschichte Serbiens, 19.–21. Jahrhundert* (Vienna: Böhlau 2007); Gale Stokes, *Politics as Development. The Emergence of Political Parties in Nineteenth-Century Serbia* (Durham, NC: Duke University Press, 1990); Alex Dragnich, *The Development of Parliamentary Government in Serbia* (New York: Columbia University Press, 1978).

84 On the brief constitutional era, see e.g. Robert Devereux, *The First Ottoman Constitutional Period: A Study of the Midhat Constitution and Parliament* (Baltimore, MD: Johns Hopkins, 1964). An overview of 'The Crisis of 1873–78 and Its Aftermath' can be found in Eric Zürcher, *Turkey: A Modern History* (London: I.B. Tauris, [1993] 2014). On the system of rule in the Abdulhamid era, see, e.g. Abdulhamit Kırmızı, *Abdülhamid'in Valileri: Osmanlı Vilayet İdaresi 1895–1908* [Abdülhamid's governors: Ottoman provincial administration, 1895–1908] (İstanbul: Klasik, 2007); François Georgeon, *Abdülhamid II: Le sultan calife 1876–1909* (Paris: Fayard, 2003); Selim Deringil, *The Well-Protect Domains: Ideology and the Legitimation of Power in the Ottoman Empire, 1876–1909* (London: I.B. Tauris, 1998).

until 1908, a national assembly in Veliko Tarnovo in April 1879 gave the young principality its own constitution, which regulated political affairs during the ensuing decades. A foreign prince was installed through the agency of the great powers, and he was to share political power with a parliament elected on the basis of universal male suffrage. Alexander of Battenberg, who came from the German high nobility, was enthroned in 1879, but soon ran afoul of the National Assembly and was overthrown a few years later. Another representative of the German high nobility, Ferdinand of Sachsen-Coburg and Gotha, was chosen as his replacement by the Bulgarian parliament and by representatives of the great powers, being named Prince Ferdinand I of Bulgaria (1887–1918, Bulgarian tsar as of 1908).[85] The second state-building project involved the tiny principality of Montenegro, which, as early as the eighteenth century, enjoyed autonomous status within the Ottoman Empire, often defended and expanded by means of warfare. Montenegro was a traditional ally of Russia, having been supported by it for decades in its efforts to achieve statehood. In the Russo-Turkish War of 1877–8, Montenegro sided with the victorious Russians, and along with Romania and Serbia, was awarded recognition as an independent state in 1878. Prince Nikola (1860–1918, king as of 1910), who largely ruled in an authoritarian manner, now became the official head of state. He was sceptical of modern forms of political participation during most of his period of rule. Only in 1906 an elected parliament (*Narodna Skupština*) received some legislative functions and replaced the earlier occasionally held general people's assemblies.[86]

With the state-building processes in Ottoman and post-Ottoman Southeastern Europe described above, new political realities were established during the so-called 'Oriental crisis'.[87] These realities were characterized by the coexistence of numerous small states, Ottoman rule still present but territorially reduced. Although such a framework in the Balkan Peninsula lasted nearly three decades with little in the way of change until 1908 and 1912–13 respectively, and although many of the abovementioned rulers were in power for a remarkably long time, their period of rule was not always indicative of internal stability. It was due, first of all, to the fact that all of these young states in the Balkans were plunged into recurrent crises: particularly, Romania in 1871, Greece in 1875 and 1893, Bulgaria in 1886–7 and Serbia on multiple occasions.[88] One highly contentious issue was the attempt to find an acceptable

---

85 Dobrinka Parusheva, *Pravitelstvenijat elit na Rumǎnia i Bǎlgarija prez vtorata polovina na XIX I načaloto na XX vek. Socialna istorija* [The governmental elite in Romania and Bulgaria during the second half of the nineteenth and early twentieth century: a social history] (Sofia: Institute of Balkan Studies 2008); Alexander Vezenkov, 'In the Service of the Sultan, in the Service of the Revolution: Local Bulgarian Notables in the 1870s', in Grandits et al., *Conflicting Loyalties in the Balkans*, 86–106; Wolfang Höpken, 'Beamte in Bulgarien: Zum Modernisierungsbeitrag der Verwaltung zwischen staatlicher Unabhängigkeit und Balkan-Kriegen, 1879–1912', *Südost-Forschungen* 54 (München, 1995): 219–50; Bernard Lory, *Le sort de l'heritage ottoman en Bulgarie: L'exemple des villes Bulgares, 1878–1900* (Istanbul: Isis, 1985); Richard Crampton, *Bulgaria 1878–1918* (Boulder, CO: East European Monographs, 1983).

86 Elisabeth Roberts, *Realm of the Black Mountains: A History of Montenegro* (London: Hurst 2007); Bogumil Hrabak, *Podgorica do početka XIX vijeka* [Podgorica until the beginning of the 19th century] (Belgrade: n.s., 2000); Caspar Heer, *Territorialentwicklung und Grenzfragen von Montenegro in der Zeit seiner Staatswerdung 1830–1887* (Bern: Lang, 1981).

87 For an overview of these state-building processes, see Konrad Clewing, 'Staatensystem und innerstaatliches Agieren im multiethnischen Raum: Südosteuropa im langen 19. Jahrhundert', in *Geschichte Südosteuropas: Vom frühen Mittelalter bis zur Gegenwart*, eds Konrad Clewing and Jens-Oliver Schmitt (Regensburg: Pustet, 2011), 432–553.

88 Edda Binder-Iijima and Ekkehard Kraft, 'The Making of States: Constitutional Monarchies in the Balkans', in *Ottomans into Europeans: State and Institution Building in South-East Europe*, eds Alina Mungiu-Pippidi and Wim van Meurs (London: Hurst 2010), 1–30.

Towards a new quality of statehood

balance of power between the monarch (all of the states mentioned became kingdoms in the nineteenth century; the last to do so was Bulgaria in 1908) and the young parliaments. The struggle between competing political parties in these states was often the source of considerable conflict. In Serbia it resulted in regicide and a change of dynasty in 1903.

But the internal political stability of these new states was also put to the test in that entry into independence was not always accompanied by economic betterment. Some of these states expanded their new state institutions with the help of large loans on international financial markets, often with high interest rates. In Greece this led to state bankruptcy in 1893 and the establishment of an international debt control commission.[89] As Michael Palairet has shown, new borders and the sudden loss or reduction of trade relations, sometimes linked to the entire Ottoman economy, often had a negative impact, especially in the case of Bulgaria.[90] Moreover, existing foreign-policy dependencies from before the time of their independence occasionally worsened once they gained independence.[91]

This brings us to an additional problem: the overwhelming influence of the great powers on foreign policy in Southeastern Europe. In simplified terms, it might be fair to say that in the era of aggressive New Imperialism, the European great powers actually created 'dependent' rather than 'independent' states in the Balkans. Russia in particular (but also Austria-Hungary), was very present in Southeastern Europe, exercising political and economic pressure on the governments of these new states. This deeply affected the newly emerging party landscape, where pro-Russian factions, for example, vigorously battled pro-Austrian ones. The other great powers as well – above all Great Britain and France, later the Kingdom of Italy and the German Empire – pursued their increasingly conflicting interests in the Balkans (and the 'Orient' in general) through an ever-expanding network of consulates.

These international pressures not only affected the politics and policies of the small Balkan states, but especially the Ottoman Empire. It was not a coincidence that Ottoman elites feared that their empire – the only remaining Muslim great power in 1900 – would (increasingly) become the object of European great-power imperialism, if not an open policy of colonialism. It was against the backdrop of this threat that Sultan Abdülhamid sought legitimacy for his autocratic government. At the same time, he endeavoured to present his government as decidedly 'European'. Selim Deringil, in his study of Abdülhamid's staging of power, summarized the situation as follows:

> The Hamidian regime sought to project the image in Europe that 'we are like you'. Just as the kaiser, the Austrian emperor, and the tsar were legitimate autocrats, so was Abdülhamid.[92]

To the outside world, the regime of Abdülhamid strove to project the image of a modern empire. Ottoman delegations were present at all international expositions and the Ottoman government took pains to modernize its technology and infrastructure throughout the empire and advertise these improvements 'in Europe'. Inwardly, Abdülhamid's representation of power

---

89 Thomas Gallant, *Modern Greece: From the War of Independence to the Present* (London: Bloomsbury, 2016), 80–2.

90 Michael Palairet, *The Balkan Economies c. 1800–1914: Evolution without Development* (Cambridge: Cambridge University Press, 1997), 2002.

91 On developments in Serbia, see Marie-Janine Calic, *Sozialgeschichte Serbiens 1815–1941: Der aufhaltsame Fortschritt während der Industrialisierung* (München: Oldenbourg, 1994).

92 Deringil, *The Well-Protected Domains*, 15.

was more complex. For one thing, his rule greatly hinged on a cult of personality. Abdülhamid was presented as the guardian of the state and the existing social order. But this image was communicated along with the claim to 'internally civilize' rural areas and modernize the state. In general, the emphasis on staging himself as the caliph and just leader of the Muslim world occupied a central place here. Yet recurrent Muslim symbolism linked to the sultan's public persona (and increasingly intertwined with Ottoman state symbols) coexisted with another focus of intense propaganda, namely, the notion of Ottomanism (*Osmanlılık*), emphasizing the equality of all imperial citizens regardless of their religion.

Ottomanism and the cult of personality around the sultan were both attempts by an autocratic ruler to offer his citizens a rallying point. But Ottoman rule was challenged in many ways, from within as well as from without. The greatest threat was posed by the various national(ist) movements demanding more 'national rights'. There also arose a variety of revolutionary splinter groups which negated the sultan's authority completely. At the turn of the twentieth century, an empire-wide underground opposition movement (the subsequent Committee of Union and Progress, popular in the army and in large parts of the state bureaucracy) was ultimately formed in opposition to the autocratic rule of the sultan.[93] The regime reacted harshly to this sometimes real, sometimes suspected threat. This was true in particular of the tragic persecution and pogroms against Armenian settlements in eastern Anatolia during the 1890s, tolerated and sometimes even initiated by the regime.[94] Macedonia was the second region in the empire in which violence escalated at the turn of the twentieth century. Various guerrilla, irregular and revolutionary groups had formed in the Macedonian vilayets to fight the Ottoman authorities and its representatives by means of sabotage and terrorist attacks.[95] Almost all of these nationalist and revolutionary groups in Macedonia, which likewise engaged in brutal internecine warfare, had connections to or stood in the direct employ of one of the respective nationalist irredenta in the neighbouring states of the region.[96]

Irredentist visions of expanding national territory were key to the respective representations of power in all of the new post-Ottoman states in the Balkans. In Greece, it was the Megali Idea; in Bulgaria, the Bulgaria of San Stefano; in Serbia, it was the struggle for a mythic Kosovo and the unification of all Serbs. Romania, too, dreamt of a Greater Romania. The respective governments

---

93 Erik Jan Zürcher, 'The Young Turks – Children of the borderlands?' *Journal of Turkish Studies* 9, 1–2 (2003): 275–83; Şükrü Hanioğlu, *Preparation for a Revolution: The Young Turks, 1902–1908* (Oxford: Oxford University Press, 2001); Şükrü Hanioğlu, *The Young Turks in Opposition* (Oxford: Oxford University Press, 1995).

94 Selim Deringil, "The Armenian Question is Finally Closed': Mass Conversions of Armenians during the Hamidian Massacres of 1894–1897', *Comparative Studies in Society and History* 51 (2009): 344–71; Hans-Lukas Kieser, *Der verpasste Friede: Mission, Ethnie und Staat in den Ostprovinzen der Türkei 1839–1938* (Zurich: Chronos, 2003); Jelle Verheij, 'Die armenischen Massaker von 1894–1896: Anatomie und Hintergründe einer Krise', in *Die armenische Frage und die Schweiz 1896–1896*, ed. Hans-Lukas Kieser (Zurich: Chronos, 1999), 69–129; Stephen Duguid, 'The Politics of Unity: Hamidian Politics in Eastern Anatolia', *Middle Eastern Studies* 9 (1973): 139–55.

95 Keith Brown, *Loyal Unto Death: Trust and Terror in Revolutionary Macedonia* (Bloomington, IN: Indiana University Press, 2013); Mehmet Hacısahlioğlu, *Die Jungtürken und die Mazedonische Frage 1890–1918* (München: Oldenbourg, 2003); Fikret Adanir, *Die Makedonische Frage: Ihre Entstehung und Entwicklung bis 1908* (Wiesbaden: Steiner, 1979).

96 See e.g. Bernard Lory, 'Schools for the Destruction of Society: School Propaganda in Bitola, 1860–1912', in Grandits et al., *Conflicting Loyalties in the Balkans*, 46–63; Ioannis Zelepos, 'Amateurs as Nation-builders? On the Significance of Associations for the Formation and Nationalization of Greek Society in the Nineteenth Sentury', in Grandits et al., *Conflicting Loyalties in the Balkans*, 64–86.

Towards a new quality of statehood

and/or political elites were often very passionate in advocating 'their' national vision and expansionist projects. Both were important for the creation of internal national unity. Domestic politics in all of the states mentioned above were frequently characterized by massive antagonisms once the euphoria of achieving an independent state subsided. Major social conflicts, which often accompanied these new states' 'entry into modernity', surfaced time and again, especially between the typically narrow circle of ruling elites and the majority rural population. Against a backdrop of political and social tensions, propaganda focusing on a 'golden future' (usually coupled with a 'golden past' that existed long before the Ottoman era) were held out as a promise for overcoming problems in the here and now – and if these problems weren't solved in the present, everything would take a turn for the better if only the vision of national greatness were achieved in the imminent future. In the age of a burgeoning press in the Balkans, the irredentist message reached an ever-greater share of the urban and – to a lesser extent – rural population.

The dream of expansion fit well with the imperial zeitgeist, with the idea prevalent in European politics that all states were vying for a 'place in the sun' and that – rather appropriately in the case of the Balkans – the small and weak ones had to reckon with being dominated by the bigger, stronger ones.

But this zeitgeist needs to be put in the context of other, competing visions and developments. The turn of the twentieth century in particular was marked by quite pluralist political dynamics. A specific turning point in Southeastern Europe could also be viewed in this context, one that in 1908 was initially linked to great hopes in many parts of Ottoman society. It was during this year that the so-called Young Turk movement put an end to the autocratic rule of Abdülhamid in the Ottoman Empire.[97] The mood was euphoric throughout the empire – and this across religious and national divides – when a parliament was elected once again, and constitutional order reinstated. This happened around the same time that 'waves of democratization' were overtaking the other 'Eastern' empires dealt with in this chapter. The introduction of universal male suffrage (1907) in the Austrian half of the Habsburg monarchy was yet another step towards parliamentarianism achieving mass democracy. As will be shown in the next section, the revolution of 1905 in the Russian Empire led to the establishment of the Duma as a place of parliamentary participation and to the palpable limitation of a hitherto all-encompassing autocracy.

The Russian Empire and the Kingdom of Poland

As indicated above, reform efforts in the Russian Empire after the Crimean War expanded the spaces for social participation while also effecting a lasting transformation in the legitimation and representation of monarchic rule. The reform era was also characterized by increasing tensions, which initially found an outlet in the form of political terrorism before new forms of resistance against the old order developed in the 1890s.

As discussed, reform-period thinking was guided by the understanding that only with the aid of social activation would state modernization succeed. The reform bureaucracy advocated extending an 'invitation' to society to have a say in certain (local) decision-making processes.

---

97 On the dynamics and mood of this revolutionary year, see especially, Aykut Kansu, *The Revolution of 1908 in Turkey* (Leiden: Brill, 1997). How these developments looked in specific contexts is shown, for example, by Bernard Lory, *La ville balkanissime: Bitola 1800–1918* (Istanbul: Isis, 2011) in the chapter 'Bitola, Foyer De La Revolution Jeune-Turque' or in Mark Mazower, *Salonica: City of Ghosts: Christians, Muslims and Jews, 1430–1950* (London: Harper, 2004) in the chapter 'The Young Turk Revolution'.

Grazhdanstvennost', or 'civicness', referring to a sense of civic duty, became a key concept of the era, whereas courts of lay assessors or rural and urban organs of self-government (zemstva or city dumas) provided the institutions for social engagement of this sort.[98] And yet, despite a liberal censorship policy, these spaces of participation were narrowly circumscribed from the very start. Autocracy – the absolute rule of the tsar – was left unchallenged as the basic principle of the political system in the Russian Empire. Thus, even under Alexander II a broadly defined field of 'political' activity remained the preserve of the autocrat and his ministers.[99] Social engagement, on the other hand, was supposed to take place in the domain of practical local tasks such as road maintenance, the establishment of welfare, health and educational facilities, or the promotion of local industry, trade and agriculture. In this respect, the era of 'counter-reforms' under Alexander III was not a fundamental transition, even though the responsibilities of organs of self-government were cut back considerably after 1881 and rights of access to them were limited, the most privileged being the nobles and urban property owners. In principle, however, the tsar and his team of advisors, who were highly sceptical of social empowerment, could no longer dispense with forums of civic participation if they wanted to maintain the pretence of being a competitive European great power.[100]

For all their limitations, these institutions set up during the reform era made a major contribution to dynamizing society. Organs of self-government not only gave rise to new job profiles that opened up spaces for new social and cultural milieus in a slowly developing middle class; a hitherto unknown politicization of broad segments of society – whether in the form of zemstvo liberalism or a radical intelligentsia – also took root here.[101] This tolerated public sphere became an important forum of opinion and field of professional activity. The growth and diversification

---

98 On the topos of 'civicness', see Baberowski, 'Auf der Suche nach Eindeutigkeit', especially 489–90; Jörg Baberowski, 'Nationalismus aus dem Geist der Inferiorität: Autokratische Modernisierung und die Anfänge muslimischer Selbstvergewisserung im östlichen Transkaukasien 1828–1914', *Geschichte und Gesellschaft* 26, no. 3 (2000): 371–406, here 380–81; Beyrau, 'Liberaler Adel und Reformbürokratie'; Kappeler, *Rußland als Vielvölkerreich*, 203–26; Andreas Kappeler, 'The Ambiguities of Russification', *Kritika: Explorations in Russian and Eurasian History* 5, 2 (2004): 291–7, here 294; Yaroshevski, 'Empire and Citizenship'. On the significance of judicial reform, see Jörg Baberowski, *Autokratie und Justiz: Zum Verhältnis von Rechtsstaatlichkeit und Rückständigkeit im ausgehenden Zarenreich 1864–1914* (Frankfurt a.M.: Klostermann, 1996); Jörg Baberowski, 'Law, the Judicial System and the Legal Profession', in *The Cambridge History of Russia*, ed. Dominic Lieven, vol. 2, *Imperial Russia, 1689–1917* (Cambridge: Cambridge University Press, 2006), 344–68; Lena Gautam, *Recht und Ordnung: Mörder, Verräter und Unruhestifter vor spätzarischen Kriminalgerichten, 1864–1917* (Wiesbaden: Harrassowitz, 2017).

99 See Walter Sperling, 'Vom Randbegriff zum Kampfbegriff: Semantiken des Politischen im ausgehenden Zarenreich (1850–1917)', in *Politik*: *Situationen eines Wortgebrauchs im Europa der Neuzeit*, ed. Willibald Steinmetz (Frankfurt a.M.: Campus, 2007), 248–88.

100 See also Matthias Stadelmann, '"Die Einladung der Gesellschaft" und ihre Ausladung: 1881 als Schicksalsjahr in Russlands politischer Geschichte', in *Schlüsseljahre: Zentrale Konstellationen der mittel- und osteuropäischen Geschichte – Festschrift für Helmut Altrichter zum 65. Geburtstag*, eds Lilia Antipow and Matthias Stadelmann (Stuttgart: Steiner, 2011), 185–201.

101 See Terence Emmons and Wayne S. Vucinich, eds, *The Zemstvo in Russia: An Experiment in Local Self-Government* (Cambridge: Cambridge University Press, 1982); Klaus Fröhlich, *The Emergence of Russian Constitutionalism, 1900–1904: The Relationship between Social Mobilization and Political Group Formation in Pre-revolutionary Russia* (The Hague: Martinus Nijhoff, 1981); Lutz Häfner, *Gesellschaft als lokale Veranstaltung: Die Wolgastädte Kazan' und Saratov (1870–1914)* (Köln: Böhlau, 2004); Guido Hausmann, ed., *Gesellschaft als lokale Veranstaltung: Selbstverwaltung, Assoziierung und Geselligkeit in den Städten des ausgehenden Zarenreiches* (Göttingen: Vandenhoeck & Ruprecht, 2002); Geoffrey Hosking, *Russia: People and Empire, 1552–1917* (Cambridge, MA: Harvard University Press, 1997), especially ch. 4; Pearson, *Russian Officialdom in Crisis*.

Towards a new quality of statehood

of the press soon followed, which even in the framework of autocracy had unexpected consequences. This was particularly evident in the run-up to the Russo–Turkish War of 1877–8, the jingoism sustained by public opinion being one of the main reasons why the Russian Empire even gambled on a war with the Ottomans in the first place.[102]

But a newly relevant public sphere that even the autocracy could not avoid manifested itself in other areas too. When the Russian autocracy saw itself challenged by a series of terrorist attacks and the subsequent founding of the *Narodnaia Volia* (People's Will) organization in 1879, with a number of social opinion makers showing a good deal of sympathy for the revolutionaries' motives, the Ministry of the Interior developed an explicit strategy for winning over public opinion. With the aid of counter-narratives in the press, it hoped to influence public sentiment in favour of autocracy. Minister of the Interior Mikhail Loris-Melikov consistently followed this approach. His contemporaries dubbed his period in office (1880–81) the 'dictatorship of the heart', marked as it was by his attempts to increasingly include the more cooperative segments of society in administrative and political decision-making processes. Loris-Melikov sought dialogue with opinion leaders in the public sphere and endeavoured to make state antiterror measures more plausible through public channels of communication. He understood better than others that terrorist acts of violence were an expression of profound social friction, and he allowed a moderate discussion of it in the Russian press. Other state officials in the Ministry of the Interior were thus quite aware that public opinion had acquired a new significance in the overall political landscape of the empire.[103]

The accession to the throne of Alexander III by no means brought an abrupt end to these new dynamics of opinion making. Censorship may have been heightened after 1881 and the universities put under tight police surveillance, but voices that endeavoured to demonstrate their loyalty still had considerable leeway in the press. This was illustrated rather clearly by the influence of Mikhail Katkov, publisher, publicist and editor of *Moskovskie vedomosti* (Moscow News), who worked his way into Alexander III's closest circle of advisors gathered around Konstantin Pobedonostsev. Katkov was instrumental in promoting the monarchy's strong Russian-nationalist tendencies.[104]

---

102 See Aleksei Miller, *The Romanov Empire and Nationalism: Essay in the Methodology of Historical Research* (Budapest: CEU Press, 2008), ch. 6; Berger and Miller, *Nationalizing Empires*; Andreas Renner, *Russischer Nationalismus und Öffentlichkeit im Zarenreich, 1855–1875* (Köln: Böhlau, 2000); Raphael Utz, *Rußlands unbrauchbare Vergangenheit: Nationalismus und Außenpolitik im Zarenreich* (Wiesbaden: Harrassowitz, 2008); M. Hakan Yavuz and Peter Sluglett, eds, *War and Diplomacy: The Russo-Turkish War of 1877–1878 and the Treaty of Berlin* (Salt Lake City, UT: University of Utah Press, 2012).

103 See Johnathan W. Daly, *Autocracy under Siege: Security Police and Opposition in Russia, 1866–1905* (DeKalb, IL: Northern Illinois University Press, 1998); Anke Hilbrenner and Frithjof Benjamin Schenk, 'Introduction: Modern Times? Terrorism in Late Tsarist Russia', *Jahrbücher für Geschichte Osteuropas* 58, 2 (2010): 161–71; Stephan Rindlisbacher, *Leben für die Sache: Vera Figner, Vera Zasulič und das radikale Milieu im späten Zarenreich* (Wiesbaden: Harrasowitz, 2014); Claudia Verhoeven, *The Odd Man Karakozov: Imperial Russia, Modernity, and the Birth of Terrorism* (Ithaca, NY: Cornell University Press, 2009); Tim-Lorenz Wurr, *Terrorismus und Autokratie: Staatliche Reaktionen auf den Russischen Terrorismus 1870–1890* (Paderborn: Ferdinand Schöningh, 2017).

104 See Martin Katz, *Mikhail N. Katkov: A Political Biography, 1818–1887* (Den Haag: Mouton, 1966); see also Mikhail Dolbilov, 'Russification and the Bureaucratic Mind in the Russian Empire's Northwestern Region in the 1860s', *Kritika: Explorations in Russian and Eurasian History* 5, 2 (2004): 245–72; Miller, *The Romanov Empire and Nationalism*; Berger and Miller, *Nationalizing Empires*; Darius Staliunas, *Making Russians: Meaning and Practices of Russification in Lithuania and Belarus after 1863* (Amsterdam: Rodopi, 2007).

This new kind of social activation soon had an effect on the representation of monarchic rule. Here, too, the strategies of legitimation of the country's autocratic rulers changed. The programmatic 'scenarios of power' of Alexander III upon acceding to the throne placed a completely new and decisive emphasis on the 'Russian' character of tsarist rule.[105] In addition to legitimizing the monarchy by its dynastical tradition and its imperial character, there was now an attempt to justify the rule of the Romanovs by linking it a Russian 'national cause'. This greater nationalization of rule had considerable effects on the social structures of the multi-ethnic empire. It is true that a supranational understanding of statehood was never abandoned, as evidenced in the adjective *rossiiskii* ('Russian' in reference to the Russian state, as opposed to *russkii* or 'Russian' in reference to its people, i.e. ethnic Russians). It is likewise true that the dynasty remained the unifying force ensuring the empire's territorial integrity. And yet, the autocracy's new self-definition as 'Russian' rule implied an unambiguous hierarchization of its subjects, one that didn't exist before. It is telling that under Alexander III Uvarov's triad – a concept dating from the 1830s and emphasizing the unity of autocracy, Orthodoxy and nationality (*narodnost'*) – underwent a reinterpretation. The nation (*narod*) was increasingly understood as the Russian nation. In this respect, the ruling powers' self-definition clearly points to a narrowed focus on Russianness, alongside the traditional mythic glorification of autocracy as the only suitable form of state and government in the Russian Empire.[106]

This attempt to give the monarchy a more nationalist underpinning was undoubtedly a reaction to the state crisis brought on by the terrorist threat of the 1870s and 1880s and the murder of Alexander II. It shows that winning over the people as a pillar of support figured prominently in the survival strategy of Russian autocracy. Even in the post-reform period, autocratic policies could not afford to ignore wider segments of society. The more narrow, national focus on Russians as the key constitutive nation can thus be interpreted as an aftereffect of society's activation in the reform era. For even in the era of counter-reforms, the Russian autocracy did not abandon the fundamental idea that autocratic politics require consensus-building legitimation. High-level state officials therefore made a conscious effort to promote an explicitly government-friendly public sphere. National-minded protagonists like Katkov had ever more leeway in interpreting political developments and saw their opportunities for (partial) participation in state decision-making processes increase.[107]

This reorientation was by no means mere programmatic lip service but was translated into specific state policies under Alexander III and Nicholas II that would fundamentally alter the character of the multi-ethnic empire. Particularly on the non-Russian peripheries of the empire, state authorities gave preference to religious, educational and symbolic policies that clearly favoured Orthodox Russians and which imposed on non-Russian subjects the professed hegemony of Russian culture and language.[108] The indigenous societies affected by these measures often perceived them as targeted efforts at Russification that went well beyond the administrative and legal unification tendencies of the reform era, since areas of culture and

---

105 For a fundamental look at tsarist 'scenarios of power', see Richard Wortman, *Scenarios of Power: Myth and Ceremony in the Russian Monarchy: From Alexander II to the Abdication of Nicholas II* (Princeton, NJ: Princeton University Press, 2000).

106 Nathaniel Knight, 'Ethnicity, Nationality, and the Masses: *Narodnost'* and Modernity in Imperial Russia', in *Russian Modernity: Politics, Knowledge, Practices*, eds David L. Hoffmann and Yanni Kotsonis (Houndmills: Palgrave Macmillan, 2000), 41–64.

107 Miller, *The Romanov Empire and Nationalism*, especially ch. 2 and ch. 6.

108 For example, Russian Orthodox churches and cathedrals were built in the centre of regional capitals on the periphery of the empire. See Karsten Brüggemann, 'Wie der Revaler Domberg zum Moskauer Kreml wurde: Zur lokalen Repräsentation imperialer Herrschaft im späten Zarenreich',

religion were now affected that were sometimes felt to be a serious danger to their national self-understanding. It was of secondary importance here that the policies of the St. Petersburg administration generally did not aim to make Russians out of non-Russian subjects but 'merely' expected them to bow to the cultural hegemony of the Russian language and Russian culture. Nevertheless, the struggle against 'Russification' became a battle cry of the era, used by local elites to counter the reach and penetration of the imperial claim to power. The de facto equating of state and Russianness promoted by St. Petersburg elicited sometimes vehement opposition on the peripheries of the empire and resulted in a long-term process of alienation of non-Russian subjects from an overall state they perceived as being Russian. Forms of resistance were quite heterogeneous, ranging from passive non-compliance to the outright obstruction of the centre's unreasonable demands (as in the case of the Baltic Germans), to underground activities against Russification measures (as in the Polish provinces) or against autocracy in general and the Russian Empire as a prison of nations. All told, the attempted nationalization of the monarchy in the 1880s and 1890s contributed significantly to the tension between nations in the multi-ethnic Russian empire.[109]

Kingdom of Poland

Along with the Baltic Sea provinces, the situation in the Kingdom of Poland first came to a head in the 1890s. The 'national question' undeniably added fuel to the fire, as the Russification measures adopted by state bureaucracy in education, religion and culture had intensified considerably in the 1880s and early 1890s. The situation was aggravated even more by the fact that the opportunities for social engagement were extremely limited in the Polish provinces compared to the core of Russia. For while an 'invitation' was extended to society in the inner-Russian provinces and some areas on the periphery, enabling the participation of citizens in administrative and legal processes in newly created organs of self-government and courts of lay assessors, the disempowerment of local society in the Polish territories was a constant of St. Petersburg rule after the January Uprising. The hegemony of state administration was oppressive in these territories, engagement in civil society was strictly regulated and there was certainly no intention of allowing the local population to participate in the affairs of public life. The almighty state (at least in its self-understanding) endeavoured to divorce itself from the claims and expectations

---

in *Imperiale Herrschaft in der Provinz: Repräsentationen politischer Macht im späten Zarenreich*, eds Jörg Baberowski, David Feest and Christoph Gumb (Frankfurt a.M.: Campus, 2008), 172–95; L.E. Gorizontov, *Paradoksy imperskoi politiki: Poliaki v Rossii i russkie v Pol'she (XIX – nachalo XX v.)* [Paradoxes in imperial politics: Poles in Russia and Russians in Poland (19th and early 20th centuries)] (Moscow: Izdatel'stvo Indrik, 1999); Piotr Paszkiewicz, 'The Russian Orthodox Cathedral of Saint Alexander Nevsky in Warsaw: From the History of Polish-Russian Relations', *Polish Art Studies* 14 (1992): 64–71; Robert L. Przygrodzki, 'Russians in Warsaw: Imperialism and National Identities, 1863–1915' (PhD diss., Northern Illinois University Press, 2007); Malte Rolf, 'Russische Herrschaft in Warschau: Die Aleksandr-Nevskij-Kathedrale im Konfliktraum politischer Kommunikation', in *Jenseits der Zarenmacht: Dimensionen des Politischen im Russischen Reich 1800–1917*, ed. Walter Sperling (Frankfurt a.M.: Campus, 2008), 163–89. This was also true of the self-presentation of the Russian Empire to the outside world. On the Russian pavilion at the Paris World's Fair of 1900 see the chapter 'Projections and Representations of Statehood' by Sabina Ferhadbegović in this volume.

109 On the Baltic Sea provinces, see especially Haltzel, 'Administrative Russification'; Michael H. Haltzel, *Der Abbau der deutschen ständischen Selbstverwaltung in den Ostseeprovinzen Russlands: Ein Beitrag zur Geschichte der russischen Unifizierungspolitik, 1855–1905* (Marburg: Herder-Institut, 1977); Thaden, 'The Russian Government'; Thaden, *Russification in the Baltic Provinces*; Thaden, *Russia's Western Borderlands*. On Finland, see Polvinen, *Imperial Borderland*; Waldron, 'Stolypin and Finland'.

of the indigenous population, and local bureaucracy tried to focus exclusively on the interests of the imperial centre.[110] The long-term exclusion of society only increased the potential conflict between the state and the indigenous population, the former being perceived as foreign rulers by the latter. The overall state had little support among the moderate middle class at the turn of the century, while a younger generation of political activists was beginning to make more radical demands for the self-determination of the Polish nation and to venture the move into illegality and a revolutionary underground movement. This step seemed all the more plausible considering that national movements were gaining momentum on other peripheries of the empire as well as internationally.[111]

The conflict-ridden situation in the Kingdom of Poland at the turn of the twentieth century illustrates the basic dilemma of social engagement in an autocratic state. In core Russia, too, there was a fundamental contradiction between the 'invitation of society' and the enabling of a public sphere on the one hand, and the conditions of limited participation on the other. This contradiction was a source of frustration and contributed to the radicalization of a portion of the intelligentsia that only emerged in the context of these new institutions of self-government. The many terrorist attacks and organizations of the 1870s and 1880s are certainly an expression of this radicalization. More recent research has rightly pointed out that no simple dichotomy existed between the state and society.[112] There were undoubtedly numerous fields of interaction and interspaces of negotiation and cooperation in which the opposition between state bureaucracy and social lobbying was not fundamental in nature. And yet there was a vital conflict between these two protagonists, a conflict deriving from the considerable difference between their respective understandings of the state. State bureaucrats, after all, were hardly prepared to accommodate their own agenda to the needs of the population. They saw themselves as representatives of state authority, and though they may have been willing to make some compromises or cooperate with society to a limited degree, they nonetheless insisted on their own, exclusive decision-making power. The notion of negotiating interests on an equal footing did not conform to their self-image; the bridges they built between the state and its people remained fragile, and access to them was strictly regulated. And so the relationship between institutions of self-government and representatives of the state was fraught with

---

110 See Rolf, *Imperiale Herrschaft im Weichselland*; Rolf, *Rządy imperialne w Kraju Nadwiślańskim*; Rolf, 'Between Imperial State-Building and Local Cooperation'; Rolf, 'What Is the "Russian Cause" and Whom Does It Serve? Russian Nationalists and Imperial Bureaucracy in the Kingdom of Poland', in *Protecting the Empire: Imperial Government and Russian Nationalist Alliance in the Western Borderlands in the Late Imperial Period*, eds Yoko Aoshima, Paul Werth and Darius Staliunas (Budapest: CEU Press, forthcoming); Wandycz, *Partitioned Poland*; Weeks, *Nation and State*.

111 See Robert E. Blobaum, *Feliks Dzierżyński and the SDKPiL: A Study of the Origins of Polish Communism* (New York: Columbia University Press, 1984); Robert E. Blobaum, *Rewolucja: Russian Poland, 1904–1907* (Ithaca, NY: Cornell University Press, 1995); Marian Kamil Dziewanowski, 'The Polish Revolutionary Movement and Russia, 1904–1907', in *Russian Thought and Politics*, eds Hugh McLean, Martin E. Malia and George Fischer (Cambridge, MA: Havard University Press, 1957), 375–94; Andrzej Garlicki, *Józef Piłsudski, 1867–1935* (London: Scolar Press, 1995); Brian A. Porter, *When Nationalism Began to Hate: Imagining Modern Politics in Nineteenth-Century Poland* (Oxford: Oxford University Press, 2000).

112 See the publications of Baberowski et al., *Imperiale Herrschaft in der Provinz*; Kirsten Bönker, *Jenseits der Metropolen: Öffentlichkeit und Lokalpolitik im Gouvernement Saratov (1890–1914)* (Köln: Böhlau, 2010); Edith W. Clowes, Samuel D. Kassow and James L. West, eds, *Between Czar and People: Educated Society in Pre-revolutionary Russia* (Princeton, NJ: Princeton University Press, 1991); Heiko Haumann and Stefan Plaggenborg, eds, *Aufbruch der Gesellschaft im verordneten Staat: Rußland in der Spätphase des Zarenreiches* (Frankfurt a.M.: Peter Lang, 1994); Walter Sperling, ed., *Jenseits der Zarenmacht: Dimensionen des Politischen im Russischen Reich 1800–1917* (Frankfurt a.M.: Campus, 2008).

Towards a new quality of statehood

tension and conflict, culminating in the revolution of 1905. A state authority without a social basis, however, would inevitably be weak, with very limited local influence. In this respect, the state in the Russian Empire up to the turn of the twentieth century suffered from the disparity between its representatives' claim to absolute power and the inability to thoroughly control its heterogeneous population and the great expanses of its territory.[113]

In this context, the revolution of 1905 and the constitutional order it forced into existence represented a profound break. The Fundamental Law of 1906 gave Russia a parliament in the form of the Duma, legalized political parties and abolished pre-censorship. The brief decade from 1906 to the outbreak of the First World War was marked by an invigoration of politics in the public sphere, reflected not only in the election campaigns for the Duma but especially in the broad spectrum of political newspapers. The conflict persisted, of course, between the state bureaucracy and government on the one hand, with their claim to total power, and social activists on the other in the form of elected representatives of the people or political publicists. The disbanding of the first two Dumas after just a few months, Pyotr Stolypin's coup d'état-like reform of electoral law in 1907, and the numerous lawsuits against newspapers on account of supposed statutory violations are a telling indication of this. And yet, a new state order existed as of 1906, safeguarded by the Fundamental Law, which granted a considerable scope of manoeuvre for political participation and freedom of speech in society. In the centre of the empire as well as on its peripheries, this contributed to the politicization of broad segments of the population, which began, to a hitherto unseen degree, showing an interest in questions concerning the entire empire. Whether this set-up would have stabilized the Russian Empire in the long run is doubtful given the national diversification of the political public sphere. For, these new opinion forums allowed a mobilization of nationality issues which heavily burdened the relationships between ethnic and religious populations, challenging the integrity of the supranational state over the medium term. Thus, the period from 1906 to 1914 was marked in the Russian Empire not only by the development of a political public sphere and the traditional confrontation between state bureaucrats and social opinion makers, but also by an unprecedented intensification of interethnic conflicts.[114]

---

113 See Haumann and Plaggenborg, *Aufbruch der Gesellschaft im verordneten Staat*; Hosking, *Russia: People and Empire*, 424–51; Dominic Lieven, *Towards the Flame: Empire, War and the End of Tsarist Russia* (London: Penguin, 2015), 46–90; Malte Rolf, 'Kooperation im Konflikt? Die zarische Verwaltung im Königreich Polen zwischen Staatsausbau und gesellschaftlicher Aktivierung (1863–1914)', in *Vom Vorrücken des Staates in die Fläche: Ein europäisches Phänomen des langen 19. Jahrhunderts*, eds Jörg Ganzenmüller and Tatjana Tönsmeyer (Köln: Böhlau, 2016), 35–64; Rolf, 'Between Imperial State-Building and Local Cooperation'.

114 See Abraham Ascher, *P.A. Stolypin: The Search for Stability in Late Imperial Russia* (Stanford, CA: Stanford University Press, 2001); Robert E. Blobaum, ed., *Antisemitism and Its Opponents in Modern Poland* (Ithaca, NY: Cornell University Press, 2005); Wayne Dowler, *Russia in 1913* (DeKalb, IL: Northern Illinois University Press, 2010); Caspar Ferenczi, 'Funktion und Bedeutung der Presse in Russland vor 1914', *Jahrbücher für Geschichte Osteuropas* 30, 1 (1980): 362–98; Felicitas Fischer v. Weikersthal, Frank Grüner, Susanne Hohler, Franziska Schedewie and Raphael Utz, eds, *The Russian Revolution of 1905 in Transcultural Perspective: Identities, Peripheries, and the Flow of Ideas* (Bloomington, IN: Slavica Publishers, 2013); Manfred Hagen, *Die Entfaltung politischer Öffentlichkeit in Rußland, 1906–1914* (Wiesbaden: Franz Steiner, 1982); Manfred Hagen, '*Obshchestvennost*: Formative Changes in Russian Society Before 1914', in *Die russische Freiheit: Wege in ein paradoxes Thema*, ed. Manfred Hagen (Stuttgart: Franz Steiner, 2002), 124–36; Alexandra Korros, *A Reluctant Parliament: Stolypin, Nationalism, and the Politics of the Russian Imperial State Council, 1906–1911* (Lanham, MD: Rowman & Littlefield, 2002); Malte Rolf, 'A Continuum of Crisis? The Kingdom of Poland in the Shadow of Revolution (1905–1915)', in Fischer v. Weikersthal et al., *The Russian Revolution of 1905*, 159–74; Pascal Trees, *Wahlen im Weichselland: Die*

A new quality of statehood? the intensification of state activity around the turn of the century

The emerging spaces of political participation for old and new social groups in the monarchies of the late nineteenth and early twentieth centuries by no means contradicted the progressive expansion of modern, bureaucratic statehood. If the reform period of the second half of the nineteenth century was marked by the replacement of the older, feudal orders with new state-administrative structures, the internal expansion of the state around the turn of the century gave rise to a new quality of statehood. Alongside the opening of forums for social participation, a new understanding of the state developed, one approaching the interventionist welfare state. Whole new fields of state activity emerged. Added to this was the pivotal process of expanding participation and self-determination in political decision-making, a heated topic of debate in these decades. By 1900 reform efforts in all three empires had produced rapid and often radical social, cultural and economic change, as well as unexpected responses from society. The elaboration of state structures and bureaucracies proceeded apace in all three empires – indeed across Europe – albeit to very different degrees in each empire and in the new Balkan states. This broader development invariably opened new areas for public participation at several levels of the state. And as that state became more directly implicated in people's daily lives, it also became more present in their consciousness. This development produced new popular expectations about the role the state should play in society, about popular participation in political decision-making, and it produced several new and different visions for how transformed states might look and function in the future. The expectations for popular participation and state intervention also triggered new tensions between imperial centres and localities, as well as new initiatives for state reform from the margins of empire. The following sections examine more closely the status of intensified state-building efforts in the decades preceding the outbreak of the First World War.

The Russian Empire and the Kingdom of Poland

The Great Reforms had already promoted the bureaucratization of rule, a process which consolidated around the turn of the century. Given the international competition between imperial powers, which in the context of colonial expansion resulted in inner state expansion as well, the Russian Empire endeavoured in a targeted way to consolidate its state bureaucracy. This race between the great powers made the bureaucratic state seem like the only 'modern' and competitive form of government. Reluctant to expand its spaces of social participation, the Russian autocracy was all the more eager to expand and streamline its state administration. This was ultimately linked to an intensification of state activity which created a new quality of statehood and gave rise to a rudimentary form of the interventionist welfare state in Russia.

Nationaldemokraten in Russisch-Polen und die Dumawahlen, 1905–1912 (Stuttgart: Franz Steiner, 2007); Weeks, *Nation and State*, especially 172–92; Anna Veronika Wendland and Andreas R. Hofmann, 'Stadt und Öffentlichkeit: Auf der Suche nach einem neuen Konzept in der Geschichte Ostmitteleuropas – Eine Einführung', in *Stadt und Öffentlichkeit in Ostmitteleuropa 1900–1939*, eds Andreas R. Hofmann and Anna Veronika Wendland (Stuttgart: Steiner, 2002), 9–25. For an overview on the nationality question, see also Theodore R. Weeks: 'Nationality, Empire, and Politics in the Russian Empire and USSR: An Overview of Recent Publications', in *H-Soz-Kult*, 29 Oct. 2012, www.hsozkult.de/literaturereview/id/forschungsberichte-1134 (retrieved on 12 February 2017).

Towards a new quality of statehood

State expansion applied to both central and local administration, drastically increasing the number of permanent posts, particularly for mid-level staff. In 1900 the tsarist bureaucracy employed more than 500,000 civil servants, the largest administrative apparatus being directly subordinate to the Ministry of the Interior. The growing importance of the Ministry of the Interior found ample expression in the expansion of centralized power at the local level of administration. Traditionally, the 'strong men' of tsarist administration in the imperial provinces were the governors or governors general. The latter were the traditional viceroys of the tsar, reporting directly to the monarch and authorized to give administrative orders. Such remnants of a premodern, direct autocratic form of rule exercised through provincial viceroys were increasingly called into question by the turn of the twentieth century. The Ministry of the Interior succeeded in curbing the influence of governors, making important decisions on staff and other administrative issues in the provinces directly through a new and powerful central authority – a development which the governors perceived as a painful marginalization.[115]

The St. Petersburg Ministry of the Interior not only made a substantial contribution to the expansion of bureaucracy in the provinces, but also accelerated the professionalization of state representatives. In no other public authority was the share of civil servants with university degrees so high. Whereas the highest posts in the provincial administration were assigned according to the traditional logic of dovetailing civil and military administration, governors general not only having a predominantly high-aristocratic pedigree but usually having a lengthy military career behind them, the average civil servant in the Ministry of the Interior had a wholly different education and socialization. The latter were generally from the low nobility, rarely looked back on a military career, and often had a university degree (especially in law). This new type of civil servant was guided more by administrative and legal questions than by military paradigms. Hence, the transformation to a modern civil service in terms of staff and mentality had already taken place by 1900 in the Ministry of the Interior and its sphere of influence.[116]

---

115 See Łukasz Chimiak, Gubernatorzy rosyjscy w Królestwie Polskim, 1863–1915: Szkic do portretu zbiorowego [Russian governors in the Kingdom of Poland, 1863–1915: outlines of a collective portrait] (Wrocław: Wydawnictwo Funna, 1999); Jörg Ganzenmüller and Tatjana Tönsmeyer, 'Einleitung, Vom Vorrücken des Staates in die Fläche: Ein europäisches Phänomen des langen 19. Jahrhunderts', in Ganzenmüller et al., Vom Vorrücken des Staates, 7–31; Orlovsky, Ministry of Internal Affairs in Imperial Russia; Robbins, The Tsar's Viceroys; Rolf, Imperiale Herrschaft im Weichselland; Rolf, Rządy imperialne w Kraju Nadwiślańskim; Rolf, 'Between Imperial State-Building and Local Cooperation'.

116 See Lieven, Russia's Rulers, especially chapters 2 and 3; Dominic Lieven, 'The Elites', in The Cambridge History of Russia, ed. Dominic Lieven (Cambridge: Cambridge University Press, 2006), 227–44; on the provincial governors, see also Robbins, The Tsar's Viceroys, 31–9. In 1913, about 50% of governors had been in the employ of the military directly prior to entering the civil service, and 46% of them had formal military training. Still, by 1913 more than half of all governors had a university degree. On the background of governors general and governors in the Kingdom of Poland, see Chimiak, Gubernatorzy rosyjscy; Malte Rolf, 'Namiestnicy Królestwa Polskiego i Generał-Gubernatorzy Warszawscy nad Wisłą po powstaniu styczniowym (do 1914 r.)' [Viceroys of the Kingdom of Poland and General Governors of Warsaw on the Vistula after the January Uprising (until 1914)], in Rosja, Europa i Polska. Walka o Niepodległość w XIX Wieku [Russia, Europe, and Poland: the struggle for independence in the 19th century], eds Łukasz Adamski and Sławomir Dębski (Warsaw: Center for Polish-Russian Dialogue and Understanding, 2016); Katya Vladimirov, The World of Provincial Bureaucracy in Late 19th and 20th Century Russian Poland (Lewiston, NY: Mellen Press, 2004). For an exemplary biography of an imperial governor, see Ulrich Hofmeister, 'Der Halbzar von Turkestan: Konstantin fon-Kaufman in Zentralasien (1867–1882)', in Elites and Empire: Imperial Biographies in Russia and Austria-Hungary (1850–1918), eds Tim Buchen and Malte Rolf (Berlin: De Gruyter Oldenbourg, 2015), 65–89.

Grandits, Judson and Rolf

And yet the tendency to disentangle civil and military administration was not uncontroversial, and neither was it ubiquitous or cross-departmental. For one thing, the provinces on the periphery of the empire were presided over by officials in the form of viceroys or governors general who not only had a military career but were often supreme commanders in their respective military districts. For another, the army was involved in internal affairs in a multitude of ways. The tsarist army had traditionally been an institution for maintaining internal order. This remained so in the late nineteenth century, meaning that locally stationed troops were still the most reliable pillar of the ancien régime in times of crisis. Whether to put down local peasant uprisings, to secure public spaces during urban protests, or during the revolutionary tumults of 1905–06, the state administration regularly called in troops to support the local police. One could even speak of a militarization of the state administration during the revolution of 1905, extending into the Duma period in the form of martial law and a state of emergency that lasted for years. The liberal opposition viewed this militarized administration as a perpetual violation of the law and an expression of premodern statehood.

Just how ambiguous the division between civil and military administration was, even in 1900, can be seen in the hybrid status accorded to the police force by state administration. In big cities, the local police force was headed by an *oberpolitsmeyster* (senior police officer) who was subordinate to the St. Petersburg Ministry of the Interior. The tasks of these police chiefs were manifold. The annual reports they wrote offer a glimpse into these activities. Apart from reporting on the 'mood of the population', they supplied data on demographic developments, the economic situation, the educational system and about public life in general in their respective towns. Crime statistics were just one part of these comprehensive data compiled by the police chief, his department being responsible not only for the police surveillance of political suspects but also for building, labour and hygiene inspection.[117] Given its abundant tasks, the police force was easily overwhelmed in crisis situations despite its considerable manpower. During the revolution of 1905, in particular, the police proved largely ineffectual, and in many instances the autocracy had to call in soldiers to handle policing tasks. And yet, the uniformed policeman was a pivotal figure, at least when it came to making statehood more visible in urban spaces.[118]

The progressive expansion of state bureaucracy, however, led to increased contacts in other domains between state institutions and local societies. The state, after all, with its growing apparatus, was an increasingly important business partner, if not an actual employer. Especially

---

117 See Felix Schnell, Ordnungshüter auf Abwegen? Herrschaft und illegitime Gewalt in Moskau, 1905–1914 (Wiesbaden: Harrassowitz Verlag, 2006); Robert W. Thurston, Liberal City, Conservative State: Moscow and Russia's Urban Crisis, 1906–1914 (New York: Oxford University Press, 1987); on the Kingdom of Poland, see Rolf, Imperiale Herrschaft im Weichselland; Rolf, Rządy imperialne w Kraju Nadwiślańskim; Rolf, 'Between Imperial State-Building and Local Cooperation'.

118 See Daly, Autocracy under Siege; Jonathan W. Daly, The Watchful State: Security Police and Opposition in Russia, 1906–1917 (DeKalb, IL: Northern Illinois University Press, 2004); William C. Fuller, Civil-Military Conflict in Imperial Russia, 1881–1914 (Princeton, NJ: Princeton University Press, 1985); Christoph Gumb, 'Drohgebärden. Repräsentationen von Herrschaft im Wandel. Warsaw, 1904–1907' (Ph.D. diss., Humboldt-Universität zu Berlin, Philosophische Fakultät I, published 6 December 2013); Jan Kusber, Krieg und Revolution in Russland 1904–1906: Das Militär im Verhältnis zu Wirtschaft, Autokratie und Gesellschaft (Stuttgart: Franz Steiner, 1997); Malte Rolf, 'Metropolen im Ausnahmezustand? Gewaltakteure und Gewalträume in den Städten des späten Zarenreichs', in Kollektive Gewalt in der Stadt: Europa, 1890–1939, ed. Friedrich Lenger (München: De Gruyter Oldenbourg, 2013), 25–49; Schnell, Ordnungshüter; Thurston, Moscow.

Towards a new quality of statehood

in urban agglomerations, state institutions served in a variety of ways as contracting authorities for the civilian sector, whether renting office space, awarding concessions for construction and infrastructure projects, or hiring companies for state and urban logistics. Entire professions – engineering, for example – were oriented towards the employment opportunities offered by state contracts. Large segments of the new bourgeois elite profited from the growing range of activities linked to the expansion of the state, especially in urban areas, around the turn of the twentieth century.

The increasing presence of the state did not necessarily lead to an increased sense of loyalty towards the overall political system, however. A liberal-oppositionist stance and critique of the administrative apparatus could easily go hand in hand with routine (business) contacts with this very bureaucracy. This was due in part to the political immobility of Russian autocracy, but also had to do with the fact that the intensification of state intervention rapidly changed people's expectations. The inherent logic of state expansion meant that more was demanded of the state in turn, so that conflicts with state institutions proliferated.

In principle, the highest officials of the tsarist administration adhered to a traditional understanding of the state, primarily defining the latter as the guarantor of law and order. This paradigm remained untouched well into the twentieth century, ensuring public order was the main business of state officials even after 1900. Added to this were traditional tasks promoting overall state or local development. At the very latest under Peter the Great, the 'well-ordered state' comprised targeted state support to trade and industry as well as the provision of educational facilities and welfare benefits for the general 'well-being of the population'.[119] The latter sector particularly saw a considerable intensification of state activities in the late nineteenth century which, at least in some areas, pointed towards the rise of an interventionist welfare state. This took place sometimes in cooperation with, sometimes in competition with, existing institutions of local government.

Thus, state economic promotion under finance ministers Nikolai Bunge (1881–87) and especially Sergei Witte (1892–1903) took on hitherto unknown proportions and, with the help of a protectionist tariff policy and massive investment in railroads as the motor of domestic production, enabled the rapid industrialization of an agrarian state shortly before the turn of the twentieth century. In this instance, as well as during the subsequent agrarian reforms under Stolypin starting in 1906, the state saw itself as a central steering agency whose extensive claims to intervention in economic affairs and a liberally interpreted right to nationalize (e.g. land) offered key impulses for the economic rise of Russia and hence its industrial (later, agricultural) modernization. The state became a pivotal actor, not only for setting the economic framework enabling the structural transformation of Russia; rather, with the help of targeted promotion and investment measures as well as the awarding of concessions, state authorities endeavoured to have a formative influence on the substance of this transformation, tailoring it to the Russian Empire's great-power ambitions.[120]

---

119 See Marc Raeff, *The Well-Ordered Police State: Social and Institutional Change through Law in the Germanies and Russia, 1600–1800* (New Haven, CT: Yale University Press, 1983).

120 See Susan P. McCaffray, *The Politics of Industrialization in Tsarist Russia: The Association of Southern Coal and Steel Producers, 1874–1914* (DeKalb, IL: Northern Illinois University Press, 1996); Anton Fedyashin, 'Sergej Witte and the Press: A Study in Careerism and Statecraft', *Kritika: Explorations in Russian and Eurasian History* 14, no. 3 (2013): 507–34; Dietrich Geyer, *Der russische Imperialismus: Studien über den Zusammenhang von innerer und auswärtiger Politik, 1860–1914* (Göttingen: Vandenhoeck & Ruprecht, 1977); Jonathan A. Grant, *Big Business in Russia: The Putilov Company in Late Imperial Russia,*

With regard to the labour question that emerged in the 1880s and 1890s, a number of state representatives saw the need to intervene and thus developed the first state social policies. Factory inspections were instituted in 1882, and by 1903 more than 250 inspectors were active throughout Russia. Certain protection clauses were issued in factory legislation, and industrial safety in general was increasingly codified into law. In 1882 child labour was restricted; from 1885 to 1890, night work was prohibited in numerous trades for both minors and women; in 1897 the workday was limited to 11 hours, and as of 1900, various legal forms of worker organization were discussed and even experimented with in Moscow. The beginnings of social-welfare legislation in the Russian Empire also predated the revolution of 1905 in the form of accident insurance and discussions about health and old-age insurance. And yet, it was after 1906 and the establishment of a new constitutional order that the process really took off. Legalized trade unions and societies or associations to articulate the interests of workers, as well as protracted debates in the Duma and its commissions about comprehensive industrial-safety legislation dynamized the field of state-interventionist social policy.[121]

But even the first measures of the 1880s and 1890s made clear that the state increasingly understood itself as a regulating authority in company internal affairs and disputes. Indeed, by the end of the nineteenth century, local state officials were being called in more and more to mediate factory disputes. Such state interventions would sometimes end in local entrepreneurs being reprimanded for neglecting their employees, which was considered tantamount to 'endangering the public order'.[122] In the paternalist worldview of higher state officials, the social dislocations brought on by industrial capitalism were quite problematic; hence, many of these officials were critical of factory owners and industrial working conditions.[123] The intervention of state officials caused the disputing parties to increasingly perceive the state as an institution fundamentally responsible for mediating conflicts. Expectations rose with regard to state interventionist policies as a consequence. The demand for an eight-hour workday, which gained traction with the revolution of 1905, was expected to be regulated and enforced by the state. Thus, dissatisfaction with the working conditions in factories was soon directed not only

---

1868–1917 (Pittsburgh, PA: University of Pittsburgh Press, 1999); Sidney Harcave, *Count Sergei Witte and the Twilight of Imperial Russia: A Biography* (Armonk: M.E. Sharpe, 2004); Th. H. v. Laue, *Sergei Witte and the Industrialization of Russia* (New York: Columbia University Press, 1974); Shilov, *Gosudarstven-nye deiateli Rossiiskoi imperii*; Francis W. Wcislo, *Tales of Imperial Russia: The Life and Times of Sergei Witte, 1849–1915* (Oxford: Oxford University Press, 2011). On Stolypin's agrarian reforms, see Ascher, *Stolypin*; Mary Schaeffer Conroy, *Peter Arkadevich Stolypin: Practical Politics in Late Tsarist Russia* (Boulder, CO: Westview Press, 1976); Judith Pallot, *Land Reform in Russia, 1906–1917: Peasant Responses to Stolypin's Project of Rural Transformation* (Oxford: Oxford University Press, 1999); Joachim von Puttkamer, 'Die Vertretung der Bauernschaft in der Dritten Duma und ihr Beitrag zur Debatte über die Stolypinschen Agrarreformen', *Jahrbücher für Geschichte Osteuropas* 41 (1993): 44–80.

121 See Joachim von Puttkamer, *Fabrikgesetzgebung in Russland vor 1905: Regierung und Unternehmerschaft beim Ausgleich ihrer Interessen in einer vorkonstitutionellen Ordnung* (Köln: Böhlau, 1996). On Zubatov's union initiative and his 'police socialism', see Orlando Figes, *A People's Tragedy: The Russian Revolution 1891–1924* (Harmondsworth: Penguin, 1998), 173–89; Thurston, *Moscow*, 105–10. On reform projects concerning industrial-safety legislation negotiated in the Duma after 1905–06, see Benjamin Beuerle, *Russlands Westen: Westorientierung und Reformgesetzgebung im ausgehenden Zarenreich 1905–1917)* (Wiesbaden: Harrassowitz, 2016).

122 Archiwum Głowne Akt Dawnych (AGAD), Kancelaria Generał-Gubernatora Warszawskiego/Kantselariia Varshavskogo General-Gubernatora, sygn. 6481, kart. 22–25 Letter of Piotrków Governor Miller to Governor General of Warsaw Gurko, 14 November 1894, here kart. 4v-6.

123 See Robbins, *The Tsar's Viceroys*, 200–3.

Towards a new quality of statehood

at their owners and operators, but at state bodies and officials in general, whose achievements lagged behind expectations.[124] The inherent logic of expanding the sphere of state activities meant that the state increasingly adopted a steering function in social interactions, making its presence felt in numerous new fields of conflict.

This new quality of state involvement and its willingness to intervene was even more pronounced in local urban contexts. In the rapidly growing cities of the late nineteenth century, state bureaucracy increasingly acted as a regulatory authority, sometimes looking to cooperate and sometimes seeking confrontation with the respective organs of self-governance. The new challenges posed by the rapid growth of cities caused by industrialization required ever more state intervention in urban affairs, beyond its traditional task of maintaining law and order. This included the broadly defined fields of police-monitored hygiene and building inspection, which gave state representatives – especially the local city prefect (*gradonachal'nik*) and senior police officer (*oberpolitsmeyster*) – considerable influence and discretionary power in the process of urbanization.[125]

If the scope of manoeuvre of state bureaucracies was limited in most Russian cities due to the parallel structures and activities of urban self-government, the situation in the western periphery of the empire was entirely different. Imperial authorities had blocked the introduction of the zemstvo and Duma in the Kingdom of Poland in the 1860s and 1870s. St. Petersburg's mistrust of the indigenous Polish and Jewish population was simply too great after the January Uprising to grant local civic communities such spaces of development. This attitude changed little in the ensuing decades. Municipal organs of self-government were not introduced in Vistula Land until the First World War.[126]

Such a policy of territorial discrimination in the late nineteenth century gave rise to the Polish self-government movement, which demanded equality for all citizens. It also made sure that in the Kingdom of Poland, state bureaucracy alone was responsible for the overall administration of municipal affairs. Thus, in metropolises like Warsaw and Lodz the state was in much greater

---

124 See esp. Abraham Ascher, *The Revolution of 1905: A Short History* (Stanford, CA: Stanford University Press, 2004); Blobaum, *Rewolucja*, 72–114; Andreas R. Hofmann, 'The Biedermanns in the 1905 Revolution: A Case Study in Entrepreneurs' Responses to Social Turmoil in Łódź', *The Slavonic and East European Review* 82 (2004): 27–49, here 32–3; Joachim von Puttkamer, 'Ziele unterschiedlicher Reichweite? Die Arbeiter in der Revolution von 1905/06: Eine Übersicht', in *Das Zarenreich, das Jahr 1905 und seine Wirkungen: Bestandsaufnahmen*, eds Jan Kusber and Andreas Frings (Münster: LIT, 2007), 105–20.

125 In 1881 St. Petersburg had 876,000 inhabitants, and by 1910, over 1.9 million. Moscow had about 750,000 inhabitants in 1886 and more than 1.6 million in 1912. Warsaw, the third-largest city in the empire, had a population of about 380,000 in 1882; by 1914 it had grown to over 880,000. See James H. Bater, *St. Petersburg: Industrialization and Change* (Montreal: McGill-Queen's University Press, 1976); Joseph Bradley, *Muzhik and Muscovite: Urbanisation in Late Imperial Russia* (Berkeley, CA: University of California Press, 1985), 141–93; Daniel R. Brower, *The Russian City Between Tradition and Modernity, 1850–1900* (Berkeley, CA: University of California Press, 1990); Michael F. Hamm, ed., *The City in Russian History* (Lexington, KY: University Press of Kentucky, 1976); Michael F. Hamm, ed., *The City in Late Imperial Russia* (Bloomington, IN: Indiana University Press, 1986); Schnell, *Ordnungshüter*; Thurston, *Moscow*; Rolf, 'Between Imperial State-Building and Local Cooperation'; Malte Rolf, 'Imperiale Herrschaft im städtischen Raum: Zarische Beamte und urbane Öffentlichkeit in Warschau (1870–1914)', in *Russlands imperiale Macht: Integrationsstrategien und ihre Reichweite in transnationaler Perspektive*, ed. Bianka Pietrow-Ennker (Köln: Böhlau, 2012), 123–53.

126 See Stephen D. Corrsin, *Warsaw before the First World War: Poles and Jews in the Third City of the Russian Empire, 1880–1914* (New York: Columbia University Press, 1989); Rolf, 'Kooperation im Konflikt'; Rolf, 'Between Imperial State-Building and Local Cooperation'; Weeks, *Nation and State*.

demand as an administrative authority than it was in the heart of Russia. Correspondingly, the circle of officials around the Warsaw mayor entrusted with the day-to-day administration of urban affairs developed extensive notions of state interventionism and rather technocratic visions of modern urbanity. In these segments of the state apparatus, a technicist form of statism emerged where these officials' willingness to invest sometimes went well beyond that of the notables assembled in elected city Dumas. Whether building water supply and sewage systems, opening municipal market halls, or expanding local transport infrastructure – tsarist officials initiated large-scale projects, advocated their financing by the central authorities in St. Petersburg, and thus made a key contribution to transforming Warsaw into a modern metropolis. They were sometimes even more successful than cities with their own institutions of self-government. This was because the authorities in Warsaw did not need to contend with the opposition of civil societies and their elected representatives, who in other places were often reluctant to assume the high costs of new infrastructure or were busy securing concessions in order to enrich themselves.[127] In a certain sense, Warsaw was a laboratory for modern administrative practices, pointing towards more interventionist state bureaucracy, often going beyond the administrative measures undertaken by the autocratic government in the centre of the empire, and – similar to the other European colonial empires – ultimately having a ripple effect from the periphery back to the centre.

To be sure, state engagement had its limits, for the guiding idea of an active and interventionist state bureaucracy was not shared by all representatives of the empire. Conservative institutions such as the governor general and his administration were often sceptical of such new approaches. But there were significant and fundamental differences within the tsarist administration of Vistula Land with regard to the scope of manoeuvre of officials and the agenda that they followed. The governors general were reluctant to commit to any long-term urban planning projects or sweeping infrastructural changes. Any transformation that threatened the urban status quo too immensely was viewed with caution by these tsarist emissaries. The notion of an interventionist state administration was largely foreign to them. There were thus a range of issues where the mayor was unable to induce the governor general to act. Leading officials in the state bureaucracy could not be convinced of the need for a state-sponsored housing programme or any form of 'interventionist health policy'.[128] Authorities were just as unwilling to take action against rampant inner-city poverty as they were against the intolerable living conditions in newly built working-class neighbourhoods.

Moreover, given the limited finances available to state authorities, the bureaucracy remained utterly dependent on cooperation with certain segments of urban society. Thus, representatives in St. Petersburg were willing, at least in Warsaw, to allow limited and controlled philanthropic

---

127 On Kiev, see Michael F. Hamm, *Kiev: A Portrait, 1800–1917* (Princeton, NJ: Princeton University Press, 1986); Michael F. Hamm, 'Continuity and Change in Late Imperial Kiev', in *The City in Late Imperial Russia*, ed. Michael F. Hamm (Bloomington, IN: Indiana University Press, 1986), 79–122. On St. Petersburg, see Sergei Glezerov, *Peterburg serebrianogo veka: Byt i nravy* [Petersburg during the Silver Age: customs and ways of life] (Moskau: Tsentrpoligraf, 2007), 136–43. Even in Riga, only one-third of the city was connected to the sewer system in 1914. Anders Henriksson, 'Riga: Growth, Conflict and the Limitations of Good Government, 1850–1914', in Hamm, *The City in Late Imperial Russia*, 177–207, here 186.

128 See Clemens Zimmermann, *Die Zeit der Metropolen: Urbanisierung und Großstadtentwicklung* (Frankfurt a.M.: Fischer, 1996), 31. On the reluctant acceptance of interventionist notions of social policy in municipal politics, see Annegret Bautz, *Sozialpolitik statt Wohltätigkeit? Der Konzeptionswandel städtischer Fürsorge in Sankt Petersburg von 1892 bis 1914* (Wiesbaden: Harrassowitz, 2007).

Towards a new quality of statehood

investments from local civil society, despite the fact that the state authorities, for political reasons, had refused to expand the municipal self-government statutes in Vistula Land.[129] Tolerating charitable private initiatives and the sale of concessions to private individuals remained the preferred method of the authorities in their attempt to combat ever more dire social problems in the industrial city of Warsaw. 'Municipal socialism' typical of big cities in Western Europe around the turn of the twentieth century, in which communal governments tried to avoid or reverse the privatization of public services, did not catch on in the Kingdom of Poland.[130]

In this regard, Russian state administration in the Polish provinces presented an ambivalent picture. As common as notions of an interventionist urban 'service administration' were among the officials responsible for the daily tasks of municipal administration, they were nonetheless not characteristic of the overall state apparatus. A comparison with other Eastern and Central European cities in this period, however, reveals that this ambivalence was quite common in the region. An urban social policy was generally lacking outside the St. Petersburg empire as well.[131]

Given this contradictory picture, we shall turn our attention now to the changing understanding of the state in the Russian Empire at the turn of the century.

Ideas about what form the state should take, what areas of life it was responsible for and what it was expected to achieve changed dramatically in the second half of the nineteenth century and were also extremely varied across different segments and groups of society. In general, however, most contemporaries had come to terms with the process of state growth and intensified bureaucratization, however varied their expectations.

State expansion did not lead to fewer conflicts between state representatives and social activists. Indeed, communication remained ambivalent between state authorities and local communities. Cooperation and conflict were cheek by jowl, situations of intense confrontation alternating with moments of collaboration. The modus vivendi of pragmatic day-to-day communication did nothing to alter the general scepticism, if not outright rejection, that many social protagonists displayed towards the organs and representatives of the state who served as the long arm of autocratic order.

One reason for this was that the state, even after 1905 and the ensuing years, was rarely prepared to hand over its decision-making powers in matters of social policy. The various camps

---

129 The most well-known example of a philanthropic private initiative is surely the 'Wawelberg Colony' workers' settlement in Warsaw. See J. Szokalski, *Institucja tanich mieszkań im. Hipolita i Ludwiki małż. Wawelbergów* [The Hipolit and Ludwika Wawelberg institute of affordable housing] (Warsaw: B. r. ok., 1904). See also Ute Caumanns, 'Mietskasernen und "Gläserne Häuser": Soziales Wohnen in Warschau zwischen Philanthropie und Genossenschaft 1900–1939', in *Wohnen in der Großstadt, 1900–1939: Wohnsituation und Modernisierung im europäischen Vergleich*, eds Alena Janatková and Hanna Kozińska-Witt (Stuttgart: Franz Steiner, 2006), 205–24; Ute Caumanns, 'Modernisierung unter den Bedingungen der Teilung: Überlegungen zur Frage strukturellen und kulturellen Wandels in Warschau am Beispiel öffentlicher Gesundheit', in *Städte im östlichen Europa: Zur Problematik von Modernisierung und Raum vom Spätmittelalter bis zum 20. Jahrhundert*, eds Carsten Goehrke and Bianka Pietrow-Ennker (Zürich: Chronos, 2006), 365–91.

130 On municipal socialism, see Zimmermann, *Die Zeit der Metropolen*, 31.

131 The idea of a service administration and interventionist municipal administration began to take hold in Western Europe in the second half of the nineteenth century. For a detailed account, see Dieter Langewiesche, '"Staat" und Kommune: Zum Wandel der Staatsaufgaben in Deutschland im 19. Jahrhundert', *Historische Zeitschrift* 248 (1989): 621–35; likewise, Adelheid von Saldern, 'Wohnen in der europäischen Großstadt 1900–1939: Eine Einführung', in Janatková, *Wohnen in der Großstadt*, 11–38; Anna Veronika Wendland, '"Europa" zivilisiert den "Osten": Stadthygienische Interventionen, Wohnen und Konsum in Wilna und Lemberg 1900–1930', in Janatková, *Wohnen in der Großstadt*, 271–96, especially 271–3.

93

in state bureaucracy were all unanimous on this point. However varied the ideas of state among elite conservative representatives of high-level bureaucracy and the more interventionist mid-level cadre in local administration, all of them viewed the inclusion of society as a means, if not a necessary evil, to achieve the aim of further state expansion. Dialogue and cooperation with organs of self-government and social initiatives were viewed in instrumental terms, as necessary means to stabilize public life in a crisis-ridden country. Rights of participation were to help make the state more efficient, and the freedoms granted could be revoked at any time by the state should its 'invited' representatives from society not stick to the rules defined by bureaucracy. It was not about the gradual inclusion of society in decision-making processes, which state authorities and their apparatuses viewed as their own prerogative. That this mentality changed very little even after the introduction of a constitutional system in 1906 can be seen in the continued preference of state officials to rule by means of administrative and emergency decrees. Whether it was Prime Minister Pyotr Stolypin (1906–11) using emergency decrees in accordance with article 87 of the Fundamental Law to implement his policies, or provincial governors in many districts using the extensive administrative rights provided them under a state of emergency, there was still a clear tendency even after 1906 for state authorities to act and make decisions autonomously.

Nevertheless, this primacy of state decision-making hegemony and the preference for administrative means was indicative of a shift towards interventionist statehood, for the scope of bureaucratic activity was permanently expanding in the self-understanding of state authorities, deeply permeating social interactions by the turn of the century. To be sure, reasons of state still prevailed among the highest representatives of central and local administration, who were mainly keen to preserve existing power relations. To their minds, the main function of the organs of state was to maintain law and order and secure the traditional hierarchies of the corporative state. The State Council, the upper house in the constitutional order of 1906, gave considerable weight to this position in the political arena. The formative prime minister of the Duma period, Pyotr Stolypin, on the other hand, preferred the vision of an interventionist state power that did not shy away from radical reform measures when it came to the much-needed modernization of the empire. This can be seen not only in the agrarian reforms that Stolypin initiated as of 1906 and that he ultimately pushed through with emergency decrees, but also in other projects such as plans for a health ministry following contemporary and strongly medicalized notions of a comprehensive hygiene and population policy.[132] Hence even central state representatives were willing to promote the bureaucratization of the state and expand its areas of responsibility, though they often met with social resistance or opposition from elite-conservative quarters, and sometimes their plans simply foundered on the state bureaucracy's chronic underfinancing.

Inherent logic in state expansion

The inherent logic of state expansion is also evident here. The more spheres of activity state authorities defined as their own, the more urgent the permanent reinforcement and expansion of the state apparatus seemed, which in turn had consequences of its own. This process was particularly evident on the imperial peripheries. The state expansion initiated and pursued during the Great Reforms, for instance, soon made clear to reform bureaucrats that it was necessary to

---

132 See Ascher, *P.A. Stolypin*; Korros, *Stolypin*; Peter Waldron, *Between Two Revolutions: Stolypin and the Politics of Renewal in Russia* (DeKalb, IL: Northern Illinois University Press, 1998).

enforce the uniform use of the 'state language' in the areas of administration, law and education. For a unified administration could only function efficiently when one official language bridged the linguistic diversity of the empire and was valid for all of its subjects. Teaching this language was a key task of state schools. Accordingly, the state bureaucracy endeavoured to restructure local educational systems on the peripheries of the empire and elevate Russian to the language of instruction while making Russian history, literature and geography core requirements of the teaching curriculum. The officials implementing these measures always pointed out that introducing Russian into the classroom was solely for the purpose of learning the 'language of the state' or 'government' and did not aim to Russify the population to such an extent that non-Russian peoples would risk losing their cultural identity.[133] As mentioned above, however, the long-term consequences of such state expansion were often perceived on the peripheries as a threat to their cultural autonomy, considerably contributing to the experience of indigenous populations feeling alienated from the state authorities in the Polish provinces, the Baltic districts and Finland in equal measure. But also in the interior, state expansion and the dynamics of its continued intensification exposed the state to myriad social conflicts. But since state representatives were hardly prepared to relinquish their authority and hence their responsibilities, they inadvertently monopolized all possible forms of social dissatisfaction. A state which claimed to be all-powerful and which raised expectations without being able to fulfil them while at the same time being unwilling to allow social participation in decision-making processes was ultimately condemned to isolation. For all its bureaucratic expansion, the Russian Empire remained a fragile construct – a government without a social basis.

The post-Ottoman and Ottoman Balkans

In the last quarter of the nineteenth century and into the twentieth century, after the watershed of the crisis years of 1875–78, 'state expansion' in the Balkans followed two general lines of development, depending on whether it was in the Ottoman Empire itself or in the context of post-Ottoman states. Whereas the latter has often been given particular attention in research on Southeastern Europe and in the respective national histories, late-Ottoman state expansion has tended to be overlooked. And yet, without a doubt, both contexts witnessed a rapid expansion of the state. A strong, centralist administrative apparatus expanded in the empire as well as in the nation states seceding from it. The expanding (higher) education system produced a new, educated class that found employment in the institutions of the state. This was especially the case in the rapidly growing capital of the Ottoman Empire as well as in the capital cities of the new Balkan states, but it was also increasingly so in provincial towns. The tasks that state institutions claimed as their responsibility expanded greatly in the empire and the new independent states alike, so that this period of more than three decades (from 1878 to 1910–11) must be taken as a formative phase in the development of modern statehood in both Ottoman and post-Ottoman Southeastern Europe.

There is, therefore, little sense in positing too strong a dichotomization between Ottoman and post-Ottoman state expansion for the period in question here. It is also misleading to support a notion commonly found in the literature that the 'entry into modernity' of these 'young' Balkan states proceeded in leaps and bounds 'after liberation from the Ottoman yoke' whereas

---

133 Gosudarstvennyi Arkhiv Rossiiskoi Federatsii (GARF), f. 215, op. 1, d. 94, ll. 55ob–58ob [Publication of the resolutions of the Committee of Ministers, 17 February 1898], l. 55–7.

the 'old' empire was stuck in a rut, stagnating in terms of its state development. On the contrary, rather similar developments were evident in both contexts. The difficulties they faced were particularly similar, as will be seen below.

There were some key differences, however, which also need to be addressed. One important distinction is between elite continuity and discontinuity within the state bureaucracy and political elites. Elite continuity in the civil service undoubtedly continued to have a strong influence on developments in the Abdülhamid era (after the Young Turk revolution of 1908, a new class of politicians took powerful positions). In the new successor states, considerable discontinuities with the previously existing Ottoman system occurred at different points in their autonomy and/or independence movements. However, these breaks weren't always massive and all-pervasive like they were, for example, in Bulgaria where in the years after 1878, the previous representatives of the administration and state lost their positions virtually overnight and a new Christian Orthodox elite (which had sometimes been active earlier in state functions such as the council of elders or *meclis*, as Alexander Vezenkov has shown) began to build up a new state.[134] This pattern of de facto expulsion of Muslim elites (and in many instances Muslim populations) was characteristic of many subsequent post-Ottoman regions, having happened in a more or less brutal manner in almost all of the so-called wars of liberation, especially in the formerly Ottoman regions incorporated into Southeastern European nation states after 1912–13 (though many of these regions retained their Muslim imprint).[135]

In those states, however, which had achieved special autonomy at an earlier point in time (the Danubian Principalities, Serbia, Montenegro and especially in 'core' Greece, the earliest to gain its independence) there had been a continuity of elites for decades throughout the nineteenth century. This is especially true of Romania, where a powerful class of boyars (established well before the nineteenth century) had a formative influence on establishing and intensifying sovereignty even after independence.[136] A class of this sort did not exist in Serbia, though local notables there had occupied powerful positions in earlier phases of autonomy, sometimes lasting for generations. As described by Stevan Pavlowitch, however, this was accompanied by structural changes:

> The fathers – the notables who were in high office with little education – had set up a state administration which they expected people to obey and respect. The sons – the junior officials with foreign degrees and the teachers in the *Lycée* – were influenced by the ideas of the general European movement of 1848.[137]

---

134 See e.g. Alexander Vezenkov, 'In the Service of the Sultan, in the Service of the Revolution: Local Bulgarian Notables in the 1870s', in Grandits et al., *Conflicting Loyalties in the Balkans*, 86–106; or, Andreas Lyberatos, 'Privileged Scapegoats: Nation-State Formation and Civil Officialdom in Bulgaria, 1878–1912', in *Society, Politics and State Formation in Southeastern Europe during the 19th Century*, eds T. Anastassiadis and N. Clayer (Athens: Alpha Bank, 2011), 66–98.

135 See Nicole Immig, *Zwischen Partizipation und Emigration: Muslime in Griechenland, 1878–1897* (Wiesbaden: Harrassowitz, 2015); Isa Blumi, *Ottoman Refugees, 1878–1939: Migration in a Post-Imperial World* (London: Bloomsbury, 2013); Justin McCarthy, *Death and Exile: The Ethnic Cleansing of Ottoman Muslims, 1821–1922* (Princeton, NJ: Princeton University Press 1996); Alexandre Toumarkine, *Les migrations des populations musulmanes balkaniques en Anatolie (1876–1913)* (Istanbul: Isis, 1995). For an excellent overview of the socio-political developments, especially with regard to the Muslim population, see Nathalie Clayer and Xavier Bougarel, *Les musulmanes de l'Europe du Sud-Est. Des Empires aux États balkaniques* (Paris: Karthala, 2013).

136 Kenneth Jowitt, ed., *Social Change in Rumania, 1860–1940: A Debate on Development in a European Nation* (Berkeley, CA: Inst. of International Studies, 1978).

137 Stevan K. Pavlowitch, *Serbia: The History Behind the Name* (London: Hurst, 2003), 43.

Towards a new quality of statehood

In general, it is important here not to take the replacement of one political generation with another too absolutely. The individual states were all marked by the more or less pronounced coexistence of 'conservative' and 'liberal' political tendencies, which influenced the expansion of statehood described above. It was often the conservative element that had the upper hand in shaping these new states. This was certainly the case in the Ottoman Empire prior to the Young Turk revolution, where the autocratic system of Abdülhamid, supported by his loyalist-conservative officials, endeavoured systematically for over three decades to exclude (overly) liberal political tendencies.[138] But in Habsburg-occupied Bosnia as well, the established conservative (Muslim) notables in positions of power were confronted by liberal or 'national' young elites.[139] Even in Greece, independent since 1830, the situation was similar for many decades.[140]

But the implementation of new developments in statehood was not solely the work of polarized elites. In the decades of transition from the nineteenth to the twentieth centuries, the idea was prevalent among ruling elites – more so than ever before – that statehood in the modern era could only be properly expanded if the 'backward rural population' was included in the process. Balkans societies were predominantly rural, with only minor regional differences. Despite the appreciable growth of numerous cities, mainly the capitals, this remained the case well into the twentieth century. Hence, the rural-urban divide was all the more pressing from the perspective of these modern elites, who considered the traditional structures of the countryside problematic. If this rural world was to enter 'modernity' – and there was no alternative from the perspective of these elites – then state-building and state expansion had to be coupled with the project of modernizing and 'civilizing' the broad mass of the population. This civilizational mission was even thought by many ruling elites to be one of the state's main tasks. In the new post-Ottoman states of Southeastern Europe, this mission became ever more indissolubly linked with the notion of 'nation-building'.[141] Holm Sundhaussen succinctly summarized this close connection between state- and nation-building in the new states of the Balkans as follows:

> The formation of the nation and nation state and the implementation of that which promised to lend the nation state its power and prestige was carried out by the newly established state bureaucracy despite the reluctance of the majority of the population, which initially had no use for the construct of nation, had always perceived the state as a potential adversary, and experienced nascent capitalism as an attack on their traditional solidarity and Roman law as a perversion of their own ideals of justice. The conflict between the envisioned 'overriding responsibility' of the state and the

---

138 Şükrü Hanioğlu, *A Brief History of the Late Ottoman Empire* (Princeton, NJ: Princeton University Press, 2008); Kırmızı, *Abdülhamid'in Valileri*.

139 Husnija Kamberović, *Begovski zemlišnji posjedi u Bosni i Hercegovini od 1878. do 1918. godine* [The landed property of Begs in Bosnia and Herzegovina from 1878 to 1918] (Sarajevo: Ibn Sina, 2005); Srećko Džaja, *Bosnien-Herzegowina in der österreichischen-ungarischen Epoche (1878–1918): die Intelligentsia zwischen Tradition und Ideologie* (München: Oldenbourg, 1994); Tomislav Kraljačić, *Kalajev režim u Bosni i Hercegovini, 1883–1903* [The Kalay regime in Bosnia and Herzegovina, 1883–1903] (Sarajevo: Veselin Masleša, 1987); Robert Donia, *Islam under the Double Eagle: The Muslims of Bosnia-Hercegovina, 1878–1914* (New York: Columbia University Press, 1981).

140 Kostas Kostis, 'The Formation of the State in Greece', in *Disrupting and Reshaping: Early Stages of Nation-Building in the Balkans*, eds Marco Dogo and Guido Franzetti (Ravenna: Longo Editore, 2002), 47–64. For more detail, see Hering, *Die politischen Parteien in Griechenland*.

141 For a critical discussion of this not-always top-down development, see, e.g. Andreas Kosmas Lyberatos, 'Through Nation and State: Reform and Nationalism "from Below" in the Late Ottoman Balkans – Introduction', in *Turkish Historical Review* 7 (2016): 121–33.

preservation of local autonomy and traditional institutions wore on for decades in every Balkan country, with varied results on both sides. The centralized nation state as the guiding principle of the ruling classes and the demiurge of development was perceived everywhere as the antithesis to the traditional norms and values of peasants.[142]

But it was not only the national idea that combined so well with a 'civilizational' and 'unifying mission' emanating from the centre and aimed at the rural and peripheral world. In the Ottoman Empire, similar processes occurred by means of strengthened links between the state and religion, or the state and imperial history. The Ottoman centre under the rule of Abdülhamid clearly endeavoured to promote Sunni-Hanafi orthodoxy even at the margins of the empire, restricting the hitherto tolerated diversity of Muslim belief in favour of more modern forms of state-compatible Islam (motivated in part by the fear of Christian missionaries, tolerated as of 1856 and who subsequently intensified their work in many areas of the empire).[143] With the vigorous expansion of primary schooling, prioritized and implemented under Abdülhamid (though mass literacy was slow in coming due to the scarcity of schools in rural areas), these policies began to have an effect among the population at large, beyond the urban centres and their elites.[144]

Religion and nationalism, however, were not necessarily contradictory state projects in the realm of state expansion in the Balkans. For the post-Ottoman Christian states in Southeastern Europe it was surely a pivotal development in the period under investigation. The growing presence of 'religiosity' was evident in the increased construction of sacred buildings and was supported by a growing network of religious institutions and an increasing number of clerics.[145]

To be sure, it is important to always weigh stated objectives against reality and assess the actual level of implementation when considering the state projects previously mentioned and the new legal frameworks. The emergence of the modern police force during this period may serve as an example: it was a central institution of modern statehood which made considerable progress in the Ottoman Empire, despite the many challenges that still stood in the way.

An independent urban and rural police force, designed to operate outside of the military command structure, was established in the Ottoman Empire during the 1840s and expanded during the Tanzimat era, so that by the 1870s it eventually consisted of nearly 38,000 men. The greatest wave of modernization, however, occurred after 1879, in the Abdülhamid era. In international comparison, the quantitative development of the Ottoman police was quite impressive by the early twentieth century. Nadir Özbek calculated that the ratio of one

---

142 Sundhaussen, Holm, 'Südosteuropäische Gesellschaft und Kultur vom Beginn des 19. bis zur Mitte des 20. Jahrhunderts', in Clewing, *Geschichte Südosteuropas*, 345–425, here 359.

143 Selim Deringil, *The Well-Protected Domains*.

144 Benjamin Fortna, *Imperial Classroom: Islam, the State, and Education in the Late Ottoman Empire* (Oxford: Oxford University Press, 2002); Norbert Reiter and Holm Sundhaussen, eds, *Allgemeinbildung als Modernisierungsfaktor: Zur Geschichte der Elementarbildung in Südosteuropa von der Aufklärung bis zum Zweiten Weltkrieg* (Berlin: Harrassowitz, 1994).

145 See, for example, Maria Todorova, *Bones of Contention: The Living Archive of Vasil Levski and the Making of Bulgaria's National Hero* (Budapest: CEU Press, 2009); Paschalis Kitromilides, *Orthodox Commonwealth: Symbolic Legacies and Cultural Encounters in Southeastern Europe* (Aldershot: Routledge, 2007); Nenad Makuljević, *Crkvena umetnost u kraljevini Srbiji, 1882–1914* [Religious art in the Kingdom of Serbia, 1882–1914] (Belgrade: Colorgrafx, 2007);Vasilios Makrides, ed., *Religion, Staat und Konfliktkonstellationen im orthodoxen Ost- und Südosteuropa: Vergleichende Perspektiven* (Bern: Peter Lang, 2005); Klaus Buchenau, *Auf russischen Spuren: orthodoxe Antiwestler in Serbien, 1850–1945* (Wiesbaden: Harrassowitz, 2011).

Towards a new quality of statehood

policeman/gendarme per thousand inhabitants in a country of 27 million people (in 1910) was even higher than in Prussia or the Habsburg Empire.[146] Indeed, the (political) police in the capital of Istanbul was so pervasive and vigilant that some contemporaries likened Abdülhamid's leadership to a police and surveillance state.[147]

However, rural and especially peripheral mountain regions were often more difficult to police. Gendarmerie units were primarily concentrated in administrative towns and hence far removed from rural settlements. The turnover rate among gendarmes was high in certain periods due to poor or unpaid salaries, occasionally resulting in strikes or the hazing of new recruits. Members of the lower classes (quite often from refugee families) predominantly served as low-ranking gendarmerie officers in rural areas. In crisis areas (and elsewhere), Ottoman governors would rely – as in the past – on their traditional 'auxiliary troops', sometimes recruited from mountain or tribal peoples (in the Kosova area, for instance, it was the Albanian Fandi[148]) even in the early twentieth century.

As in other areas, the difficulties described here were quite similar in post-Ottoman Balkan states as well. And yet, the centre expanded much more rapidly in these new states than in the Ottoman Empire, making its presence felt more intensively in their 'peripheries'. By 1900 at the latest, the newly founded small states in the Balkans (Serbia had a population of 2.5 million, Greece 2.4 million, Bulgaria 3.7 million, Romania 5.9 million and Montenegro a mere 200,000) were quite capable of implementing a programme of massive state centralization.[149] Holm Sundhaussen, neatly sums it up as follows with a view to the long nineteenth century:

> While the Ottoman Empire, and for a long time the Habsburg monarchy too, had long been 'weak' states in terms of their penetration into society, their independent successor states rapidly developed into 'strong' ones, that is to say into imposing machines that increasingly nationalized their respective societies.[150]

One area where the state machinery of these new states was particularly capable of rapidly mobilizing their societies was the military. For much of the nineteenth century, these semi-autonomous states tended to rely on rapidly mobilized militias and irregular troops. For years, independent armed forces were only permitted under Ottoman suzerainty with considerable restrictions. Once they achieved independence – or, in the case of Bulgaria, a good deal before they achieved independence – all of the new Balkan states built up their militaries over the course of roughly three decades (between 1875 and 1912), and did so to such an enormous degree and in such a comparatively short period of time that contemporary observers (e.g. in the diplomatic corps of the great powers) were astonished by what they saw. All of the armies

---

146 Nadir Özbek, 'Policing the Countryside: Gendarmes of the Late-Nineteenth-Century Ottoman Empire (1876–1908)', *International Journal of Middle East Studies* 40, 1 (2008): 47–67. See also Glen Wilfred Swanson, 'The Ottoman Police', in *Police Forces in History*, ed. George L. Mosse (London: Sage Publications, 1975), 39–56.

147 Noémi Lévy, 'Une institution en formation: la police ottomane à l'époque d'Abdülhamid II', *European Journal of Turkish Studies* 8 (2008), URL: https://ejts.revues.org/2463

148 For a vivid account, see Eva-Annes Frantz, 'Catholic Albanian Warriors for the Sultan in Late-Ottoman Kosovo: The Fandi as a Socio-Professional Group and Their Identity Patterns', in Grandits et al., *Conflicting Loyalties in the Balkans*, 182–201.

149 On population statistics and their development, see, e.g. Palairet, *The Balkan Economies*, 3–33.

150 Holm Sundhaussen, 'Südosteuropäische Gesellschaft und Kultur vom Beginn des 19. bis zur Mitte des 20. Jahrhunderts', in Clewing, *Geschichte Südosteuropas*, 361.

of the Balkan states adopted universal conscription, striving for and attaining a high degree of military mobilization. The figures for 1910 illustrate this rather impressively.

In Bulgaria, where compulsory military service was two years in the infantry and three or more in other branches of the military, recruits formed the basis of the peacetime army, along with career officers and soldiers. Reservists were regularly called upon to partake in military exercises and were mobilized in the wartime army. All told, more than 450,000 soldiers were available in case of war (with a population of only around 4 million). The situation was similar in Serbia, with an especially high number of permanent officers (3,700) and a peacetime army of 165,000 men. If reservists (in various branches of the military and classified by age groups) were mobilized as well, more than 300,000 men in arms were battle-ready should they be needed. The degree of militarization in little Montenegro was astonishingly high, with 44,000 soldiers out of a total population of less than 200,000! The Greek armed forces required all young men to serve two years on active duty, followed by ten years in the first reserves, nine in the second, and seven in the national guard reserves. With a total population of 2.5 million, about 260,000 men could be mobilized in the various branches of its armed forces. Romania, with a population of just under 6 million, could mobilize the largest army of all among the abovementioned states, with several hundred thousand men in arms depending on the degree of mobilization.[151]

As these figures demonstrate, enormous efforts were undertaken to become 'capable of modern warfare'. Huge sums were spent on armaments and military build-up. In some years, up to one-third or more of the state budget was allocated to the military in some of the aforementioned states. This high military expenditure was a decisive factor in the Bulgarian state's bankruptcy of 1905. It is no surprise that the Ottoman Empire entered this arms race in the Balkans too, expending considerable resources on the modernization of its armed forces and weapons systems (under the guidance of German military advisors). These military developments indicate that the Ottoman Empire, including all of the other Balkan states, feared being on the losing side in the event of a war in the Balkans. Guerrilla activity in the Macedonia *vilayets* – particularly feared by the Ottomans – were a harbinger of conflicts to come. But Ottoman military build-up must be viewed as well in the context of a growing international arms race that began at the turn of the twentieth century. Ottoman leaders and many Ottoman elites had forebodings of imperialist projects on the part of the European powers with a strategic or concrete interest in certain Ottoman territories. This fear was not unfounded with Italy's 1911 offensive against Ottoman Tripolitania, which unleashed subsequent wars in the Balkans.[152]

While enormous sums of money were being spent on the military capabilities of these states, considerable efforts were being made to expand modern institutional structures, and elites in positions of power in (national and regional) capitals increasingly imitated European lifestyle trends, the necessary funds were sorely lacking for infrastructure and other state services. The bulk of the population did not enjoy, or scarcely enjoyed, the benefits of a modern welfare

---

151 Edward Erickson, *Defeat in Detail: The Ottoman Army in the Balkans, 1912–1913* (Westport, CT: Praeger, 2003), esp. 69–71. See also Milić Miličević, *Reforma vojske Srbije 1897–1900* [Serbian military reform 1897–1900] (Belgrade: Vojnoizdavački Zavod, 2002); Draga Vuksanović-Anić, *Stvaranje modern srpske vojske* [The establishment of the Serbian military] (Belgrade: Srpsks književna zadruga, 1993); or the contemporary estimates of Noel Buxton and Charles Roden Buxton, *The War and the Balkans* (London: George Allen, 1915).

152 On the building-up of military infrastructure for this war, see especially Wolfgang Höpken, '"Modern Wars" and "Backward Societies": The Balkan Wars in the History of 20th Century European Warfare', in *The Wars of Yesterday: The Balkan Wars and the Emergence of Modern Military Conflict 1912–1913*, eds Kathrin Boeckh and Sabine Rutar (New York: Berghahn, 2018).

Towards a new quality of statehood

state: indeed, at that time the 'social state' was undergoing its first expansion in several European states. This was related to demographic and economic developments that can only be roughly outlined here.

The societies of Southeastern Europe were in the midst of rapid population growth in the early twentieth century, a process that had been underway since the last third of the nineteenth century. This 'demographic transition' resulted in a high rate of natural population growth.[153] Despite a strong urban influx and a growing workforce in industry and trade, the societies of Southeastern Europe nonetheless remained deeply rural and agrarian in absolute terms (70 to 90 per cent) of the overall population). Furthermore, in the decades around the turn of the century, there was massive emigration overseas which varied from region to region.[154]

Policymakers in the Balkan states and the Ottoman Empire faced virtually the same economic challenges, despite a number of regional differences (the European provinces of the Ottoman Empire had much more in common with neighbouring regions of the Balkans, for example, than they did with Anatolia or the eastern regions of the Empire). One of the main problems was limited state or private investment capital. Ottoman state finances were subject to international debt management into the 1910s (the same was true of Greece and Bulgaria) and limited in their investment opportunities. And yet, there were enormous flows of foreign capital into the Ottoman Empire. A massive expansion of the railroad network (financed by international concessions) soon connected the various regions of the empire with booming port cities such as Thessaloniki, opening up hitherto unknown possibilities.[155] But this opening up to international trade was a threat to traditional ways of doing business in many small cities. State protectionism in the Ottoman economy was only possible to a limited extent and was not necessarily an aim of the ruling elites.

Political struggles in the Balkan states were marked by debates about finding the right economic policy: that is, between a more 'open' policy and 'protectionism'. The example of Serbia can be used to illustrate this point. Serbia was greatly economically dependent on the Habsburg Empire into the early twentieth century, with almost all of its exports (mostly agrarian products) going to the Habsburg market. The majority of its imports also came from

---

153 On the (demographic and other) developments in social and family structures of Southeastern Europe, see the multi-faceted work of Siegfried Gruber, for example, 'Demographic Change and the Family', in *Demographic Changes in the Time of Industrialization (1750–1918): The Example of the Habsburg Monarchy*, eds Ioan Bolovan, Rudolf Gräf, Harald Heppner and Ioan Lumperdean (Cluj-Napoca: Center for Transylvanian Studies, 2009), 159–85; and especially see Karl Kaser's classic texts, such as Karl Kaser, ed., *Household and Family in the Balkans: Two Decades of Historical Family Research at University of Graz* (Vienna: Lit, 2012); Karl Kaser, *Macht und Erbe: Männerherrschaft, Besitz und Familie im östlichen Europa, 1500–1900* (Vienna: Böhlau, 2000); Karl Kaser, *Familie und Verwandtschaft auf dem Balkan: Analyse einer untergehenden Kultur* (Vienna: Böhlau, 1995); See also Maria Todorova, *Balkan Family Structure and the European Marriage Pattern: Demographic Developments in Ottoman Bulgaria* (Washington, DC: American University Press, 1993). For an accomplished comparative overview of social structures in transition (here with reference to the region of Yugoslavia), see the older but still quite valuable work of Jozo Tomasevich, *Peasants, Politics, and Economic Change in Yugoslavia* (Stanford, CA: Stanford University Press, 1955).

154 On emigration, see especially the recent work of Ulf Brunnbauer, *Globalizing Southeastern Europe: Emigrants, America, and the State since the Late Nineteenth Century* (Lanham, MD: Lexington Books, 2016).

155 Malte Fuhrmann and Vangelis Kechriotis, eds, *The Late Ottoman Port-Cities and Their Inhabitants: Subjectivity, Urbanity, and Conflicting Orders*, special issue of the *Mediterranean Historical Review*, 24 (2009). On Thessaloniki in particular, see Mazower, *Salonica: City of Ghosts − Christians, Muslims and Jews, 1430–1950* (London: Harper, 2004).

there. And yet for many years, the Serbian government consistently blocked an expansion of the railroad network. The only major railway project was the north-south axis – a condition stipulated by the great powers at the Congress of Berlin – which was built in the 1880s with Serbian funds and brought the state close to bankruptcy. Guild regulations in Serbia were also highly restrictive until the first decade of the twentieth century. What was meant to protect urban craftsmen was viewed by opponents of protectionism as the relic of a bygone era. With the assassination of the king and the subsequent change of dynasty in 1903, the Serbian government did everything in its power to free itself from economic dependence on Austria-Hungary. But this necessitated an alternative 'opening up' to foreign capital – from France, Russia, etc.[156] Dependencies on foreign capital and similar strains over the extent and meaningfulness of state protectionist measures in various sectors of the (urban) economy were characteristic of all states of Southeastern Europe in the decades of state expansion under investigation here. It would not be possible to discuss this in any detail here. It is evident, however, that the generally rather limited funds available for state economic policies were channelled to a narrow circle of economic elites and business sectors with close ties to the government. This promoted a dynamic economic and hence communal development, especially in capital cities and – in the Ottoman context – large port cities, without really contributing, however, to an overall industrial take-off. The problem was exacerbated in capital cities by the considerable influx of people from the countryside (most of whom did not find work) which led to a chronic housing shortage. There were scarcely any funds available to invest in social welfare in the cities to alleviate these pressures, and zero funds were available for economic intervention in the countryside. State funds went to welfare programmes for state employees, members of the military and, increasingly, to refugees. Support for refugees would eventually comprise the bulk of state-sponsored social outreach.

The Ottoman state already had to look after hundreds of thousands of refugees from the Caucasus and the Balkan states before and after the Crimean War and the Ottoman-Russian War of the 1870s. The anarchical situation in Macedonia as of the 1890s and 1900s was an additional cause of concern. But it was during and after the two Balkan wars of 1912–13 that the situation really began to unravel, when a coalition of Balkan states went to war against the Ottoman Empire and later fought amongst themselves for territory. The last post-Ottoman successor state of the pre-war era emerged in this context: the Principality of Albania, whose state- and nation-building projects mostly took place outside the focus of this chapter.[157] Albania, too, and all of the Balkan states, the Ottoman Empire included (more so than all of the others), had to deal with a large influx of refugees – a task far greater than their rudimentary welfare systems could handle.

Austria-Hungary around the turn of the century

Starting in the 1880s and continuing until 1914, Austrians and Hungarians engaged more directly with their states, as the states in turn became increasingly involved in people's everyday lives, partly through a continued growth of local and district bureaucracies. During this period,

---

156 See, for example, Holm Sundhaussen, *Geschichte Serbiens, 19.-21 Jahrhundert* (Vienna: Böhlau, 2007), 173–88; Palairet, *The Balkan Economies*, 85–128 and 298–341; Marie-Janine Calic, *Sozialgeschichte Serbiens, 1815–1941: Der aufhaltsame Fortschritt während der Industrialisierung* (München: Oldenbourg, 1994).

157 Nathalie Clayer, *Aux origines du nationalisme albanais: la naissance d'un nation majoritairement musulmane en Europe* (Paris: Karthala, 2007).

Towards a new quality of statehood

the expanding states in Austria and Hungary became far more important factors in almost every aspect of people's daily lives. From school attendance to universal military service, to their interactions with expanding and condensing networks of communication and transport services, people of all walks of life increasingly shared in common experiences of state institutions. At the same time, as more people used state services they demanded more of them. During the last decades before the war, the imperial, regional and local bureaucracies became understood as guarantors of a range of critical services on which rural and urban Austrians and Hungarians increasingly relied. In 1887 and 1889, for example, Austria had already created one of Europe's early health and accident insurance systems for workers and employees in several branches of commerce and industry.[158] Thus, as both states undertook increasing numbers of such responsibilities, their clients came to view those programmes as entitlements. Burgeoning socialist movements in both states – but especially in Austria where the socialist parties made up the largest political group in Parliament – built their own programmes in large part on demands for more ambitious and wide-ranging state programmes.[159] This increasing understanding of the role of the state as the provider of legitimate social entitlements would become critical during the First World War.

The twenty years before 1914 were also years of restless movement and rapid social, economic and cultural change throughout both monarchies. In 1910 the population of Austria stood at 28.5 million, while Hungary was close to 21 million and Bosnia Herzegovina almost 2 million. By 1900 almost 40 per cent of these Austro-Hungarians had left their place of birth to migrate to other parts of the monarchy and in only 20 years, from 1890 to 1910, the populations of both the monarchy's largest but also its many medium-sized cities expanded dramatically, experiencing 50 to 60 per cent population growth. Thanks to the growing network of railways, and to the cheaper cost of railway travel, migrants flocked in greater numbers to industrial and commercial centres. From 1876 to 1910, almost four million Austrian and Hungarian men and women not only left their place of birth, but also travelled further afield to seek work and new lives across the Atlantic in Canada, the United States or Latin America. And from 1900 to 1910, almost four hundred thousand of them came back to Austria-Hungary, returning to their villages or towns and bringing with them new experiences of a wider world, new capital, and new skills.[160]

Those who remained in Austria-Hungary saw their own lives profoundly changed by infrastructural developments, the proliferation of educational institutions and a revolution in print

---

158 On welfare provisions, Birgit Bolognese-Leuchtenmüller, *Bevölkerungsentwicklung und Berufsstruktur: Gesundheits- und Fürsorgewesen in Österreich, 1750–1918* (Vienna: Verlag für Geschichte und Politik, 1978), 328. In its earliest years, the health insurance provisions covered around 9% of the Imperial Austrian population. On infrastructure spending in Imperial Austria, Josef Wysocki, 'Die Österreichische Finanzpolitik', in *Die Habsburgermonarchie 1848–1918*, vol. 1, *Die Wirtschaftliche Entwicklung*, eds Helmut Rumpler and Peter Urbanitsch (Vienna: Verlag der Akademie der Wissenschaften, 1973) 68–104, here 92.

159 In Austria in 1906 the number of unionized workers stood at 448,270, while in Hungary it stood at 71,173 (mostly in Budapest industries). Geoffrey Drage, *Austria-Hungary* (New York: E.P. Dutton, 1909), 112, 851. See also Wolfgang Maderthaner, 'Die Entstehung einer demokratischen massenpartei: Sozialdemokratische Organisation von 1889–1918', in *Die Organisation der österreichischen Sozialdemokratie, 1889–1995*, eds Wolfgang Maderthaner and Wolfgang C. Müller (Vienna: Löcker, 1996).

160 Heinz Fassmann, 'Die Bevölkerungsentwicklung, 1850–1910', in *Die Habsburgermonarchie 1848–1918*, vol. 9, *Soziale Strukturen*, eds Helmut Rumpler and Peter Urbanitsch (Vienna: Verlag der österreichischen Akademie der Wissenschaften, 2010), 159–84; Tara Zahra, *The Great Departure: Emigration from Eastern Europe and the Making of the Free World* (New York: W.W. Norton, 2016), 23–63. On the growth of the railways, Iván Berend, *History Derailed: Central and Eastern Europe in the Long Nineteenth Century* (Berkeley, CA: University of California Press, 2003).

media, the seeds of which, it could be argued, had been planted with the major liberal reforms of the 1850s and 1860s. By 1900 even most rural villagers in Austria-Hungary had access to a local or regional newspaper, and many towns and villages boasted postal service and sometimes telephone service as well. In 1910 there were 22,386 primary schools in Austria and 16,455 in Hungary. After 1900 the lowest literacy rates – in Bukovina, Dalmatia, Galicia, Transylvania and Bosnia-Herzegovina – rapidly began to catch up with the regions with the highest rates in Austria, Bohemia and metropolitan Hungary, which had already reached close to 100 per cent literacy. In 1910 inhabitants over the age of 11 in the Austrian half of the Dual Monarchy, for example, had a literacy rate of 83.5 per cent, a figure comparable to that of France with 85 per cent. In Hungary the rate (measured for people over the age of 6) was somewhat lower, with German and Hungarian speakers reporting the highest rates (70 per cent) while for Rumanian and Ukrainian speakers, it remained quite low at around 30 per cent.[161]

Increasingly, rural youth actively sought social mobility by taking advantage of growing opportunities for post-primary school courses. The expansion of low-level white-collar employment that followed industrialization had created demand for new kinds of secretarial workers that in turn required new skills like typing, filing or stenography. Preparatory courses in these fields offered rural youth the possibility to leave agriculture and pursue a career in a town or perhaps even a city. We should also note the critical ways in which state-building at the local level produced the expansion of such low-level white-collar employment thanks to a growing need for organizing and keeping records, copying them and communicating them to the centre. In this sense, we can say that unlike the bureaucratic state-building expansion of the 1850s that radiated from the imperial centres, this phase of expansion often developed at the margins of empire, especially in the autonomous communes.

Initiatives developed by locally elected officials and the administrative experts they increasingly consulted – from public hygiene programmes and the establishment of hospitals, to the creation of parks and public swimming pools – all fuelled an expansion of bureaucratic functions in villages, towns and in the crown land governments, along with increases in hired personnel. Both the state-run and the local autonomous bureaucracies in the communes stretched to fill their mounting responsibilities to a growing clientele. They employed more men – and by the late nineteenth century, women as well – from increasingly varied social backgrounds in a range of new positions: from telegraph operators to food inspectors, to postal workers, to schoolteachers, to railway ticket sellers. The development of local postal savings banks in Austria and Hungary, for example, offered banking services to rural and small-town customers of modest means that would otherwise have been unavailable to them. Postal workers and elementary school teachers now symbolized the empire for the general public, since they represented it in the most common of daily life interactions, even in the most isolated rural settings. One historian characterized the Hungarian postal system as 'the state institution that doubtless created the greatest familiarity among ordinary people.'[162]

---

161 On the transformation of education and access in Austria, Gary B. Cohen, *Education and Middle-Class Society in Imperial Austria, 1848–1918* (West Lafayette, IN: Purdue University Press, 1996). On literacy and schools, Margaret Friedrich, Brigitte Mazohl, and Astrid von Schlachta, 'Die Bildungsrevolution', in Rumpler, *Die Habsburgermonarchie 1848–1918*, 9, 67–107; see also the tables in ibid., vol. 9, book 2 (*Kartenband*), 228–9.

162 Hungary was also one of the earliest states in Europe to introduce mail delivery by truck in 1909. Since 1896, telegrams had already been delivered by bicycle. János Szulovszky, 'Die Dienstleistungsgesellschaft in Ungarn', in Rumpler, *Die Habsburgermonarchie 1848–1918*, vol. 9, 479.

Towards a new quality of statehood

These recognizable professional sectors – postal and telegraph workers along with teachers – were noteworthy as sites of growing employment opportunities for single women in the late nineteenth century.[163] By 1911, the Austrian state employed over 15,000 women, most of them in the postal, telegraph, and telephone services, while in 1913 close to 19,000 Austrian women held certificates qualifying them to teach in primary schools.[164] Growing bureaucracies were another factor that actually tied mass nationalist, socialist and Christian social parties even more closely to the state, since those parties lobbied increasingly for the appointment of their own members or patrons to positions in the imperial bureaucracy. This was even more the case for civil servants appointed by the elected municipal governments or by the crown land governments who represented parties in the regional diets. Taken together, it is clear that the bureaucracy – or perhaps even the state at its many levels – was increasingly becoming a creature of the popular parties and no longer an institution loyal only to the dynasty and separate from society.[165]

This expansion of bureaucracies at the local, crown land and national levels, and especially the range of new and increasing services provided by the states, such as sickness and accident insurance for increasing numbers of industrial workers, are often overshadowed in historical accounts by the explosive domestic political crises that appeared to challenge the very viability of each state's political system around 1900. In Austria, boycotts and violence surrounding the so-called Badeni crisis paralyzed the imperial parliament and Bohemian Diet for several years. At the height of the crisis in 1897, thousands of Austrians marched and even rioted in the streets to demonstrate their support for, or opposition to, Prime Minister Count Kasimir Badeni's (1846–1909) proposed language ordinances for Bohemia. The ordinances would have equalized the status of the Czech and German languages in the Bohemian civil service and required that speakers of one language learn the other within a limited time. German nationalists saw the ordinances as a threat to their language's traditionally privileged position in the Austrian government, while Czech nationalists (and their allies) treated the ordinances as the next logical step in a necessary process of equalization.[166] In Hungary, meanwhile, electoral victories by the radical nationalist opposition made it impossible for the King to form a government with an acceptable programme that could command a parliamentary majority. Demanding a separate military for Hungary (with Hungarian as the language of command), the radicals challenged

---

163 Female civil servants could not be married, and in the early years, offices tended to employ the widows or daughters of existing employees. Erna Appelt, 'The Gendering of the Service Sector in Late Nineteenth-Century Austria', in *Austrian Women in the Nineteenth and Twentieth Centuries*, eds David F. Good, Margarete Grandner and Mary Jo Maynes, (New York: Berghahn, 1996), 115–31. On women as telegraph operators, Sonia Genser, 'Von Klingelfeen, Blitzmädels und dem Fräulein vom Amt: Die Geschichte der ersten Frauen im österreichischen Telefon- und telegrafenwesen 1869–1914' (PhD diss., Innsbruck, 2003).

164 Friedrich et al., 'Die Bildungsrevolution', 74. The Austrian Ministries that employed the largest numbers of women were the Ministry of Commerce and the Ministry of the Interior.

165 For examples of Czech nationalist parties and the staffing of the bureaucracies, see Martin Klečacký, 'Český ministr krajan v předlitavské vládě' [Czech 'Landsmann' ministers of the Cisleithanian government] (PhD diss., Charles University, 2016). See also Klečacký, ed., *Český 'konzul' ve Vídni: Politická korespondence c.k. ministra krajana Antonína Rezka s mladočeským předákem Bedřichem Pacákem* [A Czech 'Consul' in Vienna: the political correspondence of the Czech 'Landsmann' Minister Antonin Rezka with the young Czech leader Bedřich Pacák] (Prague: Nakladatelství Lidové noviny, 2015).

166 Berthold Sutter, *Die Badenischen Sprachverordunungen von 1897*, 2 vols. (Graz and Köln: Böhlau 1960, 1965); Markus Krzoska, 'Die Peripherie bedrängt das Zentrum: Wien, Prag, und Deutschböhmen in den Badeni-Unruhen 1897', in *Grenzregionen der Habsburgermonarchie im 18. und 19. Jahrhundert: Ihre Bedeutung und Funktion aus der Perspektive Wiens*, ed. Hans-Christian Maner (Münster: LIT, 2005), 145–65.

Francis Joseph's most cherished prerogative, his exclusive power over the military.[167] The King, in turn, used thinly veiled threats of introducing universal manhood suffrage to enforce his will on Hungarian nationalists.

Were these nationalist crises in fact signs of irrevocable structural decay in Austria-Hungary that threatened the very survival of the monarchy in the future, as many historians have thought? Or were these events more standard examples of political crises that increasingly roiled most European societies in an era of mass mobilization in society and politics? I believe the evidence points mostly to the latter. In this regard, some historians have also emphasized the performative character of these nationalist conflicts, noting that nationalist politicians around 1900 deployed increasingly radicalized rhetoric, hoping to mobilize or win supporters among the indifferent of their own language groups, while nevertheless showing a willingness to both work within the institutional system and to compromise on certain policy elements, albeit behind closed doors.[168] Moreover, within a few years, both the Austrian and Hungarian systems appear to have weathered the immediate storms as political conditions returned to a somewhat quieter status quo. However, especially among military and aristocratic elites, there developed a palpable sense of pessimism with regard to the monarchy's future, indeed its very survival. For many among these elite groups, the increasing influence of mass interest group politics and what seemed an inevitable movement toward greater democratization of the political system endangered their privileged position. Critically, it made them cling to a vision of an ideal absolutist and harmonious Monarchy before 1848 that had in fact never existed. These aristocrats and military chiefs increasingly blamed divisive popular and nationalist politics for their own loss of status, and for what they perceived to be Austria-Hungary's weakened international position in Europe, a critique to which I will return at the end of the chapter.[169]

In the Austrian half of the dual Monarchy, the post-Badeni period in fact produced creative examples of federalist and nationalist political power sharing at the level of the crown lands, experiments that often brought unexpected results. In Moravia in 1905, the Imperial government brokered an historic compromise agreement between Czech and German nationalist parties that sought to remove nationalist conflict from the realm of politics by giving national communities a legal status for the first time in order to separate them. The agreement divided the Moravian population into three distinct and legally binding groups that no longer competed against one another for political influence and financial resources. From now on, every Moravian had to belong – permanently – either to a Czech national group, a German national group or to a supranationalist group of noble large landowners. These three groups made up separate election curias, and their parties competed amongst themselves rather than against each other for representation in the Moravian Diet and in the Austrian Parliament. Each curia also received a separate share of resources for education, as well as for agriculture.[170] Children whose

---

167 László Péter, 'The Army Question in Hungarian Politics 1867–1918', *Central Europe* 4 (November 2006).

168 Lothar Höbelt, 'Bohemia 1913 – a Consensual *coup d'état*?', *Estates and Representation* 20 (November 2000): 207–14; also, Höbelt, *Kornblume und Kaiseradler: Die Deutschfreiheitliche Parteien Altösterreichs, 1882–1918* (Vienna: Verlag für Geschichte und Politik, 1993).

169 See, for example, Solomon Wank, 'Pessimism in the Austrian Establishment at the Turn of the Century', in *The Mirror of History: Essays in Honor of Fritz Fellner*, eds Solomon Wank, Heidrun Maschl, Brigitte Mazohl-Wallnig and Reinhold Wagenleitner (Santa Barbara, CA: ABC-Clio, 1988), 295–314.

170 Horst Glassl, *Nationale Autonomie im Vielvölkerstaat: Der mährische Ausgleich* (München: Sudetendeutsche Stiftung, 1977); T. Mills Kelly, 'Last Best Chance or Last Gasp? The Compromise of 1905 and Czech Politics in Moravia', *Austrian History Yearbook* 34 (2003): 279–301; Lukás Fasora, J. Hanuš and Jiří Malíř, eds, *Moravské vyrovnání z roku 1905/Der Mährische Ausgleich von 1905* (Brno: Matice Moravská pro Výkumné Středisko pro Dějiny Střední Evropy: Prameny Země Kultura, 2006).

Towards a new quality of statehood

parents belonged to one group had to attend that group's schools, unless they could prove a high level of competence in the other language. Although parents may have preferred a flexible system that allowed their children the option of attending school in either of the two crown land languages, the compromise made such choice far less possible.[171] Indeed, this Moravian Compromise caused much initial confusion among a population uncertain about its own categorization or unwilling to commit permanently to one national community. In this sense, the compromise contradicted general imperial practice, which had until now considered linguistic or national belonging to be a matter not ascribed, but best determined by individual subjects.[172]

In subsequent years two other crown lands, Bukovina and Galicia, reached their own settlements in order to remove nationalist issues as much as possible from local political and cultural life. In Bukovina the settlement included an informal attempt to create a Jewish national category in practice where none was legally allowed to exist (the courts ruled that Jews were not a nationality since they did not speak a common language, which was the measure of national belonging in Austria).[173] In Galicia, for example, the Polish elite agreed to a minimal guaranteed representation by non-Poles in the Diet, and conceded the creation of a Ukrainian-language university.[174] In practice it is important to note that all three settlements constituted examples of the Imperial government's willingness to engage in federalist or local compromises if they offered realistic solutions to the threat of nationalist conflict in politics. At the same time, in terms of state-building practices, each settlement put exorbitant new strains on crown land budgets, if only because each normalized a doubling or tripling of crown land services as well as the implementation of far greater and costlier translation bureaus.[175] An outmoded system of taxation implemented in the 1860s had assigned several responsibilities to the communes and crown land diets without giving them adequate access to resources or income. This financial strain, along with the strain caused by the general increase in services throughout the monarchy, produced some new and tentative efforts to achieve a kind of imperial federalism. Increasingly, members of individual crown land diets felt forced to communicate directly with their counterparts in other diets, bypassing the Imperial government in order to seek common solutions to the fiscal crisis. For its part, the imperial government convoked several expert boards of inquiry in Vienna to study the crown land fiscal crises and recommend possible solutions.[176] This development, as

---

171 On this element of the Moravian Compromise, see Tara Zahra, *Kidnapped Souls: National Indifference and the Battle for Children in the Bohemian Lands, 1900–1948* (Ithaca, NY: Cornell University Press, 2008).

172 Jeremy King, *Budweisers into Czechs and Germans: A Local History of Bohemian Politics, 1848–1948* (Princeton, NJ: Princeton University Press, 2002), 138–147; also, Jeremy King, 'Who is Who? Separate but equal in Imperial Austria' (unpublished manuscript, 2010).

173 Gerald Stourzh, 'The National Compromise in Bukovina 1909/1910', in *From Vienna to Chicago and Back: Essays on Intellectual History and Political Thought in Europe and America* (Chicago, IL: University of Chicago Press, 2007), 177–89.

174 Börries Kuzmany, 'Der galizische Ausgleich als Beispiel moderner Nationalitätenpolitik?', in *Galizien: Peripherie der Moderne – Moderne der Peripherie*, ed. Elisabeth Haid (Marburg: Verlag Herder Institut, 2013), 119–37.

175 Michaela Wolf, *Die vielsprachige Seele Kakaniens: Übersetzen und Dolmetschen in der Habsburgermonarchie 1848 bis 1918* (Vienna: Böhlau, 2012).

176 Deak, *Forging a Multinational State*, 226–32; 249–58; Hans Peter Hye, 'Strukturen und Probleme der Landeshaushalt', in *Die Habsburgermonarchie 1848–1918*, vol. 7, *Verfassung und Parlamentarismus 2*, eds Helmut Rumpler and Peter Urbanitsch (Vienna: Verlag der Akademie der Wissenschaften, 2000), 1545–92; Jana Osterkamp, 'Cooperative Empires: Provincial Initiatives in Imperial Austria', in *Austrian History Yearbook* 47 (2016): 128–145.

Jana Osterkamp has recently argued, demonstrates a degree of contact and cooperation among different parts of empire that contradicts the standard accounts of empire in which regions only communicate with each other through the centre.[177]

By contrast in Hungary, the ruling elite refused to countenance any type of franchise or linguistic school or administrative reform that might concede even the smallest degree of recognition – much less empowerment – to non-Hungarian nationalists. A Budapest-oriented Hungarian nationalist centralism kept non-Hungarian language groups under enormous pressure and even resulted in attempts to impose more Hungarian language on Croatian society. Hungarian educational policy increasingly required the teaching of and instruction in Hungarian in primary public and religious schools, although recent historical research has demonstrated that the practical effects of this policy were often of negligible influence.[178] At the same time, by the end of the nineteenth century, local and national administrative policy made it increasingly difficult in Hungary to use the Romanian, Serb, Slovak, or German languages in even the most local situations of public life. Ironically, and unlike its Austrian counterpart, this trend left the Hungarian half of the Dual Monarchy – with so few capable translators – completely unprepared for the demands of wartime surveillance.

The politically flexible federalizing potential of the Austrian half of the Dual Monarchy is also in evidence when we consider the somewhat contradictory status assigned to Bosnia-Herzegovina after its formal annexation in 1908. In 1910 Francis Joseph issued a provincial statute (*Landesstatut*) for Bosnia-Herzegovina modelled to some extent on the basic laws that governed the Austrian half of the Dual Monarchy. The statute provided for an elected Diet organized in curias (as in the Austrian crown lands), although the Sarajevo diet curias (urban, rural, highest taxed) were divided again by religion (Eastern Orthodox, Muslim, Catholic), and not by language use as they were in Moravia or Bukovina. Moreover, the statutes provided for the use of sharia law in civil cases involving members of the Muslim religion. Voters in the urban and rural curias were male citizens over the age of 24 and had lived in Bosnia-Herzegovina for at least a year. But unlike the situation in the other Austrian diets, voting was not limited to citizens of the crown land but was also open to members of the civil service, teaching profession, and railway employees who had emigrated there from other parts of the monarchy.[179]

The statutes did not, however, clarify Bosnia-Herzegovina's relationship to the rest of the Empire. The region remained technically neither a part of Austria nor of Hungary. For this reason, the territories were not formally represented in the common institutions of the monarchy, nor did they have a voice in either parliament. For the same reason, the Bosnian statute had to create a specifically Bosnian form of citizenship since its citizens could neither be Austrian nor Hungarian.

To some Croatian and Serb nationalists within Austria and Hungary, Bosnia-Herzegovina's separate status meant that it might someday serve as the basis for a transformation of the monarchy from dualism to a trialism made up of Austrian, Hungarian and South Slav parts. To some radical nationalists who looked to Serbia, Bosnia's constitutional position might make

---

177 Osterkamp, 'Cooperative Empires', 128–46.

178 Ágoston Berecz, *The Politics of Early Language Teaching: Hungarian in the Primary Schools of the Late Dual Monarchy* (Budapest: CEU Press, 2013). More generally on Hungarian education policy over the decades, Joachim von Puttkamer, *Schulalltag und nationale Integration in Ungarn: Slowaken, Rumänen und Siebenbürger Sachsen in der Auseinandersetzung mit der ungarischen Staatsidee, 1867–1914* (München: Oldenbourg, 2003).

179 Karl Lamp, 'Die Verfassung von Bosnia und der Herzegowina vom 17. Februar 1910', in *Jahrbuch des öffentlichen Rechts der Gegenwart*, 5 (1911): 137–229.

Towards a new quality of statehood

it more easily detachable from Austria-Hungary. To other legal experts, however, Bosnia-Herzegovina's exceptional status seemed to point to a necessary centralization of the Dual Monarchy in order to accommodate it on an equal, legal basis with the other two parts.

Perspectives

On 28 June 1914 the heir to the Austro-Hungarian throne, Archduke Franz Ferdinand and his wife Sophie were assassinated while on a summer visit to Sarajevo. The assassination was carried out by a group of politically radicalized young men belonging to the Young Bosnia secret society, several of whom – like the assassin Gavrilo Princip himself – were barely 20 years of age. This event caused a wave of shock, not only in Sarajevo, the Balkans, and Austria-Hungary, but also throughout the rest of Europe and beyond. The murder occurred at a time when most of the Balkan states found themselves in a situation of instability and were hoping to consolidate themselves after the harrowing experience of the recent Balkan wars (1912–13). These wars, in which all the parties mobilized their populations in their respective state and parastate war machines on a massive scale, resulted in territorial gains for Greece, Serbia, Montenegro, Bulgaria and Romania, all of whom annexed formerly Ottoman regions. The Ottoman Empire, despite its own massive mobilization campaign, suffered a disastrous defeat. To a certain extent this was true of Bulgaria as well, the 'loser' of the Second Balkan War.

By the summer of 1914, most governments in the region hoped for nothing more than the return of a 'new normality'. Much remained uncertain, however. To give just one example, the viability of the borders of the newly established state of Albania, were challenged and had to be supported by guarantees from the great powers. In domestic terms as well, Serbian head-of-state Nikola Pašić was concerned about stability, uncertain to what extent his government really controlled the officer corps and secret service. Much of this uncertainty among regional governments, including that of Austria-Hungary, argued against their taking up the challenge of yet another war.

From the Russian perspective, too, the summer of 1914 was not the best time to engage in war. There was general agreement among political and military leaders that a military engagement with the German Empire was inevitable in the medium term, but only in very limited military and nationalist circles was there evidence of downright war fever in 1914 Russia. The trauma of the Russo–Japanese War was too great, the Russian illusion of a 'brief, victorious war' helping to consolidate the empire's internal politics having been dashed by the harsh reality of a military fiasco in the Far East and the revolutions of 1905–6. Now, ten years after its revolutionary turmoil, Russia finally seemed to be entering a phase of internal consolidation. The Duma seemed tamed after 1907, economic growth raised hopes (despite a concomitant increase in strikes and workers' protests) of further improvement, and the military, too, was making steady advances with the adoption of new technologies and strategies of industrial warfare.

Hopes for a longer respite, allowing the Russian Empire to prepare for its confrontation with the German Empire, turned out to be illusive. A strongly nationalized public sphere in the years after 1905 limited the diplomatic scope of the tsar and his government. As much as prime ministers like Stolypin endeavoured to use the nationalist consensus as an instrument of integration, its inherent logic demanded that a great power demonstrate an aggressive foreign policy and unyieldingness in conflicts of interest such as in the Balkans.[180] In the years leading up to 1914, the nationalist public sphere in Russia revelled in fantasies of war, a war that would

---

180 See also Utz, *Nationalismus und Außenpolitik im Zarenreich.*

finally enable Russia to gain the upper hand in its 'eternal struggle' with its German enemy and assert itself as the protector of all Slavs. Numerous Russian authors had wholly subscribed to Oswald Spengler's dramatic alternative of 'world power or decline'. Such extreme positions were buoyed up by the widely shared belief in an impending war to end all wars that would sweep away the old order. St. Petersburg's Silver Age was marked by a sense of being on the eve of catastrophe and global conflagration, and many longed for the moment of conflict and the catharsis it would bring.[181]

Accordingly, an emboldened nationalist public sphere vehemently demanded active support for Serbia even before 1914 and intensified its programmatic clamour after the July crisis. There is no doubt that the inherent military logic of a race for general mobilization was ultimately responsible for the rapid developments that ensued in the summer of 1914. And yet, the importance of a nationalist, war-hungry public sphere should not be underestimated in trying to understand the Russian government's need to act. It helps us comprehend the state of autosuggestion that Russian (civil and military) leaders found themselves in, with exaggerated notions of military prowess, an aggressive feeling of imperial superiority, and the illusion of a broad social consensus, all making for an explosive combination. This mixture of self-aggrandizement and hubris, with a simultaneous and extreme pressure to act, was surely a key factor in the decision to go to war.

Not only in the Russian Empire would national mobilization for the Great War prove to be a highly flawed strategy of integration. The jingoism of the public sphere of (the newly renamed) Petrograd in 1914 quickly vanished when confronted by the harsh realities of the war and the ensuing military setbacks. As early as January 1916, the leader of the Cadets, Pavel N. Milyukov, denounced the government for its failures in his famous Duma speech, asking: Is it merely stupidity or is it treason? The trust that Milyukov and many other politicians may have once had in the government's (or even the tsar's) capacity to rule was already exhausted after two years of war. Even political leaders began to believe that the Russian state as a political entity could ultimately only be preserved without its monarch and dynasty. It is not far-fetched to interpret the subsequent February Revolution of 1917 as an expression of the new fixation on the state that had been on the rise over the preceding decades. Preservation of the state had long since gained priority over holding on to the dynasty. Monarch and state had become divisible. The war and Nicholas II's hapless role as supreme commander were not the only reasons for this. The new quality of statehood that had formed in the course of bureaucratization and state-building in the Russian Empire ever since the Great Reforms also played a part.

In Austria-Hungary, however, the events of the war would reveal a simmering conflict that divided some of the empire's military social elite from the administration and political parties. In the years before 1914, as we have seen, the growth of the state was increasingly linked in the public mind with growth in opportunities and social benefits. Here there was less clamour for war in 1914 than in Russia, although the public certainly supported the war effort at the start. However, the greater danger to Austria-Hungary in 1914 was the potential domestic power the military leadership had managed to accumulate behind the scenes in the previous decade, power it could only exercise given the opportunities presented by a war.

---

181 See, e.g. Peter Haslinger and Malte Rolf, eds, *Untergangsszenarien und Zukunftsvisionen in den Imperien des östlichen Europa* (Berlin: Metropol, 2015); on Spengler see Jannis Wagner, '"Weltmacht oder Niedergang": Wilhelminische Mentalität, extreme Emotionen und Bilder des Kommenden am Beispiel Oswald Spenglers', in Haslinger, *Untergangsszenarien und Zukunftsvisionen*, 930–48.

Towards a new quality of statehood

To understand how this became the case we need to return to the political outcomes of the 1908 annexation of Bosnia-Herzegovina. The international dimensions of the annexation crisis had not simply added to the political instability in the Balkans or increased the hopes of some south Slav nationalists within Austria-Hungary for a possible reorganization of the empire – a reorganization that the heir to the throne Archduke Franz Ferdinand was believed to support. The annexation had also enabled the military elite to increase its influence over domestic policy.

The outbreak of war between the Balkan states and the Ottoman Empire, and then among the Balkan states over the division of the spoils – especially Macedonia – caused increasing concern in Austria-Hungary's military high command. Many among that elite group saw Austria-Hungary's possible involvement in a Balkan war as an opportunity – perhaps a final opportunity – to transform decisively the domestic political systems of Austria and Hungary. War would allow the military elite to circumvent the normal constitutional channels of rule and to impose their own non-political system of governance on the monarchy. They would stifle all forms of political conflict – especially, but not exclusively, nationalist conflict. In doing so they could allegedly 'restore' a greater respect for social hierarchy and discipline that many military leaders believed mass society lacked, and that supposedly weakened Austria-Hungary's reputation in the eyes of the other powers.

In the years 1906–1914, the military high command developed secret plans for organizing the domestic front in case of war. These plans involved the imposition of a harsh dictatorship by subordinating the civil bureaucracies and the judiciary, whose members were allegedly tainted by their links to the political parties, to military power.[182] Military courts and military standards of justice would replace civil courts. Civilians would be placed under surveillance and the press would be subjected to harsh censorship. More importantly, however, the plans called for justice and administration to be implemented by men who strongly believed that several of the monarchy's language groups were, by definition, traitors to the fatherland. This presumption of guilt among a considerable segment of the population based on language use went well beyond the general suspicion of socialists present in all European combatant states. Commenting on the eventual fall of empire, Laurence Cole has recently argued, 'It was more the ruling elite that lost faith in its peoples, rather than the other way around.'[183]

By undermining the Austro-Hungarians' expectation of fair treatment at the hands of the state, not to mention the rule of law, especially by unreasonably criminalizing and persecuting certain language groups, these dictatorial measures that lasted until the death of Francis Joseph in November 1916, eventually did more to bring about the end of the monarchy than any other factors. And, as Joseph Redlich noted in his original study of the wartime military regime, these measures were extreme even by the dictatorial standards typical for all wartime

---

182 Jonathan Gumz and Tamara Scheer from different perspectives have argued cogently for this interpretation through a careful analysis of the legislation around wartime state of emergency and wartime practices of occupation in Serbia and elsewhere. Jonathan Gumz, *The Resurrection and Collapse of Empire in Habsburg Serbia, 1914–1918* (New York: Cambridge University Press, 2009); Tamara Scheer, *Die Ringstrassenfront: Österreich-Ungarn, das Kriegsüberwachungsamt und der Ausnahmezustand während des ersten Weltkrieges* (Vienna: Republik Österreich, Bundesminister für Landesverteidigung und Sport, 2010). See also Christoph Führ, *Das k.u.k. Oberarmeekommando und die Innenpolitik in Österreich, 1914–1917* (Vienna: Böhlau, 1968). For some of the worst consequences of these plans that caused a kind of local hysteria in August 1914, see Martin Moll's devastating account, *Kein Burgfrieden: Der deutsch-slowenische Nationalitätenkonflikt in der Steiermark 1900–1918* (Innsbruck: Studienverlag, 2007).

183 Cole, *Military Culture*, 322.

states during 1914–1918.[184] So strong were the fears of nationalist conflict and political instability among the socially elite military circles that, taken together with their fears about the
growing strength of Serbia, they also produced Austria-Hungary's fateful rush to war in the
summer of 1914. And despite a general consensus – even enthusiasm – for the war among most
language groups, the military would swiftly alienate the good will of the people. At the same
time, the growth of the state and its bureaucracies we have witnessed in the decades prior to
1914, also meant that during the war the citizenry would increasingly look to the state to solve
problems of food, energy and housing supply. By 1918 this trend would produce a radical
change in public expectations of the very purpose and function of the state.

Further reading

Adanır, Fikret, and Suraiya Faroqui, eds. *The Ottomans and the Balkans: A Discussion of Historiography* (Leiden: Brill, 2002).

Anastassiadis, Tassos, and Nathalie Clayer, eds. *Society, Politics and State Formation in Southeastern Europe during the 19th Century* (Athens: Alpha Bank, 2011).

Ascher, Abraham. *P.A. Stolypin: The Search for Stability in Late Imperial Russia* (Stanford, CA: Stanford University Press, 2001).

Baberowski, Jörg. *Autokratie und Justiz: Zum Verhältnis von Rechtsstaatlichkeit und Rückständigkeit im ausgehenden Zarenreich 1864–1914* (Frankfurt a.M.: Klostermann, 1996).

Barkey, Karen. *Bandits and Bureaucrats: The Ottoman Route to State Centralization* (New York: Columbia University Press, 1997).

Bautz, Annegret. *Sozialpolitik statt Wohltätigkeit? Der Konzeptionswandel städtischer Fürsorge in Sankt Petersburg von 1892 bis 1914* (Wiesbaden: Harrassowitz, 2007).

Berend, Iván. *History Derailed: Central and Eastern Europe in the Long Nineteenth Century* (Berkeley, CA: University of California Press, 2003).

Berger, Stefan, and Alexei Miller, eds. *Nationalizing Empires* (Budapest: CEU Press, 2015).

Beuerle, Benjamin. *Russlands Westen: Westorientierung und Reformgesetzgebung im ausgehenden Zarenreich 1905–1917)* (Wiesbaden: Harrassowitz, 2016).

Binder-Iijima, Edda. *Die Institutionalisierung der rumänischen Monarchie unter Carol I, 1866–1881* (München: R. Oldenbourg, 2003).

Blobaum, Robert E. *Rewolucja: Russian Poland, 1904–1907* (Ithaca, NY: Cornell University Press, 1995).

Blobaum, Robert E., ed. *Antisemitism and Its Opponents in Modern Poland* (Ithaca, NY: Cornell University Press, 2005).

Blumi, Isa. *Ottoman Refugees, 1878–1939: Migration in a Post-Imperial World* (London: Bloomsbury, 2013).

Brown, Keith. *Loyal unto Death: Trust and Terror in Revolutionary Macedonia* (Bloomington, IN: Indiana University Press, 2013).

Brunnbauer, Ulf. *Gebirgsgesellschaften auf dem Balkan: Wirtschaft und Familienstrukturen im Rhodopengebiet (19./20. Jahrhundert)* (Vienna: Böhlau, 2004).

Brunnbauer, Ulf. *Globalizing Southeastern Europe: Emigrants, America, and the State Since the Late Nineteenth Century* (Lanham, MD: Lexington Books, 2016).

Buchen, Tim, and Malte Rolf, eds. *Elites and Empire: Imperial Biographies in Russia and Austria-Hungary (1850–1918)* (Berlin: De Gruyter Oldenbourg, 2015).

Clayer, Nathalie, and Xavier Bougarel. *Les musulmanes de l'Europe du Sud-Est. Des Empires aux États balkaniques* (Paris: Karthala, 2013).

Clowes, Edith W., Samuel D. Kassow, and James L. West, eds. *Between Czar and People: Educated Society in Pre-revolutionary Russia* (Princeton, NJ: Princeton University Press, 1991).

Coen, Deborah. *The Earthquake Observers: Disaster Science from Lisbon to Richter* (Chicago, IL: University of Chicago Press, 2012).

---

184 Josef Redlich, *Österreichs Regierung und Verwaltung im Weltkrieg* (Vienna: Hölder-Pichler-Tempsky, 1925). Formally at least, the plans repeatedly ran up against stone-walling by the Hungarian govern-ment that wanted to maintain its own power to act under wartime circumstances, and this explains why conditions differed somewhat in wartime Hungary, although not by much.

Cole, Laurence. *Military Culture and Popular Patriotism in Late Imperial Austria* (Oxford: Oxford University Press, 2014).

Corrsin, Stephen D. *Warsaw before the First World War: Poles and Jews in the Third City of the Russian Empire, 1880–1914* (New York: Columbia University Press, 1989).

Daly, Jonathan W. *The Watchful State: Security Police and Opposition in Russia, 1906–1917* (DeKalb, IL: Northern Illinois University Press, 2004).

Déak, István. *The Lawful Revolution: Louis Kossuth and the Hungarians, 1848–1849* (New York: Columbia University Press, 1979).

Deak, John. *Forging a Multinational State: State Making in Imperial Austria from the Enlightenment to the First World War* (Stanford, CA: Stanford University Press, 2015).

Deringil, Selim. *The Well-Protected Domains: Ideology and the Legitimation of Power in the Ottoman Empire, 1876–1909* (London: I.B. Tauris, [1998] new edition, 2011).

Donia, Robert. *Islam under the Double Eagle: The Muslims of Bosnia-Hercegovina, 1878–1914* (New York: Columbia University Press, 1981).

Eklof, Ben, John Bushnell, and Larisa Zakharova, eds. *Russia's Great Reforms 1855–1881* (Bloomington, IN: Indiana University Press, 1994).

Erickson, Edward. *Defeat in Detail: The Ottoman Army in the Balkans, 1912–1913* (Westport, CT: Praeger, 2003).

Evans, R.J.W. *Austria, Hungary, and the Habsburgs: Essays on Central Europe c. 1683–1867* (Oxford: Oxford University Press, 2006).

Figes, Orlando. *A People's Tragedy: The Russian Revolution 1891–1924* (Harmondsworth: Penguin, 1998).

Figes, Orlando. *Crimea: The Last Crusade* (London: Penguin, 2010).

Figes, Orlando. *The Crimean War: A History* (New York: Picador, 2011).

Findley, Carter V. *Ottoman Civil Officialdom: A Social History* (Princeton, NJ: Princeton University Press, 1989).

Fortna, Benjamin. *Imperial Classroom: Islam, the State, and Education in the Late Ottoman Empire* (Oxford: Oxford University Press, 2002).

Gallant, Thomas. *Modern Greece: From the War of Independence to the Present* (London: Bloomsbury, 2016).

Ganzenmüller, Jörg, and Tatjana Tönsmeyer, eds. *Das Vorrücken des Staates in die Fläche im langen 19. Jahrhundert* (Köln: Böhlau, 2016a).

Ganzenmüller, Jörg, and Tatjana Tönsmeyer, eds. *Vom Vorrücken des Staates in die Fläche: Ein europäisches Phänomen des langen 19. Jahrhunderts* (Köln: Böhlau, 2016b).

Garlicki, Andrzej. *Józef Piłsudski, 1867–1935* (London: Scolar Press, 1995).

Gautam, Lena. *Recht und Ordnung: Mörder, Verräter und Unruhestifter vor spätzarischen Kriminalgerichten, 1864–1917* (Wiesbaden: Harrassowitz, 2017).

Göçek, Fatma Müge. *Rise of the Bourgeoisie, Demise of Empire: Ottoman Westernization and Social Change* (New York: Oxford University Press, 1996).

Good, David. *The Economic Rise of the Habsburg Monarchy 1750–1914* (Berkeley, CA: University of California Press, 1984).

Good, David F., Margarete Grandner, and Mary Jo Maynes, eds. *Austrian Women in the Nineteenth and Twentieth Centuries* (New York: Berghahn, 1996).

Grandits, Hannes. *Herrschaft und Loyalität in der spätosmanischen Gesellschaft: Das Beispiel der multikonfessionellen Herzegowina* (Weimar: Böhlau, 2008).

Grandits, Hannes, Nathalie Clayer, and Robert Pichler, eds. *Conflicting Loyalties in the Balkans: The Great Powers, the Ottoman Empire and Nation-Building* (London: I.B. Tauris, 2011).

Gumz, Jonathan. *The Resurrection and Collapse of Empire in Habsburg Serbia, 1914–1918* (New York: Cambridge University Press, 2009).

Häfner, Lutz. *Gesellschaft als lokale Veranstaltung: Die Wolgastädte Kazan' und Saratov (1870–1914)* (Köln: Böhlau, 2004).

Hagen, Manfred. *Die Entfaltung politischer Öffentlichkeit in Rußland, 1906–1914* (Wiesbaden: Franz Steiner, 1982).

Hakan, Yavuz, M., and Peter Sluglett, eds. *War and Diplomacy: The Russo-Turkish War of 1877–1878 and the Treaty of Berlin* (Salt Lake City, UT: University of Utah Press, 2012).

Haltzel, Michael H. *Der Abbau der deutschen ständischen Selbstverwaltung in den Ostseeprovinzen Russlands: Ein Beitrag zur Geschichte der russischen Unifizierungspolitik, 1855–1905* (Marburg: Herder-Institut, 1977).

Hamm, Michael F. *Kiev: A Portrait, 1800-1917* (Princeton, NJ: Princeton University Press, 1986).

Hanioğlu, Şükrü. *Preparation for a Revolution: The Young Turks, 1902–1908* (Oxford: Oxford University Press, 2001).

Hanioğlu, Şükrü. *A Brief History of the Late Ottoman Empire* (Princeton, NJ: Princeton University Press, 2008).

Haslinger, Peter, and Malte Rolf, eds. *Untergangsszenarien und Zukunftsvisionen in den Imperien des östlichen Europa* (Berlin: Metropol, 2015).

Heindl, Waltraud. *Josephinische Mandarine: Bürokratie und Beamte in Österreich* vol. 2, 1848–1914 (Vienna: Böhlau, 2013).

Hitchins, Keith. *Rumania, 1866–1947* (Oxford: Oxford University Press, 1994).

Hosking, Geoffrey. *Russia: People and Empire, 1552–1917* (Cambridge, MA: Harvard University Press, 1997).

Immig, Nicole. *Zwischen Partizipation und Emigration: Muslime in Griechenland, 1878–1897* (Wiesbaden: Harrassowitz, 2015).

Janatková, Alena, and Hanna Kozińska-Witt, eds. *Wohnen in der Großstadt, 1900–1939: Wohnsituation und Modernisierung im europäischen Vergleich* (Stuttgart: Franz Steiner, 2006).

Jelavich, Barbara. *Russia's Balkan Entanglements 1806–1914* (Cambridge: Cambridge University Press, 1993).

Judson, Pieter M. *Guardians of the Nation: Activists on the Language Frontiers of Imperial Austria* (Cambridge, MA: Harvard University Press, 2006).

Judson, Pieter M. *The Habsburg Empire: A New History* (Cambridge, MA: Harvard University Press, 2016).

Kappeler, Andreas. *The Russian Empire: A Multi-Ethnic History* (Essex: UK Pearson Education Limited, 2001).

Karpat, Kemal H. *Ottoman Population, 1830–1914: Demographic and Social Characteristics* (Madison, WI: University of Wisconsin Press, 1985).

Kasaba, Reşat. *The Ottoman Empire and the World Economy: The Nineteenth Century* (Albany, NY: State University of New York Press, 1988).

Kaser, Karl. *Hirten, Helden, Stammeskrieger: Ursprünge und Gegenwart des balkanischen Patriarchats* (Vienna: Böhlau 1992).

Kaser, Karl. *Macht und Erbe: Männerherrschaft, Besitz und Familie im östlichen Europa, 1500–1900* (Vienna: Böhlau, 2000).

Kaser, Karl, ed. *Household and Family in the Balkans: Two Decades of Historical Family Research at University of Graz* (Vienna: Lit, 2012).

Kitromilides, Paschalis. *Orthodox Commonwealth: Symbolic Legacies and Cultural Encounters in Southeastern Europe* (Aldershot: Routledge, 2007).

Leonard, Carol Scott. *Agrarian Reform in Russia: The Road from Serfdom* (New York: Cambridge University Press, 2011).

Leonhard, Jörn, and Ulrike Hirschhausen, eds. *Comparing Empires: Encounters and Transfers in the Long Nineteenth Century, Schriftenreihe der FRIAS School of History 1* (Göttingen: Vandenhoeck und Ruprecht, 2010).

Lieven, Dominic. *Russia's Rulers under the Old Regime* (New Haven, CT: Yale University Press, 1989).

Lieven, Dominic. *Towards the Flame: Empire, War and the End of Tsarist Russia* (London: Penguin, 2015).

Lincoln, W. Bruce. *The Great Reforms: Autocracy, Bureaucracy, and the Politics of Change in Imperial Russia* (DeKalb, IL: Northern Illinois University Press, 1990).

Lory, Bernard. *La ville balkanissime: Bitola 1800–1918* (Istanbul: Isis, 2011).

Macey, David A.J. *Government and Peasant in Russia, 1861–1906: The Prehistory of the Stolypin Reforms* (DeKalb, IL: Northern Illinois University Press, 1987).

Mazower, Mark. *Salonica: City of Ghosts: Christians, Muslims and Jews, 1430–1950* (London: Harper, 2004).

McCaffray, Susan P. *The Politics of Industrialization in Tsarist Russia: The Association of Southern Coal and Steel Producers, 1874–1914* (DeKalb, IL: Northern Illinois University Press, 1996).

McCarthy, Justin. *Death and Exile: The Ethnic Cleansing of Ottoman Muslims, 1821–1922* (Princeton, NJ: Princeton University Press, 1996).

Michelson, Paul. *Romanian Politics, 1859–1871: From Prince Cuza to Prince Carol* (Iaşi: Center for Romanian Studies, 1998a).

Michelson, Paul E. *Romanian Politics 1858–1871: From Prince Cuza to Prince Carol* (Iaşi: Centrul de Studii Romaneşti, 1998b).

Mišković, Nataša. *Basare und Boulevards: Belgrad im 19. Jahrhundert* (Vienna: Böhlau, 2008).

Müller, Dietmar. *Staatsbürger auf Widerruf: Juden und Muslime als Alteritätspartner im rumänischen und serbischen Nationalcode – Ethnonationale Staatsbürgerschaftskonzepte, 1871–1941* (Wiesbaden: Harrssowitz, 2005).

Okey, Robin. *Taming Balkan Nationalism: The Habsburg 'Civilizing Mission' in Bosnia, 1878–1914* (Oxford: Oxford University Press, 2007).

Pallot, Judith, ed. *Transforming Peasants: Society, State, and the Peasantry, 1861–1930* (Houndmills: Macmillan, 1998).

Pallot, Judith. *Land Reform in Russia, 1906–1917: Peasant Responses to Stolypin's Project of Rural Transformation* (Oxford: Oxford University Press, 1999).

Polvinen, Tuomo. *Imperial Borderland: Bobrikov and the Attempted Russification of Finland, 1898–1904* (London: Hurst, 1995).

Porter, Brian A. *When Nationalism Began to Hate: Imagining Modern Politics in Nineteenth-Century Poland* (Oxford: Oxford University Press, 2000).

Puttkamer, Joachim von. *Fabrikgesetzgebung in Russland vor 1905: Regierung und Unternehmerschaft beim Ausgleich ihrer Interessen in einer vorkonstitutionellen Ordnung* (Köln: Böhlau, 1996).

Puttkamer, Joachim von. *Schulalltag und nationale Integration in Ungarn: Slowaken, Rumänen und Soebenbürger Sachsen in der Auseinandersetzung mit der ungarischen Staatsidee, 1867–1914* (München: Oldenbourg, 2003).

Raeff, Marc. *The Well-Ordered Police State: Social and Institutional Change through Law in the Germanies and Russia, 1600–1800* (New Haven, CT: Yale University Press, 1983).

Reill, Dominique Kirchner. *Nationalists Who Feared The Nation: Adriatic Multinationalism in Habsburg Dalmatia, Trieste, and Venice* (Stanford, CA: Stanford University Press, 2012).

Rindlisbacher, Stephan. *Leben für die Sache: Vera Figner, Vera Zasulič und das radikale Milieu im späten Zarenreich* (Wiesbaden: Harrasowitz, 2014).

Robbins, Richard G. *The Tsar's Viceroys: Russian Provincial Governors in the Last Years of the Empire* (Ithaca, NY: Cornell University Press, 1987).

Roberts, Elisabeth. *Realm of the Black Mountains: A History of Montenegro* (London: Hurst, 2007).

Rolf, Malte. *Imperiale Herrschaft im Weichselland: Das Königreich Polen im Russischen Imperium (1864–1915)* (München: De Gruyter Oldenbourg, 2015).

Rolf, Malte. *Russian Rule in the Kingdom of Poland (1864–1915)* (Pittsburgh, PA: University of Pittsburgh Press, forthcoming).

Roman, Viorel S. *Rumänien im Spannungsfeld der Grossmächte. Teil: Bd. 1., 1774–1878: die Donaufürstentümer vom osmanischen Vasallentum zur europäischen Peripherie* (Offenbach: Falk, 1987).

Rowney, Don Karl, and Eugene Huskey, eds. *Russian Bureaucracy and the State: Officialdom from Alexander III to Vladimir Putin* (Houndmills: Palgrave Macmillan, 2009).

Ryavec, Karl W. *Russian Bureaucracy: Power and Pathology* (Lanham, MD: Rowman & Littlefield, 2003).

Sandgruber, Roman. *Ökonomie und Politik: Österreichs Wirtschaftsgeschichte vom Mittelalter bis zur Gegenwart* (Vienna: Ueberreuter, 2005).

Schattenberg, Susanne. *Die korrupte Provinz? Russische Beamte im 19. Jahrhundert* (Frankfurt a.M.: Campus Verlag, 2008).

Scheer, Tamara. *Die Ringstrassenfront: Österreich-Ungarn, das Kriegsüberwachungsamt und der Ausnahmezustand während des ersten Weltkrieges* (Vienna: Republik Österreich, Bundesminister für Landesverteidigung und Sport, 2010).

Schmitt, Jens-Oliver. *Levantiner: Lebenswelten und Identitäten einer ethnokonfessionellen Gruppe im Osmanischen Reich im 'langen 19. Jahrhundert'* (München: Oldenbourg, 2005).

Schnell, Felix. *Ordnungshüter auf Abwegen? Herrschaft und illegitime Gewalt in Moskau, 1905–1914* (Wiesbaden: Harrassowitz Verlag, 2006).

Scott, Tom, ed. *The Peasantries of Europe from the Fourteenth to the Eighteenth Centuries* (London: Longman, 1998).

Stokes, Gale. *Three Eras of Political Change in Eastern Europe* (Oxford: Oxford University Press, 1997).

Sundhaussen, Holm. *Geschichte Serbiens 19.-21. Jahrhundert* (Vienna: Böhlau, 2007).

Thaden, Edward C. *Russification in the Baltic Provinces and Finland, 1855–1914* (Princeton, NJ: Princeton University Press, 1981).

Thaden, Edward C. *Russia's Western Borderlands, 1710–1870* (Princeton, NJ: Princeton University Press, 1984).

Thurston, Robert W. *Liberal City, Conservative State: Moscow and Russia's Urban Crisis, 1906–1914* (New York: Oxford University Press, 1987).

Todorova, Maria. *Balkan Family Structure and the European Marriage Pattern: Demographic Developments in Ottoman Bulgaria* (Washington, DC: American University Press, 1993).

Unowsky, Daniel. *The Pomp and Politics of Patriotism: Imperial Celebrations in Habsburg Austria 1848–1916* (West Lafayette, IN: Purdue University Press, 2005).

Utz, Raphael. *Rußlands unbrauchbare Vergangenheit: Nationalismus und Außenpolitik im Zarenreich* (Wiesbaden: Harrassowitz, 2008).

Verhoeven, Claudia. *The Odd Man Karakozov: Imperial Russia, Modernity, and the Birth of Terrorism* (Ithaca, NY: Cornell University Press, 2009).

Vladimirov, Katya. *The World of Provincial Bureaucracy in Late 19th and 20th Century Russian Poland* (Lewiston, NY: Mellen Press, 2004).

Waldron, Peter. *Between Two Revolutions: Stolypin and the Politics of Renewal in Russia* (DeKalb, IL: Northern Illinois University Press, 1998).

Wandycz, Piotr S. *The Lands of Partitioned Poland 1795–1918* (Seattle, WA: University of Washington Press, 1974).

Wcislo, Francis W. *Tales of Imperial Russia: The Life and Times of Sergei Witte, 1849–1915* (Oxford: Oxford University Press, 2011).

Weeks, Theodore R. *Nation and State in Late Imperial Russia: Nationalism and Russification on the Western Frontier, 1863–1914* (DeKalb, IL: Northern Illinois University Press, 1996).

Weikersthal, Felicitas Fischer v., Frank Grüner, Susanne Hohler, Franziska Schedewie, and Raphael Utz, eds. *The Russian Revolution of 1905 in Transcultural Perspective: Identities, Peripheries, and the Flow of Ideas* (Bloomington, IN: Slavica Publishers, 2013).

Wolf, Michaela. *Die vielsprachige Seele Kakaniens: Übersetzen und Dolmetschen in der Habsburgermonarchie 1848 bis 1918* (Vienna: Böhlau, 2012).

Worobec, Christine D. *Peasant Russia: Family and Community in the Post-Emancipation Period* (DeKalb, IL: Northern Illinois University Press, 1995).

Wortman, Richard. *Scenarios of Power: Myth and Ceremony in the Russian Monarchy: From Alexander II to the Abdication of Nicholas II* (Princeton, NJ: Princeton University Press, 2000).

Zahra, Tara. *Kidnapped Souls: National Indifference and the Battle for Children in the Bohemian Lands, 1900–1948* (Ithaca, NY: Cornell University Press, 2008).

Zahra, Tara. *The Great Departure: Emigration from Eastern Europe and the Making of the Free World* (New York: W.W. Norton, 2016).

3

DECONSTRUCTING AND RECONSTRUCTING STATEHOOD

The impact of the World Wars (Part I) – the First World War

Jochen Böhler

Introduction

As was to be expected, the two World Wars had a tremendous impact on the manifestation and transformation of statehood in Central and Eastern Europe. For two periods during the twentieth century, the cards were completely reshuffled, destroying existing state structures and replacing them with different ones.[1] Experiences of violence, the magnitude of destruction and ubiquitous scarcity posed severely difficult problems for new governments, problems which overshadowed the years after the World Wars during which even decades of peace had a double-edged effect on statehood: on the one hand, these problems necessitated the formation of certain state structures in order to solve them. On the other hand, specific types of statehood either predetermined, furthered or hampered the very solution to these problems. The picture gets more complicated when foreign interference is taken into account, since the states of Central and Eastern Europe – on two occasions during the timeframe considered here, and not for the first time in history – were occupied and partly destroyed by their powerful neighbour states Germany and Russia and had to rely on help from abroad for their recovery.

It has been often overlooked that the first structures of self-government, which were a precursor to independent statehood in Central and Eastern Europe, were not established at the end of the war but as it was taking place. During the First World War, the warring states might have been preoccupied with fighting, but they still could not afford to ignore questions of welfare, health, provisions and – in the long term – the fairer distribution of resources, land,

---

1 The third case of major armed conflict in Central and Eastern Europe – the Yugoslav Wars of the 1990s – are not dealt with in this chapter because they only influenced statehood on a regional level. See the volume *Violence* in this series.

education and political participation among their populations. The same goes for the occupied states, which had generally already experienced hunger and destruction in the periods of war on an even larger scale and where, therefore, both the occupied and the occupiers had to react immediately by building – or allowing for – improvised forms of self-government to prevent the collapse of public welfare systems. In a different example, during the course of the First World War, the Russian and German militaries developed parastate systems for the mass control of human resources through expulsion, detention and forced labour, thus anticipating measures which Russia and Germany would perfect between the wars and carry out to extreme degrees during the Second World War, both domestically and in the occupied countries. This resulted in vast camp complexes that were often conveniently used by the Allies to deal with the deluge of prisoners of war, with both alleged and real enemies of the new state power, and with stateless persons at the war's end. While the camps were dissolved in a defeated Germany (at least in the western part of the country), they would survive during peacetime within the victorious Soviet Union as the notorious 'Gulag archipelago', which was so harrowingly described by former inmate, dissident and Nobel Prize winner Aleksandr Solzhenitsyn.

However, as I have said, the people that had been subject to imperial rule before 1914 were not completely paralyzed by occupation; on the contrary, they often even viewed it as an opportunity to prepare for long-awaited freedom and were therefore eager to establish basic parastate structures before peace was negotiated in the midst of the ongoing struggles. A similar statement can be made about the societies in Central and Eastern Europe during the Second World War. To be sure, though, the overall experience of German or Russian – and sometimes also Hungarian or Romanian – occupation was certainly very different from what the region had witnessed a quarter of a century before. It was the harshness of the foreign rulers and the desperation of the ruled that triggered a new force which had not yet surfaced during the Great War: armed resistance movements mushroomed all over Central, Eastern and Southeastern Europe, and fought not only against their oppressors but, in the long run, for the reformation of the old or the creation of new states according to their hopes and expectations, whether they were nationalist or communist in nature. These were two conflicting visions that frequently caused the partisan groups of different convictions to fight not only their common enemy with a vengeance, but each other as well. Further, the revisionist feelings (harboured against neighbour states for territories lost in the course of the First World War) and ethnic tensions that were so characteristic of interwar Central and Eastern Europe had been augmented by the traumatizing experience of ethnic cleansing and genocide, accompanied either by the National Socialist or the Soviet policy of divide and conquer. Both developments led to bloody civil wars, especially in the Ukraine, Yugoslavia and Greece, which began as early as 1943 and – in an attempt to create 'ethnically pure' nation states – served as a reminder of the post-war struggles of 1918–23.[2] Another, rather more pragmatic, option was to throw in one's lot with the occupying forces, in the hope of achieving some kind of independent statehood in the new world order; it was a hope that, in reality, as we now know well, was illusory and never wholeheartedly supported by the Nazi or Soviet rulers.

Due to the chronological structure of this volume, the topic of deconstructing and reconstructing statehood is divided into two parts (Chapters 3 and 5): the first part deals with the First World War and the second with the Second World War, with an intercalary chapter on the interwar period appearing in between. Each part contains five sub-chapters that correspond

---

2 See the volume *Violence* in this series.

The First World War

1. War and statehood – occupation and persistence (I)[4]

Prior to the outbreak of the First World War, the better part of Central and Eastern Europe had been governed for a hundred years or more by foreign powers: at the Congress of Vienna from 1814 to 1815, the Hohenzollern, Habsburg and Romanov dynasties had divided this part of the continent amongst themselves, and despite ongoing quarrels about borders and influence, this partition proved to be stable until their armies came into conflict during the course of what soon escalated from a local conflict into a global confrontation.[5]

Even before the old order underwent atomization, single states in the Balkans had proceeded to independence during a period of violent conflict with the weakened Ottoman Empire. Bulgarians and Romanians had successfully fought the sultan's troops in 1878 side by side with the Russian army and were thus rewarded with the recognition of their independence.[6] However, the Treaty of Berlin left large parts of the Bulgarian and Romanian populations outside its border, which was a continual point of contention. Serbians and Greeks had already revolted against Ottoman domination some decades earlier, actions that finally resulted in their achievement of full independence in 1832 and 1867 respectively. Conflicts, revolutions and wars of independence in the Balkans destabilized the area and were jointly responsible for the outbreak of war.[7] To the major belligerent parties, it initially looked to be the long-anticipated storm that was needed to clear the air. In reality, the Ottoman Empire was only the first to fall and was soon joined by its rivals. By the time that the fog had cleared and the weapons were put down again, independent states mushroomed all over Central and Eastern Europe.

Indeed, the new European post-war order did not appear out of thin air. The war brought a variety of shifting, short-lived regimes to the war-ridden region. From the very beginning of the war, in 1914–15, the western parts of Russia were placed under a military administration that persecuted its ethnic minorities – Germans, Poles and Jews – as much as, or even more than, a foreign occupation might have done, before they had to retreat from the offensive by the Central Powers in the summer of 1915.[8] After a failed invasion in 1914, which was accompanied by harsh repressions against the civil population, Habsburg and Bulgarian

---

3 To facilitate the second option, which implies switching back and forth between Parts I and II, at the beginning of each sub-chapter, the reader will find a page reference guide in the annotated section.

4 See the first sub-chapter in Chapter 5 of this volume, page 194, 'War and statehood – occupation and persistence (II)'.

5 Eberhard Straub, *Der Wiener Kongress: Das große Fest und die Neuordnung Europas* (Stuttgart: Klett-Cotta, 2014); and Christopher Clark, *The Sleepwalkers: How Europe Went to War in 1914* (New York: Harper, 2013).

6 In the Romanian case, de facto independence had already been obtained in 1858.

7 Alan Palmer, *The Lands Between: A History of East-Central Europe Since the Congress of Vienna* (London: Weidenfeld & Nicolson, 1970), 103–19.

8 Daniel W. Graf, 'The Reign of the Generals: Military Government in Western Russia, 1914–1915' (PhD diss., University of Nebraska, 1972). See the volume *Violence* in this series.

troops occupied Serbia in 1915 and had to build up an improvised military government from scratch since most Serbian officials had either fled, were killed or were interned. The Austrians established a military government that ran the country largely without local participation and further alienated the population through the mass internment of some 40,000 civilians, mostly men, but also women and children on occasion.[9] This development was already presaged by the way Austria-Hungary treated its minorities in the Balkans in the years preceding the First World War.[10] However, taken as a whole, the Habsburg occupation was less brutal than was often stated after the war.[11] The Bulgarians, for their part, earmarked occupied eastern Serbia for later annexation and subjugated it to a programme of firm Bulgarization, which included the replacement of nearly all former Serbian local administration officials (including priests and teachers) with Bulgarians, while Vardar Macedonia, between 1915 and 1918, became a battlefield for the Central Powers and the entente, leaving no place for any kind of Macedonian self-government.[12] Romania was occupied by General von Mackensen's troops in 1916, where a German–Austrian military government conducted the country's affairs for two years, broadly incorporating the Romanian elites, experts and structures.[13]

When the gun smoke cleared, a 'South Slavic' state (which is the English translation for the country's subsequent name, 'Yugoslavia') emerged as one of the major beneficiaries of the Great War on the terrain of what had formerly been Serbia, Montenegro and parts of the Habsburg Empire. However, this was not a process that developed in a single direction. The term 'South Slavic' was artificial and feigned a degree of cohesiveness between the competing ethnic groups within the region that was not always reflected in reality. A Serbian state, albeit occupied, already existed and its prime minister Nikola Pašić claimed that he was communicating 'South Slavic' issues to the Allies, while the Yugoslav Committee, under Ante Trumbić's leadership, could not agree about the form their future state should take. In the summer of 1917, the Serbian government and the Yugoslav Committee finally met on the Greek island of Corfu to advance the creation of a South Slavic state. The Corfu Declaration, issued on 20 July 1917, proposed a constitutional, democratic and parliamentary

---

9 Andrej Mitrović, *Serbia's Great War, 1914–1918* (London: Hurst, 2007), 228–30.

10 As Pieter Judson states: 'By undermining the Austro-Hungarians' expectation of fair treatment at the hands of the state, not to mention the rule of law, especially by unreasonably criminalizing and persecuting certain language groups, these dictatorial measures that lasted until the death of Francis Joseph in November 1916, eventually did more to bring about the end of the monarchy than any other factors.' See Chapter 2, 'Towards a new quality of statehood: Bureaucratization and state-building in empires and nation states before 1914', in this volume.

11 Jonathan E. Gumz, *The Resurrection and Collapse of Empire in Habsburg Serbia, 1914–1918* (New York: Cambridge University Press, 2009).

12 Tamara Scheer, 'Besatzungsregime im Vergleich: Serbiens Wirtschaft unter österreichisch-ungarischer und bulgarischer Herrschaft (1915–1918)', in *'Mitteleuropa' und 'Südosteuropa' als Planungsraum: Wirtschafts- und kulturpolitische Expertisen im Zeitalter der Weltkriege*, ed. Carola Sachse (Göttingen: Wallstein-Verlag, 2010), 315–39; Björn Opfer, *Im Schatten des Krieges: Besatzung oder Anschluss – Befreiung oder Unterdrückung? Eine komparative Untersuchung über die bulgarische Herrschaft in Vardar-Makedonien 1915–1918 und 1941–1944* (Münster: LIT Verlag, 2005), 57–162; Milan Ristović, 'Occupation During and After the War (South East Europe)', in *1914–1918-online: International Encyclopedia of the First World War*, eds Ute Daniel et al. (2014), doi: 10.15463/ie1418.10481, paragraph 5 (accessed 22 February 2020).

13 Lisa Mayerhofer, *Zwischen Freund und Feind – Deutsche Besatzung in Rumänien 1916–1918* (München: Meidenbauer, 2010), 373; Ristović, 'Occupation During and After the War', in *1914-1918-online*, paragraph 7.

Statehood: the First World War

monarchy with equal rights for all inhabitants, regardless of background or faith, with one coat of arms and two official languages (Serbian and Croatian) and scripts (Cyrillic and Latin). As its predecessor, while Austria-Hungary was faltering and retreating from the area, the State of Slovenes, Croats and Serbs was proclaimed on 31 October 1918. It was meant to amalgamate with Serbia and Montenegro at the earliest opportunity and did so only a few weeks later.[14]

The newly formed Kingdom of Serbs, Croats and Slovenes – or, to give it its short name, Yugoslavia – endured severe tensions between all three titular nations. The dominant Serbs, who comprised almost half of the population, propagated the idea of a central state ruled by a Serbian king, thus nipping any Croatian and Slovenian endeavours to establish a federal state system in the bud. This authoritarian act placed a strain on interethnic relations in the kingdom, which subsequently suffered from years of instability and terrorist violence after its creation. One important factor in the conflict was that Serbia had been occupied by the vanquished Habsburg Empire, whose Slavic soldiers had been predominantly Croatian, among them Sergeant Josip Broz Tito, communist partisan leader during, and head of state after, the Second World War. A new state was borne out of the war but had failed to master its future and the repercussions of its formation.[15] If one keeps in mind that its inhabitants had fought in the Great War on different sides of the front line, one at least partly understands the reasons for this.

Further to the north-west, Poles were also not spared the traumatic experiences of fratricide. As early as summer 1915, the Kingdom of Poland had been occupied by the Central Powers, who created two administrative districts called General Governments, which had their centres in Lublin (governed by Austria) and in Warsaw[16] and the military district of 'Ober Ost'[17] (both governed by Germany).[18] In these areas, tensions were often more fraught between ethnic groups than between the occupied and the occupiers. To be clear, the Central Powers' occupation of Central and Eastern Europe – especially under German rule and subject to long-term planning in Ober Ost – was harsh and increasing quotas of the production of material goods along with forced labour plagued the population.[19] However, apart from that, the majority of the inhabitants led relatively peaceful lives under their foreign masters, which, from their perspective, was heavily dependent on local participation. Therefore, various bodies of

---

14 Mitrović, *Serbia's Great War*, 289–94, 318–21.

15 Marie-Janine Calic, *Geschichte Jugoslawiens im 20. Jahrhundert* (München: Beck, 2010), 83–97; Mark Biondich, *The Balkans: Revolution, War, and Political Violence since 1878* (Oxford: Oxford University Press, 2011), 98–106; John Newman, 'Silent Liquidation? Croatian Veterans and the Margins of War Memory in Interwar Yugoslavia', in *Sacrifice and Rebirth: The Legacy of the Last Habsburg War*, eds Mark Cornwall and John Newman (New York: Berghahn Books, 2016), 197–215.

16 Stephan Lehnstaedt, 'Dwie (różne) okupacje? Polityka gospodarcza Niemiec i Austro-Węgier w Królestwie Polskim w latach 1915–1918' [Two (different) occupations? The German and Austrian Economic Policy in the Kingdom of Poland, 1915–1918], *Dzieje Najnowsze* 45 (2013): 17–33.

17 Ober Ost was the abbreviation for the area under the control of the Supreme Commander of All German Forces in the East (*Oberbefehlshaber der gesamten Deutschen Streitkräfte im Osten*), covering Courland, large parts of Lithuania and the Białystok–Grodno area.

18 Włodzimierz Borodziej, *Geschichte Polens im 20. Jahrhundert* (München: Beck, 2010), 80.

19 Christian Westerhoff, *Zwangsarbeit im Ersten Weltkrieg: Deutsche Arbeitskräftepolitik im besetzten Polen und Litauen 1914–1918* (Paderborn: Schöningh Verlag, 2011); and Christian Westerhoff, '"A Kind of Siberia": German Labour and Occupation Policies in Poland and Lithuania during the First World War', *First World War Studies* 4, no. 1 (2013): 51–63.

self-government were tolerated in order to assist the hopelessly understaffed and overworked occupation administration.[20] These clerks would form the nucleus of the new states' civil institutions, as soon as the iron grip of the Central Powers had loosened.

The Austrian General Government of Lublin was highly militarized and did not allow for an expanded system of self-governing Polish institutions to any significant degree.[21] In the General Government of Warsaw, the situation was ambiguous, as the Germans, on the one hand, 'sought to gain Polish support for the long-term goal of German domination in Central Europe after the war' while they, on the other hand, 'ruthlessly plundered Poland's economy for the short-term goal of keeping the German war effort going'.[22] Thus, Governor General Hans Hartwig von Beseler, who after 1916 suddenly became interested in establishing Polish parastate structures – a position that he had previously categorically rejected[23] – faced opposition not only from German hawks but also from Polish nationalists who did not buy into his new outlook. Nevertheless, under the German occupation, a Polish-language university was opened, which was soon followed by a nascent state-school system. In these educational establishments, the Germans sought to raise a class of apolitical Polish administrators who would run a future satellite state from within, while leaving foreign policy to a king in thrall to the Germans. Most surprisingly, elected city councils, a Polish military force, a Provisional Council of State and a Regency Council – created for the German *and* the Austrian administrative territories in 1917 – also materialized, which first and foremost built up the Polish court and state-school systems. However, the occupants 'were never interested in a shared partnership, but more or less exclusively in willing executioners'.[24] Then again, all these newly created domestic institu-

---

20 Jesse Kauffman, 'Warsaw University under German Occupation: State Building and Nation *Bildung* in Poland during the Great War', *First World War Studies* 4, no. 1 (2013): 65–79; idem, 'Schools, State-Building, and National Conflict in German Occupied Poland, 1915–1918', in *Finding Common Ground: New Directions in First World War Studies*, eds Jennifer D. Keene and Michael S. Neiberg (Leiden: Brill, 2011), 113–37; Stephan Lehnstaedt, 'Fluctuating between "Utilisation" and Exploitation: Occupied East Central Europe during the First World War', in *Legacies of Violence: Eastern Europe's First World War*, eds Jochen Böhler, Włodzimierz Borodziej and Joachim von Puttkamer (München: Oldenbourg, 2014), 89–112; Arkadiusz Stempin, 'Deutsche Besatzungsmacht und Zivilbevölkerung in Polen: Juden und Deutsche im Vergleich', in *Besetzt, interniert, deportiert: Der Erste Weltkrieg und die deutsche, jüdische, polnische und ukrainische Zivilbevölkerung im östlichen Europa*, ed. Alfred Eisfeld (Essen: Klartext, 2013), 153–72; and idem, 'Deutsche Besatzungspolitik im Kongress-Königreich 1915–1918' (Habilitation, Universität Freiburg, 2008).

21 Stephan Lehnstaedt, *Imperiale Polenpolitik in den Weltkriegen: Eine vergleichende Studie zu den Mittelmächten und zu NS-Deutschland* (Osnabrück: fibre, 2017).

22 Jesse Kauffman, 'German State-Building in Occupied Poland as an Episode in Postwar Reconstruction, 1915–1918', in *Decades of Reconstruction: Postwar Societies, State-Building, and International Relations from the Seven Years War to the Cold War*, eds James Retallack and Ute Planert (Cambridge, MA: Cambridge University Press, 2017), 239–55, here 241; Lehnstaedt, 'Dwie (różne) okupacje?'; idem, 'Fluctuating between "Utilisation" and Exploitation'; and Arkadiusz Stempin, *Próba 'moralnego podboju' Polski przez Cesarstwo Niemieckie w latach I wojny światowej* [The German Empire's attempt to achieve Poland's 'moral subjugation' during the First World War] (Warszawa: Wydawnictwo Neriton, 2013).

23 Up to 1915, Russian rule had, by and large, refused to allow the establishment of Polish self-governing institutions. See Malte Rolf, *Imperiale Herrschaft im Weichselland: Das Königreich Polen im russischen Imperium (1864–1915)* (München: Oldenbourg, 2015). In 1915, Beseler dissolved the Central Citizens Committee (*Centralny Komitet Obywatelski*), which had – funded solely by donations – successfully organized the food supply, schools, children's homes, communal kitchens and poor relief, just because he regarded it as politically unreliable. See Lehnstaedt, *Imperiale Polenpolitik*.

24 Lehnstaedt, *Imperiale Polenpolitik*, 215.

Statehood: the First World War

tions were not automatically loyal to the German and Austrian emperors either, but rather the opposite and, more importantly, they were to form the nucleus of the future Polish state when the Germans had to retreat from the area.[25] Significantly, when the constitution of the Regency Council was announced on 5 November 1916, the masses in the streets of Warsaw celebrated Józef Piłsudski as a hero – the future military leader of the Polish armed forces and the first head of the independent Polish state – rather than Wilhelm II.[26]

Even in Ober Ost – despite the bad reputation it has gained in recent historiography for being a prototype for German policies of domination and extermination before and during the Second World War[27] – the use of parastate structures as a precondition for future statehood could be observed from 1917 on. In light of the Russian Revolution and the United States' entrance into the war, the harsh occupation policy had to be revised. A Lithuanian State Council (Taryba) formed in September, but its bilingual declaration clearly mirrored the differing views of the occupier and the occupied: whereas the Lithuanian version spoke of 'working towards the reconstruction of the country', the German version only allowed the inclusion of the term 'cooperation', reducing the Lithuanians to the level of mere assistants to their German masters. From as early as the beginning of the war, the German historian Johannes Haller characterized this patronizing German world view in the following way: 'If we win – and anyone who doubts we shall is a dog – we can impose our rules on the conquered world and give things the shape necessary for our own development and for the good of the small neighbouring peoples that flock around us and look to us for protection and salvation'.[28] In October 1917, the military government even forged plans to incorporate the entire Ober Ost as New Land (*Neuland*) into Prussia and to assign it a purely German administration.[29] Shortly afterwards, the region plunged into the chaos of the Central European post-war struggles.[30] The short-lived experiment of Lithuanian self-government in the last phase of German rule in Ober Ost had not been much more than a fig leaf.

In occupied Poland and Lithuania, the Central Powers' aim to compensate for their limited manpower and strengthen their standing in the imagined European post-war order through indigenous participation was inextricably linked to the vague promise of future national sovereignty. Without it, the intended level of cooperation could not be achieved. In reality, the simultaneous need to exploit the countries' natural and human resources counteracted those

---

25 Jesse Kauffman, *Elusive Alliance: The German Occupation of Poland in World War I* (Cambridge, MA: Harvard University Press, 2015); and Kauffman, 'Warsaw University under German Occupation'. For the Provisional Council of State and the Regency Council, see also: Włodzimierz Suleja, *Tymczasowa Rada Stanu* [The provisional council of the state] (Warszawa: Wydawn. Sejmowe, 1998); and Zdisław Winnicki, *Rada Regencyjna Królestwa Polskiego i jej organy, 1917–1918* [The Regency Council of the Kingdom of Poland and its institutions, 1917–1918] (Wrocław: Wektory, 1991).

26 Werner Conze, *Polnische Nation und deutsche Politik im Ersten Weltkrieg* (Köln: Böhlau, 1958), 227.

27 Vejas G. Liulevicius, *War Land on the Eastern Front: Culture, National Identity, and German Occupation in World War I* (Cambridge: Cambridge University Press, 2000).

28 Johannes Haller in *Süddeutsche Monatshefte*, September 1914, quoted from Mark von Hagen, *War in a European Borderland: Occupations and Occupation Plans in Galicia and Ukraine, 1914–1918* (Seattle, WA: University of Washington Press, 2007), 54.

29 Abba Strazhas, *Deutsche Ostpolitik im Ersten Weltkrieg: Der Fall Ober Ost 1915–1917* (Wiesbaden: Harrassowitz, 1993), 221–75.

30 Peter Gatrell, 'War After the War: Conflicts, 1919–1923', in *A Companion to World War I*, ed. John Horne (Chichester: Wiley-Blackwell, 2010), 558–75; and Jochen Böhler, *Civil War in Central Europe, 1918–1921: The Reconstruction of Poland* (Oxford: Oxford University Press, 2018), 59–145.

efforts and alienated the Polish and Lithuanian population, whose young men, by German calculations, were ready to support the German war effort, but in the end fought in the border wars of 1918–23, occasionally even against each other. Thus, they were vital for the creation of the independent Polish and Lithuanian Republics, ruled by governments that partially originated from the provisional State Councils of Poland and Lithuania.[31]

After the disappearance of imperial power from the Central and Eastern European map in late 1918, the formation of states was contested in two different areas of activity: militarily in the region itself, where generals and warlords, revolutionaries and nation-state builders strove for their respective future states' territory;[32] and politically in Paris, where politicians, diplomats, historians, ethnologists and other experts competed to delineate the broadest boundaries and to gain international recognition for their states. This is surely not the place to recount all the debates on future forms of statehood that filled the corridors and conference rooms of the French capital in 1919, which has been done in masterful detail elsewhere.[33] Nevertheless, we should not move on without mentioning that amongst the negotiators, many of whom had been in exile for years, we find Nikola Pašić and Ante Trumbić, prime minister and foreign minister of the Kingdom of Yugoslavia respectively; Ion Brătianu and Aleksandar Stamboliyski, the Romanian and Bulgarian prime ministers; Tomáš Masaryk, president of Czechoslovakia and his right-hand man Edvard Beneš, minister of foreign affairs and later president of Czechoslovakia;[34] Roman Dmowski, leader of the National Democrats and, for a short period in 1923, minister of foreign affairs in Poland; and Oskaras Milašius, Lithuanian chargé d'affaires, to name but a few. This unique meeting of nearly all the top-ranking politicians of interwar Central and Eastern Europe impressively illustrates that in Paris in 1919, and the years that followed, it was not only peace that was achieved, but statehood that was forged, and anyone who was anyone in the political scene of that time felt he had to be present.

On their way to the official hearings for each country, the victors of the First World War would occasionally meet the losers, the representatives of envisioned states that had never existed and would not come into existence during the interwar period. The delegates from war-torn Western Ukraine were one such group. The Council of Four in Paris – Woodrow Wilson (USA), David Lloyd George (Great Britain), Vittorio Emanuele Orlando (Italy) and Georges Clemenceau (France) – were quite indifferent to the fate of the land that lay between dangerous Bolshevik Russia and extending Poland: 'I only saw a Ukrainian once', was a comment from the British prime minister in a poor display of grace. He went on, 'It is the last Ukrainian I have seen, and I am not sure that I want to see any more.'[35]

Even if they had been interested in assisting this group, they would surely have lost their way in the labyrinth of Ukraine's recent past. The chances for the development of stable structures of self-government in Ukraine were smaller than in other parts of Central and Eastern Europe,

---

31 Benjamin Conrad, *Umkämpfte Grenzen, umkämpfte Bevölkerung: Die Entstehung der Staatsgrenzen der Zweiten Polnischen Republik 1918–1923* (Stuttgart: Steiner, 2014). See the volume *Violence* in this series.

32 Jochen Böhler, 'Generals and Warlords, Revolutionaries and Nation State Builders: The First World War and its Aftermath in Central and Eastern Europe', in Böhler, Borodziej and von Puttkamer, *Legacies of Violence: Eastern Europe's First World War*, 51–66.

33 Palmer, *The Lands Between*, 150–73; Margaret MacMillan, *Paris 1919: Six Months that Changed the World* (New York: Random House, 2003).

34 See the first sub-chapter in Chapter 5 of this volume, 'War and Statehood – Occupation and Persistence (II)'.

35 MacMillan, *Paris 1919*, 226.

Statehood: the First World War

due to the fact that between 1914 and 1918 it witnessed the disorientating comings and goings of various occupation armies – Russians, German and Austrians, and later Bolsheviks and the White Army, each of them entering Ukraine several times.[36]

Nevertheless, amidst the chaos of conquest and retreat, war and revolution, different rival bodies championing Ukrainian statehood emerged from late 1917 onwards: first of all, there was the Central Council (Rada) – a coordinating centre that represented all the Ukrainian parties – which was then followed by a People's Republic, a People's Republic of Soviets and a Ukrainian State (or Hetmanate). As disparate as they were, all these institutions had one thing in common: they vanished almost as fast as they had appeared. In the wake of the Polish–Soviet War (1919–20), Poland and Russia put an end to this charade and clearly divided Ukraine between them, incorporating the western part (the former Austrian province of Galicia) into Poland and the eastern part into Bolshevik Russia, after installing a puppet regime in Kiev and baptizing the artificial state the Ukrainian Soviet Socialist Republic, which was only grudgingly recognized by the Western powers in 1923.[37] Although the Ukrainian Soviet Socialist Republic was all but independent, it is still important to emphasize that

> Ukrainian statehood mattered. For the first time in modern history, eastern Ukrainians had a territorial entity with borders closely corresponding to the ethnic boundaries of Ukrainian settlement. A part of the Soviet Union, the Ukrainian republic nonetheless provided a symbolic national homeland for generations of Soviet Ukrainians.[38]

Despite all this, an incipient form of Ukrainian independence emerged out of the Great War. Following the lead of the Kingdom of Belgium, which had established a government-in-exile between 1914 and 1918, the political leadership of the Ukrainian People's Republic left the country in 1920 and formed a government-in-exile on its own, emigrating through Poland and Vienna to Paris and claiming to represent the Ukrainian people alone. However, while the representatives of Belgium had acted as a serious negotiation partner for the Allies, the Ukrainian government-in-exile under Symon Petliura and then Andriy Livytsky was largely

---

36 Hagen, *War in a European Borderland*, 3–4.

37 Serhy Yekelchyk, *Ukraine: Birth of a Modern Nation* (Oxford: Oxford University Press, 2007), 67–84; Mark von Hagen, 'The Emergence of Kyiv as Capital of Revolutionary Ukraine, March–July 1917, with a Focus on the War and Soldiers', in *Imperienvergleich: Beispiele und Ansätze aus osteuropäischer Perspektive; Festschrift für Andreas Kappeler*, eds Guido Hausmann, Angela Rustemeyer and Andreas Kappeler (Wiesbaden: Harrassowitz, 2009), 377–402; Henry Abramson, *A Prayer for the Government: Ukrainians and Jews in Revolutionary Times, 1917–1920* (Cambridge, MA: Harvard University Press, 1999); Abraham Revutsky, ed., *Wrenching Times in Ukraine: Memoir of a Jewish Minister* (St. John's, Newfoundland, Canada: Yksuver Publications, 1998); Wolfram Dornik and Peter Lieb, 'Misconceived *Realpolitik* in a Failing State: The Political and Economical Fiasco of the Central Powers in the Ukraine, 1918', *First World War Studies* 4, no. 1 (2013): 111–24; Stephen Velychenko, *State-building in Revolutionary Ukraine: A Comparative Study of Governments and Bureaucrats, 1917–1922* (Toronto: University of Toronto Press, 2011); Caroline Milow, *Die ukrainische Frage 1917–1923 im Spannungsfeld der europäischen Diplomatie* (Wiesbaden: Harrassowitz, 2002).

38 Yekelchyk, *Ukraine*, 85. Another example of imagined rather than real Ukrainian statehood after the First World War was the idea of a 'Ukrainian Piedmont', as well as a 'Carpathian Ukraine' or 'Carpathian Rus'. See Albert S. Kotowski, '"Ukrainisches Piemont"? Die Karpatenukraine am Vorabend des Zweiten Weltkrieges', *Jahrbücher für Geschichte Osteuropas* 49, no. 1 (2001): 67–95; and Paul R. Magocsi, '"Carpathian Rus": Interethnic Coexistence without Violence', in *Shatterzone of Empires: Coexistence and Violence in the German, Habsburg, Russian, and Ottoman Borderlands*, eds Omer Bartov and Eric D. Weitz (Bloomington, IN: Indiana University Press, 2013), 449–62.

ignored in Paris, and even among many expatriate Ukrainians it was not regarded as more than another political party.[39] Although, in the wake of the First World War, Ukraine surpassed all other countries in Central and Eastern Europe in its number of governments, it proved unable to transfer from a revolutionary phase of statehood to post-war independence, as it lacked the three basic requirements for the time: a charismatic leader influential enough to unite splintered interest groups, a powerful army and support from the West.

Not surprisingly, after such disillusionment, many Western Ukrainians (in the early 1930s, they amounted to a population of seven million) who now lived within the borders of the Second Polish Republic, were not willing to accept the status quo, and were not counting on their feeble representatives in the French capital or their mainstream politicians who had passively begun to cooperate with the Polish state. In the early 1920s, young radicals, mostly veterans of the Polish–Soviet War, set up the Ukrainian Military Organization, which assassinated a number of Polish and Ukrainian officials in the following decade and claimed that independent Ukrainian statehood was their highest aim.[40] Their counterpart in Southeastern Europe was the Internal Macedonian Revolutionary Organization, which, under the Bulgarian occupation, had enjoyed de facto autonomy and had even governed parts of Macedonia. After the war, when an independent Macedonian state did not materialize, the organization went underground and tried to achieve this goal through political terror in the Greek and Yugoslav borderlands.[41]

2. War and work – forced labour and the organization of human resources (I)[42]

From the beginning of the First World War, the Russian military in the western territories of tsarist Russia pursued a scorched earth policy through mass migration and expulsion of the Russian and non-Russian populations.[43] Additionally, by the summer of 1915, hundreds of thousands of refugees were living on the streets of larger towns and cities in the Baltic coastal area, the Kingdom of Poland and Galicia. Much further to the south-east, the main victims of the Russian soldiers' large-scale offensives were Transcaucasian Muslims, while, at the same time, Ottoman soldiers triggered the Armenian genocide.[44] In Belorussia (now Belarus),

---

39 Jan J. Bruski, *Petlurowcy: Centrum Państwowe Ukraińskiej Republiki Ludowej na wychodźstwie, 1919–1924* [Petliurovians: the state centre of the Ukrainian People's Republic, 1919–1924] (Kraków: Arcana, 2000); and Paul R. Magocsi, *A History of Ukraine: The Land and its Peoples* (Toronto: University of Toronto Press, 2010), 535, 552. Tellingly, the Ukrainian government-in-exile and its main protagonists are not even mentioned in the standard volume, MacMillan, *Paris 1919*.

40 Yekelchyk, *Ukraine*, 122–28.

41 Opfer, *Im Schatten des Krieges*, 79–89, 162–87; Stefan Troebst, 'Nationalismus und Gewalt im Osteuropa der Zwischenkriegszeit: Terroristische Separatismen im Vergleich', *Berliner Jahrbuch für osteuropäische Geschichte* 3, no. 1 (1996): 273–314.

42 See the second sub-chapter in Chapter 5 of this volume, p. 199, 'War and work – forced labour and the organization of human resources (II)'.

43 Eric Lohr, 'The Russian Army and the Jews: Mass Deportation, Hostages, and Violence during World War I', *Russian Review* 60, no. 3 (2001), 404–19.

44 Alexander V. Prusin, *Nationalizing a Borderland: War, Ethnicity, and Anti-Jewish Violence in East Galicia, 1914–1920* (Tuscaloosa, AL: University of Alabama Press, 2005); Peter Holquist, 'Forms of Violence during the Russian Occupation of Ottoman Territory and in Northern Persia (Urmia and Astrabad), October 1914–December 1917', in Bartov and Weitz, *Shatterzone of Empires*, 334–61; Uğur Ümit Üngör, 'The Armenian Genocide in the Context of Twentieth-Century Paramilitarism', in *The Armenian Genocide Legacy*, ed. Alexis Demirdjian (Basingstoke: Palgrave Macmillan, 2016), 11–25.

Statehood: the First World War

refugees and expellees sometimes outnumbered the local urban population by a factor of three, and 'entire provinces adjacent to the theater of war ... were "crowded to the limit"'. For many of those who were forced out, their journey ended in Siberian forced labour camps, while their property was seized and distributed among Russian soldiers or incoming Russian settlers. By early 1917, about six million displaced persons were roaming throughout the Russian Empire.[45]

Nevertheless, such widespread flight and expulsion cannot be equated with planned ethnic cleansing. Although it had been practised by Russian authorities half a century before in the Western Caucasus, deportation and forced migration, accompanied by expropriation and resettlement, were not consistent with state policy in tsarist Russia.[46] While some generals applied such ruthless methods in 1914–15 in order to – as they saw it – 'secure' the frontier and remunerate soldiers and citizens of the titular nation at the expense of ethnic minorities, some politicians from the Duma criticized harsh measures such as these and insisted that they were counterproductive. In any case, the expulsion of millions of 'internal enemies' into the interior or even beyond resulted in the de facto Russification of those parts of the empire that were adjacent to the front.[47]

The refugees were not simply a mass to be transported or expelled from one place to another. Although the refugees were disproportionally women, old people and children, they still represented a deep reservoir of cheap labour, a resource that was conspicuously missing in a state that was unprepared for and hopelessly dysfunctional in a war of global proportions. Nevertheless, the Russian administration proved itself unable to organize the allocation of work, and thus supply and demand were rarely met. It was only the Russian agrarian sector, in which between 250,000 and 350,000 refugees were employed in 1916–17 – a small figure in relation to the total number of displaced persons – that was regarded as a success by the authorities.[48]

The employment of prisoners of war (POWs) as a labour force was more efficient and better organized: 'Beginning in the spring of 1916', one reads in the new *International Encyclopedia of the First World War,*

> Russia systematically used POW labour in agriculture, industry and the public sector. ... Within one year, half of all enlisted men were used as cheap labour. By 1917, POWs constituted 20–25 percent of Russia's workforce. For many men employed in construction, scandalous working and living conditions were life threatening. In other cases, leaving the large Siberian camps meant an improvement in their situation, especially if they worked as farm hands and lived with peasant families.[49]

According to Russian figures, 1.64 million POWs in total were employed during the war.[50]

In the German and Austrian occupation zones, military authorities did not cause the same large-scale flight and migration. The biggest movement of people west of Russia was arguably

---

45 Peter Gatrell, *A Whole Empire Walking: Refugees in Russia During World War I* (Bloomington, IN: Indiana University Press, 1999), 17–25, here 21.

46 Peter Holquist, 'Violent Russia, Deadly Marxism? Russia in the Epoch of Violence, 1905–21', *Kritika: Explorations in Russian and Eurasian History* 4, no. 3 (2003): 634–35.

47 Lohr, 'The Russian Army and the Jews'; Prusin, *Nationalizing a Borderland.*

48 Gatrell, *A Whole Empire Walking,* 128–35.

49 Reinhard Nachtigal and Lana Radauer, 'Prisoners of War (Russian Empire)', in *1914–1918-online: International Encyclopedia of the First World War,* eds Ute Daniel et al. (2014), doi: 10.15463/ie1418.10386 (accessed 22 February 2020).

50 Alon Rachamimov, *POWs and the Great War: Captivity on the Eastern Front* (Oxford: Berg, 2002), 108.

that of Eastern European Jewish refugees who fled persecution at the hands of the Russian military; they crowded into the metropolises of the hinterlands such as Budapest, Vienna and Berlin. According to Christian Westerhoff, towards the end of the war, the north-eastern parts of the front, which were governed by the military administration of Ober Ost, had turned into 'a laboratory for forced labour and total war' for at least 10,000 people. One might argue that for an area of more than 40,000 square miles in size, these figures indicate failure rather than efficiency. However, with a deplorable standard of medical care, and high levels of illness and mortality, the prevailing working conditions were a warning of things to come. Despite harsh criticism within the occupied territory, the Reichstag and the international arena, the German military 'refused to be told how to handle a population it considered incapable of self-determination'.[51] It has often been asked whether the German occupation in the East during the First World War anticipated the occupation of the Second World War. In terms of the organization and use of forced labour, this is undoubtedly the case, although these elements differed in their extent to a very great degree between those two wars.

3. War and land – the agrarian question (I)[52]

At the turn of the nineteenth to the twentieth century, a collection of social and political questions had become pressing in Central and Eastern Europe. Since the imperial rulers' willingness to accept reform was rather limited, social and political tension rose. One of the most burning questions before the outbreak of the Great War was the distribution of land. To be sure, serfdom had been abolished everywhere and the effects of industrialization, the rationalization of agriculture, a degree of distribution of labour between the rural and urban spaces and the accompanying development of new markets for farm products that were advanced in Western and Northern Europe had an impact on Central and Eastern Europe as well. In states that had gained independence before the First World War, such as Serbia, Bulgaria or Greece, smallholder agriculture was on the rise; in some areas of the Habsburg Empire, such as Bohemia, Transylvania, the Vojvodina and to some extent even Galicia, peasants that had organized cooperatively could buy out the owners of large but unprofitable estates. Nevertheless, Central and Eastern Europe lagged far behind the levels of development in the western half of the continent, and large parts of the rural population in the region were still tilling land that was in the hand of a few large landowners.[53]

Therefore, whether belligerent or occupied states would be successful or not in mobilizing the rural masses for the war effort from 1914 onwards (and the rural masses constituted the majority of the population in all European countries until well after the end of the Second World War[54]), depended to a great degree on their ability to convince this group that once the war was over they would be better off on a personal level than before. It was fundamental to the agrarian issue that any improvement of the living standards of the peasants/soldiers

---

51 Westerhoff, "'A Kind of Siberia'", here 51 and 56. For further reading, see Westerhoff, *Zwangsarbeit im Ersten Weltkrieg*.

52 See the third sub-chapter in Chapter 5 of this volume, p. 202, 'War and land – the agrarian question (II)'.

53 Iván T. Berend and György Ránki, *Economic Development in East-Central Europe in the 19th and 20th Centuries* (New York: Columbia University Press, 1974), 28–58. See the volume *Challenges of Modernity* in this series.

54 Wolfram Fischer et al., eds, *Europäische Wirtschafts- und Sozialgeschichte vom Ersten Weltkrieg bis zur Gegenwart* (Stuttgart: Klett-Cotta, 1987), 57, table 2.

Statehood: the First World War

was – at least in their own understanding – directly linked to who owned the fields that they were working in.[55]

In imperial Russia, the agrarian question fermented between the middle of the nineteenth century and the beginning of the First World War.[56] Prime Minister Pyotr Stolypin's land reforms, which in the beginning were stimulated by the 1905 revolution and aimed to pass land ownership from communal to private hands, had brought little relief, since at the outset of the war, 80 per cent of peasant households still had no entitlement to their land.[57] That it was crucial for the Russian Empire to win over its farmers and peasants can easily be confirmed by the knowledge that in 1915 this group was as large in number as the Russian armies' soldiers. According to Corinne Gaudin, 'the empire's stability, as well as the government's ability to fulfil its economic, military, and foreign policy ambitions seemed to depend on the peasant's willingness to produce, market, pay taxes, and fight'.[58] However, since the Russian state was unable to convey convincing visions of mass participation in land ownership and politics to its conscripts, both social tensions and peasant unrest troubled the armed forces of imperial Russia from the very beginning, neither of which were settled when they dissipated in 1917. At that point, the Provisional Government took over and embarked on land reform, but it was soon overthrown by the Bolshevik revolutionaries who – facing military defeat, civil war, foreign intervention and the Herculean task of restoring order at the same time – won the peasants over by finally granting them control over the countryside and allowing them to take up ownership of their land.[59] It can be justifiably assumed that without this course of action, after the colossal losses of territory after the Treaty of Brest-Litovsk in March 1918, the Bolshevik government would have suffered the fate of its predecessors.[60] 'If there was ever a period when the peasantry broadly sympathized with Soviet power', writes Donald Raleigh, 'it was now.'

The process of passing land to the people was not always a smooth one, as the case of workers' unrest in Saratov demonstrates. Finally, most of the land had not been given to individual peasants as private property, which the rural masses expected and desired, but rather to the local community within a system of collective agriculture. This was a bone of contention that made collectivization in Soviet Russia in the 1920s such a violent endeavour and hampered the peasantry's identification with the new state they were living in.[61] The situation was

---

55 Despite all their promising titles, the contributions to the book Max Sering, ed., *Die agrarischen Umwälzungen im ausserrussischen Osteuropa: Ein Sammelwerk* (Berlin: De Gruyter, 1930) skip the First World War and only deal with events leading up to and following the war.

56 Francis W. Wcislo, *Reforming Rural Russia: State, Local Society, and National Politics, 1855–1914* (Princeton, NJ: Princeton University Press, 1990).

57 Judith Pallot, *Land Reform in Russia 1906–1917: Peasant Responses to Stolypin's Project of Rural Transformation* (Oxford: Oxford University Press, 1999); percentage according to www.britannica.com/EBchecked/topic/567072/Stolypin-land-reform (accessed 22 February 2020).

58 Corinne Gaudin, *Ruling Peasants: Village and State in Late Imperial Russia* (DeKalb, IL: Northern Illinois University Press, 2007), 3, here 4.

59 See entry 'Decree on Land' in Jon Smele, ed., *Historical Dictionary of the Russian Civil Wars, 1916–1926*, 2 vols (Lanham, MD: Rowman & Littlefield, 2015), 318–9.

60 Joachim von Puttkamer, 'Collapse and Restoration: Politics and the Strains of War in Eastern Europe', in Böhler, Borodziej and von Puttkamer, *Legacies of Violence: Eastern Europe's First World War*, 9–23, here 15–20.

61 Donald J. Raleigh, *Experiencing Russia's Civil War: Politics, Society, and Revolutionary Culture in Saratov, 1917–1922* (Princeton, NJ: Princeton University Press, 2002), 312–47, here (paragraph above) 313; for more specific information on the agrarian question in revolutionary Russia in 1917, see Graeme J. Gill, *Peasants and Government in the Russian Revolution* (New York: Barnes & Noble Books, 1979); on the agrarian question during the Russian Civil War from 1917 to 1921, see Orlando Figes, *Peasant Russia, Civil War: The Volga Countryside in Revolution, 1917–1921* (Oxford: Clarendon Press, 1989).

further aggravated by the returning war veterans and city dwellers who, as a result of shrinking industry, fled to the countryside in 1918, which swelled the peasant communities: one peasant explained to the authorities that

> before the revolution it was better concerning the land. We got, you know, about five hundred *desiatin* [about 1350 acres] for our peasant commune, but there are more eaters now in the commune, about a thousand now. So you can see yourself.[62]

Be that as it may, the Bolsheviks were far from being the only ones who intended to bring hope but in the long run disappointed the rural classes of Central and Eastern Europe at the end of the First World War. In post Brest-Litovsk Ukraine, the increasing demand for grain from the German and Austrian occupation forces and their complete lack of any political vision for the country had further strengthened popular support for the socialist-revolutionary Central Council, which the foreign rulers subsequently replaced with the puppet government of Pavlo Skoropadskyi, Hetman of Ukraine.[63] As a result, large landowners were reinstalled, local communities were collectively punished for prior insubordination and expropriation, and villages were raided and pillaged.[64] As such, loyalty to the state was reduced to a minimum. Sergej Yekelchyk puts it in a nutshell: 'The chief interest of the peasants, who were far from being latent nationalists, was obtaining land. The government's failure to address this concern of its main constituency undermined popular support for the Ukrainian idea.'[65] And thus, as Wolfram Dornik and Peter Lieb summarize:

> in rural Ukraine, peasant social and political loyalty traditionally centered on local networks and societal hierarchies and not on the state. Already the Tsarist government had exercised only limited power in the villages and had experienced huge difficulties in enforcing law and order. The turbulences of the First World War and the Civil War exacerbated this. As a result, the power basis in the countryside often laid [sic] in the hands of warlords and their followers, impoverished peasants who did not shrink from robbing and terrorizing other peasants. A culture of everyday violence emerged.[66]

In this critical situation, the peasant or Green Armies were born, forming – along with the Red and White Armies – one of the major colourful parties in the Russian Civil War. But the 'Greens' neither gave the peasants control over their land nor a viable vision of future statehood for rural Ukraine – a vision under different terms than conceived by the Bolsheviks. They were small in number, badly organized, had a limited scope of action (they often only operated in or near the local regions whence they came), followed no consistent political

---

62 Vladimir Brovkin, *Behind the Front Lines of the Civil War: Political Parties and Social Movements in Russia, 1918–1922* (Princeton, NJ: Princeton University Press, 1994), 141.

63 On the continually changing governments in Ukraine between 1917 and 1920, see above.

64 Wolfram Dornik et al., eds, *Die Ukraine: Zwischen Selbstbestimmung und Fremdherrschaft 1917–1922* (Graz: Leykam, 2011); Felix Schnell, 'Ukraine 1918: Besatzer und Besetzte im Gewaltraum', in *Gewalträume: Soziale Ordnungen im Ausnahmezustand*, eds Jörg Baberowski and Gabriele Metzler (Frankfurt a.M.: Campus, 2012), 135–68, here: 144.

65 Yekelchyk, *Ukraine*, 67.

66 Dornik and Lieb, 'Misconceived *Realpolitik* in a Failing State', 115. For more detail, see Wolfram Dornik and Peter Lieb, 'Die Ukrainepolitik der Mittelmächte während des Ersten Weltkrieges', in Dornik et al., *Die Ukraine: Zwischen Selbstbestimmung*, 91–128.

Statehood: the First World War

ideology, apart from anti-Bolshevism (which did not prevent them from occasionally form-ing short-lived coalitions with the Red Army), shifted their allegiances repeatedly and used violence not only against their adversaries, but also against peasants who were unwilling to grant them food, manpower or shelter.[67] The third party in the Civil War, the 'Whites', which was led by former tsarist officers, was even less attractive to the peasantry, since its primary aim was to defeat the Red Army, and their leadership largely desired to reinstall the Russian Empire, which had, as I have shown, not been such a hospitable regime for the rural population either. The skills the Whites possessed in organization and soldiering were counteracted by their lack of ideological commitment: 'The generals were not intellectuals', Peter Kenez states flatly,

> and they did not systematically summarize their goals and beliefs. They never under-stood the importance of ideology and did not take ideas seriously. Rather stupidly, they believed that their enemies were evil and assumed that the Russian people would soon realize what to themselves seemed so obvious.[68]

Overall, the Whites, who were largely supported by the large landowners, tried to avoid the topic of who would own the land in the future. Even generals who embarked on small-scale projects of land reform, such as Pyotr Nikolayevich Wrangel, did not hesitate to rein-stall ex-tsarist functionaries. In addition, the manifesto on land reform of the commander of the Volunteer Army, Anton Denikin, which passed in 1919 due to the unexpected prolongation of the civil war, was too half-hearted to compete with the Bolsheviks' project in any serious way.[69]

All in all, it can be said that the Red Army won the Russian Civil War because they were seen as the lesser of two evils for the majority of the population, including the peasants, and because they possessed what their enemies – who were all quickly wiped out from Central and Eastern Europe – lacked in unity, organizational skill and ideological zeal. Once the fighting was over, the victorious Bolsheviks had to rethink their strategy and develop meth-ods, such as the New Economic Policy and the application of brute force, to keep the rural population in line.[70]

In the areas to the west and south of revolutionary Russia, the agrarian question was not settled by the outcome of a civil war. The starting position of the countries that were situated there differed significantly at the final stage of the Great War. Some of them had been occu-pied by the Central Powers for years, and Germany and Austria simply offered nothing to the

---

67 Brovkin, *Behind the Front Lines of the Civil War*, 127–62, 300–56; on peasant armies in Ukraine, see Fe-lix Schnell, *Räume des Schreckens: Gewalträume und Gruppenmilitanz in der Ukraine, 1905–1933* (Ham-burg: Hamburger Edition, 2012) and Christopher Gilley, 'The Ukrainian Anti-Bolshevik Risings of Spring and Summer 1919: Intellectual History in a Space of Violence', *Revolutionary Russia* 27, no. 2 (2014): 109–31; for a local study on the Greens in the Tambov region, see Oliver H. Radkey, *The Unknown Civil War in Soviet Russia: A Study of the Green Movement in the Tambov Region, 1920–1921* (Stanford, CA: Hoover Institution Press, Stanford University, 1976).

68 Peter Kenez, 'The Ideology of the White Movement', *Soviet Studies* 32, no. 1 (1980): 58–83, here 58.

69 Ibid., 70–72.

70 For further developments in the agrarian sector, see Dietmar Müller's chapter in this volume, 'State-hood in Central, Eastern and Southeastern Europe: The Interwar Period'. For collectivization in the 1920s and 1930s, see Timothy Snyder, *Bloodlands: Europe Between Hitler and Stalin* (London: Random House, 2010), 21–58.

Jochen Böhler

peasantry in any of the following places: in the Baltic region where the Germans themselves had traditionally constituted the large landowning class;[71] in Poland where the two emperors, despite their declaration of a Polish Kingdom in November 1916, never had real interest in the resurrection of an autonomous Polish state;[72] in Romania where the German occupiers marginally favoured peasants to landowners but were reluctant to alienate the latter and left the pre-war agricultural order untouched;[73] or in Serbia where the relations between the Habsburg troops and the rural masses had been poisoned in 1915 by alleged peasant participation in partisan warfare and harsh requisitions in the countryside, but which had been ameliorated during the course of the occupation.[74] Notwithstanding regional differences, the overall occupation 'policy' focused on the exploitation of labour, agriculture and natural resources, and recruiting indigenous manpower, while it completely lacked any realistic and attractive plans for a fairer distribution of land, let alone the pursuit of separate statehood. However, the Central Powers lost the war in 1918 and subsequently had to retreat completely from our area of interest, leaving devastated swathes of land behind them, which were beset by epidemics and contained millions of starving and sick people.

The same tragedy could be seen in countries that had been spared from combat and occupation, such as Croatia or Slovenia. 'The land looks as if the enemy had destroyed everything, dried up and contaminated. . . . People wander around like ghosts, dead from hunger', wrote a chemist's wife from the Istrian peninsula in autumn 1918.[75] Additionally, the whole area was destabilized by peasant unrest, since the rural classes felt that the elites who were designing national unity and statehood in Zagreb had forgotten about them and were not promoting their cause. The peasant revolts were partly enforced, partly threatened by groups called the Green cadres, who were peasant soldiers from the Habsburg armies who returned from the battlefields with socialist ideas and an even stronger inclination towards burning and looting, thus resembling the Green Armies further to the north-east. Fundamentally, according to Mark Biondich, in Croatia and Slovenia, 'the divergence of opinion between . . . middle-class intellectuals and the peasantry was painfully obvious. In 1918 the chasm that separated the two worlds was indeed great.'[76] The reason for this was that state-building and the attempt to restore order had

---

71 Liulevicius, *War Land on the Eastern Front*; Otto Korfes, 'Die Agrarrevolution in Estland und Lettland', in Sering, *Die agrarischen Umwälzungen,* 72–127, here 86–91. For the radical changes within the agrarian economy in the Baltic states *after* the Great War, see Gert von Pistohlkors, 'Tiefgreifende agrarische Umwälzungen und Umstrukturierungen in den neu gegründeten baltischen Staaten Estland, Lettland und Litauen 1919/1922: Motivationen und Ergebnisse bis 1940', in *Agrarreformen und ethnodemographische Veränderungen: Südosteuropa vom ausgehenden 18. Jahrhundert bis in die Gegenwart*, ed. Karl-Peter Krauss (Stuttgart: Franz Steiner Verlag, 2009), 175–205.

72 See footnotes 22 and 25.

73 Mayerhofer, *Zwischen Freund und Feind*, 173 and 184.

74 Gumz, *Resurrection and Collapse of Empire*.

75 Croatian nationalists, though, missed the one-time opportunity then to unite the peasants behind them. See Mark Cornwall, 'The Great War and the Yugoslav Grassroots: Popular Mobilization in the Habsburg Monarchy, 1914–18', in *New Perspectives on Yugoslavia: Key Issues and Controversies*, eds Dejan Djokić and James Ker-Lindsay (Milton Park, Abingdon, and Oxon: Routledge, 2010), 27–45, here 30. See also: Ștefan Dorondel and Stelu Șerban, 'A Missing Link: The Agrarian Question in Southeast Europe', *Martor – The Romanian Peasant Museum Journal for Social Anthropology* 19 (2014): 7–29; and Christian Giordano, 'The Ethnicization of Agrarian Reforms: The Case of Interwar Yugoslavia', *Martor – The Romanian Peasant Museum Journal for Social Anthropology* 19 (2014): 31–42.

76 Mark Biondich, *Stjepan Radić, the Croat Peasant Party, and the Politics of Mass Mobilization, 1904–1928* (Toronto: University of Toronto Press, 2000), 143–4, here 144.

Statehood: the First World War

postponed land reform instead of enforcing it. Peasants, for their part, not only requested participatory rights but ownership of land. Within the Kingdom of Yugoslavia, such antagonisms led to conditions that resembled civil war.

Hungary, as part of the Habsburg Empire, did not witness war on the home front, but the state lost every seventh soldier in battle, the war itself and two thirds of its pre-war territory. It also witnessed a short-lived Bolshevik revolution and the bloody months of White terror that ensued.[77] Initially, the revolutionary upheavals seemed to pave the way for radical land reforms. Shortly after his accession to power in March 1919, the revolutinary leader Béla Kun embarked on a project comparable to that which the Bolsheviks launched in Russia in a state of crisis:

> Land in Hungary belongs to the workers' society. Anyone who does not work is not permitted to hold on to land in his possession. All medium and large landholdings, together with all their appurtenances, live or dead stock, and agricultural workshops, are transferred with immediate effect into ownership of the proletarian state.[78]

However, no action followed these inflated promises, and only a few months later, Kun and his association fled from the Romanian army and the Hungarian White Guards.[79] As a result, the lion's share of the arable land in Hungary in the early interwar period was still in the hands of a few aristocratic owners of large estates. According to Joseph Rothschild,

> during the so-called revolutions of 1918–19, the [Hungarian] peasants had no sense of real change in agrarian or agronomic arrangements on the land, and hence they lacked leverage with which to resist the return to the latifundist system of extensive cultivation carried on by large armies of itinerant and domiciled agricultural laborers.[80]

Thus, despite its short Bolshevik experiment, Hungary was the only Eastern European country in which considerable residues of feudal agriculture had not only outlived the nineteenth

---

77 According to Joseph Rothschild, Hungary mobilized 3,614,179 troops. See Joseph Rothschild, *East Central Europe between the Two World Wars* (Seattle, WA: University of Washington Press, 1992), 138. Close to 530,000 of them died, 1.4 million were wounded and 833,000 were taken prisoner; see Ignác Romsics, *Hungary in the Twentieth Century* (Budapest: Corvina Books Ltd., 1999), 85. For ground-breaking work on the White Terror, see Béla Bodo, 'Paramilitary Violence in Hungary after the First World War', *East European Quarterly* 38, no. 2 (2004): 129–73; idem, *Pal Pronay: Paramilitary Violence and Anti-Semitism in Hungary, 1919–1921* (Pittsburgh, PA: Center for Russian and East European Studies, 2011); idem, 'Militia Violence and State Power in Hungary, 1919–1922', *Hungarian Studies Review* 33, nos. 1–2 (2006): 121–56; idem, 'Hungarian Aristocracy and the White Terror', *Journal of Contemporary History* 45, no. 4 (2010): 703–24; idem, 'Heroes or Thieves? Nepotism, Clientage and Paramilitary Violence in Hungary, 1919–1921', *Centre. Journal for Interdisciplinary Studies of Central Europe in the 19th and 20th Centuries* 7, no. 1 (2015): 66–114. See the volume *Violence* in this series.

78 *Tanácsköztársasági Törvénytár* [Legal Code of the Soviet Republic], ed. J. Pongnicz (Budapest: Magyarországi Szocialista Part, 1919), 1: 56, as cited in Ignác Romsics, *Hungary in the Twentieth Century* (Budapest: Corvina Books Ltd., 1999), 101; Béla Kenéz, 'Die Agrarreform in Ungarn', in Sering, *Die agrarischen Umwälzungen*, 255–75, here 258–9.

79 For a recent biography on Béla Kun, see Thomas L. Sakmyster, *A Communist Odyssey: The Life of József Pogány/John Pepper* (Budapest and New York: Central European University Press, 2012).

80 Rothschild, *East Central Europe*, 137–60, here 159.

century, but also the Great War.[81] 'This country has the worst system of landholding in Europe. The peasants there are as oppressed as they were in the Middle Ages, and manorial law still exists there', Lloyd George gloomily remarked in Paris.[82] Thus, the situation in Hungary differed fundamentally from that of the Baltic coast, especially with regard to Estonia and Latvia. In these countries, a German nobility, which had formed the landholding elite for centuries, was compromised by its cooperation with the German occupiers. With the defeat of the Central Powers, the land and forests of the Baltic knights were nationalized. Not all of it, though, was transferred down to the peasantry, with the two states keeping a significant part for themselves.[83]

With the notable exception of Hungary and the Baltic states, the First World War shook or even shattered the old agricultural order everywhere in Central and Eastern Europe without replacing it with a viable new order. It can be surmised that state-building, in tandem with land reform, was a process that was furthered by peace rather than war, grandiose but ultimately unfulfilled pledges made in times of crisis notwithstanding.[84] 'Agriculture and the peasants', Mihai Chioveanu concludes, 'were rather "orphans" of the national economy' at the end of the First World War.[85] However, the other newcomer states in post-war Central and Eastern Europe, which were all without exception parliamentary democracies, were now eager to define political and economic goals and to win the support of the masses along the way. Peasant parties mushroomed all over the region, which – often in alliance with social-democratic parties – had much to say in the arenas of interwar politics and economics.[86] Amongst them, Czechoslovakia, which had largely escaped war and destruction, took the pole position. According to Rothschild, 'the existence of a disciplined proletariat and an organized peasantry side by side with the experienced bourgeoisie made for a more balanced society and a more integrated polity than existed among [the] neighbors.'[87] In other words, it was the very antithesis of Hungary.

---

81 Robert Bideleux and Ian Jeffries, *A History of Eastern Europe: Crisis and Change* (London, New York: Routledge, 2007), 315. In this book, the authors argue that – alongside Hungary – a reborn Poland was the second 'reactionary' state in interwar Central Europe in which landlordism did 'survive largely intact'. This is not the case, as can be confirmed by reading Borodziej, *Geschichte Polens im 20. Jahrhundert*, 130–9.

82 MacMillan, *Paris 1919*, 258.

83 Pistohlkors, 'Tiefgreifende agrarische Umwälzungen'.

84 These conclusions can be regarded as preliminary at best. Comparative research on the relationship between war, the state and the rural economy is still marginal. When it has been conducted, it has not focused on Central and Eastern Europe, but on the West. See: Avner Offer, *The First World War: An Agrarian Interpretation* (Oxford: Clarendon Press, 1991); and more recently, Benjamin Ziemann, 'Agrarian Society', in *The State*, vol. 2, *The Cambridge History of the First World War*, ed. Jay Winter (Cambridge: Cambridge University Press, 2014), 382–407.

85 Mihai Chioveanu, 'A Fragmented World: Cooperation, Conflict and Conquest in Central East Europe', *Studia Politica* 9, no. 1 (2009): 81–104, here 86.

86 von Puttkamer, 'Collapse and Restoration', 21. For information on the further development of the agrarian sector, see Dietmar Müller's Chapter 4, 'Statehood in Central, Eastern and Southeastern Europe: The interwar period', in this volume.

87 Rothschild, *East Central Europe*, 76. See also: Joachim von Puttkamer, 'Die tschechoslowakische Bodenreform von 1919: Soziale Umgestaltung als Fundament der Republik', *Bohemia* 46, no. 2 (2005): 315–42; and the volume *Challenges of Modernity* in this series.

Statehood: the First World War

4. War and destruction – relief and reconstruction (I)[88]

At two points in the twentieth century, the area between Germany and Russia was devastated, its economic prosperity wrecked and its population displaced, wounded, widowed, orphaned or killed in the millions. These hardships had a considerable influence on the destruction and building up of state structures in the region as well. Where these structures had vanished, they had to be quickly restored or at least partly replaced in order to deal with the collateral damage of warfare and to prevent the human catastrophe assuming even greater and unimaginable proportions. More often than not, the populations of these war-ridden lands, and the states that evolved from them, depended on outside help.

Foreign relief for Central and Eastern Europe during the First World War did not come without difficulties, though. While Belgium immediately became the focus of deep sympathy for the Western Allies and was well provided for, the same did not apply to the states east and south-east of Berlin and Vienna. A team of representatives from the Rockefeller Foundation and the American Red Cross that travelled to Europe in 1915 to estimate the amount of help civilians needed did not even consider visiting the eastern part of the continent and had to be spurred into action by the Central Powers, who were not eager to solve the material problems of their occupied territories either. The neediest patient was Poland:

> Throughout the territory examined the Commission found all industries stopped and the people idle. Many of the towns had no oil for lighting and no coal for heating or cooking. In many places the people were living upon potatoes or upon small quantities of supplies given to them by the soldiers. It was estimated that about three millions of people in the occupied territory were facing famine. Everywhere the distress seemed more extreme than it had been at any time in Belgium and with far less resisting power on the part of the people.[89]

The situation worsened with the advance of the Central Powers and the Russian retreat from Congress Poland, which was accompanied by a ruthless Russian scorched earth policy. As an American relief worker noted at the time,

> one Million . . . were made homeless in about five or six weeks, and . . . approximately 400,000 of these perished . . . I motored . . . for over 230 miles with German officers . . . and devastation is almost complete everywhere . . . the country is a waste, and the people are flat on their backs.[90]

However, although the Americans and the Germans alike pushed for an easing of the situation, the United Kingdom – in contrast to its policies towards occupied Belgium – stubbornly refused to relax the economic blockade.

---

88 See the fourth sub-chapter in Chapter 5 of this volume, p, 204, 'War and destruction – relief and reconstruction (II)'.

89 The Rockefeller Foundation, ed., *Annual Report, 1915* (New York, [n.d.]), 284.

90 Mieczysław B. Biskupski, 'Strategy, Politics, and Suffering: The Wartime Relief of Belgium, Serbia, and Poland, 1914–1918', in *Ideology, Politics and Diplomacy in East Central Europe*, ed. Mieczysław B. Biskupski (Rochester, NY: University of Rochester Press, 2003), 31–57, here 48.

A similar course of action can be observed in relation to Serbia, whose infrastructure after the Austrian assault of August 1914 had gone to rack and ruin. The virtually bankrupt country had lost 200,000 from a pre-war population of 4.3 million and was beset not only by isolated cases of famine but also by disease which, by the spring of 1915, had taken the lives of 150,000 civilians. An international Sanitary Commission was dispatched and managed to contain the spread of typhus, but no further financial or material aid was added to this rather inexpensive effort from the Allied Powers. When Serbia was invaded by the Central Powers in October 1915, Great Britain again did not consent to lifting the blockade against Serbia and held the German and Austrian occupiers solely responsible for supporting the country. This stance led to disaster. In 1917, 'the number of seriously ill again reached well into six figures and, because of food shortages, the fatality rate soared to one third of the population'.[91]

Nevertheless, the suffering of the Central and Eastern European populations did not leave the Western world completely unmoved. Indeed, it was the evocation of the desperate fate of the starving Polish population that first directed the attention and empathy of the American public towards the non-existent state in the heart of Europe. Without this, the Polish expatriates in the United States, headed by the famous pianist Jan Paderewski, would have encountered much more difficulty in promoting their dreams of independence and statehood. The public mood surely encouraged President Woodrow Wilson to evoke the image of 'a united, independent, and autonomous Poland' in his 'peace without victory' speech on 22 January 1917 and to make its realization one of his Fourteen Points. Analogous to this, Western support for a post-war Yugoslav state was also a result of its compassion for the nightmarish wartime experiences of the Serbians. Perhaps Mieczysław B. Biskupski overstates things a little when summarizing that 'both nations attracted widespread sympathy that prepared the groundwork for political support of their national aspirations',[92] but he certainly has a point.

Contrary to the general Allied relief organizations, the American Jewish Joint Distribution Committee (JDC, also colloquially known as 'Joint') focused its activities first and foremost on Eastern Europe, particularly Latvia and Poland, where the vast majority of European Jews under occupation lived and which had been devastated by the war.[93] In some parts of Latvia, about six thousand farms had been completely destroyed by the war, and the country lost 20 per cent of its pre-war horse and cattle stock. Comparable figures also applied to Estonia.[94] Since it provided aid in the form of money and not goods, the JDC did not face difficulties in overcoming the British sea blockade. In the military administration zone of Ober Ost, they cooperated with German field rabbis and the Benevolent Society of German Jews in Berlin (Hilfsverein der Deutschen Juden in Berlin), which in 1916 founded the Jewish Aid Committee for Poland and Lithuania (Jüdisches Hilfskomitee für Polen und Litauen). The JDC divided the area that was controlled by the Central Powers into three districts: the General Governments of Warsaw (1) and Lublin (2), and Lithuania and Courland (Latvia), with Vilnius at the centre (3). In occupied Poland, the Jewish representative bodies – such as the Jewish Workers' Union (Bund) or the Zionists – were particularly competitive, as they realized that 'to receive money means to acquire political power. Whoever can establish one more free kitchen has thousands

---

91 Ibid., 44.

92 Mieczysław B. Biskupski, 'The Diplomacy of Wartime Relief: The United States and Poland, 1914–1918', *Diplomatic History* 19, no. 3 (1995): 431–51, here 431.

93 Rakefet Zalashik and Nadav Davidovitch, 'Taking and Giving: The Case of the JDC and OZE in Lithuania 1919–26', *East European Jewish Affairs* 29, no. 1 (2009): 57–68.

94 Otto Korfes, 'Die Agrarrevolution in Estland und Lettland', in Sering, *Die agrarischen Umwälzungen*, 86.

Statehood: the First World War

more adherents. The relief work has become a political club, even though the relief work had concerned itself only with poverty'.[95] The activities of the JDC during the war were not limited to Central Europe, as its work reached far into the Balkans and even to Palestine.[96]

Although substantial material and financial aid necessarily had to be imported into the exhausted region from abroad, indigenous organized relief structures did exist, and they can be seen as a microcosm for features of self-government that even outlived the war. The Polish case is a prime example. The Central Citizens' Committee (Centralny Komitet Obywatelski) in Warsaw was founded in 1914 when it was still under Russian control; it subsequently acted even outside the Kingdom of Poland in Galicia and was tolerated by the new German authorities. Under the name Central Welfare Council (Rada Główna Opiekuńcza), after the war it expanded its remit into Lithuania, Latvia and Estonia.[97] Analogously, with the looming prospect of a collapse of state control as the war unfolded, genuine governmental tasks, such as food supply or medical care, were taken over by self-governmental bodies from the Balkans to the Baltic Sea. The political implementations of this shift of responsibility should not be underestimated. As Joachim von Puttkamer describes:

> The various Latvian, Lithuanian, Belorussian, Polish, and Armenian national refugee committees thus helped pave the way for the emerging nation states. . . . Welfare institutions that had been established by the various nationalities during the war took over social politics from the Habsburg state und thus strengthened the progression of national segregation in everyday life.[98]

Wartime relief work thus had the power to influence political and state-building processes. This is even truer for the immediate post-war period. According to Herbert Hoover, the man whose name is linked like no other to relief work in Europe in the wake of the First World War, the new states in Central and Eastern Europe built their state structures from scratch, and there was no marked continuity between the old state governments and the new ones, which had to deal with the needs of their starving and freezing populations from the winter of 1918–19 onwards. As a consequence, chaos and violence reigned during the first months of independence:

> In the shrunken enemy areas of Germany, Austria, Hungary and Turkey the old governments collapsed in revolutions and also emerged in democratic forms. . . . There was at the start some rioting and pillaging of the countryside. The poorer people of the towns and cities were for a time much worse off than they were before the Armistice when there were rigid food controls.[99]

---

95 Chiara Tessaris, 'The War Relief Work of the American Jewish Joint Distribution Committee in Poland and Lithuania, 1915–18', *East European Jewish Affairs* 40, no. 2 (2010): 127–44, here 141, quoting a report by Bernhard Kahn who was on a journey through Poland from 25 March to 7 April 1916.

96 Jaclyn Granick, 'Waging Relief: The Politics and Logistics of American Jewish War Relief in Europe and the Near East (1914–1918)', *First World War Studies* 5, no. 1 (2014): 55–68.

97 Małgorzata Przeniosło, *Rady opiekuńcze w Galicji 1919–1921* [The Central Welfare Council in Galicia, 1919–1921] (Kielce: Wydawnictwo Uniwersytetu Jana Kochanowskiego, 2014).

98 von Puttkamer, 'Collapse and Restoration', 16.

99 Herbert Hoover, 'We'll Have to Feed the World Again', in *Organization of American Relief in Europe 1918–1919: Including Negotiations Leading up to the Establishment of the Office of Director General of Relief at Paris by the Allied and Associated Powers – Selected Documents*, eds Suda L. Bane and Ralph H. Lutz (Stanford, CA: Stanford University Press, 1943), 6–25, here 13.

Central and Eastern Europe's dependency on assistance from abroad did not cease in peacetime, when its populations were threatened by widespread death and starvation of hitherto unknown proportions.

Three main motives catalyzed the gigantic American-led relief operation headed by Hoover which, during the nine months that followed the Armistice, pumped four million tons of goods and food – one billion dollars' worth – into Central and Eastern Europe. First of all, the United States saw themselves as a world-leading moral authority, whose duty it was to provide humanitarian aid in the face of the unparalleled hardships that had plagued the European continent in the aftermath of the Great War. Secondly, instead of playing the political card against the defeated Central Powers, President Wilson – in line with his peace without victory programme – engaged in a rather pragmatic economic policy towards Central and Southeastern Europe which anticipated the restoration of the region as a functioning market for American trade and exports. Thirdly, which is, so to speak, the flip side of this particular coin, he aimed to protect this sphere of American economic interests from ideological enemies of the Western-style free-enterprise system. Since the October Revolution of 1917 installed a communist state in Moscow, all American efforts were geared towards, as Hoover phrased it, 'stem[ming] the tide of Bolshevism'. In the meantime, post-revolutionary and post-war Russia, far from being pacified, was engulfed in a civil war and suffered a terrible famine that resulted in a death toll of somewhere between one and two million. The (principally) American efforts to help the beleaguered population of Central and Eastern Europe were not executed without the more or less hidden agenda of winning the successor states of the fallen empires over to the ideals of democracy, independence, freedom and national self-determination. 'Gentlemen, food is a weapon', the Soviet assistant people's commissar of foreign affairs, Maxim Litvinov, commented upon the signing of an agreement with Hoover's recently founded American Relief Administration in reference to food supplies for his starving country in August 1921.[100] In the years between 1918 and 1921, the whole of Central, Eastern and Southeastern Europe became a giant experimental arena for Western humanitarian aid.[101] These experiences would prove crucial after a second human catastrophe occurred within a generation, the Second World War, when the former US

---

100 Bertrand M. Patenaude, *The Big Show in Bololand: The American Relief Expedition to Soviet Russia in the Famine of 1921* (Stanford, CA: Stanford University Press, 2002), figures 197–98, here 32, 41. See also Bertrand M. Patenaude, 'Food as a Weapon', *Hoover Digest*, no. 1 (2007): www.hoover.org/research/food-weapon (accessed 22 February 2020); Adam Tooze, *The Deluge: The Great War and the Remaking of Global Order 1916–1931* (London: Lane, 2014). For a contemporary essay on the image of the 'tide of Bolshevism', see the unpublished manuscript of T.T.C. Gregory, *Stemming the Red Tide: A Sketch of the Activities of Herbert Hoover and his Band of Americans in Central Europe Following the Great War* (1919).

101 The literature on these efforts is vast, although it predominantly concentrates on Central Europe. See: Suzanne Ferrière, *Les États-Unis au secours de l'Europe, 1918–1923: L'oeuvre de Hoover en Europe depuis l'armistice* (Genève: Union Internationale de Sécours aux Enfants, 1923); Frank M. Surface and Raymond L. Bland, eds, *American Food in the World War and Reconstruction Period: Operations of the Organizations Under the Direction of Herbert Hoover, 1914 to 1924* (Stanford, CA: Stanford University Press, 1931); Bane and Lutz, *Organization of American Relief in Europe 1918–1919*; William R. Grove, *War's Aftermath: Polish Relief in 1919* (New York: House of Field, Inc., 1940); Herbert Hoover, *Famine in Forty-five Nations: The Battle on the Front Line, 1914–1923* (Chicago, IL: Henry Regnery, 1961); George J. Lerski, *Herbert Hoover and Poland* (Stanford, CA: Hoover Institution Press, 1977); Matthew L. Adams, *Cadillacs to Kiev: The American Relief Administration in Poland, 1919–1922* (Savannah, GA: Kortusphere Publishing, 2017); Matthew L. Adams, 'Herbert Hoover and the Organization of the American Relief Effort in Poland, 1919–1923', *European Journal of American Studies*, no. 2 (2009), http://ejas.revues.org/7627 (accessed 22 February 2020).

director of the American Relief Administration, who in the intervening time was even elected 31st President of the United States, expressed once again the need to 'feed the world'.[102]

5. War and belonging – displaced persons and statelessness (I)[103]

The First World War uprooted millions of civilians, a development which began before shots were fired in Sarajevo. The seemingly endless lines of displaced persons were already a tragic side effect of the Balkan Wars. Members of the Carnegie Endowment's Commission reported what they saw in autumn 1913:

> No account of the sufferings of the noncombatant population in Macedonia would be complete which failed to describe the final exodus of Moslems and Greeks from the territory assigned to Bulgaria. Vast numbers of Moslems arrived on the outskirts of Salonica during our stay there. We saw them camped to the number, it is said, of 8,000, in the fields and by the roadside. They had come with their bullock carts, and whole families found their only shelter in these primitive vehicles. They had left their villages and their fields, and to all of them the future was a blank. They did not wish to go to Asia, nor did they wish to settle, they knew not how nor where, in Greek territory. They regretted their homes, and spoke with a certain passive fatalism of the events which had made them wanderers.[104]

This early picture became a deplorably common sight across the theatre of the First World War in Eastern Europe. Surprisingly, in the beginning most people were pushed into an unknown future far away from their homes, not by enemy soldiers but by their own governments. As I mentioned earlier in this chapter, in 1915 the Russian army expelled hundreds of thousands of inhabitants of the empire's western borders, who they regarded as a security risk, into the interior, namely ethnic Germans, Poles and Jews. Later, of course, the advance of the victorious German and Austrian troops exacerbated the problem.[105] The number of displaced persons in Russia grew to over three million during 1915, almost doubling again by early 1917 and was arguably a major factor in destabilizing the Russian state, which subsequently disintegrated in the chaos of revolution and civil war.[106]

It is therefore not surprising that from 1918 onwards, the term 'Russian refugees' – who in reality were refugees from former tsarist Russia with diverse ethnic backgrounds – became synonymous with the refugee problem as a whole, especially in the Western world, which a lot of those who had been uprooted viewed as their dream destination. First of all though, they had to travel westward. 'For five and a half years we have scarcely opened a morning paper without reading a head-line telling of the sufferings of some new group of victims of the war', lamented the director of the Civil Affairs Office of the American Red Cross: 'This morning – January

---

102 Hoover, 'We'll Have to Feed the World Again'.

103 See the fifth sub-chapter in Chapter 5 of this volume, p.000, 'War and belonging – displaced persons and statelessness (II)'.

104 *Report of the International Commission to Inquire into the Causes and Conduct of the Balkan Wars* (Washington, DC: Carnegie Endowment for International Peace, 1914).

105 Jochen Böhler, 'Generals and Warlords', here 52–7; Gatrell, *A Whole Empire Walking*, 15–32; and Graf, *The Reign of the Generals*.

106 Peter Holquist, *Making War, Forging Revolution: Russia's Continuum of Crisis, 1914–1921* (Cambridge, MA: Harvard University Press, 2002).

10, 1920 – it happens to be Poland, and the Red Cross reports that, of its twenty millions, four millions are refugees at this moment.'[107] Four hundred thousand Latvians left revolutionary Russia for Latvia by 1918, but their number reached its peak between 1920 and 1922 following a Latvian–Russian Refugees Re-evacuation Agreement.[108] Lithuania took 350,000 refugees from Russia between 1918 and 1924.[109] As it was at the beginning, so it was at the very end of the global conflict – with hundreds of thousands of homeless people wandering through the Balkans. Fridtjof Nansen, the famous Norwegian explorer and, after 1921, high commissioner for Russian refugees, described his impressions after arriving in Constantinople (Istanbul) during the Greco-Turkish war in late 1922: 'I saw a whole city before me with its thousands of lights – it was their [the Greek refugees'] camps spread over the plain, camp-fire by camp-fire, and there they were sleeping on the ground without shelter of any kind.'[110] The Treaty of Lausanne of 1923 put the hostilities to an end, but it further exacerbated the situation by allowing for further gigantic movements of people: Muslims (mostly Turks) had to leave Greece, and Christians (mostly Greeks) had to leave Turkey. This coordinated two-way mass deportation, unparalleled in history, produced 'the largest population exchange of the post-World War I period, involving over 1.5 million people'.[111]

The number of people in the West who had fled their homes in the course of the war was considerable – almost two million French (in France), more than 300,000 Belgian (in France) and more than 100,000 Italian refugees were officially reported in 1918[112] – but this did not equal the human catastrophe that was unfolding in Central, Eastern and Southeastern Europe at the same time, especially if one not only looks at the total numbers, but also at the living conditions that were witnessed by those assisting foreign relief organizations: 'We came presently to a house made out of half a cistern', Sidney Loch from the Society of Friends (Quakers) noted in 1919 in Eastern Poland:

> A widow, with three small children, had found her way back from Russia, leaving the husband behind her on some typhus death-bed. She had got back at last to her six *desyatinas* [about 16 acres] of ground. She had recognized it by the ups and downs. The house she expected was not standing – not one board of it. Searching round at her wits' end, she had found the half of a large galvanized-iron cistern, which one of the armies had left behind instead of the house, and she and her children had gone to live inside as a dog and its puppies go into a kennel.[113]

---

107 Homer Folks, *The Human Costs of the War* (New York: Harper & Brothers, 1920), xiii–xiv.

108 Aija Priedite, 'Latvian Refugees and the Latvian Nation State During and After World War One', in *Homelands: War, Population and Statehood in Eastern Europe and Russia, 1918–1924*, eds Nick Baron and Peter Gatrell (London: Anthem Press, 2004), 35–52, here 46–7.

109 Tomas Balkelis, 'In Search of a Native Realm: The Return of World War One Refugees to Lithuania', in Baron and Gatrell, *Homelands: War, Population and Statehood*, 74–97, here 76.

110 Bruno Cabanes, *The Great War and the Origins of Humanitarianism, 1918–1924* (Cambridge: Cambridge University Press, 2014), 174.

111 Ibid., 178. For further reading on the Greek refugee crisis, see Harry J. Psomiades, *Fridtjof Nansen and the Greek Refugee Crisis 1922–1924: A Study on the Politics of International Humanitarian Intervention and the Greek-Turkish Obligatory Population Exchange Agreement* (Bloomingdale, IL: The Asia Minor and Pontos Hellenic Research Center, 2011).

112 Peter Gatrell and Philippe Nivet, 'Refugees', in *Society*, vol. 3, *The Cambridge History of the First World War*, ed. Jay Winter (Cambridge: Cambridge University Press, 2014), 186–215, here 187–92.

113 Joice M. Nankivell and Sydney Loch, *The River of a Hundred Ways: Life in the War-Devastated Areas of Eastern Poland* (London: Allen & Unwin, 1924), 40.

Statehood: the First World War

The situation of refugees in the Baltics, Hungary and certain parts of Yugoslavia, Greece and Turkey was very similar by that time.[114] These places endured extreme hardships, lack of shelter, exhaustion, the spread of epidemics and high fatality rates; it was an experience that was more typical for Eastern and Southeastern Europe than it was for Western Europe in the wake of the First World War. However, by its very nature, the 'refugee question' was a transnational one. By 1922, most of the Russian refugees had settled outside Russia, with 'more than a quarter . . . in Germany. One-fifth lived in Poland, and most of the remainder lived in the Balkan states, France and China'.[115]

The effect of the Russian refugee problem on state-building in Central Europe was twofold. Firstly, regions such as Latvia were faced with the challenge of housing hundreds of thousands of people while having been deserted by a comparable number of people only a matter of years before. The country's total population declined during the war and post-war years by almost 30 per cent. The mortality rate among the total of roughly 700,000 Latvian refugees exceeded 40 per cent; another 20 per cent of them remained in Russia. As such, the Latvian nation state that was to emerge from the aftermath of the Great War lacked over half of the population that in 1914 spoke, and considered itself to be, Latvian. Secondly, the refugee problem in the country produced a group of managers of humanitarian aid whose male representatives joined the political elite of the newly founded Latvian state.[116]

However, it was mainly through the invention of a new category of citizenship that the Russian refugees influenced the formation of statehood at the time. The country they left behind, the Russian Empire, had gone up in smoke. The new Soviet state that had emerged regarded most of the refugees as anti-Bolshevik and a threat to its integrity, refusing to accept them as Russian citizens. As a result, millions of people in the middle of the continent had literally overnight become stateless, lacking the guarantees of legal and material protection every state's citizens should enjoy, at least in theory. Their interests now were attended by non-state institutions: the League of Nations from above, and various relief organizations from below (the latter of which was the subject of the previous sub-chapter). The founding of the League of Nations itself was a result of the inability of single states to deal with the legal challenges of displacement and statelessness, which after 1918 concerned not only refugees, but also ethnic minorities, who had not been displaced from their homes by forced expulsion but by the drastic changes in the political character or geographical shape of the state they had hitherto lived in.[117]

---

114 Tomas Balkelis, 'From Defence to Revolution: Lithuanian Paramilitary Groups in 1918 and 1919', *Acta Historica Universitatis Klaipedensis* 28 (2014): 43–56; Robert Nemes, 'Refugees and Antisemitism in Hungary During the First World War', in *Sites of European Antisemitism in the Age of Mass Politics, 1880–1918*, eds Robert Nemes and Daniel L. Unowsky (Waltham, MA: Brandeis University Press), 236–54; István I. Mócsy, *The Uprooted: Hungarian Refugees and Their Impact on Hungary's Domestic Politics, 1918–1921* (New York: Columbia University Press 1983); David Mitrany, *The Effect of the War in Southeastern Europe* (New Haven, CT: Yale University Press, 1936).

115 Peter Gatrell, 'Refugees', in *1914–1918-online: International Encyclopedia of the First World War*, eds Ute Daniel et al. (2014), https://encyclopedia.1914-1918-online.net/article/refugees (accessed 22 February 2020); and Martyn Housden, 'White Russians Crossing the Black Sea: Fridtjof Nansen, Constantinople and the First Modern Repatriation of Refugees Displaced by Civil Conflict, 1922–23', *Slavonic and East European Review* 88, no. 3 (2010): 495–524.

116 Nick Baron and Peter Gatrell, 'Population Displacement, State-Building, and Social Identity in the Lands of the Former Russian Empire, 1917–23', *Kritika: Explorations in Russian and Eurasian History* 4 (2003): 51–100, here 72–3.

117 On triangle citizenship, protection and freedom in 20th and 21st century Europe, see Dieter Gosewinkel, *Schutz und Freiheit? Staatsbürgerschaft in Europa im 20. und 21. Jahrhundert* (Berlin: Suhrkamp, 2016).

The newly drawn borders of Central and Eastern Europe had burdened the region with a bitter legacy. Due to the mix of people that had shaped the region's history, every frontier was a contact zone between two countries and, at the same time, a dividing line that ran through century-old ethnic, linguistic and religious communities with shared feelings of belonging. The borders themselves, of course, were not an invention of the nationalizing states of the early twentieth century, and the contact zones between empires had also always featured a certain amount of unrest and mobility. Up until the First World War, Mark Biondich writes,

> these borderlands never constituted a multiethnic idyll, but neither should they be understood as zones of perpetual instability and violence. Several recent studies of these borderlands suggest that violence was driven primarily by state elites and nationalizing states; over the course of the twentieth century the borderlands were moulded and transformed into relatively homogeneous spaces by various state projects.[118]

At the beginning of the 1920s, some groups that had been at least partly autonomous entities in one empire before the war found themselves spread over the territory of two, three or even more of the First World War's successor states. Prior to 1914, their affairs had been a matter of negotiation with local authorities and the imperial capital. Now, it was hard to say where they had to appeal to safeguard their group interests. Especially in places where they constituted one of the new states' minorities, there was a high risk that they would be bullied by the elite representing the majority.[119] In addition to the political unrest of the immediate post-war period, and the imminent threat of another war, this was the major reason for the great powers' attempts in Paris to establish intrastate procedures and supranational structures for the settling of current or future internal or external conflicts. These procedures were to be outlined in annexes to the peace agreements and were called the minority treaties; the structures were to be imposed through the founding of an international court of appeal called the League of Nations. However, the League of Nations was not a super state. It was 'an experiment in internationalism at a time when the counterclaims of nationalism were running powerfully in the opposite direction' and never replaced state sovereignty; on the contrary, the independence of the member states was sacrosanct, and the League's declarations were not legally binding. As a result, as Carole Fink has noted, the new international system for the protection of minorities, which had been inscribed into the peace treaties by France, Great Britain and the United States, repeatedly proved rather ineffective, mainly because it was 'born under the cloud of dictated arrangements imposed on unwilling governments on behalf of highly diverse, unnamed and largely unconsulted minorities in a devastated region of Europe',[120] and it lacked a legal institution above state level to enforce such protections.[121]

---

118 Mark Biondich, 'Eastern Borderlands and Prospective Shatter Zones: Identity and Conflict in East Central and Southeastern Europe on the Eve of the First World War', in Böhler, Borodziej and von Puttkamer, *Legacies of Violence: Eastern Europe's First World War*, 25–50, here 27.

119 Ryan Gingeras, 'Nation States, Minorities, and Refugees, 1914–1923', in *The Oxford Handbook of European History, 1914–1945*, ed. Nicholas Doumanis (Oxford: Oxford University Press, 2016), 138–59.

120 Carole Fink, 'Minority Rights as an International Question', *Contemporary European History* 9, no. 3 (2000): 385–400, here 390.

121 Zara S. Steiner, *The Lights That Failed: European International History, 1919–1933* (Oxford: Oxford University Press, 2005), 345–86, here 349.

In contrast to the problems relating to minorities, the refugee crisis, at the outset of the 1920s, was a problem the new nation states could not afford to belittle, ignore or declare a purely domestic matter. It was clearly in their own interest to seek out international agreements. While they tended to oust or assimilate minorities, if necessary by force, and ignore their alignment with areas outside their territory, in general they did not want refugees to become citizens of their respective states but to leave the country as soon as possible. The inability to cope with the refugee problem purely domestically, and the desire to pass it on to neighbouring or more remote states at the first opportunity, meant that cooperation rather than obstruction and pragmatic answers rather than diplomatic quarrels were required.

Consequently, the nomination of Nansen as high commissioner for Russian refugees in 1921 was widely welcomed. Nansen was two things in one: a powerful symbol of hope, given his own personal history of having braved the polar winter of 1895–6 without almost any resources, and a brilliant organizer. Although he tirelessly travelled the continent to accomplish his mission, the impact of his efforts was totally dependent on the refugees' host countries, since his office was not equipped with any financial means to alleviate the situation of the suffering people it represented. Thus, Nansen's greatest achievement as high commissioner was not material but judicial.

Many refugee organizations had emphasized again and again that, apart from food and shelter, what their dependents were in dire need of was the triumvirate of legality, liberty and latitude. Most of them had not only lost their home state, but also its protection. Apart from being stateless themselves, for many refugees, vital questions about crossing borders, marriage, rights of inheritance or their newborn children's citizenship remained unsolved for years and thus left hundreds of thousands in a legal grey area. To make the situation worse, a continent that had witnessed millions on the move was now sealing itself off at the same time, making passage from one country to another a bureaucratic nightmare. What Nansen was aiming for was an internationally recognized identification paper, which would be issued to refugees who had been deprived of or were unable to prove their citizenship, and which would at least partly restore their lost rights.

What he came up with in the summer of 1922 was the Nansen Certificate, better known as the 'Nansen passport', which in many ways fell short of what many refugees might have hoped for. It typically expired within the course of one year, and of all the problems mentioned above, it only addressed the legal crossing of state borders for its bearers. Issued by the state of residence, it allowed the individual to travel abroad but not necessarily to return. Its initially narrow limitation to Russian refugees meant that it was not available to other national groups, such as the Armenians who had fled the Ottoman Empire after the genocide of 1915, and who only became beneficiaries of the Nansen Certificate in 1933. Vladimir Nabokov spoke of it disparagingly in hindsight as:

> a very inferior document of a sickly green hue. Its holder was little better than a criminal on parole and had to go through most hideous ordeals every time he wished to travel from one country to another, and the smaller the countries the worse the fuss they made.[122]

Reading between these bitter lines, one can sense the humiliation that was experienced by legions of young men, such as the subsequently world-famous Russian novelist, who were

---

122 Vladimir Nabokov, *Speak, Memory: An Autobiography Revisited* (New York: Putnam, 1966), 276.

scrutinized and questioned for hours in narrow border stations by suspicious immigration officials. But despite its shortcomings, the Nansen Certificate was a novelty, since its bearers could invoke an international authority – the League of Nations – that guaranteed their rights where their states of origin did not, and in the end it was accepted by 52 states.[123] Nansen, surely deservedly, was awarded the Nobel Peace Prize for his commitment to the cause of prisoners of war and refugees in 1922, and, eight years after his death, the Nansen International Office for Refugees also won the prize in 1938 for continuously issuing the Nansen Certificate to an ever widening group of people on the run. As a side note, Nabokov narrowly missed out on the Nobel Prize in Literature a few months before his frustrations with the document quoted above were published.[124]

Apart from its material, diplomatic, political and legal implementations, the refugee experience in the wake of the First World War shocked the whole continent. By deracinating millions of people and leaving them to an uncertain future, it contributed not only to an atmosphere of restlessness and volatility, but also to the mobility and flexibility that was characteristic of European metropolises in the 1920s. In his novel *Flight Without End* from 1927, Joseph Roth describes the end of a half-Jewish, Austrian officer's odyssey from Siberia to Paris via Moscow and Vienna on a sombre note:

> It was at this hour [at 4 p.m. on 27 August 1926], that my friend Tunda, thirty-two years of age, healthy and vigorous, a strong young man of diverse talents, stood on the Place de la Madeleine, in the centre of the capital of the world, without any idea what to do. He had no occupation, no desire, no hope, no ambition, and not even any self-love. No one in the whole world was as superfluous as he.[125]

There is also another side to this story, namely the perception that the masses of refugees posed a threat to national integrity and ethnic identity, which was especially shared in ultraconservative circles. This could easily be used as an argument for propaganda, further radicalization and the destabilization of the democratic state system of the 1920s. A leaflet from a German right-wing party published in the summer of 1921 stated that

> Hardly three years have elapsed since the Jewish apostles of the Future State promised to bring men, in Russia, the paradise by way of revolution. . . . While now millions of Russian workers, worn out by hunger and despair, drag themselves from the cities to the country that equally suffers hunger, yet perishing miserably just the same, the flood of the destroyers of this Russian people, covered with diamonds, rolls towards the west of Europe, towards Germany and Switzerland.[126]

It was the year in which a certain Adolf Hitler became the leader of that very party.

---

123 Cabanes, *The Great War and the Origins of Humanitarianism, 1918–1924*, 133–73.
124 Alison Flood, 'Nabokov, Neruda and Borges Revealed as Losers of 1965 Nobel Prize', *The Guardian*, 6 January 2016, www.theguardian.com/books/2016/jan/06/borges-auden-nabokov-neruda-nobel-prize-literature-1965 (accessed 22 February 2020).
125 Joseph Roth, *Flight Without End: A Novel* (Woodstock: Overlook Press, 2003), Chapter 34.
126 Leaflet of the Nationalist Socialist German Worker's Party 'Help Soviet Russia!', undated (ca. summer 1921), printed in: Adolf Hitler, *Mein Kampf: Complete and Unabridged, Fully Annotated*, with the assistance of John Chamberlain et al., 19th ed. (Boston, MA: Houghton Mifflin Company, 1941), 537.

Statehood: the First World War

Further reading

Abramson, Henry. *A Prayer for the Government: Ukrainians and Jews in Revolutionary Times, 1917–1920* (Cambridge, MA: Harvard University Press, 1999).

Adams, Matthew L. *Cadillacs to Kiev: The American Relief Administration in Poland, 1919–1922* (Savannah, GA: Kortusphere Publishing, 2017).

Bane, Suda L., and Ralph H. Lutz, eds. *Organization of American Relief in Europe 1918–1919: Including Negotiations Leading up to the Establishment of the Office of Director General of Relief at Paris by the Allied and Associated Powers – Selected Documents* (Stanford, CA: Stanford University Press, 1943).

Bartov, Omer, and Eric D. Weitz, eds. *Shatterzone of Empires: Coexistence and Violence in the German, Habsburg, Russian, and Ottoman Borderlands* (Bloomington, IN: Indiana University Press, 2013).

Berend, Iván T., and György Ránki. *Economic Development in East-Central Europe in the 19th and 20th Centuries* (New York: Columbia University Press, 1974).

Bideleux, Robert, and Ian Jeffries. *A History of Eastern Europe: Crisis and Change* (London and New York: Routledge, 2007).

Biondich, Mark. *Stjepan Radić, the Croat Peasant Party, and the Politics of Mass Mobilization, 1904–1928* (Toronto: University of Toronto Press, 2000).

Biondich, Mark. *The Balkans: Revolution, War, and Political Violence since 1878* (Oxford: Oxford University Press, 2011).

Bodo, Béla. *The White Terror: Antisemitic and Political Violence in Hungary, 1919–1921* (Abingdon: Routledge, 2019).

Böhler, Jochen. *Civil War in Central Europe, 1918–1921: The Reconstruction of Poland* (Oxford: Oxford University Press, 2018).

Böhler, Jochen, Włodzimierz Borodziej, and Joachim von Puttkamer, eds. *Legacies of Violence: Eastern Europe's First World War* (München: Oldenbourg, 2014).

Borodziej, Włodzimierz. *Geschichte Polens im 20. Jahrhundert* (München: Beck, 2010).

Brovkin, Vladimir. *Behind the Front Lines of the Civil War: Political Parties and Social Movements in Russia, 1918–1922* (Princeton, NJ: Princeton University Press, 1994).

Bruski, Jan J. *Petlurowcy: Centrum Państwowe Ukraińskiej Republiki Ludowej na wychodźstwie, 1919–1924* [Petliurovians: The Ukrainian People's Republic Government in exile, 1919–1924] (Kraków: Arcana, 2000).

Cabanes, Bruno. *The Great War and the Origins of Humanitarianism, 1918–1924* (Cambridge: Cambridge University Press, 2014).

Calic, Marie-Janine. *Geschichte Jugoslawiens im 20. Jahrhundert* (München: Beck, 2010).

Clark, Christopher. *The Sleepwalkers: How Europe Went to War in 1914* (New York: Harper, 2013).

Conrad, Benjamin. *Umkämpfte Grenzen, umkämpfte Bevölkerung: Die Entstehung der Staatsgrenzen der Zweiten Polnischen Republik 1918–1923* (Stuttgart: Steiner, 2014).

Conze, Werner. *Polnische Nation und deutsche Politik im Ersten Weltkrieg* (Köln: Böhlau, 1958).

Cornwall, Mark, and John Newman, eds. *Sacrifice and Rebirth: The Legacy of the Last Habsburg War* (New York: Berghahn Books, 2016).

Dornik, Wolfram, Georgiy Kasianov, Hannes Leidinger, Peter Lieb, Alekseij Miller, Bogdan Musial, and Vasyl Rasevyc, eds. *Die Ukraine: Zwischen Selbstbestimmung und Fremdherrschaft 1917–1922* (Graz: Leykam, 2011).

Figes, Orlando. *Peasant Russia, Civil War: The Volga Countryside in Revolution, 1917–1921* (Oxford: Clarendon Press, 1989).

Folks, Homer. *The Human Costs of the War* (New York: Harper & Brothers, 1920).

Gatrell, Peter. *A Whole Empire Walking: Refugees in Russia During World War I* (Bloomington, IN: Indiana University Press, 1999).

Gatrell, Peter, and Philippe Nivet. 'Refugees', in *Society, vol. 3, The Cambridge History of the First World War*, ed. Jay Winter (Cambridge: Cambridge University Press, 2014), 186–215.

Gaudin, Corinne. *Ruling Peasants: Village and State in Late Imperial Russia* (DeKalb, IL: Northern Illinois University Press, 2007).

Gingeras, Ryan. 'Nation States, Minorities, and Refugees, 1914–1923', in *The Oxford Handbook of European History, 1914–1945*, ed. Nicholas Doumanis (Oxford: Oxford University Press, 2016), 138–59.

Gosewinkel, Dieter. *Schutz und Freiheit? Staatsbürgerschaft in Europa im 20. und 21. Jahrhundert* (Berlin: Suhrkamp, 2016).

Graf, Daniel W. 'The Reign of the Generals: Military Government in Western Russia, 1914–1915' (PhD diss., University of Nebraska, 1972).

Grove, William R. *War's Aftermath: Polish Relief in 1919* (New York: House of Field, Inc., 1940).

Gumz, Jonathan E. *The Resurrection and Collapse of Empire in Habsburg Serbia, 1914–1918* (New York: Cambridge University Press, 2009).

Hagen, Mark von. *War in a European Borderland: Occupations and Occupation Plans in Galicia and Ukraine, 1914–1918* (Seattle, WA: University of Washington Press, 2007).

Holquist, Peter. *Making War, Forging Revolution: Russia's Continuum of Crisis, 1914–1921* (Cambridge, MA: Harvard University Press, 2002).

Hoover, Herbert. *Famine in Forty-five Nations: The Battle on the Front Line, 1914–1923, vol. 3, An American Epic* (Chicago, IL: Henry Regnery, 1961).

Kauffman, Jesse. *Elusive Alliance: The German Occupation of Poland in World War I* (Cambridge, MA: Harvard University Press, 2015).

Lehnstaedt, Stephan. *Imperiale Polenpolitik in den Weltkriegen: Eine vergleichende Studie zu den Mittelmächten und zu NS-Deutschland* (Osnabrück: Fibre, 2017).

Lerski, George J. *Herbert Hoover and Poland* (Stanford, CA: Hoover Institution Press, 1977).

Liulevicius, Vejas G. *War Land on the Eastern Front: Culture, National Identity, and German Occupation in World War I* (Cambridge: Cambridge University Press, 2000).

MacMillan, Margaret. *Paris 1919: Six Months that Changed the World* (New York: Random House, 2003).

Magocsi, Paul R. *A History of Ukraine: The Land and its Peoples* (Toronto: University of Toronto Press, 2010).

Mayerhofer, Lisa. *Zwischen Freund und Feind – Deutsche Besatzung in Rumänien 1916–1918* (München: Meidenbauer, 2010).

Mitrany, David. *The Effect of the War in Southeastern Europe* (New Haven, CT: Yale University Press, 1936).

Mitrović, Andrej. *Serbia's Great War, 1914–1918* (London: Hurst, 2007).

Mócsy, István I. *The Uprooted: Hungarian Refugees and Their Impact on Hungary's Domestic Politics, 1918–1921* (New York: Columbia University Press, 1983).

Nachtigal, Reinhard, and Lana Radauer. 'Prisoners of War (Russian Empire)', in *1914–1918-online: International Encyclopedia of the First World War*, eds Ute Daniel, Peter Gatrell, Oliver Janz, Heather Jones, Jennifer Keene, Alan Kramer, and Bill Nasson (2014), doi:10.15463/ie1418.10386 (accessed 22 February 2020).

Nankivell, Joice M., and Sydney Loch. *The River of a Hundred Ways: Life in the War-Devastated Areas of Eastern Poland* (London: Allen & Unwin, 1924).

Nemes, Robert, and Daniel L. Unowsky, eds. *Sites of European Antisemitism in the Age of Mass Politics, 1880–1918* (Waltham, MA: Brandeis University Press, 2014).

Offer, Avner. *The First World War: An Agrarian Interpretation* (Oxford: Clarendon Press, 1991).

Opfer, Björn. *Im Schatten des Krieges: Besatzung oder Anschluss – Befreiung oder Unterdrückung? Eine komparative Untersuchung über die bulgarische Herrschaft in Vardar-Makedonien 1915–1918 und 1941–1944* (Münster: LIT Verlag, 2005).

Pallot, Judith. *Land Reform in Russia 1906–1917: Peasant Responses to Stolypin's Project of Rural Transformation* (Oxford: Oxford University Press, 1999).

Palmer, Alan. *The Lands between: A History of East-Central Europe since the Congress of Vienna* (London: Weidenfeld & Nicolson, 1970).

Patenaude, Bertrand M. *The Big Show in Bololand: The American Relief Expedition to Soviet Russia in the Famine of 1921* (Stanford, CA: Stanford University Press, 2002).

Prusin, Alexander V. *Nationalizing a Borderland: War, Ethnicity, and Anti-Jewish Violence in East Galicia, 1914–1920* (Tuscaloosa, AL: University of Alabama Press, 2005).

Przeniosło, Małgorzata. *Rady opiekuńcze w Galicji 1919–1921* [The Central Welfare Council in Galicia, 1919–1921] (Kielce: Wydawnictwo Uniwersytetu Jana Kochanowskiego, 2014).

Rachamimov, Alon. *POWs and the Great War: Captivity on the Eastern Front* (Oxford: Berg, 2002).

Revutsky, Abraham, ed. *Wrenching Times in Ukraine: Memoir of a Jewish Minister* (St. John's, Newfoundland, Canada: Yksuver Publications, 1998).

Ristović, Milan. 'Occupation During and After the War (South East Europe)', in *1914–1918-online: International Encyclopedia of the First World War*, eds Ute Daniel, Peter Gatrell, Oliver Janz, Heather Jones, Jennifer Keene, Alan Kramer, and Bill Nasson (2014), doi:10.15463/ie1418.10481 (accessed 22 February 2020).

Romsics, Ignác. *Hungary in the Twentieth Century* (Budapest: Corvina Books Ltd., 1999).

Rothschild, Joseph. *East Central Europe Between the Two World Wars* (Seattle, WA: University of Washington Press, 1992).

Statehood: the First World War

Scheer, Tamara. 'Besatzungsregime im Vergleich: Serbiens Wirtschaft unter österreichisch-ungarischer und bulgarischer Herrschaft (1915–1918)', in *'Mitteleuropa' und 'Südosteuropa' als Planungsraum: Wirtschafts- und kulturpolitische Expertisen im Zeitalter der Weltkriege*, ed. Carola Sachse (Göttingen: Wallstein-Verlag, 2010), 315–39.

Schnell, Felix. *Räume des Schreckens: Gewalträume und Gruppenmilitanz in der Ukraine, 1905–1933* (Hamburg: Hamburger Edition, 2012).

Steiner, Zara S. *The Lights That Failed: European International History, 1919–1933* (Oxford: Oxford University Press, 2005).

Stempin, Arkadiusz. *Próba 'moralnego podboju' Polski przez Cesarstwo Niemieckie w latach I wojny światowej* [The German Empire's attempt to achieve Poland's 'moral subjugation' during the First World War] (Warszawa: Wydawnictwo Neriton, 2013).

Strazhas, Abba. *Deutsche Ostpolitik im Ersten Weltkrieg: Der Fall Ober Ost 1915–1917* (Wiesbaden: Harrassowitz, 1993).

Tooze, Adam. *The Deluge: The Great War and the Remaking of Global Order 1916–1931* (London: Lane, 2014).

Velychenko, Stephen. *State-building in Revolutionary Ukraine: A Comparative Study of Governments and Bureaucrats, 1917–1922* (Toronto: University of Toronto Press, 2011).

Westerhoff, Christian. *Zwangsarbeit im Ersten Weltkrieg: Deutsche Arbeitskräftepolitik im besetzten Polen und Litauen 1914–1918* (Paderborn: Schöningh Verlag, 2011).

Yekelchyk, Serhy. *Ukraine: Birth of a Modern Nation* (Oxford: Oxford University Press, 2007).

4

STATEHOOD IN CENTRAL, EASTERN AND SOUTHEASTERN EUROPE

The interwar period

Dietmar Müller

Historiography and fields of statehood

The period between the two world wars is presented quite positively in most post-1989 Central and Eastern European historiographies as an era of successful economic modernization, state consolidation and the political as well as socio-cultural inclusion of citizens.[1] Some authors argue against the use of the term 'between-the-wars' or 'interwar period' altogether, referring as it does to the foreign-policy moments framing this period, claiming that rather than emphasizing extraneous factors, which threaten to swallow up autonomous developments in the countries of Central, Eastern and Southeastern Europe, one should try to lend greater expression to the independence, democracy and success stories of this period. Critical studies of this post-imperial and pre-socialist era, by contrast, tend to direct their primary focus towards the crisis-prone economies, fragile political systems and the precarious situation of ethnic and religious minorities in the new countries that emerged and defined themselves as nation states.[2] Beyond these

---

1 For an overview of post-communist historiography, see Ulf Brunnbauer, ed., *(Re)Writing History: Historiography in Southeastern Europe after Socialism* (Münster: LIT, 2004); Sorin Antohi et al., eds, *Narratives Unbound: Historical Studies in Post-Communist Eastern Europe* (Budapest: CEU Press, 2007).

2 Still quite relevant as an introduction, Joseph Rothschild, *East Central Europe Between the Two World Wars* (Seattle, WA: University of Washington Press, 1974). See also Hans Lemberg, ed., *Ostmitteleuropa zwischen den beiden Weltkriegen (1918–1939): Stärke und Schwäche der neuen Staaten, nationale Minderheiten* (Marburg: Verlag Herder-Institut, 1997); Boris Barth, *Europa nach dem Großen Krieg: Die Krise der Demokratie in der Zwischenkriegszeit, 1918–1938* (Frankfurt a.M.: Campus Verlag, 2016). On social and economic history, see Michael Charles Kaser and Edward Albert Radice, eds, *The Economic History of Eastern Europe*, vol. 1, *Economic Structure and Performance between the Two Wars* (Oxford: Clarendon Press, 1985); *Handbuch der europäischen Wirtschafts- und Sozialgeschichte*, vol. 6, *Europäische Wirtschafts- und Sozialgeschichte vom Ersten Weltkrieg bis zur Gegenwart* (Stuttgart: Clett-Cotta, 1987); Bogdan Murgescu, *România şi Europa: Acumularea decalajelor economice (1500–2010)* [Romania and Europe: accumulating economic lags (1500–2010)] (Bucharest: Polirom, 2010).

Statehood: the interwar period

historiographic fault lines, which nowadays are marked by a post-communist idealization of pre-communist times, more long-term lines of development can also be observed in the interwar period, some of which date back to the imperial era, and some of which continued under state socialism. An analysis of long-term social, cultural and institutional developments will have a natural predilection for continuities as opposed to discontinuities, the latter being the preferred perspective of approaches focusing on political history. In other words, the over-emphasis on a new beginning after 1918, and the harsh break with the liberal-democratic and market-economy system after 1945, encourages an idealized view of the period between the wars. Part of this chapter is a discussion as to what extent, if at all, the interwar period should be considered a distinct period of history.

The current chapter will use a comparative and systematic approach to describe the transformation of statehood in the countries of Central, Eastern and Southeastern Europe during the interwar period in the fields of agrarian reform and agricultural policy, social security, population and family policy, as well as communal housing and urbanism. Scholars have not yet systematically investigated the nature of statehood in these countries. All that exist are isolated inquiries in numerous fields. The most impressive of these have been done in the area of economic history, with evidence pointing to economic nationalism in the region, not only as a reaction to the collapse of the trade, finance and transport system that existed in the Habsburg monarchy but also as a development strategy for the newly formed nation states in the region. If the breakthrough of economic nationalism is generally linked to the Great Depression and its aftermath in the 1930s, then this is merely an instance of the much broader phenomenon of statism being reduced to economic nationalism.[3] This narrow focus fails to recognize that the options open to new elites were already undergoing a clear shift towards statism due to the pressures of an organized war economy,[4] but also as an expression of their plans to forcefully modernize all spheres of society and sectors of the economy. In this regard, their plans converged with the expectations of the population who hoped that the new states would bring them greater political representation and, not least of all, economic and social betterment. The transformation from statehood to an interventionist and sometimes planned welfare state is reflected in the partial departure from the nineteenth-century liberal-individualist concept of property in the implementation of agrarian reform, in the establishment or expansion of a social-security system to protect against major life risks, in

---

3   For classic depictions of this perspective, Alice Teichova, *Kleinstaaten im Spannungsfeld der Großmächte: Wirtschaft und Politik in Mittel- und Südosteuropa in der Zwischenkriegszeit* (München: Oldenbourg, 1988); Iván T. Berend and György Ránki, *Economic Development in East Central Europe in the 19th and 20th Centuries* (New York: Columbia University Press, 1974). See also more recent studies such as Henryk Szlajfer, ed., *Economic Nationalism in East-Central Europe and South America, 1918–1939* (Geneva: Droz, 1990), and Thomas David, *Nationalisme économique et industrialization: L'expérience des pays de l'est (1789–1939)* (Geneva: Droz, 2009).

4   It is not possible here to elaborate on this correlation. David Mitrany, in synthesizing a range of studies on the 'Economic and Social History of the World War' on behalf of the Carnegie Endowment for International Peace, came to the following conclusion: 'For what had been an unusual system of emergency measures during the War – when every field of economic life was invaded by the State – was continued in most of the countries of Central and Southeastern Europe after the War as a system of policy, though in principle and in practice the State had ceased to interfere with production and distribution.' David Mitrany, *The Effect of the War in Southeastern Europe* (New Haven, CT: Yale University Press, 1936), 190. See also Hans-Peter Ullmann, 'Kriegswirtschaft', in *Enzyklopädie Erster Weltkrieg*, ed. Gerhard Hirschfeld et al. (Paderborn: Schöningh Verlag, 2009), 220–32, as well as Chapters 3 and 5 by Jochen Böhler in this volume.

communal housing and in the attendant increase in expertise in the corresponding institutions and systems of knowledge.[5]

The research conducted to date on this shift in thinking about the legitimate tasks of the state[6] has primarily focused on immediate causes, such as the fear of social unrest, especially among the rural and proletarian milieus. Without discarding such causes altogether, this chapter would like to suggest and analyze additional motives, such as the need felt by new elites to legitimize their state as the superior alternative to the now defunct empires which they replaced. This is why the great reform projects were undertaken in the first place, the results of which – as well as their limits (ethnopolitical strictures, financial and organizational overstretch) – will be the focus of this investigation.

This analysis of the aforementioned fields of investigation regarding the character of these new states will be preceded by some general remarks on the underlying territorial and civic foundations, as well as a look at the normative framework for new statehood in the form of the states' founding constitutions and subsequent constitutional revisions. While political systems are not the focus of this chapter, parliamentarianism is nonetheless an important aspect of this new statehood; its failure, as early as the mid-1920s in some countries, marking the limits of a new beginning. On the other hand, the almost comprehensive transformation of the liberal-democratic system to authoritarian forms of government in the 1930s points to a renewed and even more sweeping transformation of statehood throughout the aftermath of the Second World War.

Territory, nationality and citizenship

The conclusion of the First World War brought the surprising collapse of all Continental European multi-ethnic and dynastic empires, which was a real boon for the national movements in Central, Eastern and Southeastern Europe. From the Baltic to the Black and Adriatic seas, many new states suddenly came into existence and others significantly expanded their territory with lands once belonging to the German, Russian, Habsburg and Ottoman empires.[7] The elites of these states were faced with the enormous challenge of making immediate comprehensive decisions and implementing regulations in ways encompassing several dimensions of statehood: state borders had to be maintained and internationally recognized; the citizen body – that is, the people as the sole legitimate source of state authority – had to be determined; and, finally, the material substance of membership in these nation states, i.e. the rights and duties of citizens, had to be defined. The 1949 publication of *Citizenship and Social Class*[8] by English sociologist Thomas Humphrey Marshall made 'citizenship' an influential model for examining

---

5 Dirk von Laak, 'Technokratie im Europa des 20. Jahrhunderts – eine einflussreiche "Hintergrundideologie"', in *Theorien und Experimente der Moderne: Europas Gesellschaften im 20. Jahrhundert*, ed. Lutz Raphael (Vienna: Böhlau, 2012), 101–28; Thomas Etzemüller, 'Strukturierter Raum – integrierte Gemeinschaft: auf den Spuren des *social engineering* im Europa des 20. Jahrhunderts', in ibid., 129–54.

6 Dieter Grimm, 'Die sozialgeschichtliche und verfassungsrechtliche Entwicklung zum Sozialstaat', in idem, *Recht und Staat der bürgerlichen Gesellschaft* (Frankfurt a.M.: Suhrkamp, 1987), 138–60; Michael Stolleis, 'Die Entstehung des Interventionsstaates und das öffentliche Recht', *Zeitschrift für Neuere Rechtsgeschichte* 11 (1989): 129–47; Franz-Xaver Kaufmann, 'Diskurse über Staatsaufgaben', in *Staatsaufgaben*, ed. Dieter Grimm (Frankfurt a.M.: Suhrkamp 1996), 15–41.

7 On the problem of empires collapsing from a comparative perspective, see Karen Barkey and Mark von Hagen, *After Empire: Multiethnic Societies and Nation-building: The Soviet Union and the Russian, Ottoman, and Habsburg Empires* (Boulder, CO: Westview Press, 1997).

8 Thomas Humphrey Marshall, *Citizenship and Social Class* (Cambridge: Cambridge University Press, 1949).

Statehood: the interwar period

these historical developments, one frequently used – and criticized – especially since the rediscovery of Marshall in the 1980s. There are many critiques of this model, however, this chapter will only look at those elements which are relevant to the period and region under investigation here. Using the example of English history, Marshall described a process of increasing inclusion of the working class and other disadvantaged social groups into the capitalist economic system and liberal order. Accordingly, the eighteenth century witnessed the breakthrough of legal claims to equality, the nineteenth century a distinct boost in the political rights of citizens, and the twentieth century a breakthrough in social equality. Apart from more general criticisms of Anglocentrism and an evolutionary logic of development, it is evident that he is only referring to male citizens, without reflecting on improvements in women's equality, which often lagged far behind. For our concerns, it is worth noting, moreover, that the certain fact of the English nation presupposed by Marshall and based on a clearly defined territory in existence since the eighteenth century has no parallel in the case of Central, Eastern and Southeastern Europe. It is not possible here to assume that the institution of citizenship has a solely inclusive function, because at the same moment the inhabitants of the state were being granted civil, political and social rights through a constitution, it also became necessary to determine the external boundaries of state territory as well as the criteria for belonging to the constitutive people. Both territorial boundaries and boundaries of citizenship include *and* exclude certain groups at the same time, the most sensitive questions being who is excluded, for which reasons and from which rights. In the interwar period however, the clear trend had been a nationalization of citizenship rights, not only in Central and Eastern Europe but the rest of Europe as well.[9]

Since ethnic diversity was, for all intents and purposes, a structural characteristic of Central, Eastern and Southeastern Europe in the 'long nineteenth century', even the greatest efforts to create ethnically homogeneous states were hardly crowned with success. To be sure, a combination of arbitrary decisions – for example, that only some ethnic groups were given the opportunity of national self-determination and that borders were often drawn according to strategic or economic calculations – led to a situation where a considerable part of the population in the new states belonged to an ethnic group other than the titular nation. In extreme cases, for instance in Poland, Romania and Czechoslovakia, minorities made up 30 per cent of the country's population, though even in the case of the latter, with two titular nations coexisting in one state, or in the example of the Kingdom of Serbs, Croats and Slovenes, the result was hardly a cohesive whole. It is also worth noting that in numerous regions the titular nation was often not even a relative majority. There were feelings of nostalgia for the old imperial days, even political and armed separatism among members of these minorities, but the strong centralist tendencies of all these new nation states, as well as the will of a titular nation to favour its own ethnic group, were admittedly ill-suited to creating new loyalties in the ranks of these minorities.[10]

The new countries of Central, Eastern and Southeastern Europe could all be described as 'nationalizing states'[11] in the sense that resolute policies in key areas of society were used to

---

9 For a masterful comparison and synthesis of citizenship in Europe in the 20th and 21st centuries, see Dieter Gosewinkel, *Schutz und Freiheit? Staatsbürgerschaft in Europa im 20. und 21. Jahrhundert* (Berlin: Suhrkamp Verlag, 2016), for the nationalization of citizenship rights, 212–40.

10 Peter Haslinger and Joachim von Puttkamer, eds, *Staat, Loyalität und Minderheiten in Ostmittel- und Südosteuropa 1918–1941* (München: R. Oldenbourg, 2007).

11 Rogers Brubaker, *Nationalism Reframed: Nationhood and the National Question in the New Europe* (Cambridge: Cambridge University Press, 1996).

strengthen the dominance of one ethnic group in the form of a (sometimes composite) titular nation. An ethnically informed concept of nation such as this naturally contradicted the political concept of nation that was routinely proclaimed in the constitutions of the interwar period. Moreover, given the League of Nations' inability to enforce its mandate, the minority-protection agreements signed by most states in the region were interpreted by the elites of these nationalizing states not as protections for minorities against discrimination, but instead as protections for the states in the region against attempts made by these minorities to prevent them from becoming nation states according to the French model.[12] These generalizations aside, the majority and minority configurations in the period between the wars were varied. They can essentially be divided into three groups: 1) minorities with an external homeland that was often a neighbouring state; 2) imperial minorities that had exercised special functions in these now defunct empires and had sometimes secured a privileged status on account of it; 3) minorities that, due to having a non-Christian religion including the cultural, economic and political characteristics attributed to that religion, were considered incompatible with the norm of European nation states.[13] Of course these categories don't account for all minorities; there are some that cannot be so neatly defined or given multiple descriptors. The Germans in western Poland, for example, were a borderland minority with the neighbouring German homeland, whereas the Germans in Yugoslavia and Romania were considered an imperial minority. The Jews and certain groups of Muslims, however, were always considered minorities that did not conform to the usual pattern of nations.[14] The Jews of Central and Eastern Europe, including those of Romania, and the Muslims in the Balkan states, were not only thought of as imperial minorities but as anational groups whose cultural assimilation was deemed a danger by forces on the extreme right and even in the political centre, supposedly undermining the Christian-ethnonational definition of the titular nation. These 'undesirable' citizens[15] who, as of the mid-1930s, were 'provisional' citizens (until such citizenship could be revoked) in the sense that the numerous disadvantages they suffered as a religious group and with respect to their access as individuals to university education, to the liberal professions and the civil-service sector, were now compounded by the deprivation of citizenship and forced emigration. Anti-semitism as a discourse and political practice was present all across Central and Eastern Europe, led by Hungary, Romania and Poland.

Once the borders were established by the peace treaties and the constitutive people were defined – processes that will not be discussed in detail here – the new states were faced with the task of determining the political and material rights and obligations of their citizens. It is quite right to argue – as some feminists did at the time – that women, the 'other half' of the

---

12 Martin Scheuermann, *Minderheitenschutz contra Konfliktverhütung? Die Minderheitenpolitik des Völkerbundes in den zwanziger Jahren* (Marburg: Verlag Herder-Institut, 2000).

13 Dietmar Müller, *Staatsbürger auf Widerruf: Juden und Muslime als Alteritätspartner im rumänischen und serbischen Nationscode – Ethnonationale Staatsbürgerschaftskonzeptionen, 1878–1941* (Wiesbaden: Harrassowitz Verlag, 2005).

14 Ezra Mendelsohn, *The Jews of East Central Europe between the World Wars* (Bloomington, IN: Indiana University Press, 1983); Dittmar Dahlmann and Anke Hilbrenner, eds, *Zwischen großen Erwartungen und bösem Erwachen: Juden, Politik und Antisemitismus in Ostmittel- und Südosteuropa 1918–1945* (Paderborn: Ferdinand Schöningh Verlag, 2007); Wolfgang Höpken, 'Flucht vor dem Kreuz? Muslimische Emigration aus Südosteuropa nach dem Ende der osmanischen Herrschaft (19./20. Jahrhundert)', *Comparativ* 1 (1996): 1–24.

15 Holm Sundhaussen, 'Unerwünschte Staatsbürger: Grundzüge des Staatsangehörigkeitsrechts in den Balkanländern und Rumänien', in *Staatsbürgerschaft in Europa: Historische Erfahrungen und aktuelle Debatten*, eds Christoph Conrad and Jürgen Kocka (Hamburg: Edition Körber, 2001), 193–215.

Statehood: the interwar period

nation, should have been given equal rights first, before the integration of the many groups (ethnic minorities, peasants, workers) into these new nations. What Karen Offen wrote about the women's rights movements of the interwar period was true for the other groups to be integrated: 'Feminisms in Europe had become deeply intertwined with the growth and development of nation-states, on both the political and economic front.'[16] Czech feminism at that time clearly interpreted the political emancipation of women in the Czechoslovak constitution of 1920 as a shift away from the 'prison of nations' of the Habsburg monarchy and as proof of the manifest modernity of the Czechoslovak state.[17] In other national movements, especially the Polish one, it was argued that emancipatory aims were legitimate in part by virtue of the special role played by women in the national struggle for independence.[18] The breakthrough of women's suffrage in Europe came only after the First World War (the exceptions were Finland in 1906, Norway in 1913 and Denmark in 1915), when the Soviet Union and the Weimar Republic introduced universal franchise, a move that most countries sought to emulate for political reasons. In rapid succession between 1919 and 1920, most of the states of Central and Eastern Europe, that is, the Baltic states, Poland and Czechoslovakia, passed regulations, laws and constitutions providing for universal female suffrage. In Hungary and Romania women were merely given the right to vote in local elections in 1920 and 1929 respectively,[19] whereas Turkey and Greece enacted universal women's suffrage in 1930. Yugoslavia and Bulgaria were the two countries in Southeastern Europe that – like France, Belgium and Italy – only enacted such laws during or after the Second World War.[20] However, in many countries of the region women were subject to further restrictions, such as not being granted active and passive suffrage simultaneously and having a higher minimum voting age than their male counterparts.[21] The proclaimed elimination of discrimination in family and marriage law and in access to education and labour markets was often delayed and generally reversed during the Great Depression. This will be discussed later in the context of population policy.

Having dwelt on the numerous challenges to the elites of these new states, like establishing the three formal pillars of modern statehood – political autonomy, territory, citizenry – little has been said thus far about the concepts and ideologies espoused by key actors and parties concerning the substance of these new states.[22] In terms of the political system, liberal democracy

---

16 Karen Offen, *European Feminisms, 1700–1950: A Political History* (Stanford, CA: Stanford University Press, 2000), 341.

17 Melissa Feinberg, *Elusive Equality: Gender, Citizenship, and the Limits of Democracy in Czechoslovakia, 1918–1950* (Pittsburgh, PA: University of Pittsburgh Press, 2006), 28–40.

18 Bianka Pietrow-Ennker, 'Frau und Nation im geteilten Polen', in *Geschlecht und Nationalismus in Mittel- und Osteuropa 1848–1918*, ed. Sophia Kemlein (Osnabrück: fibre Verlag, 2000), 125–42; Natali Stegmann, '"Wie die Soldaten im Feld": Der widersprüchliche Kampf polnischer Frauen für "Vaterland" und Frauenrechte im Ersten Weltkrieg', in Kemlein, *Geschlecht und Nationalismus*, 197–216.

19 Andrea Pető, 'Kontinuität und Wandel in der ungarischen Frauenbewegung der Zwischenkriegsperiode', in *Feminismus und Demokratie: Europäische Frauenbewegungen der 1920er Jahre*, ed. Ute Gerhard (Königstein im Taunus: Ulrike Helmer Verlag, 2001), 138–58.

20 Vlasta Jalušić, 'Frauenbewegung(en) und der Staat – Slowenien und der Staat', in Gerhard, *Feminismus und Demokratie*, 116–37.

21 For a comparative and synthesizing perspective on the interwar period, see Offen, *European Feminisms*, 251–377; Offen, 'Umstände, Unwägbarkeiten – Feministinnen der zwanziger Jahre zwischen Krieg, Revolution und neuem Wissensstreit', in Gerhard, *Feminismus und Demokratie*, 210–35.

22 Joachim von Puttkamer, *Ostmitteleuropa im 19. und 20. Jahrhundert* (München: Oldenbourg, 2010), 66–88; Dieter Segert, *Die Grenzen Osteuropas: 1918, 1945, 1989 – Drei Versuche im Westen anzukommen* (Frankfurt: Campus Verlag, 2010), 29–68.

and parliamentarianism seemed the inevitable choice, bearing in mind that the United States, Great Britain and France all backed this option. Beyond the formal organization of the political system, however, the visions of political elites were considerably varied concerning the content and development of this new statehood. In general, in Central, Eastern and Southeastern Europe, as was the case across Europe, conservative political forces and parties emerged weakened from the war, particularly due to agrarian reforms and the expansion of suffrage. Broadly speaking, liberal, peasant and in some cases social-democratic parties were powerhouses in most of these states. However, as one explanatory model from social history argues, ideological cleavages between the major European party families are not what really matters in explaining the political scene in Central, Eastern and Southeastern Europe.[23] More important was the region's lack of economic, social and other structural prerequisites for democracy and parliamentarianism. A weak entrepreneurial class would not have succeeded in establishing a bourgeois counter-culture against the landowning aristocracy, gentry and intelligentsia. Hence, the state alone emerged as the locus of political decision-making and economic progress. A civil and military state bureaucracy evolved across the region as a result, being able to absorb redundant members of the conservative gentry and left-leaning members of the intelligentsia, and it was this stratum that supplied the party members considered fit for government positions.

Paradoxically, the euphoria surrounding democracy and liberation after the First World War – made manifest by a significant increase in suffrage – only burdened the political system even more. In most countries there was no significant electoral threshold for parties entering the parliament, which inevitably resulted in dozens of parties sending representatives to parliament.[24] It was partly in response to this brand of parliamentarianism with its innate inability to generate stable governments in some countries – most notoriously in Poland, leading to the May Coup d'État – that the constitutional prerogative to elect prime ministers and governments in Southeastern Europe was disputed, with no agreement on whether it was the president, the monarch of the country or the parliament that should do so. Another instrument implemented to cope with near-universal suffrage was to introduce a second chamber of parliament whose members were either named by the president or monarch, or were reserved for traditional landowning elites. To the same end, age and gender restrictions to active and passive voting rights were instituted in Hungary and Romania, for instance, and the secret ballot was abandoned, particularly in rural areas. Furthermore, bureaucracy-run government parties all across the region tampered with the electoral process by preventing opposition candidates from running for office and blocking the voter registration of those who would elect them, or by outright election fraud.[25] While the structural perspective on the social and economic basis of democracy

---

23 Hugh Seton-Watson, *Eastern Europe Between the Wars, 1918–1941* (Cambridge: Cambridge University Press, 1945); Werner Conze, 'Die Strukturkrise des östlichen Mitteleuropas vor und nach 1919', in *Vierteljahrshefte für Zeitgeschichte* 61 (1953): 317–38. For a post-1989 resurgence of this position, see George Schöpflin, 'The Political Traditions of Eastern Europe', in *Dædalus* 119, no. 1 (1990): 55–91. For a decisive critique of this position from a comparative angle and by historicizing the interwar period, see Wolfgang Höpken, 'Strukturkrise oder verpaßte Chance? Zum Demokratiepotential der südosteuropäischen Zwischenkriegsstaaten Bulgarien, Jugoslawien und Rumänien', in Lemberg, *Ostmitteleuropa zwischen den beiden Weltkriegen*, 73–127.

24 Jörg K. Hoensch, 'Demokratie und autoritäre Systeme in Ostmitteleuropa', in Lemberg, *Ostmitteleuropa zwischen den beiden Weltkriegen*, 53–72, here 56; Barth, *Europa nach dem Großen Krieg*, 164, 182.

25 For a critical discussion of the models of political modernization and political culture as applied to the Balkans, see Alina Mungiu-Pippidi, 'Failed Institutional Transfer? Constraints on the Political Modernization of the Balkans', in *Ottomans into Europeans: State and Institution-building in South Eastern Europe*, eds Wim van Meurs and Alina Mungiu-Pippidi (London: Hurst & Company, 2010), 51–74.

Statehood: the interwar period

and parliamentarianism may explain some of the political processes in interwar Central, Eastern and Southeastern Europe, it runs the risk of reifying the notion of a 'backward and failing East' versus a 'thriving and successful West'. Much more research needs to be done to counteract this tendency, in particular through comparative studies, both within the region and across Europe because, after all, the phenomena of liberal democracies collapsing into authoritarian rule, economic and cultural nationalism – to name but a few of the symptoms – were by no means specific to Eastern Europe.

Constitutional development

Constitutions, in the tradition of nineteenth-century constitutionalism, are seen as social contracts in which, following extensive deliberations, the constitutive people represented by its elite codifies the rights and duties of its citizens and the structure of the political system, resulting in a division of powers between the legislative, executive and judicial branches. Whereas constitutionally legitimized state powers were increasingly expanded in several successive waves in the nineteenth century,[26] social and economic legislation was the last and weakest area of reform.[27] In addition to being a social contract, a constitution can serve the function of being a founding contract in historical situations where fundamental political, social or territorial changes have taken place, substantiating the founding of a new state.

In such regard, the constitutions of Central, Eastern and Southeastern Europe in the 1920s heralded a new beginning in a dual sense: numerous new sovereign states were formed – some for the first time as nation states, some after a long hiatus, and some in a considerably expanded form. However, in all of the constitutions belonging to this first wave of constitutionalization in the twentieth century, there was a noticeable emphasis on the new, in the sense of greater political and social participation. In European constitutional history of the nineteenth and twentieth centuries, the aforementioned constitutions, together with the Weimar Constitution, are the ones with the most pronounced economic and social component. To a certain extent, the more or less explicit anchoring of basic social rights in the constitution can be considered a defining characteristic of the new Central, Eastern and Southeastern European states, as well as of the Weimar Republic. In the rest of Europe, the expansion of the welfare state as a means of civic integration for coping with the challenges of industrialization and urbanization generally found no expression in constitutions during the interwar period.[28]

The following survey of the first constitutions of countries ranging from Estonia to Greece can of course not be a systematic comparison of constitutions;[29] it is merely a selective analysis

---

26 For an overview of the waves of European constitutionalization, see Peter Brandt et al., 'Einleitung', in *Handbuch der europäischen Verfassungsgeschichte im 19. Jahrhundert: Institutionen und Rechtspraxis im gesellschaftlichen Wandel*, vol. 1, *Um 1800*, eds Peter Brandt et al. (Bonn: Verlag J.H.W. Dietz, 2006), 7–118, here 42–9; Werner Daum, 'Europäische Verfassungsgeschichte 1815–1847: Eine vergleichende Synthese', in *Handbuch der europäischen Verfassungsgeschichte im 19. Jahrhundert: Institutionen und Rechtspraxis im gesellschaftlichen Wandel*, vol. 2: *1815–1847*, eds Peter Brandt et al. (Bonn: Verlag J.H.W. Dietz, 2012), 66–164.

27 See the classic text on the political sociology of citizenship by T.H. Marshall, *Citizenship and Social Class*, 1949.

28 Gabriele Metzler, 'Die sozialstaatliche Dimension der parlamentarischen Demokratie im Europa der Zwischenkriegszeit', in *Herausforderungen der parlamentarischen Demokratie: Die Weimarer Verfassung im europäischen Vergleich*, ed. Andreas Wirsching (München: R. Oldenbourg, 2007), 205–32.

29 Herbert Küpper, *Einführung in die Rechtsgeschichte Osteuropas* (Frankfurt a.M.: Peter Lang Verlag, 2005).

of categories and political ideas of order, such as property and social welfare. It will serve as a basis for investigating the areas of agrarian reform and agriculture, social security and the welfare state, as well as communal housing projects.

The prototype of the new wave of constitutionalization in the interwar period was the Weimar Constitution, passed in August 1919.[30] This document contained a separate section called 'Economic Life', made up of 15 articles (151 through 165) formulating expansive rights as well as objectives for consolidating the level of social welfare attained under Bismarck, while paving the way for new kinds of state intervention.[31] Article 153 ensured that the constitution would protect property rights,[32] their 'content and limits' defined as emanating 'from the law' and with the assurance that expropriations would only be for the public good and proceed by legislative means. The article concluded that, '[p]roperty entails responsibility. Its use should likewise serve the common good.'[33] With a view to agricultural and residential property, it was stipulated that 'properties whose acquisition are necessary to satisfy residential needs, to promote settlement and the cultivation of land, and to improve agriculture may be expropriated.'[34] Article 161 proclaimed the preservation and expansion of a comprehensive social-security system, though explicitly only to protect against the risks of sickness and old age, mentioning unemployment only in the vaguest terms (defined as 'provisions against the vicissitudes of life').[35] The character of the welfare state was described as the interplay between rights and obligations, when, for instance, the right to work (Article 163, paragraph 2: 'Every German should be given the possibility to earn his livelihood through productive labour') is contrasted with the obligation to work (Article 163, paragraph 1: 'Notwithstanding his personal freedom, every German has the moral obligation to exercise his mental and physical capacities as is required for the common good').[36] This same dynamic can be seen with regard to property rights in their linkage to the 'obligation of the landowner towards the community to work and use the land' (Article 155, paragraph 3).[37]

There is no evidence in this analysis that the Weimar Constitution had any direct influence on the constitutions of Central, Eastern and Southeastern Europe. We can assume, however, that the nation states of Southeastern Europe borrowed from one or more centres of nineteenth-century Western European constitutionalism, even though the transfer of norms and institutions was not a matter of simple imitation but adaptation in the interests of local elites and dependent on their agency in a specific political context.[38] We can also assume there were multiple influences, for instance by French, German and Austrian notions of constitutions, as well as a close observation of the constitutional developments in other parts of the region.

---

30 Christoph Gusy, *Die Weimarer Reichsverfassung* (Tübingen: Mohr Siebeck, 1997), particularly 342–69; Andreas Wirsching, *Die Weimarer Republik: Politik und Gesellschaft* (München: R. Oldenbourg, 2000).

31 For the full text of the Weimar Reich Constitution, see *Jahrbuch des Öffentlichen Rechts* 9 (1920): 53–69; art. 151–65, 66–8.

32 Herbert Langkeit, *Enteignung und normative Eigentumsbeschränkung in Artikel 153 der Weimarer Verfassung: ein Beitrag zur neueren Eigentumslehre unter besonderer Berücksichtigung der höchstrichterlichen Rechtsprechung* (Königsberg: Kröwing&Döhring, 1930); Hans Schlegel, *Der Eigentumsbegriff in den Enteignungsbestimmungen der Weimarer Verfassung* (Berlin: Walter Säuberlich, 1934).

33 Article 153, *Jahrbuch des Öffentlichen Rechts*, 66.

34 Article 155, paragraph 2, Ibid., 66–7.

35 Article 161, Ibid., 67.

36 Article 163, Ibid., 67.

37 Article 155, paragraph 3, Ibid., 67.

38 Constantin Iordachi, 'The Making of Citizenship in the Post-Ottoman Balkans: State Building, Foreign Models, and Legal-Political Transfers', in van Meurs, *Ottomans into Europeans*, 179–244.

Statehood: the interwar period

Thus, for example, the Yugoslav debate on the constitutional concept of property was particularly influenced by the reception of the solidarist notion of private law in the writings of Léon Duguit, whereas in Romania the French critique of a liberal-individualistic concept of property may have been acknowledged, but conscious reference was made, in particular, to the Weimar Constitution.[39] The myriad challenges after the war were, however, of greater importance for the general trend in the constitutions of Central, Eastern and Southeastern Europe towards an understanding of the state in which interventions in economic and social life were no longer seen as an occasional tool but something more systematic. The elites of every state in the region faced serious problems of political, social and economic legitimation, as the new nation states offered a better life than that offered by the defunct multi-ethnic empires, or that which the Bolshevist Soviet Union would later propose.

The constitutions of Estonia (1920) and Lithuania (1922) included provisions on property and the welfare state, whereas Latvian legislators were silent on these issues.[40] Estonia guaranteed the private property of every citizen (Article 24) and the 'organization of economic life' was to be commensurate to the 'guarantee of a humane way of life by means of appropriate laws': for example, by allocating land for cultivation, by enabling individuals to find a place to live and work, and by offering protections against life risks such as sickness, disability and old age.[41] The provisions in the Lithuanian constitution on the 'principles of state economic policy' and 'social welfare' posited a right to work (Article 88, paragraph 2), put property in general under special protection (Article 21), and in particular, protected small and medium-sized landholdings after agrarian reform (Article 90), and with respect to acknowledged life risks, explicitly determined that, '[t]he state protects workers in case of sickness, old age, accidents and unemployment.'[42]

In Article 99 of the Polish constitution (1921) a comparatively detailed and explicit guarantee of property rights was put forth, which was essentially described as 'one of the most important foundations of society and the legal system'. It was then followed by a passage in the second paragraph denoting property and the distribution of land as a regulatory area of special significance: 'Land, as one of the most important factors of national and state life, may not become the object of unrestricted trade.'[43] Furthermore, in articles 102 and 103 work was placed under state protection, the gainful employment of children, youth and women was regulated, and the right to insurance against the four acknowledged life hazards was asserted.[44]

Czechoslovakia and Hungary were the two states – apart from Germany and Austria, of course – that might be considered the closest successors to the German and Habsburg empires,

---

39 Dietmar Müller, 'Eigentum im öffentlichen Diskurs: Léon Duguit im Jugoslawien der Zwischenkriegszeit', *Mitropa* (2013): 22–6; Alexandru Costin, 'Concepţiile actuale ale proprietăţii şi constituţia' [Recent concepts of property and the Constitution], in: *Noua constituţie a României în dezbaterea contemporanilor* [The New Romanian Constitution in contemporaneous debate] (Bucharest: Humanitas, [no date]), 356–80.

40 Toomas Anepaio, 'Die rechtliche Entwicklung der baltischen Staaten 1918–1940', in *Modernisierung durch Transfer zwischen den Weltkriegen*, ed. Tomasz Giaro (Frankfurt a.M.: Vittorio Klostermann, 2007), 7–30.

41 'Grundgesetz der Estnischen Republik, vom 9.8.1920', *Jahrbuch des Öffentlichen Rechts der Gegenwart* 12 (1923–24): 202–6, here 203–4.

42 'Die Verfassung des Litauischen Staates, vom 1.8.1922', *Jahrbuch des Öffentlichen Rechts der Gegenwart* 16 (1928): 315–26, here 317, 321–2.

43 'Verfassung der polnischen Republik, vom 17.3.1921 (im Gesetzesblatt veröffentlicht am 1.5.1921)', *Jahrbuch des Öffentlichen Rechts der Gegenwart* 12 (1923/24): 300–10, here 308.

44 Wojciech Witkowski and Andrzej Wrzyszcz, 'Modernisierung des Rechts im unabhängigen Polen', in Giaro, *Modernisierung durch Transfer*, 249–71.

Dietmar Müller

thereby consciously continuing the legacy of the welfare state begun in the late nineteenth century.[45] It is all the more surprising then – and very much in contrast to the markedly welfare-state-oriented policies of Prague in the interwar period – that the constitution of Czechoslovakia (1920), save for the standard property guarantee (Article 109), made no specific reference to economic and social policy aims and hence, in this sense, resembled the classic liberal constitution of the nineteenth century.[46] In the case of Hungary, it is not possible to discern a transformation in statehood in its constitution during the period between the wars since the constitution of the Republic of Councils was only active for about six months in 1919 before the old laws took over again.

Of particular interest are the constitutions of the Southeastern European states of Romania and the Kingdom of Serbs, Croats and Slovenes (called Yugoslavia as of 1929 and henceforth referred to as such in this chapter), as these states achieved independence in the 1830s and 1860s and could thus build on their own constitutional traditions in the interwar period.[47] In comparison to the constitutions of Serbia and Romanian Old Kingdom, private property in Greater Romania (1923) and Yugoslavia (1921) was not regarded as an unrestricted right in the liberal-individualist sense. Whereas property was viewed as a 'sacred and inviolable' right in Article 19 of the Romanian constitution of 1866, in Article 17 of the 1923 constitution this 'guarantee' was qualified by its being assigned a 'social function'.[48] The same was the case in Yugoslavia, where the guarantee of property rights in Article 37 was immediately followed by the provision that its content, scope and limits would be regulated by simple statutes.[49] The Yugoslav public generally understood this as a limitation on property for the purpose of achieving social aims, especially considering that the guarantee of property rights was merely one of 23 articles in a separate section of the constitution called 'Social and Economic Provisions'. Compared to other Central and Eastern European constitutions, the Yugoslav provisions here are the most exhaustive of their kind, covering not only the protection of work (Article 23) and the acknowledged life risks (Article 31) but also a range of economic and social regulations. With an unusual degree of detail, articles 41–43 announced and sanctioned interventions in the ownership structure of land. Yugoslav legislators did something remarkable in that they explicitly laid out a state intervention imperative in Article 26:

> In the interest of the collective and by force of law, the state has the right and the duty to intervene in the economic affairs of its citizens in the spirit of justice and for the purpose of alleviating social contradictions.

---

45 Ladislav Lipscher, *Verfassung und politische Kultur in der Tschechoslowakei 1918–1939* (München: R. Oldenbourg, 1979); Katalin Gönczi, 'Kontinuität und Wandel im ungarischen Rechtssystem der Zwischenkriegszeit', in Giaro, *Modernisierung durch Transfer*, 69–83.

46 'Verfassung der Tschechoslowakischen Republik, vom 29.2.1920', in *Die Verfassungen in Europa 1789–1949*, eds Dieter Gosewinkel and Johannes Masing (München: C.H. Beck, 2006), 1828–50.

47 Lucian Goga, 'Politik und Rechtskultur der Zwischenkriegszeit in Rumänien', in Giaro, *Modernisierung durch Transfer*, 31–68; Srđan Šarkić and Maša Kulauzov, 'Constitutional History of Yugoslavia 1918–1941', in Ibid., 169–83. See also the comparative approach of Wolfgang Höpken, 'Strukturkrise oder verpaßte Chance?', ed. Lemberg, 73–127, here 86–100.

48 'Die Verfassung des Königreichs Rumänien, vom 29.3.1923', in Gosewinkel et al., *Die Verfassungen in Europa 1789–1949*, 1735–54. See also Ernst Schmidt, *Die verfassungsrechtliche und politische Struktur des rumänischen Staates in ihrer historischen Entwicklung* (München: Ernst Reinhardt, 1932).

49 'Verfassung des Königreiches der Serben, Kroaten und Slowenen, vom 28.6.1921', *Jahrbuch des Öffentlichen Rechts der Gegenwart* 11 (1922): 200–17, here 203–4.

Statehood: the interwar period

Romania's constitution remained more indebted to European constitutionalism of the nineteenth century in that the guarantee of property rights was subsumed under basic citizens' rights and that, furthermore, the protection of work and insurance against the four life risks in Article 21 was very brief and summary in nature. The relatively extensive interventions in the ownership structure of land in the wake of agrarian reform were all but hidden in the transitional regulations of Article 131.

The constitutionalism of the remaining three Southeastern European states gives little indication of a changing concept of state in the interwar period. No new constitution was created in Bulgaria, despite the turbulent political events of the 1920s; the constitution of 1879 remained in effect, articles 67 and 68 of which merely referred to classic property rights.[50] The same was true of the constitutions of Albania (property rights in Article 129)[51] and Greece (property rights in Article 19) from the year 1925, whereby in the case of Greece labour was placed under state protection.[52]

Apart from the aforementioned need for political legitimacy on the part of national elites, socio-economic factors in the narrow sense also played a role in generating a more active, interventionist understanding of the state. Industrialization and urbanization as well as the concomitant destabilization of traditional social relationships in families and village communities created a heightened demand for state regulations. This will be analyzed more intensively in the next section with reference to specific cases. It will not be possible here, however, to investigate the exact combination of reasons for a more active understanding of the state in each individual country. Nonetheless, we might note more generally that the programmatic ideas expressed in these constitutions were not identical to their concrete implementation in the guise of agrarian reform and the expansion of social security and communal housing schemes. Institutional and professional legacies from the German and Habsburg empires played an important role with regard to systems of social security in particular.

Agrarian reform and agricultural policy

The implementation of more or less sweeping agrarian reforms after the First World War was of utmost political, social and symbolic importance for many states in Central, Eastern and Southeastern Europe. With the exception of Czechoslovakia, more than half of the gainfully employed population in each of these countries was working in agriculture well into the interwar period. In some countries, such as Poland, Romania, Yugoslavia and Albania, the figure was as high as 80 per cent.[53] The unexpected collapse of multi-ethnic empires in a long and bloody war made it necessary, and possible, for the newly emerging nation states in this region to implement sweeping reforms in rural areas as well. The world war was the first time many peasant soldiers had left their familiar village surroundings, and many of them had either been explicitly promised, or returned with the implicit expectation that in recognition of their service to the fatherland they would be given a better position in the economy and state. Added to this were the soldiers on the

---

50 'Verfassung des Fürstentums Bulgarien vom 16.4.1879', in Gosewinkel et al., *Die Verfassungen in Europa 1789–1949*, 1772–89.

51 'Verfassungsstatut der Republik Albanien, vom 7.3.1925', in Gosewinkel et al., *Die Verfassungen in Europa 1789–1949*, 2065–78.

52 'Verfassung der Republik Griechenland, vom 29.9.1925', in ibid., 1080–1101.

53 Iván T. Berend and György Ránki, 'Polen, Ungarn, Rumänien und Albanien 1914–1980', in *Handbuch der europäischen Wirtschafts- und Sozialgeschichte*, vol. 6, 777. For a comparison with the rest of Europe, see Dudley Kirk, *Europe's Population in the Interwar Years* (New York: Gordon and Breach Science Publishers, 1967 [1946]), 13–16.

Eastern Front who had witnessed the wild expropriation of land under the banner of Bolshevism, which elites in the new states perceived as a grave danger. For purely social reasons, it was also considered important to take care of the soldiers returning as invalids as well as the many war widows.[54] Moreover, for social and economic reasons it was necessary to dissolve post-feudal property and land-use relations. Thus, in many of the new states of Central, Eastern and Southeastern Europe the dividing line between large landowners and those owning little or no land usually reflected the old power structures, the large landowners belonging to the dominant ethnic groups of the old empire and the small farmers and rural proletariat generally being members of the new titular nations. Thus, agrarian reforms in the entire region were a central element of state and nation-building, and it is not an exaggeration to describe their implications as an 'encroachment on individual property rights hitherto unprecedented in European history'.[55]

The extent, timing and implementation of agrarian reforms in the individual states of Central, Eastern and Southeastern Europe was characterized by a cluster of political motives as well as by agro-structural and agro-economic factors.[56] One of these was the question of whether a country belongs to the winners or the losers of the war – Austria, Hungary and Bulgaria being the group of countries with the smallest amount of redistributed land.[57] In Bulgaria a mere 3.2 per cent and in Hungary a mere 5.8 per cent of all land was expropriated.[58] Whereas the specific reasons for this in the case of Austria and Bulgaria are to be found in their primarily small and medium-sized ownership structure prior to 1914, in the case of Hungary the reasons were political in nature. With the suppression of Béla Kun's Republic of Councils and the authoritarian rule of Miklós Horthy, the old elites stabilized the situation in a way that left the old conditions of land ownership untouched.[59] In Lithuania and Poland (respectively, ca. 9 per cent and 6.9 per cent of land expropriated) moderate agrarian reforms were carried out in terms of

---

54 Julia Eichenberg, 'War Experience and the National State in Poland: Veterans and Welfare in the 20th Century', 50–62; Natali Stegmann, 'Veteran Status and War Victims' Policy in Czechoslovakia from the End of the First World War until the Nineteen-Fifties', 63–74, both in *Veterans and War Victims in Eastern Europe During the 20th Century: A Comparison*, eds Katrin Boeckh and Natali Stegmann (Leipzig: Leipziger Universitätsverlag, 2011).

55 Uwe Müller, 'Landreformen und Wirtschaftsnationalismus in Ostmitteleuropa', in *Soziale Konflikte und nationale Grenzen in Ostmitteleuropa: Festschrift für Helga Schultz zum 65. Geburtstag*, ed. Dagmara Jajeśniak-Quast et al. (Berlin: Berliner Wissenschafts-Verlag, 2006), 171–87, here 172.

56 For comparative overviews, see Hugh Seton-Watson, *Eastern Europe between the Wars, 1918–1941* (New York: Harper & Row, 1962 [1945]), 75–122; Wojciech Roszkowski, *Land Reforms in East Central Europe after World War One* (Warsaw: Institute of Political Studies, Polish Academy of Sciences, 1995); Wilfried Schlau, 'Die Agrarreformen und ihre Auswirkungen', in *Ostmitteleuropa zwischen den beiden Weltkriegen*, 145–59; Müller, 'Landreformen und Wirtschaftsnationalismus', 171–87.

57 On Austria, see Anton Freiherr von Pantz, 'Die Wiederbesiedlung in Österreich', in *Die agrarischen Umwälzungen im ausserrussischen Osteuropa: ein Sammelwerk*, ed. Max Sering (Berlin: De Gruyter, 1930) 240–54; Ulrich Kluge, *Bauern, Agrarkrise und Volksernährung in der europäischen Zwischenkriegszeit: Studien zur Agrargesellschaft und -wirtschaft der Republik Österreich 1918 bis 1938* (Stuttgart: Franz Steiner, 1988). On Bulgaria, see Ernst Buske, 'Die Agrarreform in Bulgarien', in *Die agrarischen Umwälzungen*, 396–446; Markus Wien, *Markt und Modernisierung: Deutsch-bulgarische Wirtschaftsbeziehungen 1918–1944 in ihren konzeptionellen Grundlagen* (München: R. Oldenbourg, 2007), 88–124.

58 For a roundup of expropriated and redistributed land in the states of Central, Eastern and Southeastern Europe, see Müller, 'Landreformen und Wirtschaftsnationalismus', 174.

59 Béla Kenéz, 'Die Agrarreform in Ungarn', in Sering, *Die agrarischen Umwälzungen*, 255–75; Zsombor Bódy, 'Weder Demokratisierung noch Diktatur: Die kontrollierte Politisierung der ländlichen Unterschichten im Ungarn der Zwischenkriegszeit', in *Agrarismus und Agrareliten in Ostmitteleuropa*, eds Eduard Kubů, Torsten Lorenz, Jiri Šouša and Uwe Müller (Berlin: BWV Berliner Wissenschafts-Verlag, 2013), 225–52.

Statehood: the interwar period

the percentage of land redistributed, though the focus in both countries was on agro-structural measures[60] – namely, land consolidation (i.e. the merging of smaller and disparate land holdings in Lithuania and Galician Poland) and the abolition of servitude in the Kresy (i.e. a clear reallocation of once divided land holdings to individuals).[61]

Czechoslovakia, Romania and Yugoslavia also belonged to the middle group, with 12.8 per cent, 12.3 per cent, and 8.3 per cent respectively, of lands expropriated. The highest percentages were in Latvia and Estonia, with 51.7 and 49.3 per cent, respectively. The middle group in particular will be further investigated in more detail.

The most salient characteristic of post-1918 agrarian reforms in Central, Eastern and Southeastern Europe is clearly the significantly increased role of the state in allocating greater resources for individual agency. It was always state actors and institutions that determined the amount of land expropriated from certain groups and, in turn, which groups would be in receipt of land, to which quantity and finally, what legal status this land would have in the future. In a clear break with the notion of the state limiting itself to the role of guaranteeing property rights as practised under the banner of liberalism in nineteenth-century Western Europe, national elites in Central, Eastern and Southeastern Europe now gave the state the additional role of being an active protagonist.

The ethnopolitical dimension and colonization projects

The ethnonational dimension of agrarian reform was the aspect most discussed by contemporaries, the result being an inexhaustible supply of apologetic literature from nation state and minority perspectives.[62] With regard to regional comparison, there is quite a bit of diversity in

---

60 On Lithuania, see Silvio Broedrich, 'Die Agrarreform in Litauen', in *Die agrarischen Umwälzungen*, 128–53; Gert von Pistohlkors, 'Tiefgreifende agrarische Umwälzungen und Umstrukturierungen in den neu gegründeten baltischen Staaten Estland, Lettland und Litauen 1919–1922: Motivationen und Ergebnisse bis 1940', in *Agrarreformen und ethnodemographische Veränderungen: Südosteuropa vom ausgehenden 18. Jahrhundert bis in die Gegenwart*, ed. Karl-Peter Krauss (Stuttgart: Franz Steiner, 2009), 175–205, here 189.

61 As a *pars pro toto* for the wealth of literature on agrarian reform in Poland, see Aleksander Matwiejew, *Die Agrarreformen Polens im XX. Jahrhundert* (Kiel: Institut für Weltwirtschaft, 1958); Isaj Lifszyc, *Die Agrarfrage in Polen*, Dissertation der Rechts- und Staatswissenschaftlichen Fakultät der Universität Zürich (Łódź, W. Schweitzera, 1928), 54–69; Gerhard Doliesen, *Die polnische Bauernpartei 'Wyzwolenie' in den Jahren 1918–1926* (Marburg: Verlag Herder-Institut, 1996), 156–176. On the embeddedness of land reform in the overall Polish context, see Antony Polonsky, *Politics in Independent Poland 1921–1939: The Crisis of Constitutional Government* (Oxford: Oxford University Press, 1972).

62 For a selection, see Sering, *Die agrarischen Umwälzungen*; Wilhelm Luig, *Agrarverhältnisse und Agrarreform in Estland* (Leipzig, 1923); Vilis Kalniņš, *Die Entwicklung der Landwirtschaft Lettlands seit der Agrarreform* (Berlin: Verlag Eugen Kehrer, 1937); Alexander von Ley, *Litauens wirtschaftliche Entwicklung unter besonderer Berücksichtigung der Agrarreform* (München, 1933); Konrad Kaschny, *Die Agrarreform in der Tschecho-Slowakei* (Breslau: Verlag Erich&Herbert Hoppe, 1933); Martin Kaiser, *Die tschechoslowakische Agrarreform als Rechtsproblem* (Leipzig: Universitätsverlag Robert Noske, 1931); Alexander Spickermann, *Agrarfrage und neustaatliche Bodenreformbestrebungen in Polen* (Lodz, 1928); Willy Wiese, *Die polnische Bodenbesitzpolitik: Untersuchungen auf dem Gebiete der Agrarreform und der landwirtschaftlichen Organisationen in Polen während der Jahre 1919 und 1926* (Berlin, 1928); Mitja Lukan, *Die Kausalität der Agrarreform in den Nachfolgestaaten der österreichisch-ungarischen Monarchie, ihre Gestaltung und Auswirkung* (Ljubljana: J. Blasniks Nachf. Universitätsdruckerei, 1931); Eugen Tenhof, *Politik der ländlichen Grundverteilung in Alt-Rumänien unter besonderer Berücksichtigung der Agrar-Reform vom 14. Juli 1921* (Osnabrück, 1925); Josef Matl, *Die Agrarreform in Jugoslawien* (Berlin: Verlag Hermann Sack, 1927); Zdenko Bruck, *Die Agrarreform des Königreiches der Serben, Kroaten und Slowenen* (Bern: Buchdruckerei Steiger, 1927); Jordan S. Petkoff, *Landwirtschaftsgestaltung und Agrarpolitik Bulgariens unter besonderer Berücksichtigung der Agrarreform der Zeit nach dem Weltkriege* (Sofija: Druckerei Isgrew, 1941).

terms of the method, implementation and the consequences of land reform after the First World War, ranging from an unavoidable structural severity for minorities to targeted discrimination; there was, however, a universal tendency to understand the new state as the property of the titular nation. Control over property was crucial, whether concretely with respect to land ownership or more abstractly in the titular nation's mythological ownership of the fatherland, symbolized by the integration of provinces previously under foreign domination. This ethnic understanding of nation found expression in land redistribution in the form of considerable discrimination against formerly dominant ethnic groups (Germans, Hungarians, Russians, Turks), against members of smaller states on the losing side of the First World War (Bulgaria), as well as against groups without a homeland (Jews, Ukrainians, Belarussians, etc.). Land redistribution was less pronounced in areas where large land holdings were already in the hands of the new titular nation, such as in the Polish Kresy, in Galicia, in the Romanian Old Kingdom and all of Hungary; it was more drastic, by contrast, in western Poland, Estonia and Lithuania or in the new Romanian provinces (Transylvania, Bessarabia, Bukovina).

The ethnopolitical bias was particularly manifest in colonization projects, as will be shown here using examples from Yugoslavia, Poland and Czechoslovakia. War veterans, in many cases members of the titular nation, were settled in strategically important regions that were often close to the border and heavily populated by minorities. They set up new farms, usually larger than those of the local population, and enjoyed generous state subsidies in return for the appropriation and defence of national territory that was both symbolic and very real.[63]

In Yugoslavia, the timing of legislation is an indication that ethnonational factors were of particular importance, decrees and laws on colonization generally being enacted prior to general agrarian regulations.[64] The colonization of Kosovo, Macedonia and Vojvodina was not merely a part of Yugoslav agrarian reform but its primary aim.[65] Comparing the colonization of Kosovo with that of Vojvodina, a common goal is discernible despite considerable differences in the

---

63 For agrarian reforms with colonization, see the examples of Dobruja and Kosovo in Müller, *Staatsbürger auf Widerruf*, 362–74 and 436–53 respectively; for Macedonia, see Nada Boškovska, *Das jugoslawische Makedonien: eine Randregion zwischen Repression und Integration* (Vienna: Böhlau, 2009), 206–18; for eastern Galicia, Volhynia and other parts of the Kresy, see Werner Benecke, *Die Ostgebiete der Polnischen Republik: Staatsmacht und öffentliche Ordnung in einer Minderheitenregion 1918–1939* (Vienna: Böhlau, 1999); Édouard Conte, 'Land und "ethnische Reinheit" im polnisch-ukrainischen Grenzgebiet', in *Es war einmal die Wende ...: Sozialer Umbruch der ländlichen Gesellschaften Mittel- und Südosteuropas*, eds Édouard Conte and Christian Giordano (Berlin: Centre Marc Bloch, 1999), 35–82; Cornelia Schenke, *Nationalstaat und nationale Frage: Polen und die Ukrainer 1921–1939* (Hamburg: Dölling und Galitz, 2004).

64 For a cataloguing of decrees and laws on agrarian reform and colonization in Kosovo, see Jusuf Osmani, 'Zakonski propisi o agrarnoj reformi i kolonizacija na Kosovo između dva svetska rata' [Legal acts on agrarian reform and colonization in Kosovo between the two World Wars], *Vjetar i arkivit të Kosovës* 20 (1985): 169–89.

65 Christian Giordano, 'Agrarreformen als Potential ethnischer Spannungen in Osteuropa: Das Beispiel Jugoslawiens – Das Prinzip der Staatsnation und der Mythos der ethnischen Reinheit', in *Nation und Nationalismus in Europa: Kulturelle Konstruktion von Identitäten*, eds Catherine Bosshart-Pfluger et al. (Frauenfeld: Huber, 2002) 463–80. The author of the standard work on Yugoslav agrarian reform in English, Jozo Tomasevich, disguises more than he analyzes the goal of colonization implicit in agrarian reform: 'the political strengthening of the Christian sector in Bosnia-Herzegovina and Macedonia'. He does not reflect at all on how the implementation of this ethnonational aim influenced, for example, the economic success of agrarian reform. See Jozo Tomasevich, *Peasants, Politics, and Economic Change in Yugoslavia* (Stanford, CA: Stanford University Press, 1955), 358–9.

Statehood: the interwar period

way it was carried out.[66] The ever greater ruthlessness with which a Slavic-Serbian majority was sought in Kosovo can be explained by Germany and Hungary's increased diplomatic and military importance when compared with Albania, even after the First World War. Similarly, the considerable publicity that ethnic Germans generated in the form of petitions at the League of Nations – with regard to either their real or supposed discrimination in the context of Polish and Czechoslovak agrarian reform and colonization – does a lot to explain why the perception of their discrimination was much greater than it actually was.[67]

In both Kosovo and Vojvodina, the state could hand out expropriated land in communities and villages that were now in its possession. The state lands available in Kosovo after 1912 were primarily the former property of religious Albanian Muslim foundations (*vakıf*) and in Vojvodina the formerly communally owned church lands of predominantly Hungarian and German religious communities once used to maintain (private) schools.[68] In urbanized Vojvodina the problem of communal lands became acute during agrarian reform, and colonizers mostly received land from the property of heavily Hungarian and German-influenced cities. This land had previously been rented out to subsidize community services.[69] All of Kosovo was essentially regarded as a potential settlement area, because once land was settled by Slavs it was never restituted to their previous Albanian owners, even if the latter could prove their rightful claim. This was specifically the case for land that was declared to be wasteland on account of its previous owners having fled during the war or being classified as insurgents (*kačaks*). In Kosovo, large land holdings were defined as being more than 50 hectares. Although the majority of Albanians owned less than this, they were nonetheless defined as large landowners and expropriated, being allowed to hold on to 5 to 15 hectares. The practice was radicalized in the mid-1930s when a wave of expropriations took place, particularly in border areas and in areas with especially large Albanian populations: the minimum amount of land that Albanians were entitled to was reduced to 0.4 hectares per person. At the same time, Yugoslav legislators had to redouble their efforts to 'Serbianize' Vojvodina. Land here was owned mostly by individual German and Hungarian farmers with medium-sized holdings and was not affected much by agrarian reform.[70] It is true that ethnic Germans and Hungarians in the province were defined, in a wholesale manner, as the representatives of erstwhile foreign rule, so that they were granted neither voting rights nor rights of co-determination in the agrarian reform committees and their

---

66 On the colonization of Kosovo, see Milovan Obradović, *Agrarna reforma i kolonizacija na Kosovo* [Agrarian reform and colonization in Kosovo] (Priština: Institut za Istoriju Kosova, 1981); Vladan Jovanović, *Jugoslovenska država i Južna Srbija 1918–1929: Makedonija, Sandžak, Kosovo i Metohija u Kraljevini SHS* [The Yugoslav state and south Serbia, 1918–1929: Macedonia, Sandžak, Kosovo and Methochia in the kingdom of SCS] (Belgrade: Inis, 2002), 208–23; Michel Roux, *Les Albanais en Yougoslavie: Minorité nationale et development* (Paris: Éditions de le Maison des Science de L'Homme, 1992), 191–203; Noel Malcolm, *Kosovo: A Short History* (London: Macmillan, 1998), 265–88; Müller, *Staatsbürger auf Widerruf*, 436–53.

67 For an analysis of minority petitions to the League of Nations, also with regard to agrarian reforms, see Scheuermann, *Minderheitenschutz contra Konfliktverhütung*; von Puttkamer, *Die tschechoslowakische Bodenreform*, 331–41.

68 *Das Schicksal der Deutschen in Jugoslawien* (München: DTV, 2004 [1961]), 20E.

69 See the document of town representatives in Novi Sad, *Predlog slobodne i kraljevske varoši Novog Sada u predmetu sprovađanja agrarne reforme* [Proposal of the free and regal city of Novi Sad for the agrarian reform] (Novi Sad: 1920).

70 Zoran Janjetović, 'Die Konflikte zwischen Serben und Donauschwaben', *Südost-Forschungen* 58 (1999): 119–68; here 141–5; idem, *Between Hitler and Tito: The Disappearance of the Vojvodina Germans* (Belgrade: self-published, 2005 [2000]), 34–6.

poor hardly benefited from land reallocation measures.[71] And yet, just a decade after agrarian reform, Yugoslav authorities were alarmed to see successful German and Hungarian farmers expanding their land holdings once again. A law was passed in February 1938 to counteract this tendency, calling for a moratorium of land sales in a 50-kilometre-wide swath along the state border.[72]

Up to that point the land being traded in Vojvodina and Kosovo was mainly land that had been allocated to colonists. Belgrade's focus had been to get the greatest possible number of Serbs and Southern Slavs to settle both provinces, making it nearly impossible to vet the suitability or intention of colonists to settle there permanently and engage in farming. Quite a few of them accepted these state concessions and immediately rented out the land illegally or sold it later to local Albanians, Germans or Hungarians.[73] Market logic – that land automatically went to the best farmer – did not prevail in the process of agrarian reform, nor in the sale of land that followed. Instead, farmers were forced to adopt illegal practices in order to expand their production or were at least made to engage in transactions that led to ambiguous property rights on their land because Yugoslavia, like Romania, rejected the Habsburg legacy of a functioning cadastral and land-register system. Even though there had been a decree in 1931 to make the land-recording system of the Vojvodina valid across the entire country, little of this was put into practice.[74]

As in the case of Romania and Transylvania, the policy of forcing farmers and agricultural labourers to resort to oral agreements or illegal measures with the looming and ever-present danger of being caught – especially in Vojvodina – was aimed not only at a 'Serbianization' of the province in ethnic terms but also its 'Šumadization'. The aim, in other words, was to transfer a clientelistic-structured political system from the heartland of Serbia, with its largely undifferentiated society, in which a homogeneous class of small farmers was essentially mobilized and integrated by populist political parties.

The implementation of colonization in Yugoslavia became the subject of increasing criticism in the second half of the 1930s. If previous criticisms had faulted the lack of a system and the enrichment of certain individuals with no real ties to agriculture, the discourse now became decidedly anti-parliamentary. According to this new line of argument, political parties and parliamentarianism were fundamentally unable to efficiently solve a task as complex as colonization. Party politicians were guilty of forgetting their duty to the nation,

---

71 Matl, *Die Agrarreform in Jugoslawien*, 101.

72 Nikola Gaćeša, 'Nemci u agrarnoj reformi i vlastništvu obradivog zemljišta u Vojvodini 1919–1941' [The Germans in agrarian reform and their landownership in Vojvodina 1919–1941], in *Radovi iz agrarne istorije i demografije*, ed. Nikola Gaćeša (Novi Sad: Matica srpska, 1995), 286–308, here 294–5.

73 It was not only potentially biased German contemporaries and direct representatives of the Germans who claimed this to be the case: see Matl, *Die Agrarreform in Jugoslawien*, 127; and Ludwig Fritscher, 'Agrarverfassung und agrarische Umwälzung in Jugoslawien', in Sering, *Die agrarischen Umwälzungen*, 267–340, here 322–3; or *Die Agrarreformen im Königreich der Serben, Kroaten und Slowenen und ihre Folgen* (Novisad: n.p., 1924), 17. Contemporary South Slavic authors also expressed very negative views on colonists' agronomic abilities and sense of national duty as well as on the expertise of the politicians and officials concerned with agrarian reform. For Kosovo see in particular Đorđe Krstić, *Kolonizacija u Južnoj Srbiji* [The colonization of south Serbia] (Sarajevo: Štamparija 'Bosanska' Počta, 1928).

74 *Zakon o izdavanju tapija na području Kasacionog Suda u Beogradu i Velikog Suda u Podgorici* [Law on Tapija for the jurisdiction of the cassation court in Belgrade and the high court in Podgorica] (Belgrade: Narodna štamparija, 1931). For an overview, albeit embellished, of the Yugoslav cadastral and land-register system, see *Le cadastre, le livre foncier et la reforme agraire en Yugoslavie* (Belgrade: Edition du Ministère de finances, Département du cadaster es des domains d'Etat, 1936).

Statehood: the interwar period

adhering to the democratic principle of majority rule and the rule of law rather than ruthlessly advancing the interests of the Serbian/South Slavic ethnonation.[75] These colonization-cum-system critiques culminated towards the end of the 1930s in publicized statements from the 'Serbian Culture Club' about how the Serbianization of Kosovo and Vojvodina could be accelerated. Đoko Perin, director of the Serbian Farm Workers' Association (*Savez srpskih zelmjoradničkih zadruga*) in Sarajevo, tallied up the dissatisfactory results of the colonization qua Serbianization of Kosovo and Vojvodina, then proposed a radical alternative: population exchange and expulsion.[76] Turks and Albanians in Kosovo and Macedonia were to be resettled against their will, an option he did not think feasible in the case of Hungarians in Vojvodina. In this case he suggested dividing the province into a northern, predominantly Hungarian settled part and a southern, mainly Serbian-occupied part that would be about twice as large. The two parts would then be homogenized by means of a population exchange and the northern part would be ceded to Hungary. The Germans of Vojvodina were evidently not perceived as a threat to the state when this plan was presented in 1937, as they only figured marginally in Perin's deliberations. In a memorandum to the Yugoslav government, presented in March 1937 at the same Serbian Culture Club, influential intellectual and historian Vasa Čubrilović pointed out that the moment was favourable for a radical solution to the 'Albanian problem':

> Nevertheless, the world today has grown used to things much worse than this and is so preoccupied with its day-to-day problems that this issue should not be a cause for concern. At a time when Germany can expel tens of thousands of Jews and Russia can shift millions of people from one part of the continent to the other, the evacuation of a hundred thousand Albanians will not set off a world war.[77]

In other words, after criticizing colonization in general and, more specifically, the introduction of a Western European concept of property applicable to the Albanian population, his policy recommendation was the mass expulsion of Albanians.

Agrarian reform and colonization in eastern Galicia and the Kresy had two salient characteristics:[78] large land holdings were in Polish hands, and the state was taking pains to maintain and consolidate Polish dominance.[79] This resulted in numerous special provisions for these regions, with repercussions for agrarian reform in general. For one thing, according to the farm

---

75 Krstić, *Kolonizacija*, 39–49.

76 Đoko Perin, 'Nacionalizovanje Vojvodine i Južne Srbije' [The nationalization of Vojvodina and South Serbia], in *Iskušenja srpske elite: Dokumenti o radu Srpskog Kulturnog Kluba*, ed. Pero Simić (Belgrade: Službeni Glasnik, 2006), 105–20.

77 Čubrilović, quoted in Robert Elsie, ed., *Kosovo in the Heart of the Powder Keg* (Boulder, CO: East European Monographs, 1977), 408.

78 In the interwar period, the voivodeships of Vilnius, Novogródek, Polesie and Volhynia were subsumed into the Kresy, whereas Lviv, Tarnopol and Stanisławów (now Ivano-Frankivsk) were considered as belonging to western Galicia. On the Kresy, see Benecke, *Die Ostgebiete der Polnischen Republik*. On eastern Galicia, see Conte, 'Land und "ethnische Reinheit"', 35–82. On Volhynia, see Schenke, *Nationalstaat und nationale Frage*.

79 For Poland's minority politics, see Winson Chu, *The German Minority in Interwar Poland* (New York: Cambridge University Press, 2012); Stephan Stach, 'Minderheitenpolitik aus der zweiten Reihe: Konzepte und Praktiken zur Einbindung nationaler und ethnoreligiöser Minderheiten in Piłsudskis Polen (1926–1939)' (PhD Diss. Halle-Wittenberg 2015); Stephan Horak, *Poland and Her National Minorities, 1919–39: A Case Study* (New York: Vantage Press, 1961).

bill of 1925, the ideal-sized farm in the eastern and western voivodeships was set at 20 hectares, as opposed to 15 hectares in the rest of Poland. For another, the maximum – until large land holdings were expropriated in the Kresy and Galicia (and until 1925 in the western voivodeships) – was set at 300 hectares, compared to 180 hectares in the remainder of Poland.[80] Tenant farmers in the voivodeships of the Kresy were entitled, in principle, to buy the land they rented, but not in the case of those who 'had expressed their hostile disposition to the Polish state' and not worked the land at a given moment or for longer than a year.[81] Contemporary Ukrainian and German accounts of the situation of minorities in eastern and western Poland after agrarian reform point to two additional aspects.[82] Observers, who were certainly arguing in their own interest, pointed out the large discretionary powers enjoyed by the local authorities, specifically by those authorities entrusted with the implementation of agrarian reform. Thus, the council of ministers could arbitrarily decide in which rural administrative district how much land from large landholders should be parcelled out, as well as which large landholders could be expropriated if they did not fulfil their annual parcellation plan. Appeals against such decisions could not be lodged with the respective authority but had to be taken to court, usually straight to the highest judicial authority, the Supreme Administrative Court.[83] The equality of all citizens proclaimed in the constitution could not prevent the coalition of interests between the authorities and elite large-parcel Polish landowners from systematically discriminating against German, Ukrainian and Belarussian minorities.

Whereas in the case of agrarian reform there were only indications of a state programme for Polonizing these regions, the existence of such a programme is obvious in connection with the settlement of military veterans in the Kresy.[84] As in Kosovo, the settlement measures in eastern Poland were justified as being civilizational and strategic. The idea was not only to reward volunteer and veteran front soldiers and officers for their services to the fatherland, but to put them in vulnerable eastern territories where they would act as a military bulwark and bring a higher degree of civilization.[85] In reality, the settlement programme steadily dwindled in the course of the interwar period, most likely due to a lack of resources and the waning interest of potential settlers, so that all together, barely ten thousand individuals were relocated there. A considerable share of them simply rented out their land to local Belarussian and Ukrainian

---

80 Rudolf Freund, 'Die polnische Agrarreform', in *Weltwirtschaftliches Archiv* 24, 2 (1926): 309–20, here 315; Anton Heinrich Hollmann, 'Die polnische Agrarreform', *Berichte über Landwirtschaft* [new series] 5, 1 (1926): 125–38, here 128–30; Conte, 'Land und "ethnische Reinheit"', 56.

81 Friedrich Hellwege, 'Agrarverfassung und Agrarreform in Polen', in Sering, *Die agrarischen Umwälzungen*, 154–204, here 180.

82 Freund, 'Die polnische Agrarreform', 314–5; Hollmann, 'Die polnische Agrarreform', 127–8; Hellwege, *Agrarverfassung und Agrarreform*, 179–81; *Ausrottung der Ukrainer in Polen* (Prague: Zentral Exekutivausschuss der Vertreter der Organisationen der Ukrainischen Emigration in der Tschechoslowakei, 1930), 22–3; Basil Paneyko, 'Galicia and the Polish-Ukrainian Problem', in *Slavonic and East European Review* 9 (1930/1931); *La situation de la population ukrainienne en Pologne* (Nendeln: Kraus, 1973 [1924]).

83 Hellwege, *Agrarverfassung und Agrarreform*, 186; Freund, *Die polnische Agrarreform*, 129.

84 Christhardt Henschel, 'Front-line Soldiers into Farmers: Military Colonization in Poland after the First and Second World Wars', in *Property in East Central Europe: Notions, Institutions and Practices of Landownership in Twentieth Century*, eds Hannes Siegrist and Dietmar Müller (New York: Berghahn Books, 2015), 144–62; Benecke, *Die Ostgebiete*, 123–33.

85 On this perspective, see Stanislaw Srokowski, 'The Ukrainian Problem in Poland: A Polish View', *Slavonic and East European Studies* 9 (1930/1931): 588–97; A.G. Macdonnell, 'East Poland After Ten Years', *Fortnightly Review* 33 (1933): 492–502; M.B. Winsch, 'Scenes in Eastern Poland', *Contemporary Review* 146 (1934): 472–9.

Statehood: the interwar period

farmers, since they themselves either lacked the capital, skills or time (as active military personnel) to run a farm. The damage done by resettling these veterans – in the form of an antagonized Belarussian and Ukrainian populace – was considerably greater than the benefit from an ethnopolitical perspective. And this is true despite the relatively small number of veterans actually relocated there, in a region as large as the Kresy, the Polish state having revealed the sizeable discrepancy between its high-flown plans and the limited means at its disposal for putting them into practice. Extrapolating from the case of colonists and veterans, we can say the same about agrarian reform: that the damage was done immediately while the medium- and long-term gains were slow in coming.

Colonization projects were implemented in Czechoslovakia too, albeit to a much lesser extent than in Yugoslavia and Poland. All together about three thousand mostly Czech and Slovak families were furnished with thirty-eight thousand hectares of land, more than two thirds of this being in Slovakia and Carpathian Ruthenia – that is to say, on the former property of Hungarian large-parcel landowners.[86] The remaining third of colonist land was allocated in Bohemian lands. As with other colonization projects – for example, in Romania, in the heavily Turkish and Bulgarian-populated Southern Dobrudja and Russian and Ukrainian Bessarabia – a tendency for revendication was clearly evident. Agrarian reform and colonization had the task of rectifying a historical wrong, i.e. a disproportionate number of 'foreigners' now considered as belonging to a minority.

The state as a protagonist: the allocation and legal status of land

Beyond the perspective of nationalizing nation states, the increasing role of the state in the implementation of agrarian reforms during the interwar period can be divided into three phases: the expropriation, the allocation and the administration of land. Given the 'wild' land expropriations towards the end of the war and during the militarily and politically unstable transition period in many parts of the region, it is no surprise that the redistribution of land did not follow the rule of law. Expropriations were generally legalized retroactively, infringements against liberal and individualist concepts of property being anchored in constitutions that were ratified after the fact. No country in Central, Eastern and Southeastern Europe entirely abolished the liberal concept of property in its constitution, but typically put a restriction on it, emphasizing the 'social function' of property.[87]

In all of these countries, the expropriation and reallocation of land in the wake of agrarian reform was entrusted to land offices, some of which were established especially for this purpose. These state agencies began by assuming all or part of the property rights on land, followed by a second phase in which it redistributed land to new owners. This gave agrarian reform the veneer of state sovereignty, largely exempting land ownership from the effects of market mechanisms. Thus, legislators could decide how much land it was necessary, useful and legitimate to own. Moreover, it was up to parliament to determine the amount of compensation payments, which were generally paid out as long-term government bonds, the inviolability of property being upheld, at least in formal terms, in the practice of indemnification. The amount varied considerably from country to country, with Czechoslovakia in the lead, paying out 15 to 25

---

86 Daniel E. Miller, 'Colonizing the Hungarian and German Border Areas during the Czechoslovak Land Reform, 1918–1938', *Austrian History Yearbook* 34 (2003): 303–17, here 305.

87 V. Alton Moody, 'Agrarian Reform before Post-War European Constituent Assemblies', *Agricultural History* 7, 2 (1933): 81–95.

per cent of the actual value, whereas countries like Romania and Yugoslavia paid less than 5 per cent: tantamount to confiscation.[88]

Just like in the case of compensation payments, there were considerable differences in how much expropriated land was redistributed, how long and under what conditions it remained in state control, and how much of it became state property altogether. Once again Czechoslovakia is the country where agrarian reform was the least statist and quickest to shift its focus from social and national policy issues to economic criteria, because it was here that no less than one third of the 1.3 million hectares of confiscated land was given back to its previous owners once about 760,000 hectares had been parcelled out, leased and sold, strengthening medium-sized farms in particular.[89] A highly efficient land office that was present in the countryside in the form of numerous local offices was quick to implement agrarian reform, giving old and new landowners full property rights to their land. Only an insignificant amount of land remained in state hands. Estonia and Latvia were at the opposite end of the spectrum, with about 2.3 and 3.4 million hectares of expropriated land, 48 and 58 per cent respectively, remaining in the possession of the state.[90] Such aggregated figures, however, disguise some significant regional differences within a given country, as evidenced by Romania, where only 7.7 per cent of expropriated land remained state property in the Romanian Old Kingdom, whereas in Transylvania it was 18.5 per cent, in Bessarabia 26.4 per cent, and in Bukovina 30.1 per cent.[91]

The speed with which expropriated land was reallocated essentially depended on two factors: the political will of the national elites to rapidly initiate and implement the reforms, and the ability of participating institutions and professions to do so effectively. The latter was quite pronounced in Bohemia, with a well-educated pool of specialists in functioning post-Habsburg institutions, e.g. the cadastral office and land register. In cases where several institutional legacies, and hence concomitant cultures of property, had to be combined into a homogeneous whole in the process of legal unification – the challenge was biggest in Poland, Romania and Yugoslavia – agrarian reform was a lengthy procedure for technical reasons alone. Here, a crosscurrent becomes evident in all the countries of the region except for Czechoslovakia. While the state's claim to control, regulate and plan the property of its citizens grew considerably, the quality of state services was less than optimal, so that the state was relatively ignorant about property relations in the countryside. In Romania, the main reason for the sluggish and incomplete implementation of agrarian reform was to be found in the 'struggle of institutions'. On one side, there were professionals from post-Habsburg institutions in Transylvania and Bukovina – land surveyors, cadastral and

---

88 Joachim von Puttkamer: 'Die tschechoslowakische Bodenreform von 1919: Soziale Umgestaltung als Fundament der Republik', *Bohemia* 46, 2 (2005): 315–42, here 324. For Romania and Yugoslavia, see the respective international and national standard works: David Mitrany, *Land & Peasant in Romania: The War and Agrarian Reform (1917–21)* (London and New Haven, CT: Oxford Universisty Press and Yale University Press, 1930); Dumitru Şandru, *Reforma agrară din 1921 în România* [The agrarian reform of 1921 in Romania] (Bucharest: Editura Acadademiei Republicii Socialiste România, 1975); Tomasevich, *Peasants, Politics, and Economic Change in Yugoslavia*; Nikola Gaćeša, *Agrarna reforma i kolonizacija u Jugoslaviji* [Agrarian reform and colonization in Yugoslavia] (Novi Sad: Matica Srpska 1984).

89 von Puttkamer, 'Die tschechoslowakische Bodenreform', 328, footnote 58.

90 von Pistohlkors, 'Tiefgreifende agrarische Umwälzungen und Umstrukturierungen', 189.

91 Mircea Georgescu: *Principii şi metode în legiuirile Române pentru reforma agrară* [Principles and methods in the Romanian laws on agrarian reform] (Bucharest: Bucovina I.E. Torouţiu, 1943), 132–3.

Statehood: the interwar period

land-registry officials as well as public notaries – lobbying to transfer these institutions to all of Greater Romania.[92] The opposing side consisted of the much more powerful class of lawyers in Old Romania, whose strong bloc of lawyer-politicians in both houses of parliament managed not only to retain the Old Kingdom's land-recording system, considered by experts to be extremely inefficient, but also to undermine the post-Habsburg system in Transylvania and Bukovina. Thus, the land-ownership system of the Old Kingdom effectively remained in place, with transactions such as purchases and sales, mortgages and inheritance being done without a cadastre and land register. The result was that land transactions were burdened with extremely high transaction costs, giving rise to contractual agreements with low legal certainty and predictability, the overall upshot of which was that precious little private capital went into agriculture due to the high risks involved.

In addition to these institutional causes for the undercapitalization of agriculture after agrarian reform, the legislators of most countries in the region provided yet another cause by imposing limits on the marketability of land distributed during reform. State land offices functioned everywhere as intermediary institutions between old and new landowners, with the land being allocated generally remaining as state property until the new peasant landowner had paid off the last instalment of the purchase price. This period could last up to fifteen years in which the new owner only had partial property rights, being allowed neither to sell, nor to mortgage, thus making it impossible to use the land as collateral for a desperately needed bank loan to modernize the farm. Moreover, in Romania and Yugoslavia the state reserved an option to buy any of the land distributed in agrarian reform even after the farmer had paid off his debts. Particularly in interwar Yugoslavia, the protection of a legal minimum of farmland – of house and garden – against market mechanisms was in keeping with the tradition of homestead legislation of the 'long nineteenth century', prohibiting land from being repossessed in the case of a farmer not being able to pay off his debts.[93] These protection measures show that, primarily in rural Southeastern Europe, the implementation of agrarian reform and the stabilization of its results was a process that was mostly concerned with securing the welfare of farmers. But even in Central and East European states, such as Poland and the Baltic states, these farmers – with a lower percentage in the overall population – were not yet integrated into existing or expanding systems of social security.[94]

We have seen that, despite a significant expansion of farmer-owned lands, agrarian reforms by no means meant the triumph of the liberal-individualist concept of property concomitant with the shaking off of post-feudal forms of property by societies, that during the interwar period, were emancipating themselves into nation states. In fact, there was a tendency of the nation and the state to reshape the liberal-individualist concept of property for its own purposes.

---

92 Dietmar Müller, 'Eigentum verwalten in Rumänien: Advokaten, Geodäten und Notare (1830–1940)', in *Professionen, Eigentum und Staat: Europäische Entwicklungen im Vergleich (19. und 20. Jahrhundert)*, eds Dietmar Müller and Hannes Siegrist (Göttingen: Wallstein Verlag, 2014), 75–132.

93 For more detail, see Dietmar Müller, 'Die Institutionalisierung von Eigentumsformen in Ostmittel- und Südosteuropa im 20. Jahrhundert: für eine Kulturgeschichte des Rechts', in *Institutionen und Kultur in Südosteuropa*, eds Wim van Meurs and Dietmar Müller (München: Verlag Otto Sagner, 2014), 119–62. On homestead legislation in Serbia, the so-called *okućje* regulations, see Marie-Janine Calic, 'Probleme nachholender Entwicklung in Serbien (1830–1941)', in *Archiv für Sozialgeschichte* 34 (1994): 63–83, here 70–1.

94 On the fruitless efforts of the ILO to integrate farmers into a system of social security, see Amalia Ribi Forclaz, 'A New Target for International Social Reform: The International Labour Organization and Working and Living Conditions in Agriculture in the Inter-War Years', *Contemporary European History* 10, 3 (2011): 307–29.

It is important to point out that traditions protecting the property of small farmers that stemmed from the 'long nineteenth century' were continued by legislators in the interwar period: in Old Romania as patriarchal policy elements, in Serbia as egalitarian ones. The social and protectionist intentions of this old homestead legislation were given a significantly new meaning in the wake of agrarian reform, newly distributed land being linked to national obligations whose definition and enforcement was the prerogative of elites in the service of the state. The exploitation of land for national purposes, as evidenced in particular in colonization projects as well as more generally in the establishment of state authorities for implementing agrarian reforms and securing their long-term results, was accompanied by a major expansion of state functions in rural areas. During the Great Depression, however, it became clear that the agricultural sector in most states of Central, Eastern and Southeastern Europe was undercapitalized and hence in need of modernization, giving rise to renewed state intervention to set moratoriums on farm debts and tax arrears. With that, the state had established itself as an active protagonist in agriculture in large parts of the region, not only in the plans made by elites but likewise in the expectations of the rural population.

Systems of social security and the welfare state

Social policy is perhaps the most appropriate field for demonstrating that the politically and historically significant years of 1918 and 1945 are not particularly well-suited as markers of a more comprehensive historical watershed. For one thing, the intensive expansion of social-security systems in Central, Eastern and Southeastern Europe during the interwar period was based, both in terms of staff and institutions, on German and Habsburg legacies; for another, new developments occurred in the period between the wars that could not be so easily abandoned after the Second World War. Apart from institutional continuity, the emergence of two international organizations after the First World War, the International Labour Organization (ILO) and the League of Nations, was a major force in transnationally structuring social policy as a field of knowledge.[95] Motives for expanding the social security system can be found, first of all, in the pressures exerted by industrialization, urbanization and equalization to rewrite the social constitution for the needs of a mass society.[96] Ideally through this process, industrial workers and the parties and unions representing them would be immunized against the Bolshevist alternative. Well-functioning social security was thought of as a powerful source of legitimation that would help lend credibility to the master narratives of new nation states, according to which these new states were more capable of serving the common good than the bygone empires had been. But legitimation can turn into delegitimization, for example when a level of care promised for political reasons is never put into practice on account of overstretch.[97]

---

95 Sandrine Kott, 'Constructing a European Social Model: The Fight for Social Insurance in the Interwar Period', in *Essays on the International Labour Organization and Its Impact on the World During the Twentieth Century*, eds Jasmien Van Daele et al. (Frankfurt a.M.: Peter Lang, 2010), 173–95; Madeleine Herren, *Internationale Organisationen seit 1865: eine Globalgeschichte der internationalen Ordnung* (Darmstadt: Wissenschaftliche Buchgesellschaft, 2009), 67–71.

96 Anselm Doering-Manteuffel, '"Soziale Demokratie" als transnationales Ordnungsmodell', in *Dimensionen internationaler Geschichte*, eds Jost Dülffer and Wilfried Loth (München: Oldenbourg, 2012), 313–33.

97 Metzler, 'Die sozialstaatliche Dimension der parlamentarischen Demokratie', 205–32.

Statehood: the interwar period

Systems of social security functioning as the institutional foundation of the welfare state have their roots in the German Empire and Austria-Hungary of the 1880s.[98] At that time, organized liberalism in both states had entered into an ideological and political crisis, prompting conservative reformers such as Reich Chancellor Otto von Bismarck and Minister-President Viscount Eduard von Taaffe to undertake the long-term project of establishing a social security system that would keep the liberals permanently out of power and socially integrate the working classes. The German Empire witnessed the adoption of health insurance (1883), workers' compensation (1884) as well as old-age and disability insurance (1889) in rapid succession. Similar legislation was soon to follow in the Transleithanian, Austrian part of the Habsburg Empire, with health insurance in 1888, accident insurance in 1887 and a relief fund with old-age and disability benefits in 1892. These types of insurance were initially just for factory workers but were eventually expanded to include other kinds of workers and salaried employees (pension insurance for salaried employees in Austria in 1906, in the German Empire in 1913). This so-called Bismarckian system of social security has four main characteristics: its compulsory nature, a three-tier contribution structure (employee, employer, state), state initiative and responsibility being transferred to organizations governed by public law, and self-management. In industrial regions and cities, in particular, the number of people insured against the three main life risks had reached several million by the eve of the First World War. This was naturally the case in Silesia and Posen, the Bohemian lands and Prague, as well as in cities and industrial regions that after the war would belong to the successor states of the German Empire and Austria-Hungary. But even states in Central, Eastern and Southeastern Europe that did not directly inherit territories from these empires had been closely following the development of social security there (and sometimes in France as well) in the waning years of the 'long nineteenth century', and they began to set up their own systems along these lines.

This long-term tendency towards increasing state intervention received an enormous impetus during the First World War due to all-encompassing state demands made on citizen-soldiers, in a way that had not been seen in Europe for a very long time. Compulsory military service may have been introduced in Austria-Hungary as early as 1868, but the link between military service and the state's obligation to provide welfare services to its citizens was not established until during the First World War.[99] Apart from civil servants and state employees working directly for the state, a second group with direct claims was added to the group of state beneficiaries: disabled veterans and the surviving dependents of fallen soldiers. The question of reintegrating invalids after the First World War was an integral, if separate, part of the welfare state in other states of the region. The benefits ranged from receiving an invalid or surviving dependent's pension to preferential employment in public service, or the issuing of state licences to run tobacco shops, etc. One source of political conflict was the question of whether or not soldiers who had served in armies of the Central Powers or associated troops were eligible for

---

98 Detlev Zöllner, 'Länderbericht Deutschland', 45–179; Herbert Hofmeister 'Landesbericht Österreich', 445–729, both in *Ein Jahrhundert Sozialversicherung in der Bundesrepublik Deutschland, Frankreich, Großbritannien, Österreich und der Schweiz*, eds Peter A. Köhler and Hans F. Zacher (Berlin: Duncker & Humblot, 1981).

99 Verena Pawlowsky and Harald Wendelin, 'Kriegsopfer und Sozialstaat: Österreich nach dem Ersten Weltkrieg', in *Die Weltkriege als symbolische Bezugspunkte: Polen, die Tschechoslowakei und Deutschland nach dem Ersten Weltkrieg*, ed. Natali Stegmann (Prague: Praha Masarykův Ústav a Archiv AV ČR, 2009), 127–46.

state benefits at all. In Warsaw and Prague, as well as in Belgrade and Bucharest, this potential problem was viewed as an opportunity to create a national master narrative in which the overwhelming majority of all combatants were to be integrated into the new titular nation.[100]

The development of Central and Eastern European social security systems can be interpreted as the interplay between inheritance and national appropriation, between social and political challenges and responses, and between expansion and contraction.[101] Poland and Czechoslovakia in particular had a pool of well-trained specialists who had worked at regional branches of the German and Austro-Hungarian social security agencies. The new elites were well aware of the potential for integration of these systems and the great personal resources at their disposal. The more or less seamless continuity of inherited social security systems, including provisions for state employees and disabled veterans, meant that not only were the old institutions themselves salvaged but a considerable number of former staff members was kept in their employ, regardless of whether these experts were Germans, Austrians, Poles or Czechs.[102] There was political pressure to expand these social security systems in the immediate post-war period in an atmosphere marked by conflicts over new state boundaries and old provincial allegiances, as well as due to the fear of Bolshevist revolution spreading to Central Europe as it did briefly in the Hungarian and the Munich Republic of Councils. But evidence of a general trend does not imply a political consensus. Roman Dmowski, for example, considered it a grave danger to Poland and Europe if the Weimar Republic became a liberal welfare state.[103] This makes it abundantly clear that, for example, from a conservative national-Catholic perspective, the expansion of the welfare state could be construed as a loss of control – the empowerment of individuals to adopt a morally dubious way of life, and sheer presumptuousness on the part of the secular state to try and institutionalize it. To be sure, it also reveals Dmowski's fear – representative for many anti-revisionist states – that the Weimar Republic and, subsequently, the Third Reich might become too economically and socially attractive, and even be perceived as another alternative system.

The further expansion of the social security system happened threefold: first, benefits were improved in the event of insurance claims; second, beneficiaries were expanded to including most wage-earning employees outside of agriculture; and third, insurance against unemployment

---

100 Natali Stegmann, *Kriegsdeutungen – Staatsgründungen – Sozialpolitik: der Helden- und Opferdiskurs in der Tschechoslowakei 1918–1948* (München: Oldenbourg, 2010); Julia Eichenberg, *Kämpfen für Frieden und Fürsorge: polnische Veteranen des Ersten Weltkriegs und ihre internationalen Kontakte, 1918–1939* (München: Oldenbourg, 2011); Katrin Boeckh and Natali Stegmann, eds, *Veterans and War Victims in Eastern Europe During the twentieth Century: A Comparison* (Leipzig: Leipziger Universitätsverlag, 2011); Heike Karge, 'Sozialpolitische Erwartungen und Erfahrungen im Königreich der Serben, Kroaten und Slowenen', in *Staatsbürgerschaft und Teilhabe: bürgerliche, politische und soziale Rechte im östlichen Europa*, eds Katrin Boeckh et al. (München: De Gruyter, 2014), 67–79.

101 Tomasz Inglot, *Welfare States in East Central Europe, 1919–2004* (Cambridge: Cambridge University Press, 2008); Béla Tomka, *Welfare in East and West: Hungarian Social Security in an International Comparison 1918–1990* (Berlin: Akademie Verlag, 2004); Béla Tomka, *A Social History of Twentieth-Century Europe* (London and New York: Routledge, 2013).

102 Ingo Loose, 'How to Run a State: The Question of Knowhow in Public Administration in the First Years after Poland's Rebirth', in *Expert Cultures in Central Eastern Europe: The Internationalization of Knowledge and the Transformation of Nation States since World War I*, eds Martin Kohlrausch, Katrin Steffen and Stefan Wiederkehr (Osnabrück: fibre Verlag, 2010), 145–59.

103 This was the opinion expressed by Roman Dmowski in a conversation with General T. Bliss, an advisor of Woodrow Wilson, in the run-up to the Paris Peace Treaties, see Kay Lundgreen-Nielsen, *The Polish Problem at the Paris Peace Conference: A Study of the Policies of the Great Powers and the Poles, 1918–1919* (Odense: Odense University Press, 1979), 105–6.

Statehood: the interwar period

was established, which did not become law in Central, Eastern and Southeastern Europe until the 1920s. Despite this general trend of expanding social security systems in the region, there were specific regional characteristics resulting from differences in social structure and political circumstances. In Czechoslovakia, for example – the state with the highest percentage of industry and workers in the entire region – the role of unions and social democracy cannot be underestimated, especially in the years from 1919 to 1922. Here only unionized workers were insured against unemployment, whereas mine and steel workers along with salaried employees were excluded from the general system. This fragmentation remained intact for the most part in the second developmental phase of social security, when from 1922 to 1935 the social-democratic influence was replaced by the *Pětka*, a corporative political system of five parties in a permanent informal coalition.[104] In Poland the discrepancies between partition areas were far more dramatic than in Czechoslovakia but the share of industry and services in the overall economy was much smaller. These circumstances, together with the political events of the Polish-Soviet war of 1920–21 and Piłsudski's putsch of 1926, resulted in the Polish social security system developing in a decidedly paternalist and centralist way. For fear of leftist influence in the self-administration of the welfare system, but also out of a sense of genuine optimism about the possibility of shaping the future on the part of the intelligentsia beholden to Józef Piłsudski, the Social Insurance Institution (*Zakład Ubezpieczeń Społecznych*) was founded in 1934 by the Sanacja regime and placed under the Ministry of Labour and Social Welfare (*Ministerstwo Pracy i Opieki Społecznej*).[105] The institutional step of setting up the Central Social Insurance Institute (*Ústřední Sociální Pojišt'ovna*) in late 1930s Czechoslovakia presumably followed the Polish example.

In the Transleithanian half of the Habsburg Empire, that is to say in the Hungarian lands, the first social security laws were passed some years after those in Austria and included mandatory health insurance for workers (1891), work injury insurance (1907) and pensions and family benefit for civil servants (1912).[106] This relatively early start was followed by years of modest, sector-related expansion of the social system that essentially lasted into the late 1930s. This was due to stagnating industrialization after the turn of the century, and with it the core target group of social security, but it was also due to the government's lax enforcement of mandatory employer coverage. In Hungary, like everywhere in the region, the bureaucrats working in the social security system were generally social-democratic or communist sympathizers, which resulted in a halting expansion of the system against the backdrop of the revolutionary and counter-revolutionary events of 1919–20. National-conservative elites gave few discretionary powers to social bureaucrats and the Ministry of Social Affairs, and the pension system introduced in 1929 included mostly state employees and miners, and very few industrial workers.

---

104 Inglot, *Welfare States*, 62–70. See also Michael J. Kopanic, 'Labor Unions in Interwar Czechoslovakia: The Case of Slovakia, 1918–1929', *East Central Europe/L'Europe du Centre-Est* 19 (1992): 26–44; Peter Heumos, 'Thesen zur sozialgeschichtlichen Dimension eines Systemzusammenbruchs: Das Beispiel der Ersten tschechoslowakischen Republik 1938/39', *Archiv für Sozialgeschichte* 34 (1994): 55–61; Natali Stegmann, 'Die Habsburgermonarchie als Fundament: Sozialpolitik in der Tschechoslowakei', in *Staatsbürgerschaft und Teilhabe*, eds Katrin Boeckh et al., 51–65.

105 Inglot, *Welfare States*, 78–90. See also Krzysztof Piątek, 'Sozialstaat in Polen: Von der Teilung Polens über den Realsozialismus zum aktuellen Transformationsprozess', in *Sozialstaat in Europa: Geschichte, Entwicklung, Perspektiven*, eds Katrin Kraus and Thomas Geisen (Wiesbaden: Westdeutscher Verlag, 2001), 201–24; Stanislas Nawrocki, *Les Assurances Sociales en Pologne* (Lille: Imprimerie G. Sauti, 1930).

106 Inglot, *Welfare States*, 97–103; Tomka, *Welfare in East and West*, 55.

Any proper assessment of the importance of these social security systems must also discuss the scope of these services. Apart from the question of which life risks were insured, it is important to know which sectors of the economy were included, how high the rate of coverage was in the overall population, what the replacement rate was for sickness, disability, unemployment and pensions, how long they were paid out, and finally what percentage of the GDP was spent on social security benefits. In general terms, workers, salaried employees and farmers were handled separately by the social security system, the latter group being excluded from the system entirely. In some instances, this fragmentation even applied to certain branches of industry. The Central European countries with Prussian and Habsburg legacies offered slightly lower benefits relative to GDP than in Western Europe. With regard to coverage and replacement rates, Béla Tomka summarized as follows: 'in Czechoslovakia, social security coverage expanded dynamically already after the First World War. In Hungary and Poland, the ratio of people covered by social security increased but still stayed at a relatively low level in the interwar years.' He continued regarding the replacement rate: 'countries of East Central Europe were lagging behind in the interwar period, the level of benefits relative to income converged markedly to those in Western Europe.'[107] One of the main impediments to the expansion of the social security system was of course the Great Depression. In the wake of the Great Depression, it was evident throughout the entire region that the increasing trend towards political and administrative centralization in the field of social security effectively rolled back elements of self-administration in favour of direct state management.

The Southeastern European countries of Romania and Yugoslavia were comparable to Hungary in terms of their poor structural preconditions for the expansion of the social security system, i.e. weak and insular industrialization and a low share of blue-collar workers in the overall population. Unlike in Hungary, but similar to Poland and to a lesser extent Czechoslovakia, Romania and Yugoslavia endeavoured to harmonize post-Habsburg regions with the rest of the country, allowing Bucharest and Belgrade to celebrate the establishment and expansion of a social insurance system as an achievement of state- and nation-building.[108] In the post-Habsburg provinces of Croatia-Slavonia, Bosnia-Herzegovina, Istria, Vojvodina and Transylvania, but also in Serbia and Romania, the first types of social insurance were mostly introduced in the first decade of the twentieth century. Hence there was little time or opportunity before the First World War to consolidate and expand these systems. Only in Bukovina, Slovenia and Dalmatia were the respective laws passed earlier, in the 1880s and 1890s. Whereas the Bismarckian character of social insurance in post-Habsburg regions was self-evident, it is worth noting that the Serbian Workshop Act (*Zakon o radnjama*) of 1910 and the Romanian Crafts, Credit and Workers' Insurance Act (*Legea pentru organizarea meseriilor, creditului şi asigurărilor muncitoreşti*) of 1912 were modelled after the German and Austrian systems as well. An all-Yugoslav Workers' Insurance Act (*Zakon o osiguranju radniku*) was passed in Belgrade in 1922, but only comprised workers' compensation and health insurance. The life risks of disability, old age and death

---

107 Tomka, *A Social History of Twentieth-Century Europe*, 169, 171.

108 Jovica Luković, 'Der ferne Staat: Transfer als Institutionalisierungsvehikel der Sozialversicherung in Jugoslawien (1919–1941)', in *Institutionen und Kultur in Südosteuropa*, eds Wim van Meurs and Dietmar Müller (München: Verlag Otto Sagner, 2014), 211–40; Ilie Marinescu, *Politica socială interbelică în România* [Social policy in interwar Romania] (Bucharest: Editura Tehnică, 1995); Georges Chiriac, *Les Assurances Sociales en Roumanie* (Paris: A. Pedone, 1932); [gh. mih.]: 'Asigurările sociale în România' [Social security in Romania], in *Enciclopedia României*. vol. 1: *Statul* (Bucharest: Imprimeria Naţională, 1938), 545–51.

Statehood: the interwar period

were signed into law in 1925, though actual coverage did not begin until 1937. At no point between the wars was unemployment insured; lawmakers must have relied on the fact that Yugoslav factory workers still had sufficient ties to the countryside and could always go back to their village if they lost their jobs in the city. Work was fundamentally defined as industrial labour, leaving other categories of labour uninsured or reliant upon more fragile systems of volunteer insurance. Under the Old Romanian law of 1912, which was extended to include the previously Russian region of Bessarabia in 1921, benefits were paid in the case of sickness, maternity, death, disability, old age and occupational accidents, whereas in post-Habsburg in Transylvania old-age and accident insurance were not covered at first. Only with two new laws in 1932 was insurance coverage for industrial workers unified at the national level following the Old Romanian model and extended to salaried employees in industry and trade to include sickness and disability insurance. In both Yugoslavia and Romania, the benefits were based on employee, employer and state contributions, although during the Great Depression, in particular, the latter two were often late with their payments or paid less than the prescribed amount.

The expansion of social security systems in Central, Eastern and Southeastern Europe was accompanied in all of these countries by a considerable increase in demand for social science and social policy expertise.[109] Expert groups calling for more assistance and state intervention in the social sphere were being formed everywhere. Social issues were being given more attention by governments everywhere after the First World War, even to the point of setting up independent ministries of social affairs, and everywhere state and public institutions were being expanded or set up to help administer social security systems. The countries in the region were thus part of a Europe-wide trend that Lutz Raphael called the 'scientification of the social' and the 'professionalization of the political'.[110] The aforementioned transfer relations between social insurance of the Bismarckian type intensified in the interwar period into a transnational network of social and labour law experts.[111] The League of Nations and the ILO were the ideal foundation for this, allowing ILO functionaries, for example, to recommend Czechoslovak experts to advise the Greek government under Eleftherios Venizelos on the expansion of its social security network.[112] There were so many Czechoslovak social experts active in the ILO

---

109 For the example of Romania, see Dietmar Müller, 'Die Institutionalisierung sozialwissenschaftlichen Wissens in der Zwischenkriegszeit: Das Rumänische Sozial-Institut und der Verein für Socialpolitik', in *Kultur und Beruf in Europa*, eds Isabella Löhr, Matthias Middell and Hannes Siegrist (Stuttgart: Franz Steiner Verlag, 2012), 197–205.

110 Lutz Raphael, 'Die Verwissenschaftlichung des Sozialen als methodische und konzeptionelle Herausforderung für eine Sozialgeschichte des 20. Jahrhunderts', *Geschichte und Gesellschaft* 22, 2 (1996): 165–93; idem, *Imperiale Gewalt und mobilisierte Nation: Europa 1914–1945* (München: C.H. Beck, 2011); Gabriele Metzler and Dirk van Laak, 'Die Konkretion der Utopie: Historische Quellen der Planungsutopien der 1920er Jahre', in *Wissenschaft – Planung – Vertreibung: Neuordnungskonzepte und Umsiedlungspolitik im 20. Jahrhundert*, eds Isabel Heinemann and Patrick Wagner (Stuttgart: Franz Steiner Verlag, 2006), 23–43.

111 On transnational cultures of expertise in the interwar period, see Martin Kohlrausch, 'Technologische Innovationen und transnationale Netzwerke: Europe zwischen den Weltkriegen', *Journal of Modern European History* 6, 2 (2008): 181–95; Martin Kohlrausch, Katrin Steffen and Stefan Wiederkehr, eds, *Expert Cultures in East Central Europe: The Internationalization of Knowledge and the Transformation of Nation States since World War I* (Osnabrück: fibre Verlag, 2010); Wolfram Kaiser and Johan Schot, eds, *Writing the Rules for Europe: Experts, Cartels, and International Organizations* (Basingstoke: Palgrave Macmillan, 2014), 49–77.

112 Kott, 'Constructing a European Social Model', 190–91; Vasiliki Rapti, 'The Postwar Greek Welfare Model within the Context of Southern European Welfare', in *Reciprocity and Redistribution: Work and Welfare Reconsidered*, ed. Gro Hagemann (Pisa: Plus-Pisa University Press, 2007), 43–60.

that it seems reasonable to assume that the Czechoslovak government had actually coordinated these efforts to increase the international visibility and legitimacy of Czechoslovakia, lending it the image of a socially progressive and economically successful state.

Demographics, eugenics and family policy

With state actors and institutions having turned away from the liberal individualism of the 'long nineteenth century' and elevated the weal and woe of their citizens to a matter of statist intervention, it is no wonder that even individual lifestyles were not immune to the planning of social engineers. The demographic and biopolitical ideas and programmes of the interwar period revealed that fears of 'ethnic' degeneration and utopias of renewal, both of which were fuelled by the First World War, were converging with the scientistic promise of translating scientifically proven laws of evolution and heredity into concrete instructions for political action. Eugenics, with its ensemble of social, biological and cultural ideas about the role of 'breeding' and 'selection' in the regeneration of the 'national body', is extremely well-suited for analyzing and gauging the paths and limits of state-sponsored social engineering.[113] According to Marius Turda, the eugenics of the 1920s up to 1940 should:

> not be treated as an extraordinary episode in the history of biological sciences removed from its social, political and national contexts, as a deviation from the norm which found its culmination in Nazi politics of genocide, but as an integral part of European modernity in which the state and the individual embarked on an unprecedented quest for the renewal of an idealized national community.[114]

Eugenically inspired ideas and policy measures are to be seen in this regard as being the most extreme form of state intervention during the period of high modernity, with experts being accorded the role of planners beyond the constraints of democratic legitimation.[115]

Eugenics is in some ways complementary to other forms of state intervention in areas of social policy such as agrarian reform, social security and housing, but in other ways, it is diametrically opposed as it is a radicalized form of statist micromanagement. All of these measures were reacting to the phenomena of urbanization, industrialization and modern warfare, which from the perspective of elites had led to social behaviours tantamount to a loss of control and anomie. The accepted diagnosis throughout Europe during the First World War was that these challenges could no longer be dealt with by applying the traditional values of liberalism. The eugenic critique of the aforementioned social reforms of the interwar period was guided to a certain extent by this diagnosis. Accordingly, it was considered a mistake from the perspective of eugenics to bestow the benefits of reforms on all citizens without first taking into consideration their biological usefulness for the nation and the state.

Since the discovery around the turn of the century of blood groups and the laws of heredity, this biologistic view of the state, nation and population resulted in a flood of eugenic

---

113 Alison Bashford and Philippa Levine, eds, *The Oxford Handbook of the History of Eugenics* (New York: Oxford University Press, 2011).

114 Marius Turda, *Modernism and Eugenics* (Basingstoke: Palgrave Macmillan 2010), 120.

115 Zygmunt Bauman, *Modernity and the Holocaust* (Cambridge: Polity Press, 1989); idem: *Modernity and Ambivalence* (Cambridge: Polity Press, 1991); James C. Scott, *Seeing Like a State: How Certain Schemes to Improve the Human Condition Have Failed* (New Haven, CT: Yale University Press, 1998).

Statehood: the interwar period

publications that supplanted or overshadowed older theories of racial anthropology.[116] But only with the millions of dead and mutilated soldiers in the First World War and the apparent drop in the birth rate did elites begin to take eugenicists' alarmist warnings about the signs of degeneration seriously and shift the focus of state intervention to family, procreation, individual lifestyles and social hygiene. Without going into the details of eugenic thinking, it will suffice here to point out the fundamental distinction between 'positive' and 'negative' eugenics. Whereas the former essentially encompassed pronatalist and family-friendly policies such as financial support and the legal protection of pregnant women, mothers and small children, the latter entailed prohibitive measures such as marriage bans and the voluntary or forced sterilization of men and women who were stigmatized as socially or biologically deviant. The prevalence of eugenic thinking in Central, Eastern and Southeastern Europe – also in the institutionalized form of associations, societies and publication platforms – was more or less synchronous with developments in Western Europe.[117] In general, eugenic thinking and practices were phenomena that were not linked to specific political, economic and social regimes, since they were widespread not only in the United States, France, Germany, England and Russia, but also in more welfare-oriented and social-democratic countries such as those of Scandinavia.[118] A number of factors, however, promoted the rapid spread of eugenic thought in the swath of Europe between Tallinn and Athens. For one thing, scenarios of degeneration, miscegenation and shrinking populations encountered fears of decline and extinction which had long been expressed in the 'small cultures' of Central, Eastern and Southeastern Europe, during the 'long nineteenth century'.[119] The scientist promise of warding off such negative scenarios by means of positive intervention correlated with the optimism of elites about the prospects of social engineering against the backdrop of newly emerging states after the First World War. As of 1913 in Prague and Vienna, 1914 in Budapest, 1917 in Poland, 1919 in Romania, 1924 in Greece and Estonia, and 1928 in Bulgaria, a range of associations were founded in rapid succession that bore the

---

116 Christian Promitzer, 'Vermessene Körper: "Rassenkundliche" Grenzziehungen im südöstlichen Europa', in *Wieser Enzyklopädie des Europäischen Ostens*, vol. 11, *Europa und die Grenzen im Kopf*, eds Karl Kaser et al. (Klagenfurt: Wieser Verlag, 2003), 365–93.

117 Maria Bucur, *Eugenics and Modernization in Interwar Romania* (Pittsburgh, PA: University of Pittsburgh Press, 2002); Marius Turda and Paul J. Weindling, eds, *'Blood and Homeland': Eugenics and Racial Nationalism in Central and Southeast Europe, 1900–1940* (Budapest: CEU Press, 2007); Maria Bucur, 'Eugenics in Eastern Europe, 1870s–1945', in Bashford and Levine, *The Oxford Handbook of the History of Eugenics*, 398–412; Christian Promitzer, Sevasti Trubeta and Marius Turda, eds, *Hygiene, Health and Eugenics in Southeastern Europe to 1945* (Budapest: CEU Press, 2010); Sevasti Trubeta, *Physical Anthropology, Race and Eugenics in Greece (1880s–1970s)* (Leiden: Brill, 2013); Marius Turda, *Eugenics and Nation in Early Twentieth Century Hungary* (Basingstoke: Palgrave Macmillan, 2014).

118 Mark B. Adams, ed., *The Wellborn Society: Eugenics in Germany, France, Brazil, and Russia* (Oxford: Oxford University Press, 1990); Stefan Kühl, *Die Internationale der Rassisten: Aufstieg und Niedergang der internationalen Bewegung für Eugenik und Rassenhygiene im 20. Jahrhundert* (Frankfurt a.M.: Campus Verlag, 1997); Nils Roll-Hansen and Gunnar Broberg, eds, *Eugenics and the Welfare State: Sterilization Policy in Norway, Sweden, Denmark, and Finland* (East Lansing, MI: Michigan State University Press, 1997).

119 The same fears and expectations led minority populations such as the Transylvanian Saxons to develop eugenic literature and a eugenic movement, both before and especially after the First World War. A good part of the proliferation and substantial integration of eugenic advocates in the established structures of Transylvanian Saxons is explained by the linking of 'new science' to old, church-based institutions such as 'neighbourhoods' (*Nachbarschaften*), which as of the mid-1930s were perpetuated, especially in towns, in the form of 'national neighbourhoods' (*völkische Nachbarschaften*). See Tudor Georgescu, 'Ethnic Minorities and the Eugenic Promise: The Transylvanian Saxon Experiment with National Renewal in Interwar Romania', *European Review of History* 17, 6 (2010): 861–80.

terms 'racial hygiene', 'population policy' and 'eugenics' in their names. The fact that Central, Eastern and Southeastern Europe caught up to Western Europe and the United States is made evident by the number of international eugenic congresses that took place in the region – in Warsaw (1922), Prague (1924), Vienna (1936) and Bucharest (1937) – with the financial and organizational support of the League of Nations Health Organization and the Rockefeller Foundation.[120]

Notwithstanding the cultural proximity of the eugenic discourse to issues addressed by national movements, and despite the transnational networking of social hygienic and eugenic professionals, very few of their policy recommendations were actually turned into law or put into practice. Nazi Germany's notorious eugenic laws and practices served as a deterrent in Central, Eastern and Southeastern Europe, as did the influence of the Catholic and Orthodox churches. The Czechoslovak eugenic movement in particular tried to distance itself from the German one as early as the 1920s, accusing it of 'aristocratic and undemocratic principles of selection'.[121] In Poland, as well as most other states in the region the positive, pronatalist and family-friendly elements predominated, whereas negative eugenic measures such as sterilization were critically discussed and largely rejected. The *Casti Connubii* encyclical on Christian marriage issued by Pope Pius XI in 1930 strengthened this line of argument in all countries where Catholicism was a political factor.[122] In Southeastern European countries with a predominantly Orthodox population the respective autocephalous Orthodox churches dampened the enthusiasm for eugenics in a similar way. To be sure, the churches were not motivated by an overall rejection of social hygienic and eugenic measures but by their desire to retain their authority in moral matters and family affairs and by their general opposition to scientist and state incursions in this field. Instead, it was their scepticism and continued resistance that effectively deterred the passing of any laws providing for negative eugenic measures in Central, Eastern and Southeastern Europe until the late 1930s. The Nazi seizure of power in Germany and the quick introduction of legislative measures calling for negative eugenics, culminating in the Nuremberg Race Laws of 1935, cemented the status quo especially in anti-revisionist states.

With a few notable exceptions, the medical profession was only partly successful in asserting its authority in the public health sector in Central, Eastern and Southeastern Europe.[123] During the war and the post-war years they increasingly pointed to social causes (malnutrition, unhygienic living and working conditions, prostitution, etc.) and they fought against epidemics. Despite the fact that eugenics was inopportune from a foreign-policy perspective and the fact that there was church resistance to it, traditional elites played no small part in resisting the self-aggrandizement of technocrats. Overall, politicians were only willing to allocate budget funds to public welfare and health that directly contributed to their incremental expansion, but never

---

120 Marius Turda and Paul J. Weindling, 'Eugenics, Race and Nation in Central and Southeast Europe, 1900–1940: A Historiographic Overview', in idem, *'Blood and Homeland'*, 1–20.

121 Michal Šimůnek, 'Eugenics, Social Genetics and Racial Hygiene: Plans for the Scientific Regulation of Human Heredity in the Czech Lands, 1900–1925', in Turda and Weindling, *'Blood and Homeland'*, 146–66, here 155.

122 Magdalena Gawin, 'Progressivism and Eugenic Thinking in Poland, 1905–1939', in Turda and Weindling, *'Blood and Homeland'*, 167–83; Magdalena Gawin, 'Early Twentieth-Century Eugenics in Europe's Peripheries: The Polish Perspectives', *East Central Europe* 38, 1 (2011): 1–15.

123 Mária M. Kovács, *Liberal Professions and Illiberal Politics: Hungary from the Habsburgs to the Holocaust* (Washington, DC and Oxford: Woodrow Wilson Center Press and Oxford University Press, 1994); Bucur, 'Eugenics in Eastern Europe', 403–4.

Statehood: the interwar period

the amount necessary to implement extensive negative eugenic measures.[124] Most popular, albeit woefully underfunded, were programmes for fighting diseases like malaria, tuberculosis and syphilis, which were framed as positive eugenics. Eugenic thinking advanced the furthest amongst the political elite of Romania, where Iuliu Moldovan, the founding father of the Romanian eugenic movement, was even appointed health minister and passed a law in 1930 on the public health system. 'Hygiene physicians' were given a public mandate to check the spread of venereal disease and to maintain and monitor hygiene standards in outdoor public places (streets and squares), in public facilities, as well as on the business and commercial premises of private companies. In addition, pronatalist benefits were provided to impoverished mothers. What is more, the Penal Code of 1936 called for considerable fines and prison sentences for men and women with venereal diseases who married with the knowledge that they were infected.[125]

The wave of authoritarianism in Central and Eastern Europe in the 1930s and the example set by the Nazi sterilization law of 1933 led to laws being passed in Estonia (1937) and Latvia (1938) that enabled forced sterilizations based on racial and social hygienic indications.[126] The real eugenic breakthrough, though, resulting in a biological definition of nation, came in the late 1930s when Hungary and Romania (1938) – followed by Bulgaria and Croatia (1940) and later Norway and France (1942) – passed legislation resembling the Nuremberg Race Laws, containing numerous elements of negative and especially anti-Semitic eugenics.[127]

The aforementioned fears of a dwindling population, both in number and in quality, played out in the area of family law too.[128] The long-term trend towards increasing female employment in industry and services, beyond the traditional roles of agricultural workers and household servants, was intensified during the First World War. Women made up a majority of the population in many countries of the region due to war casualties. This, together with women's suffrage and an egalitarian concept of citizenship in many constitutions that transcended gender boundaries, led to widespread 'moral panic'. What effect would these advances in the individualization and emancipation of women have on the birth rate and the cohesion of families, as well as on that of society and the state? Fears like these were responsible for the fact that changes

---

124 This is also suggested by the results of a comparative study of welfare history in Eastern Europe (Bulgaria, Croatia, Hungary, Latvia, Poland, Romania, Russia, Slovenia). See the bilingual edition of Sabine Hering and Berteke Waaldijk, *Guardians of the Poor – Custodians of the Public: Welfare History in Eastern Europe 1900–1960/Helfer der Armen – Hüter der Öffentlichkeit: die Wohlfahrtsgeschichte Osteuropas 1900–1960* (Opladen and Farmington Hills: Verlag Barbara Budrichs, 2006); Berteke Waaldijk, 'Beyond Social Citizenship: New Approaches in Comparative European Welfare History', in *Reciprocity and Redistribution*, ed. Hagemann, 1–21.

125 Bucur, *Eugenics and Modernization in Interwar Romania*, 196ff.

126 Ken Kalling, 'The Self-Perception of a Small Nation: The Reception of Eugenics in Interwar Estonia', in Turda and Weindling, *'Blood and Homeland'*, 253–62.

127 Turda, *Modernism and Eugenics*, 115; Christian Promitzer, 'Taking Care of the National Body: Eugenic Visions in Interwar Bulgaria, 1905–1940', in Turda and Weindling, *'Blood and Homeland'*, 223–52.

128 For an analysis of the connection between eugenic demographic policy concerns and gender in Southeastern Europe, see Maria Bucur, 'Mişcarea eugenistă şi rolurile de gen' [The eugenics movement and gender roles], in *Patriarhat şi emancipare în istoria gândirii politice româneşti*, eds Maria Bucur and Mihaela Miroiu, (Iaşi: Polirom, 2002), 107–47; Gergana Mircheva, 'Marital Health and Eugenics in Bulgaria, 1878–1940', in Promitzer, Trubeta and Turda, *Hygiene, Health and Eugenics*, 235–69; and Sevasti Trubeta, 'Eugenic Birth Control and Prenuptial Health Certification in Interwar Greece', in Promitzer, Trubeta and Turda, *Hygiene, Health and Eugenics*, 271–98.

in the economic and social structure had no real lasting effect on legislation in the area of family law. To be sure, in some countries, such as Czechoslovakia and Poland, certain discriminatory laws against women were abolished in the immediate post-war period, and this with considerable aplomb, provided it could be construed as democratic progress compared with the backward conditions prevailing in the imperial era. This was the case in the eastern Polish Kresy, where regulations in Russian law had deemed the husband the head of the family, his wife having neither a right to own property nor to be represented independently in court.[129] The same in Czechoslovakia, where the so-called *celibát* practice from the Habsburg era excluded women from public service the moment they got married.[130] These initial strides were followed by little substance. Poland and Czechoslovakia followed the European trend to still regard the man as the head of the household in the respective passages on family and marriage laws in these countries' civil codes. The woman's role in the family was still primarily a moral one, her task being to love and support her husband as well as to raise the children. Czechoslovakia introduced civil marriage and divorce, but neither was considered a mandatory legal act; churches still maintained considerable influence in matters of marriage law.

In countries with different legal systems the essential question for women was which civil code was used in attempts to harmonize the country's laws. Hungarian women's rights groups, for example, were pleased that the liberal wave in Transleithania in the last third of the nineteenth century, especially in terms of matrimonial property law, brought many advantages to Hungarian women compared with the rest of Europe.[131] In Slovenia and Croatia, women's greatest fear was that the Serbian Civil Code would be introduced in all of Yugoslavia, combining as it did all the disadvantages of Old Serbian law with those of the French Civil Code tradition, systematically discriminating, for instance, against female inheritance.[132] In Old Romania, too, a civil code was in effect that was strongly influenced by the French Civil Code, so that not only women from the post-Habsburg provinces of Transylvania and Bukovina had to fear a unification of laws following the Old Romanian system but also in the formerly Russian province of Bessarabia, where an old, sometimes female-friendly, Romanian law had remained in force in some legal areas.[133] When large land holdings were redistributed under agrarian reform, the primacy of the male line resulted in property passing over to the male head of the household.[134]

Only with the onset of the Great Depression in the late 1920s, when governments were forced to make drastic cuts in the civil service, did socio-moral prejudices against female employment really begin to work against them. If critics had previously pointed out the threat

---

129 Claudia Kraft, 'Das Eherecht in der Zweiten Polnischen Republik (1918–1939) und das gescheiterte Ideal gleichberechtigter Staatsbürgerschaft', in *Zwischen Kriegen: Nationen, Nationalismen und Geschlechterverhältnisse in Mittel- und Osteuropa*, eds Johanna Gehmacher, Elizabeth Harvey and Sophia Kemlein (Osnabrück: fibre Verlag, 2004), 63–82, here 68–70.

130 Feinberg, *Elusive Equality*, 102.

131 Claudia Papp, '*Die Kraft der weiblichen Seele': Feminismus in Ungarn, 1918–1941* (Münster: LIT Verlag, 2004), 122–4.

132 Jivoin Péritsch, 'Die Frau im serbischen Erbrecht', *Zeitschrift für Osteuropäisches Recht* 2, 1 (1926): 486–509.

133 Calypso Botez, 'Drepturile femeii în constituţia viitoare' [Women's rights in the future constitution], in *Constituţia din 1923 în dezbaterea contemporanilor* (Bucureşti: Humanitas, 1990 [reprint]), 124–66, here 140.

134 Raluca Maria Pop, 'Dimensiuni ale patriarhatului în gândirea liberală românească între 1848 şi al Doilea Război Mondial' [Patriarchal dimensions in liberal thought in Romania between 1848 and the Second World War], in Bucur and Miroiu, *Patriarhat şi emancipare*, 25–71, here 64–5.

Statehood: the interwar period

to family solidarity and childrearing posed by women in the workforce, working women, especially married women in public service, were now denounced as 'double earners' in many countries of the region and indeed Europe-wide.[135] These women were accused of increasing the problems of the unemployed 'academic proletariat' through their egotistic behaviour, destabilizing the nation and state by stealing 'bread from the mouths' of family fathers.

Urbanism and housing policy

The course and aftermath of the First World War had far-reaching consequences in Central, Eastern and Southeastern Europe on the interactions between state, cities and citizens in terms of urbanism and housing policy.[136] On the one hand, under the combined pressures of war, migration and the Great Depression, the issue of liberal housing reform suddenly seemed irrelevant, as it was replaced by an active state housing policy. On the other hand, numerous large cities suddenly became the capitals of newly created states and many elites perceived this as an opportunity to prove by means of large-scale urbanization projects that their respective countries were a permanent and respectable fixture of modern Europe. Regarding the new function of new capital cities, the countries of Central and Eastern Europe now faced many of the same challenges that Southeastern Europe did at various points during the nineteenth century.[137] The question of how post-Ottoman cities such as Athens, Belgrade, Bucharest and Sofia should be transformed into modern European cities of the kind perceived to exist in the West presented challenges that were structurally similar to, yet in other ways wholly different from the problems faced by cities like Tallinn and Warsaw or Vienna, Budapest and Prague when they became new capitals.[138]

All across Europe the outbreak of war in 1914 caused a precipitous decline in construction activities, especially residential buildings, as materials, labour and capital were diverted almost entirely from this sector of consumption into the war economy.[139] In combination with the increasingly drastic shortage of housing, inflationary tendencies and stagnating wages, there was ever-more pressure in warring states to introduce rent control, forbid evictions in the case of unpaid rent, especially in the case of the families of soldiers, and to adopt other measures

---

135 Papp, 'Die Kraft der weiblichen Seele', 357–430; Feinberg, *Elusive Equality*, 99–128. On the problem of the 'academic proletariat' in Romania, see Dragoş Sdrobiş, *Limitele meritocraţiei într-o societate agrară. Şomaj intelectual şi radicalizare politică a tineretului în România interbelică* [The limits of meritocracy in an agrarian society: intellectual unemployment and the radicalization of the youth in interwar Romania] (Iaşi: Polirom, 2015).

136 For an excellent survey of the literature in the last twenty years, see Martin Kohlrausch, 'Imperiales Erbe und Aufbruch in die Moderne: Neuere Literatur zur ostmitteleuropäischen Stadt', in *H-Soz-Kult*, www.hsozkult.de/literaturereview/id/forschungsberichte-1185 (accessed 7 November 2017).

137 Alexandra Yerolympos, 'A New City for a New State: City Planning and the Formation of National Identity in the Balkans (1820s–1920s)', *Planning Perspectives* 8 (1993): 233–57; Eleni Bastéa, *The Creation of Modern Athens: Planning the Myth* (Cambridge: Cambridge University Press, 2000); Dubravka Stojanović, *Kaldrma i asphalt: Urbanizacija i evropeizacija Beograda, 1890–1914* [Cobbles and asphalt: urbanization and the Europeanization of Belgrade, 1890–1914] (Belgrade: Čigoja Štampa, 2008).

138 Emily Gunzburger Makaš and Tanja Damljanović Conley, eds, *Capital Cities in the Aftermath of Empires: Planning in Central and Southeastern Europe* (London: Routledge, 2010); Gerhard Melinz and Susan Zimmermann, eds, *Wien, Prag, Budapest: Blütezeit der Habsburgermetropolen – Urbanisierung, Kommunalpolitik und gesellschaftliche Konflikte (1867–1918)* (Vienna: Promedia, 1996).

139 *Die Wohnungsprobleme Europas nach dem Kriege* [Internationales Arbeitsamt–Studien und Berichte–Reihe G: Wohnungs- und Wohlfahrtswesen 1] (Basel: Verlags-Druckerei G. Böhm, 1924), 9–18.

for the protection of tenants. The qualitative improvement of residential spaces, as discussed in housing reform initiatives before the war,[140] now seemed like a luxury problem in the face of intensifying housing shortages. Since these extensive tenant-protection regulations had to be kept in place in the successor states at least until the 1920s,[141] solving the housing shortage with the liberal economic policies of the nineteenth century was not an option. The residential housing built before the war was mostly apartments for the middle and upper classes, but now, with rent control in place, there was no incentive for those holding capital to build small, or miniature, apartments for workers and the lower middle class.[142] The state and local authorities in the countries of Central, Eastern and Southeastern Europe were involved in construction work after the First World War to varying degrees, but in Europe as a whole there is good reason to call the interwar period the 'big breakthrough in state intervention' in subsidized public housing.[143]

Before the war, state and local authorities only took up the cause of certain groups of people, building apartments for civil servants and the employees of state enterprises (railways, postal service, mining). In the post-war period, state institutions at various levels became involved in the construction of 'small apartments', but rarely acted as actual building contractors. Instead, they facilitated the financing of construction projects, offered tax incentives on new buildings and helped contractors find building sites.[144] From a legal perspective, an active land policy was aided by the slackening protection of property in many constitutions, the expropriation of potential building sites or public road projects being considerably easier than it was, for example, in the urbanistic endeavours of Southeastern European states during the nineteenth century.[145] All in all, these state efforts promoted the construction projects of local authorities, non-commercial building associations as well as private contractors. The state housing policy of each individual state depended on a range of factors, the basics of which will be illustrated in the following by way of a few examples.

One group of cities, the capitals in particular, was marked by a high demand for low-cost housing. Vienna, Budapest and Athens were confronted with a wave of refugees from former parts of the Habsburg Empire and Asia Minor who were now flooding to the respective political centres. Whereas the two post-Habsburg metropolises looked back on communal construction

---

140 Nicholas Bullock and James Read, *The Movement for Housing Reform in Germany and France, 1840–1914* (Cambridge: Cambridge University Press, 1985); Colin G. Pooley, ed., *Housing Strategies in Europe, 1880–1930* (Leicester: Leicester University Press, 1992); Clemens Zimmermann, ed., *Europäische Wohnungspolitik in vergleichender Perspektive 1900–1939* (Stuttgart: Fraunhofer IRB Verlag, 1997).

141 Poland and the Kingdom of Serbs, Croats and Slovenes extended their wartime tenant protection laws in 1919, and Czechoslovakia in 1920, see *Die Wohnungsprobleme Europas nach dem Kriege*, 442–71, 489–98.

142 Juan Rodríguez-Lores, *Sozialer Wohnungsbau in Europa: Die Ursprünge bis 1918 – Ideen, Programme, Gesetze* (Basel: Birkhäuser Verlag, 1994).

143 Adelheid von Saldern, 'Wohnen in der europäischen Großstadt 1900–1939: eine Einführung', in *Wohnen in der Großstadt 1900–1939*, eds Alena Janatková and Hanna Kozińska-Witt (Stuttgart: Franz Steiner Verlag, 2006), 11–38, here 21, footnote 54. See also Günther Schulz, ed., *Wohnungspolitik im Sozialstaat: deutsche und europäische Lösungen 1918–1960* (Düsseldorf: Droste Verlag, 1993).

144 *Die Wohnungspolitik in Europa: der Kleinwohnungsbau* [Internationales Arbeitsamt–Studien und Berichte–Reihe G: Wohnungs- und Wohlfahrtswesen 3] (Geneva: Internationales Arbeitsamt, 1931).

145 Dubravka Stojanović, 'Orte der Veränderung und Orte der Erinnerung: die Straßen Belgrads 1885–1914', in *Schnittstellen: Gesellschaft, Nation, Konflikt und Erinnerung in Südosteuropa – Festschrift für Holm Sundhaussen*, eds Ulf Brunnbauer, Andreas Helmedach and Stefan Troebst (München: R. Oldenbourg, 2007), 65–79, here 65–6.

Statehood: the interwar period

projects from the period before the war and were able to build on this tradition in pursuing an effective housing policy,[146] countries like Greece faced a new challenge. The population of Athens grew from barely 300,000 in 1920 to around 460,000 in 1928, with about 130,000 of these newly arriving residents having been more or less impoverished refugees from Asia Minor.[147] These individuals could not compete, of course, in an Athens housing market that had once been the product of a private construction boom. Since communal and state authorities were likewise unable to provide affordable housing due to confusion regarding responsibilities and the feeble implementation of planning, entire neighbourhoods sprouted up consisting of unauthorized shanty-style housing erected in any available public space by these new arrivals.[148]

The demand was just as high in Czechoslovak cities such as Prague and Brno, where local authorities were not positioned, like pre-war Vienna had been, to promote urban expansion in line with economic and population growth, e.g. by incorporating surrounding areas.[149] In Prague, considerable spending on prestige projects such as the National Theatre (Rudolfinum), City Hall or the Municipal House (Obecní dům), built in the spirit of Czech communal nationalism in evidence since the 1880s, had all but emptied the city's coffers.[150] The demand for small apartments in interwar Czechoslovakia was estimated at 100,000 units. Authorities tried to meet this demand by encouraging the construction of small private homes, before the impact of the Great Depression forced it to subsidize the construction of larger tenement buildings as well.[151]

The population of Bucharest more than doubled between 1920 and 1940, from 380,000 to 870,000, and yet there was no communal construction there to speak of.[152] Rather, Romanian housing policy in the capital was markedly statist, and this in a dual sense. Building plots were mostly allocated on state-owned property, but the buildings erected there were almost always houses and apartment buildings for railway employees and other state officials, as well as for officers, war invalids and war widows. While the allocation of inexpensive building sites and multi-year tax exemptions did enable considerable building activities by nominally public housing societies such as the Communal Low-Cost Housing Company and the Autonomous Company for Low-Cost Construction, the 29,000 apartments erected between 1920 and 1934 were not affordable for the lower classes.

---

146 Renate Banik-Schweitzer, 'Die Kleinwohnungsfrage in Wien um die Jahrhundertwende', in *Die Kleinwohnungsfrage: zu den Ursprüngen des Sozialen Wohnungsbaus in Europa*, eds Juan-Rodríguez-Lores and Gerhard Fehl (Hamburg: Hans Christian Verlag, 1988), 431–49; Gerhard Melinz and Susan Zimmermann, 'Wohnungspolitischer Interventionismus in Österreich und Ungarn von 1890 bis in die 1930er Jahre', in Zimmermann, *Europäische Wohnungspolitik*, 85–129.

147 Eleni Bastéa, 'Athens', in Makaš and Conley, *Capital Cities*, 29–44; Eleni Bastéa, 'Athens, 1880–1940: Transitory Modernism and National Realities', in *Races to Modernity: Metropolitan Aspirations in Eastern Europe, 1890–1940*, eds Jan C. Behrends and Martin Kohlrausch (Budapest: CEU Press, 2014), 127–52.

148 Lila Leontidou, 'Greece', in Pooley, *Housing Strategies in Europe*, 297–324.

149 Gerhard Melinz and Susan Zimmermann, 'Großstadtgeschichte und Modernisierung in der Habsburgermonarchie', in idem, *Wien–Prag–Budapest*, 15–45, here 22–3.

150 Cathleen M. Giustino, 'Prague', in Makaš and Conley, *Capital Cities*, 157–73, here 164.

151 Alena Janatková, 'Die Bauaufgabe Kleinstwohnung in der Tschechoslowakei der Zwischenkriegszeit', 315–36; Andreas R. Hofmann, 'Von der Spekulation zur Intervention: Formen des Arbeiterwohnbaus in Lodz und Brünn vor und nach dem Ersten Weltkrieg', 225–48, both in Alena Janatková and Hanna Kozińska-Witt, *Wohnen in der Großstadt* (Stuttgart: Franz Steiner Verlag, 2006).

152 Maria Raluca Popa and Emily Gunzberger Makaš, 'Bucharest', in Makaš and Conley, *Capital Cities*, 61–74; Luminiţa Machedon and Ernie Scoffham, *Romanian Modernism: The Architecture of Bucharest, 1920–1940* (Cambridge, MA: The MIT Press, 1999), 102–11.

As was previously observed of the social security system in Poland and Czechoslovakia, the construction of small (communal) apartments in Poland demonstrated a clear continuity from the pre- into the post-Habsburg era. It was Adolf Gross, a Cracow city counsellor and delegate in the Viennese Imperial Assembly, who initiated a 'law on the establishment of a housing welfare fund' for the Cisleithanian half of the empire that was signed into law in 1910.[153] This tradition of a communal push for more state responsibility in the realm of housing policy was also continued in the new Poland. An important figure here was Adolf Gross's brother, the local Cracow politician Daniel Gross. Local authorities were virtually obligated to solve the housing problem, first through the decree of 4 February 1919, defining housing policy as the task of local authorities, then with the law on urban development of 25 April 1925 (*Ustawa o rozbudowie miast*). Only from 1927 on, however, were these regulations capable of stimulating construction, once the currency was stabilized and financial resources were flowing into the local community.[154] Much to the chagrin of city representatives organized in the Polish Association of Cities, building loans mostly went to Warsaw and the new Baltic Sea port of Gdynia.[155] Warsaw was in dire need of more construction, especially of affordable apartments, the city having grown from 383,000 to 765,000 inhabitants between 1882 and 1907. By 1920 the city's population exceeded one million.[156] Due to the lack of noteworthy communal or municipal building projects in the Russian partition area, and practically none during the war and the financially unstable post-war period, the housing shortage in Warsaw had reached a critical impasse in the 1920s. As Edward Wynot put it, 'The 1924–25 fiscal reform did not rekindle investor enthusiasm, and by 1926 the situation had deteriorated to the point where Warsaw was rapidly becoming a single massive slum, with isolated pockets of decent housing.'[157] A dramatic situation gave rise to a decisive and comprehensive solution. The Sanacja regime under Józef Piłsudski attracted urban planning experts and commissioned engineer and town planner Stanisław Różański with the design of a masterplan for Warsaw that was to serve in some respects as a guideline for Polish urbanism in general. The new Warsaw urban development plan took effect in mid-1930, in October of that same year the Bureau of Regional Planning in Poland began its work, and

> by 1936, Warsaw not only possessed one of the largest and most comprehensive urban planning agencies in Europe, it also had a clearly defined, carefully outlined, and yet sufficiently flexible, grand design within which to grow and realize its optimal potential as one of Eastern Europe's premier cities.[158]

---

153 Hanna Kozińska-Witt, 'Die Krakauer kommunale Selbstverwaltung und die Frage der Kleinwohnungen 1900–1939', in Janatková et al., *Wohnen in der Großstadt*, 179–204, here 184–6.

154 *Die Wohnungspolitik in Europa*, 334.

155 For a comparison of Warsaw and Kraków, see Hanna Kozińska-Witt, *Krakau in Warschaus langem Schatten: Konkurrenzkämpfe in der polnischen Städtelandschaft 1900–1939* (Stuttgart: Franz Steiner Verlag, 2008); Patrice M. Dabrowski, 'Kraków and Warsaw', in Makaš and Conley, *Capital Cities*, 189–207. On Gdynia, see Beate Störtkuhl, 'Gdynia – Meeresmetropole der Zweiten Polnischen Republik', in *Neue Staaten – neue Bilder? Visuelle Kultur im Dienst staatlicher Selbstdarstellung in Zentral- und Osteuropa seit 1918*, eds Arnold Bartetzky, Marina Dmitrieva and Stefan Troebst (Köln: Böhlau Verlag, 2005), 33–46.

156 Ute Caumanns, 'Mietskasernen und 'Gläserne Häuser': Soziales Wohnen in Warschau zwischen Philanthropie und Genossenschaft 1900–1939', in Janatková and Kozińska-Witt, *Wohnen in der Großstadt*, 204–24, here 204–5.

157 Edward D. Wynot, Jr., *Warsaw Between the World Wars: Profile of the Capital City in a Developing Land, 1918–1939* (New York: Columbia University Press, 1983), 66.

158 Ibid, 167.

Statehood: the interwar period

With their wide-ranging and determined planning efforts and the great advances they made, particularly in solving the problem of demand for small apartments, Polish town planners in the 1930s were among the pioneers of international urbanism. '*Warszawa Funkcjonalna*' made the Polish capital a reference point of functionalist architecture, whose protagonists were organized in the Congrès Internationaux d'Architecture Moderne (CIAM).[159]

Apart from housing policy, the erection of public buildings in capital cities and important, mid-sized regional centres was a further dimension of urban self-representation through architecture.[160] The planning and design of capital cities, in particular, was a way of projecting an 'image of the state',[161] the political system and its underlying values in a visually and publicly accessible way. Since the repertoire of city planning (public squares, thoroughfares, a sometimes 'elevated government district') and architectonic elements and styles (classicism, modernism) is at once limited and international, the claims of urbanist and political elites that certain new urban forms are an immediate expression of a certain nation or particular culture must be taken with a grain of salt. Undoubtedly, processes of nationalization were significant in creating a new capital. This was especially pronounced in cities of Southeastern Europe, whose elites rarely took Istanbul as a role model and generally endeavoured to strip Balkan cities of their Ottoman influences, which they perceived as 'Oriental'. There are isolated instances of a decisive rejection of Russian urbanist legacies in Warsaw and the capitals of Estonia, Latvia and Lithuania.[162] The post-imperial rejection of Vienna and Budapest were much less emphatic by comparison, since these cities – alongside London, Paris and Berlin – were then and remain still important urbanist reference points in Central and Eastern Europe. A decidedly national architecture or a correspondingly idiosyncratic urban planning concept in the interwar period is thus not evident anywhere in the region, especially considering that no capital city in the greater region, apart from Ankara, was moved: all the other new capitals had been cultural, economic and sometimes political centres even before they were turned into capitals.

Apart from this shared negative, there are also certain developments that lend the urbanism of Central, Eastern and Southeastern Europe a distinctive feature in the period from 1900 to the start of the Second World War.[163] The development of urban planning as a discipline occurred at the turn of the twentieth century, in the very same decade in which many of the metropolises in the greater region were undergoing spectacular population growth. The most influential and productive city planners and architects had studied at the same Western European universities and were able to apply their ideas in their homelands, and elsewhere in the region, after the First World War. Alongside the great demand for representative state buildings and affordable living space, there is another factor worth mentioning that facilitated their work, namely, that statehood in all the countries of the region was characterized by a very pronounced centralism in territorial terms. Those places with a tradition of communal self-administration, e.g. in the post-Habsburg regions of Galicia, Transylvania and Vojvodina, found this tradition significantly

---

159 Martin Kohlrausch, 'Warszawa Funkcjonalna: Radical Urbanism and the International Discourse on Planning in the Interwar Period', in Behrends and Kohlrausch, *Races to Modernity*, 205–31.

160 Wolfgang Sonne, *Representing the State: Capital City Planning in the Early Twentieth Century* (München: Prestel Verlag, 2003); Ákos Moravánsky, *Die Erneuerung der Baukunst: Wege zur Moderne in Mitteleuropa 1900–1940* (Salzburg: Residenz-Verlag, 1988).

161 Wolfgang Sonne, 'Die Hauptstadt als Bilde des Staates: Planungen des frühen 20. Jahrhunderts im internationalen Vergleich', in Bartetzky, Dmitrieva and Troebst, *Neue Staaten – neue Bilder?*, 13–31.

162 Andreas Fülberth, *Tallinn – Riga – Kaunas: ihr Ausbau zu modernen Hauptstädten 1920–1940* (Köln: Böhlau, 2005).

163 Kohlrausch, 'Imperiales Erbe und Aufbruch in die Moderne'.

curtailed in the interwar period under the influence of their respective centres. Strong demand and a considerable manoeuvrability facilitated the increasing importance of technocratic expertise, which was sometimes institutionalized in the form of large planning staffs and lent expression to extensive social utopias with modernist underpinnings. Little of this was realized in the interwar period. More changes in statehood were needed first, which ultimately occurred under state socialism.

Parliamentarianism, crisis and technocratic tendencies in statehood

British historian Zara Steiner reflects a general trend with respect to periodization within the interwar period when she divides her monumental *European International History* into two volumes, *The Lights that Failed* (1919–1933) and *The Triumph of the Dark* (1933–1939).[164] The year 1933 marks both the Nazi seizure of power under Hitler, as well as the moment when the Great Depression had largely passed but a gradual awareness was developing of the consequences resulting from the political and economic measures adopted to solve it. Without discussing whether the year 1933 was equally important as a turning point in all states of Central, Eastern and Southeastern Europe, it will suffice here to point out in general that in all states of the region (once again with the exception of Czechoslovakia) parliamentarianism was perceived as unstable and replaced at some point, more or less sweepingly, with authoritarian regimes. This was accompanied by a renewed transformation of statehood, which now, in the minds of elites, was freed from the time-consuming and destructive attempts of parties to achieve political legitimation and would be shaped by visionary and spirited technocrats working within state parties and bureaucracies.[165]

This chapter focuses on political and social fields to analyze and understand the transformation of statehood in the interwar period, without focusing on the political system itself. At the same time, it is important to note that parliamentary democracy in the states of Central, Eastern and Southeastern Europe underwent a crisis and was reshaped or even abolished entirely by authoritarian tendencies and rulers well before the outbreak of the Second World War. Following the deliberations of Wolfgang Höpken[166] on these states' potential for democracy during that period, it is worth pointing out the enormous challenges they faced in building up, adapting, integrating and unifying structures and institutions in just about all areas of life. Added to this was a 'performance crisis of the political system'[167] perceived by many contemporaries, which led to a rapid decline in legitimacy. This was not specific to the region but was a Europe-wide phenomenon, and yet there was often more at stake in Central, Eastern and Southeastern Europe, no less than the very existence of these states within their new borders. Elites had been quite demanding in formulating the *raison d'être* of their new states, making a wealth of normative declarations about democracy, historical justice, social entitlements, economic prosperity, etc. Now they were faced with a dual challenge. First there was the Bolshevist alternative, palpable in the party spectrum in the form of communist parties as well as in the regions bordering

---

164 Zara S. Steiner, *The Lights that Failed: European International History 1919–1933* (Oxford: Oxford University Press, 2005); idem, *The Triumph of the Dark: European International History 1933–1939* (Oxford: Oxford University Press, 2011).

165 Andrew C. Janos, 'The One-Party-State and Social Mobilization: East Europe between the Wars', in *Authoritarian Politics in Modern Society*, eds Samuel P. Huntington and Clement H. Moore (New York: Basic Books, 1970), 204–36.

166 Wolfgang Höpken, 'Strukturkrise oder verpaßte Chance?', 73–127.

167 Ibid., 101.

Statehood: the interwar period

on the Soviet Union. Second, the anti-revisionist states had to prove that their existence was no accident of history, that their legitimacy was derived from stable domestic policy and economic prosperity. With the exception of Czechoslovakia, however, none of the political systems in the region had a stable political landscape. Politics in the region were marked by frequent cabinet reshuffling and changes of government, as well as by a parliamentary culture in which splintering parties were much more common than coalition governments. The instability of the political system was also reflected in a pronounced tendency towards 'personalism' – that is to say, in the overwhelming importance of certain individuals within parties, ministries and state institutions. Access to such key individuals was often a more important resource for championing one's interests than obeying the rule of law and the norms and procedures set up in the constitution.

Apart from the usual political cleavages in Europe (from conservative, through liberal, to socialist), the party systems in these regions showed other political orientations in considerable concentration: regional parties, parties of ethnic minorities and agrarian parties. The appearance of these parties as the representatives of new interest groups on the political stage was rarely a source of new legitimacy for the political system; more often than not they contributed to the delegitimization of parliamentarianism itself by further fragmenting the spectrum of political parties. The agrarian parties so typical of Central, Eastern and Southeastern Europe in the interwar period will serve as an example here.[168] The political representatives of peasants enjoyed a prominent position, given the strength of these parties before the war, a range of party-affiliated grass-roots organizations such as cooperatives and various peasants' circles,[169] and the overwhelmingly agrarian nature of these states' economies. Agrarian structures and the political rights granted to peasants should have meant that the agrarian parties would form governments and organize politics and economics along agrarian lines. A range of agrarianist plans and policies were evident in the region, whether agrarian-populist, those supporting a peasant middle class, or corporatist in nature, and the development of agrarian parties was correspondingly varied. Whereas a kind of peasant state was set up in Bulgaria under Aleksandar Stamboliyski in 1919 and violently suppressed in 1923,[170] the reign of the Romanian National Peasants' Party under Iuliu Maniu in the late 1920s was the long-awaited political and economic alternative to the National Liberal Party.[171] Its failure during the Great Depression heralded the end of parliamentarianism in Romania. In Poland, the country's partition-related heterogeneity was reflected in the range of agrarian parties. The PSL-Piast (Polish People's Party) under Wincenty Witos, which represented peasants with medium and large landholdings and was influential in Galicia, rarely cooperated with Wyzwolenie (Liberation), which for its part was strong in Congress Poland and envisioned

---

168 Heinz Gollwitzer, ed., *Europäische Bauernparteien im 20. Jahrhundert* (Stuttgart/New York: Gustav Fischer, 1977); Helga Schultz and Angela Harre, eds, *Bauerngesellschaften auf dem Weg in die Moderne: Agrarismus in Ostmitteleuropa 1860 bis 1960* (Wiesbaden: Harrassowitz Verlag, 2010); Kubů, Lorenz, Šouša and Müller, eds, *Agrarismus und Agrareliten in Ostmitteleuropa*.

169 As a *pars pro toto*, see the situation in Galicia: Keely Stauter-Halstad, *The Nation and the Village: The Genesis of Peasant National Identity in Austrian Poland, 1848–1914* (Ithaca, NY: Cornell University Press, 2001); Kai Struve, *Bauen und Nation in Galizien: über Zugehörigkeit und soziale Emanzipation im 19. Jahrhundert* (Göttingen: Vandenhoeck & Ruprecht, 2005).

170 John D. Bell, *Peasants in Power: Aleksander Stamboliski and the Bulgarian Agrarian National Party, 1899–1923* (Princeton, NJ: Princeton University Press, 1977).

171 Dietmar Müller, *Agrarpopulismus in Rumänien: Programmatik und Regierungspraxis der Bauernpartei und der Nationalbäuerlichen Partei Rumäniens in der Zwischenkriegszeit* (St. Augustin: gardez! Verlag, 2001).

agrarian reforms creating more equality.[172] In Czechoslovakia of all places, the most industrialized country in the region, Antonín Švehla and Milan Hodža were the most successful in making political agrarianism a stable, long-term factor in Prague politics, firmly embedding agrarian interests in the country's economic policy. In the three Baltic states, by contrast, agrarian economic interests overlapped so much with those of overall economic and foreign economic policy that it is difficult to isolate the former as an independent interest at all. The authoritarian leaders who took power in Estonia, Latvia and Lithuania all came from agrarian parties and all sought corporative solutions with strong agrarianist elements.

The first presidential dictatorship in Central and Eastern Europe[173] came in Poland in the summer of 1926 with the putsch of Marshal Józef Piłsudski, followed by Lithuania, where Antanas Smetona eradicated the parliamentary system with a coup d'état in December 1926, introducing an authoritarian regime. This was followed in turn by Konstantin Päts in Estonia and Kārlis Ulmanis in Latvia, both in 1934. Hungary is an exception in that the council-democracy experiment under Béla Kun was put to an end in 1919 by Admiral Miklós Horthy, who proceeded to set up an authoritarian regime with a strong president and a marginalized parliament. In Southeastern Europe, the authoritarian turn brought forth the phenomenon of the royal dictatorship.[174] In Albania, President Ahmet Zogu declared himself king in 1928 and ruled his country just as autocratically as King Alexander Karađorđević of Yugoslavia, King Boris III of Bulgaria and King Carol II of Romania, each of whom dissolved their parliaments, in 1929, 1934 and 1938 respectively. Greece was something of an exception in that the dictatorship set up there was led not by King George II but by General Ioannis Metaxas.

The general aspiration of authoritarian regimes was to understand problems using modern, scientific methods of analysis and find a solution that would restore the conditions prevailing before democracy. Emblematic of this is the Polish authoritarian regime that called itself 'Sanation', the word itself already implying a scientific or medical diagnosis of disease in the system and society of Poland. Some authoritarian regimes endeavoured to anchor this new understanding of nation, state and society in the constitution by adopting new constitutions. One basic feature of this second interwar wave of constitutionalism in Central, Eastern and Southeastern Europe can be found in the relationship of citizens to the nation and state, the rights of individuals having clearly been rolled back in favour of those of the collective nation and its organized form, the state. Thus, detailed articles about the rights of citizens, the protection of property and the constituent power's commitment to the social welfare state were radically curtailed in the new constitutions of Yugoslavia (1931), Poland (1935) and Romania (1938). Instead, the duties of citizens were emphasized, and private property was linked more intensively to national-collectivist ideas, whereas any mention of labour protection and expanding the welfare state either disappeared entirely or was tied, with ethnonational connotations, to a citizens' duty of loyalty.

---

172 Gerhard Doliesen, *Die polnische Bauernpartei 'Wyzwolenie' in den Jahren 1918–1926* (Marburg: Verlag Herder-Institut, 1996).

173 Erwin Oberländer, 'Die Präsidialdiktaturen in Ostmitteleuropa – "Gelenkte Demokratie"?', in *Autoritäre Regime in Ostmittel- und Südosteuropa 1919–1944*, ed. idem (Paderborn: Ferdinand Schöningh, 2001), 3–17. The volume contains essays on all of the states in the region mentioned below. See also Anthony Polonsky, *The Little Dictators: The History of Eastern Europe Since 1918* (London: Routledge & Kegan Paul Books, 1975).

174 Holm Sundhaussen, 'Die Königsdiktaturen in Südosteuropa: Umrisse einer Synthese', in Oberländer, *Autoritäre Regime*, 337–48; Edda Binder-Iijima and Ekkehard Kraft, 'The Making of States: Constitutional Monarchies in the Balkans', in *Ottomans into Europeans*, 1–29.

Periodization and long trends: concluding remarks

Until some years ago, the definition of the period under consideration here as the time between the two world wars was uncontroversial. In the historiographies of Central, Eastern and Southeastern Europe, but not exclusively there, the interwar period has been taught and researched as a clearly defined historical period. Beyond the apparent self-evidence of political-historical factors such as wars, states being founded and territorial shifts, considerable doubts have emerged about defining this period as a unique historical epoch. First, the interwar period in all states of Central, Eastern and Southeastern Europe – with the exception of Czechoslovakia – was marked by internal political watersheds in the form of 'little dictatorships' having greatly restricted free elections, parliamentarianism and democracy. In some of these states, authoritarian regimes had the new status quo recast in new constitutions. From the perspective of economic history, too, the Great Depression was a historical break whose considerable influence is beyond question. A great deal of the euphoric spirit of renewal witnessed in the 1920s faded away with the onset of bank crashes, mass unemployment and the sales crisis of agricultural products. Subsequent crisis management measures generally abolished any remnants of free trade and liberalism, replacing them with currency control, high tariff walls and export subsidies, and more generally with a high degree of economic statism. Among elites vanished the initial assurance that the attractiveness of their own culture, paired with a political notion of citizenship, would lead over the middle term to the creation of an inclusive nation. By the 1930s the political scene was dominated everywhere by nationalist parties that often pursued an anti-Semitic and anti-minority project of ethno-nationalism.

Aside from these internal watersheds, the beginning and end of the interwar period also pose a conceptual problem. As demonstrated by social security, the states of Central, Eastern and Southeastern Europe having Habsburg and German legacies often expanded the welfare state that had been in place before 1918. Conversely, the constitutionally backed encroachment on liberal-individualist property rights, implemented in the form of agrarian reforms and colonization projects aimed not least of all against the formerly dominant classes and imperial minorities, as well as the economic nationalism that followed, persisted well after 1945. A renewed wave of expropriations in the immediate aftermath of the Second World War can be interpreted as a radicalized variant of the agrarian reforms of the interwar period and to a certain extent even as laboratories of socialist nationalization. From a political perspective, too, the authoritarian wave of the 1930s seems like just another manifestation of the tendency towards a hegemonic state party that eventually came to fruition after the Second World War.

The notion that the interwar period was an independent epoch must ultimately be viewed against two parallel tendencies: the efforts of elites to increase the powers of the state and the concomitant rise in expectations among the population at large on the one hand, and the implementation of a new form of statehood in concrete policy areas on the other. For a range of reasons analyzed in this chapter, state elites were not able to fully implement their vision of efficient state planning and intervention under the conditions of liberal-democratic competition. Moreover, the infusion of social science expertise into the political process, as well as into administration and planning, did not lead to a significant increase in legitimacy by dint of efficiency, but tended rather to delegitimize the political itself, allowing it to be replaced with technocratic and centralized state intervention in society.

On the other hand, the new beginning after the First World War cannot be viewed as a mere passing event for the states of Central, Eastern and Southeastern Europe. The new sense of statehood – regained, expanded, entirely new or diminished – was an experience that informed an entire generation. The statehood of the interwar period was legitimized discursively by

Dietmar Müller

elites in the region using the notion of revolution in two respects: as a national revolution, a radical break with late-feudal and undemocratic multi-ethnic empires, and as an alternative to revolutionary Bolshevism. This positioning as democratic and free-market liberal nation states, despite frequent deviations from reality, has ultimately proven to be a rich source of historico-political legitimacy and remembrance, for all the states of the interwar period were revived at the end of the Cold War, albeit in a sometimes different territorial form or dissolved into their constituent republics.

Further reading

Antohi, Sorin, Balazs Trencsenyi and Peter Apor, eds. *Narratives Unbound: Historical Studies in Post-Communist Eastern Europe* (Budapest: CEU Press, 2007).

Barkey, Karen, and Mark von Hagen. *After Empire: Multiethnic Societies and Nation-building: The Soviet Union and the Russian, Ottoman, and Habsburg Empires* (Boulder, CO: Westview Press, 1997).

Bartetzky, Arnold, Marina Dmitrieva, and Stefan Troebst, eds. *Neue Staaten – neue Bilder? Visuelle Kultur im Dienst staatlicher Selbstdarstellung in Zentral- und Osteuropa Seit 1918* (Köln: Böhlau, 2005).

Barth, Boris. *Europa nach dem Großen Krieg: Die Krise der Demokratie in der Zwischenkriegszeit, 1918–1938* (Frankfurt a.M.: Campus Verlag, 2016).

Behrends, Jan C., and Martin Kohlrausch, eds. *Races to Modernity: Metropolitan Aspirations in Eastern Europe, 1890–1940* (Budapest: CEU Press, 2014).

Bell, John D. *Peasants in Power: Aleksander Stamboliski and the Bulgarian Agrarian National Party, 1899–1923* (Princeton, NJ: Princeton University Press, 1977).

Benecke, Werner. *Die Ostgebiete der Polnischen Republik: Staatsmacht und öffentliche Ordnung in einer Minderheitenregion 1918–1939* (Vienna: Böhlau, 1999).

Berend, Iván T., and Ránki György.. *Economic Development in East Central Europe in the 19th and 20th Centuries* (New York: Columbia University Press, 1974).

Boeckh, Katrin, and Natali Stegmann, eds. *Veterans and War Victims in Eastern Europe during the 20th Century: A Comparison* (Leipzig: Leipziger Universitätsverlag, 2011).

Boeckh, Katrin, Krisztina Busa, Antje Himmelreich, Edvin Pezo and Natali Stegmann, eds. *Staatsbürgerschaft und Teilhabe: bürgerliche, politische und soziale Rechte im östlichen Europa* (München: De Gruyter, 2014).

Boškovska, Nada. *Das jugoslawische Makedonien: eine Randregion zwischen Repression und Integration* (Vienna: Böhlau, 2009).

Brubaker, Rogers. *Nationalism Reframed: Nationhood and the National Question in the New Europe* (Cambridge: Cambridge University Press, 1996).

Brunnbauer, Ulf, ed. *(Re)writing History: Historiography in Southeastern Europe after Socialism* (Münster: LIT, 2004).

Chu, Winson. *The German Minority in Interwar Poland* (New York: Cambridge University Press, 2012).

Conte, Édouard, and Christian Giordano, eds. *Es war einmal die Wende…: Sozialer Umbruch der ländlichen Gesellschaften Mittel- und Südosteuropas* (Berlin: Centre Marc Bloch, 1999).

Dahlmann, Dittmar, and Anke Hilbrenner, eds. *Zwischen großen Erwartungen und bösem Erwachen: Juden, Politik und Antisemitismus in Ostmittel- und Südosteuropa 1918–1945* (Paderborn: Ferdinand Schöningh Verlag, 2007).

David, Thomas. *Nationalisme économique et industrialization: L'expérience des pays de l'est (1789–1939)* (Geneva: Droz, 2009).

Doliesen, Gerhard. *Die polnische Bauernpartei 'Wyzwolenie' in den Jahren 1918–1926* (Marburg: Verlag Herder-Institut, 1996).

Eichenberg, Julia. *Kämpfen für Frieden und Fürsorge: polnische Veteranen des Ersten Weltkriegs und ihre internationalen Kontakte, 1918–1939* (München: Oldenbourg, 2011).

Elsie, Robert, ed. *Kosovo in the Heart of the Powder Keg* (Boulder, CO: East European Monographs, 1977).

Feinberg, Melissa. *Elusive Equality: Gender, Citizenship, and the Limits of Democracy in Czechoslovakia, 1918–1950* (Pittsburgh, PA: University of Pittsburgh Press, 2006).

Gaćeša, Nikola. 'Nemci u agrarnoj reformi i vlastništvu obradivog zemljišta u Vojvodini 1919–1941' [The Germans in agrarian reform and their landownership in Vojvodina 1919–1941], in *Radovi iz agrarne istorije i demografije*, ed. Nikola Gaćeša (Novi Sad: Matica srpska, 1995), 286–308.

Statehood: the interwar period

Giaro, Tomasz, ed. *Modernisierung durch Transfer zwischen den Weltkriegen* (Frankfurt a.M.: Vittorio Klostermann, 2007).

Gollwitzer, Heinz, ed. *Europäische Bauernparteien im 20. Jahrhundert* (Stuttgart and New York: Gustav Fischer, 1977).

Gosewinkel, Dieter. *Schutz und Freiheit? Staatsbürgerschaft in Europa im 20. und 21. Jahrhundert* (Berlin: Suhrkamp Verlag, 2016).

Haslinger, Peter, and Joachim von Puttkamer, eds. *Staat, Loyalität und Minderheiten in Ostmittel- und Südosteuropa 1918–1941* (München: R. Oldenbourg, 2007).

Hering, Sabine, and Berteke Waaldijk. *Guardians of the Poor – Custodians of the Public: Welfare History in Eastern Europe 1900–1960 / Helfer der Armen – Hüter der Öffentlichkeit: die Wohlfahrtsgeschichte Osteuropas 1900–1960* (Opladen and Farmington Hills, MI: Verlag Barbara Budrichs, 2006).

Horak, Stephan. *Poland and Her National Minorities, 1919–39: A Case Study* (New York: Vantage Press, 1961).

Inglot, Tomasz. *Welfare States in East Central Europe, 1919–2004* (Cambridge: Cambridge University Press, 2008).

Janjetović, Zoran. *Between Hitler and Tito: The Disappearance of the Vojvodina Germans* (Belgrade: Self-Published, 2005 [2000]).

Jovanović, Vladan. *Jugoslovenska država i Južna Srbija 1918–1929: Makedonija, Sandžak, Kosovo i Metohija u Kraljevini SHS* [The Yugoslav state and south Serbia, 1918–1929: Macedonia, Sandžak, Kosovo and Methochia in the kingdom of SCS] (Belgrade: Inis, 2002).

Kaiser, Wolfram, and Johan Schot, eds. *Writing the Rules for Europe: Experts, Cartels, and International Organizations* (Basingstoke: Palgrave Macmillan, 2014).

Kaser, Michael Charles, and Edward Albert Radice, eds. *The Economic History of Eastern Europe, vol. 1, Economic Structure and Performance Between the Two Wars* (Oxford: Clarendon Press, 1985).

Kaufmann, Franz-Xaver. 'Diskurse über Staatsaufgaben', in *Staatsaufgaben*, ed. Dieter Grimm (Frankfurt a.M.: Suhrkamp, 1996), 15–41.

Kohlrausch, Martin, Katrin Steffen, and Stefan Wiederkehr, eds. *Expert Cultures in East Central Europe: The Internationalization of Knowledge and the Transformation of Nation States since World War I* (Osnabrück: fibre Verlag, 2010).

Kovács, Mária M. *Liberal Professions and Illiberal Politics: Hungary from the Habsburgs to the Holocaust* (Washington, DC and Oxford: Woodrow Wilson Center Press and Oxford University Press, 1994).

Krstić, Đorđe. *Kolonizacija u Južnoj Srbiji* [The colonization of south Serbia] (Sarajevo: Štamparija "Bosanska" Počta, 1928).

Kubů, Eduard, Torsten Lorenz, Jiri Šouša, Uwe Müller, eds. *Agrarismus und Agrareliten in Ostmitteleuropa* (Berlin: BWV Berliner Wissenschafts-Verlag, 2013).

Küpper, Herbert. *Einführung in die Rechtsgeschichte Osteuropas* (Frankfurt a.M.: Peter Lang Verlag, 2005).

L'Association de l'Ukraine Occidentale pour la Société des Nations. *La situation de la population ukrainienne en Pologne* (Nendeln: Kraus, 1973 [1924]).

Lemberg, Hans, ed. *Ostmitteleuropa zwischen den beiden Weltkriegen (1918–1939): Stärke und Schwäche der neuen Staaten, nationale Minderheiten* (Marburg: Verlag Herder-Institut, 1997).

Lipscher, Ladislav. *Verfassung und politische Kultur in der Tschechoslowakei 1918–1939* (München: R. Oldenbourg, 1979).

Lundgreen-Nielsen, Kay. *The Polish Problem at the Paris Peace Conference: A Study of the Policies of the Great Powers and the Poles, 1918–1919* (Odense: Odense University Press, 1979).

Makaš, Emily Gunzburger, and Tanja Damljanović Conley, eds. *Capital Cities in the Aftermath of Empires: Planning in Central and Southeastern Europe* (London: Routledge, 2010).

Malcolm, Noel. *Kosovo: A Short History* (London: Macmillan, 1998).

Mendelsohn, Ezra. *The Jews of East Central Europe between the World Wars* (Bloomington, IN: Indiana University Press, 1983).

Meurs, Wim van, and Dietmar Müller, eds. *Institutionen und Kultur in Südosteuropa* (München: Verlag Otto Sagner, 2014).

Meurs, Wim van, and Alina Mungiu-Pippidi, eds. *Ottomans into Europeans: State and Institution-building in South Eastern Europe* (London: Hurst & Company, 2010).

Mitrany, David. *The Effect of the War in Southeastern Europe* (New Haven, CT: Yale University Press, 1936).

Müller, Dietmar. *Agrarpopulismus in Rumänien: Programmatik und Regierungspraxis der Bauernpartei und der Nationalbäuerlichen Partei Rumäniens in der Zwischenkriegszeit* (St. Augustin: gardez! Verlag, 2001).

Müller, Dietmar. *Staatsbürger auf Widerruf: Juden und Muslime als Alteritätspartner im rumänischen und serbischen Nationscode – Ethnonationale Staatsbürgerschaftskonzeptionen, 1878–1941* (Wiesbaden: Harrassowitz Verlag, 2005).

Murgescu, Bogdan. *România şi Europa: Acumularea decalajelor economice (1500–2010)* [Romania and Europe: Accumulating economic lags (1500–2010)], (Bucharest: Polirom, 2010).

Oberländer, Erwin. 'Die Präsidialdiktaturen in Ostmitteleuropa – "Gelenkte Demokratie"?', in *Autoritäre Regime in Ostmittel- und Südosteuropa 1919–1944*, ed. idem (Paderborn: Ferdinand Schöningh, 2001), 3–17.

Offen, Karen. *European Feminisms, 1700–1950: A Political History* (Stanford, CA: Stanford University Press, 2000).

Papp, Claudia. *'Die Kraft der weiblichen Seele': Feminismus in Ungarn, 1918–1941* (Münster: LIT Verlag, 2004).

Perin, Đoko. 'Nacionalizovanje Vojvodine i Južne Srbije' [The nationalization of Vojvodina and South Serbia], in *Iskušenja srpske elite: Dokumenti o radu Srpskog Kulturnog Kluba*, ed. Pero Simić (Belgrade: Službeni Glasnik, 2006), 105–20.

Polonsky, Antony. *The Little Dictators: The History of Eastern Europe since 1918* (London: Routledge & Kegan Paul Books, 1975).

Polonsky, Antony. *Politics in Independent Poland 1921–1939: The Crisis of Constitutional Government* (Oxford: Oxford University Press, 1972).

Promitzer, Christian, Sevasti Trubeta, and Marius Turda, eds. *Hygiene, Health and Eugenics in Southeastern Europe to 1945* (Budapest: CEU Press, 2010).

Puttkamer, Joachim von. *Ostmitteleuropa im 19. und 20. Jahrhundert* (München: Oldenbourg, 2010).

Raphael, Lutz. *Imperiale Gewalt und mobilisierte Nation: Europa 1914–1945* (München: C.H. Beck, 2011).

Raphael, Lutz, ed. *Theorien und Experimente der Moderne: Europas Gesellschaften im 20. Jahrhundert* (Vienna: Böhlau, 2012).

Roszkowski, Wojciech. *Land Reforms in East Central Europe after World War One* (Warsaw: Institute of Political Studies, Polish Academy of Sciences, 1995).

Rothschild, Joseph. *East Central Europe between the Two World Wars* (Seattle, WA: University of Washington Press, 1974).

Roux, Michel. *Les Albanais en Yougoslavie: Minorité nationale et développement* (Paris: Éditions de le Maison des sciences de l'homme, 1992).

Schenke, Cornelia. *Nationalstaat und nationale Frage: Polen und die Ukrainer 1921–1939* (Hamburg: Dölling und Galitz, 2004).

Scheuermann, Martin. *Minderheitenschutz contra Konfliktverhütung? Die Minderheitenpolitik des Völkerbundes in den zwanziger Jahren* (Marburg: Verlag Herder-Institut, 2000).

Schultz, Helga, and Angela Harre, eds. *Bauerngesellschaften auf dem Weg in die Moderne: Agrarismus in Ostmitteleuropa 1860 bis 1960* (Wiesbaden: Harrassowitz Verlag, 2010).

Segert, Dieter. *Die Grenzen Osteuropas: 1918, 1945, 1989 – Drei Versuche im Westen anzukommen* (Frankfurt a.M.: Campus Verlag, 2010).

Seton-Watson, Hugh. *Eastern Europe between the Wars, 1918–1941* (New York: Harper & Row, 1962 [1945]).

Siegrist, Hannes, and Dietmar Müller, eds. *Property in East Central Europe: Notions, Institutions and Practices of Landownership in Twentieth Century* (New York: Berghahn Books, 2015).

Stach, Stephan. 'Minderheitenpolitik aus der zweiten Reihe: Konzepte und Praktiken zur Einbindung nationaler und ethnoreligiöser Minderheiten in Piłsudskis Polen (1926–1939)' (PhD Dissertation, Halle-Wittenberg 2015).

Stauter-Halstad, Keely. *The Nation and the Village: The Genesis of Peasant National Identity in Austrian Poland, 1848–1914* (Ithaca, NY: Cornell University Press, 2001).

Stegmann, Natali. *Kriegsdeutungen – Staatsgründungen – Sozialpolitik: der Helden- und Opferdiskurs in der Tschechoslowakei 1918–1948* (München: Oldenbourg, 2010).

Steiner, Zara S. *The Lights that Failed: European International History 1919–1933* (Oxford: Oxford University Press, 2005).

Steiner, Zara S. *The Triumph of the Dark: European International History 1933–1939* (Oxford: Oxford University Press, 2011).

Stojanović, Dubravka. *Kaldrma i asphalt: Urbanizacija i evropeizacija Beograda, 1890–1914* [Cobbles and asphalt: urbanization and the Europeanization of Belgrade, 1890–1914] (Belgrade: Čigoja Štampa, 2008).

Statehood: the interwar period

Szlajfer, Henryk, ed. *Economic Nationalism in East-Central Europe and South America, 1918–1939* (Geneva: Droz, 1990).

Teichova, Alice. *Kleinstaaten im Spannungsfeld der Großmächte: Wirtschaft und Politik in Mittel- und Südosteuropa in der Zwischenkriegszeit* (München: Oldenbourg, 1988).

Tomasevich, Jozo. *Peasants, Politics, and Economic Change in Yugoslavia* (Stanford, CA: Stanford University Press, 1955).

Tomka, Béla. *A Social History of Twentieth-Century Europe* (London and New York: Routledge, 2013).

Trubeta, Sevasti. *Physical Anthropology, Race and Eugenics in Greece (1880s–1970s)* (Leiden: Brill, 2013).

Turda, Marius. *Modernism and Eugenics* (Basingstoke: Palgrave Macmillan, 2010).

Turda, Marius. *Eugenics and Nation in Early Twentieth Century Hungary* (Basingstoke: Palgrave Macmillan, 2014).

Turda, Marius, and Paul J. Weindling, eds. *'Blood and Homeland': Eugenics and Racial Nationalism in Central and Southeast Europe, 1900–1940* (Budapest: CEU Press, 2007).

Ullmann, Hans-Peter. 'Kriegswirtschaft', in *Enzyklopädie Erster Weltkrieg*, Gerhard Hirschfeld et al. (Paderborn: Schöningh Verlag, 2009), 220–32.

5

DECONSTRUCTING AND RECONSTRUCTING STATEHOOD

The impact of the World Wars (Part II) – the Second World War

Jochen Böhler

The Second World War

1. War and statehood – occupation and persistence (II)[1]

During almost two decades of fragile peace between the two World Wars, the Central and Eastern European states maintained their independence but did not manage to form a confederation as a bulwark against the territorial ambitions of Russia and Germany.[2] The Second World War served as an acid test for statehood in the region, since the plans for occupation and the occupying regimes were much more radical than they had been during the First World War. From the very beginning, neither the Nazis nor the Soviets would tolerate any form of continuation of statehood in the invaded territories. Between 1939 and 1941, as a result of the Molotov–Ribbentrop Pact (Hitler–Stalin Pact), Germany and Russia were even accomplices in the dividing up of Central Europe. At this point, the fleeting appearances of the First World War-era governments in exile and various representatives of the emerging Central and Eastern European states, which orbited the Paris peace negotiations in 1918–19, reappeared on a larger, more professional and long-lasting stage.[3]

With the German attack and the Russian invasion in September 1939, the Polish state as a territorial entity was, once again in history, erased from the face of the earth. Although the Polish army disintegrated within a few weeks, the Polish state institutions and considerable parts

---

1 See the first sub-chapter in Chapter 3 of this volume, p. 119, 'War and statehood – occupation and persistence (I)'.
2 Mihai Chioveanu, 'A Fragmented World: Cooperation, Conflict and Conquest in Central East Europe', *Studia Politica* 9, no. 1 (2009): 81–104.
3 See Chapter 3 of the present volume.

Statehood: the Second World War

of the armed forces were able to leave Poland, fleeing mainly over the Polish–Romanian and Polish–Hungarian borders. At the end of that September, Władysław Raczkiewicz, the speaker of the Senate, succeeded the last Polish peacetime president Ignacy Mościcki and formed a Polish government-in-exile (Rząd Rzeczypospolitej Polskiej na Uchodźstwie) in Paris, which, during the course of the German invasion of France, was forced to move to London in June 1940. The organization that would officially represent Polish statehood for years to come suffered from hubris and a lack of legitimacy from its very beginnings. Ultimately, it was the remnant of a defeated state rather than a leadership that had been chosen: 'During 1939 and 1940 there was no divine mission in France; merely a struggle for the survival of the Polish state.' With its country placed under foreign rule, the decisive factor was to what extent the government-in-exile would be able to build up armed forces outside of the former state and to control the gathering resistance movement inside Poland in order to participate substantially in the struggle for its liberation.[4]

Amazingly enough, Polish efforts to maintain structures of statehood during the Second World War were not limited to the outlands. Though it might have appeared to be an impossible undertaking at first sight, a well-functioning and highly diverse network of clandestine state institutions – political, military, educational and provisional – was established in German-occupied Poland itself. The Polish Underground State (Polskie Państwo Podziemne) was able to organize military intelligence and armed resistance within the country against the German (and, during the course of events, also Russian) occupiers, which was obviously the most pressing task of a government without territorial sovereignty. In addition, it also taught the cities' youth in underground schools and universities, thus cultivating a new Polish elite that would in due course be able to compensate for the pre-war intelligentsia that, to a large extent, had been murdered by Nazi and Stalinist death squads, thus forming the nucleus of an independent Polish state that they envisaged for the future. Finally, it provided help, supplies and shelter for the oppressed and persecuted Polish and Jewish population, and even in 1942 informed the Western Allies about the ongoing perpetration of the Holocaust. Disastrously, these desperate warnings were deliberately ignored.[5]

It is striking that the beginnings of Polish resistance movements in the German-occupied zone were not only linked to soldiers from the defeated army, who kept on fighting as paramilitary forces, but also to state clerks who considered a transition into the illegal underground to be part of their duty: 'Contrary to the expectations of the occupiers, Polish statehood ... persisted as a reference point in the self-conception of the elites.' With their expertise and access to resources, they provided the first resistance fighters with money and forged documents.[6] At the peak of its existence, the Polish Underground State, a body that was unique in occupied Europe and which recognized the London exile government's authority, had at their disposal an army, a juridical system to sentence traitors, an educational system to teach the youth and a council to help the persecuted Jews.[7]

While the Polish government-in-exile was initially universally recognized by the Allies, the German attack on Russia and the Soviet Union's subsequent move to the anti-Nazi alliance

---

4 Evan McGilvray, *A Military Government in Exile: The Polish Government in Exile, 1939–1945, a Study of Discontent* (West Midlands: Helion & Co. Ltd., 2010), 38–55, here 44.

5 Stanisław M. Jankowski, ed., *Karski* (Poznań: Dom Wydawniczy Rebis, 2009).

6 Włodzimierz Borodziej, *Geschichte Polens im 20. Jahrhundert* (München: Beck 2010), 211.

7 Grzegorz Górski, *The Polish Underground State, 1939–1945* (Lublin: Widawnictwo KUL, 2012); Halik Kochanski, *The Eagle Unbowed: Poland and the Poles in the Second World War* (Cambridge, MA: Harvard University Press, 2012).

complicated the picture. After the German authorities published pictures of mass graves that they had discovered on former Soviet-occupied soil, which bore traces of the massacre of Polish officers near Katyn (in present-day Russia) and other sites of execution (in present-day Belarus), in April and May 1940 – and when the Poles subsequently did not buy into the Russian hoax that this was allegedly a Nazi crime – Joseph Stalin severed relations with the London proxy government. After the Red Army chased the German troops out of Poland, a Soviet regime was established. Although partisan warfare against this new occupation lasted until the late 1940s, the fate of the Polish Underground State was sealed.[8] The government-in-exile subsisted in London until the downfall of the Soviet bloc, but it only had a symbolic role. In 1990, its last president, Ryszard Kaczorowski, handed the symbols of the Polish Republic (the presidential banner, the presidential and state seals, the presidential sashes and the original text of the 1935 Constitution) over to the first president of free Poland, Lech Wałęsa. Perhaps even more symbolically, and in a bitterly ironic twist of history, 20 years later, Kaczorowski died in a plane crash in the Katyn woods on his way to commemorate the victims of the 1940 massacre.

As is widely known, the Czechoslovak state had already been dismantled in Munich a year before Germany attacked Poland in 1939, and once again, Edvard Beneš, now president of the state he had helped to build two decades before, was forced to flee his native land.[9] What he left behind were shattered remains: the Sudetenland with its large group of ethnic Germans had been annexed to Nazi Germany; the 'Protectorate of Bohemia and Moravia', with a nominal Czech government, had been established in peacetime and was in reality ruled by the Nazis; and a Slovak satellite state of Nazi Germany had joined the Axis Powers.

What part was now the heir to pre-war Czechoslovak statehood was mainly a question of perspective, since the legal situation was rather complicated. Beneš himself had resigned from office as an immediate result of the Munich Agreement, but in exile he still claimed the title of head of state of the first Czechoslovak Republic, which had been founded in 1918 and, in his eyes, never ceased to exist. His 'government' in London, which was not initially recognized by the Allies (who had compromised themselves by signing the Munich Agreement), secretly maintained relations with the Czech puppet government in Prague headed by Emil Hácha, which *was* de facto recognized. After the German attack on the Soviet Union in summer 1941 and the assassination of the then deputy Reich-protector and chief of the Reich Main Security Office, Reinhard Heydrich, barely a year later, the situation changed dramatically: Stalin was the first to recognize the Czech government-in-exile, and the Western powers soon followed his example, while neither Beneš nor Hácha would accept the other's claim to the supreme office of the state. In 1944, the Slovak National Council accepted Beneš as head of a Czechoslovak state but denied the existence of any links to the pre-war First Republic. Through his rapprochement with the Soviets in 1943, Beneš did in fact remain in power after 1945, even if only for a short time. Seriously ill, he had to resign and died in 1948, making way for the 'new order' under the Czech communist Klement Gottwald.

The Yugoslav case was a mixture of the Czech and Polish cases, but it had a very different outcome. A nascent government – formed after a military coup under King Peter II (Karađorđević), who was not yet 18, in late March 1941 – had to evacuate the country only two weeks later, fleeing the invading German army and reaching London via Greece and Egypt. The country itself was divided up: Montenegro and parts of Slovenia and Kosovo,

---

8 Anita J. Prażmowska, ed., *Civil War in Poland, 1942–1948: Challenges to Communist Rule* (Basingstoke: Palgrave Macmillan, 2004).

9 See the corresponding sub-chapter in Chapter 3, 'War and Statehood – Occupation and Persistence (I)'.

Statehood: the Second World War

the larger part of Macedonia and parts of Vojvodina became part of the Italian, Bulgarian and Hungarian spheres of influence respectively. Meanwhile, the Serbian part of the country was turned into a German occupation zone under a domestic puppet government, while the Croatian part became an independent state led by the fascist Ustashe. While both of the state's representative bodies within the country thus compromised themselves through collaboration with the Nazis, the London government disintegrated in a series of internal struggles.[10] The brutal German occupation policy in ex-Yugoslavia led to the meteoric rise of two resistance movements, a communist and a Serbian nationalist one (the Chetniks), which did not – in the same way as the Slovene Home Guard (Domobranci) – flinch from cooperating with the occupants. With the war turning against Germany, it soon became clear that a struggle for power between the competing partisan groups would decide who would govern post-war Yugoslavia. With the victory of the communists, their admired leader Josip Broz Tito became prime minister in late 1944 and de facto ruled the country for more than 30 years, even standing up to constant attempts from Moscow to patronize it.

Although questions of legal representation played an important role in the eyes of citizens from that time, as well as for their allies and their foes, it is clear that good fortune, political skill and alliances were ultimately much more influential in the preservation, mutation, abolition and resurrection of states during and after the Second World War. Of the three exiled governments from Central and Southeastern Europe that I have presented in this sub-chapter, only the Czech representative body managed to return to power for a couple of years after the Second World War. Even before the war, the political classes that dominated the Polish and the Yugoslav governments in exile had not been practising politics and had lost influence over their countries' fate.[11] Only Edvard Beneš, the political survivor who had been in the service of the Czech nation since the era of the First World War, had managed – literally with his last breath – to preserve state power into peace time. Tito, for his part, and not unlike Józef Piłsudski in Poland a quarter of a century earlier, had gained his legitimacy through charisma, the fortunes of war and his endurance and physical presence within the embattled country.

The formation of political bodies to advance and represent statehood outside the state's territory at the beginning of the war was, without a doubt, of enormous symbolic importance. Whereas the various governments in exile in London have already been studied per se,[12] the official and unofficial cooperation and interaction between these state representative bodies with each other and with the Allied governments remains uncharted. These are the subject of a promising research project by Julia Eichenberg that highlights their importance in the following way:

> The radical expansion of the Nazi Empire made London the capital of Allied Europe. France, Poland, Belgium, the Netherlands, Czechoslovakia and others were represented by exile governments, led by central figures of the 20th Century such as Charles

---

10 Stevan K. Pavlowitch, 'Yugoslavia in Exile: The London-Based Wartime Government, 1941–45', in *New Perspectives on Yugoslavia: Key Issues and Controversies*, eds Dejan Djokić and James Ker-Lindsay (New York: Routledge, 2011), 100–16.

11 McGilvray, *A Military Government in Exile*, 41–3; Pavlowitch, 'Yugoslavia in Exile', in Djokić and Ker-Lindsay, *New Perspectives on Yugoslavia*, 114–15.

12 Detlef Brandes, *Großbritannien und seine osteuropäischen Alliierten 1939–1943: Die Regierungen Polens, der Tschechoslowakei und Jugoslawiens im Londoner Exil vom Kriegsausbruch bis zur Konferenz von Teheran* (München: Oldenbourg, 1988); Martin Conway and José Gotovitch, eds, *Europe in Exile: European Exile Communities in Britain 1940–45* (New York: Berghahn, 2001).

de Gaulle, Edvard Beneš, Queen Wilhelmina of the Netherlands and Władysław Sikorski. Their goal was to maintain national interests and to participate in the planning of post-war Europe. The following years saw close cooperation between the different governments-in-exile and between them and British authorities – the 'London Moment'. They claimed statehood and sovereignty in exile and found new political and legal ways to achieve them. They worked together on a new post-war order, reflected on legal options against war criminals and eventually helped prepare the Nuremberg Trials. Political collaboration in London merged traditional diplomacy with informal transnational networking and thus changed constitutional and international law as well as the understanding of statehood and governance in Europe. The study of the London Moment shows the origin of a constructive legacy of European cooperation under the most difficult circumstances.[13]

However, the significance of the governments in exile notwithstanding, towards the war's end it was people in their individual political or military aptitude and sphere of action (or the lack of it) and not councils that decided on the transition (or non-transition) of statehood from times of war to those of peace.

Other Central European countries – as had been the case for Croatia – did at least maintain their statehood, but they became more and more dependent on and involved in the Nazi Regime's policies. Slovakia, which emerged from a dismembered Czechoslovakia in 1938, in addition to Bulgaria, Hungary, Romania and Croatia – all, to varying degrees, allowed the German genocidal programme to enter their state territory. The last two in this list of countries played the most active part in the Holocaust and other German projects of ethnic cleansing. Although, in 1944, all the satellite states tried to sever ties with the sinking German vessel, a significantly large percentage of the pre-war Jewish communities within these states did not survive the war.[14] Italy, in contrast, which had been Berlin's pre-war ally, undertook concrete steps during the war to save its Jewish citizens from certain death in the German extermination camps.[15]

Governments-in-exile, resistance groups, puppet governments – all of these formations, however different, were manifestations of statehood that had one feature in common: they all existed during the Second World War. However, in Nazi-occupied Eastern and Southeastern Europe, there was another important form of statehood that was capable of mobilizing enormous masses of manpower – this was statehood that only existed in the imagination of its would-be citizens. Between 1939 and 1942, Germany did not really consider sharing its colonial gains – which by

---

13 Julia Eichenberg, 'The London Moment: European Governments-in-Exile during the Second World War and beyond', abstract, posted on the website www.geschichte.hu-berlin.de (accessed 22 February 2020).

14 Tatjana Tönsmeyer, *Das Deutsche Reich und die Slowakei 1939–1945: Politischer Alltag zwischen Kooperation und Eigensinn* (Paderborn: Schöningh, 2003); Peter Durucz, *Ungarn in der auswärtigen Politik des Dritten Reiches 1942–1945* (Göttingen: V & R Unipress, 2006); Christian Gerlach and Götz Aly, *Das letzte Kapitel: Realpolitik, Ideologie und der Mord an den ungarischen Juden 1944/1945* (Stuttgart: Deutsche Verlags-Anstalt, 2002); Keith Hitchins, *A Concise History of Romania* (Cambridge: Cambridge University Press, 2014); Alexander Korb, *Im Schatten des Weltkriegs: Massengewalt der Ustaša gegen Serben, Juden und Roma in Kroatien 1941–1945* (Hamburg: Hamburger Edition, 2013). For more details on the involvement of Central and Eastern European states in Nazi policies and genocide, see the volume *Violence* in this series.

15 See the corresponding fifth sub-chapter, 'War and Belonging – Displaced Persons and Statelessness (II)'.

Statehood: the Second World War

that point stretched from the Pyrenees almost to the Urals – with anyone except 'ethnic Germans' (*Volksdeutsche*) or 'Germanic' people in the North who they regarded as kin, such as Norwegians or Danes. Despite this, after the disaster of Stalingrad in early 1943, and the front line moving suddenly westwards rather than eastwards, the idea of recruiting 'non-Germanic' volunteers from Eastern and Southeastern Europe to fight the Red Army became more attractive. The Ukrainians, Balts and Muslims who followed this call to arms harboured no illusions about their future role within a German Empire and consequently had to be offered something else. What made millions of them enrol in the ranks of the Wehrmacht or the Waffen SS was their determination not to let their former state territory fall into the hands of communist regimes, and the small hope of achieving independent statehood within the realms of a victorious Nazi Regime.[16] However, both hopes proved elusive. The German leadership did not at any point consider granting the nations that were fighting under their banner any form of real state independence, nor could the advance of the Red Army be halted. In 1944–5, Nazi reign in Central, Eastern and Southeastern Europe was brought to an end, leaving the area behind the Iron Curtain under Soviet rule. As a reviewer of Anne Applebaum's excellent study of the Sovietization of Eastern Europe noted, the area was 'unlucky ... to be liberated from the Nazi dictatorship by the only regime that could rival it for inhumanity'.[17] Several national resistance groups kept on fighting against the Red Army, but they did not stand a chance.[18] By the late 1940s, the Baltic States had been absorbed by the Soviet Union, while East Germany, Poland, Ukraine, Czechoslovakia, Hungary, Bulgaria and Romania had become Moscow's satellites; they were dependencies of differing degrees, to be sure, but they had no real state sovereignty to speak of.

2. War and work – forced labour and the organization of human resources (II)[19]

As the First World War had already portended, it was mainly the strong neighbours of the Central and Eastern European states – Germany and Russia – that would, first through military conquest and then through brutal coercion, mobilize vast masses as forced labourers within their respective spheres of influence. The inhumanity of the system was most clearly revealed in the fate of those who were mobilized but not considered suitable for the category 'fit for work' by Nazi Germany, as millions of them died through neglect or targeted execution. Hundreds of thousands more died while working for the enemy, who would also use exhausting work under extreme conditions as an additional means of extermination.

Both totalitarian states had already started programmes of internal forced labour organization before the war. The Soviet Solovki prison complex in the White Sea became notorious in the late 1920s amongst Ukrainian peasants and 'for the communist leadership [it] was the first place where the labor of deportees had been transformed into profit for the state'. Such 'special settlements', where deportees were efficiently turned into slaves – in a significant difference to the imperial Russian refugee policy between 1914 and 1917 – mushroomed in Siberia, European Russia and Kazakhstan until the turn of the decade, during which time they confined almost

---

16 Rolf-Dieter Müller, *An der Seite der Wehrmacht: Hitlers ausländische Helfer beim 'Kreuzzug gegen den Bolschewismus' 1941–1945* (Berlin: Links, 2007); and Jochen Böhler and Robert Gerwarth, eds, *The Waffen-SS: A European History* (Oxford: Oxford University Press, 2017).

17 Oliver Bullow, review of *Iron Curtain: The Crushing of Eastern Europe, 1944–1956*, by Anne Applebaum, *The Independent*, 29 September 2012.

18 See the volume *Violence* in this series.

19 See the second sub-chapter in Chapter 3 of this volume, p. 126, 'War and work – forced labour and the organization of human resources (I)'.

two million people. The new name for this camp system 'Gulag' – which was the acronym for the Russian name, Chief Administration for Corrective Labour Camps – spread fear and terror amongst Soviet citizens. Meanwhile in Germany, 'wild' detention and work camps, designed for people who were regarded as political or ethnic 'enemies' of the German people, had been built in the wake of Hitler's rise to power and soon spread throughout the country. In 1939, the Stalinist and the Nazi camp systems formed states within the two states. However, it would be misleading to regard them as legal vacuums, as different worlds where deviant camp guards could live out their basest instincts. On the contrary, both systems of terror were established consciously by the authorities to 'purge' domestic society in order to create the ideal German 'members of the master race' (*Herrenmensch*) or the Russian 'New Soviet Man' (*novy sovetsky chelovek*) by applying the merciless 'law' of the totalitarian state.[20]

Such measures would become more radical in wartime, especially when they were directed against people regarded as non-German or non-Soviet. From the very outset of the Second World War, Germans began to mobilize and move hundreds of thousands of people, initially as a measure for ethnic cleansing. In the parts of Poland that had been annexed to the German Reich, non-Germans were deported and ethnic Germans from abroad were resettled, while throughout German-occupied Europe, Jews were isolated in special urban areas called ghettos, pending their planned deportation to Madagascar or Siberia, megalomaniac plans that never even came close to realization. However, with the failed assault on the Soviet Union in the summer of 1941 and the ensuing prolongation of the war, Nazi Germany's plans shifted to the extensive use of forced labour and extermination within its territories. These goals were not mutually exclusive, but complementary. In the ghettos – the best example being the Lodz Ghetto – for a certain period Jews fit for work could save their lives by working for the German army, while those unfit for work were sent to extermination camps. In Belorussia in 1943, even men who had fought as partisans against Germany could avoid execution by boarding trains and joining the slave army that was operating in Germany – which had eight million members by the end of the war – while women and children were to be killed on the spot.[21] In a third German camp system, the prisoner-of-war camps for Soviet soldiers also turned into sites of mass killing through malnutrition and maltreatment, resulting in the death of about three million. For some of the Red Army soldiers who had been captured, 'work' – in probably the most perverted sense of the word – was a form of rescue, as they were recruited as so-called 'Trawniki men' to carry out the menial work in the German death camps on Polish soil.[22] Meanwhile, the Soviet Gulag system remained relatively unchanged, although of course it had a more diverse group of inmates, as now the non-Russian nationals from within Russia or the recently Soviet-occupied territories who were regarded as unreliable – such as the Balts, Poles, Belorussians, Ukrainians and Germans – flooded into the camps.[23]

Exploitation and extermination through forced labour was an undertaking that oscillated between the extremes of madness and sinister rationality. As disturbing as it sounds, recent studies have painstakingly shown that the Nazi camps and the Gulag system, at least for many years

---

20 Anne Applebaum, *Gulag: A History* (New York: Doubleday, 2003); Timothy Snyder, *Bloodlands: Europe between Hitler and Stalin* (London: Random House, 2010), 26–7.

21 Snyder, *Bloodlands*, 244; Adam Tooze, *The Wages of Destruction: The Making and Breaking of the Nazi Economy* (New York: Viking, 2007); and Michael T. Allen, *Hitler's Slave Lords: The Business of Forced Labour in Occupied Europe* (Stroud: Tempus, 2004).

22 Peter Black, 'Foot Soldiers of the Final Solution: The Trawniki Training Camp and Operation Reinhard', *Holocaust and Genocide Studies* 25, no. 1 (2011): 1–99.

23 Applebaum, *Gulag*, 411–44.

Statehood: the Second World War

of their existence, benefited the perpetrators of these atrocities.[24] The complete perversity of the system, on the other hand, manifests itself first and foremost in its unimaginably pervasive brutality, which weakened the physical and mental constitution of the inmates, but also in the arbitrariness with which victimized groups were defined. The Nazi ideology's deep-rooted disdain for Jews and Slavs was derived from an abstruse world view. The Soviet definition of 'class enemies' also did not stand up to close examination, as it was not only convicted Russian and non-Russian war criminals, but also forced labourers and prisoners of war, who had survived Nazi persecution and returned home, that often ended up in the Gulag system, the latter as 'suspicious elements'. After all, they had survived, and so, according to the Stalinist logic, they must have collaborated with the enemy in one way or another.

The Nazi and Soviet camp systems were fairly similar instruments for the mass control of alleged political or ethnic 'enemies' through isolation and exploitation. If we try to define them by their function, it is hard to say whether they were state or extra-state territories. In practice, they were fields of experimentation where the wardens were omnipotent and the inmates deprived of all their rights as citizens. And although the Nazi and Soviet camp systems were part of two totalitarian universes where the life of individuals did not count much anyhow, this still marked a new level of subjection and vulnerability. Forced labourers and camp inmates had neither advocates to talk to nor courts to appeal to. 'Time there is not like it is here on earth', the Israeli writer and Auschwitz survivor Yehiel Dinor recalled during Adolf Eichmann's trial in Jerusalem in 1961, trying to describe the sensation of absolute defencelessness:

> The inhabitants of this planet had no names, they had no parents nor did they have children. ... They breathed according to different laws of nature, they did not live, nor did they die, according to the laws of this world. Their name was the number. [25]

They were cast out into an interstitial world, where state structures were replaced by the incredibly cruel realities of the camp. Dinor later regretted having used the expression 'Planet Auschwitz' in this context, since it seemed to imply that Auschwitz had never really existed on earth. A metaphor that better fits this context is surely Aleksandr Solzhenitsyn's 'Gulag Archipelago', which depicts an isolated world of oppression and dehumanization that spread out over the entire Soviet Union.

As Timothy Snyder has recently cogently argued, the Nazi's execution programme foresaw the destruction of state structures as a prerogative for genocide.[26] On the other hand, the Nazi and Soviet machineries of persecution and destruction are difficult to imagine in a world without a state. On the contrary, these operations were vital parts of each state's control of its resources of manpower. The paradox is probably best described as the state's effort to create stateless zones in order to pursue a state-directed programme of persecuting, exploiting and destroying masses of people who had been deprived of their civil rights. The main difference between the Nazi and the Soviet camp systems was that, while both

---

24 Tooze, *The Wages of Destruction*; Tobias Wunschik, 'Ein Regenmantel für Dertinger: Das instabile 'Tauwetter' im Gefängniswesen der DDR 1956/57', in *Kommunismus in der Krise: Die Entstalinisierung 1956 und die Folgen*, eds Roger Engelmann, Thomas Großbölting and Hermann Wentker (Göttingen: Vandenhoeck & Ruprecht, 2008), 297–325, here 322.

25 Meg Jensen and Margaretta Jolly, eds, *We Shall Bear Witness: Life Narratives and Human Rights* (Madison, WI: The University of Wisconsin Press, 2014), 147.

26 Timothy Snyder, *Black Earth: The Holocaust as History and Warning* (New York: Tim Duggan Books, 2015).

unflinchingly supported the mass deaths of inmates, only the Germans built special camps for mass extermination.

The more research that is conducted on systematic forced labour under the Nazi and the Soviet Regimes, the more their myriad ramifications become apparent. Up until today, even encyclopaedic projects have only revealed the tip of the iceberg thus far, given the fact that the total number of Nazi camps probably surpassed 42,000, which means quite simply that literally every town in today's Germany has – or at least should have – a memorial for the 'Eastern workers' (*Ostarbeiter*) who suffered and often perished there.[27] The exact number of Gulag and subsidiary camps is unknown; the highest estimates state that there were 30,000 and put the number of victims between 1918 and 1953 at more than twenty million.[28] We have no figures for the German-occupied territories, but since the number of people in the black hole of the extermination camp system fell victim to 'extermination through labour' (*Vernichtung durch Arbeit*), it is safe to assume that the overall number of forced labourers killed by Germans runs high into six-digit numbers. More than 150,000 forced labourers from Russia and Poland died in work camps within the borders of the Nazi Regime alone.[29] Hundreds of thousands of forced labourers, one has to assume, deprived of the state's protection, did not die in remote corners of the continent but in plain view of the local civil population that still benefited from this protection. Indeed, statehood made a difference.

3. War and land – the agrarian question (II)[30]

When it comes to the Second World War, and its destructive transformation of whole regions into wastelands, one might be inclined to think that within this Armageddon there was not much room for the agrarian question. Far from it! In Hitler's mind, the question of where Germans would till land in the future was the starting point for all his plans of conquest. In his first book, *Mein Kampf* (1925–6), and even more so in his second unpublished book manuscript from 1928, he made it perfectly clear that, after the territorial losses of the First World War, in order to survive, the German people had to acquire new living space (*Lebensraum*) in Eastern Europe. A German propaganda song from 1940 stated that 'in the East lies our tomorrow. ... There good earth lies waiting, that carried no seed till now, there lie no farms or cattle but land crying out for the plough!'[31]

Such vague ideas were soon concretized in the Master Plan for the East (*Generalplan Ost*), which, if completed, according to Heinrich Himmler, would have been 'the greatest piece of colonization which the world will ever have seen'. It envisaged German settlements that stretched east up to the Ural mountain range, where legions of soldier peasants would defend the borders of the German Empire in an eternal struggle against 'Asiatic hordes'. The land would belong to the state and be tilled under the auspices of the SS. Since participation in

---

27 See the United States Holocaust Memorial Museum's project 'Encyclopedia of Camps and Ghettos, 1933–1945', www.ushmm.org/research/publications/encyclopedia-camps-ghettos (accessed 22 February 2020).

28 Tomasz Kizny, *Gulag: Life and Death Inside the Soviet Concentration Camps* (Richmond Hill, Ontario: Firefly Books, 2004), 30–1; and Nicholas W. Balabkins, 'Forced Labor Under the Gulag Regime (1918–1990)', in *The Liberation of the Serfs: The Economics of Unfree Labor*, ed. Jürgen G. Backhaus (New York: Springer, 2012), 65–71, here 70–71.

29 Dieter Pohl, *Verfolgung und Massenmord in der NS-Zeit 1933–1945* (Darmstadt: Wissenschaftliche Buchgesellschaft, 2003), 61.

30 See the third sub-chapter in Chapter 3 of this volume, p. 128, 'War and land – the agrarian question (I)'.

31 Mark Mazower, *Hitler's Empire: Nazi Rule in Occupied Europe* (London: Penguin, 2009), 53.

Statehood: the Second World War

this agricultural mega-project required a membership card for the German ethnic community (*Volksgemeinschaft*), the other side of the coin related to the fate of the people who lived in the projected areas and who, according to the German planners, could not be 're-Germanized'. It is hard to believe when we visualize the horrors of the one extermination programme that the Nazis actually nearly completed – the Holocaust, which murdered six million European Jews in Eastern Europe – but the planners in Berlin did actually consider removing fifty million people from these areas – a logistic endeavour that would have been absolutely unthinkable during wartime – and openly asked whether the goal was 'to permanently secure them some sort of subsistence' or whether they should 'be totally eradicated?' Fortunately for the Balts, Ukrainians, Belorussians, Poles and Czechs who would have been immediately severely affected by these measures, the Nazi occupation forces never even came close to the realization of these nightmarish visions. In contrast to their detailed, structured, utopian spatial planning, with its models of villages, farm complexes and agrarian systems that were showcased in the exhibition *Planning and Reconstruction in the East* in Poznań in October 1941, the actual German policy in Eastern Europe between 1941 and 1944 was heavy-handed, exploitative, erratic and, in the end, contributed to the downfall of the German Empire. Nevertheless, millions of people in the occupied territories lost their lives before the Wehrmacht had to retreat westwards in late 1944.[32]

In contrast to Nazi Germany, Soviet Russia preferred to shape the agricultural future of Central and Eastern Europe only after it had won the war. The whole region found itself behind the Iron Curtain, and this had long-lasting effects on the organization of agriculture. Until the end of the 1940s, Moscow's new satellite states would have to introduce the system of collectivization that was so enthusiastically promoted by technocrats and despised by peasants. However, in the immediate aftermath of the war, communist leaders were careful not to antagonize the masses before their power was fully established.[33] Shortly after the events of the war, Jozo Tomasevich described this programmatic course of action as follows:

> After World War II all Eastern European countries executed agrarian reforms. Generally speaking, the expropriations affected large estates and their remnants, land owned by churches, banks, and business corporations, land owned by the German minority and by those considered collaborators or war criminals, and the excess of land above a decreed maximum owned by big and medium peasants. Although the terms and political tone of these reforms were more radical than those following World War I, they were basically of a similar character.[34]

This is an interesting insight from the prominent Yugoslav economic historian, who emigrated to the US before the war. He means that the influence of the events of the war themselves, in this special case, were not the dominant factor. What mattered was the outcome, which in the immediate post-war period made the property of Germans, 'enemies of the people', and Jewish people, who had mostly been deported or murdered, available to them, enabling the countries of Central and Eastern Europe to pick up land reform where they had left it at an impasse in the 1920s, while Moscow, in order not to jeopardize state-building in its nascent stages, gave them the leeway they needed. Hungary meant business and expropriated one third of the owners of

---

32 Ibid., 204–11, here 205 and 208. See also the volume *Violence* in this series.

33 Applebaum, *Iron Curtain*.

34 Jozo Tomasevich, 'Agriculture in Eastern Europe', *The Annals of the American Academy of Political and Social Science* 1, 317 (May 1958): 44–52, quote 45.

large estates. Romania took one million hectares of land out of the hands of 'kulaks' and 'war criminals', while Czechoslovakia redistributed the land of the Germans and the Hungarians. Up to 1947, 'every East European country saw the creation of a large class of smallholders beholden to the new authorities for their land'.[35]

The peasants' euphoria over these developments did not last long. To say that the political outcome of the Second World War with its East–West divide predetermined the successive collectivization of Central and Eastern Europe is a rather commonplace assertion.[36] In terms of the experiences on which it drew and the methods that were applied, its policies of coercion were a continuation of what was practised by Moscow in Soviet Russia and Ukraine in the pre-war decade, but not in wartime.

4. War and destruction – relief and reconstruction (II)[37]

The devastation caused by the Second World War in Central, Eastern and Southeastern Europe even exceeded the horrors of the First World War. For the second time within a generation, the region between Germany and Russia had been turned into a gigantic graveyard, with starving masses of homeless people roaming across it, dotted with thousands of towns and cities razed to the ground by war and deliberate destruction. But although the level of destruction – apart from the Allied carpet bombings of German cities – in Central and Eastern Europe was not comparable to that in the West, any reader interested in the topic will look in vain for a compendium on post-war relief programmes and acts of reconstruction in socialist countries comparable to Alan S. Milward's *Reconstruction of Western Europe, 1945–51.*[38] This is probably owing to the fact that the European Recovery Program (or the Marshall Plan), a giant aid programme carried out by the US to kick-start the European economy, was not applied to countries within the Soviet sphere of influence. At the war's end, Moscow controlled all Central and Eastern European capitals, including Berlin, and was coming into conflict with its Western Allies, especially over economic issues. While the US was a financial superpower, the USSR had been materially exhausted by the preceding years of war and occupation and was dependent on big long-term loans. Washington, for its part, was reluctant to pump money into Eastern Europe as long as the Kremlin did not allow free trade within its political and military sphere of influence.[39]

It is not the case that the West was initially uncaring about the people that now lived behind the Iron Curtain. In Eastern Europe, death had not been halted by the ceasefires. In 1946–7, as a result of the combination of the destruction from war, a lack of manpower and a poor harvest, the whole of post-war Europe, except Sweden and Switzerland, endured food shortages, and a famine in the Soviet Union cost, as had also occurred in 1921–2, the lives of between one and two million people.[40] Material wartime losses in the area between Russia and Germany often

---

35 Tony Judt, *Postwar: A History of Europe Since 1945* (New York: Penguin Books, 2006), 78.

36 For collectivization in Central and Eastern Europe at the end of the 1940s, see the volume *Challenges of Modernity* in this series.

37 See the fourth sub-chapter in Chapter 3 of this volume, p. 135, 'War and destruction – relief and reconstruction (I)'.

38 Alan S. Milward, *The Reconstruction of Western Europe, 1945–51* (Berkeley, CA: University of California Press, 1984).

39 Gerhard Wettig, *Stalin and the Cold War in Europe: The Emergence and Development of East-West Conflict, 1939–1953* (Lanham, MD: Rowman & Littlefield, 2008), 69–73.

40 Nicholas Ganson, *The Soviet Famine of 1946–47 in Global and Historical Perspective* (Basingstoke: Palgrave Macmillan, 2009), xv.

Statehood: the Second World War

even surmounted the national pre-war gross domestic products: 370 per cent in Yugoslavia, 350 per cent in Poland, 200 per cent in Hungary, more than 100 per cent in Czechoslovakia, and 50 per cent in both Bulgaria and Romania, the two countries that had been Germany's allies and did not witness intense fighting at the end of the war.[41] When Hugh Gibson, the first US minister plenipotentiary to Poland in 1919, returned to Warsaw in March 1946, he did not recognize the capital. Asked about a new park, his driver answered that 'it wasn't a park, but a hole where the central railway station used to be'.[42]

Nevertheless, to cite the late Tony Judt's prize-winning study of the post-war era, 'the material damage suffered by Europeans in the course of the war, terrible though it had been, was insignificant when set against the human losses', which he specified as amounting to about 36.5 million people in total. In the Eastern and Southeastern part of the continent, they amounted to numbers that were unparalleled in history. While France lost about 1 in 77, and Britain 1 in 125 of their pre-war populations, the figures – which can, of course, only be educated guesses – were 1 in 5 in Poland, 1 in 8 in Yugoslavia, 1 in 11 in the Soviet Union and 1 in 14 in Greece. It is impossible to measure the psychological wounds that the survivors had to live with.[43]

The war was still raging when the United Nations Relief and Rehabilitation Administration (UNRRA) was founded to ease the situation of the Axis-occupied countries and their population as soon as there was a chance to do so.[44] Although its founding document was signed by 44 states (including the Soviet Union), it was largely dominated by the United States. The UNRRA ran the displaced persons camps in liberated Western Europe,[45] and apart from China and Italy, the lion's share of its material aid went to Central and Eastern Europe, with Poland receiving US$478 million, Yugoslavia US$416 million, Greece US$347 million, Czechoslovakia US$261 million, Ukraine US$188 million and Austria US$136 million. Of course, in a world that had been torn to pieces, help was not always granted – or received – immediately and without bias. In October 1944, Tito declined UNRRA help out of consideration for his 'brethren' from the Soviet Union, which had just sent 50,000 tons of bread to the starving country.[46] In the reverse situation, two years later British foreign correspondent George Bilainkin noted the following during his visit to Yugoslavia:

I am reminded of the published remark made by the U.S. Ambassador here, Richard Patterson, junr., during the August crisis over the shooting down of U.S.

---

41 Adrian Webb, *The Routledge Companion to Central and Eastern Europe since 1919* (London: Routledge, 2008), 247.

42 Michael Gibson, *The Food Mission Diaries of Hugh Gibson, 1946 and 1947*, vol. 1, entry from 28 March 1946, www.hoover.org/library-archives/collections/food-mission-diaries-hugh-gibson-1946-and-1947, (accessed 22 February 2020).

43 Judt, *Postwar*, 17–18, here 17.

44 Grace Fox, 'The Origins of UNRRA', *Political Science Quarterly* 65, no. 4 (1950): 561–84; and Ben Shephard, *The Long Road Home: The Aftermath of the Second World War* (London: Vintage, 2011), 31–40.

45 See the fifth sub-chapter, 'War and belonging – displaced persons and statelessness (II)' in the present chapter.

46 Letter from Tito to Edvard Kardelj, vice president of the Yugsolav National Committee, 3 October 1944, in *Zbornik dokumenata i podataka o narodnooslobodilačkom ratu naroda Jugoslavije. Dokumenti Centralnog komiteta KP Jugoslavije i Vrhovnog štaba NOV i PO Jugoslavije* [Collection of documents and information on the war of National Liberation of the Yugoslav People: documents of the Central Committee of the Communist Party of Yugoslavia and of the Supreme Staff of the National Liberation Army and Partisan Detachments of Yugoslavia], ed. Jovan Vujošević, vol. 2/14, (Beograd: Vojnoistorijski institut, 1981), 196.

airmen who had trespassed on Yugoslav territory, 'Only over my dead body will UNRRA supplies reach this country.' ... Why, I asked myself, is it necessary to bully these people, tell them what it is they do right, when there is so much needing to be done on our own doorstep?[47]

On the other hand, the mere fact that the Ukrainian Soviet Socialist Republic was on the list of recipients is remarkable, notwithstanding the Soviet Union's signing of the UNRRA agreement in 1943. Politics aside, for the survivors of the Nazi camps and the starving people within the occupied countries, the relief workers with the letters UNRRA on their sleeves and a stylized red globe on their caps were nothing short of guardian angels. While, due to its ephemeral character, some historians tend to downplay the significance of the organization, William I. Hitchcock points out that it was never designed to be a permanent institution, that 'in an increasingly divided world, it was a genuinely international enterprise' and that, in the end, it only 'fell short as a vehicle for American foreign economic interests'.[48]

In the second half of the 1940s, after a short period of jubilation following the end of combat, the global mood changed significantly. In the summer of 1946, Herbert Hoover, a hero in the arena of foreign relief to Eastern Europe after the First World War, headed President Harry S. Truman's Famine Emergency Committee (often referred to simply as the Food Mission), which on its tour around the globe also stopped off in Czechoslovakia, Poland and Yugoslavia, and the diary of his right-hand man Gibson clearly registers both their deep contempt for the communist nomenklatura they met at every step.[49]

Post-war relief and reconstruction was – again – a powerful weapon, and this time, when the short marriage of convenience between the United States and the Soviet Union ended in divorce, America decided to use it. Secretary of State George C. Marshall's plan for the recovery of Europe was not an emergency relief programme anymore, but rather a long-term measure to build up markets for US products and ensure free trade. Theoretically, it was an offer open to the countries in Central and Eastern Europe as well, and at least the Czechoslovak government considered taking part in transatlantic economic negotiations in Paris in July 1947 and was only prevented from doing so at the last minute by a resolute intervention from Moscow.[50] But was the American offer really unconditional, impartial and intended for Russia's participation? Given our extensive knowledge of Stalin's paranoid vision of strictly separated Western and Eastern spheres of influence – both political *and* economic – such doubts are surely justified. Only one week after Marshall had publicly outlined his programme at Harvard University, and before the USSR's 'stop' command for the Eastern bloc countries, Hoover bluntly stated in a letter to the chairman of the American Committee on Appropriations that 'Upwards of a billion people in the war-torn areas of Western Europe and Asia are asking for help. ... We should concentrate our limited resources in the areas where Western Civilization can be preserved'.[51] The war had not ended, it had just turned cold.

---

47 George Bilainkin, *Four Weeks in Yugoslavia* (London, New York: R. Tuck, 1947), 31, 34.
48 William I. Hitchcock, *The Bitter Road to Freedom: A New History of the Liberation of Europe* (New York: Free Press, 2009), 215–48, figures 220, quotes 247. More critical on the UNRRA's achievements is Shephard, *Long Road Home*, 47–59.
49 Gibson, *Food Mission Diaries*, vol. 1. For more on the Famine Emergency Committee and its political significance at the beginning of the Cold War, see Ganson, *The Soviet Famine*.
50 Judt, *Postwar*, 90–3.
51 Letter from Hoover to Senator Styles Bridges, 13 June 1947, in *Addresses Upon the American Road*, vol. 5, *1945–1948*, ed. Herbert Hoover (Toronto: D. van Nostrand, 1949), 109–18, quote 109, 118.

Statehood: the Second World War

On the other hand, Stalin's empathy for the countries between Russia and (the Federal Republic of) Germany was somewhat limited as well. While Western Europe was slowly recovering from wartime destruction, the Soviet Union unwaveringly demanded enormous compensation for its losses in war from former enemies and allies alike. It is estimated that the net transfer of 'reparations' Moscow received between 1945 and 1953 from Central and Eastern European countries roughly equalled the equivalent net transfer Western European countries received from Washington over the same period. The Iron Curtain thus functioned like a gigantic mirror, reversing western aid in eastern exploitation.[52]

What this all amounts to is the following: the effects wartime destruction and post-war reconstruction had on state-building in Central and Eastern Europe were diametrically opposed across the two global conflicts. After 1918, war had enabled the creation of a buffer zone between the East and the West. After 1945, it wiped away this same buffer zone. 'If one is looking for a single overwhelming cause of communist revolution', writes Stephan A. Smith,

> it was war rather than the systemic crisis of capitalism. The Bolsheviks were able to seize power [within Russia] because the Provisional Government in 1917 opted to continue to participate in the First World War. Similarly, it was the massive destruction caused by the Second World War that enabled the Soviet Union to install communist states in Eastern Europe ...[53]

5. War and belonging – displaced persons and statelessness (II)[54]

With the Treaty of Sèvres in 1923, the state-coordinated movement of millions of people had become an internationally accepted method for creating ethnically homogeneous nation states.[55] However, the 'exchange' of Muslim Turks and Christian Greeks in the wake of the Greco–Turkish War was the last large-scale programme in peacetime to ease ethnic tensions in Central and Eastern Europe. Subsequently, within the Soviet Union, Stalin would perfect the technique of mass deportation to the Gulag Archipelago as a punishment for allegedly defiant Soviet citizens, but his guiding criterion was class, and not ethnicity, and prior to the Second World War, only Soviet citizens were affected.[56]

It was Hitler who put a demographic policy defined by race, nationality and statehood on the agenda. After he came to power, during the 1930s he pursued a two-fold course of action that would seal the fate of millions. Firstly, in the Nuremberg Laws of 1936, he deprived German Jews of equal civil rights. Secondly, from 1938 onwards, he merged territories that added a large portion of ethnic Germans – Austria and the Sudetenland in 1938 and the remaining Czech territories (*Rest-Tschechei*) in 1939 – to the Nazi Regime's territory and granted them German citizenship. The message was clear: 'foreign races' (*Fremdvölkische*) were to be isolated

---

52 Robert Bideleux and Ian Jeffries, *A History of Eastern Europe: Crisis and Change* (London and New York: Routledge, 2007), 460–1.

53 Stephen A. Smith, 'Introduction: Towards a Global History of Communism', in *The Oxford Handbook of the History of Communism*, ed. Stephen A. Smith (New York: Oxford University Press, 2014), 1–34, here 5.

54 See the fifth sub-chapter in Chapter 3 of this volume, p. 000, 'War and belonging – displaced persons and statelessness (I)'.

55 See the volume *Violence* in this series.

56 Snyder, *Bloodlands*, 26–111. See also the sub-chapter, 'Forced labor and the organization of human resources (II)'.

and would vanish from German-controlled areas in the long term, whereas 'ethnic Germans' were to come 'back home to the Reich' ('*heim ins Reich*'), or rather: the Reich came to *them*.

The first to experience the negative effects of this policy were the tens of thousands of Polish Jews and their families, who had lived on the territory of the Nazi Regime for decades but who now, enduring persecution from the Nazi authorities, longed to leave for the country for which they held passports. In order to curb the influx of Jews after the annexation (Anschluss) of Austria, the Consular Section of the Polish Foreign Office decided to allow Polish nationals living abroad to enter Poland only in exceptional cases. A corresponding law was passed at the beginning of April 1938 and a supplementary passport regulation at the beginning of October 1938. According to these guidelines, nearly every Pole living abroad could lose citizenship or be denied return to Poland. In spite of their deliberately generalizing character, they were supposed in particular to dam the return of Polish Jews. In the 1930s, other European states also closed their borders to refugees from the national-socialist sphere of domination. Poland's response, however, alarmed the Nazi German government, which feared that 'tens of thousands of Polish Jews living in the Reich area would soon have to be tolerated in Germany', at a time when the German Jews were already largely deprived and expropriated, persecuted and compelled to emigrate. At the end of October 1938, the Gestapo summarily detained 17,000 Polish Jews, many of whom had been living in Germany for two or three generations. They had to leave behind all their possessions and, with the use of brutal force, were deported and forced to cross the German–Polish border 50 miles west of Poznań. Thousands of them spent the winter months of 1938–9 along the border strip under life-threatening conditions facing an uncertain future.[57]

One of the deportees, Marcel Reich-Ranicki, who after 1945 was for decades the leading literary critic in the Federal Republic of Germany, described the shock he felt at this sudden loss of his civil rights. For many years, his family of assimilated Polish Jews had lived undisturbed in Berlin. Now, 'in the early morning of 28 October 1938, it was not yet seven o'clock', the then eighteen-year-old recounts:

> [I] was vigorously awakened by a policeman who looked no different from those who controlled the traffic in the streets. Having carefully examined my passport, he handed me a document. It said that I was being expelled from the German Reich. The policeman ordered me to get dressed at once and to come along with him. But I asked to be allowed to read the document again. This was allowed. I then took the liberty of objecting, a little timidly, that the paper said I had to leave the Reich within a fortnight – and, moreover, I had the right to appeal. Such subtleties did not move the rather impassive policemen. 'No, come along at once.'[58]

At the same time, a man the same age as Ranicki, Herschel Grynszpan, who was living in Paris without valid documents, learned that his parents and siblings had been deported in the same transports. As a motive for his assassination of the German embassy diplomat Ernst vom Rath on 7 November 1938, he named the first mass deportation of Jews by the National Socialist regime. However, his act provided a welcome pretext for the pogrom, euphemistically referred to as *Reichskristallnacht* ('Night of the Broken Glass') on 9–10 November. All across Germany,

---

57 Jerzy Tomaszewski, *Auftakt zur Vernichtung: Die Vertreibung polnischer Juden aus Deutschland im Jahre 1938* (Osnabrück: Fibre Verlag, 2002); quote: Hans G. Adler, *Der verwaltete Mensch: Studien zur Deportation der Juden aus Deutschland* (Tübingen: Mohr, 1974), 93.

58 Marcel Reich-Ranicki, *The Author of Himself: The Life of Marcel Reich-Ranicki* (Princeton, NJ: Princeton University Press, 2001), 106–7.

Statehood: the Second World War

the windows of Jewish shops were smashed, synagogues burned, Jews humiliated in the streets, arrested, battered and murdered.[59] Denying full citizenship to the Jews both in- and outside Germany was the first step in the German extermination programme, and the subsequent denaturalization of Jews who had fled the Nazi Regime its logical consequence.[60]

With the onset of the Second World War, other ethnic groups also got caught up in the confusion created by violent ethno-political interventions. After the German army defeated the Polish army in September 1939 and the Red Army entered the country from the east, Central Europe, after two decades of deceptive calm, was on the move again. Lithuania regained the Vilna region, which the country had lost to Poland in 1920 and, as an act of revenge, disenfranchised the roughly 83,000 Poles who lived in the area by denying them citizenship rights, thus reducing their status to that of the approximately 20,000 other refugees who had fled invaded Poland to the north.[61] Nazi Germany divided its share of the country into two parts: the first was the General Government (*Generalgouvernement*) in central Poland (a legally undefined land) into which it henceforth deported about 400,000 Poles and Jews from western Poland, which was now labelled 'incorporated territory' and annexed by Nazi Germany. The 'Germanization' of this zone was seen as a failure in the eyes of the Germans since they had anticipated to deport ten times more non-Germans and to replace them with ethnic Germans. In their sphere of influence, the Soviets, for their part, started to deport hundreds of thousands of inhabitants who were regarded as unreliable further to the east.[62]

As was the case with forced labour, in terms of the Holocaust, the level of state protection and questions of belonging would often be a matter of life or death. To be sure, this does not apply to the German-occupied territories in Central and Eastern Europe where the destruction of statehood was an integral part of the persecution and extermination of the European Jews.[63] However, it certainly does apply to states that were allied with Germany in Southeastern Europe, such as Romania, Bulgaria, Croatia or Italy. For the Jews under their authority, their respective stances towards the German elimination programme would tip the scales. From 1941 onwards, Romania would also itself murder Jews outside the 'Romanian Old Kingdom', specifically the Jews of Bukovina and Bessarabia, who had lost their Romanian citizenship through Russia's annexation of these very territories the previous year, and the Jews of Transnistria (which Romania had received as bounty for its participation in the German attack on the Soviet Union) who had never been Romanian citizens.[64] After Germany occupied Yugoslavia and Greece in 1941, Bulgaria assumed full administrative control of Eastern Macedonia and Western Thrace, making all people who lived there Bulgarian citizens, except the more than 10,000 Jews who were subsequently deported and killed in the Auschwitz and Treblinka death camps in German-occupied Poland.[65] Further to the South, though, another ally of Germany

---

59 Saul Friedländer, *The Years of Persecution, 1933–1939*, vol. 1, *Nazi Germany and the Jews* (London: Phoenix, 1997), 269–305.

60 Irith Dublon-Knebel, 'Das Auswärtige Amt im Krieg', in *Das Amt und die Vergangenheit: Deutsche Diplomaten im Dritten Reich und in der Bundesrepublik*, eds Eckart Conze, Norbert Frei, Peter Hayes and Moshe Zimmermann (München: Blessing, 2010), 167–220, here 179–80.

61 Tomas Balkelis, 'Nation State, Ethnic Conflict, and Refugees in Lithuania, 1939–1940', in Bartov and Weitz, *Shatterzone of Empires*, 243–57.

62 Snyder, *Bloodlands*, 119–54; see also the volume *Violence* in this series.

63 Snyder, *Black Earth*.

64 Mazower, *Hitler's Empire*, 330–40.

65 Rossen Vassilev, 'The Rescue of Bulgaria's Jews in World War II', *New Politics* 12, no. 4 (2010), http://newpol.org/content/rescue-bulgarias-jews-world-war-ii (accessed 22 February 2020).

demonstrated how the diplomatic instrument of citizenship could be a lifesaver. Within its occupation zone, Italy summarily declared that the Greek Jews whose ancestors had emigrated centuries before from Italy to be Italian subjects, thus exempting them from deportation and certain death. With the fall of Benito Mussolini in autumn 1943, this last resort for the Greek Jews went up in smoke, along with independent Italian statehood.[66] What all these examples vividly demonstrate is that, even in times of total war and fully fledged extermination programmes, the question of whether the victims who were targeted could appeal to the protection of a state or not was one of life and death.

While the elimination of stateless people was a new feature of the Second World War, the masses of stateless people it produced through flight and displacement was clearly reminiscent of the First World War. In 1943, the sociologist Eugene Kulischer estimated that 'more than thirty million of the inhabitants of the continent of Europe have been transplanted or torn from their homes since the beginning of the war'. He knew whereof he spoke. Born in 1881, he first fled revolutionary Russia in 1920, then Nazi Germany in 1935, whence his odyssey took him via Denmark and France, to the United States, turning him into the category of person he dedicated most of his academic career to studying: the 'displaced person' (DP), a term which, by the way, he himself coined.[67]

The fact that not all the millions of people, who after the Second World War found themselves in another place than they had lived before, were stateless in the word's strictest sense caused problems that were already visible after 1918, when only refugees from Russia were the children of sorrow from High Commissar Fridtjof Nansen, while others, who also needed legal protection, were excluded.[68] This time, the successor institution of the League of Nations – the United Nations (UN) – would not again permit a much too narrow, legalistic definition of the status of millions of refugees, but would follow a more flexible approach. In their *Study of Statelessness*, published in 1949, a person could be defined as stateless de jure or de facto, the latter applying to:

> persons who, having left the country of which they were nationals, no longer enjoy the protection and assistance of their national authorities, either because these authorities refuse to grant them assistance and protection, or because they themselves renounce the assistance and protection of the countries of which they are nationals.[69]

This shift in the international community's approach was a reaction to the moral disaster and human catastrophe of total war, persecution and mass killing. People not only needed the UN's protection if their state had disowned them, they also needed it when their state had persecuted them or would probably persecute them upon their return. Nevertheless, mainly due to political considerations, many DP groups found themselves with poor advocacy after Germany's unconditional surrender. About two million Russian prisoners of war, forced workers and camp inmates were forcefully repatriated from Western countries to the Soviet Union, regardless of the fate that awaited them if they had, or were merely suspected of having

---

66 Mark Mazower, *Inside Hitler's Greece: The Experience of Occupation, 1941–44* (New Haven, CT: Yale University Press, 2001), 235–61.

67 Abraham J. Jaffe, 'Notes on the Population Theory of Eugene M. Kulischer', *The Milbank Memorial Fund Quarterly* 40, no. 2 (1962): 187–206; quote: Gerard D. Cohen, *In War's Wake: Europe's Displaced Persons in the Postwar Order* (Oxford: Oxford University Press, 2012), 4.

68 See the corresponding sub-chapter in Part I, 'War and belonging – displaced persons and statelessness'.

69 United Nations, eds, *Study of Statelessness* (New York, 1949), 8–9.

Statehood: the Second World War

(due to the simple fact that they survived forced labour and imprisonment), collaborated with Nazi Germany. Instead of taking the traumatic experience hundreds of thousands of them had suffered into consideration, these people were passed from one totalitarian system to another or, more precisely, from Nazi camps to Soviet camps via DP camps, a fate that awaited one in four of them. In the immediate post-war world, when the USA and Russia were still allies, their destiny was not taken into consideration.[70]

Furthermore, in UN language, the term 'German refugee' only applied to people who had fled Hitler's Germany before 1945, not the roughly 14 million Germans who had fled or were forcefully expelled from Poland and Czechoslovakia in the wake of the war. Since most Nazis who were guilty of heinous crimes against the Jewish and Slavic populations fled before the arrival of the advancing Red Army, these measures initially affected millions of innocent women, old people and children. It is estimated that hundreds of thousands lost their lives during this exodus. In Western Germany, the expellees were met with a cold welcome.[71] Two million Poles, Belarussians, Ukrainians and Lithuanians were deported in order to keep them within the shifting borders of post-war Central Europe. In the end, after 1946 the label of stateless people applied only to a 'last million' of DPs, a 'multinational group of Jewish and non-Jewish asylum seekers unwilling or unable to go home'.[72]

The camps that these DPs populated were mainly found in Germany and Italy. As a result of repatriation and emigration, the number of ethnic Poles declined constantly (in 1946, there were 422,000; 1948, 210,000; 1949, 113,000).[73] From 1946 onwards, only the lot of the roughly 400,000 'extraterritorial' Jewish inmates of DP camps touches upon questions of statehood and citizenship that are connected to our area of interest. The majority of these DPs had resided in Poland before the war, but with the trauma of having lost relatives and anti-Semitic sentiment growing in the country, which culminated in the Kielce Pogrom of July 1946, for many of them returning was not a practical option.[74] As an immediate reaction to the bitter experiences of war and genocide, in the post-war years, Jewish survivors from Central and Eastern Europe developed an enhanced consciousness concerning nationality, with Zionism as its major political expression. Consequently, the majority of these survivors engaged themselves in building the State of Israel, emigrating illegally before and legally after 1948.[75]

Conclusion

The five thematic sub-chapters of this contribution aimed to address the issues one is confronted with when studying the impact the two World Wars had on statehood in our region of interest. Naturally, additional or alternative topics could have been selected. Here, they

---

70 Mark R. Elliott, *Pawns of Yalta: Soviet Refugees and America's Role in Their Repatriation* (Urbana, IL: University of Illinois Press, 1982); and Ulrike Goeken-Haidl, *Der Weg zurück: Die Repatriierung sowjetischer Kriegsgefangener und Zwangsarbeiter während und nach dem Zweiten Weltkrieg* (Essen: Klartext-Verlag, 2006).

71 Andreas Kossert, *Kalte Heimat: Die Geschichte der deutschen Vertriebenen nach 1945* (München: Siedler, 2008).

72 Cohen, *In War's Wake*, 4–7, quote 5.

73 Krzysztof Ruchniewicz, *Polskie zabiegi o odszkodowania niemieckie w latach 1944/46–1975* [Polish activities for German recompense 1944/46–1975] (Wrocław: Wydawnictwo Uniwersytetu Wrocławskiego, 2007), 53.

74 Jan T. Gross, *Fear: Anti-Semitism in Poland after Auschwitz – An Essay in Historical Interpretation* (Princeton, NJ: Princeton University Press, 2006).

75 Cohen, *In War's Wake*, 126–49.

shall at least be named. Both World Wars were accompanied by hardship and the mass killing of soldiers and civilians, which, although it reached different levels in the two wars, grew to a hitherto unknown dimension in both cases. Twice within one century, post-war Europe, even the post-war world, eagerly sought out solutions to cope with the horrors of the past and to prevent their recurrence in the future. New forms of mourning and new strategies for memorializing the dead evolved, which – since the experience of violence and death had not respected any borders – often tended to transcend the new state frontiers as well. A similar effect could be observed in the prosecution of those who were considered to be the culprits responsible for both the outbreak of the wars and the perpetration of war crimes; indeed, without close international cooperation among national police forces and high courts prosecution was impossible. Finally, since the pre-war systems of international cooperation had proved completely insufficient in preventing mass slaughter, idealistic visions of an effective and just world order emerged – especially during the first years of peace in which people lived with the immediate effects of the destructive wars – giving birth to the League of Nations in 1920 and the United Nations in 1945. In tracing the impact of the two World Wars on individual state-building, it is advisable not to overlook how they influenced transnational and international cooperation in Central and Eastern Europe. Thus, the non-governmental initiatives and international organizations that were founded to address the legacies of war often resulted in structures that rivalled or exceeded the newly established structures of the states in the region.

Twice within the twentieth century war had destroyed and re-erected the states of Central and Eastern Europe. In the wake of war, the structures of old states would vanish, and the structures of new states would emerge. War, in this regard, became a transitional phase during which statehood would undergo continual metamorphosis and perpetually redefine itself. Throughout this process, the political and societal composition of the Central and Eastern European states changed with a speed that was unimaginable in peacetime. War was the largest accelerator of statehood. Notwithstanding the enormous loss of human life and suffering, from a bird's-eye view, the two World Wars might even be regarded as an interesting continental experiment in the transformation of states.

For many ethnic groups in Central and Eastern Europe, who had developed independence movements under imperial rule, the First World War, especially in its final stage, provided the one chance to channel their energies into the building of autonomous states. The Second World War, especially in its final stage, witnessed the abrupt end of this autonomy and its replacement with imperial rule from Moscow. This complete and almost unhindered hostile takeover would not have been possible if the pre-war state structures of the occupied countries had not been completely destroyed. In addition, all over Central, Eastern and Southeastern Europe, the state elites had fled, had been deported or were liquidated. Where they had maintained power, they discredited themselves irreversibly by giving their allegiance to the Nazis, a tactic which proved to be a verdict rather than an asset, while wartime collaboration with the victorious Soviets was potentially rewarded with membership in the new communist nomenklatura.

For the people living in the lands between Germany and Russia between 1939 and 1945 that were on Hitler's or Stalin's target lists, the evaporation of their state's protection proved fatal. Detention, deportation and death hung over their heads in both occupation zones like not one, but three swords above Damocles. So, as I highlighted earlier, Timothy Snyder is absolutely right when he states the obvious point that has nevertheless so often been overlooked: the Nazi programme of persecution and annihilation necessitated the destruction of state structures.[76] Two addenda, however, seem appropriate here. First, it is also clear that such an organized

---

76 Snyder, *Black Earth*.

Statehood: the Second World War

programme necessitated the existence of state structures as well, specifically those structures that would execute this very programme. Second, as Snyder has masterfully shown in his book *Bloodlands*, between 1939 and 1941, there were *two* totalitarian dictatorships that had such an agenda for the region we are considering.[77] There were even points of contact and entanglement over population transfer and processes of persecution between these two dictatorships. Ethnic Germans or Russians would cross the border west- or eastwards and political enemies would be extradited, exchanges that automatically prompted questions of citizenship and state protection – or the lack of it; and stuck in the middle were the Jews. Towards the end of 1939, 150,000 of them managed to flee from German-occupied Poland to the Soviet Union, where they were offered citizenship; those who declined awaited deportation to northern Russia or Siberia. In early 1940, Stalin refused to extend his state's protection to the German Jews that Hitler had 'offered' to transport to the Soviet Union for naturalization and resettlement in Western Ukraine and East Asia. Their fate – along with almost all Jews who were still living in Europe – was sealed.[78]

As might have also become clear, statehood during war and its aftermath was not something that one could label with moral attributes such as 'good' or 'bad' per se. It would either save or destroy, provide shelter or make life a living hell, send aid packages or artillery shells and poison gas. War – even in its total manifestation – did not mean the absence of the state. Statehood mattered in wartime.

Further reading

Allen, Michael T. *Hitler's Slave Lords: The Business of Forced Labour in Occupied Europe* (Stroud: Tempus, 2004).

Applebaum, Anne. *Gulag: A History* (New York: Doubleday, 2003).

Böhler, Jochen, and Robert Gerwarth, eds. *The Waffen-SS: A European History* (Oxford: Oxford University Press, 2017).

Brandes, Detlef. *Großbritannien und seine osteuropäischen Alliierten 1939–1943: Die Regierungen Polens, der Tschechoslowakei und Jugoslawiens im Londoner Exil vom Kriegsausbruch bis zur Konferenz von Teheran* (München: Oldenbourg, 1988).

Cohen, Gerard D. *In War's Wake: Europe's Displaced Persons in the Postwar Order* (Oxford: Oxford University Press, 2012).

Conway, Martin, and José Gotovitch, eds. *Europe in Exile: European Exile Communities in Britain 1940–45* (New York: Berghahn, 2001).

Elliott, Mark R. *Pawns of Yalta: Soviet Refugees and America's Role in Their Repatriation* (Urbana, IL: University of Illinois Press, 1982).

Friedländer, Saul. *The Years of Persecution, 1933–1939, vol. 1, Nazi Germany and the Jews* (London: Phoenix, 1997).

Ganson, Nicholas. *The Soviet Famine of 1946–47 in Global and Historical Perspective* (Basingstoke: Palgrave Macmillan, 2009).

Gerlach, Christian, and Götz Aly. *Das letzte Kapitel: Realpolitik, Ideologie und der Mord an den ungarischen Juden 1944/1945* (Stuttgart: Deutsche Verlags-Anstalt, 2002).

Goeken-Haidl, Ulrike. *Der Weg zurück: Die Repatriierung sowjetischer Kriegsgefangener und Zwangsarbeiter während und nach dem Zweiten Weltkrieg* (Essen: Klartext-Verlag, 2006).

Górski, Grzegorz. *The Polish Underground State, 1939–1945* (Lublin: Widawnictwo KUL, 2012).

---

77 Snyder, *Bloodlands*, in particular the chapter 'Molotov–Ribbentrop Europe'.

78 Pavel Polian, 'Hätte der Holocaust beinahe nicht stattgefunden? Überlegungen zu einem Schriftwechsel im Wert von zwei Millionen Menschenleben', in *Besatzung, Kollaboration, Holocaust: Neue Studien zur Verfolgung und Ermordung der europäischen Juden*, eds Johannes Hürter and Jürgen Zarusky (München: Oldenbourg, 2008), 1–19.

Gross, Jan T. *Fear: Anti-Semitism in Poland after Auschwitz – An Essay in Historical Interpretation* (Princeton, NJ: Princeton University Press, 2006).

Hitchcock, William I. *The Bitter Road to Freedom: A New History of the Liberation of Europe* (New York: Free Press, 2009).

Hitchins, Keith. *A Concise History of Romania* (Cambridge: Cambridge University Press, 2014).

Judt, Tony. *Postwar: A History of Europe since 1945* (New York: Penguin Books, 2006).

Kizny, Tomasz. *Gulag: Life and Death Inside the Soviet Concentration Camps* (Richmond Hill, Ontario: Firefly Books, 2004).

Kochanski, Halik. *The Eagle Unbowed: Poland and the Poles in the Second World War* (Cambridge, MA: Harvard University Press, 2012).

Korb, Alexander. *Im Schatten des Weltkriegs: Massengewalt der Ustaša gegen Serben, Juden und Roma in Kroatien 1941–1945* (Hamburg: Hamburger Edition, 2013).

Kossert, Andreas. *Kalte Heimat: Die Geschichte der deutschen Vertriebenen nach 1945* (München: Siedler, 2008).

Mazower, Mark. *Inside Hitler's Greece: The Experience of Occupation, 1941–44* (New Haven, CT: Yale University Press, 2001).

Mazower, Mark. *Hitler's Empire: Nazi Rule in Occupied Europe* (London: Penguin, 2009).

Milward, Alan S. *The Reconstruction of Western Europe, 1945–51* (Berkeley, CA: University of California Press, 1984).

Müller, Rolf-Dieter. *An der Seite der Wehrmacht: Hitlers ausländische Helfer beim 'Kreuzzug gegen den Bolschewismus' 1941–1945* (Berlin: Links, 2007).

Pohl, Dieter. *Verfolgung und Massenmord in der NS-Zeit 1933–1945* (Darmstadt: Wissenschaftliche Buchgesellschaft, 2003).

Prażmowska, Anita J., ed. *Civil War in Poland, 1942–1948: Challenges to Communist Rule* (Basingstoke: Palgrave Macmillan, 2004).

Shephard, Ben. *The Long Road Home: The Aftermath of the Second World War* (London: Vintage, 2011), 31–40.

Snyder, Timothy. *Bloodlands: Europe between Hitler and Stalin* (London: Random House, 2010).

Snyder, Timothy. *Black Earth: The Holocaust as History and Warning* (New York: Tim Duggan Books, 2015).

Tönsmeyer, Tatjana. *Das Deutsche Reich und die Slowakei 1939–1945: Politischer Alltag zwischen Kooperation und Eigensinn* (Paderborn: Schöningh, 2003).

Tooze, Adam. *The Wages of Destruction: The Making and Breaking of the Nazi Economy* (New York: Viking, 2007).

Wettig, Gerhard. *Stalin and the Cold War in Europe: The Emergence and Development of East-West Conflict, 1939–1953* (Lanham, MD: Rowman & Littlefield, 2008).

Wunschik, Tobias. 'Ein Regenmantel für Dertinger: Das instabile "Tauwetter" im Gefängniswesen der DDR 1956/57', in *Kommunismus in der Krise: Die Entstalinisierung 1956 und die Folgen*, eds Roger Engelmann, Thomas Großbölting and Hermann Wentker (Göttingen: Vandenhoeck & Ruprecht, 2008), 297–325.

6

STATEHOOD IN SOCIALISM

Ulf Brunnbauer and Claudia Kraft

Introduction

Alf Lüdtke has called 'violence by the state and love for the state' a 'political sentiment of the modern age'.[1] Lüdtke refers here to the Janus-faced nature of the state as an institution that represents, on the one hand, coercive action and control and, on the other, the promise of welfare and participation. From this perspective, the state in socialism can be seen as a sub-category in a typology of the modern state. In this chapter, we will attempt to classify the self-understanding and actions of the state in state socialism within a typology of the modern state and to identify the specific characteristics of state socialist models before the backdrop of the changing political and social parameters during the more than four decades of communist rule in Eastern Europe.

Our initial focus will be on the establishment and justification of state rule in socialism. Then, we will examine who was able to profit from state provisions and how access to welfare-state benefits and political participation was regulated. Carl Schmitt's concept of the political, according to which the state is able to function only through exclusion, is relevant here; Hannah Arendt's reflection about the state being overwhelmed by the nation is also interesting in this context: to what extent was the 'nation' during the period of state socialism conceived in national terms or in socialist terms? In this context, we will also trace the (specific) violent dimension of state action in socialism. To what extent does the socialist state model accord with sociologist Heinrich Popitz's observation that social order curbs violence, but that at the same time violence is necessary to maintain social order?[2] Was there perhaps beyond this a 'surplus' of state violence in socialism that would require a special explanation?

One characteristic of the modern state is its increasing penetration into all domains of citizen life. This phenomenon is the focus of the third section. Here it becomes clear that the socialist welfare state is particularly well suited to demonstrate the close interaction between welfare and discipline (also in the sense of a Foucauldian biopolitics). The fourth section examines the ways in which the legitimacy of socialist statehood (in the Weberian sense of participants' belief in the legitimacy of a regime) was produced in practice, as well as how this was gradually called into

---

1 Alf Lüdtke, 'Gewalt des Staates – Liebe zum Staat: Annäherungen an ein politisches Gefühl der Neuzeit', in *Rationalitäten der Gewalt: Staatliche Neuordnungen vom 19. bis zum 21. Jahrhundert*, eds Susanne Krasmann and Jürgen Martschukat (Bielefeld: transcript, 2007), 197–213.
2 Heinrich Popitz, *Phänomene der Macht*, 2nd rev. ed. (Tübingen: Mohr Siebeck, 1992), 63.

215

question – not only in the open rejection of dissidents, but was also successively undermined by practices of Eigen-Sinn in the sense used by Alf Lüdtke – or collapsed due to the state's inability to realize its own objectives.

Survey of political events

A systematic consideration of the various facets of statehood within state socialism is best preceded by a review of the essentials of the political history of communist regimes.[3] The overarching framework was the Cold War, with its ups and downs corresponding to the intensity of the confrontation between the blocs. One peculiarity of the Cold War was the close relationship between domestic and foreign policy along with the high propensity for ideologically charged politics. Especially at first, the opponents in the Cold War saw themselves in a conflict between absolute good and absolute evil – an existential struggle. The Soviet Union presumed the right to intervene, even militarily, in 'brother states' to safeguard the socialist order, as it did to defeat the revolution in Hungary in 1956 and, in cooperation with the other states of the Warsaw Pact (except Romania), to put an end to the Prague Spring of 1968. Furthermore, the imposition of martial law in Poland in 1981 followed (at the very least) an implicit threat of Soviet military intervention. But the Cold War also signified a security guarantee: the allies of the Soviet Union could rely on its protection, a fact of particular importance for countries along the 'front' facing NATO and Poland, which had shifted westward at the conclusion of the Second World War.

Even the seizure of power by communists in Eastern Europe was the result – as well as a strengthening factor – of the Cold War, and less a long-held master plan of Joseph Stalin. The Soviet leadership maintained that only communist governments ultimately displayed loyalty sufficient to guarantee its security interests. Overall, two patterns of power seizure emerged, with one in between: in Poland, Romania, Hungary, Bulgaria and the Soviet occupation zone in Germany (the GDR as of 1949), the establishment of communist one-party dictatorships, which were more or less in place by 1947 and into 1948, can largely be attributed to the presence of the Soviet army and massive Soviet intervention; in Yugoslavia and Albania, however, communists came to power primarily as a result of their successful liberation struggle against German occupation during the Second World War. Communist power in Yugoslavia stemmed from a particularly broad-based movement (which is not to say that communists in other states were not also able to build upon local support). Czechoslovakia exhibited a somewhat hybrid form. On one hand, the communist party enjoyed considerable popularity at the ballot box – in 1946 it was the country's strongest party, receiving around 40 per cent of votes in Bohemia and Moravia and filling the post of prime minister in a coalition government. On the other hand, the party only achieved full control of the country in February 1948 by means of a coup d'état coordinated with Moscow.

---

3 A concise overview of the political history of the region after 1945 can be found in Richard J. Crampton, *Eastern Europe in the Twentieth Century* (London: Routledge, 1994); Joseph Rothschild and Nancy Merriwether Wingfield, *Return to Diversity: A Political History of East Central Europe since World War II*, 3rd ed. (New York: Oxford University Press, 2000); Richard Crampton and Ben Crampton, *Atlas of Eastern Europe in the Twentieth Century*, reprinted (London: Routledge, 2001); Ivan T. Berend, *Central and Eastern Europe, 1944–1993: Detour from the Periphery to the Periphery*, reprinted, *Cambridge Studies in Modern Economic History*, vol. 1 (Cambridge: Cambridge University Press, 2001); Wojciech Roszkowski, *East Central Europe: A Concise History* (Warsaw: Instytut Studiów Politycznych Polskiej Akademii Nauk, 2015); Mark Pittaway, *Eastern Europe 1939–2000, Brief Histories* (London: Bloomsbury Academic, 2010). Literature on the individual countries is cited below in the analytical subchapters.

Statehood in socialism

The establishment of one-party rule (where other parties could exist, like in the GDR and Bulgaria, they played no actual role) was accompanied by the first stages of the Sovietization of the political and societal system, as expressed at the end of the 1940s in new constitutions based on the Soviet constitution of 1936.[4] Political opposition was eliminated, frequently through state repression or even the execution of prominent opposition figures (such as Nikola Petkov, the leader of Bulgaria's peasant party, in September 1947). Social democratic parties were forced to merge with the communist party. The structure of the political system and its particular communist party, as well as the official ideology, largely correlated to the Soviet orthodoxy under Stalin. Large, powerful security apparatuses, partly with roots in the authoritarian regimes of the interwar period, were careful to toe the party line. Comprehensive propaganda was to convey this to the population from early on. Borders were massively fortified (those facing the West were increasingly installed with landmines), voluntary emigration was prohibited, and the issuance of passports and travel visas was severely restricted.

The level of political repression was newly intensified from June 1948 onward, after which the Soviet Union and its allies had broken with Yugoslavia. The leaders of the regimes loyal to Stalin now eliminated their opponents, whether actual or perceived, from within the party, while in Yugoslavia thousands of Stalin's supporters, either real or presumed, were detained. The show trial and execution of the prominent Hungarian communist, László Rajk, in October 1949 is a typical case of such a party cleansing. In Romania, around 40,000 people considered by the state to be disloyal were deported in 1951 from the regions bordering Yugoslavia to the inhospitable steppe in the east of the country. Yugoslavia, in contrast, would follow a unique path to socialism after a realignment with the Soviet Union would appear to be wishful thinking. The Yugoslav '*Sonderweg*' was evident in the far-reaching decentralization of its federation, the introduction of workers' self-management, the freedom to travel, a liberal cultural policy and close ties to the West.

The year 1948 was not the only caesura in the development of the state socialist countries; the period from 1953 to 1956 marked another, as the death of Stalin, workers' protests in the GDR, Poland and Czechoslovakia as well as the revolution in Hungary forced party leadership to rethink their strategies. Although the upheaval precipitated violence in each case (in Hungary by Soviet troops), in the second half of the 1950s the regimes focused more intently on a policy of material concessions to the populace and the establishment of bearable living conditions. The 'Goulash Communism' under Hungary's party leader János Kádár became indeed a literal description. This went hand in hand with de-Stalinization under the banner of Khrushchev's thaw (only Albania forwent this development altogether). The class struggle, terror and mass mobilization that had characterized Stalinism were over; in the future, the governments would give stronger emphasis to the micromanagement of social relations. If the principles of the communist monopoly on power were questioned, as during the Prague Spring of 1968, the strike movement in Poland in 1970 and the Croatian national mobilization (*maspok*) at the end of the 1960s and start of the 1970s, the Soviet Union or the regime itself relied on large-scale repression. This assumed a peculiar form in the GDR, where the Berlin Wall was built in 1961 to thwart the tide of East German citizens voting with their feet by emigrating across town to West Germany.

Repression was not the only reaction of the communist regime to the repeated symptoms of dissatisfaction, which more often were countered with reforms. However, through

---

4 Cf. Balázs Apor, Péter Apor and E.A. Rees, eds, *The Sovietization of Eastern Europe: New Perspectives on the Postwar Period* (Washington, DC: New Academia Publishing, 2008).

the end of the 1980s these reforms never went so far as to threaten the regime's monopoly on power, and thus the fundamental structural problems could never be sufficiently addressed. In Czechoslovakia, for instance, the defeat of the Prague Spring was followed by a period of 'normalization' that, although it failed to bring about any political liberalization, was designed to guarantee the populace a 'calm', materially secure life and did indeed succeed in creating again a certain legitimacy for the communist party. In Yugoslavia, the cleansing of the liberal party leaders at the beginning of the 1970s was followed in 1974 with far-reaching constitutional reforms, which resulted in the country bearing the traits of a true confederation. In the GDR, the SED regime under Erich Honecker attempted to promote compliance by way of a generous social policy. On two occasions in Poland, workers' protests resulted in the party leader being replaced by a more popular candidate (1956 and 1970).

As economic problems worsened significantly in the 1960s and 1970s, the regimes reacted with reforms intended to decentralize economic decision-making and create more leeway for market forces. However, only Yugoslavia and, to a lesser extent, Hungary actually saw the development of a 'socialist market economy', while the overwhelming majority of business in these two countries remained in government hands. Governments in the other countries ran a zig-zag course, making do in the 1970s with loans from the West; in the 1980s, Romania ultimately opted on a radical downsizing of its foreign debt, which wreaked catastrophic results for its citizens' standard of living; only the Stalinist leadership in Albania forwent all economic reforms, which resulted in the country soon becoming the poorest in Europe.

Just as the development in domestic policy continued to fluctuate and showed every greater variation between countries, the foreign policy of state socialist countries would also fail to remain unchanged. This was most pronounced in individual countries' positions vis-à-vis the USSR or the West, as the policies of each country were strongly influenced by that country's security considerations. Beginning in 1948, Yugoslavia carved its own path between the two blocs *nolens volens*, achieving international significance as part of the Non-Aligned Movement (formally established at a 1961 summit in Belgrade) it was essential in helping to initiate. At the same time, Yugoslavia cultivated close relations with the West (to where Yugoslav labourers could migrate as of 1964) and normalized its relations with the Soviet Union after the death of Stalin. Josip Broz Tito was among the most travelled heads of state of his era, and his international prestige was an essential component of his charisma. As mentioned above, Albania – positioned geographically in the shadow of Yugoslavia and bordering no states of the Warsaw Pact – proceeded along its own path and indeed in an opposite direction, resulting in near-complete isolation: in 1961 it broke away from the Soviet Union and its allies, and in 1977 from the People's Republic of China. Romania under Nicolae Ceauşescu conducted policy that was increasingly independent from the Soviet Union and did not accept the primacy of the Communist Party of the Soviet Union (CPSU) over the other national communist parties. The country thus did not participate in the Warsaw Pact intervention in Czechoslovakia. While Ceauşescu's sympathies lay not with the Prague reformers, his staunch nationalism dictated his embrace of the sacred principle of non-intervention in the domestic affairs of another country. Bulgaria, which shared borders with two NATO members, followed a different path; it ostentatiously underscored its close friendship with the Soviet Union, which allowed the country to profit economically and otherwise. For the northern countries of the Warsaw Pact, the recognition of their western borders was once again a central question, especially for Poland. The conclusion of the Treaty of Warsaw in 1970, in which West Germany acknowledged the Oder-Neisse line, proved a milestone in Polish foreign policy.

One international event of great importance to the Eastern bloc was the signing of the Helsinki Accords at the Conference on Security and Cooperation in Europe (CSCE) in Helsinki

Statehood in socialism

in 1975, which succeeded in achieving international recognition for the borders drawn after the Second World War as well as the political order of the post-war period. At the same time, the socialist states (as well as the countries of the Western bloc) pledged to observe human and civil rights as well as foment the increase of cultural and interpersonal exchange between the blocs. In the long term, the Helsinki Accords proved an important document to which opposition parties in state socialist countries could point (see below). Although dissidents in most countries were few in number and isolated from society for prolonged periods of time, they laid important roots for the eventual toppling of the communist regimes in 1989.

In Poland, a broad opposition movement was able to emerge, as critical intellectuals joined forces with opposition labourers after the strike movements of 1956, 1970 and 1976. In 1980, this would culminate – amid a renewal of mass strikes – in the founding of the first alternative mass movement in the Eastern bloc, the Solidarity (Solidarność) trade union. At the end of the 1960s and beginning of the 1970s, Yugoslavia was witness to a similarly broad cross-class mobilization of opposition. In each case, one reason was the existence of relatively autonomous realms that had withstood the reach of the party. In Poland this was, above all, the Catholic church, which had enjoyed a high degree of independence since 1956 (and whose prestige increased enormously with the election of a Pole, Karol Wojtyła, as pope in 1978), while universities and cultural institutions filled a similar role in Yugoslavia. By the end of the 1980s in countries like the GDR, Romania and Bulgaria, state security isolated dissidents to a great extent, in extreme cases resorting to murder (e.g. the Bulgarian dissident in exile, Georgi Markov, 1978) or expatriation (above all in the GDR). In multinational states (especially in Yugoslavia, but also in Bulgaria, with its large Turkish minority) opposition to communist control came also from national movements or minority activists. The hard line taken by the Yugoslav state against the Albanian protest movement in Kosovo, as well as the attempted forced assimilation of Turks in Bulgaria and their resistance to it in the 1980s, were essential causes of the erosion of the system's legitimacy and stability.

The diverse opposition to communist domination, which criticized the regime from a multitude of ideological positions while articulating various political visions, accompanied important factors that created the conditions for the downfall of the regime.[5] Its most important contributions included sustaining the belief in a possible alternative and, above all, the provision of a reservoir of politicians in several countries for the time after communism. The election of the prominent ex-dissidents Václav Havel as president of Czechoslovakia on 19 December 1989 and Želju Želev as president of Bulgaria on 1 August 1990, are good illustrations. An even more decisive factor for the end of communist domination was the multiple organ failure suffered by the state socialist systems due to an accumulation of political, social and economic troubles by the end of the 1980s (see section below titled 'Processes and practices of (de-)legitimation'). Another significant factor was the reform policies of the Soviet Union under Mikhail Gorbachev, who became general secretary of the CPSU in 1985. *Perestroika* and *Glasnost* not only raised the pressure to reform among the reform-averse Eastern bloc states, whose party leaders had taken office long before Gorbachev had; it ushered in profound changes to the political opportunity structures, as Gorbachev publicly shelved the so-called Brezhnev Doctrine that had served as the basis for Soviet intervention in its allied states to safeguard socialism.

The concrete form of the end of communist domination varied from country to country; a true revolution with excessive violence and numerous casualties transpired only in Romania,

---

5 See Padraic Kenney, *A Carnival of Revolution: Central Europe 1989* (Princeton, NJ: Princeton University Press, 2002).

where even the dictator and his wife lost their lives. In the other countries, the governing communists submitted to the inevitable and, unlike their Chinese comrades, forwent the deployment of heavy weaponry to quash the mass protests. Not only did police attempts at a violent dissolution of demonstrations over the course of 1989 fail to achieve the expected effect of deterrence, they actually led to an increase in protests. Within a very short period of time the countries underwent what may be referred to as a political 'bank run'.[6] Highly symbolic yet also politically significant acts like the dismantling of the fortifications at the border between Hungary and Austria, the Polish Round Table Talks and the opening of the Berlin Wall mark the year 1989 as a turning point. Only in the two Balkan *maverick* socialist states outside the Soviet bloc did this transformation take a different course: in Albania, one-party rule lingered until 1991; in Yugoslavia, it persisted until 1990 at the level of the constituent republics, and in terms of the federal state as a whole, until 1991 (but in this case, not only did communist rule disappear, but the entire state was dismantled in a brutal war). And with that, the epoch of state socialism in Europe ultimately came to an end, yet not without far-reaching legacies that continue today.

Self-understanding of the state in transformation

In the classical perspective of Marxism-Leninism, the state was conceived as a coercive apparatus that would be overcome by the proletarian revolution. The state, however, by no means disappeared in Eastern Europe, even after the new state parties had successfully established themselves over their competitors following the Second World War and a transitional phase in which bourgeois and socialist conceptions of the state co-existed. The phase of 'transforming socialist statehood into communist self-administration', which the CPSU proclaimed at its twenty-first party congress in 1959,[7] never even entered the discursive purview of Eastern European state socialism – except for Yugoslavia, where worker self-administration and constitutional decentralization were conceived by Yugoslav ideologues as steps toward the Marxist withering away of the state. Instead, the state appropriated ever more domains of political, economic and social life. It is also important in this context to clarify the relationship between state and party; the significance of the party – as Pavel Kolář has impressively demonstrated – continued to grow even during the long post-Stalinist phase.[8] It is telling that the term 'state socialism' has been adopted both as a periodic and a systemic designation, underscoring the statist nature of real existing socialism, in contrast to the ideological projections of Karl Marx and Friedrich Engels.

If we situate our examination of the state in socialism within a broader panorama of the development of modern statehood, we note with astonishment that the central domains of statehood since the emergence of the modern territorial state in the early modern period continue to be relevant in outlining the parameters of state action. One doesn't have to accept Wolfgang Reinhard's thesis that the 'modern social interventionist state [can be regarded] as the

---

6 See Stephen Kotkin, *Uncivil Society: 1989 and the Implosion of the Communist Establishment*, 1st ed. (New York: Modern Library, 2009), as well as unmodified editions published later.

7 Kazimierz Grzybowski, 'Staat', in *Sowjetsystem und demokratische Gesellschaft: Eine vergleichende Enzyklopädie*, vol. 6, *Sozialrevolutionäre bis Zufall*, ed. C.D. Kernig (Freiburg: Herder, 1972), 144–68, here 161.

8 Pavel Kolář, 'The Party as a New Utopia: Reshaping Communist Identity after Stalinism', *Social History* 37, no. 4 (2012): 402–24.

return of the authoritarian police state [*obrigkeitlicher Policeystaat*].'[9] Nevertheless, the persistence of the most important responsibilities of the state is surprising. There is, on the one hand, the monopoly on use of force, through which the political and social order are maintained and which implies a permanent, more or less open threat of violence by the state. On the other hand, the state acts as the institution that guarantees welfare and (not only social) security. If we restrict our perspective to the second half of the twentieth century, a further aspect becomes prominent, namely, the state as the institution best suited to organize complex and functionally differentiated industrial and post-industrial societies. In Eastern and Southeastern Europe, the state also assumed a protagonist role in a belated industrialization, in which the state compensated for the lack of private capital through state investment allocations and through the political mobilization of economic resources. Finally, we have to take into consideration the close relationship between the institution of the state and multiple nation-building processes that possessed a special dynamic in Eastern Europe during the twentieth century due to repeated border shifts.

Ideal-typical socialist statehood and the cultural history of the political

Before turning to a history of the state in socialism against the background of the changing contexts and immense regional differences, let us begin with an outline of ideal-typical socialist statehood as a template. Drawing on Klaus von Beyme, three basic characteristics of this ideal type can be identified here:[10] in the sphere of production, the nationalization of the means of production and the ex-ante regulation of the economy through planning, rather than the predominance of private property and the ex-post regulation of the economy by the market; in the sphere of distribution, social engineering by the state through interventions in wage and employment structures, rather than the acceptance of persisting inequalities of income and life possibilities; and finally, in the sphere of political legitimation, the integration of citizens through ideology, coercion, organization and gratification (in that order of significance), whereas integration in capitalist states occurred primarily through gratification and organization, and only secondarily through coercion and ideology. Critics of socialism such as János Kornai have argued that this kind of 'classical socialism' was repressive and ineffective as a system, but nevertheless quite coherent in itself, in contrast to the reform socialisms that arose after de-Stalinization and that were unstable per se due to 'internal contradictions'.[11] Such a position, however, which emphasizes political coercion and economic dysfunctionality, fails to recognize that state socialism was also a social order that can be considered partially successful 'catch-up' modernization.[12] This latter perspective shifts the focus especially onto sustained social transformation, thereby analyzing the state as an instrument of social modernization.[13]

To explain how this historical transformation occurred during the four decades of state socialist rule, our investigation cannot remain purely 'systemic', but also has to focus on the

---

9 Wolfgang Reinhard, *Geschichte der Staatsgewalt: Eine vergleichende Verfassungsgeschichte Europas von den Anfängen bis zur Gegenwart* (München: C.H. Beck, 1999), 467.

10 Klaus von Beyme, *Ökonomie und Politik im Sozialismus: Ein Vergleich der Entwicklung in den sozialistischen Ländern* (München: Piper, 1975), 18–19.

11 János Kornai, *The Socialist System: The Political Economy of Communism* (Oxford: Clarendon Press, 1992), XXIV–XXV.

12 Dieter Segert, 'Der Staatssozialismus war mehr als nur ein politisches Herrschaftssystem: Anmerkungen zu einem theoretischen Defizit des Totalitarismuskonzepts', *Bohemia* 49, no. 2 (2009): 412–20.

13 Dieter Segert, *Transformationen in Osteuropa im 20. Jahrhundert* (Vienna: UTB, 2013), 63.

dynamic interplay between state and society. Beyond the totalitarian paradigm we also have to examine the shared values and satisfied interests, and thus the connection between 'leadership and self-leadership'. In this respect, there is certainly a proximity between culturalist approaches such as the 'micro-politics' of Michel Foucault and the self-descriptions of Eastern European dissidents.[14] Václav Havel, for example, characterized society in the post-totalitarian era in his book 'The Power of the Powerless': '[T]his line runs *de facto* through each person, for everyone in his or her own way is both a victim and a supporter of the system.'[15] There is, in other words, no longer a clear separation between the oppressors and the oppressed: the objects of control are simultaneously its subjects. This interpretation is quite compatible with Foucault's analysis of power: 'How simple and easy it would be, no doubt, to dismantle power, if it only worked to supervise, spy upon, to sneak up on, to prohibit and to punish; but it incites, instigates, produces; it isn't simply eye and ear; it brings about speech and action.'[16] Thus in order to understand the persistence of socialist rule it is necessary to adopt this kind of cultural-historical perspective on statehood parallel to an investigation of institutional orders.[17]

(Re-)building statehood: continuities and changes

An examination of the socialist state must be synchronic as well diachronic. A nuanced description, in other words, requires that we take into account the historical conditions upon which the state was built in socialism as well as the situational context of the long European 'post-war' (Tony Judt) from a comparative perspective. During the interwar period there was already an increase in state expenditures and a crisis of parliamentary democracy in the states of Eastern and Southeastern Europe.[18] The violence with which political conflicts were carried out in the interwar period, especially the experiences of occupation and civil war during the Second World War, reinforced a friend-or-foe attitude in societies. This produced a specific relationship to 'state power', which was regarded, on the one hand, as an authority to be opposed, while, on the other hand, there were always great expectations about the state in terms of security and prosperity.

The experiences of the future socialist countries during the Second World War not only differed significantly with regard to their position in the struggle between the two totalitarian powers, Nazi Germany and the Stalinist Soviet Union, but also with respect to the role that the Soviet Union played directly or indirectly in establishing the new system. Yugoslavia and Albania were able to liberate themselves on their own from Axis occupation and push forward systemic reconfiguration without or even against Soviet influence. Poland and Czechoslovakia had been important components of the anti-Hitler coalition beginning in 1939, although the respective political elites in exile had markedly different attitudes toward the Soviet Union, their de facto ally since 1941. Other states such as Hungary, Romania and Bulgaria had collabo-

---

14 Jonathan Arac, 'Foucault and Central Europe: A Polemical Speculation', *Boundary 2* 21, no. 3 (autumn, 1994): 197–210, here 201.

15 Václav Havel et al., *The Power of the Powerless*, ed. John Keane (Armonk, NY: Sharpe 1985), 19.

16 Michel Foucault, 'The Life of Infamous Men', in *Power, Truth, Strategy*, eds Meaghan Morris and Paul Patton (Sydney: Feral, 1979), 89.

17 Alexei Yurchak, *Everything Was Forever, Until It Was No More: The Last Soviet Generation* (Princeton, NJ: Princeton University Press, 2005); Martin Sabrow, 'Sozialismus als Sinnwelt: Diktatorische Herrschaft in kulturhistorischer Perspektive', *Potsdamer Bulletin für Zeithistorische Studien* 40/41 (2007): 9–23.

18 Dieter Segert, *Die Grenzen Osteuropas: 1918, 1945, 1989 – Drei Versuche im Westen anzukommen* (Frankfurt a.M.: Campus, 2002), 34–54.

Statehood in socialism

rated at times with Nazi Germany. In each case, the collaboration or resistance contributed in different ways to a broad spectrum of possibilities for discrediting the old elites. In Poland, the size and social prestige of the non-communist underground meant that initial conditions for the communists were difficult. In none of these nations should we underestimate the connection between dealing with the consequences of war and establishing a new political order. Justified as well as spurious accusations of collaboration with occupying Axis troops significantly affected and enhanced legitimation and de-legitimation processes.

We should bear in mind that it was not only political opponents who lost their reputations in this way. Equally significant was the fact that the experiences of war undermined the authority of the state itself as an institution capable of guaranteeing security on the basis of its monopoly on the use of force. At the same time, communist parties made use of this state – which was no longer the guarantor of the old order it had been unable to protect during the war – as an instrument of comprehensive social transformation. The years of physical violence (at times extreme) as well as the permanent disregard for existing legal orders in a war economy that blatantly violated property rights, also contributed to this altered perception of statehood.

The effect of these war experiences, however, was not only destabilizing. It might seem obvious at first glance to regard the legal prosecution of both actual and ostensible 'collaborators' after the war as a means for the emerging political forces of the left to eliminate political opponents, or to understand notions of an ethnically based 'collective guilt', and the reversal of the legal presumption of innocence as part of the continuous undermining of constitutional principles through juridical practices during and after the war. Nevertheless, political justice was also a specific way of dealing with extremely heterogeneous war experiences that could not be forced into the simple schema of collaboration and resistance. Constructing heroic self-images and dictating an unambiguous conception of friend and foe also made it possible to neutralize existing potentials for social conflict. Thus, the collective accusation that Sudeten Germans had acted 'subversively' diverted attention away from the quite varied courses of action available to the Czech population in the Protectorate; and Yugoslav opinion makers in the People's Front dominated by Tito, simplified and streamlined the perception of very heterogeneous resistance groups in Yugoslavia. If we take into account this tendency to myth-make (which can also be observed in Western Europe), we can confirm Tony Judt's assertion that the war had a stabilizing effect on European post-war states and enabled reconstruction among populations deeply divided by their different experiences during the war.[19] The social levelling effects of occupation policies and the war economy also contributed, if more indirectly, to the reconstruction and to a certain homogenization of the 'societies of collapse' (a term Christoph Kleßmann uses for German society, but which could also be applied to Eastern and Southeastern Europe) at the end of the war.[20] The war-related material losses were immense: between 1938 and 1946 gross domestic product sank around 50 per cent in Poland and Yugoslavia, around 40 per cent in Hungary and around 25 per cent in Czechoslovakia.[21]

---

19 See Judt's chapter 'Retribution' in *Postwar: A History of Europe since 1945* (London: Penguin, 2005); see also István Deák, Jan T. Gross and Tony Judt, eds, *The Politics of Retribution in Europe: World War II and Its Aftermath* (Princeton, NJ: Princeton University Press, 2000).

20 Mark Mazower, Jessica Reinisch and David Feldman, eds, *Post-War Reconstruction in Europe: International Perspective, 1945–1949* (Oxford: Oxford University Press, 2011); Christoph Kleßmann, *Die doppelte Staatsgründung: Deutsche Geschichte 1945–1955*, 5th ed. (Göttingen: Vandenhoeck & Ruprecht, 1991), 37–65.

21 Barry J. Eichengreen, *The European Economy Since 1945: Coordinated Capitalism and Beyond* (Princeton, NJ: Princeton University Press, 2007), 131.

With regard to the character of statehood examined here, there were continuities as well as discontinuities in the international system re-established after the end of the Second World War. Of great symbolic value was the restoration of the national sovereignty of those states that had been occupied or whose territorial integrity had been violated during the war. This was underlined, for instance, by the fact that Yugoslavia, Poland and Czechoslovakia were founding members of the United Nations and thus representatives of a conception of international order committed to the permanent stabilization of international relations and to a more successful peacekeeping than its predecessor, the League of Nations, had been able to achieve. The most important instrument of this stabilization mission was not extensive international legislation, but sovereign nations that were as homogeneous as possible.[22] At the same time, however, the discord within the anti-Hitler coalition that had become visible during the war meant that another model of international order was established quasi parallel to this, one whose interpretation of fixed spheres of influence (determined by ideology, or rather by power politics) lay at odds with the premises of national sovereignty.[23] This model became significant at the latest with the founding of the Communist Information Bureau (Cominform) at a conference in Szklarska Poręba in 1947. Its influence lasted far beyond the actual existence of Cominform, which was dissolved in 1956. With the 'two camp theory' and especially with the prerogative it claimed for the form and speed of Sovietization, the Soviet Union marked out its sphere of influence and set clear boundaries to the sovereignty of those nation states within this space.

This claim to power was felt especially by those countries that wanted to leave due to their advanced revolutionary domestic transformation in expanding and consolidating their communist power base, such as Bulgaria and Yugoslavia, which had planned a federation of Balkan and Danube countries. After the condemnation and exclusion of Yugoslavia (which Stalin viewed as especially insubordinate), there were purges in all of the other states remaining within the Soviet sphere of influence. As a result, adherents of a national sovereignty that encompassed not only the preservation of borders, but also the configuration of the domestic political system, were radically removed from power, at least until the end of Stalinism. Long after Stalinism, however, the guarantee of the integrity of national borders within the Soviet sphere of power – which were constantly seen as threatened by Western and, especially, West German efforts to revise the post-war order – remained coupled to a minimum of ideological loyalty to the party line. The Brezhnev Doctrine of 1968 once again underlined the fragility of national borders.

Even before 1948, when communist state parties established a monopoly of power in all of the countries of the region, important strategic decisions had been made during the period of coalition governments with bourgeois political parties that were central to an expanded and powerfully altered (if not entirely new) understanding of the state. The redistribution of large estates, the nationalization of important key industries, power supply, transportation and the banking sector and large-scale plans to expand the welfare state (the implementation of which,

---

22 Mark Mazower, *No Enchanted Palace: The End of Empire and the Ideological Origins of the United Nations* (Princeton, NJ: Princeton University Press, 2009).

23 The extent to which the political division of the world was already affecting the functioning of the UN at the beginning of the East–West conflict can be seen in the clash between the two blocs in the run-up to the passage of the Genocide Convention in 1948, in which the historic experiences of the Second World War – the impetus for the convention – took a back seat to the political interests of the two new superpowers and the ideologies of their various camps. This dynamic would steer the course of discussions and ultimately lead to a diminished scope for the convention. See Matthew Lippmann, 'A Road Map to the 1948 Convention of the Punishment of the Crime of Genocide', *Journal of Genocide Research* 4, no. 2 (2002): 177–95.

Statehood in socialism

however, had to be partially delayed due to the economic weakness of the state) pointed to the past as well as to the future. These were reactions to historical experiences of global economic crisis and to social emergencies triggered by the war; at the same time, they were also supposed to ensure security for societies in the future, a promise that the market economy had evidently been incapable of fulfilling. The two-year plans for reconstruction introduced in several countries after the end of the war were similarly Janus-faced: they were initially intended to deal ad hoc with the consequences of the war, but then triggered a domino effect that made further planning interventions necessary.[24]

Even if this already implied a qualitative transformation, we should not forget that after the Second World War an expansion of state functions was also the rule in Western Europe; for instance, the expansion of the British welfare state following the Beveridge Report, the nationalization of French energy companies and Italian infrastructural and energy companies. The French Constitution of 1946 included the social rights of workers, while Article 1 of the Italian Constitution of 1948 declared, 'Italy is a republic founded on labour.' Even during the 'second wave' of democratization on the Iberian Peninsula, a corresponding conception of the state is evident in the Portuguese Constitution of 1976 which declared that Portugal is a 'democratic state based on ... the sovereignty of the people' and that the state was committed to 'a transition to socialism'.[25]

The re-establishment of the state in Eastern Europe was marked by a strong continuity of nation state traditions. The sole exception was Yugoslavia, which was founded as a federal state with six equal republics under the motto of 'brotherhood and unity'. (Except for Bosnia-Herzegovina, all of the republics bore the characteristics of a nation state *in nuce*.) Even when Soviet influence became increasingly noticeable, the nationalist anchoring of the communist parties continued, which fitted well with Stalin's interests. Different legitimatizing strategies were employed, all of which underlined the sovereignty of the nation state as well as the role of the communist party as its authentic defender. Contributing to this were also the experiences of the war and the post-war era, where ethno-national homogeneity had played a central role as a racist value (for instance, in Nazi Germany), as a security issue (in the USSR) and as geopolitical stabilizing element (for the Western allies). This was also confirmed by the fact that – in contrast to after the First World War and with the exception of Poland – the borders in the region remained more or less stable and territorialization processes of nation states (despite the genocide and mass evacuations) aimed more clearly than ever at a congruence between the people of a state and the territory of that state.

Here, it becomes quite clear that in post-war rhetoric social revolution and national revolution were fused together and that in the transformative propaganda of the communist powers 'ethnically defined plebs' were set against the 'traditional hierarchical social order'.[26] Older ethnic conflicts and recent war experiences also played a role. Even when, beginning in 1947–48, communist state parties emphasized their revolutionary transformative potential, they left no doubt that the path to a classless society had to take place within the nation state. This was the case

---

24 Jaromír Balcar and Jaroslav Kučera, 'Von der Gestaltung der Zukunft zu der Verwaltung des Mangels: Wirtschaftsplanung in der Tschechoslowakei von der Befreiung bis in die frühen fünfziger Jahre', in *Zukunftsvorstellungen und staatliche Planung im Sozialismus: Die Tschechoslowakei im ostmitteleuropäischen Kontext 1945–1989*, eds Martin Schulze Wessel and Christiane Brenner (München: Oldenbourg, 2010), 187–203.

25 Judt, *Postwar*, 515–6.

26 Pavel Kolář, 'Communism in Eastern Europe', in *The Oxford Handbook of the History of Communism*, ed. Stephen A. Smith (Oxford: Oxford University Press, 2014), 203–19, here 205.

not so much because special value was placed on state institutions, but rather because the policies of socialist transformation required national topoi in order to communicate with society – whether the anti-German card was played, as in the Polish or Czechoslovak case (at the latest since Jan Hus, the Czechoslovak nation had been imagined as a democratic counter-model to Germany), or whether a national genealogy reaching back to antiquity was invoked, as in the case of Albania or Romania.[27] The state as a nation state remained untouched by the Marxist critique of the state as an instrument of the exploitative class. On the contrary, communist parties, which by and large had been fundamentally opposed to the state during the interwar period, presented themselves after the Second World War as state-bearing organizations.[28]

If the material and non-material destruction caused by the war as well as the continuing relevance of statehood organized as a nation state can be regarded as pan-European phenomena, specific characteristics of the socialist state also emerged clearly and contributed to a homogenization within the Eastern bloc at the latest beginning around 1948 with the elimination of non-communist political parties and the adoption of the Stalinist political model. This period was characterized not only by socialization measures extending far beyond large industry and the vigorously pursued collectivization of agriculture, but also by a permanent social mobilization evident in the educational system. Just when the supremacy of the communists had been attained in reality and been legally anchored in the new constitutions starting in the late 1940s, the specific character of state political parties became clear and was reflected in the rhetoric and practice of permanently combatting enemies, whether this be tracking down economic 'sabotage' or political 'diversion'. From a diachronic perspective, the experience of persecution that all Eastern European communist parties had had during the interwar period played as much a role as the cadre principle borrowed from the Soviet model. A pronounced friend-or-foe attitude and this strict cadre principle, however, made state parties and their members as well as all other institutions into instruments of permanent mobilization and all-encompassing mistrust. In Hungary and Czechoslovakia, for instance, around one-quarter to one-third of all party members were subject to expulsion proceedings.[29]

The 'de-Stalinization crises' that began after Stalin's death and the distancing from the previous phase of permanent mobilization thus led in a certain way to a re-establishment or consolidation of party rule, which state security agencies had called into question during Stalinism.[30] Characteristic for post-Stalinism was the party's comprehensive claim to formulate policy, established now for the first time, which no longer appeared to allow any clear separation between societal sub-systems and which overrode intermediary organizations and producers of alternative norms. The repositioning of Eastern Europe as a result of Stalin's death in 1953

---

27 On Czechoslovakia, see Benjamin Frommer, *National Cleansing: Retribution Against Nazi Collaborators in Postwar Czechoslovakia* (Cambridge: Cambridge University Press, 2005); on Poland, see Marcin Zaremba, *Im nationalen Gewande: Strategien kommunistischer Herrschaftslegitimation in Polen 1944–1980* (Osnabrück: Fibre, 2011); Jan C. Behrends, 'The Stalinist Volonté Générale: Legitimizing Communist Statehood (1935–1952) – A Comparative Perspective on the USSR, Poland, Czechoslovakia, and Germany', *East Central Europe* 40, no. 1–2 (2013): 37–73.

28 Jan C. Behrends, '"Heben wir einen neuen Staat als den Ausdruck einer neuen Ordnung aus der Taufe": Zur Legitimation von Staatlichkeit in Polen, der Tschechoslowakei und der SBZ/DDR (1943–1952)', in *Sozialistische Staatlichkeit*, eds Jana Osterkamp and Joachim von Puttkamer (München: Oldenbourg, 2012), 45–71, here 54–5.

29 Ivan T. Berend, *Central and Eastern Europe 1944–1993: Detour from the Periphery to the Periphery* (Cambridge: Cambridge University Press, 1996), 50.

30 Kolář, 'Communism in Eastern Europe', 209; idem, *Der Poststalinismus: Ideologie und Utopie einer Epoche* (Köln: Böhlau, 2016).

Statehood in socialism

and Nikita Khrushchev's secret speech in 1956[31] made it necessary in all of the countries to renegotiate socialist legitimacy, which now equally stigmatized Stalinist deviation as the enemy which had to be overcome.

The search for legitimacy did not cease until the end of state socialism and contributed to the instability of the political orders, not least because state parties frequently stimulated perceptions of crisis within society through their own reform efforts. Thus, reforms in part preceded social protests, rather than reacting to them. One consequence of the now closer communicative ties between state parties and the respective societies was that after 1953/56 a clear diversification in strategies of problem solving emerged. In Czechoslovakia, accelerated economic modernization through the scientific-technological revolution served as the new basis for legitimation after 1956; in Poland and Romania, it was the 'national paths' to communism; and in all of the states, there was also an increased focus on social security and consumption. At the same time, legitimation was also supposed to be produced discursively by proclaiming the 'victory of socialism', for instance, in Bulgaria in 1958. Here, Bulgaria assumed a leading role in the socialist camp, irrespective of the 'really existing' living standards there. Nevertheless, other states followed: the second wave of socialist constitutions beginning in the 1960s reiterated the success of socialism and referred to the 'socialist people', instead of the 'workers'.

State and economy

Recent literature on European post-war history has emphasized the similarities of developments in the East and West especially during the first two post-war decades. In both parts of Europe, the state was considered the eminently important actor in overcoming the immense war damage. This implied a general acceptance for state interventions in the areas of infrastructure and energy supply, as well as in banking. These interventions were justified in particular by the need to ensure macro-economic stability, which had been repeatedly undermined beginning in the 1920s. Economic historians point out that after the Second World War the socialist states were by no means a special case, but rather one variety of growing state interventionism. For this reason, Barry Eichengreen has designated the economic history of post-war Europe as 'coordinated capitalism', which was based on powerful corporatist institutions and on the state as the influential actor in setting wages and prices. From this perspective, Eichengreen identifies gradual distinctions between Eastern and Western Europe, especially for the period of extensive growth into the 1960s. Not only in retrospect, but even during the division into blocs, legal historians (as well as others) questioned the extent to which private property could be diametrically opposed to state property, and asked whether it was not more appropriate to speak of gradual distinctions in conceptions of property, which existed in the East in terms of state, social and personal property, and in the West in terms of differentiated rights of access and interest groups (shareholders, management, works councils and trade unions).[32]

Living conditions in the countries of the Eastern bloc had in fact changed significantly. Precisely in light of the clearly lower standards of living (with the exception of Czechoslovakia)

---

31 Carole Fink, Frank Hadler and Thomas Schramm, eds, *1956: European and Global Perspectives* (Leipzig: Leipziger Universitätsverlag, 2006).
32 Georg Brunner, 'Was ist sozialistisch am "sozialistischen" Recht?' in *Festschrift für Klemens Pleyer zum 65. Geburtstag*, eds Paul Hofmann, Ulrich Meyer-Cording and Herbert Wiedemann (Köln: C. Heymann, 1986), 187–205, here 196–7.

and the powerful agrarian influence prior to the Second World War, there were enormous growth rates in the Eastern bloc for the first fifteen years after the war: over 10 per cent in the first half of the 1950s in Bulgaria and Romania, around 8 per cent in Poland and the ČSSR and 6 per cent in Hungary; in the second half of the decade, growth rates were still around 6 or 7 per cent.[33] The economic structural transformation was considerable: in the late 1960s over 50 per cent of the net domestic product was earned in industry even in the Balkan states, which previously had had little industrialization. For all of these countries, the accelerated expansion of heavy industry came at the cost of the consumer goods industry, residential construction and energy supply for private households.

When the initially immense growth rates began to stagnate starting in the 1960s, the role of the state in consumer socialism increased, as did the expectations placed upon it. The state responded with new elements of (scientific) planning. Similar to Western Europe, a notion of planning based on theories of cybernetics predominated in the Eastern bloc in the early 1960s, according to which the state was seen as a feedback loop, whose capacity could be optimized through accurate control. Especially for economic reformers, cybernetics was a welcome concept that provided a connection between state planning and elements of economic self-administration, giving enterprises greater manoeuvring room.[34] The easing of centralized planning favoured by economic reformers such as Oskar Lange in Poland and reform communists affiliated with the Prague Spring, however, ran up against the limits of the ideological elasticity of state-party socialism.

The pressure on economic planning increased in the second half of the 1960s because modernization measures had become urgently necessary with the structural transformation 'after the boom' and these required increased investments. At the same time, however, the growing consumption demands of the population had to be taken into consideration. This made necessary a costly dual strategy that was difficult to implement in terms of financing as well practical planning. The individual nations took quite different approaches to this. Whereas Romania implemented a five-year plan of accelerated industrialization without socio-political cushioning between 1971 and 1975, Hungarian Kádárism permitted elements of the market economy and virtually promoted a broad consumerism among the population. For the most part, however, the state parties vacillated between consumption and investment policies, for example during the phase of 'small stabilization' under Władysław Gomułka in Poland in the 1960s, the 'dynamic development' under Edward Gierek in the first half of the 1970s and the 'consolidation' under Gustáv Husák in Czechoslovakia in the 1970s.[35]

Considering the growing economic problems of the socialist countries that began in the 1960s and ran counter to the apparent convergence of East and West after the Second World War, socialist states clearly had more difficulty adapting to new socio-economic developments than the comparatively flexible Western economies. Seen in this light, the year 1973 can

---

33 Eichengreen, *The European Economy Since 1945*, 139–40.

34 Jakob Tanner, 'Komplexität, Kybernetik und Kalter Krieg: "Information" im Systemantagonismus von Markt und Plan', in *Die Transformation des Humanen: Beiträge zur Kulturgeschichte der Kybernetik*, eds Michael Hagner and Erich Hörl (Frankfurt a.M.: Suhrkamp, 2008), 377–413. For a contemporary perspective, see Herbert Biermann, 'Die Kybernetik als Hilfsmittel zur Planung in sozialistischen Volkswirtschaften', *Jahrbuch der Wirtschaft Osteuropas* 3 (1972): 13–43.

35 Peter Hübner, '1970 und die Folgen: Sozialpolitisches Krisenmanagement im sowjetischen Ostblock', in *Das Ende der Zuversicht? Die siebziger Jahre als Geschichte*, ed. Konrad Jarausch (Göttingen: Vandenhoeck & Ruprecht 2008), 261–78.

certainly be regarded as a turning point comparable to 1989.[36] The first oil crisis marked the end of a quantitatively driven economic growth and contributed significantly to the emergence of a new kind of network capitalism. A rethinking of social benefits from the state was also necessary in order to address the structural crisis, evident, for example, in a stable level of systemic unemployment. Around this time the Conference on Security and Co-operation in Europe posed a serious challenge to the legitimacy of socialist states by introducing a sustained human rights discourse into international relations.[37] The socialist states, which had responded to social dissatisfaction with a strategy of patriarchal consumerism, were now confronted by this crisis in two respects: they were unable to satisfy the steadily growing consumer needs of their own populations, and they were in no position to promote necessary economic innovations. The policies of secrecy and the concealment of actual economic problems impeded a public discussion among economic experts.[38]

Attempts to connect investment and consumption policies increasingly overburdened the socialist states. Beginning in the 1970s, the high growth rates resulting from the necessities of reconstruction and the industrialization carried out initially at the cost of consumption policy could no longer be maintained. The increase in commodity prices due to the oil crisis and the technological revolution of the dawning computer age caused financial bottlenecks in state budgets that could be alleviated only temporarily by cheap crude oil deliveries from the USSR and by Western loans. Instead of fundamentally adapting to new structures of production and labour, the socialist countries focused one-sidedly on industrial growth even in the 1970s and 80s, with continuing emphasis on heavy industry. For this reason, they were unable to overcome the scarcity of consumer goods despite industrial expansion. From 1970 to 1988, industrial output doubled in Poland, Hungary, Czechoslovakia and Yugoslavia; it increased 300 per cent in Bulgaria and 500 per cent in Romania. Beginning in the late 1960s, the policy of detente helped to facilitate the import of modern Western investment goods and technologies. As a result, however, essential innovation efforts were not carried out with the necessary consistency. The introduction of the American IBM System/360 in the USSR in 1970, and then subsequently in the German Democratic Republic (GDR), Poland, Romania, Bulgaria, Hungary and Czechoslovakia through the Council for Mutual Economic Assistance (Comecon) was exemplary in this regard.[39] Efforts to innovate on one's own, such as the Zastava automobile factory in Yugoslav Kragujevac – where the Yugo, an inexpensive car, was produced in the 1980s and even shipped to the US market – failed.

This low productivity growth required steadily increasing capital in order to continue to grow at all. Foreign loans were the means of choice – except in Romania, which aimed at autarky – and were also available at favourable conditions because inefficiency could not be cushioned by taxes (as in the West) or by price increases, since these would have resulted in social protests, which such measures were meant to prevent in the first place. Western lenders were probably not farsighted enough to believe that they could weaken the socialist

---

36 For an introduction to the relevant debate, see the Andreas Wirsching, Göran Therborn, Geoff Eley, Hartmut Kaelble and Philippe Chassaigne, 'The 1970s and 1980s as a Turning Point in European History?', *Journal of Modern European History* 9 (2011): 8–26; see also Anselm Doering-Manteuffel and Lutz Raphael, eds, *Nach dem Boom: Perspektiven auf die Zeitgeschichte seit 1970* (Göttingen:Vandenhoeck & Ruprecht 2012, 3rd edition); Jarausch, *Das Ende der Zuversicht*.

37 Daniel C. Thomas, *The Helsinki Effect: International Norms, Human Rights, and the Demise of Communism* (Princeton, NJ: Princeton University Press, 2001).

38 Eichengreen, *The European Economy Since 1945*, 294–5.

39 Peter Hübner, '1970 und die Folgen', 276.

economic system by granting loans, but presumed instead that Moscow would offer its satellite states not only military, but also financial guarantees. Due to the global debt crisis, the International Monetary Fund (IMF) has been involved with somewhat loose credit policies since the 1970s, likewise in its few socialist member states (Yugoslavia since 1945, Romania since 1972, Hungary since 1982, Poland since 1986). Yet, this cooperation has met with little success due to the incompatibility of the IMF's macro-economic policies with the planned economic governance in Eastern Europe (except with regard to Hungary and Yugoslavia, whose economic systems had had market-related elements for years).[40]

Position of the law and procedurality

In the Marxist reading, law – like the state – was considered to be an instrument of oppression for the ruling class. Nevertheless, the notion of a socialist law was actually established in socialism and possessed two functions in particular: it served as an instrument for transforming existing conditions and implementing social-policy goals; and it was a justificatory discourse intended to legitimate political decisions. In a systems-theoretical reading, Rainer M. Lepsius has identified the central characteristics of socialist states as the 'under-institutionalization of two essential rationality criteria', which he described as 'economic efficiency' and 'legal admissibility'.[41] It is unlikely, however, that such an overly ideal-typical contrast to liberal-democratic institutional orders is useful here, especially if we bear in mind that, at least since the onset of industrialization, the increasingly powerful interventions of the state into the social order have rendered untenable calls to separate the administration of the state from its political organization, or to regard social and economic questions as distinct from a public order regulated by law. Even in capitalist societies the state does not act as a 'neutral referee of the social order', as postulated by classical liberalism.[42]

The idea of an order serving both the interests of the working class and the implementation of a revolutionary agenda did, however, affect legal reality. This was evident in the politicization of the courts, which were seen as instruments in the political struggle and not as defenders of 'socialist legality'. This legal conception was expressed, for instance, in the Czechoslovak Constitution of 1948: 'The new constitution should contribute to transforming the law from a conservative, retarding, or even reactionary element into an element of development and progress and into a factor of the reconstruction efforts.'[43] Socialist legality, on the one hand, served 'socialist objectives' or 'the will of the working class'. Especially after the injustices of the Stalinist judiciary became known, the courts were supposed to ensure adherence to the rules of socialist legality. On the other hand, however, socialist legality also established the param-

---

40 Alfred Schüller and Hannelore Hamel 'On the Membership of Socialist Countries in the International Monetary Fund', *Acta Oeconomica* 34, nos. 1–2 (1985): 113–30; Petra Pisulla, 'Zur Rolle von IWF, Weltbank und Gatt in den Ost-West-Wirtschaftsbeziehungen', *Berichte des Bundesinstituts für ostwissenschaftliche und internationale Studien* 16 (1991).

41 Rainer M. Lepsius, 'Die Institutionenordnung als Rahmenbedingung der Sozialgeschichte der DDR', in *Sozialgeschichte der DDR*, eds Hartmut Kaelble, Jürgen Kocka and Hartmut Zwahr (Stuttgart: Klett-Cotta, 1994), 17–30.

42 Kazimierz Grzybowski, 'Staat', in *Sowjetsystem und demokratische Gesellschaft: Eine vergleichende Enzyklopädie*, vol. 6, *Sozialrevolutionäre bis Zufall*, ed. C.D. Kernig (Freiburg: Herder, 1972), 144–68.

43 Cited in Karel Malý, 'Vom Rechtsstaat zur sozialistischen Gesetzlichkeit in der Tschechoslowakischen Republik', in *Recht im Sozialismus: Analysen zur Normdurchsetzung in osteuropäischen Nachkriegsgesellschaften (1944/45–1989)*, vol. 3, *Sozialistische Gesetzlichkeit*, eds Gerd Bender and Ulrich Falk (Frankfurt a.M.: Klostermann, 1999), 27–40, here 34.

Statehood in socialism

eters for rather 'apolitical domains', as is evident if we consider that 10,000 landlord and tenant cases, 27,000 divorce cases and 45,000 fare evasion cases were heard in Czechoslovak courts in 1980.[44] The varying degree of politicization of the justice system is also evident in the fact that around 70 per cent of state prosecutors in Poland were members of the Polish United Workers' Party, whereas only 43 per cent of Polish judges were.[45]

Neither the division of powers nor a superordinate judicial review guaranteeing such a division played a role in this instrumental understanding of law as a means of social transformation, as illustrated by the absence of any constitutional jurisdiction. Yugoslavia was only an apparent exception in this regard. Constitutional courts were introduced in Yugoslavia on both the federal level and that of the republics in 1963. These courts, however, had a purely instrumental character: the new constitution emphasized strengthening self-administration in factories and regional bodies. The constitutional courts were supposed to protect especially the activities of these bodies and were thus created as state organs with the task supporting organs of self-administration that were supposed to overcome forms of classical statehood.[46] Attempts to limit the dominance of the executive emerged only in the 1980s, for instance, when administrative jurisdiction was introduced in Poland in 1980.[47] Judicial review became a component of discourses about legitimacy and socialist legality only in the 1980s as well: a constitutional court (with significantly less authority) was introduced in Poland in 1982 (but whose activity began in 1986) and in Hungary in 1989 – at a time when the revolutionary legitimacy of the system had already been significantly damaged and could hardly be replaced by strengthening formal legality.[48]

One important characteristic in the understanding of basic rights in socialist states was that rights were always coupled with duties. Socialist citizenship meant affiliation to a community of workers, which implied a prioritization of social rights that were always seen as the result of realizing social objectives or as specific 'status rights of workers'.[49] These social rights, however, were not regarded as enforceable individual rights of citizens in the sense of T.H. Marshall's theory.[50] Nevertheless, it should be noted that in Western welfare states there were also tensions of redistribution and recognition among citizen groups with varying status, as is evident, for instance, in the dichotomy between working people paying taxes and 'welfare mothers' collecting social benefits.[51] The notion of an authoritarian-paternalistic character of granting material benefits suggests interesting parallels between socialist and capitalist states that could be discussed in terms of state paternalism. In both socialism and capitalism, the pre-modern *pater*

---

44 Ibid., 38.

45 Andrzej Rzepliński, 'Principles and Practices of Socialist Justice in Poland', in Bender and Falk, *Recht im Sozialismus*, vol. 3, 1–26, here 25–6.

46 Vojin Dimitrijević, 'Verfassungsgerichtsbarkeit in Jugoslawien', *Zeitschrift für ausländisches öffentliches Recht und Völkerrecht* 28 (1968): 170–98.

47 Rzepliński, 'Principles and Practices of Socialist Justice in Poland', 9.

48 Matthias Hartwig, 'The Institutionalization of the Rule of Law: The Establishment of Constitutional Courts in the Eastern European Countries', *American University International Law Review* 7, no. 3 (1992): 449–70, for Poland, see 453–6, for Hungary 460–3.

49 Ulrike Götting, *Transformationen der Wohlfahrtsstaaten in Mittel- und Osteuropa: Eine Zwischenbilanz* (Opladen: Verlag für Sozialwissenschaften, 1998), 60–1.

50 Thomas H. Marshall, *Citizenship and Social Classes and Other Essays* (Cambridge: Cambridge University Press, 1950).

51 Nancy Fraser and Linda Gordon, 'A Genealogy of *Dependency*: Tracing a Keyword of the U.S. Welfare State', *Signs: Journal of Women in Culture and Society* 19, no. 2 (1994): 309–36.

familias became 'father state'. Wendy Brown's examination of the welfare system in the United States and Katherine Verdery's analysis of the 'zadruga state' in Southeastern Europe come to similar conclusions: by addressing especially women as the recipients of social benefits, the state bureaucracy created subordinate, feminized subjects, not least because care work was essentialized as feminine.[52] Even in the 1950s, socialist states regarded social policy as superfluous. A citizen's 'right to work' was the dominant element in socialist constitutions. The claim that good social policy could be found only in socialism first arose with de-Stalinization and was then increasingly heard beginning in the 1960s.[53]

In general, the close coupling of industrial labour and entitlements to welfare-state benefits reflected a mixture of socialist ideology and institutional heritages, since the neglect of people beyond industrial wage labour was based on the socialist fixation on industrialization as well as on traditions of the Prusso-German and Habsburg welfare systems. These Central-European-conservative, income-based social security systems, which were established in predecessor states or empires and were primarily oriented around wage earners and their incomes, functioned over the long-term as a model for the social security systems in the successor states and was one reason that maintaining the status of the working population continued to be a focus.[54] The expansion of state welfare programmes to include a growing number of eligible people is thus comparable to social policymakers in West Germany formulating a 'new social question' in the 1970s. For both the socialist states and liberal-democratic and capitalist states, the historical meaning of citizenship can be determined only if we include the axes of gender, class and ethnicity (bearing in mind that an ethnically homogenizing political model continued to be relevant in socialism).

Where the state acted: land reform, the nationalization of property and planning

The appropriation and distribution of property as well as economic planning became central domains of state action. With the exception of Yugoslavia – where beginning in the 1950s the privileging of social property meant that organs of (economic) self-administration, rather than the state, became the most important motor of social transformation – socialist states created three hierarchical forms of property by distinguishing between state, social or collective and personal property. These forms of property were identified in the constitution and ascribed distinct qualities, as was evident, for instance, in the criminal prosecution of property violations, with offences against state property being punished most severely.[55] In general, the state monopolized the available economic resources as extensively as possible, became contracting authority and purchaser in one and positioned itself, as planning authority, between producers and consumers.

---

52 Wendy Brown, 'Finding the Man in the State', *Feminist Studies* 18, no. 1 (Spring 1992): 7–34; Katherine Verdery, 'From Parent-State to Family Patriarchs: Gender and Nation in Contemporary Eastern Europe', in *What Was Socialism and What Comes Next?* (Princeton, NJ: Princeton University Press, 1996), 61–82.
53 Götting, *Transformationen der Wohlfahrtsstaaten*, 59.
54 Tomasz Inglot, *Welfare States in East Central Europe, 1919–2004* (Cambridge: Cambridge University Press, 2008), 7.
55 Herbert Küpper, 'Property in East Central European Legal Culture', in *Property in East Central Europe: Notions, Institutions and Practices of Landownership in the Twentieth Century*, eds Hannes Siegrist and Dietmar Müller (New York: Berghahn, 2015), 65–99, here 77–80.

Statehood in socialism

Land reform

The transformation of land ownership began very early and focused on the still powerfully agrarian character of states of the region – even before the communist parties had attained their dominant position. Cooperating closely, communist, socialist and agrarian parties initiated a redistribution of land in all of the countries of Eastern and Southeastern Europe in 1944 and 1945. This redistribution began with the confiscation of lands exceeding a certain size and with the state appropriation of abandoned properties in territories affected by ethnic cleansing both during and after the war. Given the ethno-national justifications and the proclaimed goal of creating a property-owning stratum of small farmers, this redistribution appeared to be more closely tied to agrarian-political projects of the pre-war period than to the dawning of a state socialist transformation. Distinctions to the interwar period arose from the fact that massive violations of property rights during war had further undermined the notion of individual property and that the state was now regarded not only by leftist political parties but by all of society as a much more important factor in economic life than it had been in the pre-war period.[56]

Hungarian land reform had the broadest scope. As a rule, property over 57.6 hectares was confiscated. Profitable self-run farmers were allowed a maximum of 115 hectares, and recognized anti-Fascist fighters were even allowed 158 hectares. In the area around Budapest, 29 hectares was the maximum for individual ownership. In Poland and Romania, property of more than 50 hectares was confiscated (with higher limits of up to 100 hectares in some regions of Poland). In Yugoslavia, the limit was set between 20 and 45 hectares of arable land depending on the region. In Bulgaria, where comprehensive agrarian reform had already taken place during the interwar period and a significantly lower percentage of sizeable land holdings existed, the maximum was 20 hectares. In contrast to the countries mentioned above, this first phase of land reform in Bulgaria had no significant influence on rural property structures. The situation was different in Albania, where the limit was also set at 20 hectares: here there was still extensive large property ownership. Only in Czechoslovakia were there no confiscations based on quantitative criteria at this early point in time; the land fund initiated by the Košice Government Programme in 1945 contained only the real estate of ethnically 'foreign' people (Germans and Hungarians) as well as people accused of being political collaborators. The territories affected by ethnic cleansing were seen as laboratories for an economic-political transformation, and experiments with forms of nationalized property were carried out early on. In general, the redistribution of rural property was an opportunity for communist parties, which had enjoyed little support in the countryside, to increase their popularity.[57]

In many places, the redistribution created a sizeable group of potentially successful property-owning farmers for the first time. Thus, it is hardly surprising that the history of collectivization, which was massively promoted starting in 1948 and which aimed at socializing agricultural production and subordinating it to state planning, must be narrated as a history of delays and partial failures. With the exception of the GDR, there were interruptions everywhere between 1953 and 1955, concomitant to de-Stalinization. Collectivization was halted in Yugoslavia in 1953 in part because of a major peasant uprising in north-eastern Bosnia, and in Poland in 1956 due to immense social opposition. Even where authorities defied agrarian opposition (in part

---

56 On these lines of continuities, see the contributions in Siegrist and Müller, *Property in East Central Europe*.

57 Hannes Siegrist and Dietmar Müller, 'Introduction: Property in East Central Europe: Notions, Institutions and Practices of Landownership in the Twentieth Century', in Siegrist and Müller, *Property in East Central Europe*, 1–20.

with the massive use of force), the transformation of rural property relations dragged on for years. It was considered completed in Bulgaria in 1959, in Czechoslovakia and the GDR in 1961, in Romania in 1962 and in Albania in 1967. In this regard as well, there was enormous heterogeneity among the countries examined here. Although the agrarian sectors in Poland and Romania were comparable in terms of size and significance, collectivization efforts proceeded quite differently in the two countries. Collectivization was carried out very rigorously in Albania, where the significance of collectivized agriculture appeared more important for autarky within the Soviet bloc than as the adaptation to a new understanding of property. In Bulgaria, in contrast, agrarian opposition drew on radical peasant-populist traditions from the pre-war period. The new communist rulers responded with a brutally expedited collectivization campaign between 1948 and 1951, which was unable to completely break the farmers' resistance. Between 1956 and 1961 there was a kind of stalemate and the state had to content itself with the stabilization of existing cooperative farms, before continuing the collectivization in a second phase in 1956 with the help of political and social pressure. Comparatively little resistance was offered to collectivization in Czechoslovakia, where there had been a tradition of state-owned farms and collectives in the pre-war period.[58]

It is not surprising that the changes to the agrarian ownership structure occurred very differently in the individual countries. In 1960, only 10 per cent of agrarian land was owned by the state or by collectives in Yugoslavia, and only 13 per cent in Poland. In Hungary, in contrast, the figure was 77 per cent, in Romania 84 per cent, in Albania 85 per cent, in Czechoslovakia 87 per cent and in Bulgaria 91 per cent.[59] Recent studies have noted that the history of collectivization cannot be told exclusively as a history of resistance by farmers and coercion by the state: there were tenacious negotiation processes involving a new functionary group that was largely unestablished in the countryside, traditional strategic manoeuvring by village leaders and resistance from a previously sub-peasant strata that had become land owners only after 1944–45.[60]

Nationalization

The nationalizations after the war initially encompassed key industries, energy and transportation companies, as well as banks and insurance companies. In general, this development (which also occurred in a number of Western European countries) can be seen as the state's attempt to assume control of basic public services for a population that had suffered through six years of war. However, it should also be noted that, in addition to arguments about political economy, the principle of ethnicity played an important role here, a development

---

58 Constantin Iordachi and Arnd Bauerkämper, eds, *The Collectivization of Agriculture in Communist Eastern Europe: Comparison and Entanglements* (Budapest: CEU Press, 2014); Frederic L. Pryor, *The Red and the Green: The Rise and Fall of Collectivized Agriculture in Marxist Regimes* (Princeton, NJ: Princeton University Press, 1992).

59 Mark Harrison, 'Communism and Economic Modernization', in Smith, *The Oxford Handbook of the History of Communism*, 387–406, here 396, table 22.3.

60 On Romania, for instance, see Gail Kligman and Katherine Verdery, *Peasants Under Siege: The Collectivization of Romanian Agriculture, 1949–1962* (Princeton, NJ: Princeton University Press, 2011); on Yugoslavia, see Jovica Luković, 'The Country Road to Revolution: Transforming Individual Peasant Property into Socialist Property in Yugoslavia, 1945–1953', in Siegrist and Müller, *Property in East Central Europe*, 164–90; on Poland, see Dariusz Jarosz, 'The Collectivization of Agriculture in Poland: Causes of Defeat', in Iordachi and Bauerkämper, *The Collectivization of Agriculture*, 113–46.

Statehood in socialism

that was closely coupled to wartime events. In Poland, a comprehensive nationalization of companies with more than 50 people was carried out very early on the basis of a decree issued on 3 January 1946. Companies owned by Germans were identified in this decree as well as in subsequent ones as 'abandoned' property with absent owners – a result of the Nazi's mass murder of most of the Polish Jews as well as the flight or the forced resettlement of the German population. Here the redistribution was accelerated by radical demographic changes.[61] In Czechoslovakia the transfer of German property to state administration also played an important role. The fact that the nationalization here affected former Czechoslovak citizens was especially significant. In other countries as well, the state confiscated property belonging to 'enemies of the people' and to 'collaborators'.

The speed of nationalization also depended on constellations that had existed during the Second World War. In countries that had already been allied with the Soviet Union during the war, nationalization proceeded more rapidly than in former 'enemy states'. By the end of 1946, state-owned enterprises in Albania were responsible for 89 per cent of the country's industrial production, in Yugoslavia 82 per cent, in Poland and Czechoslovakia 80 per cent; in contrast, the figure was only 45 per cent in Hungary, 16 per cent in Bulgaria, and 11 per cent in Romania.[62] If we consider total production (agrarian as well as non-agrarian), it becomes clear that the initial differences regarding the role of the state in economic life subsequently levelled out: in 1960, 100 per cent of the national income in Bulgaria was produced by state-owned or collective enterprises, in Czechoslovakia 99 per cent, in Hungary 91 per cent, in Albania 88 per cent, and in Romania 83 per cent. In Yugoslavia and Poland, where the state was never able to establish itself as the principal owner, especially in agriculture, the numbers were significantly lower: 73 per cent in Yugoslavia and 63 per cent in Poland.[63]

Nevertheless, a diversity of property forms continued to exist during the entire socialist period, and new hybrid forms of ownership also developed. It is important to consider not only property rights, but also the various forms of property relations. In Yugoslavia, for instance, the self-administration of enterprises emerged as a special form of 'social property'; and in the countryside, property relations can only be understood if the close interlinking and mutual interdependency of continuing private land ownership with the cooperatives is taken into account.[64] Over the course of the political reforms, new property relations developed, for example, in Hungary, where 'economic working communities within enterprises' were established in 1982: workers were provided with a workshop they could use within an enterprise, but that enterprise continued to be state property.[65] Especially during the crisis-ridden later phase, executives assumed an increasingly important role in the larger state enterprises, which has led scholars to argue that in late socialism the state was only the pro forma owner of enterprises, while the role of the executives increasingly became similar to that of 'company managers'.[66] Finally there were also multiple forms of informal control over property that contradicted the formal system of ownership.

---

61 Matthias Barelkowski and Claudia Kraft, 'La Pologne et les biens allemands et juifs après 1945', *Revue de l'histoire moderne et contemporaine* 61, no. 1 (2014): 62–96.

62 Berend, *Central and Eastern Europe*, 72–3.

63 Harrison, 'Communism and Economic Modernization', 396, table 22.3.

64 Luković, 'The Country Road to Revolution'.

65 Brunner, 'Was ist sozialistisch am "sozialistischen" Recht?', 192–7.

66 Segert, 'Der Staatssozialismus war mehr als nur ein politisches Herrschaftssystem', 419–20.

Planned economy

Besides state-owned property, the centrally planned economy was the most important pillar of socio-economic transformation in Eastern Europe, a transformation that was closely based on the Soviet model of accelerated accumulation and thus promoted the expansion of heavy industry (especially the armaments industry) at the cost of agriculture. This produced high growth rates, especially in countries that had had little industrialization to begin with, and brought about a rapid transformation of the economic structure from agricultural work to industrial labour (on average around 40 to 50 per cent of the population in the countries examined here moved from the countryside to the cities starting in the 1950s). The planned economy was able to produce significant growth during the initial post-war decade, when the elimination of war damage, the industrialization of the traditionally agrarian-centred political economies of Eastern Europe and thus extensive growth were the focus. However, the lack of efficiency criteria, the notorious information deficits and a weakly developed incentive system were structural problems of this economic form that became increasingly evident as the demand for consumer goods grew, central state planning restricted the capacity to innovate and an economy of scarcity prevented urgently needed modernization investments. State planning authorities placed themselves between producers and consumers, which meant that neither the desires of consumers nor the successes and failures of producers had any consequences.[67]

The concept of state planning thus had a modernizing effect, especially in poorer countries such as Bulgaria and Romania, where the creation of a modern social structure was accelerated in this way. Matters were different in countries that already possessed a stronger and more differentiated economic infrastructure, especially Czechoslovakia or the GDR. While the strategies of state planning authorities that aimed at quantitative growth did produce high growth rates here as well, these national economies fell behind the formerly comparable national economies in Western Europe due to planning miscalculations regarding their technological innovation capacities.

The system of central planning was inherently static and hostile to innovation,[68] which became increasingly apparent following the radical structural transformation of industrial societies to post-Fordist service societies, especially after digital technology assumed a central significance for modern national economies. The service sector, which became the motor of growth in post-industrial societies in the West, remained weak in the Eastern bloc, both in terms of investment and employment figures. Eastern European states were less capable of dealing with the 'dual crises' – the crisis of (industrial) production and the crisis of the welfare state – than more flexible and more functionally differentiated economies.[69] These crises in production and distribution, which sharpened beginning in the 1970s, also increased the susceptibility to crises of political legitimation.

In general, we can distinguish between two forms of modern state planning: planning and transformation with an open future; and planning in order to avert threats.[70] This second form

---

67 Harrison, 'Communism and Economic Modernization', 396–7.

68 Eichengreen, *The European Economy Since 1945*, 154–5.

69 Christoph Boyer, 'Zwischen Pfadabhängigkeit und Zäsur: Ost- und westeuropäische Sozialstaaten seit den siebziger Jahren des 20. Jahrhunderts', in Jarausch, *Das Ende der Zuversicht?*, 103–19.

70 Martin Schulze Wessel, 'Zukunftsentwürfe und Planungspraktiken in der Sowjetunion und der sozialistischen Tschechoslowakei: Zur Einleitung', in Schulze Wessel and Brenner, *Zukunftsvorstellungen und staatliche Planung*, 1–18; Thomas Etzemüller, 'Strukturierter Raum – integrierte Gemeinschaft: Auf den Spuren des *social engineering* im Europa des 20. Jahrhunderts', in *Theorien und Experimente der Moderne: Europas Gesellschaften im 20. Jahrhundert*, ed. Lutz Raphael (Köln: Böhlau, 2012) 129–54.

Statehood in socialism

is entirely compatible with the preventative planning of social engineering in Western welfare states.[71] The variant of a centralized state-planned economy in the Soviet sphere of power was clearly different. There, the central planning commission or supreme economic council (as the executive organ of the party or of the politburo and the central committee) determined planning numbers for all economic branches, for the distribution of raw materials as well as for the goods to be produced. The planning commission then passed these figures on to the industrial ministers responsible for the individual branches of the economy; they then passed them on to the individual industrial sectors, which passed them on to the individual enterprises. In this way, a cumbersome vertical system developed that allowed little communication between the individual economic sectors. Prices were determined by planning authorities, with heavy industrial goods placed at the top of the pyramid, followed by consumer goods and, significantly thereafter, agricultural products.

Since target figures and prices were set in advance, enterprises were de-coupled from the market and any market-based price development. An incentive system consisted solely in the (over)fulfilment of the plan. Enterprises were continually obligated to report to the superior authorities, which gave rise to an extensive bureaucratic apparatus. In order to guarantee the fulfilment of plans, central authorities issued ad hoc corrective measures, but in doing so were dependent on cooperation from 'below'. Thus, negotiation processes developed between the state planning bureaucracies and company directors, in which the planners' central focus was the fulfilment of planned targets, whereas directors focused on increasing investments as much as possible and maximizing raw material allocations, while simultaneously minimizing planned targets. A specific form of profit maximizing developed in enterprises in the sense that production was performed as cheaply as possible, which was one reason that it was difficult to expand the range of consumer goods. Furthermore, since investments could not be written off in socialist accounting, enterprises had an interest in maintaining existing equipment and machinery at the expense of technological innovation. Although enterprises certainly did have some manoeuvring room in this regard, the planned economy was nevertheless characterized by bureaucratization and discipline: the primary objective was the fulfilment of the plan. Especially into the mid-1950s, deviations from the plan were subject to criminal prosecution as 'diversion' and 'sabotage'.[72]

The example of Czechoslovakia – that is, a planned economy in a country with the structures of a relatively modern industrial society – illustrates the internal dynamics that developed with central state planning. Economic planning was already introduced in Czechoslovakia between 1945 and 1947 (and not in the late 1940s or early 1950s, as in other countries) and not under pressure from the Soviet Union. A two-year plan was adopted in October 1946. The plan was initially designated as 'an economic reconstruction plan', although the objective quickly shifted to the 'development of socialism'. As a result of the rapid nationalization, which began in the autumn of 1945 with the nationalization of banks and key industries, the state owned about two-thirds of Czechoslovak industry in 1947. This development made necessary increased regulatory authority by the state. The first five-year plan was adopted at the end of 1947. As in the other Eastern bloc countries, the state pushed the transformation of the economy: heavy industry and the capital goods industry were privileged over the consumer goods industry, thereby restricting social consumption. Because consumer goods were scarce as a result, price regulations were introduced for consumer goods. In 1949, planning also included

---

71 Etzemüller, 'Strukturierter Raum – integrierte Gemeinschaft', 129–54.
72 Berend, *Central and Eastern Europe*, 74–9; Eichengreen, *The European Economy Since 1945*, 133–46.

prices and wages, since wages had risen more rapidly than work productivity. The introduction of company wage funds was supposed to alleviate this. The wage funds, however, required anticipating the labour power needed and estimating work productivity, which meant that ever more domains of company life were included in the superordinate planning.[73]

Beginning in the mid-1950s a counter-trend developed that was supposed to reform the planning process and prevent the dysfunctional internal dynamics of planning. In Poland, an economic council headed by economist Oskar Lange was established after the 'Polish October'. The council called for more freedoms for enterprises as well as flexibility in determining prices and wages, and also recommended that central authorities concern themselves only with long-term planning. In Hungary, there were experiments beginning in 1965 with a 'new economic mechanism' that included a partial liberalization of many prices (controls were removed for half of consumer goods prices in 1968, and domestic prices were coupled to global market prices in 1979–80). In contrast to this, however, there was little incentive for workers and managers in terms of wages. Furthermore, central planning authorities maintained their influence over investment allocation. In Yugoslavia, the workers' councils played an important role in determining wages beginning in the 1950s, although the state continued to be predominant in the allocation of resources. In Yugoslavia in the second half of the 1960s, free price setting was allowed for many items; factories were allowed to engage in foreign trade; and workers were able to increase their influence through the election of management. In addition, investment decisions were decentralized and banks were commercialized. As a consequence of these developments, there were fears among workforces that enterprises could go bankrupt; in response, workers generously raised their own wages. The ČSSR responded to the inefficiency of the economic system by liberalizing the price system beginning in the 1960s and setting prices only for energy and raw materials. The suppression of the Prague Spring, however, marked the end of these reform efforts. Countries such as Bulgaria, Romania and Albania did not even seriously attempt such measures.

This reluctance to reform the planned economy, however, was evident not only among conservative party elites: because reform socialism also undermined at least in part the ideals of workplace security and economic equality, workers also frequently opposed reforms. In Czechoslovakia, for example, workers criticized the reform plans of the Communist Party of Czechoslovakia (CPC) because they feared a loss of status as well as stricter controls and discipline in enterprises.[74] In Yugoslavia, decentralization made regional differences more visible and led to nationalism and worker unrest (for example, because commercialized banks invested above all in the most prosperous parts of the country). In Hungary in the 1980s, industrial workers criticized reforms legalizing private sector activities that had previously been illegal and that reinforced social inequalities.

Relation between the state and the party

Although the legislative, executive and judicial branches of government did continue to be mentioned in the constitutions of socialist countries, the leading role of the party was a fundamental distinction to other forms of statehood and was successively written into socialist con-

---

73 Balcar and Kučera, 'Von der Gestaltung der Zukunft zu der Verwaltung des Mangels'.

74 Peter Heumos, 'Arbeitermacht im Staatssozialismus: Das Beispiel Tschechoslowakei 1968', in *Die letzte Chance? 1968 in Osteuropa: Analysen und Berichte über ein Schlüsseljahr*, ed. Angelika Ebbinghaus (Hamburg: VSA, 2008), 51–60.

stitutions (in Albania in 1950, in Romania in 1952, in Czechoslovakia in 1960, but in Bulgaria only in 1970, in Hungary in 1972 and in Poland in 1976; the role of the party was least explicit in the Yugoslav constitutions of 1963 and 1974). In this way, the party was attributed the sole monopoly on knowledge and leadership, rendering superfluous the principle of the division of powers. For this reason, the party has been a central focus for scholars not only with regard to constitutional structures, but also in characterizing the substance of the socialist state: 'The general will was embodied by the party which served as the metaphysical and hidden, yet obvious, core of communist statehood.'[75]

During the interwar period, the communist parties of Eastern Europe (with the exception of Czechoslovakia) had been small groupings on the margins of the political system and had frequently been declared illegal. Within a few years after the war, they had transformed themselves from the 'pariah of the old order'[76] into mass organizations. By 1949, they had developed in mass political parties, in part through the persecution and elimination of their former allies during a transitional phase in the establishment of socialism that intensified starting in 1947. In Czechoslovakia, the party had 2,310,000 members, in Poland 1,370,000, in Hungary 1,200,000, in Romania 940,000, in Yugoslavia 780,000 and in Bulgaria 500,000.[77] Corresponding to their mass character and their claim to lead society, the party congresses assumed de jure an outstanding significance as the representation of the entire party membership, but were held only every four or five years. During the interim, the central committee (consisting of 80 to 150 members) represented the will of the party. The actual power lay with the elected party secretaries or the politburo as the even smaller leading circle (usually 10 to 15 members), with the first or general secretary at the top. This led to an enormous concentration of power among a very few communist functionaries.[78]

The party was able to assert its claim to leadership in a sustained way because it imposed itself more or less on the state and its institutions. Although socialist states did resemble other models of modern statehood with legislative, administrative and judicial branches, these were responsible first and foremost for the implementation of decisions made by the party committees. The system of the nomenklatura (see the next section) guaranteed that party members occupied the leading positions in state and social institutions as well as in economic enterprises. Departments were created in the general secretariat of the central committee that matched state authorities, in other words, departments for certain political sectors or realms of the national economy such as education, mining or agriculture, which were headed by party secretaries and which set the guidelines in the respective branches and also drew up economic plans for the individual branches. The ministries were then merely responsible for implementing the guidelines or the economic planning targets. Thus, the most important executive organs were not the government and the ministries, but the secretariats responsible for the individual political realms. Parliaments were also relieved of their actual function as legislative bodies. As a rule, they met only two or three times a year and were responsible for reformulating party resolutions into legislation and then adopting them. The vertically organized state administration also lost its regional and local independence because here too party members held the most important (administrative) functions. The discipline of these party members guaranteed the principle of democratic centralism, through which every party committee remained subordinate to the one

---

75 Behrends, 'The Stalinist volonté générale', 65; see also Kornai, *The Socialist System* 55–7.

76 According to Segert, *Die Grenzen Osteuropas*, 72.

77 Figures in Berend, *Central and Eastern Europe*, 49.

78 Ibid., 48–50.

above it. Not only the vertical administration (all the way down to the village level), but also institutions such as universities and major enterprises had their own party organizations, which meant that the organizational principles of the strictly hierarchical party were evident in all realms of the state. This close interconnectedness meant that when one spoke of the 'cadre', often both state and party functionaries were meant.

Given this intimate connection there is also little point in speaking of a division of labour in the sense that the state had administrative functions and that the party, in contrast, had political functions. We can affirm rather that in state socialism there was no area of public life that was free from politics. János Kornai writes: 'In fact, the existence of the "party-state" and the blending of political and administrative functions is one of the main characteristics of the system.'[79] At the same time, however, older institutions continued to exist or were upgraded to state structures because more and more societal sub-systems came under state control. Transportation, social security agencies and energy supply facilities became part of the state bureaucracy. Through their monopoly position, trade unions and artists associations, as well as women's and youth organizations acquired a semi-state character.[80]

The strict hierarchy described above and the enormous control of superordinate over subordinate levels in the hierarchy were rooted in part in communist functionaries' experiences of persecution during the war and contributed to a habitus of militarization and conspiracy within state parties. Yet despite the hierarchical configuration of state parties and their authority to appoint functionaries at all levels and in all politically and socially relevant domains, political life by no means froze into pure ritual. Precisely because the party was omnipresent and was represented all the way down to the local level, it also possessed the most important function in a hierarchically organized system: that of communicating interests from the ground upwards. Many party members were committed communists and dedicated themselves to the success of the communist project. Furthermore, the fact that the party was a mass organization meant that very different group interests were represented within party organizations. For this reason, state parties were 'heterogeneous communication structures with ... consensus-creating integration mechanisms.'[81] In the 1960s state parties had large memberships, and the party had high approval ratings among the population, particularly during times of political upheaval. Especially after 1956, the 'good' party was frequently defended against the excesses of the police and the judiciary during Stalinism.[82] Finally, for many people the party was an essential vehicle for a successful professional career.

Actors: bureaucrats – technocrats – experts

The stability of state socialism was based not least on the loyalty[83] of the functionaries active in party and state institutions. To this end, the centrally organized state parties used the nomenklatura to develop a rigid selection system that was intended to guarantee the reliability and loyalty

---

79 Kornai, *The Socialist System*, 39.

80 Berend, *Central and Eastern Europe*, 49–52; Kornai, *The Socialist System*, 33–9.

81 Pavel Kolář, 'Kommunistische Identitäten im Streit: Politisierung und Herrschaftslegitimation in den kommunistischen Parteien in Ostmitteleuropa nach dem Stalinismus', in *Zeitschrift für Ostmitteleuropa-Forschung* 60 (2011): 232–66, here 238.

82 Kolář, 'The Party as a New Utopia'.

83 The concept of loyalty appears well suited for examining communication relations among the political elite, the bureaucratic service class, as well as the population. On this, see Volker Zimmermann, Peter Haslinger and Tomáš Nigrin, eds, *Loyalitäten im Staatssozialismus: DDR, Tschechoslowakei, Polen* (Marburg: Herder, 2010).

Statehood in socialism

of people in positions of responsibility. However, given the party's enormous permeation into all areas of state and social life, it is clear that this was not a manageable group of ideologically committed cadre, but rather a very heterogeneous and quite sizeable 'sub-elite', which inserted itself as the new 'service class' between the party elite and society.[84] The congruence between advancement possibilities enabled by party rule, on the one hand, and the pursuit of positive life goals, on the other, resulted in an overlapping between the personal interests and world views of many citizens and the ideology of the socialist system. This was a source of stability as well as instability.[85]

The demand for trained administrative personnel increased enormously with the centrally planned economy and the transformation of trade unions, cultural institutions and interest groups into representative organs with semi-official character predominated by the party state. Significant segments of society that had already been mobilized socially to a great extent through collectivization, industrialization, urbanization and educational policies were presented with advancement opportunities that served as the basis for institutionally produced ties to the political system. The rapidly expanding bureaucracy had for this reason a Janus-faced character. It drew criticism precisely from reform communists, who argued that capitalist exploiters had simply been replaced by a new class that had wedged itself between workers and the means of production.[86] At the same time, it offered a significant part of the population attractive advancement opportunities.[87] At the latest, beginning in the 1960s, however, there was a deceleration of vertical social mobility: once a social position had been attained, it was frequently 'passed on' within the family.[88] The prestige of bureaucracy possessed special significance because – in contrast to capitalism, which also valued social success and property – it was an important 'currency', in which social distinction could be expressed. 'Privileges' were more important than differences in income and provided above all access to goods and services.[89]

Contemporary social scientists had already argued in the 1950s and 60s that the modern industrial societies of the East and West were faced with quite comparable requirements (for instance, a highly differentiated division of labour, enormous demands for investments as well as the continuing need to improve efficiency). The first two post-war decades can be seen as the climax of the belief that politics could be planned and that expert knowledge can be trusted. In this context, 'bureaucratic dirigisme' became a feature of statehood irrespective of the surrounding socialist or capitalist economic system, as Polish sociologist Maria Hirszowicz shrewdly observed.[90] The importance of political planning along with the scienticization of politics gave rise to a caste of confident experts who understood their task to be intervention in political and economic processes. In the West, they regarded themselves primarily as non-ideological specialists and saw society as a system, or in the language of cybernetics popular at the time, as 'techno-structure'. In the East, trust in expert planning as well as planning in gen-

---

84 In Hungary, for instance, there were an estimated 450,000 posts in the 1970s, if the nomenklatura are included down to the local level; see Segert, *Die Grenzen Osteuropas*, 119, footnote 92 (which cites Rudolf L. Tökés, *Hungary's Negotiated Revolution: Economic Reform, Social Change and Political Succession* [Cambridge: Cambridge University Press, 1996], 143).

85 Segert, *Die Grenzen Osteuropas*, 103, 117–21.

86 Milovan Djilas, *The New Class: An Analysis of the Communist System* (San Diego, CA: Harcourt Brace Jovanovich, 1957).

87 Segert, *Die Grenzen Osteuropas*, 119–20.

88 Béla Tomka, *A Social History of Twentieth-Century Europe* (London: Routledge, 2013), 137–44.

89 Kornai, *The Socialist System*, 322–3; Donald Filtzer, 'Privilege and Inequality in Communist Society', in Smith, *The Oxford Handbook of the History of Communism*, 505–21.

90 Maria Hirszowicz, *The Bureaucratic Leviathan: A Study in the Sociology of Communism* (Oxford: Martin Robertson, 1980), 5–6.

eral was rather limited, since party functionaries considered the experts to be politically unreliable due to their apolitical stance.

In the 1960s, paradoxically, the belief in the ability to plan processes in highly complex modern societies appears to have been much more widespread among the technocratic elite in Western Europe than in Eastern Europe, where cybernetics lost favour already during this decade due to its ostensible ideological incompatibility with socialism. Perhaps even more significant than this political stigmatization, however, was the fact that in the economies of scarcity in the socialist bloc, planning was frequently rendered impossible by the necessity of permanent improvisation. Thus, precisely in the heyday of convergence theory, scientific planning created, especially in the West, a confident stratum of experts and politically influential technocrats. In Eastern Europe, these experts and technocrats lost their influence at the latest by the end of 1960s to the group frequently described by critics of bureaucracy as the 'service class'. As managers of state-owned enterprises or as party and trade-union functionaries, they were much more influential than scientific experts. Their position was based less on expert knowledge than on ideology: the arbitrary interventions made necessary by the limits of planning were guaranteed by the state party's power monopoly and secured their prominent role in a system that ultimately placed political calculus over expertise.

Nevertheless, beginning in the last third of the nineteenth century, the belief in the capacity to plan social processes and turn them into objects of science constituted an important characteristic of modern statehood. The term 'social engineering,' which has been used to describe this characteristic, is regarded as formative for 'high modernity'.[91] Authoritarian states with weakly developed civil societies, onto which a schematic social order was imposed without regard for flexible, often chaotic local practices, were considered especially susceptible to this form of politics based on the belief in planning.[92] Another interpretation of modern statehood emphasizes, in contrast, less the social-disciplining, coercive character than a specific rationality that allowed societies to become the object of planning euphoria, and experts and technocrats to become decisive political actors, irrespective of the political system. The Cold War can be seen as the heyday and final phase of technocratic thinking, since in the competition for efficiency between the two systems the predominant understanding was that 'humanity [should be] defined by social indicators in an ostensibly value-free and objective way.'[93] From this perspective, the twentieth century can be interpreted as a process of normalization, in which social grievances were to be diagnosed less through ideology than through a strict belief in empirical reality and then treated by means of learning processes and prevention.[94]

Ideas about the 'scienticization of the social' (Lutz Raphael) undoubtedly also played an important role in the emergence of an expertocracy that was influential, at least at times. Exemplary for this was Czech biologist Ivan Málek, who in the 1950s advocated cultivating the 'new human', but then increasingly focused in the 1960s on preventative measures regarding

---

91 Ulrich Herbert, 'Europe in High Modernity: Reflections on a Theory of the 20th Century', *Journal of Modern European History* 5 (2007): 5–20; Lutz Raphael, 'Ordnungsmuster der Hochmoderne: Die Theorie der Moderne und die Geschichte der europäischen Gesellschaften im 20. Jahrhundert', in *Dimensionen der Moderne: Festschrift für Christoph Dipper*, eds Lutz Raphael and Ute Schneider (Frankfurt a.M.: Peter Lang, 2008), 73–91.

92 James C. Scott, *Seeing Like a State: How Certain Schemes to Improve the Human Condition Have Failed* (New Haven, CT: Yale University Press, 1998), 4–6.

93 Dirk van Laak, 'Technokratie im Europa des 20. Jahrhunderts – eine einflussreiche "Hintergrundideologie"', in Raphael, *Theorien und Experimente der Moderne*, 101–28, here 120.

94 Etzemüller, 'Strukturierter Raum – integrierte Gemeinschaft', 132–5.

Statehood in socialism

human living conditions. In 1968, Málek fell victim to the Czechoslovak normalization regime, since his notion of 'creative prevention' – a scientifically developed human creativity – ran counter to the new political realities.[95] Here the similarities and differences in the East and the West regarding expert knowledge and political praxis become clear. When in the 1960s Málek supported increasingly powerful social preventative methods that seemed to leave more room for individuality, there was no longer any place for him in a political order with fixed ideological horizons (which were reflected in the self-understanding of the state party as the organ responsible for establishing the common good and implementing the laws of history).

Policymakers in state socialism were generally sceptical about either ostensible or actual apolitical scientific experts. Technological innovations often fell victim to the primacy of politics. Models of society that employed technology comprehensively such as cybernetics were deprecated in socialism even before the planning euphoria had abated in the West because the comprehensive claims of these models to regulate and explain society ran counter to the opinion monopoly of the state party.[96] In contrast to functionally differentiated societies – where new models of describing society (e.g. more ecologically oriented ones) arose after the belief in scientific social planning had dwindled – planned-economy and centralized state-party systems were increasingly confronted with innovation deficits. It is certainly possible to identify counter examples here, that is, experts who refused to subordinate their work to ideological premises at certain times or in certain ways. For instance, Polish social experts Jan Rosner and Antoni Rajkiewicz argued that a new phase of state-interventionist policies was emerging in the 1970s, in which social progress and economic growth would be better coordinated. They argued that planning was difficult precisely in the realm of social policies and that while economic growth was easier to plan, even here the changing needs of the population had to be taken into account. According to Rosner and Rajkiewicz, social policy should counteract the 'technocrat-manager mentality'. Measuring 'social progress', they continued, was problematic since this would have to include post-materialist values that played no significant role at the time, much to their disappointment.[97]

Starting in the 1970s, support for the idea of macro-social (scientific) planning declined for a number of reasons: one was the obvious weakness of adjusting planning targets to changing social and economic contexts; another was the fundamental critique that such an approach disenfranchised society, reducing it to an object of bureaucratic planning.[98] This critique contributed to the idea among dissidents of counter-society, which ultimately led to a fundamental questioning of the state socialist system and its institutions.[99]

The use of force and the socialist state's monopoly on violence

The communist parties of Eastern Europe underwent a radical transformation during the postwar era. In the period between the two world wars they had been forced to the margins of society or even had to operate underground. Their very existence had been threatened

---

95 Martin Franc, 'Biologiediskurse über den "neuen Menschen" in der Tschechoslowakei der fünfziger Jahre am Beispiel des Biologen Ivan Málek', in Schulze Wessel and Brenner, *Zukunftsvorstellungen und staatliche Planung*, 63–77.

96 Jakob Tanner, 'Komplexität, Kybernetik und Kalter Krieg', 377–413.

97 Antoni Rajkiewicz und Jan Rosner, 'Sozialpolitik im Aufbau des entwickelten Sozialismus', *Polnische Perspektiven* 6, no. 7/8 (1976): 12–22, here 13–14.

98 Hirszowicz, *The Bureaucratic Leviathan*, 6–7.

99 Barbara J. Falk, *The Dilemmas of Dissidence in East Central Europe: Citizen Intellectuals and Philosopher Kings* (Budapest: CEU Press, 2003).

even before the outbreak of the war, not least through Stalinist purges. During the Second World War, the Nazis' radical and exterminatory anti-communism had intensified this threat in many locations. The 1930s and 40s were a permanent state of emergency for communist parties, which was reflected in the establishment of a conspiratorial habitus relying on militancy. However, it was not only communist parties, but also populations in general that were subject to violence on an unprecedented scale during the war and in the immediate post-war period. The dissolution of existing political and social orders created a climate of social anomie.[100]

This anomie and the concurrent radical transformation of property ownership and population demographics led to an atmosphere in which historical actors – even beyond (para)military organizations – were increasingly willing to engage in mass violence.[101] Leftist political parties, establishing themselves only now in the aftermath of pre-war and wartime experiences, conceived the construction of the new system in terms of battle and invoked the omnipresence of 'enemies'.[102] Another contributing factor was that broad parts of the population in several countries, even the overwhelming majority, rejected communism. The massive display and use of physical force reached its climax during the communist seizure of power and during Stalinism.[103] The special agencies, which were created at the time to suppress the opposition, would later be transformed into bureaucratic state security apparatuses.

After the end of Stalinism, however, an older line of tradition became increasingly important: in state socialism as well, state rule was legitimated first and foremost through the establishment and preservation of security.[104] The habitus of the permanent fighter was replaced by the image of the law enforcement official ensuring public safety and order.[105] The use of force continued to be an integral component of statehood, but in a form markedly different than during the initial phase of state socialism influence by the military. The state guaranteed above all the preservation of public order and understood itself as the guarantor of social security. In comparison to states in which private property was the predominant form of ownership, the socialist state enormously expanded the space in which it exercised its functions of order and security. The introduction of a centrally planned economy and of nationalization meant that the state's monopoly on violence extended to ever more domains.[106]

Another specific feature of the socialist state's monopoly on violence was the secret police, which as 'the party's shield and sword' were supposed to ensure the establishment of the socialist order, combatting foreign and especially domestic enemies. In all Eastern bloc countries, there were apparatuses with sizeable personnel and sophisticated technological equipment to

---

100 For Poland, see for instance, Marcin Zaremba, *Wielka Trwoga, Polska 1944–1947: ludowa reakcja na kryzys* [The great fear: Poland 1944–1947 – the people's reaction to crisis] (Kraków: Znak, 2012).

101 Christian Gerlach has noted that the affinity to violence in societies increases during periods of comprehensive material redistribution; see *Extremely Violent Societies: Mass Violence in the Twentieth Century World* (Cambridge: Cambridge University Press, 2010).

102 Julia Strauss, 'Communist Revolution and Political Terror', in Smith, *The Oxford Handbook of the History of Communism*, 355–70; Silke Satjukow and Rainer Gries, eds, *Unsere Feinde: Konstruktionen des Anderen im Sozialismus* (Leipzig: Leipziger Universitätsverlag, 2004).

103 Kevin McDermott and Andrew Stibbe, eds, *Stalinist Terror in Eastern Europe: Elite Purges and Mass Repression* (Manchester: Manchester University Press, 2010).

104 Thomas Lindenberger, 'Öffentliche Sicherheit und normale Abläufe: Überlegungen zum zeitweiligen Gelingen kommunistischer Herrschaft in der DDR', in *Ordnung und Sicherheit, Devianz und Kriminalität im Staatssozialismus: Tschechoslowakei und DDR 1948/49–1989*, eds Volker Zimmermann and Michal Pullmann (Göttingen: Vandenhoeck & Ruprecht, 2014), 15–38, here 17–22.

105 Marco Albeltrato, 'The Life of a Communist Militant,' in Smith, *The Oxford Handbook of the History of Communism*, 441–54, here 442.

106 Lindenberger, 'Öffentliche Sicherheit und normale Abläufe', 37.

Statehood in socialism

spy on and discipline both actual and ostensible 'opponents of the system'.[107] Although the security services represented the most negative side of socialist statehood, they also offered citizens an opportunity to get involved: when people made denunciations, they did not always act out of ideological conviction, but also did so because it allowed them to take part in state rule and thus exercise power themselves on a minor scale.[108]

In addition to this expansion of the monopoly on violence resulting from the specific configuration of socialist states, however, the question also arises: were socialist states characterized beyond this by a special affinity to violence? One could examine the situational significance of specific acts of violence in historical-anthropological terms by describing them as a means for realizing respective interests or as social constructs through which historical actors reinforced their own perceptions of themselves. Such an approach would seem to be appropriate especially for the immediate post-war period and the initial consolidation phase of socialism. During this time, an enormous amount of physical violence was used against 'enemies of the people' – a frequently changing group – whether these were members of ethnic minorities, citizens with the 'wrong' class affiliation, or other 'internal' enemies of the socialist system. Until the end of Stalinism all of them were confronted with an enormous amount of state violence. After Stalinism, the use of physical force occurred in a more regulated form, as a component of the social contract between citizens and the socialist state.

Nevertheless, until the very end, socialist regimes were characterized by a multiplicity of paramilitary organizations that citizens unavoidably encountered, whether at school, university or the workplace.[109] This militarization of many domains of life was the result of a sense of continuous threat from internal and external enemies. In the constitutions of socialist states, the use of force was regulated imprecisely; especially in the realm of penal law, general phrases predominated that insufficiently restricted the penal powers of the state. Without meaning to relativize the comparatively precarious position of legal certainty in state socialism, we can nevertheless raise the following question: considering Carl Schmitt's dictum that the sovereign is he who decides on the state of emergency, to what extent is the legality of modern statehood in general, fundamentally threatened? In 1961, the police killed 200 French Algerians at a demonstration in Paris. When Polish communist party leader Władysław Gomułka believed that striking workers in Polish coastal cities in 1970 threatened the Polish state, he criticized the Polish militia for their indecision and pointed to the actions of the French Police in 1961 as an example to be emulated.[110] Although the arbitrary use of violence by state security forces in socialist states was significantly more frequent than in Western European societies, a fundamental discomfort regarding the state's monopoly of violence remains. Alf Lüdtke has described this as follows: 'The ritual dimension of suspending regulated normality that does not thereby suspend statehood, but rather strengthens it – this points to a blind spot that characterizes "Western notions" of the state.'[111]

---

107 Krzysztof Persak and Łukasz Kamiński, eds, *A Handbook of the Communist Security Apparatus in East Central Europe, 1944–1989* (Warsaw: Instytut Pamieci Narodowej, 2005).

108 Sándor Horváth, 'Life of an Agent: Re-Energizing Stalinism and Learning the Language of Collaboration after 1956 in Hungary', *Hungarian Historical Review (New Series of Acta Historica Academiae Scientiarium Hungaricae)* 4, no. 1 (2015): 56–81; Lüdtke, *Gewalt des Staates*, 207.

109 Péter Gosztony, ed., *Paramilitärische Organisationen im Sowjetblock* (Bonn: Hohwacht, 1977).

110 Włodzimierz Borodziej, 'Gewalt in Volkspolen (1944–1989)', *Osteuropa* 50, no. 12 (2000): 1364–84, here 1381.

111 Alf Lüdtke, '17. Juni 1953 in Erfurt: Ausnahmezustand und staatliche Gewaltrituale', in *Staats-Gewalt: Ausnahmezustand und Sicherheitsregimes: Historische Perspektiven*, eds Alf Lüdtke and Michael Wildt (Göttingen: Wallstein, 2008), 241–73, 256.

State and international organizations, systems and networks

Statehood did not develop in a vacuum, but rather within an international system that presupposed the existence of sovereign states and – with few exceptions – considered only these states to be constituent entities of international law. This system gave rise to certain requirements that socialist states also had to fulfil and that helped shape their character, while generating international recognition and new potential for interest-driven politics. The most far-reaching framework was the United Nations, which all countries in the region joined; each member committed itself to the observance of human rights and to the UN charter. Yugoslavia, Poland and Czechoslovakia were among the founding members of the United Nations (24 October 1945); Albania, Bulgaria, Romania and Hungary joined in 1955, and the GDR followed in 1973.[112]

Within the UN, the socialist countries succeeded in forcing the inclusion of social and economic content in human rights documents. Specifically in terms of developing countries, as well as in their promotion of women's rights as human rights, the socialist countries strove to present themselves as role models. It is no wonder that the initiative for an International Women's Year (as the year preceding the UN's Decade for Women from 1976 to 1985) was introduced by the Women's International Democratic Federation (WIDF), which had closer affiliation with the Eastern bloc. The year and decade were actively promoted by the socialist states, such that women's rights were always associated with other foreign policy themes like peace and disarmament, and were seen as social rights within state modernization projects.[113] Furthermore, Yugoslavia pushed for the inclusion of collective rights for minorities in the catalogue of human rights with its 1978 submission to the UN Human Rights Council of a proposal for minority rights protection.[114] Moreover, the communist states were vehement supporters of decolonization while campaigning for the establishment of new states. Romania became highly involved in the United Nations Conference on Trade and Development after the country itself officially acquired 'developing nation' status at the beginning of the 1970s.

Socialist countries were also members of the IMF (Yugoslavia since 1945, Romania since 1972, Hungary since 1982, and Poland since 1986), a factor that had ramifications for a central aspect of their statehood, i.e. the autonomy of their fiscal policy. While Yugoslavia was forced to accept IMF cutbacks at the beginning of the 1980s in order to rein in its debt, Romania avoided such measures by means of an independent, radical austerity policy. Yugoslavia's austere budgetary policy contributed to the de-legitimation of its entire federation of states.[115]

Beyond the international organizations, the state socialist countries developed their own formats for intensifying their cooperation with one another, yet the boundaries of sovereignty (vis-à-vis the Soviet Union) were only tested in military matters; otherwise, the countries held the principle of non-intervention and national sovereignty in high regard, even in cases when

---

112 Member States of the United Nations, Wikipedia page: http://en.wikipedia.org/wiki/Member_states_of_the_United_Nations (accessed 8 January 2015).

113 Kirsten Ghodsee, 'Rethinking State Socialist Mass Women's Organizations: The Committee of the Bulgarian Women's Movement and the United Nations Decade for Women, 1975–1985', in *Journal of Women's History* 24, no. 4 (Winter 2012): 49–73; Celia Donert, 'Wessen Utopie? Frauenrechte und Staatssozialismus im internationalen Jahr der Frau 1975', in *Moral für die Welt? Menschenrechtspolitik in den 1970er Jahren*, eds Jan Eckel and Samuel Moyn (Göttingen: Vandenhoeck & Ruprecht, 2012), 367–93.

114 Li-Ann Thio, *Managing Babel: The International Legal Protection of Minorities in the Twentieth Century* (Leiden: Martinus Nijhoff, 2005), 127.

115 Branka Magaš, *The Destruction of Yugoslavia: Tracking the Break-up 1980–1992* (London: Verso, 1993), 96.

Statehood in socialism

the primacy of the Soviet communists and the interests of the Soviet Union were not a factor. As mentioned earlier, a first organ of multilateral cooperation, the Information Bureau of the Communist and Workers' Parties – known as Cominform in the West – was founded in September 1947 in Szklarska Poręba, Poland.[116] This body did not represent the states themselves, but rather the communist parties within them, which, as far as the Eastern bloc countries were concerned, amounted to more or less the same thing. In contrast to Comintern (Communist International), which was dissolved in 1943, Cominform's decisions were not intended to be binding for the member parties; indeed, their intention was to establish an exchange of experiences and coordinate policy amongst its members. Cominform gained particular notoriety by virtue of the conflict between the Soviet and the Yugoslav communists, which ended with the latter being expelled from the body in June 1948. Stalin fell out with Tito essentially because the Yugoslav communists were not ready to accept their expected submission to the interests of the Communist Party of the Soviet Union. Especially in important foreign policy issues, like the plans of a Balkan Federation of socialist states, the Yugoslavs had shown their own will, not seeking the Kremlin's consent beforehand. Subsequently, Cominform failed to develop any more substantial activities and was dissolved in April 1956.[117]

Of greater importance, although falling equally short of expectations, was the Council for Mutual Economic Assistance (CMEA) founded in 1949 as a response to the Marshall Plan (an initiative which, due to Soviet pressure, Eastern European countries were prevented from taking part in). The CMEA encompassed no long-term integration plans; its function was rather to ensure the USSR's economic control over its satellite states and to promote regional cooperation as compensation for the limited foreign commerce that resulted from the system of planned economies. In the first years of its existence, the CMEA was largely meaningless; until 1959 it possessed none of its own statutes and convened for a summit only once under Stalin.[118] Under Khrushchev, the CMEA underwent a gradual revival; a 1954 meeting of the council included the recommendation to coordinate the national economic plans and the establishment of 'permanent commissions' for individual economic sectors that had their seats in capital cities of the member countries.[119]

The international socialist division of labour aspired to by the CMEA – and thus above all by the USSR – failed not in small part due to the least economically developed members (Bulgaria and Romania), which feared they would become downgraded to producing only raw materials and foodstuffs.[120] The successes of the CMEA were modest, yet they did include benefits gained through standardization as well an improved coordination in terms of infrastructure. However, individual countries retained various commercial tariffs and regulations. Trade between CMEA

---

116 Günter Nollau, 'Kominform', in *Die kommunistischen Parteien der Welt: Sowjetsystem und demokratische Gesellschaft*, ed. Claus D. Kernig (Freiburg: Herder, 1969), 32–37.

117 Svetozar Rajak, 'The Cold War in the Balkans, 1945–1956', in *The Cambridge History of the Cold War*, vol. 1, *Origins, 1945–1962*, eds Melvyn P. Leffler and Odd A. Westad (Cambridge: Cambridge University Press, 2010), 198–220, 217–8.

118 Douglas Selvage, 'The Truth about Friendship Treaties: Behind the Iron Curtain', in *The Oxford Handbook of Postwar European History*, ed. Dan Stone, 1st ed., *Oxford Handbooks in History* (Oxford: Oxford University Press, 2012), 319–36, particularly 323.

119 Richard Felix Staar, *Communist Regimes in Eastern Europe*, 4th ed., 3rd print, *Hoover Press Publication* 269 (Stanford, CA: Hoover Institution Press, 1984), 300.

120 Balázs Szalontai, 'Political and Economic Relations between Communist States', in *The Oxford Handbook of the History of Communism*, ed. Stephen A. Smith (Oxford: Oxford University Press, 2014), 305–21, here 310–2.

members was largely carried out on the basis of bilateral agreements and not as part of a multilateral framework.[121] Furthermore, it was intended that the bank of the CMEA (Bank for International Economic Cooperation) play only a subordinate role.

The CMEA failed – almost necessarily – due to the contradictions inherent in a supranational integration of countries that persistently practised national economic planning. The member countries, including the Soviet Union, which accounted for almost three quarters of the economic output of the CMEA, were not ready to accept supranational planning organs with governing authority. Nor was there any dynamic comparable to European integration, in which the sharing of sovereignty concerning economic policy was expanded to reach other political realms. Overall, among CMEA member countries, even the amount of foreign trade with the CMEA decreased over time compared to figures from 1949. Recent research on the CMEA has concluded that the Soviet allies accrued more advantages through the council than did the USSR itself, as the CMEA presented an implicit trade subsidy on the side of the Soviet Union. The USSR was an unlimited ready market for products of poor quality and supplied its allies with cheap petroleum and natural gas until the late 1980s.[122] New studies indicate that the economic cooperation between East and West did not necessarily halt at the Iron Curtain, and that the Eastern European economic policymakers looked more towards the West than the East in the 1970s due to critical imports such as technology goods.[123]

While the CMEA aimed – yet ultimately failed – to coordinate economic planning for the Eastern bloc, the Warsaw Pact, signed in 1955, had significantly greater success in defence policy, one of the most important aspects of modern statehood.[124] The signatory powers were Albania, Bulgaria, the GDR, Poland, Romania, the Soviet Union, Czechoslovakia and Hungary. This treaty was an immediate reaction to the remilitarization of West Germany and its admittance into NATO the same year. The members of the Warsaw Pact were committed to mutual assistance in case of an attack by a third party and to non-intervention in the domestic affairs of fellow pact members. This latter principle was violated by the pact's intervention in Czechoslovakia in August 1968. The Warsaw Pact was organized such that it was dominated by the Soviet army, which reflected the members' relative military capacities. Thus, the supreme commander of the united armed forces was always a Soviet colonel, who was also a deputy to the Soviet defence minister, while all of the highest command positions within the Warsaw Pact were occupied by the Soviet military.[125]

The CMEA and Warsaw Pact served to strengthen and defend communist hegemony and its specific understanding of the state, although from the 1960s onward these efforts at de-

---

121 Staar, *Communist Regimes in Eastern Europe*, 320; Eichengreen, *The European Economy Since 1945*, 155–60.
122 Randall W. Stone, *Satellites and Commissars: Strategy and Conflict in the Politics of Soviet Bloc Trade* (Princeton, NJ: Princeton University Press, 1996).
123 Dagmara Jaješniak-Quast, '"Hidden Integration": RGW-Wirtschaftsexperten in europäischen Netzwerken', in *Jahrbuch für Wirtschaftsgeschichte/Economic History Yearbook*, 2014/1, 79–95; idem, 'Iron and Steel Permeating through the Iron Curtain: Poland, Czechoslovakia, the GDR and Neutral States', in *Gaps in the Iron Curtain: Economic Relations between Neutral and Socialist Countries in Cold War Europe*, eds Gertrude Enderel-Burcel, Piotr Franaszek, Dieter Stiefel, Alice Teichová (Cracow: Jagiellonian University Press, 2009), 270–87.
124 Cf. the short presentation of the pact, its structure and development in Staar, *Communist Regimes in Eastern Europe*, 270–99. The official designation for the pact was 'Agreement of Friendship, Cooperation, and Mutual Assistance'.
125 Staar, *Communist Regimes in Eastern Europe*, 280.

Statehood in socialism

escalating tensions ultimately had the opposite effect. In this context, it is particularly instructive to mention the CSCE, which the communist governments (with the exception of Albania) actively helped shape. The Helsinki Accords, signed in 1975 in Helsinki as the final act of the CSCE, committed the socialist countries to the observation of human rights (Basket III) as well as a scaling-back of the constraints on contact between the blocs. Among other measures, the communist governments subsequently ceased efforts to obstruct the reception of Western radio and television signals. For dissidents, the Helsinki Accords became an effective means of discourse in their interactions with their regimes,[126] not only in Czechoslovakia (Charter 77), but in countries like Bulgaria (Declaration 78) and Romania as well (author Paul Goma's exhortation in defence of human rights). Overall, the CSCE 'thrust human rights onto the agenda of international politics and the communist regimes into the enduring spotlight.'[127] The subsequent transnational discourse on human rights established an important recourse for appeal.[128] However, the Soviet Union and its allies believed that this price was worth paying, as the CSCE accord also entailed the acknowledgement of the new borders drawn after the Second World War. In this respect, they traded the external protection of their statehood for the risk of its internal erosion.

Circles of inclusion and exclusion

As emphasized in the first section of this chapter, the aspirations to reconfigure society according to concrete ideological specifications were characteristic of real socialist statehood. This resulted not only in a decidedly interventionist political *dispositif*, but also in specific patterns of inclusion as well as exclusion intended and practised by the state. The party leadership formulated clear notions about who was allowed to belong to the new socialist community and who was not, as well as how the latter might qualify for membership if they could credibly demonstrate the successful cathartic purification through self-improvement. The specific criteria that served as arguments for the inclusion in the socialist community were quite varied and depended on concrete historical circumstances, although a stable element can be identified: work was fundamental to notions of participating in citizenship, together with the rights and duties of individuals tied to this. Beyond this, variations arose not only through changes in the ideological system, but also through the unintended consequences of particular policies, which, for example, reinforced existing inequalities without this being their actual objective and which frequently gave rise to new political reactions. Jens Gieseke has emphasized that '"unwanted" inequality effects' were also the result of insufficient steering capacities of the

---

126 Sarah Snyder, *Human Rights Activism and the End of the Cold War: A Transnational History of the Helsinki Network* (Cambridge: Cambridge University Press, 2013); Helmut Altrichter, ed., *Der KSZE-Prozess: vom Kalten Krieg zu einem neuen Europa* (München: Oldenbourg, 2011); Thomas, *The Helsinki Effect.*

127 Wilfried Loth, 'Der KSZE-Prozess 1975–1990: Eine Bilanz', in *Die KSZE im Ost-West-Konflikt: Internationale Politik und gesellschaftliche Transformation 1975–1990*, eds Matthias Peter and Hermann Wentker, Schriftenreihe der Vierteljahrshefte für Zeitgeschichte Sondernummer series (München: Oldenbourg, 2012), 323–31, here 330. Cf. Anthony Kemp-Welch, 'Eastern Europe: Stalinism to Solidarity', in *The Cambridge History of the Cold War*, vol. 2, *Crises and Détente*, eds Melvyn P. Leffler and Odd A. Westad (Cambridge: Cambridge University Press, 2010), 219–37, here 233.

128 Samuel Moyn, 'Die Rückkehr des verlorenen Sohnes: Einleitung – Die 1970er Jahre als Umbruchsphase in der Menschenrechtsgeschichte', in *Moral für die Welt? Menschenrechtspolitik in den 1970er Jahren*, eds Jan Eckel and Samuel Moyn (Göttingen: Vandenhoeck und Ruprecht, 2012), 7–21.

state, whose all-encompassing claim to shape society and whose enormous political powers were nevertheless often disrupted by the internal logic of social sub-systems as well as by external influences.[129]

The mechanisms and boundaries of inclusion and exclusion by the state could be very different and were also implemented with varying degrees of clarity and severity, which in turn allowed those individuals and groups affected either more or less manoeuvring room. The clearest form of exclusion from the socialist community was physical removal from society, whether by arrest, ban, expulsion, or, in extreme cases, execution. This form of exclusion was typical especially for the early years of communist rule, although it was by no means limited to them, and it included the expulsion of undesirable ethnic minorities as well as the exile of family members of former elites from capital cities to the countryside. These forms of repression often included the loss of civil rights, a punishment that was at times applied to other family members as well, especially during Stalinism. This was a further feature of repressive social policy in state socialism: the imputation of collective responsibility for primary social groups, especially family and kinship.[130] Family heritage was also important for access to education and advancement opportunities.

The production of inequality

Although these criteria of inclusion and exclusion were usually articulated openly and at times even formalized, there were also numerous categorizations that impeded the full enjoyment of socialist citizenship that were not clearly fixed, often remained implicit and were not always set by the central state. These included being part of an ethnic minority, having a physical or mental disability and belonging to certain social groups. We can identify the patterns of producing such inequality by examining the eligibility criteria for certain state benefits and the state's administrative practices in regard to people with different social positions. Finally, state socialist economies were also characterized by economic inequality, which resulted in unequal life opportunities.[131] Since the state had, as the central economic actor, a much greater significance than in the West, responsibility for economic inequality in state socialism must be sought primarily in state policies. An analysis of the mechanisms of inequality production is thus essential for an interpretation of socialist statehood since it was not a collateral effect of political action but constituted the very self-understanding of the state. The political salience of inequality in a system of rule committed to the basic values of egalitarianism (although with clear, self-imposed limitations) is also evident in the fact that opposition movements in state socialism frequently invoked inequality in radical critiques of communist rule.

---

129 Jens Gieseke, 'Soziale Ungleichheit im Staatssozialismus: Eine Skizze', *Zeithistorische Forschungen/ Studies in Contemporary History* 10, no. 2 (2013): 3, www.zeithistorische-forschungen.de/16126041-Gieseke-2-2013.

130 See the extreme, but nevertheless paradigmatic Albanian case: Georgia Kretsi, *Verfolgung und Gedächtnis in Albanien: Eine Analyse postsozialistischer Erinnerungsstrategien* (Wiesbaden: Harrassowitz, 2007).

131 The primarily contemporary literature on inequality and its various dimensions in state socialism is extensive. See, for example, David Stuart Lane, *The End of Inequality? Stratification under State Socialism* (Harmondsworth: Penguin, 1971); Tamás Kolosi and Edmund Wnuk-Lipiński, *Equality and Inequality under Socialism: Poland and Hungary Compared*, Sage Studies in International Sociology 29 (London: Sage Publications, 1983). See also the special issue of *Zeithistorischen Forschungen* 10, no. 2 (2013) on social inequality in state socialism, edited by Jens Gieseke, Klaus Gestwa and Jan-Holger Kirsch.

Statehood in socialism

The socialist state produced inequality – in principle no different than the capitalist state – through two frequently related kinds of policies: redistribution and recognition. Redistribution, for instance through the nationalization of property, state-determined wages and the establishment of extensive funds for social consumption, was one of the central objectives of communist rule. While the creation of a classless and thus egalitarian society was also an objective, the state itself undermined its realization by tying redistribution to identity politics. The socialist state recognized and honoured certain status and identity groups, but not others. According to the political logic of the communists, policies of recognition also served to redress past injustices, for instance, by giving preference to workers or in certain (rare) situations to members of ethnic minorities. Individuals could justify claims against the state by emphasizing their membership in those groups that the state regarded as essential to a common identity. Indeed, only through reference to affiliations of identity could their claims bear the seal of ideological conformity, since a politics of class could not be articulated in a society that was by definition classless and in which an authoritarian state claimed to guarantee the satisfaction of all material interests. When a politics of class was articulated, it led to repression, as the left experienced in Yugoslavia in the late 1960s and early 1970s.[132] Sociologist Zsusza Gille has written in this regard:

> In fact, demands for larger shares of the pie were anathema because of the official expropriation of any and all arguments about economic inequalities, so that asking for higher wages or better provisions from one's employer or the municipal government had to be couched not in terms of class or economic contribution but in terms of status (motherhood, proletarian origins, etc.) or political loyalty (membership in various official organisations).[133]

The politics of recognition that communist regimes employed as a means of social policy affected the identifications and subjectivities of socialist citizens. The official categories of social differentiation and status ascription can be found in numerous 'ego-documents'. In petitions and complaints – a frequently used and formalized channel for articulating dissatisfaction – complainants and petitioners regularly framed their lives in official terms in order to lend weight to their claims. They emphasized their political heritage, the contribution their families had made to the fight against Fascism and for the proletarian revolution, their long-time membership in communist organizations, etc. In this way, they made use of the positive integration opportunities provided by the regime, and if they had more precise knowledge, they also employed the regime's logic of sanctions. The use of these tropes in self-presentation followed a strategic calculus: to paraphrase Stephen Kotkin, the population had learned to 'speak Bolshevik'.[134] This pragmatic calculus, however, was often grounded in actual convictions that had resulted from an appropriation of official ideology, which the state disseminated at every possible opportunity through an extensive propaganda apparatus. Scholars have already examined these internalization processes for the Soviet Union in the 1920s and 1930s by analyzing diaries.[135] Golfo

---

132 Boris Kanzleiter, *'Rote Universität': Studentenbewegung und Linksopposition in Belgrad 1964–1975* (Hamburg: VSA, 2011).

133 Zsuzsa Gille, 'Is there a Global Postsocialist Condition?', *Global Society* 24, no. 1 (2010): 9–30, here 18.

134 Stephen Kotkin, *Magnetic Mountain: Stalinism as a Civilization* (Berkeley, CA: University of California Press, 1995), 198–227.

135 Jochen Hellbeck, *Revolution on My Mind: Writing a Diary under Stalin* (Cambridge, MA: Harvard University Press: 2006); Irina Paperno, *Stories of the Soviet Experience: Memoirs, Diaries, Dreams* (Ithaca, NY: Cornell University Press, 2009).

Alexopoulous has also used material from the period of Soviet Stalinism to demonstrate that people whose civil rights had been revoked because of (ostensible) political disloyalty or 'false' class affiliation (so-called *lishentsy*) regularly portrayed their heritage and lives in their own petitions for rehabilitation using the models that the regime had presented as the ideal type of a 'Soviet citizen'.[136] Diaries and petitions, as well as interviews made after the end of socialism indicate analogous processes in other socialist countries.

The official policies of distinction that defined specific identity groups and assigned them different spaces within (or even outside) the socialist social order were among the fundamental determining factors of socialist statehood. They determined how the state acted towards its own citizens and how it treated them differently; at the same time, they also greatly influenced how people understood the state and how they acted towards it. For citizens interacting with the state, it was enormously important whom they perceive as the state. Furthermore, status ascriptions gave rise to inequalities in terms of economic resources and – perhaps even more importantly – social resources, which could maximize or minimize an individual's manoeuvring room even with regard to the state. These patterns of interaction, however, should not be understood as stable and rigid arrangements, not merely because the recognition practices set by the regime changed over time, but also because there was a learning process among the people, who used the knowledge they had gained through daily experience to exploit the numerous aporia within the state order for their own purposes. Social anthropologist Gerald Creed coined the phrase 'domesticating the revolution' to describe this appropriation process.[137] As a result of such domestication, the actual social relations never corresponded with the original intentions. This chasm between political goals and social realities, characteristic of every modern state, was also evident in socialist states.

Citizenship

Our interpretation of state socialist statehood thus requires an analysis of the regulations and practices through which the state divided the population and granted different possibilities – formally established or tacitly implemented – for enjoying the fruits of citizenship (in the sense of T.H. Marshall's 'social citizenship').[138] The state itself regarded the concept of citizenship as an extensive bundle of relations between citizens and the state, as is evident in the Law on Romanian Citizenship of 1971, the first article of which reads:

> In the Socialist Republic of Romania, a sovereign, independent and unitary state, Romanian citizenship is the expression of socio-economic, political and juridical relations between the physical persons and the socialist state and constitutes an attribute of honour and of great civic responsibility.[139]

One central issue regarding the inclusive and exclusive dimensions of the dominant conception of citizenship concerns the legal aspect: who was entitled to protection from the state and to

---

136 Golfo Alexopoulos, *Stalin's Outcasts: Aliens, Citizens, and the Soviet State, 1926–1936* (Ithaca, NY: Cornell University Press, 2003).

137 Gerald W. Creed, *Domesticating Revolution: From Socialist Reform to Ambivalent Transition in a Bulgarian Village* (University Park, PA: Pennsylvania State University Press, 1998).

138 Marshall, *Citizenship and Social Class.*

139 Günther Tontsch, *Die Rechtsstellung des Ausländers in Rumänien*, Schriftenreihe zur Rechtsstellung des Ausländers in den sozialistischen Staaten 2 (Baden-Baden: Nomos, 1975), 97. Original law: Legea nr.24 din 17 decembrie 1971 privind cetățenia română, *Monitorul Oficial*. nr. 157, 17 December 1971.

Statehood in socialism

state benefits? Who was allowed to vote? There has not as yet been any systematic and comparative analysis of citizenship laws in socialist states; nevertheless, we can confirm in general that these laws were quite restrictive in granting state citizenship to non-citizens, which was also an expression of the general scepticism among communist regimes toward international immigrants. The principle of *ius sanguinis* (right of blood), for instance, was used in Czechoslovakia, which unified its laws on gaining and losing citizenship in 1949.[140] In Romania, citizenship was also acquired primarily at birth and, as stated in the Romanian citizenship law, was 'as an expression of the ties between parents and children, the uninterrupted continuity of generations on the ancestral soil who fought for the fulfilment of the ideals of social and national freedom.'[141] The legal systems of communist countries also recognized the possibility of expatriation, to which dissidents and refugees, for example, were subject. The most radical measures excluding entire groups from citizenship were the legal regulations expelling Germans from Poland, Yugoslavia and Czechoslovakia immediately after the Second World War (in Czechoslovakia this occurred before the communists established their monopoly of power).[142] Italians in Yugoslavia and Hungarians in Czechoslovakia suffered similar fates.

Ethnic affiliation

Ethnic affiliation was also one of the essential criteria in state socialism that determined the relationship between state and citizen. The salience of ethnicity in organizing relations between the state and its citizens underscores the fact that socialist states were nation-building states. Although the communist regimes all had different starting points, they nevertheless pursued the common goal of integrating society according to nationality (or within specific national territories beneath the state level) – a process that by definition also implied exclusionary practices. This accorded with the contemporary ideological mainstream of the communist movement, which saw the world as composed of nations. It also implied the establishment of nations where none yet existed, for instance, the Macedonians and the Bosnian Muslims in Yugoslavia, whereby Yugoslav communists primarily used the instruments of nation-building developed by the Bolshevists in the 1920s.[143] Both Poland and Czechoslovakia launched enormous propaganda campaigns depicting the territories that they had recently acquired, or from which Germans had recently been expelled, as always having been Polish or Czechoslovak.

These discourses can be seen as representative of efforts by socialist states to situate themselves within a long continuity (despite the emphasis on the revolutionary transformation initiated by the communist seizure of power), whereby the state was attributed a timeless dimension. In Albania and Romania, the genealogies produced by official agencies extended back into early antiquity, although the issue was imagining not only a prolonged history, but also a specific state form. Nicolae Ceaușescu, for instance, presented himself in the tradition of a Dacian and medi-

---

140 Karin Schmid, *Staatsangehörigkeitsprobleme der Tschechoslowakei: Eine Untersuchung sowie Dokumente zur Staatsangehörigkeit der deutschen Volkszugehörigen* (Berlin: Berlin-Verlag, 1979), 51.

141 Tontsch, *Die Rechtsstellung des Ausländers in Rumänien*, 98.

142 For the corresponding legal provisions in the ČSSR, see Schmid, *Staatsangehörigkeitsprobleme der Tschechoslowakei*, 39–41; for Poland, see Georg Geilke, *Das Staatsangehörigkeitsrecht von Polen* (Frankfurt a.M.: Metzler, 1952); for Yugoslavia, see Michael Portmann, *Die kommunistische Revolution in der Vojvodina 1944–1952: Politik, Gesellschaft, Wirtschaft, Kultur*, 1st ed. (Vienna: Verlag der Österreichischen Akademie der Wissenschaft, 2008), 225–57.

143 See Ulf Brunnbauer and Hannes Grandits, eds, *The Ambiguous Nation: Case Studies from Southeastern Europe in the Twentieth Century* (München: Oldenbourg, 2013).

eval prince ruling an ostensibly unified Romanian state.[144] In the self-representations of socialist countries, state and nation coincided as a rule (although in the federations this was the case only as long as Unitarian conceptions predominated, that is, in Yugoslavia until the late 1950s and in the ČSSR until 1968). Open questions about recognizing post-war borders (especially Poland's western border) and bilateral conflicts (for example, between Bulgaria and Yugoslavia or Romania and Hungary) also reinforced tendencies of national separation and self-assertion, especially in academic disciplines susceptible to this, such as history and ethnology.[145] If governments suspected that certain minorities might potentially have loyalties to another state, that is, to another ostensible 'motherland', then a clear correlation usually developed between the condition of bilateral relations between these two countries and the treatment of the minority in question.

While communist regimes did espouse the equality of all nationalities, they understood very different things by this and did not shy away from abandoning this principle when they thought it politically opportune. The policy of recognizing ethnic difference was characterized by great ambivalence, which was due, on the one hand, to the discrepancy between ideological claims and political reality, and, on the other, to fundamental policy changes and the accompanying differences of opinion within the power apparatus. The intensity of this ambiguity is evident in the fact that socialist states adopted very different paths in this realm of policy. One tendency can be seen in Czechoslovakia and Yugoslavia, where federal structures were reinforced significantly in the late 1960s and early 1970s: whereas Yugoslavia assumed features of a confederation following the constitution of 1974, the federation in Czechoslovakia had Unitarian features. The constitutive units of the two federations possessed legislative capacities in different areas which, particularly in Yugoslavia, led to clear distinctions in the legal systems of the individual republics and provinces.[146] Decentralization, however, by no means meant democratization. On the contrary, the process of (con)federation occurred in both countries during a period of increased political repression. On the one hand, power was supposed to be more diffused institutionally in order to impede imputations of responsibility and the mobilization of political opposition to the centre. On the other hand, party leadership hoped that strengthening decentralized authorities would lead citizens to identify more strongly with their regional bodies and promote the incorporation of local elites. From this point onwards in the ČSSR and the Socialist Federal Republic of Yugoslavia (SFRY), people were citizens of their respective republic and – through this – of the entire nation. The official expectation was that people would identify with both levels of federal statehood.[147]

---

144 Katherine Verdery, *National Ideology under Socialism: Identity and Cultural Politics in Ceausescu's Romania* (Berkeley, CA: University of California Press, 1991).

145 See for instance Stefan Troebst, *Die bulgarisch-jugoslawische Kontroverse um Makedonien 1967–1982* (München: Oldenbourg, 1983); Wim P. van Meurs, *The Bessarabian Question in Communist Historiography: Nationalist and Communist Politics and History-Writing* (New York: East European Monographs; Distributed by Columbia University Press, 1994); László Kürti, *The Remote Borderland: Transylvania in the Hungarian Imagination* (Albany, NY: SUNY Press, 2001).

146 The literature on Yugoslav federalism is extensive. See, for example, Sabrina Ramet, *Nationalism and Federalism in Yugoslavia, 1963–1983* (Bloomington, IN: Indiana University Press, 1984); Monika Beckmann-Petey, *Der jugoslawische Föderalismus* (München: Oldenbourg, 1990). On the ČSSR see Joachim Amm, *Die Föderalversammlung der CSSR: Sozialistischer Parlamentarismus im unitarischen Föderalismus 1969–1989* (Wiesbaden: Westdeutscher Verlag, 2001).

147 See Christine Kreuzer, *Staatsangehörigkeit und Staatensukzession: Die Bedeutung der Staatensukzession für die staatsangehörigkeitsrechtlichen Regelungen in den Staaten der ehemaligen Sowjetunion Jugoslawiens und der Tschechoslowakei* (Berlin: Duncker & Humblot, 1998).

Statehood in socialism

Especially in Yugoslavia, state and party leadership sought to provide a coherent ideological justification for the federal organization of the state, which was constructed as the expression of a hierarchy of rights qua nationality: members of a 'people' (*narod*) were entitled to their own republic, whereas 'nationalities' (*narodnost*) and 'ethnic groups' (*etnička grupa*) were not, but were also granted specific nationality rights. Entirely in the tradition of Soviet nationality policies, the rights of the different national groups in Yugoslavia were closely tied to language use and adequate representation in the state apparatus: for example, Albanians living in Kosovo were granted very different rights on the basis of their nationality than Albanians living in Slovenia. Ethnicity was an important, formalized administrative category that, depending on the region, (co-)determined access and opportunities to jobs, positions of power and education. Another peculiarity of Yugoslav decentralization was that it was driven not only by nationality policies, but also followed the ideological logic of self-administration that had marked the independent Yugoslav path to socialism since its break with the Soviet Union in 1948. Yugoslav communists regarded self-administration as a way of overcoming traditional statehood while simultaneously maintaining their monopoly on power.[148] All social institutions and economic enterprises were organized as 'self-administered' entities that made contracts among themselves. Here the Yugoslav leadership deviated from the principle of the planned economy and yet organized responsibilities in such a complicated way that social and economic reproduction was increasingly dependent on informal relations.

In contrast to Yugoslavia and Czechoslovakia, the trend to an increasingly rigid interpretation of minority rights was evident in Romania and Bulgaria. In both of these countries, the communist government had implemented liberal policies toward minorities during its initial years of rule, in part to distinguish itself from the previous regime. In Romania, the areas settled by Hungarians were even granted regional autonomy. In Bulgaria, the regime created a Soviet-style secular Turkish intelligentsia. However, in Romania beginning in the mid-1950s and in Bulgaria beginning in the early 1960s, leaders of the two countries increasingly pushed nationalist discourses intended to bolster their legitimacy; this was also evident in Romania in foreign policy which sought to emancipate the country from the Soviet Union. One clear expression of this policy change was the successive reduction of autonomy for the Hungarian territory, before it was completely revoked in 1968. The Romanian secret police, Securitate, monitored particularly closely those minorities that continued to enjoy particular rights (e.g. regarding the use of language). Beginning in the 1970s the Romanian government also promoted the emigration of Germans and Jews.[149] In Bulgaria the regime went even further, subjecting Muslim minorities in the country to a radical assimilation policy after the Bulgarian Constitution of 1971 had formalized the concept of a 'unified socialist nation' and no longer even mentioned minorities. In 1984 the Turkish minority in Bulgaria (around 10 per cent of the total population) was suddenly declared ethnically Bulgarian: they were not allowed to use the Turkish language and were forbidden from practising their religion. Members of this minority, whose existence the party leadership now denied, were issued new personal documents in which their Turkish-Arabic names had been changed to Bulgarian ones.

---

148 Wolfgang Höpken, *Sozialismus und Pluralismus in Jugoslawien: Entwicklung und Demokratiepotential des Selbstverwaltungssystems* (München: Oldenbourg, 1984).

149 Rainer Ohliger and Cătălin Turliuc, 'Minorities into Migrants: Emigration and Ethnic Unmixing in Twentieth-Century Romania', in *European Encounters: Migrants, Migration and European Societies since 1945*, eds Reiner Ohlinger, Karen Schönwälder and Triadafilos Triadafilopoulos (Aldershot: Ashgate, 2003), 53–70.

Ethnic discrimination was not always as overt as in Bulgaria. Frequently it was also the result of social policy measures that affected various ethnic groups differently. One example of this – also typical because it concerned a population group with specific experiences of marginalization throughout the entire region – was the regulation of childcare leave in Hungary in 1967: women who could prove they had worked full-time for at least twelve months were entitled to childcare leave. Since only a minority of Romany women had any kind of employment, the majority of them did not receive paid childcare leave.[150] Although such inequalities were not always intentional, the consequences nevertheless point to a political agenda that was clearly oriented around an ideal constructed in terms of majority society and did not take into account the fact that the planned measures would necessarily have different consequences on population groups that did not accord with this ideal.

Social policy

Communist regimes used nation building and the associated practices of representation and intervention as an instrument to shape society according to their ideals. This also led to manifestations of the state in everyday contexts of interaction and communication as well as the production of inclusion and exclusion. Social policy was another means with similar goals and consequences. Despite significant common ground, there was also great variation in social policy among the individual socialist states resulting from different institutional and conceptual heritages, social structures and political styles.[151] Communist social policy possessed a dual nature: it was part of a long-term societal policy that aimed at transforming structures of social reproduction; but it was also a means for the state to provide short-term assistance for what decision makers and experts perceived as social problems.[152] Which of these two goals had priority changed over time and varied from country to country. Through social policy measures, the state made clear its explicit or implicit orientations by granting specific categories of people greater or fewer rights. Social policy was also a powerful instrument for expanding the presence of the state into the everyday lives of individuals. From the perspective of citizens, the state was not only an authority that established norms and sanctions, but also a powerful and virtually omnipresent social actor. By inserting itself into the lives of its citizens, the state achieved social legitimation, since at least those groups privileged by the state developed their own interest in the state's continued existence, or so the party leadership hoped.

At the same time, social policy illustrates the inherent heterogeneity and ambivalence of socialist statehood, as the state was not a monolithic actor: through the nationalization of the economy – which varied from country to country, but nevertheless left but little manoeuvring room for formal private-sector activities – the state became by far the most important employer or even the exclusive employer. Many social services were not supplied directly by state institutions, but rather by state-owned enterprises (in Yugoslavia the situation was even more complicated because enterprises there were not state-owned but 'social property', and

---

150 Eszter Varsa, 'Class, Ethnicity and Gender – Structures of Differentiation in State Socialist Employment and Welfare Politics, 1960–1980: The Issue of Women's Employment and the Introduction of the First Maternity Leave Regulation in Hungary', in *Need and Care – Glimpses into the Beginnings of Eastern Europe's Professional Welfare*, eds Kurt Schilde and Dagmar Schulte (Opladen: Budrich, 2005), 197–217, here 213.

151 Inglot, *Welfare States in East Central Europe*, 119–210.

152 See Zsuzsa Ferge, *A Society in the Making* (Harmondsworth: Penguin, 1979), 47.

Statehood in socialism

over time the principle of self-administration was expanded from industrial enterprises to every kind of institution). The nationalization of the providers of diverse welfare benefits also meant a unification of social policy into the hands of the government, but at the same time, increased the number of state actors in this domain (Yugoslavia was also an exception in this respect due to the successive transfer of social welfare to municipalities starting in the 1960s).[153] Given the diversity of nominal state actors, an analysis of the inclusionary and exclusionary dimensions of social policy in socialist states cannot focus solely on the classical instruments of social policy, such as social insurance and social transfers, but also has to include the level of enterprises. In state socialism, enterprises were much more than merely employers; they were central institutions of socialization. However, the social benefits and opportunities they could offer their employees depended greatly on their size and their position in the politically defined allocation hierarchy of state investments and subsidies.[154]

The centrality of enterprises for social policy reflects the overriding significance that the communists attributed to labour as the basis for social participation and for claims made on the state. What Lynne Haney has written about Hungary can be generalized: 'At the heart of the Hungarian societal policy regime were its full employment provisions.'[155] It is telling that after the reorganization of governmental authorities at the end of the 1940s, labour ministries were responsible for social welfare in countries such as Poland, Romania and Bulgaria.[156] Marx's principle 'from each according to his abilities, to each according to his needs'[157] held sway, although determining which needs the state should recognize depended on changing political priorities. For example, in times of pronatalism (see section below titled 'Life trajectories and the state') motherhood – in comparison to employment – played an increasingly significant role in the allocation of social benefits.

The workers' state

During the first two decades of communist rule, state social policy in the broader sense was clearly oriented around the ideal of the industrial worker, who was seen as the embodiment of the vision of the 'new man'. In order to realize this vision, the state implemented a variety of concrete measures, from education and propaganda to the configuration of wages and social benefits. Especially during the initial years of communist rule, regimes focused on an intensive and extensive mobilization of all forces in order to establish and expand industry. Through propaganda, coercion and wage policies that made the single income model untenable for 'nor-

---

153 Marina Ajduković and Vanja Branica, 'Some Reflections on Social Work in Croatia (1945–1989)', in *Social Care Under State Socialism (1945–1989): Ambitions, Ambiguities, and Mismanagement*, ed. Sabine Hering (Opladen: Budrich, 2009), 249–64, here 255.

154 See Lynne A. Haney, *Inventing the Needy: Gender and the Politics of Welfare in Hungary* (Berkeley, CA: University of California Press, 2002), 108–10; Dagmara Jajeśniak-Quast, *Stahlgiganten in der sozialistischen Transformation: Nowa Huta in Krakau, EKO in Eisenhüttenstadt und Kunčice in Ostrava* (Wiesbaden: Harrassowitz, 2010).

155 Lynne Haney, 'Familial Welfare: Building the Hungarian Welfare Society, 1948–1968', *Social Politics* 7, no. 1 (2000): 101–22, here 105.

156 Kristina Popova, 'The Development of Social Care in Bulgaria (1945–1989)', in Hering, *Social Care Under State Socialism*, 24–34, here 25; Lenka Kalinová, 'Conditions and Stages of Change in the Social Security System in Czechoslovakia (1945–1989)', in Hering, *Social Care Under State Socialism*, 65–78, here 68; Maria Roth et al., 'The Romanian Social System between 1945 and 1989', in Hering, *Social Care Under State Socialism*, 189–200, here 190.

157 Gieseke, 'Soziale Ungleichheit im Staatssozialismus', 4.

mal' employees, the state was in fact able to incorporate labour resources into wage employment within a relatively short time and thereby approach its goal of transforming society into a body working for the triumph of communism. All adults capable of work were obligated to engage in paid labour until they reached retirement age; and states, in turn, guaranteed the right to work in their constitutions. For this reason, governments saw no need to provide special support benefits for the unemployed, who instead were stigmatized as asocial (the exception was Yugoslavia, where steadily rising unemployment was officially recognized starting in the early 1960s). The safeguards for people who for various reasons were unemployed were completely inadequate.

The paternalistic care of the state focused on people with jobs since the socialist welfare state was guided by the assumption of full employment and regarded achieving this as its primary objective.[158] For some social groups that had been poorly integrated into wage labour – such as women or members of the large Romany minority in the region – the massive pressure from the state to participate in wage labour marked an important step toward social inclusion, measured by access to civil rights acquired through wage labour. Precisely in regard to the female population, the socialist state considered its promise of emancipation, which was legally guaranteed in the constitution, to be essentially fulfilled by the integration of women into wage labour. To achieve this, the state created numerous specific benefits, especially in the realm of childcare. As a result, women were particularly dependent on the state to maintain their employment – a politically intended consequence in the sense of cultivating a particular social group's interest in preserving the existing system.[159] At the same time, state-driven proletarianization also worked to exclude or render déclassé former bourgeois elites: elites and their progeny were often denied access to university study, for example, during the initial period of communist rule, in order to harmonize the social composition of future educated elites with the self-image of a workers' and peasants' state.

This revolutionary vector of communist labour policy, which had largely replaced social policy in the classical sense, gradually diminished beginning in the 1950s and gave way to societal regulation aiming at stability and micromanagement. One significant reason for this was the desire of new elites, who had in fact been recruited in many cases from (former) workers and peasants, to maintain their social position. This is the reason that social mobility declined significantly in the 1970s and 1980s. The individual strata of society began to reproduce itself on its own, as sociologists in socialist countries noted at the time.[160]

The centrality of employment in generating claims to social benefits was due primarily, but not exclusively, to the communist ideological tradition. Also evident was the heritage

---

158 Bob Deacon, ed., *The New Eastern Europe: Social Policy Past, Present and Future* (London: Sage, 1992), 4, 70.

159 Susan Gal and Gail Kligman, eds, *Reproducing Gender: Politics, Publics, and Everyday Life after Socialism* (Princeton, NJ: Princeton University Press, 2000); Susan Gal and Gail Kligman, *The Politics of Gender after Socialism: A Comparative Historical Essay* (Princeton, NJ: Princeton University Press, 2000).

160 For example, Krăstju Petkov, 'Socialnata mobilnost i văzproizvodstvoto na socialno-klasovata struktura v NRB' [Social mobility and the reproduction of the social class structure in the People's Republic of Bulgaria], *Sociologičeski problemi* 13, no. 4 (1981): 31–41; Stane Saksida, Andrej Caserman and Krešo Pretrović, 'Društvena stratifikacija i pokretljivost u jugoslovenskom društvu' [Social stratification and mobility in Yugoslav society], in *Elementi strukture jugoslavenskog društva: Klase i slojevi. Prilozi izučavanju društvenog sistema* (Zagreb: Filozofski fakultet, 1977), 53–92. See Raymond Sin-Kwok Wong and Robert Mason Hauser, *Trends in Occupational Mobility in Hungary under Socialism* (Madison, 1992: Center for Demography and Ecology, CDE, Working Paper, 3).

of a Bismarckian social insurance system, which had been predominant in Central and Eastern Europe and in which social benefits had been based on the payment of premiums that were usually tied to employment. In this respect, the initial exclusion of the farming population from retirement and health insurance was not only a manifestation of communist apathy toward farmers, but also the consistent continuation of a premiums-based social insurance model. Vocational groups that did not fit into the communist worldview, such as freelancers and – to the extent they still existed – small private entrepreneurs, were also excluded from social insurance benefits, not least to encourage them to adopt ideologically endorsed vocations.[161]

Pensions and social benefits

The heritage of the Bismarckian social insurance system was thus well suited for implementing social policy objectives. Employment alone was no longer decisive for determining entitlement claims, but rather the kind of employment: the party leadership made clear that social safeguards were to be understood as the 'reward for hard work'. In Czechoslovakia beginning in the early 1950s, for example, recently retired miners and workers in heavy industry received higher pensions than white-collar workers.[162] Through such measures the new regime sought to alter societal stratification through social policy. To this end party leadership used not only state benefits, but also taxes, which in fact were supposed to fulfil a steering function. For example, the massive tax increases on independent farmers were a way to encourage them to join agricultural cooperatives. Only when this failed to have the desired effect did regimes turn to forced collectivization.[163]

The development of the social insurance system during the era of state socialism reveals much about changes in the self-understanding of the state and the problems perceived by its ruling elite. The general trend in socialist states was to gradually expand the circle of recipients of social insurance benefits as well as the benefits paid out. There were several reasons for this expansion, which was by no means specific to socialist countries, but rather a general European trend. First of all, the restrictions on social benefits and the focus on mobilizing workers during the immediate post-war years had been due to specific (re)construction necessities after the war, along with the Stalinist push for class warfare under the motto 'dictatorship of the proletariat'. The mass protests in several countries of the region in the mid-1950s had arisen primarily in response to this austerity policy aimed at industrialization, which had resulted in lower living standards around 1950 than before the war in countries such as Hungary and Czechoslovakia, in part because a number of social benefits from the state were lower in 1950 than they had been in the 1930s.[164] With the end of reconstruction and the beginning of (in part very substantial) economic growth in the 1950s and 60s, the fiscal scope for social policy expanded. Furthermore, the party leadership and their experts had learned from experience that the communist revolution and the implementation of a planned economy did not render obsolete all of

---

161 On Hungary see, for example, Hanna Szemző, 'The Hungarian Pension System, 1948–1990: Welfare and Politics in a Socialist Country in its European Context' (PhD diss., Central European University, 2012), www.etd.ceu.hu/2013/hphszh01.pdf, 40.

162 Inglot, *Welfare States in East Central Europe*, 135.

163 The paradigmatic and best investigated case is Romania; see Gail Kligman and Katherine Verdery, eds, *Peasants Under Siege: The Collectivization of Romanian Agriculture, 1949–1962* (Princeton, NJ: Princeton University Press, 2011).

164 Dorottya Szikra, 'Social Policy Under State Socialism in Hungary (1949–1956)', in Hering, *Social Care Under State Socialism*, 141–8, here 144.

the traditional objectives of social policy; rather they perceived different social problems, which they sought to alleviate through specific social policy measures.[165]

During this period, the extension of social benefits and the harmonization of entitlements were essential means for (re)establishing the legitimacy of communist rule. The expansion of the circle of people entitled to social insurance benefits followed the employment-oriented logic of the system. This was particularly evident in the successive inclusion of the agricultural population, which after the collectivization of agriculture was no longer regarded as consisting of individual farmers, but rather wage-earning cooperative members who were therefore qualified for social insurance benefits such as old-age pensions. In Hungary, for example, this process began in 1949, when cooperative members became entitled to family allowances and ended in 1975 with a new social security law that unified the pension funds for industrial workers, clerical workers and members of agricultural cooperatives. In 1980 the retirement age for cooperative members was finally lowered to the standard level.[166] The expansion of social benefits to collectivized farmers, however, was also the result of efforts to halt the rural exodus by improving living conditions in the countryside. In Poland, on the contrary, where agriculture was not collectivized, independent farmers were not included in the pension system until 1965 and even then only at a very modest pension level.[167] Social benefits for blue- and white-collar workers became equal in Poland in 1968.[168] Despite this general trend toward more equality in the realm of social insurance benefits, privileges continued to exist to varying extents from country to country, for example, special pensions for certain groups that were particularly cherished by the regime, such as the military or 'commendable fighters' (e.g. Second World War resistance veterans). There was also unequal access to scarce goods that was positively correlated to proximity to the power centre; the state, in other words, privileged those people who ensured its rule, that is, the 'power-securing elite'.[169]

The socialist pension systems showed some parallels with the pension systems of continental Western Europe, leading to a rising share of pensions among state welfare expenditure. Although pensions remained below the average levels of the Organisation for Economic Co-operation and Development (OECD) countries – with the exception of Hungary – average replacement rates increased overall: in the ČSSR in 1982 they were approximately 45 per cent of the average salary, and in Hungary approximately 52 per cent.[170] The expanding group of people entitled to pension claims combined with demographic developments led to a clear increase in the total amounts paid out for pensions by the state or by social insurance. While expenditures for pensions in Poland, Czechoslovakia and Hungary were between 1 and 3 per cent of the gross social product in the late 1940s, these figures rose to between 10 and 15 per cent in the 1980s, with an increasingly large portion coming from the state budget because pension contributions from employers were insufficient (since most enterprises were state-owned, the state played a significantly greater role overall in social insurance than in Western coun-

---

165 See Peter Hübner, Christa Hübner and Christoph Boyer, *Sozialismus als soziale Frage: Sozialpolitik in der DDR und Polen, 1968–1976* (Köln: Böhlau, 2008), 474.

166 Szemző, 'The Hungarian Pension System', 157–8; Béla Tomka, *Welfare in East and West: Hungarian Social Security in an International Comparison 1918–1990* (Berlin: Akademie Verlag, 2004), 82.

167 Inglot, *Welfare States in East Central Europe*, 160.

168 Hübner, Hübner and Boyer, *Sozialismus als soziale Frage*, 51.

169 Gieseke, 'Soziale Ungleichheit im Staatssozialismus', 6.

170 Tomka, *Welfare in East and West*, 82.

171 Inglot, *Welfare States in East Central Europe*, 123.

tries).[171] In Hungary the state directly financed 43.6 per cent of pension payments in 1980.[172] A significant factor in this development was the low retirement age (usually, 60 for men and 55 for women, but in Czechoslovakia, the ages were 57 and 53 for men and women, respectively; in Yugoslavia it was even lower at 55 and 50).[173] Despite the increasing life expectancy rate, retirement ages were not adjusted upwards. Thus, the number of pensioners rose considerably: for example, in Czechoslovakia from 2.2 million in 1960 to 3 million a decade later.[174]

Despite the evident shortfall in welfare provisions, total expenditures continued to rise to increasingly large sums: money transfers for families, which especially expanded in the 1960s; the cost of non-financial social benefits (childcare, medical care); as well as subsidies for food that were also subsumed under 'social consumption'. These were financed in part through growing debt to the West. Some political elites and especially social and fiscal policy experts warned that this was not a burden the state could carry long-term. Such fears were exacerbated by demographic projections, for example in Czechoslovakia, where in the mid-1960s it was estimated that people of retirement age would increase to about 23 per cent of the entire population by 2000.[175] Company managers also complained about the great burden on enterprises due to the money and other means they had to have available for a broad range of social benefits: childcare centres, vacation homes and sanatoriums, living quarters, facilities and materials for diverse recreational activities and at times, even monetary payments for employees with special emergencies.[176] Given the repeated problems in plan fulfilment, many enterprises would have preferred to use these funds for investments (in contrast, large, well-financed enterprises regarded the social benefits they were able to offer as an attractive recruitment tool given the scarcity of workers in most of the socialist economies beginning in the 1960s and the accompanying workforce fluctuations).[177]

In the course of the 1980s there were increasing calls in socialist countries for a reduction of social benefits, in part because the option of loans from the West was no longer available and the economic outlook became increasingly bleak. Extensive cuts, however, were implemented only by Romanian dictator Nicolae Ceauşescu, who pushed through a radical austerity policy with the goal of early foreign debt relief. As a result, consumption levels and social benefits declined significantly in Romania in the 1980s, as did pension levels (a development that seriously undermined the legitimacy of the system).[178] In Poland there were also calls for

---

172 Tomka, *Welfare in East and West*, 93.

173 Inglot, *Welfare States in East Central Europe*, 75; Diana Auth, 'Welfare States and Gender in Central and Eastern Europe: The Current State of Research and Prospective Research', in *Welfare States and Gender Inequality in Central and Eastern Europe: Continuity and Post-Socialist Transformation in the EU Member States*, eds Christina Klenner and Simone Leiber (Brussels: ETUI, 2010), 33–56, here 48; Hannes Grandits, 'Kinship and the Welfare State in Twentieth-Century Croatian Transitions', in *Family, Kinship and State in Contemporary Europe*, vol. 1, *The Century of Welfare: Eight Countries*, ed. Hannes Grandits (Frankfurt a.M.: Campus, 2010), 249–82, here 253.

174 Kalinová, 'Conditions and Stages of Change', 74.

175 Hübner, Hübner and Boyer, *Sozialismus als soziale Frage*, 489.

176 Éva Bicskei, "Our Greatest Treasure, the Child': The Politics of Child Care in Hungary, 1945–1956', *Social Politics* 13, no. 2 (2006): 151–88, here 174; Barbara Klich-Kluczewska, 'Social Policy and Social Practice in the People's Republic of Poland', in Hering, *Social Care Under State Socialism*, 161–73, here 166.

177 On fluctuations in the workforce, see Charles F. Sabel and David Stark, 'Planning, Politics, and Shop-Floor Power: Hidden Forms of Bargaining in Soviet-Imposed State-Socialist Societies', *Politics and Society* 11, no. 4 (1982): 439–75.

178 C. Ban, 'Sovereign Debt, Austerity, and Regime Change: The Case of Nicolae Ceausescu's Romania', *East European Politics & Societies* 26, no. 4 (2012): 743–76. Even the doctored data in the statistical yearbook of Romania registered a decline in living standards in the 1980s.

a reduction as well as stricter needs assessment for social benefits, but ultimately the Jaruzelski regime limited such cuts for obvious reasons, and those cuts that were made affected relatively insignificant programmes for weaker population groups. It was not until early 1989 that a comprehensive reform bill on social security was passed by the ministerial council. In Hungary and Czechoslovakia in the second half of the 1980s, a growing number of experts called for a reform of the welfare state (which would imply a reduction in benefits) and thereby discursively paved the way for the rapid dismantling of the welfare state that occurred after the end of communist rule.[179] Even in Bulgaria, state and party leader Todor Zhivkov complained at the end of the 1980s about the sense of entitlement among the population, which expected everything from the state, but could not be mobilized for the advocated reconstruction (*preustrojstvo*). At the end of communist rule, the state had lost its aura of unquestionability, at least among reform-oriented communists.[180]

Life trajectories and the state

As became evident in the preceding remarks about social policy, the ideologues of communist regimes and their bureaucrats had a clear notion about how the lives of 'normal' citizens should be organized. The ideas and administrative practices of the ideal socialist life trajectory incorporated attenuated versions of the Soviet vision of the 'new man' adapted to each country as well as to the local traditions of preceding *Lebensreform* movements.[181] Norms and administrative categories typical of modern states were also established, including attempts to legally regulate intra-familial relations. As Daniela Koleva has emphasized, given the widespread absence of intermediary social organizations and the instrumentalization of existing social organizations by the state, citizens, in almost all of their roles, were supposed to refer to the state and to the rules it set for them.[182] Even people's needs were defined by the state, which promised to satisfy them in turn.[183] The goal of policies regarding an ideal life trajectory was to shape the citizens of the socialist state, make them dependent on the state and subordinate them to the state's development objectives. The ruling regimes hoped that the population would internalize the values of socialism or communism – the terms changed over time and from country to country – and would thus know without much thought what the 'correct' – that is, 'socialist' or 'communist' – decision would be in any particular situation. The issue was thus producing legitimacy in the sense that actual citizen's lives were supposed to align with the ideological structures of the regime.

An extensive administrative and ideological apparatus conveyed to citizens the state's views about the ideal life of an individual and ensured that deviations from the postulated norms were stigmatized and sanctioned. It goes without saying that the school system was one of the most

---

179 On these debates, see Inglot, *Welfare States in East Central Europe*, 146, 173, 193.

180 Johanna Bockman takes this further and argues that predominance of neo-liberalism after 1989 was rooted in part in market-oriented reform debates during state socialism; see Johanna Bockman, *Markets in the Name of Socialism: The Left-Wing Origins of Neoliberalism* (Stanford, CA: Stanford University Press, 2011).

181 On Soviet debates about the 'new man' that articulated and developed ideas that also proved significant for further communist regimes, see Stefan Plaggenborg, *Revolutionskultur: Menschenbilder und kulturelle Praxis in Sowjetrußland zwischen Oktoberrevolution und Stalinismus* (Köln: Böhlau, 1996).

182 Daniela Koleva, ed., *Negotiating Normality: Everyday Lives in Socialist Institutions* (New Brunswick: Transaction, 2012), xiv.

183 Ferenc Fehér, Agnes Heller and György Márkus, *Dictatorship over Needs* (Oxford: Blackwell, 1983).

Statehood in socialism

important institutions in creating the model citizen, as schools in general have served the modern state not only as transmitters of knowledge but also as shaping and disciplining authorities. In addition to schools, there was a broad network of further education programmes – organized especially by mass organizations active in the workplace and in residential areas – that translated ideological goals and norms into concrete, everyday guidelines. Although the political dimension of these educational events may have inspired little enthusiasm among the intended addressees,[184] the events nevertheless brought the population closer to contemporary ideological trends, making citizens aware of the official frame of reference for their actions. The diverse educational and recreational programmes of mass organizations also provided citizens with an opportunity to take part in activities that were not explicitly ideological and thus to engage in the performance of participation.[185]

It was important for the socialist state to maintain the ideological chimera that citizens actively participated in the continuing development of socialism as well as in their own self-improvement. The work *for* socialism was always also supposed to be work *on* one's self. Finally, it should also be noted that the state tended to mark its own presence in peoples' lives, for instance, by suppressing or even prohibiting religious life-cycle ceremonies, since the state claimed a monopoly on the loyalty of its population. Functionaries of the state, the party and mass organizations were supposed to replace priests at baptism (naming), marriage and burial ceremonies – a policy that different countries engaged in with varying degrees of success and with varying degrees of intensity, and through which regimes sought to symbolically colonize people's lives.

Values and norms

The values and ideals underlying official notions of the correct way of life were relatively homogeneous in socialist states, although there were also clear differences of focus in ideology and practice over time and in different countries. The characteristics of the ideal socialist citizen that were typically emphasized by party and state ideologues throughout the socialist bloc included: subordination of individual interests to those of the collective; discipline, orderliness and responsibility; cleanliness and morality; education and social engagement; industriousness and ambition; and restraint and solidarity. Overall, the policies of standardizing one's life trajectory were based on petty-bourgeois notions that left no room for non-traditional ways of life. The most significant change at the ideological-normative level occurred in the 1950s, when the ascetic ideal – replete with battle metaphors – of the worker sacrificing himself for communism was replaced by a more civil model focusing on family, vocation and civic engagement as well as individual self-improvement.

---

184 On the modest popularity of political education by trade unions in the GDR, see for example, Anette Schumann, '"Macht die Betriebe zu Zentren der Kulturarbeit": Gewerkschaftlich organisierte Kulturarbeit in den Industriebetrieben der DDR in den fünfziger Jahren – Sozialhistorisches Novum oder Modifizierung betrieblicher Traditionen', in *Arbeiter im Staatssozialismus: ideologischer Anspruch und soziale Wirklichkeit*, eds Peter Hübner, Christoph Klessmann and Klaus Tenfelde (Vienna: Böhlau, 2005), 271–90; Jiři Pokorný, 'Die Betriebsklubs in der Tschechoslowakei 1945–1968: Zur Organisation sozialistischer Erziehung, Kultur und Erholung der Arbeiterschaft', in *Sozialgeschichtliche Kommunismusforschung: Tschechoslowakei, Polen, Ungarn, DDR 1945–1968*, eds Christiane Brenner and Peter Heumos (München: Oldenbourg, 2005), 263–76.

185 See Karin Taylor, *Let's Twist Again: Youth and Leisure in Socialist Bulgaria* (Vienna: LIT, 2006).

This change reflected the transformation from an economic and social policy that, in light of the necessities of reconstruction after the devastations of the Second World War and during the revolutionary transformation following the communist takeover, had emphasized the mobilization of all forces, intensive class warfare and mandatory reduced consumption to a policy that was, in its own words, oriented increasingly around the needs of the people and raising the general standard of living.[186] Finally, the state had realized that a permanently mobilized society was compatible neither with the ideal of planning nor with the establishment of normality. The riots and uprising in several socialist countries between 1953 and 1956 had also made clear to party leadership how little support they had among broad sections of society because their policies of austerity and physical violence had alienated the much-touted masses.

Hungarian intellectuals and dissidents György Konrád and Ivan Szelényi described this transformation of the communist party's vision of human beings as follows:

> The ideologues of the post-Stalin era are hard put to discern the revolutionary in this socialist private man and to demonstrate how he is the new human being of the new society, qualitatively different from every earlier type of personality. Their answer is the 'revolutionary of everyday life', to whom all radical or negative criticism is foreign, a constructive revolutionary distinguished from the average citizen by his steadiness and sense of responsibility in every area of life. He works harder, is more exemplary in his family life, drives his car more carefully, cultivates his garden more conscientiously, studies to get ahead, and never forgets that everything he has he owes to society; indeed, if others forget that, he will be quick to remind them of it.[187]

Although in post-Stalinism the state did not abandon its goal of shaping human beings according to its ideals, the intervention into personal life occurred less directly through parameters established by laws and social policies. There was a greater focus on peoples' needs and problems, which led in part to a renunciation of far-reaching transformations that exceeded social values and existing expectations. For instance, there were trends beginning in the mid-1950s (which will be described below) to articulate once again more traditional family ideals and gender notions.[188] During the course of 'normalization' in Czechoslovakia after the suppression of the Prague Spring, the official promise of a 'tranquil life' that the state guaranteed to citizens became the leitmotif of Czechoslovak communists' attempt to re-establish their own legitimacy and to publicly stigmatize dissidents as troublemakers.[189] Konrád and Szelényi described the Hungarian case as follows:

> In the post-Stalin era politics no longer comes in through the citizen's front door; the doorbell-ringing agitator has given way to the television screen. The total politicization of daily life has come to an end, and the sanctity of private life has been restored. Working hours are for working, not politics, and in your free time you can do what

---

186 For the example of the ČSSR, see Hübner, Hübner and Boyer, *Sozialismus als soziale Frage*, 474.

187 György Konrád and Ivan Szelényi, *The Intellectuals on the Road to Class Power*, translated by Andrew Arato and Richard E. Allen (Brighton: Harvester, 1979), 200–1.

188 Malgorzata Fidelis, 'Equality Through Protection: The Politics of Women's Employment in Postwar Poland 1945–1956', *Slavic Review* 63, no. 2 (2004): 301–24.

189 Paulina Bren, *The Greengrocer and his TV: The Culture of Communism after the 1968 Prague Spring* (Ithaca, NY: Cornell University Press, 2010).

you like. You can still get into trouble easily enough if you talk politics in your private life, but no harm will befall you if instead of politicking you take an interest in football, music, stamp-collecting, or pigeon-raising.[190]

However, even after the end of Stalinism the state by no means abandoned its objective of transforming society according to its ideals, which implied the establishment of particular life models. Social policy has always had socio-political objectives, which means that attempts to resolve concrete social problems, as they were perceived and defined by the state, was usually tied to transforming social structures permanently. The present was no longer entirely subordinated to achieving a bright communist future, but at the same time addressing problems in the here and now also meant working on the future.[191] Communist social policy makers abandoned the idea that the communist takeover and the nationalization of the economy – that is, material transformations – would automatically resolve social grievances of the past, and they rediscovered the necessity of social policy in the narrower sense. This proved to be a distinctly more sensitive instrument of steering and intervention than mass mobilization and terror.

The socialist state and the family

The family became both the central instrument and field of communist societal and social policy. For this reason, it is well suited for demonstrating the difficulty of distinguishing between the public and the private spheres in state socialism. In contrast to the view that what is public and what is private can be clearly distinguished, an analysis of family policy shows the political dimension of notions of the private, as well as the ways in which personalized relations permeated the public sphere. As Lynne Haney has emphasized in her case study of women in Hungary, when individuals articulated their claims, demands and desires, they drew a connection between their public and private roles, thereby expressing an awareness of the reciprocal interdependence of these role expectations.[192] Susan Gal and Gail Kligman argue in their analysis of the socialist gender roles:

> Rather than any clear-cut 'us' versus 'them' or 'private' versus 'public,' there was a ubiquitous self-embedding or interweaving of these categories. Everyone was to some extent complicit in the system of patronage, lying, theft, hedging, and duplicity through which the system operated.[193]

We can postulate the existence in state socialist societies of what Pierre Bourdieu has identified in the Western order:

> A social history of the process of state institutionalization of the family – which would be much more radical than ethnomethodological critique – would show that the traditional opposition between the public and the private conceals the extent to which the public is present in the private, and in the very notion of *privacy*. Being the product of a sustained effort of juridical and political construction culminating in the modern

---

190 Konrád and Szelényi, *The Intellectuals on the Road*, 199–200.
191 See Ferge, *A Society in the Making*, 47.
192 Haney, *Inventing the Needy*, 67.
193 Gal and Kligman, *The Politics of Gender after Socialism*, 51.

family, the private is a public matter. The public vision (the *nomos*, this time in the sense of *law*) is deeply involved in our vision of domestic things, and our most private behaviors themselves depend on public actions, such as housing policy or, more directly, family policy.[194]

As the central field of social policy in state socialism, the family was the object of transformative policies oriented around specific ideological goals. At the same time, communist regimes regarded the family as a resource for social welfare beyond the state or other public services. Despite contemporary clichés in the West, communist governments by no means sought to destroy the family or render it obsolete. On the contrary, they massively affirmed the family as a social institution.[195] The Polish Constitution of 1952 proclaimed in Article 79, paragraph 1, that 'marriage, motherhood and family shall be safeguarded and protected by the Republic of Poland', whereby 'the state shall extend special protection to families with many children.'[196] Article 1 of the Family Code of the People's Republic of Romania of 1953 obligated the state to protect both marriage and the family and to safeguard the interests of mothers and children. The Romanian state also had a specific conception of the character of marriage and the responsibilities of parents, since 'men and women are equal in their mutual relations as well as in the exercise of rights regarding children', and 'parental rights are exercised only for the welfare of the children.' Article 2 stated that 'family relations are based on the mutual friendship and affection of their members' (similar definitions can be found in the other socialist countries).[197] This dialectic of affirmation and aspiration is also evident in the Family Code of the People's Republic of Albania of 1965, the first article of which declares the family to be the 'basic unit of our society', but also states that marriage 'should be conducted according to the principles of communist morality.' Article 3 promises marriages and families special protection from the state, whereby parents should raise their children to be 'responsible citizens of the People's Republic of Albania' (Article 4).[198]

A plethora of handbooks and propaganda brochures translated these legal norms into guiding principles for everyday life, since the socialist state provided protection for the family not only as an end in itself, but also to instrumentalize the family in order to resolve social problems and to transform society. This required that families adhere to certain standards. A booklet published in Bulgaria in 1973 depicted the prevailing vision of the ideal typical family:

> Let's visit the D. Bonev family in Sofia. Besides the parents, there are two university students and one high school student. The love and respect, mutual support, orderliness and personal responsibility of each member transform this family into an outstanding little collective, in which everyone tries to live and work as communists. A 'family

---

194 Pierre Bourdieu, *Practical Reason: On the Theory of Action* (Stanford, CA: Stanford University Press, 1998), 72 (emphasis in original).

195 Natali Stegmann, 'Die Aufwertung der Familie in der Volksrepublik Polen der siebziger Jahre', *Jahrbücher für Geschichte Osteuropas* 43, no. 4 (2005): 523–44.

196 See the text (in German) of the Constitution of 1952, as of 1976: www.verfassungen.eu/pl/verf76-i.htm; See L. Dyczewski, *Rodzina. Społeczeństwo. Państwo* [Family, society, and the state] (Lublin: Towarzystwo Naukowe Katolickiego Uniwersytetu Lubelskiego, 1994); Stegmann, 'Die Aufwertung der Familie'.

197 Anita Grandke, *Familiengesetze sozialistischer Länder* (Berlin: VEB Deutscher Zentralverlag, 1959), 123.

198 Gustav-Adolf Lübchen, *Familiengesetze sozialistischer Länder: Textsammlung der Familiengesetzbücher der europäischen sozialistischen Staaten in deutscher Sprache* (Berlin: Staatsverlag der Deutschen Demokratischen Republik, 1971), 172.

program' hangs framed on the wall in this apartment on G. Dimitrov Boulevard and attracts the curiosity of the casual visitor. ... All questions concerning the family are settled together. Personal issues, insofar as they do not concern the dignity and honour of the family, are resolved by the individual members themselves. All decisions of the family are carried out only after each family member has been convinced of their correctness and necessity. At the request of any family member, the family council can discuss and decide personal and general questions at any time. ... Each family member is obligated to work hard, to live as frugally as possible and to constantly keep accounts; to respect and support the work of the others; to keep the apartment in good order; to become more cultured and to internalize the principles of Marxist-Leninism.[199]

These normative guidelines and the accompanying propaganda formed the basis of a policy that made the socialist state into a 'pseudo family', as Haney has called it in her analysis of maternity policies in Hungary.[200] In this context, Gal and Kligman argue that the paternalistic state assumed the traditional role of the male head of the family.[201] The significance of the family as a model for perceiving social relations also became clear in the widespread political practice of making family heritage a criterion for certain state actions toward individuals. Especially in the first years after the communist takeover, the state discriminated against people whom it considered to have a tainted family tree, for instance, impeding their access to university studies and the job market. Political repression during Stalinism – and in Albania, even beyond Stalinism – incorporated the principle of collective family liability.[202] Families were frequently held collectively responsible for the deviant behaviour of their members. In the eyes of the regime, the official state affirmation of the family meant that the family could be used to curb tendencies to individualism.

Given the significance the family possessed for social practice and as a category of political action, an analysis of family policy provides important insights into characteristics specific to socialist statehood as well as into those elements that were part of general developments in post-war Europe. What appears to be specific to state socialism is the ideological overstretch evident in the discrepancy between far-reaching goals and insufficient (material) funds that ultimately forced communist regimes to adapt both the ideological superstructure and concrete political measures to popular practices. What can be generalized for all of European post-war history, however, is the tendency to use the family as an instrument to stabilize both state and society following the devastations of the Second World War and during the massive social transformation of the post-war era.[203] The instrumentalization of the family for social and demographic policy goals was also not unique to socialism – communist regimes only articulated this connection more directly and explicitly than liberal Western governments typically did (conservatives were equally outspoken). In any case, the socialist state was eminently interventionist, and at least the intention of these interventions was aimed at an ideological objective and not merely the repair of immediate shortcomings.

---

199 S. Bakiš and S. Halova, *Da rabotim i živeem po komunističeski* (Sofia: Otečestven front, 1963), 8–9.

200 Haney, *Inventing the Needy*, 82.

201 Gal and Kligman, *The Politics of Gender*, 78.

202 On the Albanian case, see Kretsi, *Verfolgung und Gedächtnis*, 132–8. Even into the 1980s, the opportunities available to individuals in Albania depended significantly on whether the regime regarded their family as 'good' or 'bad'.

203 Cf. Mark Mazower, *After the War was Over: Reconstructing the Family, Nation and State in Greece, 1943–1960* (Princeton, NJ: Princeton University Press, 2000).

Family policy constituted one of the direct interfaces between the ideological apparatus and concrete policy on the one hand, and popular expectations and social practices on the other. The contradictions and aporia of communist statehood are evident here in paradigmatic clarity. This includes, for example, the contrast between a rhetoric of equality and a political practice of difference, which resulted in varying benefits for female and male citizens, determined according to criteria that changed with the specific political objectives. Thus, in several countries not all children were considered equally valuable: child benefits increased per child with the number of children. In Bulgaria benefits then fell again with the fourth child, as it was primarily families of ethnic minorities (Romanies, Turks) that had this many children and the party leadership regarded them as less valuable members of society.[204]

It was typical of the heterogeneity of socialist statehood that the nationalization and centralization of welfare policy through the exclusion of non-state actors did not lead to a uniformity of social policy. The state was by no means a homogeneous actor in terms of family policy; it engaged not only as administrative institutions and agencies of professional social work, but also as economic enterprises, each of which had different internal logics and concrete interests.[205] Special attention must be paid here to enterprises as providers of social benefits for families. These enterprises also represented the state indirectly since they were usually owned by the state or by society. Nevertheless, they had access to different material resources, which is why the significance of enterprises for social policy that was so typical for state socialist societies gave rise to new inequalities. People employed in branches privileged by state investments usually received more support from their employers than people who worked in marginal sectors such as the service sector and light industry. This distinction had an unmistakeable gender dimension, since men were more likely to be employed in the privileged sectors of the economy than women. In Hungary, for instance, family assistance payments were distributed at the works level. The amount was calculated according to the salary of a child's father, even if the child no longer lived in the father's household.[206] The central role that socialism attributed to wage labour as the basis of citizenship and source of both rights and duties is once again evident in the significance of enterprises as actors of social and family policy. However, there were shifts in the 1960s, as the state increasingly constructed women as a special target group and recognized their claims qua maternity independent of their concrete social circumstances.[207]

Despite national differences, the development of family policy in real socialist states can be divided into five periods.[208] (1) During the immediate post-war years, the reconstruction of families was the centre of focus, especially in countries that had suffered massive war losses; this focus included care for orphans and the reintegration of displaced persons.[209] (2) During Stalinism the rhetoric of revolutionary transformation, including that of the family, predominated in the sense of equality and collectivism; nevertheless, social policy benefits were very meagre given the priority placed on investment in heavy industry; state policy regarding the family aimed especially at integrating women into wage labour, for instance, through the expansion of childcare centres, but also through restrictive wage policies that undermined the

---

204 Ulf Brunnbauer, *'Die sozialistische Lebensweise': Ideologie, Gesellschaft, Familie und Politik in Bulgarien (1944–1989)* (Vienna: Böhlau, 2007), 648.

205 See, for example, Bicskei, "'Our Greatest Treasure, the Child'".

206 Haney, *Inventing the Needy*, 43.

207 See Haney, *Inventing the Needy*.

208 See Inglot, *Welfare States in East Central Europe*, 122; Tomka, *Welfare in East and West*.

209 See Tara Zahra, *The Lost Children: Reconstructing Europe's Families after World War II* (Cambridge: Harvard University Press, 2011).

model of the sole male breadwinner. (3) Beginning in the mid-1950s, social benefits for families were expanded as communist regimes attempted to restore their shaken legitimacy by increasing material standards of living; family benefits were supposed to increase the compatibility of vocation and family for women. (4) In the second half of the 1960s, family and social policy underwent a pronatalist shift manifest in both repressive and supportive measures. Parallel to this, family policy increasingly became the micromanagement of social relations, evident in the professionalization of social work as well as parent and family counselling. (5) In the 1960s and 70s, social-policy measures were in part expanded, and in part adjusted; in the 1980s, debates arose about the need to reduce social-policy benefits in light of economic difficulties.

In evaluating the range of family benefits from the state, we should always bear in mind that family policy encompassed not only 'classical' social benefits such as money transfers for minor children and legal regulations affecting the family, but was also embedded in a plethora of material, normative and organizational measures, through which the state directly or indirectly influenced the forms, relations and practices of the family. These included subsidies for consumer goods, which was an essential component of socialist welfare policies, as well as the expansion of professionalized counselling services, for instance, to protect the welfare of children. The multiplicity of influencing factors and their specific combinations were one of the central reasons for the significant differences in actual family policies among socialist countries. In addition, there were also differences in institutional arrangements and in the pre-socialist heritages regarding social policy, which emerged more clearly again after Stalinism and the end of the far-reaching emulation of Soviet models.[210]

Reproductive policy and images of women

The similarities as well as differences (especially in implementing political objectives) become particularly clear in the pronatalist turn in family and social policy during the second half of the 1960s.[211] All socialist states were affected by this new orientation, which was not a complete break, but rather built upon state measures to increase birth rates that had already existed in part in the pre-socialist era. The reason for this development is easy to identify: there was a decline in birth rates everywhere after the baby boom of the immediate post-war years, resulting in a marked reduction of natural population growth. At the same time, the decline in mortality rates also came to an end (in the words of demography: the 'demographic transition' was complete). This gave rise to demographic fears among politicians and experts. A central fear was the imminent scarcity of workers, since at that point in time almost all labour reserves (women) had been mobilized for industrial expansion, while economic planners had not succeeded in shifting the economies from extensive growth to intensive growth based on productivity gains. Paradoxically, this fear was a consequence of the idea of planning: economic planners and social technologies remained focused firmly on the future and on the resources for planned growth.

Population policy was thus a form of socialist sustainability. Significantly, in Yugoslavia, where no pronounced pronatalist social policy would be implemented, there had been steadily increasing unemployment since the 1960s. There were other reasons as well, differing in each country, that caused party leaderships to be concerned with the altered demographics of their populations. In Romania, for instance, Ceauşescu drew a direct connection between the coun-

---

210 Inglot, *Welfare states in East Central Europe*, 136–7.
211 Robert J. McIntyre, 'Pronatalist Programmes in Eastern Europe', *Soviet Studies* 27, no. 3 (1975): 366–80.

try's military potential, its position on the international stage and the size of the population.[212] In Bulgaria, the birth rate of Muslim minorities – especially the Turkish minority, which was clearly higher than that of the ethnic Bulgarian population – attracted the attention of party leadership, which feared that an increase in the Turkish minority would lead to demands for autonomy.[213]

The concrete measures to stimulate fertility all earmarked the family as the central recipient of the corresponding benefits. This decision was consistent with statistical findings that the fertility of married women was higher than that of unmarried or divorced women. Furthermore, family experts postulated that an intact family was an important prerequisite for children's well-being. In Bulgaria and Romania, for example, the state made divorce more difficult in order to promote family stability. In all of the socialist countries there were diverse financial benefits intended to motivate families to have more children. These included increasing child-birth bonuses and family assistance, which frequently rose with the number of children. In the ČSSR, for example, monthly child benefits ranged from 95 korunas for one child to 1,230 korunas for four children.[214] The length of paid as well as unpaid childcare leave was consistently expanded, along with generous rules for mothers returning to their original professions. In Czechoslovakia, for example, beginning in 1968 mothers had the right to a 26-week maternity leave with 90 per cent of their salary.[215] Developments in Hungary were typical: here childcare allowances were extended to three years, while the circle of recipients was expanded to include non-working women. In this way maternity, rather than labour, became the central factor generating entitlement to certain state benefits – based on the opinion of experts that 'mothers had special needs and the welfare state should be reorganized in such way that these are met.'[216]

In most countries the monetary benefits for families with children, which were supplemented with additional privileges such as preferential access to residential housing, amounted to significant sums (in relation to average wages). At the end of the 1960s, the average family assistance for a family with two children in Czechoslovakia and Bulgaria was around 20 per cent of the average wage, in Hungary around 17 per cent.[217] In the 1970s and 80s, a number of these social benefits were even augmented, since the desired demographic results – an increase in the birth rate – had been only short-term. In Bulgaria, for instance, monthly child benefits for a family with two children increased to one-quarter of the average salary by the late 1980s.[218] In Czechoslovakia as well, the government significantly increased family support in the early 1980s. These social benefits contributed to a significant rise in the percentage of social expenditure in the state budget, causing reform-oriented experts in the course of the 1980s to call for a reduction of entitlements (by focusing, for instance, on particularly vulnerable people) in order to avoid overburdening the state (see above).[219]

In addition to financial stimuli and the corresponding propaganda, governments also used repressive measures to reverse the decline in birth rates. Romania went the furthest in this regard. In 1966 the Romanian government issued a radical ban on abortion, although material

---

212 Kligman, *The Politics of Duplicity*.
213 Brunnbauer, 'Die sozialistische Lebensweise', 622–3.
214 Kalinová, 'Conditions and Stages of Change', 71.
215 Inglot, *Welfare States in East Central Europe*, 140.
216 Haney, *Inventing the Needy*, 91; see Inglot, *Welfare States in East Central Europe*, 188.
217 Brunnbauer, 'Die sozialistische Lebensweise', 645–6; Inglot, *Welfare States in East Central Europe*, 183.
218 Brunnbauer, 'Die sozialistische Lebensweise', 646.
219 See Inglot, *Welfare States in East Central Europe*, 205–6.

Statehood in socialism

support for maternity in Romania remained below the level of other countries.[220] In Bulgaria as well, there were severe restrictions on abortion rights, although these were not implemented as rigidly or consistently as in Romania.[221] Thus, the pronounced pronatalism also marked a turn in the relationship of the socialist state to the bodies of its citizens (the female body, of course, was especially affected by these policies). In Romania state security forces began to keep track of pregnancies early on in order to prevent illegal abortions.

Overall, the pronatalist social policies had powerful implications for gender relations. The significant increase and expansion of financial support from the state for families and especially for mothers marked a reversal of earlier attempts to support the family through the creation of a public offering of household support. Significant and extended child benefits in Hungary, for example, meant that women there had a real choice between remaining at home or returning early to the workplace without having to accept financial losses.[222] This did signify, however, the definitive capitulation of the state to unequal intra-familial roles: almost all of the benefits identified here were for mothers, which was also evident in the official propaganda. In Bulgaria, for example, the role of the mother clearly became the central focus of all the functions that the state attributed to women. In visual propaganda in Bulgaria women were no longer depicted as workers operating huge machines, but instead primarily as mothers.[223] The state thus actively reinforced a naturalist understanding of gender roles that clearly ran counter to the emancipatory promise of the communist ideology.

Both experts and social policy makers were aware that the work of family reproduction lay largely on the shoulders of women. Sociological studies in all of the countries at the time provided unambiguous findings. With the pronatalist turn of the 1960s, regimes accepted this and stopped intervening in intra-familial relations as long as the well-being of the children was not concerned. Ultimately, this arrangement proved to be beneficial to the state since women performed unpaid reproductive labour – labour that the communist party had originally promised to socialize, but for which the state lacked financial means. The state did support the family by assuming responsibility for vital welfare expenditures, for instance in Poland by providing support payments to employees when they cared for sick children or allowing working grandparents to take leave in order to care for their grandchildren (a measure introduced in Bulgaria in the mid-1980s).[224] In Bulgaria the functions of the family were even included in the Family Code and became thereby the basis for claims that the state made on families and vice versa.[225]

Through the official affirmation of the family reinforced by laws, social policy benefits and moralizing propaganda, state and party leaders hoped to make the family into an instrument of their policies. In addition to demographic motives, their concern was maintaining social stability. The essentialization of the family through policies was also reflected in the behaviour of the

---

220 Kligman, *The Politics of Duplicity*; Roth et al., 'The Romanian Social System', 196.

221 Dimiter Vassilev, *From Abortion to Contraception: A Resource to Public Policies and Reproductive Behavior in Central and Eastern Europe from 1917 to the Present*, ed. Henry P. David (London: Greenwood Press 1999), 69–89.

222 Szikra, 'Social Policy Under State Socialism in Hungary', 146.

223 Anelia Kasabova-Dintcheva, 'Neue alte Normen: Die versuchte Normierung der Sexualität im sozialistischen Bulgarien', *Ethnologia Balkanica*, no. 8 (2004): 155–78.

224 Hübner, Hübner and Boyer, *Sozialismus als soziale Frage*, 290; Ilija Iliev, 'Familie, Ideologie und Politik: Die Großmutter in der städtischen Familie seit 1945', in *Vom Nutzen der Verwandten. Soziale Netzwerke in Bulgarien (19. und 20. Jahrhundert)*, eds Ulf Brunnbauer and Karl Kaser (Vienna: Böhlau 2001), 89–112.

225 Iliev, 'Familie, Ideologie und Politik', 111.

population, which acted in explicitly family-oriented ways. This can be seen in basic demographic data: the average age of marriage remained low, as marriage was the prerequisite for numerous state benefits and privileges. In Hungary, Poland and Bulgaria in 1980, for instance, the average age at which women married for the first time was 22 years or younger.[226] The percentage of people who never married in their adult lives was also low – another clear indication of the normative strength of the institutions of marriage and the family. In state socialist countries in the early 1980s, between 4.8 per cent (Albania) and 11.6 per cent (Poland) of men between the ages of 35 to 39 were unmarried. Around 2010 the figures in these countries lay between 11 per cent (Albania) and 35 per cent (Hungary), indicating a marked increase since the end of socialism in men who never married or married very late.[227] The significance of marriage as a prerequisite for state benefits became less important after 1989, in part because social benefits from the state decreased.

Processes and practices of (de-)legitimation

For the socialist states and the communist parties dominating them, social policy was central to the creation of their legitimacy, as well as to their dissolution. It was also true that the ongoing functioning of the institutions of state socialist hegemony was to a certain degree reliant on legitimacy. A system of government must ultimately be underpinned by more than just violence and force; even a far-reaching surveillance apparatus cannot control every citizen, day in and day out. As the so-called revisionist research on Stalinism has determined (Sheila Fitzpatrick, Jochen Hellbeck, etc.), even this extreme repressive manifestation of communist domination cannot be reduced only to terror and violence. Essential elements of Stalinist ideology resonated among certain social groups of Soviet citizens.

An understanding of the nature of the state in real socialism therefore requires addressing the question of the acceptance of rule. If there was at least partial legitimacy, on which roots and practices did it rely? If there were an affective identification with the norms and conceptions of the order of the state, was this the result of internalization by the citizens (as per Pierre Bourdieu, Émile Durkheim and Antonio Gramsci) or was it based only in pragmatism and strategy? What role did the methods, traditions and the charisma of the sovereign play in the degree of recognition of the power system? Where do state socialist systems position themselves in the Weberian typology of domination and how do these patterns change over time?

Patterns of legitimation

Legitimacy does not necessarily intimate an enthusiastic agreement or an emotional identification with the state and with communist domination – although perhaps some did feel that way – but rather it requires little more than an acceptance that the given order is lacking in alternatives or that it is useful in an entirely pragmatic sense. Different societal groups could be placed at various points along the scale of legitimacy, ranging from ideological enthusiasm

---

226 UNECE Statistical Division Database (http://w3.unece.org/pxweb/): Gender Statistics/Fertility, familiesandhouseholds/Mean age at first marriage by sex.

227 United Nations, Department of Economic and Social Affairs: World Marriage Data 2012, www.un.org/esa/population/publications/WMD2012/Data/UNPD_WMD_2012_MARITAL_STATUS.xls.

Statehood in socialism

to profound reluctance. Martin Sabrow, for example, has indicated the broad spectrum of attitudes towards the legitimacy of party rule in the GDR.[228] He argues that the task of ruling institutions was to convince an adequately large portion of the populace of their significance, and to control, exclude from participation, isolate, and in extreme cases, physically eliminate those who remained unconvinced. Thus, communist policy comprised not only terror and violence – in emergency situations – but also various strategies of incorporation and persuasion. The party wanted to secure its claim to power by creating some overlap between the interests of the populace and the development goals of the state, and by cementing the central elements of its ideology in the consciousness and collective identities of the citizens. Society should be brought to share the regime's conceptions of order and to award institutions with the right to assert rules by force, if necessary.[229]

As a consequence, policy measures were neither merely a means to implement certain interests nor a reaction to constantly changing circumstances; but rather, they served to ever further the production of legitimacy that in turn created the possibility for political control in the first place. The central actor in this process was the communist party and its diverse spectrum of mass organizations, which in one form or another targeted the entire population beginning at an early age. The party certainly used violence in its physical and symbolic dimensions to discipline society, but it also used a broad range of offers for participation and co-opting in order to mobilize people towards its goals and to connect them to the state as a whole. This strategy relied on a meticulously formulated ideological apparatus as a system of convictions for perceiving and explaining the world and as a reservoir of guiding principles.[230] Ideology was at the very centre of the creation of cultural hegemony; without it, Antonio Gramsci tells us, political order can only exist through force. This was – to anticipate the end – one of the structural sources of the weakness of the communist regimes: they were habitually unable to accept social practices contravening their ideology and, therefore, politicized even the most banal digressions. Their constant talk of 'vigilance' and 'relentless struggle' against ideological diversions were not displays of strength but of weakness.

Over time, the concrete practices of legitimation as well as its rhetorical foundation underwent critical changes, as will be shown. One essential feature of the legitimacy of communist rule that both determined its fragility and distinguished it from Western systems remained in place: the rationale for the claim to legitimacy of the communist order was based on the achievement of concrete goals. At best, this concept of state and the expectation of legitimacy that flowed from it can be summarized by the Soviet constitution of 1977. The Soviet state – as a 'new form of state' – saw itself 'as a key instrument in the protection of revolutionary successes and the expansion of socialism and communism'.[231] In relation to state socialism, T.H. Rigby speaks of a legitimacy that relies on 'goal-rationality', while the regulations inherent to liberal

---

228 Martin Sabrow, 'Der künstliche Konsens: Überlegungen zum Legitimationscharakter sozialistischer Herrschaftssysteme', in *Jahrbuch für historische Kommunismusforschung 1999*, 191–224, here 202.

229 On the fundamental questions of the legitimacy of state ordinances, cf. Bruce Gilley, *The Right to Rule: How States Win and Lose Legitimacy* (New York: Columbia University Press, 2009).

230 As a reference work on the fundamentals of the communist system of rule, including a conceptual analysis replete with guidance categories, cf. C.D. Kernig, ed., *Sowjetsystem und demokratische Gesellschaft:Eine vergleichende Enzyklopädie*, 6 vols (Freiburg: Herder, 1966–72).

231 For a comprehensive compilation of contemporary and historical constitutions see 'Konstitutsiia (osnovnoy zakon) Soyuza Sovetskih Sotsialisticheskih Respublik' available in the Russian original and in German translation at: www.verfassungen.net/su/udssr77.htm

democracy present themselves primarily as formal and legal rationale.[232] Ideally, in Western societies the state exists to create a reliable framework based on the rule of law for societal actors to pursue their goals, which are not prescribed by the state. Under state socialism, it conducts itself in a fundamentally different way with serious consequences for the nature of administrative action:

> Here the political authorities *do* set out not only to prescribe the goals and specific tasks of the constituent units of society but indeed directly to manage their implementation through official bureaucracies. ... The predominant bureaucratic mode is the task-achieving mode. Accordingly, the central role in the political system is played by institutions concerned with formulating the goals and tasks of the constituent units of society and supervising their execution.[233]

The validity of the legitimacy claims of the political system would ultimately result from communism's final goal and the degree to which it was attained – a success measured by the meeting of milestones proclaimed by the political leadership. It recalls a typical project funded by the EU, which includes milestones and deliverables, and functions similarly to a state socialist policy, always with a concrete goal clearly in view (and by producing the paperwork, they could make it seem as if they had met these goals). The party and the state's expectation that the regulations they set would be met with compliance was grounded in the assertion of a rational relationship between the following: the specific tasks ascribed to organizations and individuals; the establishment of a socialist society; and the attainment of the end goal, communism. Bureaucracy in the state socialist system was thus 'task-oriented' and not 'rule-oriented'.[234]

From Stalinism to post-Stalinism

The embedding of state goals into the hegemonic master narrative changed over time, just as the collective was variably defined as a bearer of the body politic. As was true regarding social policy – and in close relation to it – the year 1956, i.e. the beginning of de-Stalinization, represents a certain caesura. As Martin Sabrow determined, Stalinism was dominated by a sense of *futurity*,[235] which was associated with the mobilization of the masses to create the great leap into communism in the shortest amount of time possible. The official propaganda of the late 1940s and early 1950s looked determinedly forward, betting against 'class enemies' and 'enemies of the people' who blocked the path to progress.

It is generally known that, with the exception of Yugoslavia and Albania, communists primarily came to power thanks to the Soviet army; their weak or even absent support among the population, which was of course officially denied, was sought to be compensated for by a particular will towards social transformation, and through the use of coercive measures to

---

232 T.H. Rigby, 'Introduction: Political Legitimacy, Weber and Communist Mono-organisational Systems', in *Political Legitimation in Communist States*, eds T.H. Rigby and Ferenc Fehér (London: Macmillan, 1982), 1–26, here 10.

233 Rigby, 'Introduction', 11f.

234 Rigby, 'Introduction', 14.

235 Martin Sabrow, 'Auf der Suche nach dem materialistischen Meisterton: Bauformen einer nationalen Geschichtserzählung in der DDR', in *Die historische Meistererzählung*, eds Konrad H. Jarausch and Martin Sabrow (Göttingen: Vandenhoeck & Ruprecht, 20,002), 33–77, here 64–5; see also Sabrow, 'Der künstliche Konsens', 191–224.

Statehood in socialism

subject society to their objectives. The communist agenda was firmly anchored in the drive to fulfil an historic mission, which is why the party's authority was not legitimated through a majority vote, but through the historic laws they embodied. The mission's focus was on the future that would become the present. This strategy of creating a new world in order to breed consent – and thus validate the righteousness of the vision – found its most meaningful expression in the construction of new 'socialist' cities. These were based on Soviet models (especially Magnitogorsk, a 1930s steel city built in the Urals) and embraced the prevalent traditions of modern urban development, which focused on the rational, tabula rasa design of cities that reflected the needs of modern industry. This was connected to the aspiration to establish a new society with industry at its centre. The main streets of the new East German city, Stalinstadt (now Eisenhüttenstadt), terminated at the gates of the newly constructed steelworks.

Bulgaria's version of the socialist city, Dimitrovgrad, whose construction began in 1947, illustrates the importance of these major, socialist construction sites[236] for the justification of communist domination (other cities like Nowa Huta in Poland or Sztálinváros in Hungary are similarly illustrative).[237] The communist state was one in which mere willpower could break all opposition – even those of a temporal nature – and create new realities within a short period of time: 'One can feel most clearly in Dimitrovgrad how dreams become reality', one observer exclaimed.[238] Indeed, the city became a metaphor for heroism and socialist progress, as the construction workers and brigadiers were prepared to sacrifice themselves for the construction of the city, and thus for socialism, and do so as quickly as possible. From a booklet published in German:

> In Dimitrovgrad, on the banks of the Maritsa, the dreams of a heroic party have transformed, and are transforming, into reality – a party that was informed and ignited by Stalin and Dimitrov, who live and breathe within every piece of this wonderful construction.

This belief in progress also served as a reference point for distinguishing itself from the West: 'Nowhere in the capitalist world can one dream of such great things; nowhere in the capitalist world can youths dream of their future, knowing that if they are strong and want something, they can achieve it.' Dimitrovgrad and the other socialist cities were not only the manifestation of an unseen will to build and an instrument towards the pursuit of industrialization; these cities also held subjective value as a means to churn out model socialist citizens: 'One becomes ever more convinced that the growth of this enormous plant and thermoelectric centre was accompanied by the emergence of hundreds of new, wonderful people – dedicated constructors of the new life.'[239]

---

236 Cf. Klaus Gestwa, *Die Stalinschen Großbauten des Kommunismus: Sowjetische Technik- und Umweltgeschichte, 1948–1967* (München: Oldenbourg, 2010).

237 On Dimitrovgrad, cf. Ulf Brunnbauer, '"The Town of the Youth": Dimitrovgrad and Bulgarian Socialism', *Ethnologia Balkanica* 9 (2005). On other planned socialist cities or socialist city planning, cf. Katherine Anne Lebow, *Unfinished Utopia: Nowa Huta Stalinism and Polish Society 1949–56* (Ithaca, NY: Cornell University Press, 2013); Sándor Horváth, *A kapu és a határ: Mindennapi Sztálinváros* [The gate and the border: everyday Sztálinváros] (Budapest: MTA Történettudományi Intézete, 2004); or the revised English edition: Sándor Horváth, *Stalinism Reloaded: Everyday Life in Stalin-City, Hungary* (Bloomington, IN: Indiana University Press, 2017); Brigitte Le Normand, *Designing Tito's Capital: Urban Planning, Modernism, and Socialism* (Pittsburgh, PA: University of Pittsburgh Press, 2014).

238 And for the following quotations: Brunnbauer, *Die sozialistische Lebensweise*, 127.

239 Krum Walkov, ed., *Dimitrovgrad: Die Stadt der Jugend* (Sofia: Pressedirektion, 1951), 9, 10 and 25.

The construction of this socialist city elucidates the political programme of the communist party, which linked a new, material reality to the hope for the emergence of a new populace loyal to this city and to socialism. Susan Reid and David Crowley write about the ideological point of departure of such urban development utopias: 'To change how a person thought and behaved one must change his or her material surroundings. Thus the architectural form of the city and planning of urban space were vested with a social-transformative role in the lives of its residents.'[240] In the 1940s and 1950s, the ideologues envisioned an austere sort of person who would subordinate himself or herself to the collective and with enthusiasm and determination dedicate all strength to the construction of socialism. This ideal rationalized the material limitations of war-damaged Eastern Europe, whereby state investment's privileging of heavy industry further compromised living standards. This new sort of person would have been someone who configured his or her life around the ideological guidelines of communism and internalized them. The legitimacy of governance would have automatically been accommodated by the perfect congruence between the orientation of the state and the individual. The values propagated by the new communist regimes in Eastern Europe generally followed the moral system of Stalinism.[241]

As we now know through the analysis of diaries, oral history interviews and other first-hand accounts, attempts by the communist parties to forge acceptance of mass mobilization and coerced enthusiasm were not entirely successful. The enormous amount of propaganda, the staging of massive parades, indoctrination in schools as well as the possibilities for social advancement – all features of the transformative policies under Stalinism – resulted in at least partial identification with a communist regime among a portion of the population, the size of which is difficult to assess. The state enjoyed particular legitimacy in segments of the population that were essential to the management of industry and administration, for it acted as an agent of both reconstruction and modernization.

Whatever had fomented the people's identification with, loyalty to, or at least acceptance of, the communist regime was soon to be tested: in 1953 and 1956 in Poland, the GDR and Czechoslovakia, mass protests – carried out predominantly by workers and triggered by dissatisfaction with living conditions – shook the foundation of communist domination. In Hungary in the fall of 1956, it went as far as revolution, which for a time thrust the country out of the Soviet orbit – until Soviet troops subdued the mass upheaval with bloody force. Not only did these protests make the communists anxious, but after the death of Stalin and the onset of de-Stalinization, they found themselves in a phase of ideological disorientation. This continued until a post-Stalinist ideological consensus could be established, yet not without resistance.[242] Among the essential characteristics of the new ideological orientation was a strong turn to both the present and the past, and a de-emphasis on creating the forward vision of communism, even if it was never rhetorically abandoned. Pavel Kolář speaks of a 'procedural utopia':

> After 1956, the communists perhaps lost their belief in the achievability of the communist future. But they did not cease to believe in the right of the party to lead the people, in order to search for a non-defined alternative to both Stalinism and capitalism. [243]

---

240 David Crowley and Susan E. Reid, eds, *Socialist Spaces: Sites of Everyday Life in the Eastern Bloc* (Oxford: Berg, 2002), 11.

241 Cf. David L. Hoffmann, *Stalinist Values: The Cultural Norms of Soviet Modernity, 1917–1941* (Ithaca, NY: Cornell University Press, 2003).

242 Kolář, *Der Poststalinismus*.

243 Pavel Kolář, 'The Party as a New Utopia: Reshaping Communist Identity after Stalinism', *Social History* 37, no. 4 (2012): 424.

Statehood in socialism

The identity of the party came to rely ever more on history, and thus on the proliferation of institutions dedicated to the history of the communist party and the workers' movement. But how could a large, publicly alienated share of the populace be reconciled with the communist rulers? Of the myriad concrete measures aimed at strengthening the legitimacy of power, two that were employed in most of the states, albeit to varying degrees of intensity, stand out above all: the attempt to raise living standards and the emphasis on national rhetoric.

The social and the national

The promise of raising living standards in the here and now – and not just in a distant communist utopia – became the centrepiece of the communists' legitimation policy as of the mid-1950s. Khrushchev's famous dictum that the East would reach and indeed overtake the United States economically in the foreseeable future pertained to supplying the populace with the consumer goods required to meet their daily needs.[244] As described above, the governments – with the exception of Albania – revised their economic policy by increasing investment in the consumer goods industry (yet without de-prioritizing heavy industry, which then continued to grow more quickly than light industry). Along with private consumption, 'social' consumption experienced particularly strong growth in terms of an expansion of social services (see above). As a result, the entire region observed an increase in living standards in the 1960s and 70s (in Poland, however, this process had already come to a halt by the mid-1970s). In socialist Yugoslavia, consumption became nothing less than the essential feature of the country's collective everyday culture.[245] The regimes hoped this policy would disseminate a feeling amongst the populace that they would directly benefit from the existing system and would also have something to lose through upheaval.[246] This time of burgeoning prosperity – when compared with the economic misery of the 1990s – has created a critical foundation for the widespread nostalgia for state socialism, indicating again that the new social contract justified by the policy of living standards was not without popular consensus.[247]

However, the communists' official rehabilitation of consumption opened a Pandora's box that they could no longer close, for the consequences of this change of course posed insurmountable problems: the people's expectations for consumption, fuelled by promises from party leaders, rose significantly faster than the economic possibilities of fulfilling them. The unproductive socialist economies were unable to structurally manufacture consumer goods with sufficient quantity or quality to keep pace with Western progress. An ideological expression of the problem can be seen in the constant attempts by communist ideologues to reshape con-

---

244 Hans-Hermann Höhmann and Gertraud Seidenstecher, *Zurück zu Chruschtschow? Zur sowjetischen Parole vom 'Einholen und Überholen' der amerikanischen Wirtschaft*, Bundesinstitut für Ostwissenschaftliche und Internationale Studien: Berichte des Bundesinstituts für Ostwissenschaftliche und Internationale Studien 1971.59 (Köln: Bundesinst. für Ostwiss. und Internat. Studien, 1971), http://nbn-resolving. de/urn/resolver.pl?urn=urn:nbn:de:bvb:12-bsb00058741-1.

245 Patrick Hyder Patterson, *Bought and Sold: Living and Losing the Good Life in Socialist Yugoslavia* (Ithaca, NY: Cornell University Press, 2012); Igor Duda, *Pronađeno blagostanje: Svakodnevni život i potrošačka kultura u Hrvatskoj 1970-ih i 1980-ih* [Well-being found: everyday life and consumer culture in Croatia in the 1970s and 1980s] (Zagreb: Srednja Europa, 2010), summary in English under the title: 'Well-being found'.

246 Paulina Bren and Mary Neuburger, 'Introduction', in *Communism Unwrapped: Consumption in Cold War Eastern Europe*, eds Paulina Bren and Mary Neuburger (Oxford: Oxford University Press, 2012), 3–26, 11.

247 Ibid., 14.

sumption from a moral perspective. It was to serve the noble goal of improving the individual and the attainment of a modern lifestyle, yet not equate to status or egotistical self-affirmation. Hungarian intellectuals created the memorable image of a 'dictatorship over needs',[248] except that this dictatorship never came to fruition, for in reality, the people did not accept any prescription of what they should consume and why. Rather, they became increasingly frustrated that their ambitions as consumers were constantly thwarted by the harsh realities of the 'economy of scarcity' (another term coined by a Hungarian academic). The consumption policy allowed the regimes to revamp their legitimacy for a variable amount of time yet created new ideological ambiguities that would ultimately undermine this legitimacy, for it was substantiated by a large segment of the population in a purely practical way. As long as the governments delivered, most people were prepared to tolerate the staged consensus, but only to a certain degree, as there was no true emotional identification with the ideas of the system and the goals of the regime.[249]

If the promotion of consumption could at most create instrumental identification with the state socialist system, the party leaders hoped to achieve a more emotionally based consensus through the increased use of national rhetoric. In one form or another, all the state socialist countries underwent an intensification of patriotic discourse, while Albania and Romania implemented explicitly nationalist policies. The year 1956 marked a significant reversal in this regard; under Stalin, insisting on national sovereignty would have been considered an act of disloyalty toward the Soviet Union. In fact, in 1948 it led directly to the break with Yugoslavia. However, even before 1956, communist leaders also made an effort to employ decidedly nationalist rhetoric when it came to justifying the expulsion of Germans from Czechoslovakia and Poland. Especially in Czechoslovakia, the communist party, which enjoyed an undeniably broad appeal after the end of the war, was in a position to present itself as the best guarantor of regained independence and the defender of the country against German revisionism.[250] In any case, the death of Stalin widened the possibilities for party ideologues to formulate their own national version of socialism. In political terms, national communism essentially comprised the emphasis of the interests of the respective nation, along with the necessity and possibility of tailoring socialism to that country's specific national traditions and conditions.[251] In a way, it was a fitting ideology for a political system that was wary of movement across its borders and had an economy that was predicated on import substitution and central planning.

Romania provides an excellent – albeit extreme – illustration of this orientation towards national communism. Until the beginning of the 1950s, Romanian cultural policy stressed the country's proximity to the Soviet Union, and especially to the Russian people, in the sense of the frequently invoked proletarian internationalism. Scholarship on the Romanian language emphasized the many Slavic loan words, historical treatises extolled the close relationship between Romania and Russia.[252] This was perhaps not particularly credible in the eyes of the people, who for the most part received communism as foreign ideology and associated it

---

248 Fehér, Heller and Márkus, *Dictatorship over Needs*.

249 Sabrow, 'Der künstliche Konsens'.

250 Christiane Brenner, '*Zwischen Ost und West': Tschechische politische Diskurse 1945–1948* (München: Oldenbourg, 2009).

251 Cf. Thomas T. Hammond, 'The Origins of National Communism', *Virginia Quarterly Review* 34, no. 2 (1958): 277–91.

252 Şerban Papacostea, 'Captive Clio: Romanian Historiography under Communist Rule', *European History Quarterly*, 26 (1996): 181–208.

Statehood in socialism

with the Soviet Union, particularly with the Soviet absorption of territories between 1940 and 1944. At the end of the 1950s (i.e. still under Gheorghe Gheorghiu-Dej, yet even stronger under his successor, Nicolae Ceauşescu), Romanian cultural policy experienced a radical shift; historiography was now focusing on the elaboration of the Romanians' settlement continuity since antiquity, and the relentless unification efforts of Romanians while positive references to Russia disappeared.[253] The new party programme of 1974 began with a long introduction that included an apotheosis of the Dacian kings Burebista and Decebalus. The party presented itself as the 'culmination of Romania's national history'.[254] Grand film productions depicted epic historical myths such as that of Prince Michael the Brave.[255] The public realm was saturated with symbols from the history of the Romanian people and its states as well as Romanian 'folk culture'. In terms of foreign policy, the turn towards national communism was expressed in the country's increasing independence. Romania repeatedly spurned the Soviet Union and for a time, was very well received by the West – even US President Nixon visited Romania. The consequences of nationalism for domestic policy included the limiting of minority rights for Hungarians. Not only among intellectuals but also in broad swaths of the population, Ceauşescu's nationalist course actually seemed to increase, at least temporarily, the degree of people's approval of the regime.[256]

Other socialist states also experienced an upswing in nationalist rhetoric and policy after 1956, although generally to a lesser degree than Romania, especially regarding the implications to their foreign policy, while only Albania surpassed Romania in terms of its nationalist tendencies. Beginning in 1948, Yugoslavia found itself following a course that was independent from the Soviet Union. However, in the two federations (Yugoslavia and Czechoslovakia), the balance of nationality-specific policies meant that there were clear boundaries as to how far the articulation of ethnic nationalism could go. The GDR presented a most peculiar case. Although the rejection of German nationalism was one of the GDR's founding principles, it considered itself a decidedly German – but even better – state. Moreover, in the 1980s, East Germany's increasingly positive appreciation of Prussian heritage soon led to Frederick the Great's image hanging in an ancestral portrait hall that included the likeness of Erich Honecker.[257]

Overall, national communism was particularly visible in the politics of memory, which increasingly emphasized the 'national' past preceding the heroic period of anti-fascism. A series of elaborate feature-length films in Bulgaria, which focused on medieval czars and the struggle for freedom from the Ottomans, illustrates the deeper endowment of historical meaning. Under the aegis of Lyudmila Zhivkova – daughter of the head of state and of the party while she herself was chairperson of the committee for culture, and thus de facto minister of culture – Bulgarian culture's historical contribution to world civilization was highlighted and presented abroad in elaborate exhibitions.[258] In Albania, the medieval folk hero Skanderbeg dominated

---

253 Keith Hitchins, 'Historiography of the Countries of Eastern Europe: Romania', *American Historical Review* 97, no. 4 (1992): 1064–83.

254 Dionisie Ghermani, *Die nationale Souveränitätspolitik der SR Rumänien* (München: Oldenbourg, 1981).

255 Dragos Petrescu, 'Building the Nation, Instrumentalizing Nationalism: Revisiting Romanian National-Communism, 1956–1989', *Nationalities Papers* 37, no. 4 (2009): 523–44, here 534f.

256 Cf. Verdery, *National Ideology under Socialism.*

257 Jan Herman Brinks, *Die DDR-Geschichtswissenschaft auf dem Weg zur deutschen Einheit: Luther, Friedrich II und Bismarck als Paradigmen politischen Wandels* (Frankfurt a.M.: Campus Verlag, 1992).

258 Ivanka Nedeva Atanasova, 'Lyudmila Zhivkova and the Paradox of Ideology and Identity in Communist Bulgaria', *East European Politics and Societies* 18, no. 2 (2004): 278–315.

the historical scenery. It need hardly be stressed that these images were extremely broad-brush. The strengthened efforts to preserve architectural heritage, as well as monasteries and churches, can be seen as a positive aspect of the nationalization of culture, which contributed to the legitimation of the state.

The efficacy of national symbols in the creation of loyalty lay in their emotional power and their ability to appeal to established symbols. Following Michael Billig's idea of a 'banal' nationalism,[259] a constant presence of national symbolism can be observed alongside, sometimes in excess of, or even in place of party symbols. The insistent promotion of folklore as an allegedly apolitical commendation of folk culture belongs in this context, especially as it triggered – in addition to scholarly research – numerous opportunities for laymen to be able to take part in the creation of folk culture. The nation, therefore, possessed a highly performative aspect. Even more than the proletarian production of culture, socialism furthered the folkloric production of culture, as manifested in the proliferation of relevant folk dance troupes, music groups and festivals. The GDR had a state folklore ensemble after 1954, yet they were not the only socialist country to do so; there was hardly a public party event in Bulgaria that did not also feature women dressed in folk costume or a staging of traditional round dance. A sanitized and standardized version – or vision – of folk culture was thus performed as well as promoted as a basis for manufacturing socialist culture. As a consequence, even those who may have been at odds with communist ideology, such as patriotically inclined intellectuals and creative artists, could be integrated into the socialist nation.

The national rhetoric (and specifically the folklore) was a strategy to foment unity, both discursively and practically, in times of increasing societal differentiation and fragmentation.[260] The communist ideologues struggled to accept diversity, hence their tendency towards the homologation of state, society and culture. In Albania, for example, the indigenous nationalism propagated by Enver Hoxha and those surrounding him was part of a massive attempt at nation building through the eradication of the tribal and regional divisions within the Albanian state. Another such example is Albania's 1967 declaration that it was an atheist country, for the effect of having religious affiliation was more of a separation than a unification.[261] In Bulgaria, the official affirmation of a nationalist mind-set stood in direct correlation to its attempt to assimilate its large Muslim minorities in the 1970s and 80s. In Poland in the late 1960s, the party's official anti-Semitic rhetoric was intended to create a scapegoat for economic woes and strengthen the unity of the Polish nation. As part of an 'anti-Zionist' campaign operated by the state, many members of the Polish United Workers' Party were barred in 1968, and several were expelled from university positions; around 13,000 Poles of Jewish descent emigrated as a result. National ideology offered the great advantage of clearly identifying the enemies of the state who would be blamed for the current inconveniences suffered by citizens. Thus, nationalism ideally suited the siege mentality of the communist regimes – and the fact that the Yugoslav communists affirmed it least was a good indicator of their more open attitude towards the non-socialist world.

---

259 Cf. Michael Billig, *Banal Nationalism* (London: Sage, 1995).

260 Verdery, *National Ideology under Socialism*, 131.

261 On the ideological roots of Enver Hoxha, see Bernhard Tönnes, *Sonderfall Albanien: Enver Hoxas 'eigener Weg' und die historischen Ursprünge seiner Ideologie* (München: Oldenbourg, 1980), 35–248; Cf. B.J. Fischer, 'Albania as Political Laboratory: The Development of the Albanian State During the 20th Century', *Österreichische Osthefte* 45 (2003): 177–93.

Statehood in socialism

One reason that national ideology is a suitable justification for power relations lay in the extensive use of kinship metaphors, which was much more firmly anchored in the population's horizon of experience than the abstract concepts of Marxism and Leninism. The party presented itself as the loving mother of society and presented the general secretary as *pater familias*. The best expression of the orchestration of the party leader as a father figure was Tito's godparenthood of the ninth-born child in every Yugoslav family. The pan-Yugoslav Relay of Youth, which toured the entire federation before descending on a Belgrade stadium to hand the baton to Tito on 25 May, the Day of Youth, constituted an additional, mass-impact form of presenting Tito as the father figure of the Yugoslav nation(s).[262] In this way, the life paths of young people were symbolically – as well as practically for tens of thousands of youths – interwoven with the leadership personality of the party state. The grounding of legitimacy in the charisma of the party leader and the diligent staging of this charisma were thus closely tied to the discursive construction of a national community.

It was no accident, but rather due to the logic of national ideology, that the two most extreme forms of personality cult in European state socialism were seen in the two countries in which national communist propaganda was wrought most extensively: Romania and Albania. In the 1970s and 1980s, both Ceaușescu and Hoxha had themselves portrayed as the apotheoses of their nations. Hoxha fashioned himself as the reincarnation of Skanderbeg (or it was staged as such), while Ceaușescu played the wise 'leader' (*conducător*), a title that had existed under the Antonescu dictatorship. Critical to maintaining a personality cult was the claim to extraordinary brilliance: Ceaușescu had himself praised as the 'Genius of the Carpathians', and the 71 volumes of the complete works of Enver Hoxha constitute the most comprehensive body of texts ever written by an Albanian author.[263]

The political and social function of the personality cult exists in linking the dictator directly to the party apparatus and the people.[264] However, as Daniel Ursprung has emphasized, the personality cult also bore danger for the sovereign, as the social expectations were concentrated on him: 'Instead of displaying polite reservation in passing responsibility for grievances, such as catastrophic supply shortages, onto the bureaucracy, the permanent public presence of Ceaușescu's actual person effectuated its illegitimacy.'[265] Overall, the enormous effort the communist regimes invested in ideological production, and thus in the control of the discursive realm, ultimately highlighted their weaknesses, not their strengths. They sensed that their bureaucratic control mechanisms had not been adequately routinized.[266]

Similar to the affirmation of consumption, the affirmation of nationalism had a long-term destabilizing effect, as it created expectations that could not be met by the existing system. With the exception of the Romanian, Albanian and Yugoslav regimes, all others remained too overtly subordinate to the Soviet Union for the rhetoric of national independence to be fully convincing. In Yugoslavia there were clear limits to explicit nationalist declarations. However, beginning in the 1950s and particularly with the constitution of 1974, educational, cultural and media policy grew so starkly decentralized that the constituent republics increasingly became central

---

262 Halder, *Der Titokult*, 193–214.

263 Ibid., 163.

264 On communist personality cults, cf. Klaus Heller and Jan Plamper, eds, *Personality Cults in Stalinism* (Göttingen:V&R Unipress, 2004).

265 Daniel Ursprung, 'Inszeniertes Charisma: Personenkult im Sozialismus', in *Charisma und Herrschaft: Führung und Verführung in der Politik*, eds Berit Bliesemann de Guevara and Tatjana Reiber (Frankfurt a.M.: Campus Verlag, 2011), 151–76, 168.

266 Cf. Verdery, *National Ideology under Socialism*, 307.

points of reference for collective identities and public communication. With the Macedonians and the Bosnian Muslims, the Yugoslav communists went so far as to create two new nations, while the idea of an overriding Yugoslav national identity had officially been shelved by the end of the 1950s.[267] In this respect, Yugoslavia experienced a solidification of the institutional framework of its (ethnic) nations, which could be filled with nationalist content during the political and economic crisis of the late 1980s. On the whole, Pavel Kolář's verdict on the coherence of official nationalism to system stability seems plausible: 'It is difficult to come to a clear conclusion on whether national beliefs underpinned or undermined communist rule.'[268]

Consumption and nationalism as legitimation strategies could not ensure long-term stability in communist rule (only the Chinese communists have demonstrated how this may function – but first, they had to use mass violence to suppress dissent in 1989); however, these strategies did succeed in contributing to the reinforcement of statehood. This became particularly clear in the late 1980s, for, as the party seemed to have failed, the state remained. Moreover, the state was the central recipient for claims to the realization of social justice, material redistribution and national recognition – expectations that were propagated in the previous decades by the ruling communists. When the communist parties lost their power, a 'petty-bourgeois, socialist orientation' prevailed among the general public. Only a minority championed private property and a market economy, while the majority advocated pluralism, freedom and prosperity coupled with a strong socio-political and economic role for the state.[269] During the Solidarity protests in Poland in the 1980s, for instance, the resilience of the national state was easy to see. The strikers saw the state 'as not only socialist, but Polish as well, as – at least according to expectations – an institution of the Polish people.'[270] The party's attempts to re-appropriate the state as a means of legitimation, after it had expanded its dominant role in the lives of the people over so many years, were bound to fail.[271]

Yugoslavia's federal institutions underwent a radical loss of legitimacy, but not those of the constituent republics, which since 1974 had practically operated as national states within the federation. Their institutions were more strongly present in the everyday lives of the people, as they were responsible for education, health and social policy. In this respect, titles such as 'State Collapse in South-Eastern Europe'[272] are somewhat misleading, because the disintegration of Yugoslavia did not mean the collapse of statehood, but the collapse of the collective federation; as of 1990, the actual attack on statehood would emanate from violent secessionist groups within the individual successor states. 'Real socialism' had succeeded in turning Marx and Engels' vision of the withering away of the state upside down: it was socialism that withered away and the structures of modern statehood that proved to be resilient.

---

267 Cf. Hilde Katrine Haug, *Creating a Socialist Yugoslavia: Tito, Communist Leadership and the National Question* (London: Tauris, 2012); Sabrina P. Ramet, *Nationalism and Federalism in Yugoslavia, 1962–1991*, 2nd ed. (Bloomington, IN: Indiana University Press, 1992).

268 Kolář, 'Communism in Eastern Europe', 207.

269 Jolanta Polakowska-Kujawa, 'Soziale Konflikte in Polen und die Legitimierung der Macht, 1945–1994', in *Jahrbuch für Historische Kommunismusforschung 1996*, 69–83.

270 Natali Stegmann, '"Für Brot und Freiheit": Zum Verhältnis von materiellen und ideellen Erwartungen im "Langen Sommer der Solidarność"', in *Sozialistische Staatlichkeit*, eds Jana Osterkamp and Joachim von Puttkamer (München: Oldenbourg, 2012), 161–74, here 165.

271 Jan Kubik, *The Power of Symbols against the Symbols of Power: The Rise of Solidarity and the Fall of State Socialism in Poland* (University Park, PA: Pennsylvania State University Press, 1994).

272 Lenard J. Cohen and Jasna Dragović-Soso, eds, *State Collapse in South-eastern Europe: New Perspectives on Yugoslavia's Disintegration* (West Lafayette, IN: Purdue University Press, 2008).

Statehood in socialism

Erosion of legitimation

In the 1980s, it became clear that the language of legitimation, which still functioned tolerably well in the years of post-Stalinism, no longer applied.[273] The ruling parties could not develop a viable alternative; they suffered a comprehensive loss of legitimacy, which in 1989–90 culminated in the end of their rule. This was caused by a series of mutually reinforcing factors that in the final analysis made it impossible for the communists to enforce compliance with their policies; the attempt in Romania to halt this process with a massive use of force failed. Among the relevant processes are external as well as internal ones that, in their combination, dissolved the people's confidence in the problem-solving capacities of the ruling party and its organs. This jeopardized the ruling party's constitutionally legitimated claim to omnipotence, as the people knew whom they had to hold responsible for their suffering. In the state socialist system there were no alternative channels for disapproval, like that of blaming anonymous market forces for economic difficulties. An example of one such inherent contradiction is the communist governments' commitment to environmental protection which began in the 1970s. However, they simultaneously promoted an extremely resource-intensive economic policy and were tolerant when enterprises ignored environmental regulations, as growth was always more important than the protection of nature.[274] Yet many people, thanks in part to official rhetoric, developed an increasing sensitivity towards environmental problems. In several state socialist countries – for instance, in Hungary, Bulgaria as well as the Baltic Soviet republics – environmental movements were among the first, truly broad-based opposition movements.

The economic problems that intensified in the 1980s were a crucial factor in the delegitimization of state socialism. The communist governments' answers to the crisis were both inadequate and inconsistent. In Romania, Ceaușescu's austerity policy led to a rapid drop in living standards and thus growing dissatisfaction while the country lacked the funds for much-needed investments. In Yugoslavia, cost-cutting policies demanded by international donors caused the population to suffer a severe drop in real wages and spending power, thereby dismantling an important pillar of the people's approval of the system and triggering rapidly rising unemployment. The economic crisis also led to major disagreements between the republics as their respective economic situations noticeably differed. The persistent economic misery in Poland was at the root of the 1980s-strike movement, which gave rise to Solidarity, the independent labour union that quickly became a mass movement and challenged the communist party's monopoly on power. Martial law imposed in December 1981 was unable to solve the country's economic woes; indeed, Poles were forced to become accustomed to a consistent scarcity of fundamental consumer goods throughout the 1980s. While elsewhere the supply of goods may not have been so dramatically low (such as in Hungary, Bulgaria, the GDR and Czechoslovakia), disparities in comparison to neighbours in capitalist countries were irrefutable, as most people were keenly aware of them through their increasing contact with the West. In Albania, the regime never rehabilitated consumption,

---

273 Kolář, 'Kommunistische Identitäten im Streit', 265–6.

274 See Arnošt Štanzel, *Wasserträume und Wasserräume im Staatssozialismus. Ein umwelthistorischer Vergleich anhand der tschechoslowakischen und rumänischen Wasserwirtschaft 1948–1989* (Göttingen:Vandenhoeck & Ruprecht, 2017).

having chosen instead to favour heavy industry; 1990 saw thousands revolt against this policy of de-emphasizing consumption.[275]

The communist economies collapsed because of their inability to shift from a strategy of extensive growth, which focuses on a constant increase of input-factors, to one based on intensive growth, which focuses on constantly improving efficiency. The productivity gap vis-à-vis the West was growing ever more severe; their economies were mired in old-style assembly-line production cycles, while the West was embracing a computerized technology revolution and increasingly directing resources into the service sector. Then came the second oil price shock of 1979, which had a devastating effect on the energy-intensive industries in state socialist countries, especially when the Soviet Union began demanding higher prices for crude oil deliveries to its 'satellites' in the 1980s. The promises made by communist party leaders rang ever hollower, which had far-reaching consequences for a political system whose acceptance was essentially dependent on fulfilling concrete promises regarding living standards. At the same time, ideas of radical liberalization and economic reforms found little favour among the majority of the working population, as they had internalized ideals of equality as well as the state's promises of prosperity.[276]

The governments found themselves in a catch-22 predicament. Without fundamental reform they were heading for economic collapse; at the same time, radical reform would have cost the communist party the approval of essential social groups who would see their financial situation jeopardized. This correlation first became clear in Hungary, when skilled workers – a social bedrock of the Kadar regime – complained of rising inequality stemming from the widespread informal private sector jobs that were gradually being legalized by the state.[277] In Yugoslavia, it was the largely autonomous constituent republics that prevented, through vetoes, the painful measures pushed by the federal government, as they did not wish to assume responsibility for the social costs and rather pursued a policy of 'everyone for themselves'. The reforms by the governments of Milka Planinc (1982–1986), Branko Mikulić (1986–1988) and particularly the last Yugoslav premier, Ante Marković (1989–1991), which all seemed promising at the outset, were condemned to failure due to both the institutional obstinacy of the republics and the resistance presented by opponents of reform within the League of Communists.[278]

Economic stagnation and the clientelistic structure of power relations were closely connected to the abandonment of another promise made by the communist leadership, namely the possibility for social advancement. As early as the 1970s, sociological studies indicated an increasing encrustation of the social stratification and tendency towards the self-reproduction of individual social classes. The baby boomers flooding the labour market were better educated on average than their parents' generation, yet frequently lacked an attractive job

---

275 An interesting contemporary analysis from 1990 can be found in Franz-Lothar Altmann and Robert Elsie, eds, *Albanien im Umbruch: Eine Bestandsaufnahme* (München: Oldenbourg, 1990); Südost-Institut/Article in Ger. and Eng., http://nbn-resolving.de/urn/resolver.pl?urn=urn:nbn:de:bvb:12-bsb00088482-7; Cf. Michael Schmidt-Neke, 'Innenpolitik', in *Albanien*, ed. Klaus-Detlev Grothusen (Göttingen:Vandenhoeck & Ruprecht, 1993), 57–85, here 80–4.

276 At the beginning of the 1980s, the Croatian sociologist Josip Županov coined the term 'syndrome of radical egalitarianism' for this condition; Cited in Dejan Jović, *Yugoslavia: A State That Withered Away* (West Lafayette, IN: Purdue University Press, 2009), 162.

277 Mark Pittaway, *The Workers' State: Industrial Labor and the Making of Socialist Hungary, 1944–1958* (Pittsburgh, PA: University of Pittsburgh Press, 2012).

278 Jović, *Yugoslavia*, 152, 205.

prospect. They often saw their advancement opportunities blocked by people who gained influential positions for political reasons, not due to their qualifications or achievements. In the 1970s and 80s, social inequality was on the rise, and not only in Yugoslavia where it could openly be problematized by social scientists.[279] At the same time, despite somewhat elaborately staged rituals, the official master narratives lost cohesive force among young people, who were drawn more to international pop culture than to the old myths of class struggle and the revolution. As Alexei Yurchak has maintained, ideology in late socialism had lost its verifying function, and was left only with a performative one.[280] As Mikhail Gorbachev assumed power in March 1985, the external reference point for the inevitability of communist rule began to fade.

Internally, the communist regimes became victims of the governance practices they had developed over 40 years, which were characterized by far-reaching, informal negotiation mechanisms as well as a high degree of nepotism and duplicity. The party leaders ultimately never knew what would result from a political decision that had been forged through a range of various informal interactions.[281] As there was neither a democratic balancing of interests nor an open shaping of public opinion, and because subordinate bodies were fraught with systemic incentives to lie to superior authorities about actual conditions in the country, the system lacked functioning feedback mechanisms. Despite hypertrophic secret services and a statutory system of grievances, party leaders suffered under an acute information deficit, as the entities lacked the participants' trust that is necessary to garner accurate information.[282] In a situation marked by mounting internal tensions and external challenges, such as it was at the end of the 1980s, the allegedly stable communist dictatorships proved to be decidedly dysfunctional political systems. And this applied not only to Yugoslavia, where the more than 80,000 Basic Organizations of Associated Labour (BOALs) existing in the 1980s made coherent policy structurally impossible.

Conclusion

As a first conclusion, we want to argue that the state as addressee for claims of social justice, welfare and security as well as the organizational framework of modern society survived the end of communist rule. In a way, the concepts of statehood as propagated by communists during their reign proved successful and also guided political preferences after 1989. As of today, the Eastern European populations show on average a higher acceptance of state property and a redistributive role of the state in the economy than most Western European populations. This was also conditioned by the fact that the Eastern European communists had made their peace with the state early on, never contemplating policies that would 'wither away the state', as originally envisioned by Marx and Engels. Only the Yugoslav communists embarked on this path – and succeeded in destroying their state, although in a radically different manner than originally envisioned. Yugoslavia and, two years later, Czechoslovakia were replaced by nation states, which ultimately highlights the salience of concepts of statehood predicated upon the

---

279 Rory Archer, Igor Duda and Paul Stubbs, eds, *Social Inequalities and Discontent in Yugoslav Socialism* (London: Routledge, 2016).

280 Yurchak, *Everything Was Forever*.

281 Cf. Gerald W. Creed, *Domesticating Revolution: From Socialist Reform to Ambivalent Transition in a Bulgarian Village* (University Park, PA: Pennsylvania State University Press, 1998).

282 Martin K. Dimitrov, 'What the Party Wanted to Know: Citizen Complaints as a "Barometer of Public Opinion" in Communist Bulgaria', *East European Politics & Societies* 28, no. 2 (2014): 271–95.

nation.[283] Communist economic policies, focused on national autarky and state-wide planning as they were, were actually more supportive of the principle of the nation state than Western Europe, where nation states in the 1950s began to share sovereignty and whose economies were much more strongly integrated into the international division of labour.

The state socialist period, hence, witnessed the climax of Europe's epoch of the nation state – the memories of which inform nationalist reactions against globalization and European integration today. Socialist statehood not only fits into the model of modern (or 'high-modernist') statehood but represents its apogee. The communist strive for homogeneity was combined with the availability of modern tools of policing. The growing discontent in the state socialist countries was, therefore, not directed against the state per se but against the party bureaucracy that failed to fulfil its part of the social contract. Since the communist parties were occupying all fields of politically relevant decision-making, the social discontent was channelled towards them as representatives of power but not against state institutions as such.

A second conclusion might be that the state really has no essence as an 'it', as observed by Wendy Brown:

> Despite the almost unavoidable tendency to speak of the state as an 'it', the domain we call the state is not a thing, system, or subject but a significantly unbounded terrain of powers and techniques, an ensemble of discourse, rules and practices, cohabiting in limited tension-ridden, often contradictory relation with one another.[284]

This is also true when we try to integrate our findings into a pan-European context. Here it becomes clear that also in the West, the ideal type of modern statehood never existed in its pure form. This is, of course, no revelation to students of Western European political history. But to sharpen this argument, we claim that concepts of state in Western and Eastern Europe were changing in a process of mutual observation. To give an example: the dominance of neo-liberalism in Western Europe (especially the United Kingdom) and the United States since around 1980 cannot be understood without the interrelatedness of the two blocs during the Cold War. The strange mix between condemnation and admiration of the market economy by reform communists and economists in Eastern Europe fuelled transnational expert discourses about economic reforms in both parts of the world. Johanna Bockman even identifies an Eastern European pedigree of neo-liberal thinking.[285] The realization of the West's superiority in economic productivity spurred Eastern European reformers to rethink the role of the state. In a similar manner in the decades before, Western governments had also extended welfare provisions in response to the communists' ambitious welfare policies. It is indicative that welfare cuts became politically acceptable in the West at a time when the East did not present any viable alternative any more. Cold War competition thus contributed largely to the changes in the dominant notions of state and its responsibilities in the East and the West, both in times of expansion and retrenchment of the state's economic and social role.[286]

---

283 It is indicative that the only federal state to emerge from these federations, Bosnia-Herzegovina, is widely acknowledged as being dysfunctional as a state.
284 Wendy Brown, 'Finding the Man in the State', *Feminist Studies* 18, no. 1 (Spring 1992): 7–34, here 12.
285 Bockman, *Markets in the Name of Socialism*.
286 Cf. Sharad Chari/Katherine Verdery, 'Thinking between the Posts: Postcolonialism, Postsocialism, and Ethnography after the Cold War', *Comparative Studies in Society and History* 51, no. 1 (2009): 6–34.

Statehood in socialism

This complex interference is continuing. Eastern European societies in the 1990s unwillingly became a laboratory for radical welfare system transformations. The popular preference for a strong welfare state could not be translated into respective policies after the end of communism: economic realities – a strong reduction of the cake to be distributed – and the hegemony of international financial institutions, which at that time propagated neo-liberal reform recipes, prevented a welfare-state oriented transformation in most countries. Instead, privatization was conducted in an often haphazard (and corrupt) manner. It is indicative that the two economically most developed countries of the region (Slovenia and the Czech Republic) paid only lip-service to neo-liberalism, while the state retained a strong economic position (often mediated through state-controlled banks and investment funds) and welfare provisions remained on a high level, at least until the financial crisis of 2008. Welfare reforms tested in Eastern Europe were also applied in Western Europe, which – according to Philipp Ther – resulted in a process of co-transformation.[287] The privatization of economic resources was also not an exclusively 'Eastern' development: wide-ranging, state-owned or controlled property, such as in heavy industry and infrastructure, was also delegitimized in Western Europe in the 1980s and 1990s, leading to massive sell-offs.

Statehood, thus, provides a common framework to link distinct European histories in time and space. The Cold War not only resulted in divisions, but also in new connections – real and imagined ones. And 1989 was not only a rupture, but also a linkage. The post-war state in Europe became the main locus of claims for social protection, welfare, personal safety and – in continental Europe at least – also individual as well as collective advancement. In Eastern Europe, this was mainly a result of communist policies (which is not to deny the importance of pre-war traditions of redistributive statehood). In some parts of the region, where the state had traditionally either been far away or was associated with foreign rule, the state actually became an accepted principle of order only under state socialism (think of Albania, for example, where interwar governments had struggled to create recognition of the state as an abstract institution). In the many underdeveloped regions of Eastern and Southeastern Europe, it was the state that mobilized the necessary resources for industrialization and modernization. Whatever the social and environmental costs of that might have been (and they were enormous), many people associate the advancement of their country with modernity, and they associate their family's social ascent from crushing rural poverty with the state socialist period. This might help to explain why so many people today look towards the state for protection from the dislocating forces of globalization. It is ironic, but also consequential, that rabidly anti-communist political forces in the region nowadays lead a rehabilitation of the strong and illiberal state, using rhetoric that must sound familiar to those who had lived through state socialism.

Further reading

Alexopoulos, Golfo. *Stalin's Outcasts: Aliens, Citizens, and the Soviet State, 1926–1936* (Ithaca, NY: Cornell University Press, 2003).

Altrichter, Helmut, ed. *Der KSZE-Prozess: vom Kalten Krieg zu einem neuen Europa* (München: Oldenbourg, 2011).

Amm, Joachim. *Die Föderalversammlung der CSSR: Sozialistischer Parlamentarismus im unitarischen Föderalismus 1969–1989* (Wiesbaden: Westdeutscher Verlag, 2001).

---

287 Philipp Ther, *Europe since 1989: A History*, translated by Charlotte Hughes-Kreutzmüller (Princeton, NJ: Princeton University Press, 2016).

Apor, Balázs, Péter Apor, and E.A. Rees, eds. *The Sovietization of Eastern Europe: New Perspectives on the Postwar Period* (Washington, DC: New Academia Publishing, 2008).

Archer, Rory, Igor Duda, and Paul Stubbs, eds. *Social Inequalities and Discontent in Yugoslav Socialism* (London: Routledge, 2016).

Beckmann-Petey, Monika. *Der jugoslawische Föderalismus* (München: Oldenbourg, 1990).

Berend, Ivan T. *Central and Eastern Europe, 1944–1993: Detour from the Periphery to the Periphery, reprinted, Cambridge Studies in Modern Economic History* vol. 1 (Cambridge: Cambridge University Press, 2001).

Billig, Michael. *Banal Nationalism* (London: Sage, 1995).

Bockman, Johanna. *Markets in the Name of Socialism: The Left-Wing Origins of Neoliberalism* (Stanford, CA: Stanford University Press, 2011).

Bourdieu, Pierre. *Practical Reason: On the Theory of Action* (Stanford, CA: Stanford University Press, 1998).

Bren, Paulina. *The Greengrocer and his TV: The Culture of Communism after the 1968 Prague Spring* (Ithaca, NY: Cornell University Press, 2010).

Bren, Paulina, and Mary Neuburger, eds. *Communism Unwrapped: Consumption in Cold War Eastern Europe* (Oxford: Oxford University Press, 2012).

Brunnbauer, Ulf. *'Die sozialistische Lebensweise': Ideologie, Gesellschaft, Familie und Politik in Bulgarien (1944–1989)* (Vienna: Böhlau, 2007).

Brunnbauer, Ulf, and Hannes Grandits, eds. *The Ambiguous Nation: Case Studies from Southeastern Europe in the 20th Century* (München: Oldenbourg, 2013).

Cohen, Lenard J., and Jasna Dragović-Soso, eds. *State Collapse in South-eastern Europe: New Perspectives on Yugoslavia's Disintegration* (West Lafayette, IN: Purdue University Press, 2008).

Connelly, John. *From Peoples Into Nations: A History of Eastern Europe* (Princeton, NJ: Princeton University Press, 2020).

Creed, Gerald W. *Domesticating Revolution: From Socialist Reform to Ambivalent Transition in a Bulgarian Village* (University Park, PA: Pennsylvania State University Press, 1998).

Crowley, David, and Susan E. Reid, eds. *Socialist Spaces: Sites of Everyday Life in the Eastern Bloc* (Oxford: Berg, 2002).

Deák, István, Jan T. Gross, and Tony Judt, eds. *The Politics of Retribution in Europe: World War II and Its Aftermath* (Princeton, NJ: Princeton University Press, 2000).

Djilas, Milovan. *The New Class: An Analysis of the Communist System* (San Diego, CA: Harcourt Brace Jovanovich, 1957).

Duda, Igor. *Pronađeno blagostanje: Svakodnevni život i potrošačka kultura u Hrvatskoj 1970-ih i 1980-ih* [Well-being found: everyday life and consumer culture in Croatia in the 1970s and 1980s] (Zagreb: Srednja Europa, 2010).

Dyczewski, L. *Rodzina. Społeczeństwo. Państwo* [Family, society, and the state] (Lublin: Towarzystwo Naukowe Katolickiego Uniwersytetu Lubelskiego, 1994).

Falk, Barbara J. *The Dilemmas of Dissidence in East Central Europe: Citizen Intellectuals and Philosopher Kings* (Budapest: CEU Press, 2003).

Fehér, Ferenc, Agnes Heller, and György Márkus. *Dictatorship over Needs* (Oxford: Blackwell, 1983).

Frommer, Benjamin. *National Cleansing: Retribution Against Nazi Collaborators in Postwar Czechoslovakia* (Cambridge: Cambridge University Press, 2005).

Gal, Susan, and Gail Kligman, eds. *Reproducing Gender: Politics, Publics, and Everyday Life after Socialism* (Princeton, NJ: Princeton University Press, 2000a).

Gal, Susan, and Gail Kligman. *The Politics of Gender after Socialism: A Comparative Historical Essay* (Princeton, NJ: Princeton University Press, 2000b).

Geilke, Georg. *Das Staatsangehörigkeitsrecht von Polen* (Frankfurt a.M.: Metzler, 1952).

Gerlach, Christian. *Extremely Violent Societies: Mass Violence in the 20th Century World* (Cambridge: Cambridge University Press, 2010).

Gestwa, Klaus. *Die Stalinschen Großbauten des Kommunismus: Sowjetische Technik- und Umweltgeschichte, 1948–1967* (München: Oldenbourg, 2010).

Gilley, Bruce. *The Right to Rule: How States Win and Lose Legitimacy* (New York: Columbia University Press, 2009).

Götting, Ulrike. *Transformationen der Wohlfahrtsstaaten in Mittel- und Osteuropa: Eine Zwischenbilanz* (Opladen: Verlag für Sozialwissenschaften, 1998).

Haney, Lynne A. *Inventing the Needy: Gender and the Politics of Welfare in Hungary* (Berkeley, CA: University of California Press, 2002).

Haug, Hilde Katrine. *Creating a Socialist Yugoslavia: Tito, Communist Leadership and the National Question* (London: Tauris, 2012).

Statehood in socialism

Havel, Václav, et al. *The Power of the Powerless, ed. John Keane* (Armonk, NY: Sharpe, 1985).

Heller, Klaus, and Jan Plamper, eds. *Personality Cults in Stalinism* (Göttingen: V&R Unipress, 2004).

Hering, Sabine, ed. *Social Care Under State Socialism (1945–1989): Ambitions, Ambiguities, and Mismanagement* (Opladen: Budrich, 2009).

Hirszowicz, Maria. *The Bureaucratic Leviathan: A Study in the Sociology of Communism* (Oxford: Martin Robertson, 1980).

Horváth, Sándor. *Stalinism Reloaded: Everyday Life in Stalin-City, Hungary* (Bloomington, IN: Indiana University Press, 2017).

Inglot, Tomasz. *Welfare States in East Central Europe, 1919–2004* (Cambridge: Cambridge University Press, 2008).

Iordachi, Constantin, and Arnd Bauerkämper, eds. *The Collectivization of Agriculture in Communist Eastern Europe: Comparison and Entanglements* (Budapest: CEU Press, 2014).

Jović, Dejan. *Yugoslavia: A State That Withered Away* (West Lafayette, IN: Purdue University Press, 2009).

Judt, Tony. *Postwar: A History of Europe since 1945* (London: Penguin, 2005).

Kenney, Padraic. *A Carnival of Revolution: Central Europe 1989* (Princeton, NJ: Princeton University Press, 2002).

Klenner, Christina, and Simone Leiber, eds. *Welfare States and Gender Inequality in Central and Eastern Europe: Continuity and Post-Socialist Transformation in the EU Member States* (Brussels: ETUI, 2010).

Kligman, Gail, and Katherine Verdery, eds. *Peasants Under Siege: The Collectivization of Romanian Agriculture, 1949–1962* (Princeton, NJ: Princeton University Press, 2011).

Kolář, Pavel. *Der Poststalinismus: Ideologie und Utopie einer Epoche* (Köln: Böhlau, 2016).

Koleva, Daniela, ed. *Negotiating Normality: Everyday Lives in Socialist Institutions* (New Brunswick, NJ: Transaction, 2012).

Kotkin, Stephen. *Uncivil Society: 1989 and the Implosion of the Communist Establishment* (New York: Modern Library, 2009).

Kretsi, Georgia. *Verfolgung und Gedächtnis in Albanien: Eine Analyse postsozialistischer Erinnerungsstrategien* (Wiesbaden: Harrassowitz, 2007).

Kubik, Jan. *The Power of Symbols against the Symbols of Power: The Rise of Solidarity and the Fall of State Socialism in Poland* (University Park, PA: Pennsylvania State University Press, 1994).

Le Normand, Brigitte. *Designing Tito's Capital: Urban Planning, Modernism, and Socialism* (Pittsburgh, PA: University of Pittsburgh Press, 2014).

Lebow, Katherine Anne. *Unfinished Utopia: Nowa Huta Stalinism and Polish Society 1949–56* (Ithaca, NY: Cornell University Press, 2013).

Lüdtke, Alf, and Michael Wildt, eds. *Staats-Gewalt: Ausnahmezustand und Sicherheitsregimes: Historische Perspektiven* (Göttingen: Wallstein, 2008).

Magaš, Branka. *The Destruction of Yugoslavia: Tracking the Break-up 1980–1992* (London: Verso, 1993).

Marshall, Thomas H. *Citizenship and Social Classes and Other Essays* (Cambridge: Cambridge University Press, 1950).

Mazower, Mark. *No Enchanted Palace: The End of Empire and the Ideological Origins of the United Nations* (Princeton, NJ: Princeton University Press, 2009).

Mazower, Mark, Jessica Reinisch, and David Feldman, eds. *Post-War Reconstruction in Europe: International Perspectives, 1945–1949* (Oxford: Oxford University Press, 2011).

McDermott, Kevin, and Andrew Stibbe, eds. *Stalinist Terror in Eastern Europe: Elite Purges and Mass Repression* (Manchester: Manchester University Press, 2010).

Osterkamp, Jana, and Joachim von Puttkamer, eds. *Sozialistische Staatlichkeit* (München: Oldenbourg, 2012).

Persak, Krzysztof, and Łukasz Kamiński, eds. *A Handbook of the Communist Security Apparatus in East Central Europe, 1944–1989* (Warsaw: Instytut Pamieci Narodowej, 2005).

Pittaway, Mark. *Eastern Europe 1939–2000, Brief Histories* (London: Bloomsbury Academic, 2010).

Pittaway, Mark. *The Workers' State: Industrial Labor and the Making of Socialist Hungary, 1944–1958* (Pittsburgh, PA: University of Pittsburgh Press, 2012).

Pryor, Frederic L. *The Red and the Green: The Rise and Fall of Collectivized Agriculture in Marxist Regimes* (Princeton, NJ: Princeton University Press, 1992).

Ramet, Sabrina P. *Nationalism and Federalism in Yugoslavia, 1962–1991*, 2nd ed. (Bloomington, IN: Indiana University Press, 1992).

Reinhard, Wolfgang. *Geschichte der Staatsgewalt: Eine vergleichende Verfassungsgeschichte Europas von den Anfängen bis zur Gegenwart* (München: C.H. Beck, 1999).

Rothschild, Joseph, and Nancy Merriwether Wingfield. *Return to Diversity: A Political History of East Central Europe since World War II*, 3rd ed. (New York: Oxford University Press, 2000).

Satjukow, Silke, and Rainer Gries, eds. *Unsere Feinde: Konstruktionen des Anderen im Sozialismus* (Leipzig: Leipziger Universitätsverlag, 2004).

Schulze Wessel, Martin, and Christiane Brenner, eds. *Zukunftsvorstellungen und staatliche Planung im Sozialismus: Die Tschechoslowakei im ostmitteleuropäischen Kontext 1945–1989* (München: Oldenbourg, 2010).

Segert, Dieter. *Transformationen in Osteuropa im 20. Jahrhundert* (Vienna: UTB, 2013).

Snyder, Sarah. *Human Rights Activism and the End of the Cold War: A Transnational History of the Helsinki Network* (Cambridge: Cambridge University Press, 2013).

Taylor, Karin. *Let's Twist Again: Youth and Leisure in Socialist Bulgaria* (Vienna: LIT, 2006).

Ther, Philipp. *Europe since 1989: A History*. Translated by Charlotte Hughes-Kreutzmüller (Princeton, NJ: Princeton University Press, 2016).

Tomka, Béla. *A Social History of Twentieth-Century Europe* (London: Routledge, 2013).

Verdery, Katherine. *National Ideology under Socialism: Identity and Cultural Politics in Ceausescu's Romania* (Berkeley, CA: University of California Press, 1991).

Yurchak, Alexei. *Everything Was Forever, Until It Was No More: The Last Soviet Generation* (Princeton, NJ: Princeton University Press, 2005).

Zahra, Tara. *The Lost Children: Reconstructing Europe's Families after World War II* (Cambridge: Harvard University Press, 2011).

Zaremba, Marcin. *Wielka Trwoga, Polska 1944–1947: ludowa reakcja na kryzys* [The great fear: Poland 1944–1947 – the people's reaction to crisis] (Kraków: Znak, 2012).

Zimmermann, Volker, Peter Haslinger and Tomáš Nigrin, eds. *Loyalitäten im Staatssozialismus: DDR, Tschechoslowakei, Polen* (Marburg: Herder, 2010).

7

1989 AND BEYOND

Joachim von Puttkamer

Ottomanization rather than Finlandization – since 1986, this was Timothy Garton Ash's prospect for the Soviet bloc in the light of a re-emerging idea of Central Europe.[1] He imagined an empire crumbling away and nation states gradually claiming full independence rather than a geopolitical rearrangement of hegemonic spheres. His remark was meant to make the Western reader aware of intellectual revival in the region, of the erosion of the communist regimes in the face of increasingly self-assertive populations, and of the potential changes that Mikhail Gorbachev's rise to power held in store. Historical analogy served this purpose, awkward as the comparison might seem. The Soviet Union was much different from the late Ottoman Empire, both in terms of military power and in terms of its almost omnipresent bureaucracy. It had signed the CSCE agreements on its own accord, and surely it was not going to yield to outward pressure. Finland's guided parliamentary democracy, modelled on the Scandinavian welfare state, seemed much closer to the aspirations of Central European intellectuals than the inefficient state building of the post-Ottoman nation states in the Balkans. In the late 1980s, the Soviet Union still seemed like it would last forever, so that implementing a fair degree of autonomy within its hegemonic sphere along Finnish lines seemed the best option available for its constituent states. Yet the alternative notion of Ottomanization used by Garton Ash hinted at the fact that there was more at stake than Soviet hegemony. It evoked spectres of political instability, national conflict and authoritarian rule that had risen out of the debris of demolished empires, not only in the Balkans, but in all of interwar Central Europe. Restoring Central Europe would be as much about state building and national emancipation, rebuilding economies in rapid decline, establishing trust and tackling corruption, promoting democracy and resisting populist temptations, and last but not least, would be a test of Western commitment to its brethren further to the East.

Promises of democracy: dissident concepts and the 1989 revolutions

Dissidents themselves had seldom explicitly named Finland as a model for Central Europe, but it did figure in their political conceptions. In November 1976, Jacek Kuroń had found 'Finlandization' to be a worthy goal, sufficiently moderate to appear attainable, ambitious

---

1 Timothy Garton Ash, 'Does Central Europe Exist?' in *The Uses of Adversity: Essays on the Fate of Central Europe*, ed. Timothy Garton Ash (New York: Random House, 1989), 179–213, here 209 [first published 1986]; Timothy Garton Ash, 'Reform or Revolution?' in Garton Ash, *The Uses of Adversity*, 242–303, here 252–5.

enough to motivate social movements in Poland to organize and enter into dialogue with the communist government. With the Brezhnev Doctrine in mind, he claimed that parliamentary democracy within the Soviet sphere would have to safeguard the individual against the totalitarian ambitions of the state. It was the utmost political aim, he wrote, beyond which further aspirations could only be irresponsible dreams. Just a few weeks earlier, Adam Michnik had outlined a 'New Evolutionism' along similar lines.[2] These two essays marked a departure from Marxist revisionism and with it a departure from the hope that socialism could be reformed from within the party. Since the Soviet Union would not allow socialism to take on a human face, Michnik wrote, society would have to defend itself against dictatorship and force the party state to soften repression and allow space for independent political activity. Evolutionism was a formula that called for patience while Soviet power was still in place. From then on, political opposition became a moral stance, and the public defence of human rights became its most visible expression.

In hindsight, this break with revisionism and the concomitant desire to supplant the old, Marxist utopia with the new and much more practicable utopia of human rights marked a major step towards the rise of Western democracy in Central and Eastern Europe, even if it could not yet be fully spelled out at the time. But this development was hardly straightforward or inevitable. Until 1989, oppositional thought bore many revisionist traces, and when the communist regimes came down in the autumn of 1989, the notion of taking socialist democracy seriously no longer offered a viable alternative. Western democracy, long banned from political thought, now seemed within reach, and within the next decade, it mostly won out against populist temptations of a more authoritarian nature. These developments can be traced back to dissident thought, but they had not been clearly staked out prior to 1989.

Criticizing alleged distortions of the communist party state had been at the very core of revisionist thinking since its beginnings in the 1950s. Throughout the region, intellectuals as much as the party rank and file had been horrified at the dimensions of violence that were disclosed after Joseph Stalin's death and in the wake of Nikita Khrushchev's secret speech in March 1956.[3] Most disturbing for them was the fact that party members themselves had fallen victim to fabricated charges made by a security apparatus that seemed to have spun out of control. Such discontent among party members had triggered the Hungarian Revolution of 1956. Throughout the Soviet bloc, leftist intellectuals, mostly party members themselves, argued that socialism, once triumphant, should be able to afford a retreat from violence and avoid the mistakes of the past. Such calls echoed the arguments of the late 1940s that each country should develop its own path towards socialism and avoid the horrors of protracted civil war along the Soviet model. Legal scholars then condensed these notions into theories of socialist legality.

---

2 Jacek Kuroń, 'Myśli o programie działania', in Jacek Kuroń, *Zasady ideowe* (Paris: Instytut Literacki), 11–33, in English: idem and Krystyna Aytoun, 'Document on Contemporary Poland: Reflections on a Program of Action', *The Polish Review* 22, no. 3 (1977): 51–69, www.jstor.org/stable/25777499; Jacek Kuroń, 'Zasady ideowe' [Ideological principles], in Kuroń, *Zasady ideowe*, 45–81; Adam Michnik, 'Le nouvel évolutionnisme', in *1956 Varsovie-Budapest: La deuxième révolution d'Octobre*, eds Pierre Kende and Krzysztof Pomian (Paris: Seuil, 1978), 201–14 [Polish translation in Adam Michnik, *Szanse polskiej demokracji* (London: Aneks 1984), 77–87].

3 Michal Kopeček, *Hledání ztraceného smyslu revoluce: Zrod a počátky marxistického revizionismu ve střední Evropě 1953–1960* (Prague: Argo, 2009), 293–304, forthcoming in English: *Quest for the Revolution's Lost Meaning: The Origins of Marxist Revisionism in East Central Europe 1953–1960* (Leiden: Brill Academic Publishers); George Schöpflin, *Politics in Eastern Europe: 1945–1992* (Oxford: Blackwell, 1993), 104–26.

1989 and beyond

In Czechoslovakia, ideas of a non-antagonistic, creative socialism had sparked the reformist movement, which culminated in the Prague Spring of 1968 and had been utterly disappointed.[4] Violent repression against strikers and demonstrators blatantly contradicted the party state's claim that it enjoyed overwhelming popular support.

So when opposition circles started to monitor the violation of human rights and summoned the state to adhere to its own legal principles, they tapped into widespread disquietude and transformed it into an effective political strategy. By taking recourse to the newly emerging international language of human rights, dissidents parted with Marxism while retaining a utopian element that transcended bloc confrontation. Yet the idea of the rule of law – held high by the founders of the KOR (Komitet Obrony Robotników/Workers' Defence Committee), Charter 77 and the contributors to the journal *Beszélő*, by opposition groups in the GDR and Soviet dissenters (*inakomysljashchie*) – firmly pointed towards the West. In the 1975 Helsinki Accords, dissidents found the public support that secured their moral standing at home and, often enough, protected them against arrest and incarceration.[5] Publishing abroad, as dissidents had practised it since the 1950s, generally supported the development of an alternative public sphere far beyond the human rights discourse.[6] For the small number of Romanian dissident intellectuals who were unable to build stable networks within their home country, Western attention was crucial for being heard at all.[7]

But there was more to this shift away from Marxist revisionism and towards a seemingly non-ideological political strategy supported by new transnational networks that reached out across the Iron Curtain and connected the various dissident groups with one another. In calling for outspoken resistance against the totalitarian ambitions of the party state, dissidents backed down from the utopian transformation of society and rather aimed for its emancipation. Emancipation was not just an empty slogan. Curbing political violence implied opening up spaces of civic responsibility. By drawing attention to human rights violations, underground publications – 'samizdat', 'tamizdat' (in exile) or '*drugi obieg*' – formed an alternative public sphere. These activities demanded courage, civic engagement and creativity, and were the most effective way of maintaining links with fellow activists in exile. Anti-politics, as promoted by the Hungarian writer György Konrád and the Czech playwright Václav Havel, and Václav Benda's notion of a 'parallel polis' substantiated this claim and served to defend civic activism against the ideological charge of promoting bourgeois capitalism or a 'Third Way' between capitalism and socialism. The state should care for its own affairs and leave society to itself; György Konrád defined the essence of anti-political opposition: 'its essential activity is to work for destatification'.[8] This disclaimer, however, did not make the question of what a future political order would look like

---

4 Kieran Williams, *The Prague Spring and its Aftermath: Czechoslovak Politics, 1968–1970* (Cambridge: Cambridge University Press, 1997), 3–28; Vladimir V. Kusin, *The Intellectual Origins of the Prague Spring: The Development of Reformist Ideas in Czechoslovakia 1956–1967* (Cambridge: Cambridge University Press, 1971).

5 Robert Brier, ed., *Entangled Protest: Transnational Approaches to the History of Dissent in Eastern Europe and the Soviet Union* (Osnabrück: Fibre, 2013); Friederike Kind-Kovács and Jessie Labov, eds, *Samizdat, Tamizdat, and Beyond: Transnational Media During and After Socialism* (New York: Berghahn Books, 2013).

6 Friederike Kind-Kovács, *Written Here, Published There: How Underground Literature Crossed the Iron Curtain* (Budapest: CEU Press, 2014).

7 Cristina Petrescu, *From Robin Hood to Don Quixote: Resistance and Dissent in Communist Romania* (București: Ed. Enciclopedică, 2013).

8 György Konrád, *Antipolitics: An Essay* (San Diego, CA: Harcourt Brace Jovanovich, 1984), 229.

go away. In Poland in December of 1975, Edward Lipiński, Jacek Kuroń and other signatories of the 'Letter of the 59' demanded free elections and the separation of powers as a consequence flowing directly from those civil rights that had been guaranteed in the Helsinki agreement. In contrast, the Václav Havel of 1978 saw traditional parliamentary democracy as a transitory means for recovering the self-esteem of society at best, but certainly not as a long-term solution to the deep crisis of global technological civilization.[9]

Havel, Michnik and other prominent dissidents were soon to be credited with having reintroduced the idea of civil society into European political thought. But after 1989, they were equally reproached for having allegedly overburdened the new democracies with unattainable moral standards.[10] In truth, these are two sides of the same coin, and both concern the afterlife of a concept that had its origins in a specific historical situation. Originally, the idea of anti-politics or 'living in truth' had offered a moral stance that claimed to transcend ideological confrontations. The idea's proponents sought to translate it into social activity without risking violence and bloodshed. When it became clear in the summer of 1989 that the Brezhnev Doctrine was coming to an end, anti-politics lost its validity. But it had indeed helped pave the way for political pluralism and for the politics of consensus and compromise. And for the pivotal moment of 1989, it had imbued its authors with moral credibility, which the old regime utterly lacked. In this respect, it had served its purpose well.

In economic and social thought, revisionist concepts were more persistent and less prone to conform to the shifts that had taken place in political thought. Notions of market socialism had been widespread among reformist economists throughout Eastern Europe since the de-Stalinization of the late 1950s and generally followed the arguments Oskar Lange had already made before the Second World War. Coordinating state-owned enterprises via the market combined the anti-totalitarian impetus of decentralization with the prospect of true worker control over the means of production. In these debates, however, ideological and theoretical elements outweighed the rather disenchanting results that different forms of market socialism had achieved – in Hungary after 1968, the somewhat cosmetic gains in Wojciech Jaruzelski's Poland, and the particularly disappointing fiasco of workers' self-management in Yugoslavia.[11] It has been argued that the neoclassical background of the debates on market socialism ultimately paved the way for the breakthrough to radical market capitalism and neo-liberal 'shock therapy' after 1989/90, which was imposed most radically on Poland and Czechoslovakia.[12]

---

9 Andrzej Friszke, *Czas KOR-u. Jacek Kuroń a geneza Solidarności* [The time of KOR: Jacek Kuroń and the origins of Solidarity] (Kraków: Wydawnictwo Znak, 2011), 83–9; Václav Havel, *The Power of the Powerless*, ed. John Keane (Armonk, NY: M. E. Sharpe, 1985), 89–92 [first published as *Moc bezmocných* (London: Londýnské listy, 1978)].

10 Barbara J. Falk, *The Dilemmas of Dissidence in East-Central Europe: Citizen Intellectuals and Philosopher Kings* (Budapest: CEU Press, 2003), 313–64; Jean L. Cohen and Andrew Arato, *Civil Society and Political Theory* (Cambridge, MA: MIT Press: 1992), 31–6; Milan Znoj, 'Václav Havel, His Idea of Civil Society, and the Czech Liberal Tradition', in *Thinking Through Transition: Liberal Democracy, Authoritarian Pasts, and Intellectual History in East Central Europe after 1989*, eds Michal Kopeček and Piotr Wciślik (Budapest: CEU Press, 2015), 109–37.

11 Iván T. Berend, *Central and Eastern Europe 1944–1993: Detour from the Periphery to the Periphery* (Cambridge: Cambridge University Press, 1996), 96–8, 146–52, 162–238 and 263–4; Christoph Boyer, ed., *Zur Physiognomie sozialistischer Wirtschaftsreformen. Die Sowjetunion, Polen, die Tschechoslowakei, Ungarn, die DDR und Jugoslawien im Vergleich* (Frankfurt a.M.: Vittorio Klostermann, 2007).

12 Johanna Bockman, *Markets in the Name of Socialism: The Left-Wing Origins of Neoliberalism* (Stanford, CA: Stanford University Press, 2011).

Until the autumn of 1989, the ideal of workers' self-management remained prominent even in Poland, and a return to capitalism via privatization was almost anathema. In Poland, as in Hungary and Gorbachev's Russia, private entrepreneurship remained confined to small firms primarily working in trade and service. Full-scale privatization within an authoritarian framework following the Latin American model, as advocated by the Polish liberal thinker Mirosław Dzielski, remained a marginal position.[13] Again, the political corset of state socialism defined the limits of oppositionist thought, and when this corset had been cast off, the now victorious opposition had to sail in largely uncharted waters.

The one element of revisionist thinking that held sway from the 1950s all the way through the revolutions of 1989 was the biting critique of the bureaucratic usurpation of power by the nomenklatura. Ever since Milovan Djilas' *New Class* was published in 1954, turning incisive class analysis against the ruling party itself had been a recurrent motive of oppositionist thought, its most prominent practitioners being Kuroń and Karol Modzelewski in Poland and Konrád and Iván Szelényi in Hungary.[14] Throughout these decades, communist party elites had done little to counter the appearance of clientelism, privilege, corruption and arbitrariness, and had forfeited all credibility.[15] The urge now to actually oust the nomenklatura might be regarded as the most powerful legacy of revisionist thought. It gave a voice to widespread discontent with the existing order, and when the moment came, it left behind its reformist origins and helped unite masses of demonstrators out on the streets behind previously marginal intellectual oppositionist groups. But it held no guiding principle in itself that would have been capable of creating a new political order. Drawing on strong moral overtones, in the long run it came to feed populist anti-elitism and resentment.

Set on challenging the totalitarian aspirations of the communist party state, on peacefully wringing power from the communists and on overcoming the bloc divide without provoking another Soviet military intervention, the vaguely defined blend of human rights, pluralism, market economy and anti-nomenklatura sentiments within dissident political thought could not provide a blueprint for politics and society in a post-communist world. New dividing lines began to unfold, with positions on national sovereignty being the most important. According to staunchly anti-communist groups like Fidesz in Hungary or the Confederation of Independent Poland (KPN), national freedom could only be achieved through the restoration of full sovereignty. For them, overcoming the global division of the Cold War was equivalent to breaking free from Soviet military domination. In his memoirs, Jacek Kuroń recalls how Leszek Moczulski sharply attacked him for not having called for full national independence in the 'Letter of the 59'.[16] Oppositionist circles engaged in vivid debates on the nation's past and future, and while these debates certainly

---

13 Mirosław Dzielski, *Bóg, wolność, własność* [God, liberty, property], ed. Miłowit Kuniński (Kraków: Księgarnia Akademicka, 2001); Joachim von Puttkamer, 'Der schwere Abschied vom Volkseigentum. Privatisierungsdebatten in Polen und Ostmitteleuropa in den 1980er Jahren', in *Privatisierung. Idee und Praxis seit den 1970er Jahren*, eds Norbert Frei and Dietmar Süß (Göttingen: Wallstein Verlag, 2012), 158–83.

14 Milovan Djilas, *The New Class: An Analysis of the Communist System* (New York: Praeger, 1957); Jacek Kuroń and Karol Modzelewski, *An Open Letter to the Party: A Revolutionary Socialist Manifesto Written in a Polish Prison* (London: International Socialism, 1965); György Konrád and Iván Szelényi, *The Intellectuals on the Road to Class Power: A Sociological Study of the Role of the Intelligentsia in Socialism* (Brighton: Harvester Press, 1979).

15 Leslie Holmes, *The End of Communist Power: Anti-Corruption Campaigns and Legitimation Crisis* (Cambridge: Polity, 1993).

16 Jacek Kuroń, *Autobiografia*, 2nd ed. (Warsaw: Wydawn. Krytyki Politycznej, 2011), 384–5 [from Jacek Kuroń, *Gwiezdny Czas* (London: Aneks, 1991)].

caused some division, they helped to further the development of an alternative public sphere.[17] The fear of a re-emerging National Democracy began to haunt the left opposition in Poland. In Hungary, populist voices within the opposition had taken the lead over liberal intellectuals by addressing the dire conditions of Magyar minorities in Romania and Slovakia. In 1985, István Csurka called the spiritual renewal of the Magyar nation a most noble task that entitled Hungary to take a leading role in the Carpathian Basin.[18] Adam Michnik and Jan-Józef Lipski, Jan Patočka, Petr Pithart and János Kis and others responded early on to the revival of national thought along interwar lines by calling for truthful reflection on national history.[19] Critical voices such as Ján Mlynárik even called for a reassessment of the expulsion of the German population.[20] In a similar vein, intellectuals throughout the region conceived of Central Europe as a space of heterogeneity, hybridity and ambivalence rather than of homogeneous nations. In this, they offered an Eastern contribution to the Western debate on post-modernity as much as an implicit argument against right-wing nationalism at home. The controversial debates on national sovereignty, character and identity accounted in part for the relative weakness of dissent in Romania, where the opposition could barely play the national card against a communist regime that had based its own propaganda on asserting a certain degree of national autonomy.

In 1979, Czech dissident Milan Šimečka argued that the communist dictatorship had already lost all means of reforming itself, so that any bold reform would only come after its inevitable collapse. For Šimečka, the only possible outcome of 'normalization' in Czechoslovakia would be a democratic system that restored legitimate authority and workers' control.[21] One year later, Solidarity (Solidarność) opted for workers' control as the primary goal and the first step towards the long-term prospect of pluralist democracy. The focus on self-government in all spheres of society preserved utopian features of revisionism. The formula of the 'self-limiting revolution' hinted at the difficulties activists faced in spelling out a coherent platform that might reconcile socialism with pluralist democracy while still working within the Soviet sphere of influence.[22] For many months, evolutionism as propagated by Adam Michnik and Jacek Kuroń served as a safeguard against the temptations of premature radicalism, and it would do so again after the suspension of military law. In this respect, evolutionism might actually be seen as the major dissident achievement, no less important than challenging dictatorship itself. Keeping in mind the experience of military crackdown in December 1970 and military law in December 1981, the recourse to evolutionism in Poland restrained public discontent as long as the communist regime was still able to crush the opposition physically, backed by Soviet military might as it was. It would do so again during the Round Table Talks in Poland and Hungary in 1989. Later on, the notion that building democracy demanded patience instilled intellectual elites throughout the region with confidence in the face of disinterest and apathy among the population and provided

---

17 Gregor Feindt, *Auf der Suche nach politischer Gemeinschaft. Oppositionelles Denken zur Nation im ostmitteleuropäischen Samizdat 1976–1992* (Berlin: De Gruyter Oldenbourg, 2015).

18 István Csurka, 'Uj magyar önépités' [New Hungarian self-development], in *A Monori Tanácskozás 1985 június 14–16*, ed. János M. Rainer (Budapest: 1956-os Intézet, 2005), 28–42.

19 Michal Kopeček, 'Human Rights Facing a National Past: Dissident 'Civic Patriotism' and the Return of History in East Central Europe, 1968–1989', *Geschichte und Gesellschaft* 38 (2012): 573–602.

20 Ján Mlynárik, *Thesen zur Aussiedlung der Deutschen aus der Tschechoslowakei 1945–1947* (Waldkraiburg: Danubius, 1985).

21 Milan Šimečka, *The Restoration of Order: The Normalization of Czechoslovakia, 1969–1976* (London: Verso, 1984), 146–52 [first published as *Obnovení pořádku. Příspěvek k typologii reálného socialismu* (Köln: Index, 1979)].

22 Jadwiga Staniszkis, *Poland's Self-Limiting Revolution*, ed. Jan T. Gross (Princeton, NJ: Princeton University Press, 1984).

them with an argument against populist urgings. To develop the values and institutions of an open society was not to be achieved with a single liberating stroke. Once the communists had been brought down, the far-sightedness of the intellectuals for more than a decade helped safeguard the democratic process against disappointment and the menaces of apathy and populism.[23]

The legacy of dissident thought for the emerging democracies was manifold.[24] The general consensus about key goals of implementing civil rights and safeguarding pluralism provided political guidelines for negotiating transitions to parliamentary democracy. Economic reforms, an exchange of elites and a reassertion of national sovereignty had been defined as the most pressing issues, though open debate on how to take them on had only just begun in 1989. The revolutions of 1989 would be guided as much by immediate necessities as they were by political ideas. Revolutions can hardly be planned in advance. The revolutionary situation itself would bring about revolutionary mentalities, the spontaneity of which would quickly transcend earlier concepts. And yet, Czech dissident Jiřína Šiklová soon sparked awareness that it might not even be these former dissidents who would shape the new democracies, but rather professionals who had hitherto remained in a somewhat amorphous 'gray zone'.[25]

The revolutions of 1989

In 1989, Central Europe's communist regimes collapsed one by one in rapid succession.[26] The domino theory by which Eisenhower had characterized communist takeovers in Southeast Asia in 1954 now played out in the opposite direction. Though many arguments have been made in an attempt to identify specific causes and trajectories in each country, the events of 1989 were closely intertwined. Poland's Round Table Talks immediately turned into a model for negotiations in Hungary.[27] The Hungarian transformation caused mass flight from the GDR and the downfall of the Berlin Wall. This, in turn, sparked mass demonstrations in Czechoslovakia, violent unrest in Romania and the less spectacular surrender of the Bulgarian communist regime. Gorbachev's *perestroika* had encouraged the opposition and dispelled fears of a revived Brezhnev Doctrine. Events in Eastern Europe soon played out on the Soviet periphery itself, most notably in the Baltic Republics and the Caucasus.

It has been argued that the domino theory overstresses the importance of mass mobilization and obscures the diversity of the 1989 revolutions.[28] Yet viewing the course of events as

---

23 Katarzyna Chimiak, *ROAD: Polityka czasu przełomu. Ruch Obywatelski – Akcja Demokratyczna, 1990–1991* [ROAD: politics in the time of transition – the Citizens' Action, 1990–1991] (Płock: Fundacja Lorga, 2010), 33–8.

24 Kopeček and Wciślik, *Thinking Through Transition*; András Bozóki, ed., *Intellectuals and Politics in Central Europe* (Budapest: CEU Press, 1999).

25 Jiřina Šiklová, 'The "Gray Zone" and the Future of the Dissidents in Czechoslovakia', *Social Research* 57, no. 2 (1990): 348–63.

26 Gale Stokes, *The Walls Came Tumbling Down: The Collapse of Communism in Eastern Europe* (Oxford: Oxford University Press, 1993); Petr Blažek and Jaroslav Pažout, *Dominový efekt. Opoziční hnutí v zemích střední Evropy a pád komunistických režimu v roce 1989* [The domino effect: opposition movements in the countries of Central Europe and the fall of the Communist regimes in 1989] (Prague: Ústav pro soudobé dějiny AV ČR, 2013); Dragoş Petrescu, *Entangled Revolutions: The Breakdown of the Communist Regimes in East-Central Europe* (Bucureşti: Editura Enciclopedică, 2014).

27 András Bozóki, ed., *The Roundtable Talks of 1989: The Genesis of Hungarian Democracy: Analysis and Documents* (Budapest: CEU Press, 2002).

28 Krishan Kumar, *1989: Revolutionary Ideas and Ideals* (Minneapolis, MN: University of Minnesota Press, 2001), 26 and 31–70; Philipp Ther, *Europe since 1989: A History* (Princeton, NJ: Princeton University Press, 2016), 54–6.

a chain-reaction might also serve to highlight their similarities and entanglements. The compromises struck first by the exhausted Polish communists and then by their reform-minded Hungarian comrades sparked more radical action in the neighbouring countries. In the GDR and Czechoslovakia, mass protest on the streets forced the more obstinate communist regimes to surrender. After the Berlin Wall fell and a communist parliament elected Václav Havel president of Czechoslovakia, both regimes embarked on round table negotiations that sealed their fates. The round tables, to quote Jerzy Holzer, turned into a universal instrument.[29] They shaped non-violent, peaceful transitions and gave communists the faint hope that they might preserve a share in power or at least be credited for having surrendered of their own accord. At first sight, developments in Southeastern Europe looked somewhat different. Within Yugoslavia, the reform-minded Croatian and Slovenian Communist Parties announced in early December 1989 that free parliamentary elections would be held the following spring with the aim of taking advantage of massive opposition sentiment and countering the centralizing pressure exerted by Slobodan Milošević and the Serbian political leadership. Influenced by mass demonstrations, the newly installed Bulgarian party leader Petür Mladenov also announced multi-party elections in mid-December. In Romania, the regime was toppled in an outburst of violence, some of which was carefully staged so as to secure power to a reformist group within the state apparatus. In turn, these events throughout the Soviet sphere reflected back on developments in Poland and Hungary, where the remaining strongholds of communist power rapidly melted away. In the end, most transitions were negotiated. Once the ruling party had taken a seat at the round table, the question was simply how to determine the role that their socialist successors would be allowed to play in the ensuing decade. Romania and Bulgaria were exceptional only in the sense that the opposition was far too weak to force the communist regime into outright negotiations but allowed it to define the conditions of transformation largely by themselves. Serbia was exceptional in that it took another decade to force the communists to step down in 2000, after the first demonstrations had failed in 1997.

Events in Romania aptly demonstrated that massive police violence or an outright military crackdown following the model of the 'Chinese solution', though seriously considered by both Erich Honecker and Nicolae Ceaușescu, was no longer a viable option in Central Europe.[30] Armed clashes in the streets of Timișoara and elsewhere created a power vacuum which the quickly-formed National Salvation Front (Frontul Salvării Naționale) had to fill for lack of an established opposition with which to negotiate a peaceful transition.[31] In Bulgaria, Mladenov resigned after only seven months in office due to allegations that he had seriously considered sending tanks against demonstrators in December.[32] Throughout the Soviet bloc, events of the previous two decades had amply demonstrated that communist regimes might be upheld by the use of brute force against the vast majority of the population, but that they could no longer solve internal problems with the use of violence. An additional aspect should be kept

---

29 Jerzy Holzer, 'Der Runde Tisch. Internationale Geschichte eines politischen Möbels', in *Das Revolutionsjahr 1989. Die demokratische Revolution in Osteuropa als transnationale Zäsur*, ed. Bernd Florath (Göttingen: Vandenhoeck & Ruprecht, 2011), 226–32.

30 Ther, *Europe since 1989*, 71–3; Martin Sabrow, ed., *1989 und die Rolle der Gewalt* (Göttingen: Wallstein Verlag, 2012).

31 Peter Siani-Davies, *The Romanian Revolution of December 1989* (Ithaca, NY: Cornell University Press, 2005); Dragoș Petrescu, *Explaining the Romanian Revolution of 1989: Culture, Structure, and Contingency* (București: Editura Enciclopedică, 2010).

32 Richard J. Crampton, *A Concise History of Bulgaria* (Cambridge: Cambridge University Press, 1997), 219.

in mind. In most countries of the region, the territory of the state was not contested during or immediately after the revolutions. Yugoslavia as well as the Baltic and Caucasian fringes of the Soviet Union were the obvious exceptions, and it is in these places that the struggle for power and territory turned violent. Only Estonia, which seemed largely irrelevant in political and economic terms, was allowed to leave the Soviet Union peacefully. Federations were vulnerable, but their constituent republics equally served the purpose of providing a stable institutional framework. In general, territorial stability made it possible to channel revolutionary change into free parliamentary elections, which could in turn quickly legitimize the new order or, as in the case of the GDR, substantiate the claims for unification with West Germany. It was the basic precondition for legal continuity that allowed for transitions without rupture, and in most cases the brief power vacuum was quickly filled.

The general consensus on how to instil the state with new political legitimacy was easily defined and quickly exhausted. Round table talks, at whatever stage of the process they took place, generally agreed on a similar set of measures. Civil rights were to be reasserted, police violence to be curbed and political pluralism allowed to develop freely. Elections to parliament were to restore the body politic. Communists' attempts to preserve their self-respect and to safeguard a smooth transition by securing the office of the head of state were successful in Poland, where the Sejm had elected General Jaruzelski to the newly-created office of President in July 1989 with the tacit support of the victorious Solidarity opposition. This compromise lasted little more than a year and quickly turned into a liability for the new democracy. The Hungarian communists tried to strike a similar agreement in vain, only to deepen the emerging split between moderate populists and radical anti-communists within the opposition. In Czechoslovakia, on the other hand, the Communist Party had given in to popular demands for Václav Havel to preside over revolutionary transition while the government was formally still headed by a Communist Party member. In contrast, Romania's Ion Iliescu, Bulgaria's Petŭr Mladenov, Slovenia's Milan Kučan and, most of all, Serbia's Slobodan Milošević demonstrated that the presidency could indeed help former communists hold on to political power.

The carnivalesque subversion of the existing order and the rapid spread of spontaneous self-organization were indispensable preconditions for peaceful transition. But in the long run, they also became a liability. The 4 June elections in Poland and the reburial of Imre Nagy in Hungary, the fall of the Berlin Wall half a year later and the subsequent general strike in Czechoslovakia each marked the rapid expansion of public spheres and an explosion of political expression.[33] Everything suddenly seemed possible and within reach. The creation of a revolutionary community with a romantic ethos of harmony, most visible in Czechoslovakia, took an iconoclastic turn and raised popular expectations for a moral purge. More sober natures warned against the witch-hunts they believed were imminent. But even without such warnings it was obvious that disillusionment was soon to follow when merry public happenings would have to give way to formal, legalistic procedures.

Once power had been wrested from the communists, pressure rose to oust them at all levels, from government administration and the judiciary all the way down to the workplace and educational institutions. This process was not easy to control and sometimes became chaotic. In Poland, throughout the winter of 1989/90, radical demonstrators frequently beleaguered militia and state security offices, though without being able to secure their files as civic

---

33 Padraic Kenney, *A Carnival of Revolution: Central Europe 1989* (Princeton, NJ: Princeton University Press, 2002); James Krapfl, *Revolution with a Human Face: Politics, Culture, and Community in Czechoslovakia, 1989–1992* (Ithaca, NY: Cornell University Press, 2013).

committees had done in East Germany. In the first months of 1990, the newly emerging police trade unions in Poland fervently purged the regional militia leadership. Elections to the newly-created institutions of local self-government were precipitated so as to sweep away the nomenklatura and bring new people to power. At the same time, the new minister of justice actually had to urge the judiciary to elect new judges as presidents of the voivodeship courts rather than stick to the old guard. Similar developments could be observed in Czechoslovakia and Hungary. In all three countries, the question of how harshly the new state should deal with the protagonists of the old regime became a major dividing line within the emerging political spectrum, if not a major rift. The 'Dunagate scandal' in Hungary in January 1990 uncovered the continued activities of the secret police and poisoned the ongoing electoral campaign.[34] In Czechoslovakia, the new democratic elite feared that old secret-police networks might corrupt the political process by blackmailing former informants. In East Germany, the charge of having informally cooperated with state security services first brought down the leader of the conservatives, then the head of the Social Democratic Party.[35] This issue would last for decades, and it would poison political competition. The dissolution of the former communist parties (with the exception of Czechoslovakia) and their reorganization into a socialist left only fuelled suspicions that the old nomenklatura was planning to hold on to its position. Romania and Bulgaria, where the democratic opposition had been too weak to wrest power from the communists and where the latter had effected the transformation largely by themselves, fared even worse in this respect.

In Yugoslavia, events took a different turn. With hindsight, developments have often been described as taking the precipitous path towards disintegration and ethnic war, preceded by national mobilization in the constituent republics since the late 1970s.[36] Though the picture is much more complex, and the institutional weaknesses of socialist Yugoslavia, the social dynamics and the external factors have to be taken into account, ethnic nationalism was indeed a powerful element which shaped the transition to multi-party systems in the constituent republics. In response to the rise of the communist-turned-nationalist Slobodan Milošević and his 'anti-bureaucratic revolution' in Serbia, Slovenia's reform-minded communists took a national turn themselves, whereas their Croat and Bosnian counterparts gave way to staunch oppositionists like Franjo Tuđman and Alija Izetbegović. In this course of events, one feature sticks out as exceptional. Unlike in Central Europe, the rhetoric of national unity in disintegrating Yugoslavia served to curb anti-communist sentiment rather than to fuel it. As Armina Galijaš has demonstrated for Banja Luka, national unity was not just a trope used to incite fear of one's neighbour, but an appeal to overcome previous cleavages between communists and their former opponents which dated back to the Second World War. Such an appeal for national reconciliation, inconceivable as it was to nationalists in countries further to the north, reflected the soft nature of Yugoslav communism, which

---

34 Rudolf L. Tőkés, *Hungary's Negotiated Revolution: Economic Reform, Social Change and Political Succession, 1957–1990* (Cambridge: Cambridge University Press, 1996), 378.

35 Krapfl, *Revolution with a Human Face*, 153–84; Jens Gieseke, *The History of the Stasi: East Germany's Secret Police, 1945–1990* (New York: Berghahn Books, 2014), 201–2.

36 Sabrina P. Ramet, *The Three Yugoslavias: State-Building and Legitimation, 1918–2005* (Washington, DC: Woodrow Wilson Center Press, 2006), 285–379; Jasna Dragović-Soso, 'Why did Yugoslavia Disintegrate? An Overview of Contending Explanations', in *State Collapse in South-Eastern Europe: New Perspectives on Yugoslavia's Disintegration*, eds Lenard J. Cohen and Jasna Dragović-Soso (West Lafayette, IN: Purdue University Press, 2008), 1–39; Florian Bieber, Armina Galijaš and Rory Archer, eds, *Debating the End of Yugoslavia* (Farnham: Ashgate, 2014).

had not been built on Soviet occupation and where mass repression had largely receded into distant memory.[37] Josip Broz Tito's towering figure was beginning to be demystified, but he could hardly be demonized. The reinterpretations of the Second World War allowed Serbian Chetniks, Bosnian Young Muslims and even Croatian Ustashe to reassume their place in national memory without ousting their former communist opponents. Since the mid-1980s, Serbian nationalists had directed their charge of genocide against the Serbian nation towards the Jasenovac concentration camp and its Croatian masters. In return, memorializing the post-war massacres of Croatian fighters at Bleiburg served more to underline their presumed innocence in an apologetic reassessment of the Ustasha state than to charge communist partisans with genocide.[38] As a result, the re-emergence of a public sphere founded in free parliamentary and presidential elections in disintegrating Yugoslavia did not deepen political cleavages as it did elsewhere, but rather brought about an upsurge of national mobilization along ethnic lines that had hitherto seemed almost unthinkable.

Newly installed democratic governments were soon faced with a challenge that many successful revolutionaries in history have had to face: namely, how to reassert and secure public order responsibly without taking recourse to violence themselves and thus betraying their ideals. Throughout the region, one of the key public demands was to curb police repression. Special units like the ZOMO in Poland were quickly dismantled. Indeed, the legal foundations of the police in Poland had already been changed in the wake of the Round Table negotiations. Yet such measures did not suffice to restore the authority of the police once the opposition had taken control. In Poland, it took a series of prison revolts to persuade the Mazowiecki government in November 1989 that it could not restore its monopoly on violence simply by negotiating with the rioting inmates. Police also began taking action against street blockades in early 1990. Since the government party had itself emerged out of a trade union that had been outlawed for more than seven years, it risked its authority and reputation when it turned against ongoing strikes. In the Romanian city of Târgu Mureş, a weakened police failed to intervene on time in the ethnic clashes between Romanians and Hungarian Széklers in March 1990, which ultimately led to several deaths and briefly evoked the spectre of ethnic war in the region. Three months later, newly elected president Ion Iliescu called in miners from the Jiu Valley to put down anticommunist demonstrations in Bucharest. The ensuing eruption of violence did considerable damage to the credibility of the new parliamentary elites.[39] In Sofia, protest ran high throughout the summer after the former communists had secured victory at the polls, and in late August, demonstrators set the former party headquarters on fire.[40] In Budapest, a massive blockade by taxi drivers in October 1990 tested the ability of the Antall government to secure public order without resorting to violence. Restoring a minimum of acceptance for police activity which had long been considered deeply immoral, became possible only after revolutionary fervour began to die down. It was, no doubt, part of the disillusionment that came with the return to

---

37 Armina Galijaš, *Eine bosnische Stadt im Zeichen des Krieges. Ethnopolitik und Alltag in Banja Luka (1990–1995)* (München: Oldenbourg, 2015); Stevo Đurašković, *The Politics of History in Croatia and Slovakia in the 1990s* (Zagreb: Srednja Europa, 2016).

38 Liljana Radonic, *Krieg um die Erinnerung. Kroatische Vergangenheitspolitik zwischen Revisionismus und europäischen Standards* (Frankfurt a.M.: Campus, 2010).

39 Henry F. Carey, ed., *Romania since 1989: Politics, Economics, and Society* (Lanham, MD: Lexington Books, 2004).

40 Crampton, *A Concise History of Bulgaria*, 219; Stefan Troebst, 'Bulgarien 1989: Gewaltarmer Regimewandel in gewaltträchtigem Umfeld', in Sabrow, *1989 und die Rolle der Gewalt*, 357–83, here 380–1.

Joachim von Puttkamer

normality. By the end of 1990, government authority throughout the region was again uncontested, with the fateful exception of the Serbian-populated areas in Croatia's Knin region.

It soon became obvious that throughout Central Europe, the largely peaceful transitions had caused divisions among the winners. Observers from both inside and outside had predicted early on the inevitability of their separation into rival political groups. Yet the rift ran deeper. Diverging ideological visions and political agendas were underpinned by harsh disputes over the very nature of the outcome of the revolutions, of what exactly had been achieved. Privatization ultimately settled the ambiguity as to whether the commitment to freedom, political participation, justice and humanity would remove the obstacles to true socialism with a human face, or whether socialism had finally been discarded. Nevertheless, this dispute left behind a legacy of vagueness as to the true aims of the revolutions, which fed disappointment as much as the charge of undue compromise with the old elites. In Hungary, this rift had already become visible during the Round Table Talks in the fall of 1989. While the populist MDF pled for a more compromising stance towards the receding communist party, the more radical Free Democrats and even more so the Fidesz used explicitly anti-communist positions to mobilize their constituencies. In Poland, the first hints at a rift within the former Solidarity camp became visible in the autumn of 1989 and developed into a full-scale 'war at the top' with Lech Wałęsa's presidential campaign in the fall of 1990.

A similar constellation emerged roughly one year later in Czechoslovakia, when Václav Klaus' rise to power split the Czech Civic Forum and Vladimír Mečiar left its Slovak counterpart. There was more at stake in these rifts than the transition to competitive pluralism. Throughout the region, power politicians challenged the crumbling hegemony of dissident intellectuals, whom they suspected of maintaining leftist leanings. In political terms, an emerging populist right, while trying to preserve the idea of moral purity within a revolutionary community turned national, began to challenge the institutional order which it had helped shape in 1989/90. The effects of this were to be felt only much later.

For most of the countries concerned, the events of 1989 were quickly condensed into a series of iconic images which help underscore the features shared by all of the revolutions and can help us better understand their long-term impact. The images of mass demonstrations, as in the reburial of Imre Nagy in Budapest or the protests that brought Václav Havel to power, show nations that were taking their fate into their own hands and shaking off unwanted regimes. The contemporary perception of 'peaceful revolution' has its origin in Prague where the notion of a 'Velvet Revolution' originally served to link the events of 1989 to the thwarted attempt of the Prague Spring and its fight for 'socialism with a human face', and also with the Masarykian tradition of a presumably specific Czech mission towards humanism and democracy.[41] The peaceful character of the revolution was equally underlined by the image of the round table which would come to epitomize the Polish transition. Neither image could keep at bay the notion of a revolution that was presumably hijacked by a radical minority, exemplified so clearly in the image of the Romanian dictator fleeing from his own people in a helicopter, only to be tried and executed within four days by an improvised and shady military tribunal.[42] But in Poland,

---

41 James Krapfl, *Revolution with a Human Face: Politics, Culture, and Community in Czechoslovakia, 1989–1992* (Ithaca, NY: Cornell University Press, 2013); Jiří Suk, *Labyrintem revoluce: Aktéři, zápletky a křižovatky jedné politické krize (od listopadu 1989 do června 1990)* [Through the labyrinth of revolution: the actors, storylines and crossroads of a political crisis (from November 1989 to June 1990)] (Prague: Prostor, 2003).

42 Siani-Davies, *The Romanian Revolution of December 1989*, 134–43.

1989 and beyond

Czechoslovakia and Hungary, the course of events left notions of a civic obligation towards the common good, whereas in Romania and Bulgaria, they tended to deepen long-standing popular distrust not only in the political elites, but in the state itself.

In a far-sighted essay, Timothy Garton Ash captured the revolutionary nature of evolutionary reforms in Poland and Hungary with his famously coined term, 'refolutions'.[43] In the long run, these evolutionary beginnings did not have a direct impact on specific institutional outcomes. Yet they are crucial for understanding the onset of the events of 1989 as much as they are for grasping the impact that the ensuing polemics had on their outcome. Negotiated revolutions, the argument runs, came at the price of being unduly regulated and therefore limited.[44] In a reformist scenario, it is much easier to argue that the revolution remained 'unfinished' and to lament the allegedly smooth transition of the old elites into the new order.[45] Once peaceful transition had been safely secured, the evolutionary approach became a liability and a burden. Yet debates of this nature were not at all limited to these two countries.

The debate on the character of the 1989 revolutions is relevant here only insofar as it helps to demarcate different regional patterns. In the countries of Central Europe, the much longed-for triumph of civil society and the sudden collapse of uncivil society, as Stephen Kotkin has argued, were actually two sides of the same coin.[46] But further to the south and further to the east, the old elites did not collapse; if anything, they simply retreated. Unchallenged by dissident movements, they managed to mobilize nationalist sentiments against the notions of hardship, decline and marginalization that were associated with capitalism and Western-style democracy. Here, national independence did not promise a rapprochement to the West, but rather to keep a safe distance. The fault-line ran straight through Yugoslavia, where top institutions had nearly withered away since Tito's death in 1980 and the People's Army quickly began pursuing a Serbian nationalist agenda in the name of Yugoslav political unity. This rift became the major cause for the national secessions and ensuing ethnic warfare, which other countries in the region had happily avoided. Federations proved vulnerable. Alongside the Soviet Union, Yugoslavia was the only country in the region where the existing state itself would be challenged in competing acts of national emancipation from a weak central government that had almost entirely dissolved. Elsewhere, the nation states remained surprisingly unchallenged. But to expect that civil society could effect a smooth takeover of state institutions in successive acts of self-liberation was naïve.

Political democratization

In 2003, when the first balance sheets of transformation were being set up, Grzegorz Ekiert argued that it would be a mistake to believe that communism left behind a strong and efficient state. The Leviathan had turned out to be feeble, since despotic capacity did not translate into infrastructural power. In the words of Ralf Dahrendorf's famous 'Letter on the Revolution in

---

43 Timothy Garton Ash, 'Refolution', in Garton Ash, *The Uses of Adversity*, 276–88.

44 Tőkés, *Hungary's Negotiated Revolution*; Zoltán Ripp, *Rendszerváltás Magyarországon 1987–1990* [System change in Hungary 1987–1989] (Budapest: Napvilág Kiadó, 2006); Antoni Dudek, *Reglamentowana Rewolucja. Rozkład dyktatury komunistycznej w Polsce 1988–1990* [A regulated revolution: the dissolution of the communist dictatorship in Poland 1988–1990] (Kraków: Arcana, 2004).

45 James Mark, *The Unfinished Revolution: Making Sense of the Communist Past in Central Eastern Europe* (New Haven, CT: Yale University Press, 2010).

46 Stephen Kotkin, *Uncivil Society: 1989 and the Implosion of the Communist Establishment* (New York: Modern Library, 2009).

Europe': 'Nomenklatura socialism has left the state weakened and corrupted.'[47] Reforming the state thus became crucial for successful transformation, and indeed, the response to this challenge was quite diverse.[48]

The Central European revolutions of 1989 were quickly said to have been quite unimaginative in their political aims, they were 'rectifying revolution(s)', in the words of Jürgen Habermas, which failed to offer any grand alternative and plainly sought to catch up with the capitalist, bourgeois West, mopping up the revolutionary tradition of 1789 rather than adding another chapter to it.[49] They were indeed guided less by utopian visions and more by a transition consensus that was based on a broad commitment to non-violence, to the rule of law and the separation of powers, to pluralism and broad participation, and to a vague notion of morality and humanity. In this respect, long-standing dissident debates did have a major impact in shaping the mentality of the revolutions more than any neatly defined goals.[50] Nevertheless, these notions were translated directly into far-reaching political change. The solemn declaration of December 1989 that Poland was now governed by the democratic rule of law (*demokratycznym państwem prawnym*) was the least controversial of constitutional amendments. It not only linked up to dissident demands, but also to an ongoing reformist debate on how to strengthen socialist legality, the nature of which was increasingly blurred. Simply dropping the moniker 'socialist' was an easy way out of this vagueness, but it had major consequences. Safeguarding the law became the overriding obligation of all state institutions in Poland. The constitutional tribunal, which had already been set up in 1985, became the supreme arbiter in constitutional matters.[51] Aside from Poland, only Yugoslavia had known a constitutional court before 1989. Elsewhere in the region, constitutional courts were quickly installed in the transition to democracy, with only Ukraine, Latvia and Bosnia-Herzegovina lagging somewhat behind. They soon shared the same problems faced by Western democracies, namely whether a strong judicial review of political decisions actually tends to undermine rather than to strengthen the acceptance of the parliamentary system.[52]

Pluralism, though it could not directly be derived from the notion of anti-politics, had long been on the dissident agenda. The idea of a multi-party system, as Hungary had experienced it for a few days in late October 1956, and which was again sketched by Kuroń and Modzelewski in their 1964 'Open Letter' had been a focal point of oppositional thought throughout Central Europe. It remained central even if contested or, as Kuroń himself suggested in 1981, even if its implementation had to be postponed for strategic considerations. The commitment to civil

---

47 Ralf Dahrendorf, *Reflections on the Revolution in Europe: In a Letter Intended to Have Been Sent to a Gentleman in Warsaw* (New Brunswick: Transaction Publishers, 2005), from the postscript to this edition, 170.

48 Grzegorz Ekiert, 'The State after State-Socialism? Poland in Comparative Perspective', in *The Nation-State in Question*, eds T.V. Paul, G. John Ikenberry, and John A. Hall (Princeton, NJ: Princeton University Press, 2003), 291–320.

49 Jürgen Habermas, 'What Does Socialism Mean Today? The Rectifying Revolution and the Need for New Thinking on the Left', *New Left Review* 183 (1990): 3–21, here 5; Dahrendorf, *Reflections on the Revolution in Europe*, 27 (quoting François Furet).

50 Kumar, *1989: Revolutionary Ideas and Ideals*; Krapfl, *Revolution with a Human Face*, 74–110; Jiří Přibáň and James Young, eds, *The Rule of Law in Central Europe: The Reconstruction of Legality, Constitutionalism and Civil Society in the Post-Communist Countries* (Aldershot: Ashgate, 1999).

51 Ustawa z dnia 29 grudnia 1989 r. o zmianie Konstytucji Polskiej Rzeczypospolitej Ludowej (Dz. U. 1989, Nr. 75, Poz. 444) [Act of 29 December 1989 on the Amendments to the Constitution of the Polish People's Republic].

52 Wojciech Sadurski, *Rights before Courts: A Study of Constitutional Courts in Postcommunist States of Central and Eastern Europe* (Dordrecht: Springer, 2005).

rights was equally strong and their institutional reaffirmation was facilitated by the fact that they had had some sort of formal position within the socialist constitutions all along. They simply needed to be ascertained, and the old idea that restricting or even violating them in the name of protecting socialism needed to be abolished; and so did the leading role of the communist party.

Thus, the first step to be taken in the institutional transition was to eliminate the political limits placed on constitutional law under socialism and to reinstall it as the normative framework of party politics. Poland and Hungary, where the transitions had begun, at first accommodated institutional changes by amending the existing constitutions. The newly independent Baltic countries, the Czech and Slovak republics, Slovenia and Croatia, and even Romania and Bulgaria wrote new constitutions. Poland followed suit in 1997.

The institutional order which was thus established largely remained within the framework of parliamentary republics. In Hungary, Prime Minister József Antall and opposition leader Péter Tölgyessy explicitly referred to the West German model of *Kanzlerdemokratie* when in May 1991, they strengthened the role of the prime minister at the expense of parliament and the state president. Poland, the Czech Republic and Romania were less successful in assigning clearly defined powers to the head of state. Leaning somewhat more towards the French model and picking up on traditions from the interwar period, the role of the head of state could be interpreted by ambitious figures such as Lech Wałęsa and Lech Kaczyński, or Václav Havel and later Václav Klaus, in a more ambitious way. Conflicts with parliament and the cabinet became inevitable in periods of co-habitation. As a result, the heads of state remained within the framework of party competition rather than establishing themselves as moral figures detached from party politics (with the possible exception of Václav Havel). But even though Central Europe came to be haunted by some of the spectres of the interwar period, fears of a shift towards some form of authoritarian rule mostly proved to be groundless for the time being. Despite symbolic revivals in military uniforms and political naming, in institutional terms the interwar period was assigned to history much more quickly than hesitant observers had feared. Though it received some popular support, the restoration of monarchy in Southeastern Europe, contemplated as a means to accommodate authoritarian leanings and to ease the transition to democracy along the Spanish model, was never seriously considered. The experience of Tsar Simeon II, who served as Prime Minister of Bulgaria from 2001 to 2005, demonstrated both the popular expectations invested in such figures as well as their almost inevitable disappointment. In the end, Bulgaria's abortive experiment in reviving monarchic traditions only enhanced the distrust in the new and not-so-new political elites that it was meant to disperse.

Croatia and Serbia were again the conspicuous outliers in this overall picture of emerging liberal democracy. Slobodan Milošević, who had thwarted the transition to parliamentary democracy in Serbia by marginalizing the regional elites in the 'anti-bureaucratic revolution' of 1987–89, installed himself as a national leader who would staunchly defend Serbian interests during Yugoslavia's imminent disintegration. The presidential regime which he established in 1990 was characterized as an 'ethnic semi-democracy' that allowed for some elements of political pluralism, but on a strictly nationalist basis.[53] Croatia experienced a somewhat similar development during the 1990s when war rallied the majority of the population behind the nationalist Croatian Democratic Union HDZ (*Hrvatska Demokratska Zajednica*). Limited pluralism was corrupted by President Franjo Tuđman's authoritarian leanings as the military president of a nation at war. Tuđman managed to model himself as a successor to Tito while playing on the traditions

---

53 Florian Bieber, *Nationalismus in Serbien vom Tode Titos bis zum Ende der Ära Milosevic* (Vienna: LIT, 2005); Ramet, *The Three Yugoslavias*, 341–62.

of the fascist Ustasha state of the Second World War.[54] Looking back at his presidency in early 2000, the Zagreb weekly *Nacional* pointedly termed Croatia a 'gangster state'.[55]

The genocidal collapse of Yugoslavia was in part driven by tendencies towards authoritarian rule, which were in turn strengthened by the collapse itself. Within a Yugoslav context, it has been convincingly argued that the weak institutions of a multi-ethnic state were being destroyed by nationalist elites who were willing and prepared to wage war over the future status of the Serbian population in Eastern Slavonia, Krajina, Bosnia, and finally, Kosovo. Slovenia, which lacked a substantial Serbian population, narrowly escaped a protracted war and embarked on the trajectory towards EU membership. Elsewhere, the effects of war and ethno-national mobilization overshadowed the development of democratic institutions and fed massive corruption.[56]

The return to parliamentary systems in the region paved the arduous path towards democratization, which was supported by the negotiations for EU membership. Since 2000, Croatia has seen several democratic changes of government and serious, though not entirely successful, attempts to push back against corruption.[57] In Belgrade, the downfall of Slobodan Milošević in October 2000 opened the prospect for Serbia (in its increasingly fragile federation with Montenegro) to shift towards a parliamentary democracy as well. But democratic mobilization collapsed into resignation and apathy when Serbian Prime Minister Zoran Đinđić was murdered in 2003. Since then, the legacy of illiberal nationalism and its potential to undermine the institutions of liberal democracy has remained strong.[58] Elsewhere throughout the Balkans, the power of European institutions to support democratic institution-building has been equally put into question, particularly in Bosnia and Macedonia. The Dayton Agreement of 1995 and the Ohrid Framework Agreement of 2001 curtailed ethnic warfare, but at the price of fracturing the states involved into national entities and turning them over to corrupt elites. In 2006, Sabrina P. Ramet remarked that the Dayton Peace Accords had so far 'failed to generate fully legitimate sovereign institutions'.[59] Macedonia fared somewhat better, but any stabilizing developments have been massively impeded by the ongoing Greek blockade of Macedonian integration into NATO and the EU.[60]

The peaceful dissolution of Czechoslovakia, often favourably contrasted with that of Yugoslavia, aptly demonstrated that ethnic war and a political blockade were not inevitable. The difference lay in the relative weakness of Slovak nationalism. The Czech and Slovak republics parted ways in 1993 when prime ministers Václav Klaus and Vladimír Mečiar realized that they could only actualize contrasting political ideas by separating the two diverging entities. Slovak nationalism supported Mečiar's populist authoritarianism. Once it became obvious that this development isolated the country and threatened to jeopardize its accession to the

---

54 Sabrina P. Ramet, Konrad Clewing and Renéo Lukić, eds, *Croatia since Independence: War, Politics, Society, Foreign Relations* (München: Oldenbourg, 2008); Sabrina P. Ramet, 'Politics in Croatia since 1990', in *Central and Southeast European Politics since 1989*, ed. Sabrina P. Ramet (Cambridge: Cambridge University Press, 2010), 258–85.

55 Ramet, *The Three Yugoslavias*, 587.

56 Holm Sundhaussen, *Jugoslawien und seine Nachfolgestaaten 1943–2011: Eine ungewöhnliche Geschichte des Gewöhnlichen* (Köln: Böhlau, 2012), 511–4.

57 Ramet, 'Politics in Croatia', 266–72.

58 Ramet, *The Three Yugoslavias*, 517–35; Sabrina P. Ramet, 'Serbia and Montenegro since 1989', in Ramet, *Central and Southeast European Politics*, 286–310.

59 Ramet, *The Three Yugoslavias*, 494; David Chandler, ed., *Peace without Politics? Ten Years of International State-Building in Bosnia* (London: Routledge, 2005); Florian Bieber, 'Bosnia and Herzegovina since 1990', in Ramet, *Central and Southeast European Politics*, 311–27.

60 Zachary T. Irwin, 'Macedonia since 1989', in Ramet, *Central and Southeast European Politics*, 328–57.

European Union, his successor Mikuláš Dzurinda, picking up on the liberal traditions within Slovak nationalism, radically changed course and for several years turned Slovakia into a model of pro-market democratic reforms.[61]

The reintroduction of local self-government played a key role in the formation of new democratic states in Central Europe. Most of the countries in the region had known noble and municipal, or even peasant, self-government for centuries. In former Habsburg lands such as the Czech lands or Slovenia, the tradition of efficient and self-assertive local self-government went back to the revolutions of 1848, and in the Baltic region and the former Tsarist Empire it could be traced to the 1860s. Centralization and authoritarian rule had subordinated local administration to the central government in many countries during the interwar period, especially in the Balkans. But the states of Central Europe were only able to wrest power from established local elites with the introduction of communist rule. Poland was the first post-communist country to rush towards the democratization of local administration, namely in May 1990. The primary motives were to conquer one of the strongholds of the old elites with democratic elections and to invest the protagonists of the civic committees with official responsibility for local affairs.[62] One- or two-tiered self-government was to provide the link between civil society and the state. Other countries quickly followed suit, and their degree of success was measured by their ability to draw on common Central European traditions.[63] As members of the Council of Europe, all countries of the region (with the exception of Belarus) have subscribed to the principles that were laid down in the European Charter of Local Self-Government.

Organizing free elections was one thing, defining vested powers and providing for appropriate funding was another. In most countries, local self-government was made responsible for things like housing, medical and social services, education, and in some countries such as Poland, the local police. Slovenia was one of the few countries that implemented taxes to specifically fund local administrations. From 1998 onward, local self-government in Poland has received about half of the country's overall tax revenue.[64] In countries like Latvia, income from local taxes amounted to 25 per cent of the local budget at most; in these places, local self-government has remained largely dependent on central funding.[65] Government remittances were and still are rarely sufficient to sustain local services, let alone to secure necessary investments. A 1999 investigation in Bulgaria revealed that more than half of Bulgarian municipalities spent their limited resources on construction and renovations rather than on social and medical services. The city of Ruse was only able to provide its schools with electricity and heating for just about half of the year. Some 80 smaller municipalities failed to pay wages for several months.[66] Electoral turnout throughout the region has generally been much lower than in national elections and barely exceeded 50 per cent

---

61 Erika Harris, 'Slovakia since 1989', in Ramet, *Central and Southeast European Politics*, 182–203.

62 'Czas wielkiej próby. Dyskusja redakcyjna', *Więź* 11–12 (373–374), November/December 1989, 7–32; Klaus Ziemer and Claudia-Yvette Matthes, 'Das politische System Polens', in *Die politischen Systeme Osteuropas*, ed. Wolfgang Ismayr, 3rd ed. (Wiesbaden: Verlag für Sozialwissenschaft, 2010), 209–73, here 265–7.

63 Armin Stolz, 'Die Verwaltungsorganisation im Vergleich', in *Vergleichendes Verwaltungsrecht in Ostmitteleuropa. Grundriss der Verwaltungsordnungen Polens, Tschechiens, der Slowakei und Ungarns*, eds Bernd Wieser and Armin Stolz (Vienna, Berlin: Verlag Österreich; BWV Berliner Wissenschaftsverlag, 2004), 159–95.

64 Ekiert, 'The State after State-Socialism?', 307.

65 Thomas Schmidt, 'Das politische System Lettlands', in Ismayr, *Die politischen Systeme Osteuropas*, 123–70, here 165.

66 Sabine Riedel, 'Das politische System Bulgariens', in *Die politischen Systeme Osteuropas*, 677–728, here 720–2.

of the electorate. In Slovakia, turnout dropped to a record-breaking low of less than 20 per cent in the regional elections in November 2005.[67] Against this background, it is not surprising that in some countries, corruption seems to be strongest in local administration, especially where it is still dominated by the old guard. At the same time, strong mayors such as Lech Kaczyński in Warsaw, Gábor Demszky in Budapest and Edi Rama in Tirana managed to gain substantial political reputations for themselves and exert considerable influence in national politics. In spite of its shortcomings, local self-government in Lithuania, Poland, Hungary and even Moldova enjoyed a relatively high rate of public trust according to opinion polls conducted throughout the 1990s and 2000s.[68]

In hindsight, the constitutional setup, which had been established during the revolutionary months of 1989/90, displayed an inherent tendency towards parliamentary democracy of the continental Western European type. For some, this harboured a potential for disappointment, but it did not come as much of a surprise. For years to come, the institutional order that was established throughout Central and Southeastern Europe during the 1990s provided a fairly stable framework for not so stable party systems. Party competition on the other hand supported institution-building, since mutual monitoring could put a brake on patronage and corruption.[69]

Yet, the nature of this stability came to be disputed in the light of later developments. The broad transition consensus did not compel major political forces to commit to upholding its pluralistic, democratic principles. Rather than providing a generally accepted framework of parliamentary democracy, the constitutions of Central Europe remained controversial, and the rule of law, corrupted as it had been before 1989, did not take firm roots evenly throughout the region. Structural features inherited from communism, such as the firm hold of clientele networks on weak institutions, seem to be tenaciously persistent in some places, particularly in large parts of Southeastern Europe. In a more optimistic, if not slightly euphemistic vein, one might maintain that Eastern Europe came to display a broad range of different understandings of democracy, which cannot be reduced to its liberal interpretation.[70] As it has been argued in the case of Hungary, the lack of confidence in a strong state curbed populist demagogy throughout the 1990s, while distrust in formal institutions grew and fed the longing for quick and simple solutions to complicated problems. The failure to vote on the principles of a new constitution in 1996/97 marked the erosion of consensual politics and began the path towards eventual breakdown. Henceforth, only the weakness of rivalling political camps has ensured the persistence of the constitutional order in an increasingly conflictual understanding of politics.[71] Once Fidesz

---

67 Rüdiger Kipke, 'Das politische System der Slowakei', in *Die politischen Systeme Osteuropas*, 317–56, here 349.

68 Joachim Tauber, 'Das politische System Litauens', in *Die politischen Systeme Osteuropas*, 171–208, here 204; Ziemer and Matthes, 'Das politische System Polens', 259; András Körösényi, Gábor G. Fodor and Jürgen Dieringer, 'Das politische System Ungarns', in *Die politischen Systeme Osteuropas*, 357–418, here 403; Klemens Büscher, 'Das politische System Moldovas', in *Die politischen Systeme Osteuropas*, 583–627, here 610.

69 Anna Maria Grzymała-Busse, *Rebuilding Leviathan: Party Competition and State Exploitation in Post-Communist Democracies* (Cambridge: Cambridge University Press, 2007).

70 Paul Blokker, *Multiple Democracies in Europe: Political Culture in New Member States* (New York: Routledge, 2010).

71 András Bozóki, 'The Illusion of Inclusion: Configurations of Populism in Hungary', in Kopeček and Wciślik, *Thinking through Transition*, 275–311; Zoltán Gábor Szűcs, 'The Abortion of a "Conservative" Constitution-Making: A Discourse Analysis of the 1994–1998 Failed Hungarian Constitution-Making Enterprise', in Kopeček and Wciślik, *Thinking through Transition*, 237–55; Ellen Bos, *Verfassungsgebung und Systemwechsel. Die Institutionalisierung von Demokratie im postsozialistischen Osteuropa* (Wiesbaden: Verlag für Sozialwissenschaften, 2004), 277–8.

finally scored a sweeping victory at the polls in 2008, the state that had been built over more than a decade fell prey to the party's authoritarian leanings.

In part, this development had to do with the high-running expectations to which the revolutions had given rise. But it also had to do with inevitable disappointment in the way the new democracies performed their basic functions. Unlike Hungary, Poland introduced a new constitution in 1997, but the notion that democratic revolution had remained unfinished continued to persist there as well. Even where democracy was successful, the painful task of catching up with European standards did not guarantee political stability.

In 2003, Grzegorz Ekiert came to the conclusion that the Polish state 'seems to possess more "infrastructural power" than its communist predecessor ever had'.[72] This was debatable, and it was certainly not true throughout the region. Soon afterwards, Ralf Dahrendorf admitted that he had 'underestimated the difficulty of setting up effective public institutions. ... The new political class operated in a kind of vacuum.'[73] State institutions and political values were closely intertwined, but they hardly overlapped.

From post-communist to anti-communist democracy

Liberalism in Poland and Eastern Europe, sociologist Jerzy Szacki argued in 1993, faced two fundamental challenges: either it would be reduced to a cold, technocratic economic doctrine, or it would be crowded out by appeals to the state to take sides in conflicts over morality. In either case, the state would become merely instrumental in the service of higher aims. His outlook was gloomy. He believed that pleas to refrain from debates on the presumed need for morality, instead of discussing the possibilities and limits of politics in a pluralistic society, would most likely go unheard. For Szacki, political liberalism remained an alien Western doctrine that would lose out against those traditions of political thought that were much more deeply rooted in the traditions of Eastern Europe.[74]

Szacki wrote his highly acclaimed, far-sighted book in the summer of 1993 under the impact of the electoral campaign in Poland, which saw the scattered and estranged parties of the once mighty Solidarity camp come in third place, losing out against the re-emerging post-communist left. Cold doctrines vs. hot morals – born out of the disappointment with the prospects of liberalism, his analysis outlined the basic conflicts over the nature of politics and the state that would shape the new democracies of Central and Eastern Europe in the decades to come.

Capitalism and the state

When the Polish Sejm commissioned the Catholic oppositionist Tadeusz Mazowiecki to form a government in August 1989, it was clear that radical economic reform would be its most urgent task. Within less than four months, the new minister of finance Leszek Balcerowicz, an advocate of monetarism in a market economy, outlined a set of measures unheard of in socialism. The laws adopted by the Sejm on 31 December 1989 forbade deficit spending, radically cut back state influence on the banking sector and opened the path for state-owned enterprises to either go bankrupt or be privatized.[75] The state's abrupt withdrawal from steering

---

72 Ekiert, 'The State after State-Socialism?', 309.

73 Dahrendorf, *Reflections on the Revolution in Europe*, 170–1.

74 Jerzy Szacki, *Liberalism after Communism* (Budapest: CEU Press, 1995), 194–205.

75 Jeffrey Sachs, *Poland's Jump to the Market Economy* (Cambridge, MA: MIT Press, 1993), 35–78; Leszek Balcerowicz, *Socialism, Capitalism, Transformation* (Budapest: CEU Press, 1995), 290–7.

the economy, soon labelled 'shock therapy', drew strong criticism not only because it caused a massive increase in poverty and social inequality, but also because it was guided by a neo-liberal ideology that mistook market economy for capitalism and treated the latter as the natural successor to communism. 'If capitalism is a system, then it needs to be fought as hard as communism had to be fought', Ralf Dahrendorf wrote, warning against the return of the minimal state which would restrain itself to guarding 'certain rules of the game discovered by a mysterious sect of economic advisers'.[76] Along the lines of classical liberal thought, Dahrendorf tried to reintroduce the distinction between constitutional politics, which is supposed to set the general rules of an open society and parliamentary democracy, and the broad range of economic and social policies that are open to political debate and democratic contestation. This distinction could not obscure the fact that in Western countries, the century-long development of capitalist market-economies could be seen as a condition that had brought about political democracy, whereas the opposite was now true in the former socialist dictatorships: democratic governments were needed to re-establish the legal and institutional framework of market economies.[77]

Historical research on the return of capitalism to Eastern Europe has primarily focused on the diverse strategies of privatization in different countries and on its economic balance-sheet. 'Shock therapy' as in Poland and Czechoslovakia has been contrasted with the more gradual approaches taken in Hungary and Southeastern Europe, the strictly market-based sale of shares and entire firms to private bidders in Poland, Hungary and East Germany, and voucher privatization implemented in the Czech Republic, Slovenia, Romania and most notably, Russia. Dorothee Bohle and Béla Greskovits summarized the different approaches in a typology that distinguished between neo-liberal-capitalist transformation in the Baltic states, embedded neo-liberalism that sought to balance market transformation with social cohesion in the four Visegrád countries, and neo-corporatism in Slovenia, while weak state institutions in Romania and Bulgaria failed to secure any sort of macroeconomic stability.[78] Philipp Ther has added a fourth type to the model: the oligarchic-neo-liberal approach taken in Romania, Ukraine, Belarus and Moldova.[79] Though Ther is far from telling a straightforward success story, his findings generally support the notion that large-scale privatization played a key role in restructuring and increasing the efficiency and competitiveness of the economies of Central Europe and, to a lesser extent, those of Southeastern Europe.

As previously mentioned, scholars throughout Central and Eastern Europe had been debating the prospects of competitive market relations in socialist economies since the 1950s.[80] It was only a small step from deregulating centralized economies to the restoration of private business ownership. The last communist government of Poland had been encouraging

---

76 Dahrendorf, *Reflections on the Revolution in Europe*, 41.

77 Klaus von Beyme, 'Ansätze zu einer Theorie der Transformation der ex-sozialistischen Länder Osteuropas', in *Systemwechsel 1: Theorien, Ansätze und Konzeptionen*, ed. Wolfgang Merkel (Opladen: Leske und Budrich, 1994), 141–71, here 155–8; Klaus von Beyme, *Transition to Democracy in Eastern Europe* (Basingstoke: Macmillan, 1996).

78 Dorothee Bohle and Béla Greskovits, *Capitalist Diversity on Europe's Periphery* (Ithaca, NY: Cornell University Press, 2012); William L. Megginson and Jeffrey M. Netter, 'From State to Market: A Survey of Empirical Studies on Privatization', *Journal of Economic Literature* 39, no. 2 (2001): 321–89.

79 Ther, *Europe since 1989*, 27–8.

80 Bockman, *Markets in the Name of Socialism*; Paul Dragos Aligica and Anthony J. Evans, *The Neoliberal Revolution in Eastern Europe: Economic Ideas in the Transition from Communism* (Cheltenham: Edward Elgar, 2009), 13–79.

individual entrepreneurs as early as 1988 by drawing on Catholic discourse on the social responsibilities of entrepreneurs.[81] But privatizing existing state-owned companies involved moral questions of a different sort. How could the population benefit from the sale of companies that had been propagated for decades as the property of the people? How could foreign investment be attracted without raising fears of a national sell-out? How to allow for the bankruptcy of entire industrial sectors, accommodate massive structural change and keep unemployment low all at the same time? Debates on the strategies of how best to buffer against economic crisis and achieve economic prosperity were highly controversial throughout the region. Employee ownership was mostly dismissed, since it smacked too much of market socialism and a 'Third Way'. But regardless of how these issues were being addressed in detail and codified in legislation, success depended on strong government institutions with strong regulatory power in a reform process that was similar in scope to the emancipation of the peasantry more than a century earlier. The existing state institutions were both ill-prepared and ill-equipped for this task.

If entrepreneurial agency and functioning markets could only be restored on the basis of clearly defined property rights, as the neo-liberal wisdom of the 1990 Washington Consensus stipulated, a strong state was needed to define and protect these property rights.[82] In Poland, the quick and fairly successful reform of state institutions became one of the pillars of long-term economic success. Political delays allowed Poland to avoid the mistakes of rash voucher privatization as practised in the Czech Republic.[83] Hungary and Romania followed the German model in outsourcing the entire procedure of privatization to national property agencies that had been established solely for this purpose (e.g. Állami Vagyonügynökség, Fondul Proprietății de Stat).[84] Most countries made a distinction between 'small' privatization involving the auctioning-off of local enterprises, real estate and assets, and the 'big' privatization of major industrial firms. The efficiency of local self-government played an important role in this process. At the same time, the reformed local institutions claimed to gain control of public utilities as much as of profitable enterprises on their territory, but the distinctions between the two were not always easy to draw. Whether the bodies of local self-government should be allowed to engage in economic activity, e.g. by taking over touristic enterprises for which they were responsible under socialism, was hotly debated in the Polish Sejm. The issue was finally decided in favour of local self-government.[85] At the other end of the spectrum, local institutions in Bulgaria had to sell off communal enterprises during the 1990s in order to cover expenses in education and health services.[86]

We still know little about the practical implementation of the various forms of privatization. The task of the authorities in assessing the value of real estate and business property, setting minimum prices, inviting bidders and overseeing public auctions must have been enormous. New businesses had to be properly registered, as well as property claims and restitution of property to its previous owner. Mistrust was rife where inexperienced and ill-equipped local

---

81 Puttkamer, 'Der schwere Abschied vom Volkseigentum', 158–83.

82 Bockman, *Markets in the Name of Socialism*, 171–2.

83 Ekiert, 'The State after State-Socialism?', 305; Ther, *Europe since 1989*, 79–95.

84 Árpád von Klimó, *Ungarn seit 1945* (Göttingen: Vandenhoeck & Ruprecht, 2006), 219.

85 Archiwum Sejmu [Sejm Archives]. Sejm PRL/RP – X Kadencja (1989–1991). Protokóły Komisji Sejmowych. Komisja Nadzwyczajna do rozpatrzenia projektów ustaw dotyczących samorządu terytorialnego. Nr. 1–6. 25.I. 1990–3.III.1990. Tom I. Protokół 4 posiedzenia Komisji Nadzwyczajnej do rozpatrzenia projektów ustaw dotyczących samorządu terytorialnego, 1. marca 1990, 161–2.

86 Riedel, 'Das politische System Bulgariens', 721.

administrations had to improvise, and the door to outright corruption was wide-open. Former directors of state enterprises cannibalized erstwhile firms by transforming profitable departments into their own private businesses.[87] Foreign investors plotted with managers and local officials in similar schemes. Where voucher privatization came into play, wily investors could make a fortune by buying up large numbers of shares from ignorant citizens. In Prague, privatization threatened to come to a halt when vice-minister Jaroslav Muroň failed to report an attempted bribery.[88] Scandals fed the popular image that there was something fishy about privatization.

Hungarian sociologist Elemér Hankiss was one of the first to argue that leaving the old elites a chance to gain a socio-economic foothold in the new democratic order might be the price that would have to be paid for a smooth transition.[89] To Jarosław Kaczyński, this was a serious political concern made known in his criticism of the results of the Round Table Talks.[90] But considerations of this sort did not translate directly into government policies, quite the contrary. In Czechoslovakia, Poland and Hungary, one of the main motives in pushing for privatization, aside from economic concerns, had been to curb so-called spontaneous privatization – chaotic sell-outs that mostly benefited the nomenklatura. In Hungary, where company law had been reformed in 1988, some 10 per cent of all firms had already passed into private hands before 1990.[91] But even in those countries where newly elected democratic governments quickly managed to actively control the privatization process, the old nomenklatura seemed to have got the best of it. Former Czech Prime Minister Petr Pithart lamented in hindsight that rapid privatization in the Czech Republic had been intended to prevent 'agony', but it ultimately resulted in disillusionment – the Washington Consensus had simply underestimated the power of informal practices.[92] In 2004, the year of its accession to the EU, the Czech Republic, along with El Salvador, ranked 51st in the Corruption Perception Index, just behind Greece but slightly better than Bulgaria, Slovakia and Latvia.[93] Paradoxically, while the point of rapid privatization was to wrest the people's property from the nomenklatura, the old elites ended up profiting the most due to their positions, networks and knowledge.[94]

In the privatization of land, the aspect of restitution to former owners whose property had been expropriated under communist rule raised further issues. In rural areas, traditional notions of land ownership and inheritance still prevailed or were revived after the end of communism. Land registers and cadastres, which were traditionally weak in Southeastern Europe

---

87 Jan Szomburg, 'The Political Constraints on Polish Privatization', in *Monitoring Economic Transition: The Polish Case*, eds George Blazyca and Janusz M. Dąbrowski (Aldershot: Avebury, 1995), 75–85.

88 Petr Husák, *Budování kapitalismu v Čechách. Rozhovory s Tomášem Ježkem* [Building capitalism in the Czech Lands: interviews with Tomáš Ježek] (Prague: Volvox Globator, 1997), 171–4.

89 Elemér Hankiss, *East European Alternatives* (Oxford: Clarendon Press, 1990), 233.

90 Jacek Tittenbrun, *The Collapse of Real Socialism in Poland* (London: Janus, 1993), 210–11.

91 Károly Kiss, 'Privatisation in Hungary', *Communist Economies and Economic Transformation* 3, no. 3 (1991): 305–25, here 310; Tittenbrun, *The Collapse of Real Socialism in Poland*, 176–98.

92 Petr Pithart, '1969–1989: Fehlt ein Begriff oder eher der Wille zu verstehen?' *Bohemia* 49, no. 2 (2009): 399–411, here 405–7.

93 Transparency International, Corruption Perceptions Index 2004, www.transparency.org/research/cpi/cpi_2004/0/#results (accessed 14 February 2016). Among the new EU member states, Estonia and Slovenia ranked highest (31), followed by Hungary (42), Lithuania (44), Latvia and Slovakia (57), and Poland (67). Among South European countries Bulgaria ranked highest (54), followed by Croatia (67), Bosnia (82), Romania (87), Macedonia, Serbia and Montenegro (97), Albania (108) and Moldova (114). 146 countries worldwide were ranked.

94 Gil Eyal, Iván Szelényi, and Eleanor R. Townsley, *Making Capitalism without Capitalists: Class Formation and Elite Struggles in Post-Communist Central Europe* (London: Verso, 2000).

and had been curtailed or even discontinued under communist rule, were largely restored as credible legal evidence of property ownership and mortgages.[95] In economic terms, granting members of cooperatives or their heirs the right to reclaim their former land as private property raised the prospect of the re-emergence of peasant agriculture in those countries where smallholdings had been largely eliminated by collectivization. But would it also imply a return to agrarian politics? In Romania, as Daniel Barbu lamented, the wholesale restitution of farmland paradoxically fostered the exclusion of the new owners from the body politic, since they got what they wanted without obligation and therefore without responsibility.[96] In Hungary, the historical Smallholders Party returned to the scene to focus on this issue, and in 1990 it joined the first democratic coalition government. In the end, Hungarian legislation favoured partial compensation over restitution so as to avoid the return of large noble estates, and it only allowed compensation claims to be made on property that had not been given up or expropriated before June 1948. Only the churches were to be restored part of their former landholdings so as to enable them to resume their traditional social, educational and monastic activities.[97] The Catholic Church in Poland reclaimed about one fourth of its previous landholdings.[98] In Poland, Slovakia and the Czech Republic, restitution also raised the question as to what extent German landholders who had been forced out of the country at the end of the Second World War might have a claim to their former property. This fear touched directly on the issue of national sovereignty, even more so since in Germany, the Federation of Expellees (Bund der Vertriebenen) fuelled the issue. For a brief moment, the accession of the Czech Republic to the European Union seemed to hinge on this question. In the end, while membership of the EU implied granting the expellees the right to move freely and settle in their former regions of origin, they were excluded from restitution and compensation. A formal declaration by Czech president Václav Klaus that deplored the historical 'events' as both unalterable and unacceptable was drafted with cautious vagueness.[99] This approach caused bitterness among some organized expellees, but it ultimately proved a pragmatic compromise and largely settled the issue.

Ten years after the revolutions of 1989, the reshaping of property relations had been largely accomplished in most countries of Central and Eastern Europe and the institutions of market economy were largely in place. Serbia and Montenegro lagged somewhat behind, only beginning full-on, 'unblocked', privatization in 2001.[100] Immediate economic results were mixed and the social costs were high. Most countries exacted massive cuts in social services and benefits, reduced state support for basic needs and referred issues such as unemployment, senior care,

---

95 Hannes Siegrist and Dietmar Müller, eds, *Property in East Central Europe: Notions, Institutions, and Practices of Landownership in the Twentieth Century* (New York: Berghahn Books, 2015).

96 Daniel Barbu, *Die abwesende Republik* (Berlin: Frank & Timme, 2009), 263–68 [published originally as *Republica absentă. Politică şi societate în România postcomunistă* (Bucharest: ARLD, 1999)].

97 Kiss, 'Privatisation in Hungary', 312; Ignác Romsics, *Hungary in the Twentieth Century* (Budapest: Corvina, 1999), 446–50; Tomislav Borić, *Eigentum und Privatisierung in Kroatien und Ungarn: Wandel des Eigentumsrechtssystems und Entwicklung der Privatisierungsgesetzgebung* (Berlin: Berlin Verlag, 1996), 224–5.

98 Frances Millard, *Polish Politics and Society* (London and New York: Routledge, 1999), 129.

99 Christian Domnitz, *Die Beneš-Dekrete in parlamentarischer Debatte: Kontroversen im Europäischen Parlament und im tschechischen Abgeordnetenhaus vor dem EU-Beitritt der Tschechischen Republik* (Berlin: Lit Verlag, 2007), 75 and 108.

100 Mladen Lazić and Jelena Pešić, *Making and Unmaking State-Centered Capitalism in Serbia* (Belgrade: Čigoja Štampa, 2012), 55–74.

child care and other forms of poverty back to the individual or the family. Privatized enterprises were equally quick to cut back social support and relinquish the pivotal role of their state-owned predecessors in providing social security to their employees. Yet both social democratic as well as conservative welfare regimes proved deeply entrenched, and the anticipated neo-liberal-style dismantling of social security largely failed to materialize.[101]

Little attention has been given to the fact that a historical process of reshaping notions of property in society to conform to the requirements of market economies was now coming to a close. If popular support for and the political legitimacy of large-scale privatization had been weak in the first place, its implementation did considerable damage to the approval of parliamentary democracy, regardless of economic performance.

Civil society and national sovereignty

In February 1990, Timothy Garton Ash remarked that 1989 was 'a springtime of nations, but not necessarily of nationalism; of societies aspiring to be civil; and above all, of citizens'.[102] The enthusiastic embrace of civil society took the nation state as its natural framework for granted, and rather vaguely identified nationalism as its major threat. It turned out that the two were closely intertwined, and sometimes, just two sides of the same coin.

As had been visible early on in dissident discourse, national sovereignty became a key issue in the revolutions of 1989. At the reburial of Imre Nagy in June 1989, Fidesz leader Viktor Orbán provokingly called for the withdrawal of Soviet troops. To him, as to other anti-communists throughout the region, every political arrangement that did not immediately satisfy this demand smacked of rotten compromise. This was indeed the testing ground by which the achievements of democracy were to be measured, and it was one of the main arguments in support of the rapid and radical dismantling of the totalitarian system. Once achieved, the notion that the democratic revolution was yet unfinished inspired other kinds of action, mostly lustration (see below).

The issue of national sovereignty re-emerged with many countries' accession to NATO and the European Union. As early as 1991, Poland, the Czech Republic, Slovakia and Hungary formed the Visegrád group to harmonize their efforts to closely cooperate with European institutions and develop a coordinated approach.[103] The prospect of becoming part of the Western Alliance, of erecting military defences against potential Russian aggression and participating in NATO's intervention in neighbouring former Yugoslavia played out in different ways on the issue of NATO membership, and the process of accession was far from uniform. For most countries of the region, NATO's Partnership for Peace Program turned out to be only a transitory stage. Poland, the Czech Republic and Hungary were formally invited to join NATO

---

101 Tomasz Inglot, *Welfare States in East Central Europe, 1919–2004* (Cambridge: Cambridge University Press, 2008), 211–305; Ther, *Europe since 1989*, 115–20; Béla Tomka, *A Social History of Twentieth-Century Europe* (London: Routledge, 2013), 190–1. See the contribution by Béla Tomka to the volume *Challenges of Modernity* in this series.

102 Timothy Garton Ash, 'Eastern Europe: The Year of Truth', in *The Magic Lantern: The Revolution of '89 Witnessed in Warsaw, Budapest, Berlin, and Prague* (New York: Random House, 1990), 131–56, here 149 [first published in *The New York Review of Books*, 15 February 1990].

103 Declaration on Cooperation between the Czech and Slovak Federal Republic, the Republic of Poland and the Republic of Hungary in Striving for European Integration (Visegrád Declaration): web.archive.org/web/20140419203940/www.visegradgroup.eu/documents/visegrad-declarations/visegrad-declaration-110412 [accessed 3 March 2017].

at the Madrid summit in 1997, while Slovakia and Romania were turned down for the time being. Whereas Slovak support for NATO-membership had been rather lukewarm, disappointment ran high in Romania, where the rejection was perceived as a violation of national dignity.[104] The admission of both states in 2004 together with Bulgaria, Slovenia and the Baltic states dispelled, at least for the time being, the prospect of a 'dependent intermediate zone of weak states'.[105] The re-emergence of *Zwischeneuropa*, which Garton Ash had feared in 1990, was replaced by hopes for a 'New Europe' whose members rushed to prove themselves particularly reliable partners.

Accession to the European Union had an even greater impact on national sovereignty. The Copenhagen criteria of 1993 committed the new member states to the principles of democracy, market economy and the protection of national minorities. But adopting the *acquis communautaire* with its 3,000 directives left little room for national peculiarities. It had an enormous impact on streamlining state institutions and administration throughout the region, rendering them more effective and evening out diverse historical roots and trajectories. Whether merely formal adherence to European norms and practices will prevail over committed and reliable implementation in individual countries remains to be seen.[106] Romania and Bulgaria, which were admitted in 2007 under the provision of conditionality, still have to undergo regular reports on their measures against corruption. The effects remain to be seen. In general, turning over substantial elements of national sovereignty to Brussels was largely accepted throughout the countries of the region. The 'yes' votes in the referendums ranged between almost 94 per cent in Slovakia to 67 per cent in Estonia and Latvia and 66 per cent in Croatia.

Nevertheless, turnout to accession referendums was low, and in hindsight, it seems that this might have been an early sign of insidious exhaustion with the idea of a unified Europe, the merits of parliamentary democracy in general and the emancipatory idea of civil society in particular. When dissidents stressed the concept of civil society, they were aiming to erode the communist regime rather than provide a blueprint for future democratic transition.[107] Václav Havel and Adam Michnik's repeated pleas for civil society and the virtues of civic responsibility were an emphatic attempt to preserve the legacy of dissidence and turn it into the moral foundation of the new democracies. But it can equally be seen as the defence of a middle ground between the cold technicality of the neo-liberal state and the mobilizing simplifications of national populism, be it of a rightist or leftist hue.[108]

Scholars throughout the region soon realized that in spite of such efforts to instil open society with civic moral values, the nation remained the relevant community. In Hungary, where dissidence had been fairly weak, liberal intellectuals had early on voiced the concern that political democracy might not survive the shocks brought along by social problems and the loss of

---

104 Zoltan D. Barany, *The Future of NATO Expansion: Four Case Studies* (Cambridge: Cambridge University Press, 2003), 61–7 and 144–51; Alexandra Gheciu, *NATO in the 'New Europe': The Politics of International Socialization after the Cold War* (Stanford, CA: Stanford University Press, 2005), 75.

105 Garton Ash, 'Eastern Europe: The Year of Truth', 155.

106 Frank Schimmelfennig and Ulrich Sedelmeier, eds, *The Europeanization of Central and Eastern Europe* (Ithaca, NY: Cornell University Press, 2005); Geoffrey Pridham, *Designing Democracy: EU Enlargement and Regime Change in Post-Communist Europe* (Basingstoke: Palgrave Macmillan, 2005).

107 von Beyme, 'Ansätze zu einer Theorie der Transformation', 149.

108 Václav Havel, *Summer Meditations* (New York: A.A. Knopf, 1992); Adam Michnik, *Letters from Freedom: Post-Cold War Realities and Perspectives*, ed. Irena Grudzińska-Gross (Berkeley, CA: University of California Press, 1998).

traditional values.[109] North of Yugoslavia, Hungary was the first among the new democracies of Eastern Europe to face the emergence of right-wing nationalism as a political force, and was also one of the first to engage in serious debates about it. In 1992, the writer and politician István Csurka condensed the vague idea of an unfinished democratic transformation into a programme of ethnic mobilization that questioned the 1920 Treaty of Trianon while not shying away from anti-Semitic rhetoric and fascist notions of national recovery and renewal.[110] In Romania, Corneliu Vadim Tudor and his Greater Romania Party (Partidul România Mare) followed suit.

At the time, such ideas were vehemently rejected. The prospect of accession to the European Union committed all future member states to respect minority rights and pass minority legislation along the principles that had been laid down in the Framework Convention for the Protection of National Minorities and in the European Charter for Regional or Minority Languages. In 1995, Hungary signed a treaty of good neighbourhood and friendly cooperation with Slovakia and in the following year signed a similar treaty with Romania. But the genie of Hungarian nationalism was out of the bottle. The notion of a Hungarian trans-border national community, a 'unitary Hungarian nation', underpinned the so-called status law of 2001, which conferred citizenship rights to ethnic Hungarians in the neighbouring states.[111]

Dual citizenship became a critical issue in a number of states, mostly with Croats in Bosnia and Romanians in Moldova. In the Baltic states, the collapse of the Soviet Union left a large Russian population stateless, with highly restricted access to Estonian, Latvian or Lithuanian citizenship and to respective minority rights. Bosnia's Dayton Agreement of 1995 stressed the importance of minority rights while breaking sharply with the international sanctioning of forced migration and ethnic cleansing. As mentioned above, the Bosnian government's treatment of minorities since 1995 equally demonstrates that turning over the state to uncontested ethnic elites cannot support the construction of efficient institutions and instead simply paves the way for patronage and clientelism.[112]

Finally, the Central European states' accession to the European Union brought the situation of the Roma population back onto the political agenda, since it at once raised Western European fears of Roma migration and heightened public awareness of discrimination and violence within the region. In the Czech Republic, Slovak-born Roma had been denied citizenship and faced expulsion throughout the 1990s, regardless of whether they had

---

109 István Eörsi, 'Der Schock der Freiheit', in *Der Schock der Freiheit: Ungarn auf dem Weg in die Demokratie*, eds József Bayer and Rainer Deppe (Frankfurt a.M.: Suhrkamp), 67–76 [first published as 'A szabadság sokkja', *Népszabadság*, October 19, 1991]; Attila Ágh, 'Citizenship and Civil Society in Eastern Europe', in *The Condition of Citizenship*, ed. Bart van Steenbergen (London: SAGE Publications, 1994), 108–26.

110 István Csurka, 'A Few Thoughts', in *From Stalinism to Pluralism: A Documentary History of Eastern Europe since 1945*, ed. Gale Stokes, 2nd ed. (Oxford: Oxford University Press, 1996), 265–9. For the full text see 'Nehány Gondolat a rendszerváltás két esztendeje és az MDF új programja kapcsán', *Magyar Fórum*, 20 August 1992, web.archive.org/web/20021114113758/www.miep.hu/csiforum/gondolat1. htm (accessed 16 February 2016).

111 Zoltán Kántor, Balázs Majtényi, Osamu Ieda, Balázs Vizi and Iván Halász, eds, *The Hungarian Status Law: Nation Building and/or Minority Protection* (Sapporo: Slavic Research Center, Hokkaido University, 2004), x.

112 Joseph Marko, 'Ethnopolitics and Constitutional Reform in Bosnia-Herzegovina', in *Bosnia-Herzegovina since Dayton: Civic and Uncivic Values*, eds Ola Listhaug and Sabrina P. Ramet (Ravenna: Longo editore, 2013), 49–80; Boris Divjak and Michael Pugh, 'The Political Economy of Corruption in Bosnia and Herzegovina', in Listhaug and Ramet, *Bosnia-Herzegovina since Dayton*, 80–97; Sofia Sebastián-Aparicio, *Post-War Statebuilding and Constitutional Reform in Divided Societies: Beyond Dayton in Bosnia* (Basingstoke: Palgrave Macmillan, 2014).

held long-term residency.[113] Human rights activists' continued lobbying finally secured their legal status, but it did not put an end to discrimination. When the local authorities of Ustí nad Labem built a wall to separate Roma communal flats from Czech family houses in 1999, European media was rife with indignation. The tension between a society of citizens and ethnic exclusiveness tended to become more visible, but it remained unresolved.

Debates on abortion in Romania and Poland

General expectations that people would try to redefine the state as a moral institution in order to remedy the distortions of communism came out most clearly in debates on abortion and gender equality.[114] Throughout Eastern Europe, the issue of abortion had largely been settled by the communist regimes. Ranging from more liberal approaches, such as in Poland or Czechoslovakia, or moderately restrictive ones, such as in Hungary or Bulgaria, most social states had allowed access to abortion and promoted contraception as the primary instrument of family planning.[115] Only socialist Romania stuck out with its radical 1966 ban on abortion.[116] The consequences of this extreme pro-natalism and the pressure that it exerted on women were dramatic. Illegal abortions skyrocketed, infant mortality in the 1980s was nearly twice as high as in neighbouring Hungary and Bulgaria and maternal mortality was the highest in Europe.[117] The living conditions in orphanages, let alone of abandoned street children, were miserable, and once they became public, they caused shock and indignation throughout Europe. One of the very first measures that the newly formed government took on 26 December 1989, the very day after Ceauşescu was executed, was to lift the ban on abortion. Repressive pro-natalism was considered a shame, unworthy of any civilized European country, and radical change a pledge for democracy, on the same level as free elections and minority rights.

Poland, on the contrary, had followed a fairly liberal abortion policy when compared with the other socialist countries. Among Catholic oppositionists, abortion had been an issue early on, though initially it was a rather marginal one. Non-partisan Catholic deputies had already submitted draft legislation to the Sejm in 1988.[118] In the 1989 electoral campaign, individual candidates made vague pledges to remedy the social and economic causes for abortions.[119] Conflict arose in December 1989 when 37 senators introduced a motion that would permit

---

113 Oksana Shevel, *Migration, Refugee Policy, and State Building in Postcommunist Europe* (New York: Cambridge University Press, 2011), 210–11.

114 Susan Gal and Gail Kligman, *The Politics of Gender after Socialism: A Comparative Historical Essay* (Princeton, NJ: Princeton University Press, 2000).

115 See the chapter by Claudia Kraft and Ulf Brunnbauer in this volume.

116 Gail Kligman, *The Politics of Duplicity: Controlling Reproduction in Ceauşescu's Romania* (Berkeley, CA: University of California Press, 1998); Corina Doboş, Luciana M. Jinga and Florin S. Soare, eds, *Politica pronatalistă a regimului Ceauşescu. O perspectivă comparativă* [The pro-natalist policy of the Ceauşescu regime: a comparative perspective] (Bucharest: Polirom, 2010).

117 Kligman, *The Politics of Duplicity*, 206–21.

118 Polski Związek Katolicko-Społeczny [The Polish Catholic Association], www.pzks.org.pl/ (accessed 13 February 2016); Małgorzata Fuszara, 'Abortion and the Formation of the Public Sphere in Poland', in *Gender Politics and Post-Communism: Reflections from Eastern Europe and the Former Soviet Union*, eds Nanette Funk and Magda Mueller (London: Routledge, 1993), 241–52; Eleonora Zielińska, 'Between Ideology, Politics, and Common Sense: The Discourse of Reproductive Rights in Poland', in *Reproducing Gender: Politics, Publics, and Everyday Life after Socialism*, eds Susan Gal and Gail Kligman (Princeton, NJ: Princeton University Press, 2000), 23–57.

119 *Gazeta Wyborcza* 1 (8 May 1989): 3, particularly, candidate Marek Rusakiewicz.

abortion only if the life and health of the mother were in danger or if the pregnancy had been the result of a criminal offence.[120] This was the first political issue that seriously divided the former Solidarity opposition, and it came at the very moment when it had scored its greatest victory and the Sejm had voted through Balcerowicz's package of economic liberalization. The debate on abortion tended to divide Catholicism rather than reassert it, as Kazimierz Wóycicki wrote in early 1990.[121] This remark proved to be prophetic. Whereas the motion won a majority in the senate, it was rejected by the Sejm after months of controversial debate and mass demonstrations. The parliament's rejection of the motion by a margin of nearly 60 per cent reflected opinion polls.[122] On the issue of abortion, the fear of the conservatives that their former fellow oppositionists would side with the post-communist left came true.

Debates on abortion dominated political life in Poland for a number of years. In January 1993, a conservative majority in the Sejm voted to ban abortion except for cases in which it was medically necessary. The Democratic Left Alliance (Sojusz Lewicy Demokratycznej), headed by social democrats, tried to return to a more permissive approach in 1996, but its legislation was overturned by the constitutional court, which argued that the state had a moral obligation to protect human life. But even this court ruling only settled the issue for a short time. In 2002, one hundred prominent Polish women, among them actress Krystyna Janda, film director Agnieszka Holland, art historian Anda Rottenberg and Nobel laureate Wisława Szymborska, sent an open letter to the European Parliament demanding an open and democratic debate on abortion. For its part, the government sided with the Catholic clergy in order to secure its support for Poland's accession to the European Union.[123] Appealing to a European audience and European values did not bring any direct results, but it did show to what extent the Polish state deviated from the general European stance on the issue.

Both the Romanian and the Polish legislation on abortion were telling as to the role of the church in society and its influence on politics and the state. While their stances were at opposite ends of the spectrum, debates in both countries were deeply grounded in moral arguments. Born out of the desire to return to a normal state of things after the deformations caused by the communist regimes, abortion legislation in both countries was meant to prove the new states' moral superiority over defeated communism.[124] But while the Romanian state sought to cast off the most visible burden of Stalinism's continued grip on the individual and society in order to join in with European modernity, the Polish legislation was driven by the reassertion of presumed national values that had to be defended against the kinds of modern liberalism and moral relativism they associated with Europe and the West. The Hungarian case, finally, is particularly telling. Hungarian politicians argued that even if the substance of old legislation on abortion should remain unchanged, it should be codified in a new law so as to assert its democratic character and dispel the notion that the state was still patronizing its population on matters of birth

---

120 Antoni Dudek, *Historia polityczna Polski 1989–2012* [The political history of Poland 1989–2012] (Kraków: Wydawnictwo Znak, 2013), 171–2.
121 Kaziemierz Wóycicki, 'Polskość jest zmęczona' [Polishness is wearied], in *Spór o Polskę. Wybór tekstów prasowych*, ed. Paweł Śpiewak (Warsaw: Wydawnictwo Naukowe PWN, 2000), 45–47, here 47 (originally published in *Więź* 1 (1990)).
122 Dudek, *Historia polityczna Polski 1989–2012*, 172.
123 Women's Alliance March 8, 'Letter from One Hundred Women', www.zgapa.pl/zgapedia/List_Stu_Kobiet.html (accessed 4 March 2017).
124 Gal and Kligman, *The Politics of Gender*, 30–31; Joanna Mishtal, *The Politics of Morality: The Church, the State, and Reproductive Rights in Postsocialist Poland* (Athens, OH: Ohio University Press, 2015).

control. The abortion debate became a site where broader political arguments were rehearsed and different moral visions propagated. It was not only about abortion, 'but also an argument in absentia with communism'.[125] Similar debates took place in other countries. Political authority, as Susan Gal and Gail Kligman argued in an influential essay, was partially being 'reconstituted through arguments about reproduction'.[126]

Within a broader framework, debates on abortion gave expression to conflicting claims on how to reshape gender relations in general after the end of communism. Since the 1990s, a large body of literature has demonstrated how state institutions and government politics actively propagated or facilitated a reversal towards more traditional roles.[127] In many cases, this was the direct result of attempts to break with communist-inspired forms of female emancipation, as in the 1996 Hungarian debate on parental leave.[128] But even without overt political action, it is a simple fact that women were more likely than men to slip into unemployment and suffer the effects of the erosion of social security in crumbling economies. Seemingly unrestrained capitalism and illiberal nationalism equally worsened gender inequalities, and in the light of their effects, the oft lamented failure of communist female emancipation to fulfil its promises actually seems less critical. In this highly-contested field, the shadow of communism still looms large.

Lustration and decommunization

'Is democracy a process or an outcome?' asked New York journalist Tina Rosenberg in 1995. What she had in mind was a radical approach to lustration in former Czechoslovakia, in Poland and East Germany, the urge to purify the new democracies of all those individuals who at some stage in their lives had cooperated with the secret police, a stain that would remain forever, regardless of the complexities of life. Too much justice might be injustice, she warned.[129] Unlike Latin America, Eastern Europe did not need trials to break the cycle of dictatorship and impunity; rather, she claimed, it needed a society-wide examination of how communist regimes had maintained their power for more than four decades.[130]

Rosenberg's question reflected the debates on the nature of an open society and whether capitalism could simply be implemented with the stroke of a pen. She feared that the advocates of lustration viewed democracy as the simple negation of communism in a worldview that knew only black and white. And the course that things took proved her right. Various approaches to deal with the legacy of communist dictatorship and its crimes might have been inevitable and even politically productive, but they all left behind a nasty aftertaste: none of them fulfilled the expectation that blatant crimes would finally be punished and that members

---

125 Susan Gal, 'Gender in the Post-Socialist Transition: The Abortion Debate in Hungary', *East European Politics and Societies* 8, no. 2 (1994): 256–87, here 260; Barbara Einhorn, *Cinderella Goes to Market: Citizenship, Gender and Women's Movements in East Central Europe* (London: Verso, 1993), 74–112.
126 Gal and Kligman, *The Politics of Gender*, 15.
127 Gal and Kligman, *Reproducing Gender*; Edith Saurer, Margareth Lanzinger and Elisabeth Frysak, eds, *Women's Movements: Networks and Debates in Post-Communist Countries in the Nineteenth and Twentieth Centuries* (Köln: Böhlau, 2006), 31–288.
128 Joanna Goven, 'New Parliament, Old Discourse? The Parental Leave Debate in Hungary', in Gal and Kligman, *Reproducing Gender*, 286–306.
129 Tina Rosenberg, *The Haunted Land: Facing Europe's Ghosts after Communism* (New York: Vintage Books, 1995), 6 and xix.
130 Rosenberg, *The Haunted Land*, 404–5.

of the nomenklatura would be forever prevented from gaining a foothold in the new democratic order. The expectation that moral purity could be achieved was itself flawed. In the long run, it became a heavy burden.[131]

Parliaments rather than governments took the lead in establishing institutions which would shed light on the legacies of communist dictatorship. In Poland, it only took Solidarity deputies of the newly elected contract Sejm a few weeks to set up a commission to investigate more than 100 alleged political murders. Within two years, the commission had initiated 78 criminal investigations against some 100-state security and police (Citizen's Militia) officers. More than 70 state prosecutors were dismissed for having covered up crimes involving the security forces.[132] But what might have been a success was squandered. Sifting through the procurators' files was a tedious task. 'We want to hold accountable all those officials who have abused their powers', the commission's chairman Jan Rokita declared in March 1990.[133] In many cases, such abuses, though highly probable, could no longer be proven in court. The rule of law that had been so hard to win imposed unexpected restrictions. Impatience grew, first with anti-communist extremists and later with Rokita himself. The blame for the commission's failures was all too easily placed on the shoulders of those former communist deputies who had quickly lost interest in this work.

A similar fate, though on a much broader scale, befell the parliamentary commission that had been established in Czechoslovakia after the elections of June 1990 to investigate the events of 17 November 1989, when violent police action against peaceful demonstrators had sparked the 'Velvet Revolution'. The commission, chaired by the former dissident journalist Jiří Ruml, also took up the task of investigating the moral credentials of the newly elected fellow deputies.[134] The categories which it developed to establish the guilt of those who had cooperated with the state security apparatus in one way or another were driven by the same all-encompassing urge for moral purity that motivated their colleagues in Poland. And, indeed, the commission was flawed by the same assumption that it would be easy to make judgments about individual guilt and innocence. 'I thought it was possible to tell who was a collaborator', parliamentary deputy and student activist Jiři Dienstbier, Jr. recalled. 'We found out that it was not so straightforward.'[135] Yet the moral urge gained the upper hand. Even more, the lustration law of October 1991 extended the procedures that had been developed to screen parliamentary deputies to a broad range of public officials. Within a year, more than one out of four judges in Czechoslovakia had lost their position, to give the most striking example of

---

131 Monika Nalepa, *Skeletons in the Closet: Transitional Justice in Post-Communist Europe* (Cambridge: Cambridge University Press, 2010); Katherine Verdery, 'Postsocialist Cleansing in Eastern Europe: Purity and Danger in Transitional Justice', in *Socialism Vanquished, Socialism Challenged: Eastern Europe and China, 1989–2009*, eds Nina Bandelj and Dorothy J. Solinger (Oxford: Oxford University Press, 2012), 63–82.

132 Antoni Dudek, ed., *Raport Rokity. Sprawozdanie Sejmowej Komisji Nadzwyczajnej do Zbadania Działalności MSW* [Rokita's report: report of the extraordinary commission for the investigation of the activities of the Ministry of the Interior] (Kraków: Wydawnictwo ARCANA, 2005), 33–34.

133 Archiwum Sejmu. Sejm PRL/RP – X Kadencja (1989–1991). Protokóły Komisji Sejmowych. Komisja Nadzwyczajna do rozpatrzenia projektów ustaw dotyczących samorządu terytorialnego. Nr. 1–6. 25.I. 1990–3.III.1990. Tom I. Protokół 5 posiedzenia Komisji Nadzwyczajnej do rozpatrzenia projektów ustaw dotyczących samorządu terytorialnego, 13. marca 1990, 130.

134 Závěrečná zpráva vyšetřovací komise Federálního shromáždění pro objasnění událostí 17. listopadu 1989 [Final Report of the Federal Assembly's Commission to investigate the events of 17 November 1989] (Praha: Futura, 1992).

135 Rosenberg, *The Haunted Land*, 85.

the law's effects.[136] This margin was only surpassed in the former GDR. For Jiřina Šiklová, lustration as she came to know it in the Czech Republic was simply a tragicomic farce.[137] The issue of former secret informers haunted the entire region for more than a decade. Impatient anti-communists pressed for the proverbial witch-hunts. Where legal investigations and the rule of law failed to bring the desired results, they suspected conspiracy. Some of them could not resist the temptation to publish lists that named tens, even hundreds of thousands of names of people who were allegedly implicated with the detested security services, the most infamous case being the lists published by Petr Cibulka in 1993 in the Czech Republic, and by Bronisław Wildstein in Poland in 2000.[138] In Hungary, which had been quite reluctant to embark on broad-scale lustration, the newly elected Prime Minister Péter Medgyessy nearly had to step down in June 2002 after his work for communist counter-espionage became public. The scandal briefly brought lustration back onto the agenda.[139]

By that time, Poland had already passed a lustration law of its own. It was less severe and more balanced than its Czech predecessor, since it asked former informers and agents to come out on their own. Poland also established its Institute of National Remembrance (Instytut Pamięci Narodowej – IPN), a special archive to hold and research the vast shadow empire of state security files and, next to the former GDR, the first of its kind in the region. Unlike its East German model, the Polish IPN was invested with far-reaching judicial powers to investigate and prosecute crimes of the former communist regime.[140] Slovakia, Hungary and the Czech Republic established similar institutions between 2002 and 2007, though with less investigative powers.

Political scientists have grappled with the broad range of legislation on lustration throughout Central and Eastern Europe, grouping them according to the severity of their approaches, whether legislation came early or late, whether they used incentive- or evidence-based procedures and whether they worked with principles of endogenous or exogenous retroactive justice.[141] Political competition and outright power struggles accounted for much of the precise shape which legal provisions took in individual countries. Anthropologist Katherine Verdery has rightfully pointed out that the urge for purification also tended to transcend the political sphere and reached into various fields of society.[142]

---

136 Ibid., 100.
137 Jiřina Šiklová, 'Lustration or the Czech Way of Screening', *East European Constitutional Review* 5, no. 1 (1996): 57–62; David Kosař, 'Lustration and Lapse of Time', *European Constitutional Law Review* 4, no. 3 (2008): 460–87.
138 Saygun Gökariksel, 'In the Free Market of Names: Polish Secret Service Files and Authoritarian Populism', *Anthropology of East Europe Review* 31, no. 2 (2013): 30–45.
139 Csilla Kiss, 'The Misuses of Manipulation: The Failure of Transitional Justice in Post-Communist Hungary', *Europe-Asia Studies* 58, no. 6 (2006): 925–40.
140 Antoni Dudek, *Instytut. Osobista historia IPN* [The Institute: A personal history of the IPN] (Warszawa: Czerwone i Czarne, 2011), 12–65.
141 Marek M. Kaminski and Monika Nalepa, 'Judging Transitional Justice: A New Criterion for Evaluating Truth Revelation Procedures', *Journal of Conflict Resolution* 50, no. 3 (2006): 383–408; Nalepa, *Skeletons in the Closet*; Lavinia Stan, ed., *Transitional Justice in Eastern Europe and the Former Soviet Union: Reckoning with the Communist Past* (London: Routledge, 2009); Lavinia Stan and Nadya Nedelsky, eds, *Post-Communist Transitional Justice: Lessons from Twenty-Five Years of Experience* (Cambridge: Cambridge University Press, 2015).
142 Katherine Verdery, 'Postsocialist Cleansing in Eastern Europe: Purity and Danger in Transitional Justice', in Bandelj and Solinger, *Socialism Vanquished, Socialism Challenged*, 63–82; Kieran Williams, Brigid Fowler, and Aleks Szczerbiak, 'Explaining Lustration in Eastern Europe: A "Post-Communist-Politics" Approach', *Democratization* 12, no. 1 (2005): 22–43.

Putting lustration on firm legal footing, encouraging nuanced judgments and allowing for appeals did much to build trust in new government institutions and establish the rule of law as their highest principle. At the same time, by their mere existence, these institutions became the strongholds of the anti-totalitarian urge to oust the nomenklatura and to purify the state. At times, they became almost obsessive. They fuelled the perception that far too much still remained to be done in this respect, even more so since they had no means to prevent high-ranking communists and their networks from taking hold outside the public sector, mostly in the media or the economy.

Adverse approaches to lustration tended to produce similar effects in Southeastern Europe. Rabid anti-communists were few in Romania and nearly non-existent in Bulgaria, Serbia and Albania. In Romania, it took the National Council for the Study of Securitate Files (CNSAS) six years to achieve the transfer of the bulk of the files, which it did in 2005, only to see its lustration powers redefined and partly curtailed three years later.[143] Lustration was late to come in Romania, and even more so among its Balkan neighbours. The Bulgarian files were made fully accessible only with accession to the EU in 2007.[144] In countries where trust in the state and its institutions were traditionally weak, the nomenklatura's nearly unhampered hold on power for more than a decade after 1989 tended to spur resignation rather than anti-communist fury.

Broad-scale lustration was a corollary to the manifold attempts to put top-ranking communists on trial for their deeds. The court martial against Nicolae and Elena Ceauşescu in December 1989 was intended to be shocking and sensational, a symbolic break with the crumbling communist regime, not an attempt to reinstall justice. A gross violation of judicial procedures seemed necessary to bring about a quick and harsh verdict. In this respect, the Ceauşescu trial anticipated future disappointments. Nowhere in Central and Eastern Europe did criminal procedures against former top communist officials produce the results that their supporters had hoped for. Among the communist leaders, only Bulgarian Todor Zhivkov was sentenced to jail, and even he was only sentenced for corruption. The sentence was later reduced to house arrest and was finally suspended. In Poland, Wojciech Jaruzelski and some of his generals faced trial because of the bloodshed in Gdańsk in December 1970 and for having declared martial law in 1981. After a whole series of trials on these and other matters, including a renewed trial against the superiors of the murderers of priest Jerzy Popiełuszko, only three mid-ranking officers were actually convicted. All the others, including former first secretary Jaruzelski, never received a final verdict or were legally acquitted, and if they were convicted of something like former Minister of the Interior Czesław Kiszczak, they were spared having to serve the sentence. They were simply too old.[145] Only in the Baltic states were communist parties actually outlawed.

---

143 Dragoş Petrescu, 'The Resistance that Wasn't: Romanian Intellectuals, the Securitate, and "Resistance through Culture"', in *Die Securitate in Siebenbürgen*, eds Joachim von Puttkamer, Stefan Sienerth, and Ulrich A. Wien (Köln: Böhlau, 2014), 11–35; Bogdan Iancu, 'Post-Accession Constitutionalism with a Human Face: Judicial Reform and Lustration in Romania', in *European Constitutional Law Review* 6, no. 1 (2010): 28–58.

144 Jordan Baev and Kostadin Grozev, 'Bulgaria', in *A Handbook of the Communist Security Apparatus in East Central Europe, 1944–1989*, eds Krzysztof Persak and Łukasz Kamiński (Warsaw: Institute of National Remembrance, 2005), 37–86; Björn Opfer-Klinger, 'Die bulgarische Staatssicherheit vom Kalten Krieg bis zur gescheiterten Vergangenheitsbewältigung', *Halbjahresschrift für südosteuropäische Geschichte, Literatur und Politik* 22, no. 1 (2010): 90–111, here 109–10.

145 Joachim von Puttkamer, 'Enttäuschte Erwartungen: Die strafrechtliche Aufarbeitung kommunistischer Diktatur in Polen', in *Recht und Gerechtigkeit. Die strafrechtliche Aufarbeitung von Diktaturen in Europa*, ed. Jörg Ganzenmüller (Köln: Böhlau Verlag, 2017), 173–94; Noel Calhoun, *Dilemmas of Justice in Eastern Europe's Democratic Transitions* (New York: Palgrave Macmillan, 2014), 93–132.

According to Jerzy Turowicz, decommunization in all its dimensions, in the political system, the economy and the restoration of social bonds, should serve the return to normal life and ultimately to reconciliation. It was supposed to be an instrument of justice, not of revenge. But this call largely went unheard.[146] In Poland and elsewhere, even after ritual purges, the notion that the state had been and still was in the hands of the wrong people did not simply vanish.

Conclusion

In 2004, Leszek Miller, Vladimír Špidla and Péter Medgyessy resigned from their posts as prime ministers of Poland, the Czech Republic and Hungary. They had all guided their countries into the European Union and they all belonged to a social democratic left. To be sure, accession to the EU had not been solely a social democratic, let alone post-communist project. The triumphant enlargement of the European Union by eight former communist countries continued in 2007 with the accession of Romania and Bulgaria and in 2013 with the accession of Croatia. This triumphant enlargement can be seen as the fortunate result of dissident thought and activity, an outcome that would have hardly been foreseeable three decades earlier. In hindsight, it was the end of an epoch in the development of state institutions and political systems throughout the region. In an optimistic reading, parliamentary democracy was firmly in place throughout the region by the beginning of the twenty-first century and its institutional form largely fell in line with general developments throughout Europe.[147] Though persistent corruption in parts of the region tainted the overall picture of efficient administrative institution-building, the general course seemed set.

But viewed from the vantage point of 2016, these years also marked the end of an epoch that had been shaped by the notion that democratic, social and national emancipation should go hand in hand and that the state would provide the institutions that would help them along. With the decline of emancipatory ideas, the polarization which Jerzy Szacki had predicted in 1993 seemed to have come true. The liberal idea of civil society, responsibility and the peaceful resolution of conflicts of interest as the foundations of parliamentary democracy began to lose out against the enemy camps of technocratic realism and national populism of either leftist or rightist origins.

Opinion polls in the Czech Republic during the first years of the new century showed that democracy was accepted in principle, but that its practical functioning was perceived to be massively flawed by corruption and a lack of opportunity for civic participation.[148] Elsewhere, investigations into political expectations offered a similar picture. In countries as different as Poland and Serbia, the president and the church met with the highest confidence among the population, whereas the reputation of parliament and the judiciary was abominably low.[149] This in part reflects the legacy of dissident thought, which had paired moral rigour with an anti-elitist rejection of the nomenklatura. Once transferred from civil society onto the state, the dissident

---

146 Jerzy Turowicz, 'Dekomunizacja, ale jaka?' [Which decommunization?], *Tygodnik Powszechny*, 21 February 1993; Magdalena Zolkos, 'The Conceptual Nexus of Human Rights and Democracy in the Polish Lustration Debates 1989–97', *Journal of Communist Studies and Transition Politics* 22, no. 2 (2006): 228–48.

147 Andreas Wirsching, *Der Preis der Freiheit: Geschichte Europas in unserer Zeit* (München: C.H. Beck, 2012), 78–152.

148 Karel Vodička, 'Das politische System Tschechiens', in *Die politischen Systeme Osteuropas*, 275–316, here 300–1.

149 Ziemer and Matthes, 'Das politische System Polens', 259; Irena Ristić, 'Das politische System Serbiens', in *Die politischen Systeme Osteuropas*, 897–940, here 932.

notion of a moral polity was almost inevitably disappointed, even more so since achievements in building parliamentary democracy, efficient state-institutions, market economies and European integration were generally ascribed to technocratic elites who were perceived as being insensitive towards the social needs of the great majority. Legislation on gender equality might be seen as a case in point. It was the prospect of EU membership that forced even right-wing parties, as in Poland, to subscribe to anti-discrimination laws and equal opportunity programmes. But once membership had been achieved, the EU lost much of its coercive powers. It was now mostly up to domestic social pressure to achieve anything more than superficial enforcement of the new laws. Only a few countries such as Lithuania and Slovenia sustained a strong social commitment to gender equality beyond 2004.[150]

In 1995, Gale Stokes argued that the communist regimes' moral hollowness had brought them down. The dissidents had gained the moral high ground over the Marxists, who had occupied it for such a long time, and they had assumed the role of moral leadership for themselves.[151] But tensions between national and liberal thought within the opposition that had become visible in the 1970s remained unresolved. This turned out to be a double-edged sword. Euphoria for the advent of parliamentary democracy, civil society and the rule of law began to fade in the course of the 1990s and left the field to nationalism, which has been on the rise since the 2000s. Under the conditions of the twenty-first century, the state might turn out to be equally ill-equipped to serve as the embodiment of national identity and its main safeguard. But the picture might not be all that bleak. Though hopes for general prosperity have remained unfulfilled, state institutions throughout Eastern Europe – with all their flaws – have demonstrated a remarkable capacity to moderate and stabilize the transition to market economies. This comes out clearly if we compare developments in Eastern Europe since 1989 with the outcomes of the 'Arab Spring' in 2010. It is as yet unclear whether we are today witnessing a long decline of liberal democracy, which had celebrated its late and unexpected triumph in Eastern Europe in 1989. But as parliamentary democracy has since then come under pressure in various countries throughout the so-called Western world, the state seems more relevant than ever for ensuring relative prosperity, social stability and, hopefully, the rule of law.

Further reading

Ágh, Attila. 'Citizenship and Civil Society in Eastern Europe', in *The Condition of Citizenship*, ed. Bart van Steenbergen (London: SAGE Publications, 1994), 108–26.

Aligica, Paul Dragos, and Anthony J. Evans. *The Neoliberal Revolution in Eastern Europe: Economic Ideas in the Transition from Communism* (Cheltenham: Edward Elgar, 2009).

Ash, Timothy Garton. *The Uses of Adversity: Essays on the Fate of Central Europe* (New York: Random House, 1989 [1986]).

Ash, Timothy Garton. 'Eastern Europe: The Year of Truth',in *The Magic Lantern: The Revolution of '89 Witnessed in Warsaw, Budapest, Berlin, and Prague*, ed. Timothy Garton Ash (New York: Random House, 1990), 131–56. [first published in *The New York Review of Books*, 15 February 1990].

Avdeyeva, Olga A. *Defending Women's Rights in Europe: Gender Equality and EU Enlargement* (New York: State University of New York Press, 2015).

---

150 Olga A. Avdeyeva, *Defending Women's Rights in Europe: Gender Equality and EU Enlargement* (New York: State University of New York Press, 2015).

151 Gale Stokes, 'Modes of Opposition Leading to Revolution in Eastern Europe', in *Social Construction of Democracy, 1870–1990*, eds George Reid Andrews and Herrick Chapman (New York: New York University Press, 1995), 241–63, here 261–2; Stokes, *The Walls Came Tumbling Down*, 23; Kumar, *1989: Revolutionary Ideas and Ideals*, 133.

Baev, Jordan, and Kostadin Grozev. 'Bulgaria', in *A Handbook of the Communist Security Apparatus in East Central Europe, 1944–1989*, eds Krzysztof Persak and Łukasz Kamiński (Warsaw: Institute of National Remembrance, 2005), 37–86.

Balcerowicz, Leszek. *Socialism, Capitalism, Transformation* (Budapest: CEU Press, 1995).

Bandelj, Nina, and Dorothy J. Solinger, eds. *Socialism Vanquished, Socialism Challenged: Eastern Europe and China, 1989–2009* (Oxford: Oxford University Press, 2012).

Barany, Zoltan D. *The Future of NATO Expansion: Four Case Studies* (Cambridge: Cambridge University Press, 2003).

Berend, Iván T. *Central and Eastern Europe 1944–1993: Detour from the Periphery to the Periphery* (Cambridge: Cambridge University Press, 1996).

Beyme, Klaus von. *Transition to Democracy in Eastern Europe* (Basingstoke: Macmillan, 1996).

Bieber, Florian, Armina Galijaš, and Rory Archer, eds. *Debating the End of Yugoslavia* (Farnham: Ashgate, 2014).

Blokker, Paul. *Multiple Democracies in Europe: Political Culture in New Member States* (New York: Routledge, 2010).

Bockman, Johanna. *Markets in the Name of Socialism: The Left-Wing Origins of Neoliberalism* (Stanford, CA: Stanford University Press, 2011).

Bohle, Dorothee, and Béla Greskovits. *Capitalist Diversity on Europe's Periphery* (Ithaca, NY: Cornell University Press, 2012).

Bozóki, András, ed. *Intellectuals and Politics in Central Europe* (Budapest: CEU Press, 1999).

Bozóki, András, ed. *The Roundtable Talks of 1989: The Genesis of Hungarian Democracy: Analysis and Documents* (Budapest: CEU Press, 2002).

Brier, Robert, ed. *Entangled Protest: Transnational Approaches to the History of Dissent in Eastern Europe and the Soviet Union* (Osnabrück: Fibre, 2013).

Calhoun, Noel. *Dilemmas of Justice in Eastern Europe's Democratic Transitions* (New York: Palgrave Macmillan, 2014).

Carey, Henry F., ed. *Romania since 1989: Politics, Economics, and Society* (Lanham, MD: Lexington Books, 2004).

Chandler, David, ed. *Peace without Politics? Ten Years of International State-Building in Bosnia* (London: Routledge, 2005).

Cohen, Jean L., and Andrew Arato. *Civil Society and Political Theory* (Cambridge, MA: MIT Press, 1992).

Csurka, István. 'A Few Thoughts', in *From Stalinism to Pluralism: A Documentary History of Eastern Europe since 1945*, ed. Gale Stokes, 2nd ed. (Oxford: Oxford University Press, 1996), 265–69.

Dahrendorf, Ralf. *Reflections on the Revolution in Europe: In a Letter Intended to Have Been Sent to a Gentleman in Warsaw* (New Brunswick: Transaction Publishers, 2005).

Djilas, Milovan. *The New Class: An Analysis of the Communist System* (New York: Praeger, 1957).

Ðurašković, Stevo. *The Politics of History in Croatia and Slovakia in the 1990s* (Zagreb: Srednja Europa, 2016).

Einhorn, Barbara. *Cinderella Goes to Market: Citizenship, Gender and Women's Movements in East Central Europe* (London: Verso, 1993).

Eyal, Gil, Iván Szelényi, and Eleanor R. Townsley. *Making Capitalism without Capitalists: Class Formation and Elite Struggles in Post-Communist Central Europe* (London: Verso, 2000).

Falk, Barbara J. *The Dilemmas of Dissidence in East-Central Europe: Citizen Intellectuals and Philosopher Kings* (Budapest: CEU Press, 2003).

Feindt, Gregor. *Auf der Suche nach politischer Gemeinschaft. Oppositionelles Denken zur Nation im ostmitteleuropäischen Samizdat 1976–1992* (Berlin: De Gruyter Oldenbourg, 2015).

Funk, Nanette, and Magda Mueller, eds. *Gender Politics and Post-Communism: Reflections from Eastern Europe and the Former Soviet Union* (London: Routledge, 1993).

Gal, Susan, and Gail Kligman, ed. *Reproducing Gender: Politics, Publics, and Everyday Life after Socialism* (Princeton, NJ: Princeton University Press, 2000a).

Gal, Susan, and Gail Kligman. *The Politics of Gender after Socialism: A Comparative Historical Essay* (Princeton, NJ: Princeton University Press, 2000b).

Gheciu, Alexandra. *NATO in the 'New Europe': The Politics of International Socialization after the Cold War* (Stanford, CA: Stanford University Press, 2005).

Gieseke, Jens. *The History of the Stasi: East Germany's Secret Police, 1945–1990* (New York: Berghahn Books, 2014).

Grzymała-Busse, Anna. *Rebuilding Leviathan: Party Competition and State Exploitation in Post-Communist Democracies* (Cambridge: Cambridge University Press, 2007).

Hankiss, Elemér. *East European Alternatives* (Oxford: Clarendon Press, 1990).

Havel, Václav. *The Power of the Powerless*, ed. John Keane (Armonk, NY: M.E. Sharpe, 1985). [first published as *Moc bezmocných* (London: Londýnské listy, 1978)].

Havel, Václav. *Summer Meditations* (New York: A.A. Knopf, 1992).

Holmes, Leslie. *The End of Communist Power: Anti-Corruption Campaigns and Legitimation Crisis* (Cambridge: Polity, 1993).

Inglot, Tomasz. *Welfare States in East Central Europe, 1919–2004* (Cambridge: Cambridge University Press, 2008).

Ismayr, Wolfgang, ed. *Die politischen Systeme Osteuropas*, 3rd ed. (Wiesbaden: Verlag für Sozialwissenschaft, 2010).

Kántor, Zoltán,Balázs Majtényi, Osamu Ieda, Balázs Vizi and Iván Halász, eds. *The Hungarian Status Law: Nation Building and/or Minority Protection* (Sapporo: Slavic Research Center, Hokkaido University, 2004).

Kenney, Padraic. *A Carnival of Revolution: Central Europe 1989* (Princeton, NJ: Princeton University Press, 2002).

Kind-Kovács, Friederike. *Written Here, Published There: How Underground Literature Crossed the Iron Curtain* (Budapest: CEU Press, 2014).

Kind-Kovács, Friederike, and Jessie Labov, eds. *Samizdat, Tamizdat, and Beyond: Transnational Media During and After Socialism* (New York: Berghahn Books, 2013).

Kligman, Gail. *The Politics of Duplicity: Controlling Reproduction in Ceauşescu's Romania* (Berkeley, CA: University of California Press, 1998).

Konrád, György. *Antipolitics: An Essay* (San Diego, CA: Harcourt Brace Jovanovich, 1984).

Konrád, György, and Iván Szelényi. *The Intellectuals on the Road to Class Power: A Sociological Study of the Role of the Intelligentsia in Socialism* (Brighton: Harvester Press, 1979).

Kopeček, Michal. *Hledání ztraceného smyslu revoluce: Zrod a počátky marxistického revizionismu ve střední Evropě 1953–1960* (Prague: Argo, 2009), 293–304. Forthcoming in English: *Quest for the Revolution's Lost Meaning: The Origins of Marxist Revisionism in East Central Europe 1953–1960* (Leiden: Brill Academic Publishers).

Kopeček, Michal, and Piotr Wciślik, ed. *Thinking Through Transition: Liberal Democracy, Authoritarian Pasts, and Intellectual History in East Central Europe after 1989* (Budapest: CEU Press, 2015).

Kotkin, Stephen. *Uncivil Society: 1989 and the Implosion of the Communist Establishment* (New York: Modern Library, 2009).

Krapfl, James. *Revolution with a Human Face: Politics, Culture, and Community in Czechoslovakia, 1989–1992* (Ithaca, NY: Cornell University Press, 2013).

Kumar, Krishan. *1989: Revolutionary Ideas and Ideals* (Minneapolis, MN: University of Minnesota Press, 2001).

Kuroń, Jacek, and Karol Modzelewski. *An Open Letter to the Party: A Revolutionary Socialist Manifesto Written in a Polish Prison* (London: International Socialism, 1965).

Kusin, Vladimir V. *The Intellectual Origins of the Prague Spring: The Development of Reformist Ideas in Czechoslovakia 1956–1967* (Cambridge: Cambridge University Press, 1971).

Lazić, Mladen, and Jelena Pešić. *Making and Unmaking State-Centered Capitalism in Serbia* (Belgrade: Čigoja Štampa, 2012).

Listhaug, Ola, and Sabrina P. Ramet, eds. *Bosnia-Herzegovina since Dayton: Civic and Uncivic Values* (Ravenna: Longo editore, 2013).

Mark, James. *The Unfinished Revolution: Making Sense of the Communist Past in Central Eastern Europe* (New Haven, CT: Yale University Press, 2010).

Michnik, Adam. *Letters from Freedom: Post-Cold War Realities and Perspectives*, ed. Irena Grudzińska-Gross (Berkeley, CA: University of California Press, 1998).

Millard, Frances. *Polish Politics and Society* (London and New York: Routledge, 1999).

Mishtal, Joanna. *The Politics of Morality: The Church, the State, and Reproductive Rights in Postsocialist Poland* (Athens, OH: Ohio University Press, 2015).

Nalepa, Monika. *Skeletons in the Closet: Transitional Justice in Post-Communist Europe* (Cambridge: Cambridge University Press, 2010).

Petrescu, Cristina. *From Robin Hood to Don Quixote: Resistance and Dissent in Communist Romania* (Bucureşti: Ed. Enciclopedică, 2013).

Petrescu, Dragoş. *Explaining the Romanian Revolution of 1989: Culture, Structure, and Contingency* (Bucureşti: Editura Enciclopedică, 2010).

1989 and beyond

Petrescu, Dragoş. *Entangled Revolutions: The Breakdown of the Communist Regimes in East-Central Europe* (Bucureşti: Editura Enciclopedică, 2014).

Přibáň, Jiri, and James Young, eds. *The Rule of Law in Central Europe: The Reconstruction of Legality, Constitutionalism and Civil Society in the Post-Communist Countries* (Aldershot: Ashgate, 1999).

Pridham, Geoffrey. *Designing Democracy: EU Enlargement and Regime Change in Post-Communist Europe* (Basingstoke: Palgrave Macmillan, 2005).

Radonic, Liljana. *Krieg um die Erinnerung: Kroatische Vergangenheitspolitik zwischen Revisionismus und europäischen Standards* (Frankfurt a.M.: Campus, 2010).

Ramet, Sabrina P., ed. *Central and Southeast European Politics since 1989* (Cambridge: Cambridge University Press, 2010).

Ramet, Sabrina P. *The Three Yugoslavias: State-Building and Legitimation, 1918–2005* (Washington, DC: Woodrow Wilson Center Press, 2006).

Ramet, Sabrina P., Konrad Clewing, and Renéo Lukić, eds. *Croatia since Independence: War, Politics, Society, Foreign Relations* (München: Oldenbourg, 2008).

Romsics, Ignác. *Hungary in the Twentieth Century* (Budapest: Corvina, 1999).

Rosenberg, Tina. *The Haunted Land: Facing Europe's Ghosts after Communism* (New York: Vintage Books, 1995).

Sabrow, Martin, ed. *1989 und die Rolle der Gewalt* (Göttingen: Wallstein Verlag, 2012).

Sachs, Jeffrey. *Poland's Jump to the Market Economy* (Cambridge, MA: MIT Press, 1993).

Sadurski, Wojciech. *Rights before Courts: A Study of Constitutional Courts in Postcommunist States of Central and Eastern Europe* (Dordrecht: Springer, 2005).

Saurer, Edith, Margareth Lanzinger, and Elisabeth Frysak, eds. *Women's Movements: Networks and Debates in Post-Communist Countries in the 19th and 20th Centuries* (Köln: Böhlau, 2006).

Schimmelfennig, Frank, and Ulrich Sedelmeier, eds. *The Europeanization of Central and Eastern Europe* (Ithaca, NY: Cornell University Press, 2005).

Schöpflin, George. *Politics in Eastern Europe: 1945–1992* (Oxford: Blackwell, 1993).

Sebastián-Aparicio, Sofia. *Post-War Statebuilding and Constitutional Reform in Divided Societies: Beyond Dayton in Bosnia* (Basingstoke: Palgrave Macmillan, 2014).

Shevel, Oksana. *Migration, Refugee Policy, and State Building in Postcommunist Europe* (New York: Cambridge University Press, 2011).

Siani-Davies, Peter. *The Romanian Revolution of December 1989* (Ithaca, NY: Cornell University Press, 2005).

Siegrist, Hannes, and Dietmar Müller, eds. *Property in East Central Europe: Notions, Institutions, and Practices of Landownership in the Twentieth Century* (New York: Berghahn Books, 2015).

Šimečka, Milan. *The Restoration of Order: The Normalization of Czechoslovakia, 1969–1976* (London: Verso, 1984). [first published as *Obnovení pořádku. Příspěvek k typologii reálného socialismu* (Köln: Index, 1979)].

Stan, Lavinia, ed. *Transitional Justice in Eastern Europe and the Former Soviet Union: Reckoning with the Communist Past* (London: Routledge, 2009).

Stan, Lavinia, and Nadya Nedelsky, eds. *Post-Communist Transitional Justice: Lessons from Twenty-Five Years of Experience* (Cambridge: Cambridge University Press, 2015).

Staniszkis, Jadwiga. *Poland's Self-Limiting Revolution*, ed. Jan T. Gross (Princeton, NJ: Princeton University Press, 1984).

Stokes, Gale. *The Walls Came Tumbling Down: The Collapse of Communism in Eastern Europe* (Oxford: Oxford University Press, 1993).

Sundhaussen, Holm. *Jugoslawien und seine Nachfolgestaaten 1943–2011: Eine ungewöhnliche Geschichte des Gewöhnlichen* (Köln: Böhlau, 2012).

Szacki, Jerzy. *Liberalism after Communism* (Budapest: CEU Press, 1995).

Ther, Philipp. *Europe since 1989: A History* (Princeton, NJ: Princeton University Press, 2016).

Tittenbrun, Jacek. *The Collapse of Real Socialism in Poland* (London: Janus, 1993).

Tőkés, Rudolf L. *Hungary's Negotiated Revolution: Economic Reform, Social Change and Political Succession, 1957–1990* (Cambridge: Cambridge University Press, 1996).

Tomka, Béla. *A Social History of Twentieth-Century Europe* (London: Routledge, 2013).

Williams, Kieran. *The Prague Spring and its Aftermath: Czechoslovak Politics, 1968–1970* (Cambridge: Cambridge University Press, 1997).

Wirsching, Andreas. *Der Preis der Freiheit: Geschichte Europas in unserer Zeit* (München: C.H. Beck, 2012).

INDEX

Abdülaziz, Ottoman Sultan 71, 75
Abdülhamid II, Ottoman Sultan 53, 71–2, 75, 77–9, 96–9
Abdülmecid I, Ottoman Sultan 59, 71
Alexander I (of Battenberg), Prince of Bulgaria 76
Alexander I, King of Yugoslavia (Karađorđević dynasty) 24
Alexander II, Emperor of Russia 47–9, 59, 80, 82
Alexander III, Emperor of Russia 48–51, 80–2
Antall, József 301, 305
Arendt, Hannah 215

Bach, Alexander von 63, 65
Badeni, Kasimir Felix 105–6
Balcerowicz, Leszek 309, 318
Begović, Miroslav 38
Benda, Václav 293
Beneš, Edvard 124, 196–8
Berg, Fyodor Fyodorovich fon 51
Beseler, Hans Hartwig von 122
Bibó, István xv, xvii
Bilainkin, George 205
Bismarck, Otto von 156, 171
Boris III, King of Bulgaria 188
Brătianu, Ion 124
Bruck, Karl Ludwig von 64–5
Bunge, Nikolai 89
Burebista, King of Dacia 279

Carol I, King of Romania 74
Carol II, King of Romania 35, 188
Ceaușescu, Elena 322
Ceaușescu, Nicolae 35–7, 218, 253, 261, 269, 279, 281, 283, 298, 317, 322
Cibulka, Petr 321
Clemenceau, Georges 124

Csurka, István 296, 316
Cubr, František 32
Čubrilović, Vasa 165
Cuza, Alexander Ion 74

Dahrendorf, Ralf 303, 309–10
Decebalus, King of Dacia 279
Demszky, Gábor 308
Denikin, Anton 131
Dienstbier, Jiří (Jr.) 320
Dimitrijević, Braco 31
Đinđić, Zoran 306
Dinor, Yehiel 201
Djilas, Milovan 295
Dmowski, Roman 124, 172
Duguit, Léon 157
Dzielski, Mirosław 295
Dzurinda, Mikuláš 307

Eichmann, Adolf 201
Engels, Friedrich 220, 282, 285

Ferdinand I, King of Bulgaria 60
Findley, Carter V. 56
Francis Joseph I, Emperor of Austria, King of Hungary 60, 108, 111, 120n10
Francis Stadion, Count von Warthausen 60
Frangeš, Robert 22
Franz Ferdinand, Archduke of Austria 109, 111
Frederick II, King of Prussia (a.k.a. Frederick the Great) 279

George I, King of Greece 74
George II, King of Greece 188
Gheorghiu-Dej, Gheorghe 279
Gibson, Hugh 205–6

Index

Gierek, Edward 228
Goma, Paul 249
Gomułka, Władysław 228, 245
Gorbachev, Mikhail 219, 285, 291, 295, 297
Gottwald, Klement 196
Gross, Adolf 184
Gross, Daniel 184
Grynszpan, Herschel 208

Habermas, Jürgen 304
Hácha, Emil 196
Hankiss, Elemér 312
Hansen, Theophil 20
Hauszmann, Alajos 16
Havel, Václav 219, 222, 293–4, 298–9, 302, 305, 315
Heydrich, Reinhard 196
Himmler, Heinrich 202
Hodža, Milan 188
Holland, Agnieszka 318
Honecker, Erich 218, 279, 298
Hoover, Herbert 137–8, 206
Horthy, Miklós 160, 188
Hoxha, Enver 280–1
Hrubý, Josef 32
Hus, Jan 226
Husák, Gustáv 228

Iliescu, Ion 299, 301
Ilkić, Jovan 20, 22
Izetbegović, Alija 300

Janda, Krystyna 318
Jaruzelski, Wojciech 262, 294, 299, 322
Joseph II, Holy Roman Emperor 61, 70
Jovanović, Konstantin 20

Kaczorowski, Ryszard 196
Kaczyński, Jarosław 312
Kaczyński, Lech 305, 308
Kádár, János 217, 284
Kadare, Ismael 28
Kállay, Benjámin von 1–2
Katkov, Mikhail 81–2
Khrushchev, Nikita 217, 227, 247, 277, 292
Kis, János 296
Kiszczak, Czesław 322
Klaus, Václav 302, 305–6, 313
Konrád, György 264, 293, 295
Kornai, János 221, 240
Kossuth, Louis 60
Krasnov, Nikolaj 22, 24, 36
Krleža, Miroslav 16, 18–20
Kučan, Milan 299
Kulischer, Eugene 210
Kun, Béla 133, 160, 188
Kuroń, Jacek 291, 294–6, 304

Lange, Oskar 228, 238, 294
Le Corbusier (a.k.a. Charles-Édouard Jeanneret) 27
Leopold II, Holy Roman Emperor 61
Lipiński, Edward 294
Lipski, Jan-Józef 296
Litvinov, Maxim 138
Livytsky, Andriy 125
Lloyd George, David 124, 134
Loris-Melikov, Mikhail 81

Mackensen, August von 120
Mahmud II, Ottoman Sultan 71
Málek, Ivan 242–3
Maniu, Iuliu 187
Maria Theresa, Queen of Hungary, Holy Roman Empress Consort 8, 61
Markov, Georgi 219
Marković, Ante 284
Marshall, George C. 206
Marshall, Thomas Humphrey 150–1, 231, 252
Marx, Karl 220, 257, 282, 285
Masaryk, Tomáš 17, 124
Mazowiecki, Tadeusz 301, 309
Mečiar, Vladimír 302, 306
Medgyessy, Péter 321, 323
Medvedkin, Aleksandr 27
Metaxas, Ioannis 188
Metternich, Clemens von 62
Michnik, Adam 292, 294, 296, 315
Midhat Pasha, Ahmed Şefik 54, 75
Mikulić, Branko 284
Milan I, King of Serbia (Obrenović dynasty) 75
Milašius, Oskaras 124
Miller, Leszek 323
Milošević, Slobodan 25, 298–300, 305–6
Milyukov, Pavel N. 110
Mladenov, Petŭr 298–9
Mlynárik, Ján 296
Moczulski, Leszek 295
Moldovan, Iuliu 179
Mościcki, Ignacy 195
Murad V, Ottoman Sultan 75
Muroń, Jaroslav 312
Mussolini, Benito 210

Nabokov, Vladimir 143–4
Nagy, Imre 299, 302, 314
Nansen, Fridtjof 140, 143–4, 210
Napoleon III, French Emperor 47
Nevsky, Alexander 11, 17, 25
Nicholas I, Emperor of Russia 49
Nicholas II, Emperor of Russia 9, 51, 82, 110
Niemeyer, Oscar 30
Nikola I, King of Montenegro 76
Nikolić, Živojin 22
Nixon, Richard 279

Index

Obrenović, Mihailo, Prince of Serbia (Obrenović dynasty) 75
Obrenović, Miloš, Prince of Serbia (Obrenović dynasty) 19
Orbán, Viktor 314
Orlando, Vittorio Emanuele 124
Otto I, King of Greece 74

Paderewski, Jan 136
Palacký, František 60
Pašić, Nikola 109, 120, 124
Patočka, Jan 296
Päts, Konstantin 188
Perin, Đoko 165
Peter I, Emperor of Russia (a.k.a. Peter the Great) 89
Peter I, King of Serbia (Karađorđević dynasty) 20
Peter II, King of Yugoslavia (Karađorđević dynasty) 196
Petkov, Nikola 217
Petliura, Symon 125
Petrescu, Anca 36
Piłsudski, Józef 123, 173, 184, 188, 197
Pithart, Petr 296, 312
Pius XI, Pope 178
Planinc, Milka 284
Plečnik, Jože 18, 36
Pobedonostsev, Konstantin 81
Pokorný, Zdeněk 32
Popiełuszko, Jerzy 322
Prager, Karel 33–4
Princip, Gavrilo 109

Raczkiewicz, Władysław 195
Rajk, László 217
Rajkiewicz, Antoni 243
Rajkiewicz, Antoni 243
Rama, Edi 308
Rath, Ernst vom 208
Reich-Ranicki, Marcel 208
Rokita, Jan 320
Rosner, Jan 243
Rössler, Jaroslav 33
Roth, Joseph 144
Rothschild, Joseph 133–4
Rottenberg, Anda 318
Różański, Stanisław 184
Ruml, Jiří 320

Schmidt, Friedrich von 13
Schwarzenberg, Felix Prince of 65
Schwechten, Franz Heinrich 12
Sempers, Gottfried 20
Šiklová, Jiřina 297, 321
Šimečka, Milan 296
Simeon II, King of Bulgaria 305

Skanderbeg (a.k.a. George Castriot) 279, 281
Skoropadskyi, Pavlo 130
Smetona, Antanas 188
Solzhenitsyn, Aleksandr 118, 201
Sophie, Duchess of Hohenberg 109
Spengler, Oswald 110
Špidla, Vladimír 323
Stalin, Joseph 30, 194, 196, 206–7, 212–13, 216–18, 224–6, 247, 275–6, 278, 292
Stamboliyski, Aleksandar 124, 187
Steindl, Imre 13–15
Stolypin, Pyotr A. 85, 89, 94, 109, 129
Švehla, Antonín 188
Szacki, Jerzy 309, 323
Szelényi, Ivan 264, 295
Szymborska, Wisława 318

Taaffe, Eduard von 171
Tito, Josip Broz 25, 30–1, 121, 197, 205, 218, 223, 247, 281, 301, 303, 305
Tölgyessy, Péter 305
Tommaseo, Niccolò 60
Truman, Harry S. 206
Trumbić, Ante 120, 124
Tuđman, Franjo 300, 305
Tudor, Corneliu Vadim 316
Turowicz, Jerzy 323

Ujica, Andrei 35
Ulmanis, Kārlis 188
Urşianu, Valerian 41

Vancaš, Josip 1–2, 13
Venizelos, Eleftherios 175
Vezenkov, Alexander 96
Vitić, Ivan 34

Wagner, Otto 18
Wałęsa, Lech 196, 302, 305
Wildstein, Bronisław 321
Wilhelm II, German Emperor and King of Prussia 12, 123
Wilson, Woodrow 124, 136, 138, 172n103
Witos, Wincenty 187
Witte, Sergei 89
Wojtyła, Karol (later, Pope John Paul II) 219
Woods, Lebbeus 37–8
Wóycicki, Kazimierz 318
Wrangel, Pyotr Nikolayevich 131

Ybl, Miklós 16

Želev, Želju 219
Zhivkov, Todor 262, 322
Zhivkova, Lyudmila 279
Zogu, Ahmet (ruled as Zog I, King of Albania) 188